Propaganda, Communication, and Public Opinion

Propaganda, Communication, and Public Opinion

A Comprehensive Reference Guide

BRUCE LANNES SMITH,
HAROLD D. LASSWELL, AND
RALPH D. CASEY

PRINCETON
PRINCETON UNIVERSITY PRESS
1946

London: Geoffrey Cumberlege, Oxford University Press

PREFACE

THIS Reference Guide is a continuation of the work begun in *Propaganda and Promotional Activities: An Annotated Bibliography*, compiled by Lasswell, Casey, and Smith and published by the University of Minnesota Press in 1935.

The present volume consists of four introductory essays and an annotated bibliography. The purpose of the essays is to survey briefly some aspects of the currently available scientific knowledge concerning the effects on world society of communication, and particularly of one special kind of communication: deliberate propaganda. ("Propaganda" is here taken to mean the calculated selection and circulation of symbols, with a view to influencing mass behavior.) The purpose of the bibliography is to show in detail where most of the scientific information can be found, who its authors are, and (so far as space permits) what questions it has sought to answer.

It is believed that the titles of the introductory essays are self-explanatory. A brief explanation of the bibliographic section may be in order.

Scope of the Bibliographic Section

On this occasion, as in 1935 when the previous book was published, it has been necessary to curtail our selection of material severely. In the available space we can include only the most representative titles from the great stream of writing on the subject by advertisers, educators, journalists, lawyers, political leaders, psychologists, public administrators, public relations counselors, and the several varieties of social scientists: anthropologists, economists, historians, political scientists, sociologists, and others.

As before, the bibliography is limited, in principle, to objective studies and analyses rather than examples of propaganda; but every effort has been made to include titles from every field in which conscious promotion is prominent, and from every scientific discipline which has contributed to its objectified analysis. Although it has been necessary to represent many such fields and disciplines by citing only their most characteristic documentation, the goal throughout has been inclusive scope and adequate sampling.

Titles Included

The titles here listed are: (1) Books, periodicals and articles which appeared between mid-1934 (when the previous bibliography went to press) and about March 1943. (2) A very small number of leading titles which were inadvertently omitted from the previous book. (3) A special list of "Outstanding Titles on the Art and Science of Popularization" (see p. 122 below). (4) A special list of "One Hundred and Fifty Outstanding Titles on Propaganda, Communication, and Public Opinion" (see p. 121 below).

Plan of Classification

With certain alterations among the subclasses, the plan of classification adopted in the previous volume has proved to be reasonably serviceable as a tool of research. Consequently, the main classes in the present book are the same as before, but subclasses have been altered to conform with shifts in the focus of attention of investigators, or for the sake of greater simplicity.

Obviously, the overlapping of subjects complicates the problem of arranging titles according to a logic useful to all readers. To save space, each citation has been entered only once—at the point where it seemed to fit the main plan of classification most neatly.

Cross References and Indexes

To offset the limits imposed by any one system of classification, recourse may be had to the rather detailed Table of Contents, and to the Author and Subject Index. In addition to the names of authors of titles listed in the bibliographic section, the Index includes the names of translators, authors of forewords, and authors cited in the annotations. The indexing of subjects will be found to be much more comprehensive than in our previous volume.

Identification of Authors and Observational Standpoints

The activities, connections, and backers of a writer are of the highest importance in evaluating his analytic contributions in a field as highly controversial as that of propaganda, communication, and public opinion. It would be advisable to have a *vita* or life sketch of each of our 3,000 or more authors, so that the reader might bear in mind the social strata, the income groups, the skill groups, the attitude groups, the nationality groups, the educational groups, whose standpoints may have been adopted or whose interests may have been served by these writers.

Space and the compilers' time being severely limited, the preparation of such identifying data has proved to be impossible. However, an effort has been made to provide clues to sources from which the reader may obtain further information. In the annotations, the nationalities and the principal occupations of writers have been indicated briefly, and in a number of cases other data indicating their observational standpoints have been given. In addition, initials have been placed after the names of authors of the "One Hundred and Fifty Outstanding Titles" (see p. 121, below) and also after the names of authors of titles in Part 1 and Part 4, the Parts in which the major theoretical and historical treatises and monographs are listed. These initials indicate that the author in question is listed in one or more of the following readily accessible directories:

CB '40, '41, '42, '43 = *Current Biography* for the indicated
year (up to May 1943)
D = *Directory of American Scholars*
(1942)
ESS = *Encyclopedia of the Social Sciences*
W = *Who's Who in America, 1942-1943*

It is hoped that this feature, together with the introductory essays, the intensive indexing, and the relatively full annotations, may enable the reader to use this volume not merely as a list of readings but as a kind of treatise and reference guide in its own right—at once comprehensive in scope and specific in its citations of articles, books, and authors.

Authorship

The selection and annotation of nearly all titles in the bibliography section of this volume was carried out by Bruce L. Smith, with occasional suggestions or editorial revisions by his two colleagues. He also chose the select list of titles on "The Art and Science of Popularization." Responsibility for the selection and annotation of the "One Hundred and Fifty Outstanding Titles" is equally shared by the three compilers. The essays on "The Science of Mass Communication," while signed by individual writers, are to a great extent the product of joint planning.

BRUCE LANNES SMITH
Department of Economics,
New York University

HAROLD D. LASSWELL
Director of War Communications Research,
Library of Congress

RALPH D. CASEY
School of Journalism,
University of Minnesota

ACKNOWLEDGMENTS

The making of a book like this is not without its fatiguing moments. They have been lightened by Ralph D. Casey and Harold D. Lasswell with more than ten years of discriminating scientific advice and with every sort of personal kindness; by George Biderman, Elinor Hopkinson, Morris Janowitz and Edith C. Strickland with assistance and many valued ideas; by the staff of Princeton University Press, with expert technical and editorial counsel; and by a charming and infallible secretary, Viola C. Johnson.

B. L. S.

TABLE OF CONTENTS

The Science of
Mass Communication: Four Essays

INTRODUCTION

A WRITER once dreamed of a Utopia in the year ten thousand, in which speech no longer exists and people merely read one another's thoughts.[1] In the meanwhile we are compelled to rely upon the "clumsy vehicle of words."

It staggers the imagination to think of the daily flow of words. An all-inclusive census of the stream of public communication would survey all programs of all broadcasting stations in the world, all issues of all newspapers and periodicals, all newsreels, documentary and feature films, all posters, leaflets, emblems, insignia, all trade books, textbooks and lesson guides, to say nothing of all speeches, songs, theatrical performances, ceremonies, lectures, formal discussions, demonstrations and celebrations, and architectural and monumental expressions.

The control of public communication is one of the policy objectives of a multitude of governmental and private groups and persons. Every government on the globe, whether despotism or democracy, whether at war or at peace, relies upon propaganda—more or less efficiently harmonized with strategy, diplomacy, and economics—to accomplish its ends. Private individuals and associations—political parties, pressure groups, trade associations, trade unions, and other organizations—may be prevented by the government from resorting to violence and in consequence be made particularly dependent upon propaganda.

Not all use of language is *propaganda*. When language is used in negotiations between diplomats, employer-employee representatives, and other accredited agents, the act is one of *diplomacy*, not propaganda. *Propaganda is language aimed at large masses*: it sends words, and other symbols such as pictures, through the radio, press, and film, where they reach huge audiences. *The intention of the propagandist is to influence mass attitudes on controversial issues*. The use of language in diplomacy is to conclude agreements or to expose their impossibility. Again, when words are used in teaching how to read, write, and figure, the process is not to be confused with propaganda; rather it is *education*, primarily concerned with transmitting skill or insight, not attitude. (The definition of education may be extended to include the transmission of *noncontroversial* attitudes as well as skills.) When language is used only to affirm loyalty to an accepted

[1] Will N. Harben, "In the Year Ten Thousand," *Arena* (November, 1892).

symbol or institution, again the act is not propagandistic; it is part of the *ceremonial* life of those involved.

We are not justified in making the hasty assumption that whatever appears in the channels of mass communication, even in a despotism, is propaganda. Some of it is wholly artistic and self-expressive and is not deliberately slanted toward strengthening or weakening controversial attitudes.

Propaganda is one means by which large numbers of people are induced to act together. In a relatively free society, each step of the process can be more readily observed. Initiatives may arise anywhere, ranging from simple local matters like paving the street to complex global problems of permanent peace. Many initiatives die away, leaving no discernible change. Others culminate in reform or even revolution. When societies are despotically run, public initiatives are not so freely tolerated, and criticism of a given group (party, government, church) may be treason. In a despotism there is propaganda—but it is monopolized as far as possible in the hands of the despot.

The content and control of propaganda are directly related to social structure. (By "structure" is meant the basic values of a given society and the pattern followed in distributing them. Among the most distinctive values are income; physical safety; respect; and power, by which is meant the making of important decisions.) Propaganda at once reflects, criticizes, and partially modifies the social structure. Where power, income, and other values are held in a few hands, the means of communication will be owned or regulated by the few and hence subject to the conceptions of interest and sentiment current among them. When the social structure is more democratic there is easier access to public media for every constituent group of society, and the channels of communication reveal a broad variety of interest and sentiment.

In every society, however, limits are put upon the public media by the attitudinal standards of the community as a whole, which include morality, loyalties, expectations. Propaganda must necessarily adapt itself to the accepted attitudes and vocabulary of public life. Successful propaganda in America will speak reverently of the Constitution, of the Bill of Rights and of the Declaration of Independence. Only in a late stage of internal reintegration would it be possible successfully to abandon this vocabulary.

Much of the literature of propaganda is devoted to strategy and tactics. Like other instruments of policy (war, diplomacy, economics), propaganda is bound by the strategic principles of precaution, concentration, and surprise. According to the principle of precaution the propagandist is careful to lull the unfavorable elements into passivity, until they are no longer able to block the attainment of his objective. In conformity with the idea of concentration, the successful propagandist reinforces those who are predisposed toward his goal, nullifies the unfavorable, seeks to win the neutral or indifferent. Within this framework the propagandist weighs and balances his tactical decisions about the use of slogans and symbols. If scientific and objective, he pretests and postaudits his assumptions about the relative advantages of repetition and variety, universal and local symbols, truth and deception, optimism and pessimism, public or private appeals, presentations of himself or opponent as strong or weak, presentation as moral or immoral.

All principles of propaganda depend upon certain assumptions about the nature of the process of communication. In the introductory essay to the authors' earlier book, *Propaganda and Promotional Activities: An Annotated Bibliography*, a cursory view was given of the meaning of the term "propaganda" and of the nature of propaganda strategy and technique as then understood. The authors believe that the usefulness of the present volume will be greatest if special attention is directed to the structure of the emerging science of communication.

In recent years the expansion of scientific observation on the behavior of animals, infants, primitives, the psychopathic, and the average citizen has continually redefined the laws of psychology, and this in turn has modified the principles of propaganda activity. It is beyond the scope of the following essays to review this entire development. It is, however, timely to consider the field of scientific work most immediately related to propaganda, namely, the direct study of mass communication. As developed in the past few years, the scientific study of communication centers around the four successive phases of any act of communication: In what channels do communications take place? Who communicates? What is communicated? Who is affected by the communication and how?

Hence four essays have been presented in the present work. One is devoted to each of the divisions of the field mentioned above: channels, communicators, contents, effect.

COMMUNICATION CHANNELS

BY RALPH D. CASEY

THREE major trends have shaped the character and ordered the development of American communications. The first has been the rise of democracy. The second is the technological and industrial revolution that has taken place in this country in the past hundred years. The third is the urbanization of America. The assumption that the communication channels have been molded by these three influences can be tested in the case of the newspaper, with incidental reference to other communication agencies.

The news and editorial pattern of daily newspapers is a reflection of the character of a population which reads and buys them. Ours is a land whose culture is largely dominated by the democratic middle class. Its tastes, interests, and demands have shaped the communication channels. The type of content, the range of the circulation, and the influence daily newspapers and even the popular magazines enjoy are linked with the democratic movement which goes back at least to the Jacksonian era.

The Democratic Movement

When the common man won the ballot and created the free public school, influences were set at work which altered the press through the succeeding century, just as they changed government, society, education, the arts, and other phases of life. It was in America that elementary education first became universal. Democracy enfranchised new classes and enlarged the literate public. The acquisition of both letters and political power whetted the appetite of artisans, mechanics, and farmers for reading matter directed at their interests, and stimulated their curiosity about life and affairs. The cheap popular press was born to meet these needs and in the following decades the press has responded to the changing social interests and intellectual standards of its mass audience.

In the 1830's the New York *Sun* and the New York *Herald* boldly challenged the post-Revolutionary tradition of a "class" journalism, largely founded on political party subsidy and published for politicians, well-to-do traders, business men, and well-bred planters. Benjamin Day, the founder of the *Sun*, projected his popular penny newspaper into a field theretofore dominated by the "respectable" six-cent dailies which filled their columns with matters of political and factional controversy and which were "beyond the interest, understanding and means of the plain people." Day introduced news of police courts and crime and as he won readers he and his followers, notably James Gordon Bennett, greatly increased the volume of local news. They also developed the universally understandable "human interest" story—the tale of persons "interesting merely as human beings, and not for their connection with either signifi- cant or sensational news."[1] All this was revolutionary in the journalism of that day.

When Bennett founded the *Herald* in 1835, he publicly proclaimed his paper free from the support of every political clique or faction. As significant as the creation of a new reading public was the break of the penny press with the established tradition of newspaper dependence on political favor and patronage, and the substitution of advertising and to some extent mass circulation revenue to provide the financial support of newspapers.[2]

The success of the popular papers was immediate. Within four years the *Sun*, primarily designed as it was to interest "mechanics" and other work- ers, could boast of a circulation of 30,000 copies a day. Imitators sprang up in Boston, Philadelphia, Baltimore, and elsewhere. Here was a press which based its strength upon the broad base of mass readers and the advertising such circulation could attract. Here was a press which dared to free itself from political power and which could afford to be independent of special interests. Though the pioneers in this democratic movement may not have been fully aware of the implications of their work, they ineluctably molded the press along democratic rather than "class" lines.[3]

The democratization of journalism in the great cities, while producing popular, well-balanced and sober newspapers, also led in its extreme form to the exploitation of a circulation area hitherto unsought by the popular newspapers. The "yellow journals" of Hearst and Pulitzer reached down in the 'nineties to a substratum of readers. Again, in the 'twenties the

---

[1] See Frank Luther Mott, *American Journalism*, p. 243.

[2] Walter Lippmann's remarks on this epoch of American journalism are pertinent here: "It could be demonstrated, I think, that however much the laws may seem to grant political freedom, they are ineffective until a country has for some considerable time accustomed itself to news- papers which are highly profitable and immediately powerful because of their skill in enlisting, in holding, and in influencing a great mass of readers. When there is no prosperous and popular press the liberty of publication is precarious. Publications are likely to be either controlled or venal, or else they eke out a miserable and fairly negligible existence. It will be found, I think, that the area of free publication in the world today is on the whole coterminous with the area in which commercial newspapers circulate widely." See "Two Revolutions in the American Press," *Yale Review*, March, 1931, pp. 433-441.

[3] ". . . almost without exception the penny papers published paragraphs from time to time set- ting forth their creed, which may be summarized as follows: (1) The great common people should have a realistic view of the contemporary scene, and this in spite of taboos; (2) abuses in churches, courts, banks, stockmarkets, etc., should be exposed; (3) the newspaper's first duty is to give its readers the news, and not support a party or mercantile class; and (4) local and human- interest news is important. To these doctrines Horace Greeley later added, when he founded the penny *Tribune*, the reformer's ideal of social amelioration." Mott, *ibid.*, pp. 242-243.

tabloids tapped lower levels of taste and intelligence than other papers cared to reach. The "yellows" and the "tabs" exploited the ignorance, repressions, and emotions of the masses. It should be recalled, however, that Pulitzer—and also Hearst in his early days—did advocate and support popular causes, even though they were guilty of playing upon the passions of readers.

But while the democratization of journalism reached its nadir in the periods of extreme sensationalism, both the "yellows" and the "tabs," each in their own era of apparent popularity, were compelled to modify the extremes of their editorial methods. There were editorial practices to which Demos would not eternally respond. The "yellow" press, in the sense that the term was used in the early 'nineties, does not survive today.[4] Even the revival by the tabloids of a slavish appeal to the morbid and sensational carried within itself "the seeds of its own dissolution."[5]

Throughout the heyday of sensationalism, both in the 'nineties and early twentieth century, there always were sober and intelligent newspapers. The "yellow" and tabloid press has never been the dominant pattern of American journalism the country over. The 'thirties brought in as sober and as seriously intelligent a press as we have had in our history, with a broadly based and democratic circulation.

That the democratic movement has been a more important influence than any other in shaping editorial practices is seen in the desire of publishers to appeal primarily, not to minority groups, but to the average public, albeit a public with needs, demands, and viewpoints widened by expanding educational opportunity[6] and economic pressure. Publishers and controllers of other communication channels are acutely aware of the fact that in an economy in which the communication agencies are operated for profit, with commercial advertising as the chief revenue producer, appeals to sections of society that have the greatest numbers will still ensure the greatest stability for the agency and the greatest income for the communications chan-

---

[4] Robert E. Park, "The Yellow Press," *Sociology and Social Research*, September-October, 1927, p. 11.

[5] See Lippmann, *ibid.*: "As the readers of this [sensational] press live longer in the world, and as their personal responsibilities increase, they begin to feel the need of being genuinely informed rather than of being merely amused and excited. Gradually they discover that things do not happen as they are made to appear in the human interest stories. The realization begins to dawn on them that they are getting not the news but a species of romantic fiction which they can get much better out of the movies and the magazines . . . the most impressive event of the last decade in the history of newspapers has been the demonstration that objective, orderly, and comprehensive presentation of news is a far more successful type of journalism today than the dramatic, disorderly, episodic type. . . ."

[6] The number of pupils enrolled in secondary schools in the continental United States in 1890 was 357,813. The number enrolled per 100 population, 14 to 17 years of age inclusive, was 7. The number enrolled per 100 population in 1940 was 73. See *Statistical Abstract of the United States*, 1942.

nel entrepreneur.[7] The result is that newspapers and periodicals of today remain the journals of the average man, and the radio and motion picture direct their appeal to mass constituencies. "The average man's interests, his pleasures, his good deeds—his evil deeds," are mirrored in the popular printed media of 1945 and to a considerable extent in the other channels as well.

The radio and the motion picture arrived on the scene when the democratic movement was running full tide. Neither had roots in the past. No background of "class" tradition guided their behavior or restricted their operation. If they were uncouth in their beginnings, it was a reflection of the lusty and confident democratic period that gave them birth. The nickelodeon was the progenitor of the movie theater, and any man, no matter what his status, could pick up the first radio broadcasts on a cheap crystal set.

Most of the faults which we deplore in the communications media, and many of the strong points which we applaud, are the results of the effort of those who control and manage the communication channels to satisfy the great majority, rather than the select minority. Some may prefer a level of communication agencies which appeals only to the "wisest and best"; others may show that the communication agencies do not yet approach real democratic fulfillment. The fact remains that democracy has made a powerful impression on the agencies that carry news, ideas, opinions, counsel, and entertainment to the ultimate reader or listener.

Technological and Economic Change

The technological and economic changes in the past half century have been no less influential on the newspaper and periodical as well as on the younger instrumentalities, the radio and motion picture. "Inventions point the way we are going," remarked Professor Ogburn. "We adopt them for the immediate use we make of them. But, once adopted, there are hundreds of social effects, as distinct from uses, that flow more or less inevitably."[8]

Fundamental changes in the pattern, circulation, and influence of the newspaper have come about as a result of more than a hundred years of technological progress. It has increased the scope, range, and speed of the

[7] This is not to say that newspapers are edited and radio programs are planned without regard for special levels of interest and intelligence within the public. See the section on "Departmentalized News and the Small Publics" in Helen McGill Hughes' article, "The Social Interpretation of News" in the *Annals of the American Academy of Political and Social Science*, January, 1942. New York supports "class" newspapers; the New York *Times* for one. Radio stations attempt to build their fare for all classes of listeners; in the case of the radio stations supported by universities and colleges, most of them make little effort to escape intellectual class consciousness. The names of "class" periodicals with national circulation will occur at once to the reader. Documentary films are usually aimed at discriminating movie-goers.

[8] William F. Ogburn, *Machines and Tomorrow's World*, p. 1.

distribution of symbols. It has improved the efficiency of the agencies of mass impression and greatly expanded the contacts between individuals and groups. It has brought the motion picture, the radio, television, and facsimile transmission into being within the last half century.

Prior to the invention of new printing machines, the discovery of the telegraph, and the construction of railroads—all sired by technology—newspapers were relatively insignificant in news volume and circulation, and they were costly in terms of average income. Printing presses before 1814 could produce only a few hundred impressions an hour; the use of steam-powered presses in the same year quadrupled the output. The advent of penny newspapers in 1833 led to further significant developments in printing machinery. Hoe took type from the flatbed press and put it on a revolving cylinder. This development of the rotary press, the invention of stereotyping with the attendant multiplication of plates by a quick process, and the successful use of typesetting machines revolutionized the news pattern and the economy of American journalism.

As new printing machinery duplicated thousands and later tens of thousands of copies of a newspaper at high speed, inventions in electrical transmission provided arteries which carried the blood of the news into the heart of the printing press. News in increasing quantity and speed could be transmitted from the far corners of the globe when the telegraph, cable, and telephone arrived on the scene, to be supplemented later by wireless, radio, and other devices.

In brief, technology provided the means by which millions of widely scattered persons could share information and ideas about matters of general interest. Technological communication devices are the channels for symbols that knit together social groups and widen and deepen social life.[9] They affect many aspects of life, creating new problems in the domestic field and in international relations.[10] But, in addition to these effects, technology has made a significant impress on the economy of communications. Today's use of machines in all lines of production is a commonplace, in the communications industry no less than in other lines of enterprise. Machines that transmit symbols represent a generous investment of capital.

The glamorous days of the pioneer printer who could drive into a village with a press mounted on a buckboard and a "shirt-tail full of type" and start a newspaper overnight are long past. A heavy item of capital expense is now required in publishing even a nonmetropolitan daily, and in a

---

[9] See the comment of Malcolm M. Willey and Stuart A. Rice, *Communication Agencies and Social Life*, "Introduction."

[10] The use of radio by the Great Powers in fomenting international discord and carrying on propaganda is an obvious example.

country shop the machine inventory alone may involve a sizable outlay.[11]

A few years ago the late William Allen White wrote: "In the last 50 years the cost of printing machinery—by that I mean press, linotypes, stereotypes, and photoengraving machinery—has risen so that a publisher has to be a capitalist with real standing at the town or city bank. For instance, the machinery to publish a paper in a village of 1,000 would cost, if bought new, $3,000 or $4,000. The machinery necessary to print a decent little daily newspaper in a town of 10,000 would cost between $25,000 to $40,000. The machinery to publish a daily newspaper in a town of 50,000 would cost nearly $100,000 and as towns grow into cities these figures advance until the publisher of a daily newspaper in a town of half a million needs an investment in machinery and working capital of two or three million dollars if he expects to compete with an established daily. . . ."

Mr. White's estimate of the cost of equipping even "a decent little daily newspaper" rises proportionately in the case of the metropolitan paper. In a city of 500,000 population, $1,000,000 will be invested in presses by a dominant daily journal. Stereotyping equipment will cost between $75,-000 and $100,000. Thirty-five typesetting machines will total $280,000. A good engraving camera runs to $5,000. This incomplete list of items of equipment gives some picture of investment costs for the reproduction of newspapers.

Back of presses and other equipment on a metropolitan daily newspaper is the "technology" of news production and transmission, a veritable web of telephones, telegraph wires, wireless, cable, radio, telephoto, printer teletypewriters, photoengraving equipment, and so on. Add to this a distribution system that requires a fleet of fast trucks and the use of railways and sometimes airplanes for delivery of newspapers to subscribers.

And printing machinery has its counterpart in apparatus for broadcasting and motion picture production.

Industrial Trends and Communications

Technology has led to industrial changes which have exerted still another pressure on the newspaper and periodical and molded the radio and motion picture. Industrialization stimulated the growth of cities and made it possible for the metropolitan newspaper greatly to increase its circulation and volume of advertising. The past fifty years have been marked by the organization of huge units of production and distribution to facilitate mass manufacture of commodities and to ensure the widest dissemination of machine-made, standardized products. The growth of big producing com-

[11] More than fifteen years ago Frank Parker Stockbridge estimated that the average investment in country weeklies then ran well over $15,000 "and it is increasing all the time." See "Small-Town Papers," *Saturday Evening Post*, February 25, 1928.

panies and the spread of banking, jobbing, and retail chains—these trends have been characteristic of the era. As private business enterprises, the communication agencies have not been immune from economic changes.

As William Preston Beazell, formerly of the New York *World*, has remarked: The newspaper "touches upon and is touched by too many aspects of business to have escaped so pervasive an influence."[12]

Increased business costs in other sectors of the industrial world have been paralleled in the field of communications. Newspaper production outlays have made steep ascents since the middle of the last century. Greeley founded the New York *Tribune* in 1841 with $3,000. Ten years later it was necessary to set aside a sum of between $50,000 and $75,000 to establish the New York *Times* and the paper was capitalized at $100,000. Increasing costs of production—equipment, materials, and salary outlays—caused steady advances in capitalization from that time forward. E. W. Scripps and other publishers were able to establish papers as late as the turn of the century on a relatively modest expenditure, but the New York *Herald* was sold for $5,000,000 in 1924 and a few years later the Scripps-Howard interests laid down a like sum for the New York *World*. The Kansas City *Star* was sold in 1927 for $11,000,000.

A similar curve appears in a comparison of early and current capitalization in other communication channels. The Kinetoscope Company, which distributed Edison's Kinetoscope machine and his early films, was a modest enterprise. Films for the early peephole shows in shooting galleries and arcades were sold outright to exhibitors for prices ranging from $10 to $25 a film.[13] The cost of an average screen feature production forty years later averaged between $170,000 and $250,000, with all companies producing pictures which greatly exceeded the latter figure. More than forty pictures cost more than $1,000,000 each during the boom season of 1936-1937.[14] Leo C. Rosten reported that the movie industry has "a capital investment in the United States alone of approximately two billion dollars—in movie production, theatres, and distribution."[15] The gross assets of the eight major producer-distributor-exhibitor motion picture companies in 1939 approximated, respectively, $90,000,000, $150,000,000, $60,000,000, $150,000,-000, $40,000,000, $10,000,000, $15,000,000, and $12,000,000.[16]

In the early days of radio, an independent radio station of sufficient power to enable it to blanket a local community could be built at compara-

[12] "Tomorrow's Newspaper," *The Atlantic Monthly*, July, 1930.

[13] Howard T. Lewis, *The Motion Picture Industry*, p. 3.

[14] Louis R. Reid, "Amusement: Radio and Movies" in Harold E. Stearns (ed.) *America Now*, p. 26.

[15] See his *Hollywood—The Movie Colony—The Movie Makers*, p. 3.

[16] "The Motion Picture Industry—a Pattern of Control," Monograph No. 43, Temporary National Economic Committee, U.S. Senate, 76th Congress, 3rd Session, 1941.

tively low cost. Stations depended largely upon phonograph records to build an audience which would listen to these pioneer programs because of the sheer novelty of radio. Costs were increased when stations felt compelled to pay talent fees to outstanding performers to hold listeners. When incomes mounted after advertisers agreed to sponsor programs, station owners were able to build more expensive stations of greater power. The curve of installation and operation costs shot sharply upward. The early entrance into broadcasting of big corporations—Westinghouse, the Radio Corporation of America, and other companies—set the pace. When the National Broadcasting Company, the first great chain, was created with the backing of the strongly financed RCA, the days when stations could operate on a shoe-string had disappeared.

Recent sales of radio stations to new owners indicate the change that has taken place in the economics of radio. The Washington *Post* paid $500,000 for station WINX; the Philadelphia *Bulletin*, $600,000 for station WPEN, and it cost Marshall Field $750,000 to acquire station WJJD. The New York *Times* acquired WQXR and WQXQ, a frequency modulation outlet, for a reported expenditure of a million dollars.[17] All these sales were approved by a majority of the Federal Communications Commission.[18]

The advent of frequency modulation (FM), which permits a large number of stations to operate on a single frequency if properly spaced geographically, aroused the hope that FM could be installed and operated with small capital outlay. By way of illustration, rural publishers who are fearful that the further extension of radio broadcasting will increase the difficulty of sustaining the nonmetropolitan press have investigated the cost of establishing stations. After learning that a single rural publisher could hardly afford to establish an FM station, it was suggested at state editorial meetings that newspapers in a single region could jointly organize a company for the purpose of raising funds to install a station in their region and begin an impressive campaign for regional advertising support.

These early hopes now seem illusory to rural publishers. Ownership of

---

[17] Bernard B. Smith, "The People's Stake in Radio," *New Republic*, July 3, 1944, p. 12.

[18] Clifford J. Durr, a member of the FCC, disapproved of the sale of the stations to the Washington *Post* and the New York *Times*. Commissioner Durr revealed that the purchase price of WINX was ten times its net worth and more than twenty-four times its net profit before taxes were charged. A somewhat similar situation held in the case of the charges for WQXR and WQXQ. Durr raised the question whether the "inflationary" prices were charged by owners who were "selling something they do not own and have no right to sell, namely, the use of a radio channel." He added: "The present inflationary trend in the price of radio stations, if continued, will tend not only to increase still further the already tremendous pressure on sustaining programs but also to push radio broadcasting more and more beyond the reach of any but the well-to-do. Certainly the inflationary trend should not be encouraged by permitting the capitalization of licenses." See "Durr Questions Large Prices for Radio Stations," *Editor & Publisher*, July 29, 1944, p. 42.

an FM station seems to be out of reach of either a single publisher or a group. While the expenses of operation of a station, including technical, program, and business costs, will vary with the community, as well as with the power of the station and the amount and kind of broadcast service for an area, it now seems obvious that costs to get a station started will run between $25,000 and $40,000.[19]

One expert estimates that after installation the local area must be in a position to support the station with a minimum of $15,000 worth of advertising,[20] and the station probably would be compelled to join an FM network to increase its revenue for operation.

Present AM radio interests are likely to develop FM stations since they have the resources required for the expansion of FM. Moreover, since 600 of the present 900 standard broadcasting stations are affiliated with one or more of the four national networks and since FM chains will, in all probability, tie in with the present AM ownerships, concentration of radio is likely to continue.

Effects of Standardization

While the machine age has increased production costs, our modern economy has developed standardization of products as a counterweight in fixing the prices of commodities for masses of consumers. Since standardization is part and parcel of our modern economy, it is not surprising that the standardized automobile, refrigerator, suit of clothes, and suite of furniture find their counterpart in the standardized motion picture, radio program, press association news report, syndicated feature and photograph. Even the book publisher has succumbed to the book club, which establishes "chain reading" habits.

In the case of the newspaper, three great press associations, with correspondents all over the country and in foreign capitals, supply all American daily newspapers with news in the same or similar form. Under this system of mass production and transmission, standardized news can be furnished in much larger quantities and at much lower cost than individual papers could possibly obtain for themselves. The national feature syndicates follow similar lines. Oswald Garrison Villard presents the two sides to this picture:

"Today when one travels through the country on a Sunday on a fast

---

[19] Present cost estimates vary. Ernest L. Owen in *The Newspapers and FM Radio* (Bulletin of the Syracuse University School of Journalism, 1944) reports that a 250- to 500-watt station, covering an area of twenty-seven to thirty miles in range, would cost approximately $15,000 to $20,000, and a 50,000-watt station, with a range of sixty miles and up, would cost more than $100,000.

[20] Don Robinson, "FM—Its Cost and Practicality for Newspaper Publishers," *American Press*, July, 1944, p. 8. Robinson tells the rural publishers that "the facts I have been able to gather all add up to the conclusion that you should FORGET FM."

train and buys successively the Buffalo, Cleveland, Chicago, Indianapolis, Toledo, and St. Louis Sunday papers it is hardly possible to tell which city is represented in a given mass of printed pages without careful scanning of the page headings. One finds the same 'comics,' the same Sunday magazines, the same special 'features' in almost all of them and, of course, in most of them precisely the same Associated Press news. . . .

"There is, of course, another side to syndication which, in all fairness, must be set forth. Without the syndicate, small town newspapers would be much duller and much less informed than they are. They could not print any news pictures; they could not broaden their pages; they could not have much—if any—news of New York, Washington, or other centers; their foreign features would probably almost disappear, except insofar as they were brought to them by the news associations. Some of the syndicated Washington and European correspondence is of genuine educational value."[21]

The reader can make his own analogies as far as radio broadcasting is concerned. While one of the reasons for the growth of the standardized chain program was the desire of chain owners to expand the size of radio audiences in order to increase the coverage for advertisers, there was in addition incessant pressure from the public for programs originating in great population centers. The highest-priced talent could not be moved to the studio of each independent station, even if the local outlet could afford the funds for expensive programs. Standardization and chain distribution solved the problem, while at the same time they decreased the amount of local material broadcast. Villard's comment on the usefulness of syndicate services for the press applies equally to the local radio station. Like the home-town newspaper, the station must rely on the national press associations and a chain's own foreign and Washington staff for superior news service.

It should be remembered, however, that the insistence of national advertisers that their programs monopolize the air in the evening hours has driven many "public service" programs off the air between 7:30 and 11 p.m., and has forced them to accept the less desirable morning and afternoon hours. Standardization in the field of advertising, coupled with chain distribution of programs, has thus affected the content of radio.[22]

Urbanization and Communications

Urbanization was another powerful influence which paralleled the growth of democracy and technological and industrial change in shaping the press. The significance of urbanization in connection with the historical

[21] "The Press Today," *The Nation*, June, 1930, pp. 646-647.
[22] Bernard B. Smith, *op. cit.*

increase in the number of newspapers and in their circulations is fairly obvious. Urbanization also affected the contents and tone of the newspaper.

The first American newspaper of continuous publication was the Boston *News-Letter* which first appeared on April 24, 1704. From 1720 to 1820, newspapers spread fairly rapidly over the colonies, "a phenomenon closely related to the growth of population and of trade and commerce."[23] In 1800 less than 4 per cent of the population lived in communities of more than 8,000. In 1850 this figure had risen to 12.5 per cent.[24] During this period of town development, many dailies were established, total publications rose to 2,303, and the press underwent marked transformation— changes in content and in techniques of writing and displaying the news.

Sociologists have attempted to explain this change by attributing it to the necessary adjustment of a social institution to urban conditions. Robert E. Park remarks:

"It is not practicable, in a city of three million and more, to mention everybody's name. For that reason attention is focused upon a few prominent figures. In a city where everything happens every day, it is not possible to record every petty incident, every variation from the routine of city life. It is possible, however, to select certain particularly picturesque or romantic incidents and treat them symbolically, for their human interest rather than their individual and personal significance. In this way news ceases to be wholly personal and assumes the form of art. It ceases to be the record of the doings of individual men and women and becomes an impersonal account of manners and life."[25]

Willey attributes the matter-of-fact writing of the early newspapers to the group intimacy and face-to-face contacts of the nonurban community. But when the emotion of a situation comes first to the reader through the printed word, the effect is achieved through the lively and intimate style of writing of the newspaper account. He concludes:

"It may be said that the function of the modern newspaper—at least one of its important functions—is to provide primary group experiences to people who live in groups where the majority of their contacts are secondary in nature. Further, with face-to-face intimacy gone, the old primary group mores no longer hold, and the topics that formerly were banned for public discussion and publication may now be published without fear of general offense."[26]

Circulation figures reveal the response to the techniques and methods

[23] Alfred McClung Lee, *The Daily Newspaper in America*, p. 18.

[24] These data from Willey, "The Influence of Social Change on Newspaper Style," *Sociology and Social Research*, September-October, 1928.

[25] "The Natural History of the Newspaper," Chapter IV in Park, Burgess and McKenzie, *The City*.

[26] Willey, *op. cit.*

of the urban press. These procedures found imitators in the successful magazines and when the motion picture and radio came into being, they too adjusted their "style" and "contents" to meet secondary-group demands.

Today the urban region is beset with problems of direct and fundamental concern to city dwellers. The economic, social and political difficulties brought on by depression and war demand, in addition to a lively news presentation and the "humanizing" of the news, a serious and sober presentation of today's occurrences. Editors realize today that intrinsically important news has a market value.

In precisely what manner have these forces—democratization, technological and industrial change, and urbanization—affected the communication agencies?

Two marked trends can be traced to the basic influences already discussed. A tendency common to all communication agencies is the unprecedented increase in the size of their audiences. A second common tendency is the trend toward large organizations. This has taken the various forms of consolidation, standardization, and chain operation.

Public Utilization of Media

The increased utilization of the agencies of mass impression is clearly shown in the widespread reading of newspapers. Circulation of daily English-language newspapers of general circulation stands at 45,954,838, an all-time record.[27] The public demand for newspapers has continued to increase steadily since the depression in the early 'thirties and only the wartime newsprint restrictions have held down circulation to its present peak level of close to 46,000,000.[28] Approximately one and one-third daily newspapers are made and sold for each family in the country. Interest in the war news does not account for all of these gains. Expansion of the field of interests catered to by the press in its news, feature, and editorial columns has helped to develop "the newspaper habit."[29]

[27] 1945 International Year Book Number, *Editor & Publisher*, p. 15.

[28] The demand for newspapers is characteristic of other countries also. The people of the British Commonwealth are omnivorous newspaper readers; see *Report on the British Press*, published by Political and Economic Planning Group. Before the war several of the popular dailies of Paris had larger circulations than any New York paper except the *Daily News*. In Japan "the very skies rain newspapers"; see "The Journalism of Japan," *University of Missouri School of Journalism Bulletin*, 1918. The increase in literacy has greatly increased newspaper reading in the USSR.

[29] See Douglas Waples, "Communication," *American Journal of Sociology*, May, 1942, pp. 910-911: "Since 1920 the total circulation of the English-language dailies rose from twenty-seven to forty-one million. The increase has been steady except for a sag of some four million during the depression years 1931-35. The year 1936 topped the year 1930 by 700,000 and the following year produced an all-time peak of nearly forty-one and a half million copies. The upswing since the war year 1939 will doubtless continue for the visible future."

The growth of radio listening is another phenomenon of our time. The first radio broadcast was made in 1920. Two years later it was estimated that there were fewer than 500,000 families owning radio receiving sets, but when the federal census made its first tabulation of radio set ownership in 1930, the enumeration showed that 12,078,345 families possessed sets. Something more than 35,000,000 families maintain homes in the United States. Of these, 33,716,000 have radio sets, according to an April, 1944, field study of the Bureau of the Census.

In 1900 there were no motion picture theaters in the country. The early 1900's saw the advent of the "nickelodeon." When the motion picture was transferred to a stage screen, the response of the public was immediate. By 1910, about 9,000 theaters and other amusement places were exhibiting pictures. The Motion Picture Division of the Department of Commerce estimated in 1931 that there were 22,731 picture houses in the United States, with an aggregate seating capacity of 11,300,000.[30]

Rosten reports[31] that "there are 15,115 movie theaters operating in the United States today—one movie theater for every 2,306 families, or for every 8,700 Americans." And he adds: "There are more movie theaters in the country than banks (14,952). There are twice as many movie houses as there are hotels with fifty or more rooms (7,478). There are three times as many movie theaters as there are department stores (4,201). There are almost as many movie theaters as there are cigar stores and cigarette stands."[32]

Available estimates of movie attendance are not wholly reliable. The Hays office reported a weekly attendance of 40,000,000 in 1922. The 1930 estimate was 100,000,000. Reports for subsequent years follow: 1931, 90,000,000; 1932, 85,000,000; 1933, 80,000,000; 1934, 77,000,000; 1935, 87,000,000; 1936, 82,000,000; 1937, 85,000,000; 1941, 85,000,-000;[33] 1942, 87,000,000; 1943, 93,000,000.[34]

Consolidations in the Communications Industry

A second common tendency among the communication agencies is the trend toward consolidations, standardization, and chain operation. In the newspaper field there is a striking trend toward the elimination of competitive newspaper situations, especially in cities of fewer than 50,000 resi-

[30] Willey and Rice, op. cit., p. 178.

[31] In Hollywood—The Movie Colony—The Movie Makers (1941), pp. 3-4.

[32] Ibid.

[33] This 1943 total is at variance with the estimate made by Donald Slesinger, who reports 60,000,000; see "The Film and Public Opinion," in Print, Radio and Film, edited by Douglas Waples. Rosten's estimate in 1941 is between 52,000,000 and 55,000,000.

[34] These estimates take no account of age groups. It was estimated in 1940 that two-thirds of those who visit motion picture theaters are under 30 years of age.

dents. While the total circulation of English-language daily newspapers has shown a steady increase, the number of daily newspapers has steadily declined. World War II has accelerated the number of suspensions. The peak in the total of daily newspapers was reached in 1909 with 2,600 publications. The total dropped to 2,580 in 1914 and to 2,441 in 1919, the latter decrease probably as a result of publication difficulties brought on by our participation in World War I.[35] In 1926 morning papers totaled 429, but fell to 384 at the end of 1931. Evening papers decreased from 1,576 to 1,539 in the same period. At the beginning of 1932, 1,923 daily newspapers of general circulation were published with an aggregate circulation of about 39,000,000.[36] The decrease in numbers of dailies continued in succeeding years. According to *Editor & Publisher's* estimate in October, 1943, the total in the latter part of that year was 1,754, although Dr. Raymond B. Nixon, director of the Emory University school of journalism, who has made the most scholarly study of recent changes in the basic newspaper pattern, fixed the total at 1,759. There were 27 casualties in the war year of 1943, according to Dr. Nixon's figures. At the end of 1944, the total number of English-language dailies was 1,744, ten below 1943, according to *Editor & Publisher's* report in its *1945 International Year Book Number*.

A noteworthy fact in connection with the decrease in number of dailies, which was sharp in 1942 and 1943 as a result of war influences on the publishing industry, was the record circulation attained by the newspapers that remained in operation. The circulation of English-language daily newspapers of general circulation in 1943 showed a gain of 1,017,979 copies daily or 2.3 per cent over the preceding year. The gain in 1944 over 1943 was 3.4 per cent. Though their number decreases, the daily newspapers that hold the field gather to themselves greater circulations and presumably increase their influence over readers.

The trend toward consolidation in the newspaper field is a second significant fact. Contrary to common belief, consolidation of newspapers is not a recent tendency, but can be found in all periods of the history of American journalism.[37] The rise in publication costs, however, has been a strong influence since 1914 in bringing about suspensions and consolidations.[38] Dr. Nixon's data reveal a trend toward one-newspaper cities, especially in cities under 50,000. His data are of interest in light of the

[35] See Alfred McClung Lee, *The Daily Newspaper in America*, p. 65.

[36] These data from Malcolm M. Willey and Stuart A. Rice, *Communication Agencies and Social Life*.

[37] See Frank Luther Mott, "History of the American Newspaper" in *Freedom of the Press* (Newspaper-Radio Committee, 1942).

[38] See Lee and also Willey and Rice, *op. cit.*, for data on amalgamations.

findings of two other students of communication problems who made earlier studies.

In December, 1933, Dr. Bleyer estimated that of 1,305 cities under 100,000 in population, only 163 had competing dailies published by independent companies. In 1,142 cities (87 per cent of the total) one paper or one company had a monopoly.[39] Dr. Bleyer cited 29 large cities of more than 100,000 population in which only one morning paper was published. In 1940 Professor George L. Bird of the Syracuse University school of journalism cited data to show that there were 1,201 cities with only one daily newspaper or with all newspapers in the community under a single ownership.[40] In 1942 Dr. Lee was of the opinion "that the trend toward an expansion of local monopolies and the contraction of cities with competing dailies has apparently persisted over a long period and will probably continue somewhat further." According to his data, the number of cities having only one English-language daily newspaper had risen from 981 in 1929 to 1,002 in 1930, 1,056 in 1936, and 1,092 in 1940.[41]

Dr. Nixon found that while there is a trend toward single ownership of two daily newspapers in cities between 50,000 and 500,000, there is on the other hand a clear competitive situation in cities of more than 500,000 population.[42] All five cities of more than 1,000,000 have three or more competing dailies. Dr. Nixon reveals that of the 1,384 cities which in 1944 possess daily newspapers, 1,093 have only one paper. In eleven entire states competitive ownership of daily newspapers in local communities has disappeared.

While the number of communities having two or more daily English-language newspapers has decreased during the past forty years, this phenomenon has not affected the total number of communities having daily papers. The number of *communities* possessing dailies has been on the increase.

A study of the trend toward one-publisher communities by Paul Neurath reveals the following phenomena:

During the period from 1930 to 1941, the total number of communities having two unallied papers, or papers with different publishers, decreased at about the same rate in cities of all sizes. The decrease was smallest in cities between 10,000 and 25,000. Fast growing communities have a better chance of acquiring a new second unallied newspaper, while stagnating communities have a better chance of losing a daily. There is more fluctua-

[39] See Willard G. Bleyer, "Freedom of the Press," *Journalism Quarterly*, March, 1934, pp. 22-35.

[40] George L. Bird, "Newspaper Monopoly and Political Independence," *Journalism Quarterly*, September, 1940, pp. 207-214.

[41] See Lee, *The Annals*, January, 1942, p. 46.

[42] Only two cities of more than 500,000 have a noncompetitive newspaper situation.

tion in the agricultural parts of the country in this process—more newspapers lost and more new ones established.

The metropolitan centers and all satellites of such centers have a lower rate of disappearance of dailies than the agricultural areas, but practically no new papers are established in satellite regions. The rate of disappearance of marginal papers was greatest at the beginning of the decade studied, when the depression was at its height. At the end of the depression the trend toward elimination of papers leveled off. It became high again at the close of the decade. Local radio stations and newspaper-radio affiliations do not seem to affect the trend toward one-publisher communities, Neurath found.[43]

The trend toward consolidation of newspapers is not limited to the United States. Shortly after the turn of the last century, the trend began in the British Isles. The changing structure of the press took the form largely of "combines" or chains. A reversal of the consolidation process began ten years ago and Wilson Harris, editor of the *Spectator* and author of a recent volume on the British press, believes that "further concentrations of ownership so far as the London papers are concerned do not seem to be foreshadowed."[44] Daily newspapers outside of London may be forced into further consolidations, however.

The trend toward newspaper consolidation can be accounted for as a phase of the economic force that has shaped other American institutions.[45] The desire for profit is, of course, evident. The desire for economic stability in a field where the publisher is dependent upon both the good will of the advertiser and the daily confidence and support of a sometimes fickle

---

[43] "The Trend Toward One-Publisher Communities 1930-1941," *Journalism Quarterly*, September, 1944. The study is part of a project which the Office of Radio Research, Columbia University, conducted under the direction of Dr. Paul F. Lazarsfeld.

[44] *The Daily Press.*

[45] Mott in *American Journalism* (pp. 635-666) has stressed the following factors that made consolidation seem desirable in the period prior to the depression:

(1) The wish to have opposition parties and cliques represented had resulted in the establishment of more papers than were necessary to serve their communities in the purveying of either news or advertising; and with the decline of partisan feeling as a dominant force in journalism it became possible to reduce the number of papers.

(2) Advertisers found it cheaper to buy space in one newspaper with general circulation, even at increased rates, than in two with overlapping coverage.

(3) Combination of a morning with an evening paper, allowing twenty-four-hour operation of a single plant, made for economy.

(4) Mounting costs, caused partly by the necessity of producing better modern papers, forced the elimination of unnecessary competition.

(5) The rules of the Associated Press in regard to new memberships, which made it virtually impossible to obtain a "franchise" except by the purchase of a paper that already held one, occasionally caused the absorption of a weak AP member by a paper with strong financial backing.

public imposes hazards which are sometimes not evident to analysts of the press.[46]

The sharp decline in newspaper advertising during the depression was unquestionably a factor in some of the suspensions and mergers that took place between 1930 and 1934. The competition of radio for the advertising dollar has adversely affected some of the weaker papers and compelled them to seek amalgamation with stronger rivals.

The criticism of one-newspaper situations, or the ownership of all the newspapers in a community by a single publisher, or absentee ownership as contrasted with "home" ownership of any newspaper, are well known to the reader. The ideal social situation is the publication in a single community of more than one independent newspaper. Monopolistic or semi-monopolistic situations give no assurance of a free play of diverse views in the columns of the newspaper except in the cases of publishers who realize that the public trust reposed in them demands in the one-newspaper situation more than ordinary scrupulousness in throwing open their columns to varied opinions.

The view that an economically independent press is to be preferred to a number of struggling and ineffective newspapers is recognized by trained analysts of the press.

Dr. Fred S. Siebert, Director of the School of Journalism, University of Illinois, testified in the Newspaper-Radio hearings before the Federal Communications Commission in 1941:

"I approve of a large number of avenues of communication: that is, I would rather have more than less. I would rather have seven papers in Washington, D.C., than three. I would rather have, in my own community, two papers than one.

"On the other hand, I would rather have a sound financially independent newspaper, one that could be operated at a profit, so as to be independent from all sorts of influence—I would rather have one of that kind of newspaper in a community, than six papers that were struggling to get

[46] The layman judges newspaper profits from reports of the fortunes obtained by certain publishers of great metropolitan newspapers. The yearly net profit of a great many nonmetropolitan dailies and the income from weekly newspapers is a good deal less than the public suspects.

The comment of Henry Luce bears repetition here: "Now the astounding thing is that all of this [referring to newspapers and magazines] is not a notably big business. The entire amount spent on advertising in newspapers and magazines in the great expansive year of 1929 was little more than a billion dollars. So that the whole newspaper and magazine business is not more than a billion and a half dollars per year at the very outside. That is apparently equal to the gross business of the General Motors Company alone. The entire press of the country cost less than the gasoline used by this country last year. And if the cost of the press be equally divided between males and females, we find that the amount spent by females on cosmetics was larger than their share of the cost of the press, including all the advertising of all American business." See Luce, "The Press is Peculiar," *Saturday Review of Literature*, March 7, 1931.

along, that were unable to give complete service, and that were subject to outside influences.

"That is the difference between our press and the European press. In many of the European countries, a small community would have six or seven newspapers, representing all shades of opinion. The community was usually unable to support them economically, as there weren't enough subscribers, and there wasn't enough advertising. As a result, they collapsed very easily.

"I would rather have a smaller number of financially independent newspapers than I would a mere number. . . .

"To me a multiplicity or large number of avenues or outlets doesn't necessarily mean diversification or diversity of outlets. By that I mean that in this country if you had six newspapers in one community, you would not necessarily have six different points of view, or six different accounts of an event."[47]

As Dr. Siebert's testimony indicates, multiplicity of newspapers in European countries in past decades has been based on subserviency to the point of view expressed by political parties or other interest groups that helped underwrite newspaper costs and losses. The basis of support of newspapers in the Anglo-American world provides them with a sounder base on which to operate and protects them more effectively against both outside pressure and "internal" dictation. The American public is not likely to prefer the counterpart of the European press to the economically stable newspapers of our own cities and towns, even though the average community prefers competing rival newspapers to single newspapers or single ownership situations. Production costs and the increased public demand for newspaper service of high quality, both in news and other editorial matter, are such that while a community can afford one good newspaper, it cannot afford two or more. This is an economic fact rarely considered by lay critics of the merger movement in the publishing field.

Chain Ownership and Standardization

Part of the economic trend which brought about newspaper mergers is the growth of newspaper chains since the turn of the century. Chain stores have their parallel in chain newspapers. Today many newspapers are linked up in chains owned by a single publisher or publishing company, a phenomenon of control and management which is present in the British Isles and Canada and which had a counterpart in the creation of newspaper chains in Germany during the Weimar Republic.

The chain movement was arrested in this country before World War II.

[47] See Fred S. Siebert, "The Meaning of the First Amendment" in *Freedom of the Press* (Newspaper-Radio Committee, 1942).

Chain owners disposed of weaker links in the 'thirties, partly because it became apparent that, unless a newspaper member of the chain was the dominant daily in a town, there was neither profit nor saving in such an affiliation. A changed provision in the income tax law was also an influence in the folding up of chain dailies. "Chronic losers" were dropped when unprofitable chain units could no longer be used to lower taxes by offsetting their losses against the profitable members of a chain.[48] Although the numbers in their chains have been curtailed, the Scripps-Howard, Hearst, and other chains have maintained strong influence in the newspaper picture.

The early Hearst and Scripps-McRae chains were the progenitors of the later groupings that arose about the time of the end of World War I. Robb[49] listed 30 different chain groups in 1924, a sharp increase over the thirteen chains operating in 1910.[50] The growth of chains in the ten-year period, 1923-1933, was marked, the number of chains increasing from 31 to 63. A total of 153 newspapers were included in the aggregate ownerships in 1923. In 1933 the total number of chain newspapers was 361.[51]

The chain movement seems to have reached a plateau in 1934 when both the number of chains and the number of newspapers in the groups stood at the highest total and a slow recession has taken place in the last decade. The significance of chains, however, is not alone in their total or the aggregate number of daily newspapers controlled by chains, but also in the geographical spread of the groups and in the circulation dominated by chains.

In 1923 the total daily chain circulation had reached 9,767,047 copies per diem,[52] or one-third of the total daily circulation in the United States. A little more than 42 per cent of all Sunday circulation was chain circulation. Chain circulation increased steadily from 1923 to 1930, dropped off during the depression, and then followed the upward curve of all circulations in 1934. Weinfeld's study reveals that daily chain circulation in 1935 was 41.6 per cent of the circulation for all dailies, and Sunday chain circulation a fraction more than 52 per cent of all Sunday circulation.

Chain circulation is concentrated in the largest cities. In a number of cities of 100,000 population or more only chain newspapers are available to readers.

Usually analysts have arbitrarily defined chains as consisting of two or

[48] Richard M. Boeckel, "New Influences on the Daily Newspaper," Paul Block Foundation Lecture, Yale University, November 15, 1938.

[49] Arthur T. Robb, *Editor & Publisher*, February 16, 1924.

[50] Alfred McClung Lee, "The Basic Newspaper Pattern," *The Annals of the American Academy of Political and Social Science*, January, 1942.

[51] *Ibid.* Lee's tabulations are based chiefly upon *Editor & Publisher* lists.

[52] William Weinfeld, "The Growth of Daily Newspaper Chains in the United States: 1923, 1926-35," *Journalism Quarterly*, December, 1936.

more English-language papers published in one or more places and owned and controlled by one individual, group of individuals, or corporation. Eleven chains listed in the 1945 *Editor & Publisher* Year Book comprise two dailies each. The fifteen or sixteen major groupings comprising five or more dailies each obviously are of greatest significance. The degree to which these larger chains standardize the news and follow a single line of editorial policy is the important problem.

Some of the dailies under common ownership are conducted in almost complete independence of one another. Some permit independence on the part of the editor or resident publisher, others exercise control over editorial policy on occasion, advising editors of the "central office" attitude on a major public question. Still others, as in the case of Hearst, demand uniformity on political matters.

Standardization of chain newspapers may take the form of physical appearance or policy or both. Hearst newspapers are easily recognized no matter in what city they are published. Some chain owners, however, do little to change the individuality of a paper when it is brought into a chain.

There can be little question that the superior resources of a chain have sometimes provided a superior service to a local newspaper after its incorporation into a group. Foreign and Washington news coverage, more authoritative special articles and special features may be available to a newspaper which once depended on one wire service and a limited budget of syndicate material. The argument against the chains is that the editor too often must "defer" to "New York" or "San Simeon" or some other center; that the chain unit does not adapt itself adequately to the community and serve its particular interest; that there is insufficient pride in parochialism, and that the recognition of local editors and reporters is slow.

The principal criticism of chain ownership, however, is that usually a number of independent voices become merged in one voice.

Communications Integration

Contemporary integration within the communications industry is illustrated in the case of newspaper ownership of radio stations. Although other examples of integration are not so advanced, there are indications of interest in television on the part of motion picture production companies and one newsmagazine publisher has launched into radio following an earlier production of documentary films. Two newspaper publishers have shown a recent interest in book publishing. Newspaper and press association management of several of the newspaper syndicates is nothing novel.

International Communications

The growth and development of the media of mass impression and the physical network of communications within the domestic area of the United States is matched by an extension of the American network in the international field. This external structure consists of the news-gathering agencies with their bureaus abroad, the privately owned international communication channels, the government owned or operated communications, and the American publishing companies which possess plants and distribution systems in foreign areas.

The American news-gathering agencies occupy a dominant position in the hierarchy of such organizations in the world and today they have only one serious rival in Reuters, the British agency. The United States is a news-minded nation and the American press possesses the resources to satisfy the demand for foreign as well as domestic news. In the past forty odd years, the American agencies have steadily expanded their news coverage and influence abroad.

In the period from 1900 to 1910, the Associated Press made great strides in advancing its position in the foreign field. After the Spanish-American War, when the interest of newspaper readers in this country was quickened and heightened in foreign events, the Associated Press determined to set up a more independent arrangement for covering the news abroad than existed at the turn of the century.[53] In 1902-1903 independent AP bureaus were established in France and Germany, obviating the necessity of relying upon London as the principal European news outlet. In the light of present news coverage, even these early advances were modest. The total expenses for AP foreign service in 1905 were $381,590 and monthly salaries ran to only $7,656. The AP later added bureaus in St. Petersburg, Vienna, Tokyo, Peking, Mexico City, and other capitals, all manned by trained American newspapermen. By 1910, the number of AP outlets in Europe had increased to sixteen and the total cost of foreign service was $279,616 in contrast to $2,316,071, the outlay for domestic news.

In 1927, the association had 29 foreign bureau points and boasted in addition many regular correspondents not attached to bureaus. There were further developments in the 'thirties and while World War II forced the withdrawal of men from important news centers, the AP, along with other American newspaper and news-gathering agencies, continued to maintain well equipped staffs at major foreign centers and on the battlefront.

The foreign expansion of the AP over the years can be illustrated by the listing of expenditures since 1900 for the coverage of foreign news: 1900,

[53] Oliver Gramling, *AP: The Story of News*, pp. 137-147.

$288,578; 1910, $277,102; 1914, $430,362; 1917, $564,604; 1922, $730,337; 1930, $813,093; 1935, $779,593; 1940, $1,047,383.

While the United Press entered the foreign field later than its rival, it made rapid advances abroad. UP began in 1909 a brief file of news across the Pacific to Nippon Dempo Tsushin Sha (Japanese News Telegraph Agency) and to the British agency, Exchange Telegraph, and shortly thereafter Roy W. Howard, then general manager, began the task of organizing agency bureaus in London, Paris, Berlin, and Rome, each in charge of a trained American correspondent.[54] UP invaded Latin-American areas in World War I and became the dominant American agency there. By 1921, it began to serve European papers and in 1929 boasted of thirty bureaus in foreign countries. This number increased in foreign territory until the "news blackout" of World War II forced the closing of bureaus in belligerent totalitarian and occupied countries.

The International News Service is the third American agency with foreign coverage by its own correspondents.

The strength of the American agencies has made it possible in late years for them to compete in the sale of their news with rival foreign agencies within the latter's own borders. The AP has its subsidiary organizations, the Associated Press of Great Britain, Ltd., an administrative organization which delivers news and news pictures to British newspapers, and La Prensa Asociada, which administers the AP service in Latin America. The United Press has its subsidiaries in Great Britain, in Canada, and in Latin America for the sale of news to foreign clients.

The expansion of American news-gathering agencies into foreign areas is not simply an interesting example of journalistic enterprise. It has importance in relation to our diplomacy, our trade and commerce, and the spread of our culture. In crises, news can become a weapon of propaganda. Historically, Great Britain was quick to realize the great importance to its commercial, financial, and diplomatic interests of carrying British news to its colonies and territories and to non-British areas as well. The British development of its communication channels and the support given to Reuters is a striking example of farsightedness in the protection of the national self-interest. Up to World War I, Reuters was gathering and disseminating the news of the world in a manner unrivaled by the combined efforts of all other non-British news agencies combined. This lesson apparently has not been lost on Americans.

American supremacy in the foreign news-gathering field raises a problem which will be difficult of solution. Except in a few countries like our own, where the press is financially strong enough to maintain strong independent news agencies, the gathering and distribution of foreign news is not

[54] Victor Rosewater, *The History of Coöperative Newsgathering in the United States.*

a profitable enterprise and must be supported either by a subsidy from the government or the leading banks in the country where the agency operates.[55] In the postwar world American press associations will be compelled to compete with government-controlled news agencies in other national states. Moreover, it is likely that keener rivalry than before will develop between American and British agencies for dominance in various world areas. It is no doubt a realization of future developments on the news front in continental countries that has stimulated the State Department, Congress, and the American press to favor international agreements guaranteeing freedom of the press and the right of journalists to gather news anywhere and also to write and transmit the news out of any country without hindrance.

International Physical Channels

Although American technologists were quick to bind a young nation together by setting up telegraph lines, linking up the country with telephones and producing printing presses for newspapers in every village and town, our most important developments in international communication are historically recent. World War I, however, greatly stimulated American interest in the creation of new channels reaching overseas.

Today nine or ten great privately owned companies have a stake in communication by cable, radio, radiotelephone, and radiotelegraph and upon them, as *Fortune* magazine remarked,[56] "depends whether the U.S. will grow in the future, as Great Britain has in the past, as a center of world thought and trade." *Fortune* might have added that self-defense and the success of American diplomacy are keyed with our communications position vis-à-vis other national states.

The major American companies possess facilities valued at $62,538,000 and their revenues in 1943 totaled $41,000,000.[57] The International Telephone and Telegraph Company is a holding organization whose business is divided among All American Cables & Radio, Inc., which operates 28,000 miles of cable between this country and Latin-American points; the Commercial Cable Company, operating six cables between this country and Great Britain; the Mackay Radio and Telegraph Company, with circuits to thirty-four cities in twenty-four countries; and the Commercial Pacific Cable Company, which operates a cable to Midway. Before the Japanese success in the Pacific, the circuit operated to Shanghai.

[55] See Ralph O. Nafziger, "International News Coverage and Foreign News Communication," *The Annals of the American Academy of Political and Social Science*, January, 1942; also the "Introduction" in his *International News and the Press*.

[56] "U.S. and World Communications," May, 1944, p. 129.

[57] *Ibid.*, p. 130.

The Radio Corporation of America, which was organized at the instance of the Navy Department at the close of World War I, is one of the great radio traffic corporations with broadcasting interests and direct radiotelegraph service to forty-five countries. The American Telephone & Telegraph Company (Bell System), which enjoys a great domestic business, also has a few score radiotelephone circuits in the international field. The Western Union Telegraph Company, which acquired the Postal Telegraph two years ago, operates eleven trans-Atlantic cables, five of which are leased from the British, and three cables to Cuba.

Press Wireless, Inc., owned by several large American newspapers and press services, is a carrier of press messages and overseas broadcasts and has connection with approximately ten countries. Tropical Radio Telegraph Company, a subsidiary of the United Fruit Company, does business largely in the Caribbean area where it pioneered radio. Other small organizations include the Globe Wireless, Ltd., owned by the Robert Dollar Company and used during the war for military purposes, which has Pacific and Caribbean radio telegraph circuits; the United States-Liberia Radio Corporation, a Firestone Rubber company subsidiary, with circuits to Liberia, and the South Porto Rico Sugar Company, with communication lines in the Caribbean and to Venezuela.

Both the Federal Communications Commission and the Navy Department champion the unification of all American international communication facilities, including radiotelephone, into "one government-regulated, government-aided, but not government-owned monopoly"[58] in order to meet unified foreign monopolies. It is argued by government spokesmen that American companies, dealing separately and competitively, are at a disadvantage especially in facing the powerful British monopoly, Cable and Wireless, Ltd. The British company has the most extensive cable service in the world, a system embracing 165,000 nautical miles, as well as extensive radio facilities. It provides special rates for intra-Imperial traffic. Proponents of the merger plan also argue that the merger would be more economic than cutthroat competition and would result in reduced rates to users of international channels. The introduction of radiotelegraphy and radiotelephony and the advent of international airmail has introduced a complex and confused situation from the point of view of our national self-interest in the view of one communications expert[59] and war developments in electronics will not simplify the problem. These developments have brought about a situation in which the government can seriously propose a complete reexamination of American communications policy and seek an integration of effort in the public interest. The merger plan is apparently up to the government since a concerted plan devised by the companies themselves might

[58] *Ibid*, p. 130.   [59] Ralph O. Nafziger.

be interpreted as an attempt to violate the Sherman Act. No one has yet offered immunity against this threat.[60]

The American government's own communications facilities and channels have expanded enormously since this country entered World War II and serious problems will be faced at the termination of the conflict regarding the disposition of this communications armament. Shall the structure built up in wartime be maintained in time of peace as part of a close-knit, all-embracing system with which our present privately owned international communications may be merged? Or shall the facilities be leased to private interests, or operated under a pooling arrangement with one or more of the United Nations which possess, like ourselves, strategic telecommunications bases? Is it wise to reduce the wartime structure to a mere skeleton? One of the most crucial political problems will be the decision on what to do with the new high frequency transmitters built for the Office of War Information for information and propaganda purposes and whether to dispose of that agency's news, newsreel, newsphoto and other channels which were opened up during the war in its twenty-seven or more outposts in almost as many countries. Aside from the government's facilities which were set up by civilian agencies, there remain the telecommunications of both Army and Navy which were greatly expanded during the war. What future policy will determine their operation and use?

At the outbreak of the war, the Army communications system, under command of the Signal Corps, consisted of half a dozen teleprinters and a radio network connected principally to stations in the United States and its possessions. Today it spreads out from Washington "like an immense spiderweb reaching to every corner of the globe"—the most far-flung communications system in the history of the world. Brigadier-General Frank E. Stoner pictures the amplitude and operations of this service: "Some ten million words a day, necessary to keep the nation's war machine in high gear, flash over the vast radio and wire channels of the Army Communications Service of the Signal Corps.

"Known familiarly as 'A. Com.,' the Army Communications Service itself extends throughout the country and overseas to the headquarters of the various Theaters of Operations—whether they be in London, Brisbane, Asmara, or Algiers. From these centers the system fans out through secondary networks of wire, radio, and submarine cable to American fighting men in tanks, planes, and the farthest outposts, as well as to the lonely Arctic, jungle, and desert stations along the widespread air-ferry supply routes."[61]

[60] "U.S. Now in Challenging Role for Communications Leadership," *Newsweek*, February 21, 1944, p. 102.
[61] "Army Communications," U.S. Signal Corps issue of *Radio News*, February, 1944, pp. 157-158.

Allied war correspondents made liberal use of Army facilities in both the African and Italian campaigns when other channels were not available and civilian agencies of the government utilized Army channels under similar circumstances.

While there is likely to be a sharp contraction of Army communications when land and air operations end, there may be a different outcome in the case of the Navy. The extensive world-wide system of Navy telecommunications, which has been used by civilian governmental agencies and the press since World War I is likely to suffer little curtailment at the close of World War II.

American Media Abroad

The wartime delivery of American books, periodicals, and newspapers to foreign areas and the establishment of printing plants by American companies for the production of printed media is a development of great significance in the field of communications. There is every likelihood that even after the return of Army, Navy, and Marine personnel to this country, many of the publishing houses will continue the distribution of periodical literature on a large scale to readers in alien lands who got their taste of the American printed product either as neutrals or as allies.

While the Special Services Division of the Army, including its Library Service Section, encouraged the export of American reading matter to the overseas post exchanges, hospitals, rest camps, outposts, Red Cross canteens and billets, enterprising publishers in some cases had already begun distribution of special editions of their periodicals and newspapers before the outbreak of World War II. More recently others established their own plants in foreign countries to insure speedy distribution or to avoid the heavy charges for intercontinental or overseas airmail delivery of the printed product.

In the spring of 1944, twenty-seven magazines and two newspapers were printing overseas editions, largely for American fighting personnel.[62] These editions, examples of which have been the "Battle Baby" edition of *Newsweek* and the "Overseas" edition of *Time*, are not limited in some instances to troop or navy areas, but are aimed at foreign civilian readers also. According to a release by *Time* in the summer of 1944, it printed editions in Cairo, Teheran, Calcutta, Sydney, and Honolulu, largely for Army readers, but it had established plants in Mexico City, Bogota, Sao Paulo, Buenos Aires and Stockholm for civilian readers. It prints a Canadian edition, and in Jersey City produces a special issue for air express destined for the West Indies, the northern parts of South America, and other areas.

[62] See article by Philip Schuyler in *Editor & Publisher*, April 15, 1944, pp. 11 and 46.

Newsweek was publishing editions of its magazine in Teheran, New Delhi, Honolulu, and Sydney in the summer of 1944 and three other special editions were sent from the United States to foreign shores. The *Reader's Digest* has its Latin-American edition and its overseas edition for American fighting personnel.

Both the New York *Times* and the Chicago *Tribune* print overseas editions in Honolulu and special "midget editions" of other newspapers are sent by first or second class mail to members of the armed forces. The London *Daily Mail* entered the international field with a weekly trans-Atlantic edition printed in New York which contains a digest of a week's issue of the British edition.

There are clear indications that American publishing companies will not surrender the niches they have gained in the international field at the close of the war, and that British publishers will attempt to follow the example set by publishers in this country. Moreover, signs point to an increase around the world in the number of news bureaus, and in the number of overseas personnel, established by American newspapers and periodicals, outmatching the set-ups of 1939.

January, 1945

THE POLITICAL COMMUNICATION
SPECIALIST OF OUR TIMES

BY BRUCE LANNES SMITH

WHO are the major propagandists and other communication specialists of our times in the field of politics? From what strata or
circles in society are they drawn? How and where were they
educated? What special education have they had outside the schools? In
what jobs did they make their starts in life? Whence come their skills in
binding or arousing other men? What can be done to ensure the use of their
skills for the welfare of the many, within an ordered framework of society?

Concern with these questions and their like is now widespread among
thoughtful men. It derives from a wave of "propaganda-consciousness"
that appears to have spread across the world in the past generation. Much
of it is due to the discovery in the 'twenties that a large part of the emotion
of the years of World War I was "manufactured." "This tremendous
chaos [the first World War]," says Mussolini, "gave birth among the
defeated nations to the dissolving intellectual skepticism from which
sprang the philosophy of realities."[1]

To skepticism there was added consternation when the Fascist and Old
Bolshevist regimes made open proclamation of their intent to employ the
"scientific" techniques of propaganda. Fear of the "Machiavellian" propagandist is deeply felt by many. A loss of faith in the older religious moral-
ities and a failure to develop a rational secular morality with world-wide
mass appeal has left millions deeply uncertain, both as to their own aims
and as to those of others. A deep sense of apprehensiveness and futility
arises from certainty of having been duped in the past; certainty that men
in high places today are seeking to continue that dupery; and *un*certainty
as to what one's own goals would have been had the dupery not taken place.
The specter of the omnipotent but amoral propagandist now haunts the
educated and semieducated strata of society—and worries even those strata
who are but dimly informed of the propagandist activities of recent decades.

Yet the mass political propagandist is not a specter in whose presence the
nervous can do nothing but shudder. He is a human being, product of a
family, of school days, of everyday surroundings, of job opportunities, of
opportunities to practice special skills. All these can be studied and, if
studied, perhaps altered in such a way as to make him what others desire
him to be.

[1] *My Autobiography* (London: Hutchinson, 1939), p. 40.

Background of the Inquiry

The first wave of twentieth century efforts to think out the social problem of controlling the propagandist came not in the form of biographical analysis but in the form of studies of "propaganda technique." Especially in the 1920's and 1930's, a heavy shelf of books appeared which called attention to the rhetorical and psychological devices used by the propagandist. Lippmann's *Public Opinion* (224a),[2] Chakhotin's *The Rape of the Masses* (6), Doob's *Psychology of Propaganda* (11), Cantril's *Psychology of Social Movements* (158), Lasswell's *Propaganda Technique in the World War* (14a), and Rogerson's *Propaganda Technique in the Next War* (21) may serve to remind us of these. In the United States, an Institute for Propaganda Analysis was founded, run mainly by journalists, with the general collaboration of professors. Its broad aim was to advise its subscribers whenever a propagandist used a "glittering generality," a "card-stacking device," or some other of those persuasive techniques that were generally known to the successful public speaker even before Aristotle pointed most of them out in his *Rhetoric* (138a).

It was not until late in the 'thirties that attention began to shift from *what* was said (content analysis), and *how* it was phrased for different parts of the public (technique analysis), to the study of *who* was saying it (the propagandist and his backers). It is true that there have always been books about "great" men, some of whom were propagandists; but until this time there appear to have been no deeply specialized efforts to determine the special characteristics of those classes of men whose "greatness" consists in their ability to manipulate the key political and economic symbols that have emerged thus far in the twentieth century.

Efforts in the direction of careful scientific investigations of this sort may be said to have begun with such works as Lasswell's *Psychopathology and Politics* (213), which contained provisional characterizations of some of the psychological traits of the political agitator, the public administrator, and the social theorist—all of whom, to some extent, may engage in propaganda. Leo C. Rosten published in 1937 an elaborate field study of political reporters, *The Washington Correspondents* (1508)—most of whom, by the nature of their occupation, are obliged to "slant" their writing to such an extent that mass propaganda becomes a significant part of their job.

Parliament, the U.S. Congress, the Nazi Reichstag and the Russian Communist Party have been sociologically studied in some degree.[3] How-

---

[2] Numbers in parentheses in this article are references to titles listed in the bibliography section of the present book.

[3] For a careful quantitative and qualitative study of Parliament, see James Frederick Stanley Ross, *Parliamentary Representation* (1341a). On a very recent Congress, Madge McKinney (1318). On "The Nazi Reichstag: Its Social Composition," see an article of that title by Ernest

ever, none of the published studies has been drawn up in such a way as to identify the social differentials between those who have greatly specialized in propaganda and those whose ascent is due to other social techniques, such as economic and legislative pressure on behalf of an economic interest group (the usual road to power in Parliament and Congress) or intimidation in the name of a political party (a frequent success formula in the Nazi Reichstag and the Russian Communist Party).

Up to this time, no factual analysis whatever appears to have been published on the social origins and careers of the principal governmental propagandists of the world. This is the more surprising in view of the highly dramatic careers of these men, and the fact that, as heads of state or as highly placed administrators, legislators, and publicists, they have so important a voice in the fate of Great Power nations. This essay represents a very limited attempt to fill the gap.

Preliminary Data on Governmental Propagandists

Table 1 provides a few preliminary data on a group of the world's principal propagandists in the period of World War II: the heads and propaganda ministers of some of the larger nations.

For obvious reasons the complete story of these men is not available, or publishable, at present. The information given here can be only a very modest attempt to indicate some of the directions a later inquiry might take. Whatever is deduced in this essay from this information must be viewed by the reader as in no sense a conclusion or an established "scientific fact." It is simply a provisional classification of highly insufficient data. These data are but the beginning of a scientific quest whose successful completion would call for many highly specialized investigators over a period of years. It is believed, however, that in most cases the data given are reliable. Most of the sources available in the Library of Congress have been exhausted in the course of this study. Wherever possible, statements made by the man himself were compared with statements by one or more presumably disinterested observers.

The presence of the propaganda ministers in Table 1 is no doubt self-explanatory: presumably they are superspecialists in political propaganda, or at least are thought to have paid special attention to it. The heads of state, while they may not devote so large a part of their time exclusively

M. Doblin and Claire Pohly (publication anticipated in *American Journal of Sociology*, 1945). On the Nazi Party, Hans Gerth (493). On the Russian Communist Party, Jerome Davis, "A Study of One Hundred and Sixty-three Outstanding [Russian] Communist Leaders," *Publication of the American Sociological Society*, 24, no. 2:42-55 (May, 1930); also N. S. Timasheff, "Vertical Social Mobility in Communist Society," *American Journal of Sociology*, 50:9-21 (July, 1944); and Barrington Moore, Jr., "The Communist Party of the Soviet Union, 1928-44," *American Sociological Review*, 9:267-278 (June, 1944).

to propaganda problems, may be (and perhaps usually are) even greater propagandists than the ministers. The very fact that a man is head of state requires him to accept tremendous propaganda responsibilities, both in getting and in keeping office. Moreover, it requires him to grasp and administer the coordination of propaganda with the basic economic and military functions of the state. Again, the head of state is usually the man who appoints the propaganda minister, so that a study of the two taken together may be expected to produce a better-rounded picture of the top propaganda personnel of the nation than would either alone.

In each case, the propaganda minister was chosen who held office in that capacity longest during the period of World War II. There has been a considerable turnover among propaganda ministers during this war. However, in each country for which data are given, one man, or at most two, seems to have carried the main ministerial responsibility for governmental propaganda during the greater part of the war period.

Of course we may ask ourselves whether a study of these heads of state and their propaganda ministers alone will furnish a sufficient basis for conclusive generalizations on the mass-political propaganda specialist of our times. Obviously, the answer is "No." Below these men in the social pyramid are numerous others who rival or exceed them in skill, and some of these will no doubt succeed to the power. Still others who never will have the power, but who are or will be leaders of the loyal (or disloyal) oppositions, may be equally influential in shaping the course of world events.

Finally, we may remind ourselves that the total complex of public opinion is not formed by political leaders alone. Indeed, these often have to steer a course along the channel or athwart the rocks created by other opinion leaders such as editors, publishers, radio publicists, teachers, the clergy, philosophers—and even, it is said, by scientists.

None the less, the top political leaders are generally the men who have the most to say in whatever our society does. They are specialists. Naked power and carefully cultivated fame are their deepest preoccupations, and this specialization gains them the mass support that enables them to keep the upper hand over most of the other important opinion leaders most of the time.

The fact that they have survived a ruthless competition and remained for many years at the top of the social pyramid of the western world suggests that they embody values that are deeply cherished by the populace at large. For this reason also they deserve analysis.

Consequently, the first part of this essay is mainly concerned with them; but in our later pages mention will be made of their relations to rival types of leaders.

Occupational Origins of Heads of State and Propaganda Ministers

Table 1 gives a number of clues to the social origins of the men in our sample.

Usually the most important single indicator of a man's social origins is the occupation of his father; or if there is no father, the occupation of the family in which he was raised. It determines to an overwhelming extent, in most cases, the type of neighborhood in which he will grow up—and hence, his personal manners, his tastes, his tone of voice, the words he can use, and many other traits that will determine his prospects of ascent or descent in the social pyramid. It probably will determine the type of education he desires and can most readily acquire, and almost certainly it will limit the type of education he can afford.

Because the family occupation lays down the pattern of the home, it deeply affects the son's potential skill with symbols. In the childhood home, the presence or absence of specialized varieties of books, of "highbrow" magazines, of music, conversation, and highly educated or entertaining guests, may sharply define the configurations within which the adult can later grapple with the complexities of culture. If the mother as well as the father is employed, and if this is manifested by a second set of cultural norms in the home, additional deepening and structuring of the child's tastes and aptitudes occurs. Mussolini's mother was a teacher, and his father a political agitator as well as a blacksmith. Remarkable contradictions in Mussolini's political repertory may stem from this. The coolly calculated and rather elaborate pedagogical techniques of the Fascist Youth Movement are one part of his repertory. The grotesque shoutings and struttings of his agitational public addresses are another.

How, then, do we classify the occupations of our subjects' families? Occupations could best be understood by means of a job classification that would list all the main types of gainful employment in world society. For present purposes, however, it was not thought necessary to classify *all* jobs in society, but only the broad *types* of jobs that exist in the Great Power nations. For the remainder of this century, industrial and military power, and power over the channels of mass communication, will probably be concentrated overwhelmingly in the Great Power states—especially the United States and Russia. It is scarcely necessary for the present analysis to concern itself with any social entities except Great Power nations, however interesting or ethically preferable they may be.

Seven social strata which are found in all of the Great Power nations form the basis of our classification. Table 1 is arranged in terms of these. Under the name of each stratum, various data are given.

The first figure is the approximate percentage of the gainfully employed who are in the stratum in a hypothetical but representative industrialized Great Power nation. This is a rounded figure taking into account the censuses of occupations in the United States, Germany, and USSR, all of which have many more similarities than differences in their total social structure, despite popular beliefs to the contrary.[4]

The second figure gives the percentage of the *heads of state* in our sample whose fathers spent most of their adult lives in the stratum in question. Very little movement from stratum to stratum was noted, incidentally, among this group of fathers.[5]

The third figure gives the percentage of *propaganda ministers* in our sample whose fathers spent most of their adult lives in the stratum. The fourth figure is the percentage of the total group—heads of state *plus* ministers—whose fathers belonged to the stratum.

Finally, there is a characterization of the career of the father, and the career of the head of state or minister himself. This will enable the reader to arrange the data in any other way that pleases him.

TABLE 1

HEADS OF STATE, AND PROPAGANDA MINISTERS, OF EIGHT GREAT POWER NATIONS, ARRANGED ACCORDING TO THE OCCUPATIONS OF THEIR FATHERS

STRATUM 1: Policy makers of monopolistic and basic business (including attorneys, public relations specialists, and other high policy advisers closely attached thereto; also persons receiving extremely large incomes therefrom).

(In USSR this stratum includes Five Year Plan executives and heads of large state enterprises.)

Per cent of the gainfully employed	0.3
Per cent of heads of state in this sample whose fathers were in this stratum	12.5
Per cent of propaganda ministers in this sample whose fathers were in this stratum	0
Per cent of heads of state plus propaganda ministers whose fathers were in this stratum	6.25

ROOSEVELT, FRANKLIN DELANO

President of the United States, 1933-

Born: 1882[1,2]

Father: Wealthy gentleman farmer, vice-president of Louisville and Albany Rail-

[4] U.S. data are from the 1930 and 1940 Censuses of the United States; *also* H. Dewey Anderson and Percy Davidson, *Occupational Trends in the United States* (Stanford University Press, 1942). USSR data are from *Socialist Construction in the USSR: Statistical Abstract* (Moscow: Soyuzorguchet, 1936); *also* N. S. Timasheff, "Vertical Social Mobility in Communist Society," *American Journal of Sociology*, 50:9-21 (July, 1944), in which p. 20 gives 1937-1939 census figures. German data are from Statistisches Reichsamt, *Statistisches Jahrbuch für das Deutsche Reich*, 1937, pp. 20-29.

[5] Owing to a truly startling oversight on the part of journalists and other biographers, data on the mothers were not sufficient for use in this table.

road and director of various corporations;[4] married daughter of a wealthy merchant.[2, 4]

Career: A.B., Harvard (majored in history and government);[4] attended Columbia University Law School (no degree); law practice, New York City, 1907-; member New York State Senate, 1910-13; Undersecretary of Navy, 1913-20; Governor of New York, 1929-33.[1, 2, 3, 4]

Sources: [1] *Who's Who in America*, 1942-43.
[2] *Current Biography*, 1942.
[3] Unofficial Observer (pseud. of Jay Franklin), *The New Dealers* (1934).
[4] Ernest K. Lindley, *Franklin D. Roosevelt* (1931), pp. 44, 46, 53.

STRATUM 2: Public officials (including legislators and permanent army, navy, and air force officers).	
Per cent of the gainfully employed	0.2
Per cent of heads of state in this sample whose fathers were in this stratum	50.0
Per cent of propaganda ministers in this sample whose fathers were in this stratum	0
Per cent of heads of state plus propaganda ministers whose fathers were in this stratum	25.0

CHURCHILL, WINSTON

Prime Minister of Great Britain, 1940-

Born: 1874[3, 4]

Father: Lord Randolph C——, M.P., Conservative Party leader, son of seventh Duke of Marlborough, who was also Viceroy of Ireland;[1, 2] married an American heiress.[2]

Career: Educated at Harrow and Sandhurst (military academy); entered Army 1895; fought actively in numerous campaigns, simultaneously acting as newspaper correspondent; Member of Parliament since 1900; numerous sub-Cabinet and Cabinet positions since 1906; author of a dozen historical and autobiographical books.[3, 4]

Sources: [1] "Churchill, Lord Randolph," *Dictionary of National Biography*, Supp. vol. 22.
[2] Winston Churchill, *Lord Randolph Churchill* (1906), pp. 3, 39-57.
[3] *Who's Who* (England), 1944.
[4] *Current Biography*, 1942.

FRANCO, FRANCISCO

Dictator of Spain, 1936-
Head of Falange, Sept. 1942-

Born: 1892[1, 2, 3]

Father: Commandant in Spanish Navy, who married daughter of another commandant.[1, 2]

Career: Attended Sacred Heart School at El Ferrol Naval Base; then studied at Naval preparatory school; had planned to attend National Naval Academy, but was unable to do so because entrance examinations had been temporarily suspended; graduated from Toledo Military Academy as 2d lieutenant in Spanish Army at 18; fought with Spanish army in Morocco at intervals until outbreak of Spanish Civil War; head of Nationalist Government, 1936-;[1,2] President, Political Junta of Falange, Sept. 1942-.[3,4]

Sources: [1] *Current Biography*, 1942.
[2] Johannes Steel, *Men Behind the War* (1943).
[3] *International Who's Who*, 1943-44.
[4] New York *Times*, 4 Sept. 1942, p. 1.

Hitler, Adolf

Führer of Germany, 1933-

Born: 1889[1,2]

Father: Cobbler's apprentice, later customs guard on German-Austrian border; retired to a small farm when Hitler was 4 years old;[1,2] thrice married: first to daughter of a customs collector, then to a tavern cook, then to a farm girl (Adolf Hitler's mother was the third wife).[1]

Career: Attended common schools until 16, when a lung ailment caused him to withdraw; later tried to enter art academy but was rejected as not able to draw well enough; after death of his mother (1908), lived in poverty in the slums of Vienna for 5 years; after spending some 2 years in Munich, also in poverty, served 6 years in German Army; wounded in front fighting; demobilized in 1920, he at once became an agitator on behalf of a "greater Germany," against Jews and Marxists, for a strong Reich government, abolition of unearned incomes, nationalization of trusts, etc., etc.; has agitated unceasingly since that time.[1,2]

Sources: [1] Konrad Heiden, *Der Führer* (1944 ed.).
[2] *Current Biography*, 1942.

Tojo, Eiki (Hideki)

Premier of Japan, 18 Oct. 1941-18 July 1944[4]

Born: 1884[2,3]

Father: Lieutenant General Eikyo (or Hidenori) Tojo,[1,2,4] a samurai[3] and "a leading strategist of the Russo-Japanese War."[5]

Career: Attended military schools until 1905;[1,5] graduated Military Staff College, 1915;[1,2,3] military attache, Germany, 1919;[1,2,3] returned to Japan, became instructor in various army positions and head of military gendarmerie, "the army's powerful secret police organization, which frequently supersedes the civilian police";[1,3,5] Chief of staff of Kwantung Army, 1937;[1,2,5] Vice Minister of War, 1938;[1,2,3,5] transferred from Vice Minister of War to head of army's air force, 1938;[1,2,3,5] Minister of War, July 1940[1,3,5]-July 1944.[4]

Sources: [1] New York *Times*, 18 October 1941, p. 5.
[2] *Who's Who in Japan*, 1939-40.
[3] *Current Biography*, 1941.
[4] New York *Times*, 20 July 1944, p. 1.
[5] *Time*, 3 November 1941, p. 24.

STRATUM 3: Enterprisers in medium and small business.	Per cent of the gainfully employed	in USA, about 6; in USSR, perhaps 0.5
	Per cent of heads of state in this sample whose fathers were in this stratum	0
	Per cent of propaganda ministers in this sample whose fathers were in this stratum	12.5
	Per cent of heads of state plus propaganda ministers whose fathers were in this stratum	6.25

DAVIS, ELMER

Director, U.S. Office of War Information, 1942-

Born: 1890[1, 2, 3]

Father: Small town banker in Indiana.[2]

Career: A.B., Franklin College (Ind.); Rhodes scholar; joined New York *Times* as reporter at 24; rose to be one of its chief political writers; author of many novels and short stories; CBS news analyst, 1939-42.[1, 2, 3]

Sources: [1] *Who's Who in America*, 1942-43.
[2] *Current Biography*, 1940.
[3] *Twentieth Century Authors*, 1942.

STRATUM 4: Professionals (except military and naval) and semi-professionals (journalists, trained social workers, etc.).	Per cent of the gainfully employed	4 to 5
	Per cent of heads of state in this sample whose fathers were in this stratum	12.5
	Per cent of propaganda ministers in this sample whose fathers were in this stratum	25.0
	Per cent of heads of state plus propaganda ministers whose fathers were in this stratum	18.75

De Gaulle, Charles

Leader of Free French (later Fighting French and French Committee of National Liberation), June 1940-

Born: 1890[2, 3, 7]

Father: Professor of philosophy and literature in the Jesuit College in rue de Vaugirard, Paris,[2, 3] who is said to have come from a line of the "petty aristocracy, provincial squires,"[5] and also to have "belonged not to the aristocracy nor even to the top strata of the middle class but to the intellectual branch of the white-collar class."[4]

Career: Educated at Saint-Cyr ("the West Point of France");[2, 3, 4, 5, 7] served at the front two years during World War I and became a captain;[2, 3, 4] wounded three times, won three medals;[6] prisoner of Germans, March 1916 to end of war;[2, 3, 4, 6] after war, served in Poland and Rhineland until 1924, then returned to teach in Saint-Cyr; studied further at Army Staff College and wrote books on the philosophy of leadership (*Le Fil de l'Epée*, 1932), *The Army of the Future* (1934) and *France and Her Army* (1938);[2, 3, 4, 6, 7] then held a series of important staff positions in French Army;[2, 6, 7] Undersecretary of State for War, June 1940;[3, 4] escaped to London in the same month and became leader of the Free French movement.[1, 2, 3, 6, 7]

Sources: [1] Helen L. Scanlon, *European Governments in Exile* (Carnegie Endowment for International Peace, Memoranda Series, 1943, no. 3), p. 7.
[2] Philippe Barrès, *Charles de Gaulle* (French edition, New York: Brentano, 1941).
[3] Johannes Steel, *Men Behind the War* (New York: Sheridan House, 1943), pp. 229-36.
[4] Busch, Noel F., "De Gaulle, the Prophet," *Life*, 13 Nov. 1944, pp. 100-15.
[5] *Time*, 29 May 1944, pp. 33-38.
[6] *Current Biography*, 1940.
[7] *International Who's Who*, 1943-44.

Pavolini, Alessandro

Italian Minister of Popular Culture, 1939-Feb. 1943[6]
Secretary General, Republican Fascist Party, 15 Sept. 1943-[7]

Born: 1903[3, 4, 5]

Father: Paolo Emilio Pavolini, Ph.D., professor of philology, University of Florence;[1, 2, 3] sufficiently prominent to be subject of article in *Enciclopedia Italiana* (1935);[2] member of Royal Academy of Italy.[2, 3]

Career: "Educated in Florence";[3] apparently has "Laureate" (i.e., bachelor's) degree in law and social sciences;[4, 5] took part in March on Rome, 1922; Secretary, Fascist Provincial Federation, Florence, 1929; member, National Directorate of Fascist Party, 1932-43; editor *Il Bargello*; editor *Il Messagero*, 1943; author of half a dozen books.[3, 4, 5]

Sources: [1] *Chi è?*, 1928.
[2] *Enciclopedia Italiana*, 1935, article on "Pavolini, Paolo Emilio."
[3] *International Who's Who*, 1943-44.
[4] *Chi è?*, 1940.
[5] *Who's Who Monthly Supp.*, March 1943.
[6] New York *Times*, 6 Feb. 1943, p. 3.
[7] New York *Times*, 16 Sept. 1943, p. 4.

ZHDANOV, ANDREI A.

Head of Propaganda and Agitation Section of Central Committee, Communist Party of USSR, 1938-[1, 4, 5]

Born: 1896[1, 2]

Father: Variously described as "an inspector of public schools"[1] and as "a priest."[3, 6]

Career: Attended secondary school in Tver and then spent about 1 year in Moscow Agricultural Institute;[1] left to work in underground revolutionary organizations; fought in Russian Army 1916-17;[1, 2, 3] engaged in military and political work in Tver and Gorky regions, 1917-34;[1, 2] 1930, became member of Central Committee, CPSU;[2] secretary of Central Committee, 1934-;[2, 4] member of Executive Committee of Comintern;[2, 4] reorganized Propaganda and Agitation Section of Central Committee, 1938;[5] secretary, Leningrad Provincial and City Committees of CP, 1934-;[2] headed defense of Leningrad in World War II;[3] said to be intimate friend of Stalin.[3]

Sources: [1] *Istoriko-revolutionni kalendar* (1941), pp. 105-106.
[2] *Politichki slovar* (1940), p. 189.
[3] *Time*, 25 Oct. 1943, p. 30.
[4] *Political Handbook of the World*, 1942, p. 163 and 1943, p. 161.
[5] Werner Markert in *Osteuropa*, 14: 289 (January 1939).
[6] Richard E. Lauterbach, associate editor of *Life*, in *Life*, 1 Jan. 1945, p. 65.

STRATUM 5: Skilled nonfarm manual laborers; artisans.

Per cent of the gainfully employed	about 25
Per cent of heads of state in this sample whose fathers were in this stratum	25.0
Per cent of propaganda ministers in this sample whose fathers were in this stratum	12.5
Per cent of heads of state plus propaganda ministers whose fathers were in this stratum	18.75

GOEBBELS, PAUL JOSEPH

German Minister of Propaganda, April 1933-

Born: 1897[1, 2, 3]

Father: Factory worker, then a foreman and later a manager; married daughter of
a smith;[1, 2] both families said to be descended from farmers and small business folk.[3]

Career: Attended Catholic *Volksschule, Gymnasium,* six major German universities;
Ph.D. (philology, literature), Heidelberg, 1921; Nazi agitator and journalist since 1922; editor and founder of several principal Nazi newspapers
and magazines.[1, 2, 3]

Sources: [1] *Current Biography,* 1941.
[2] Oswald Dutch, *Hitler's Twelve Apostles* (1940), p. 68.
[3] *Deutsche Führerlexikon,* 1934-35.

MUSSOLINI, BENITO

Duce of Italy, 1922-

Born: 1883[1, 2, 3]

Father: Village blacksmith and labor leader, who married teacher in village elementary school;[1, 3] became tavern keeper later in life.[3]

Career: Elementary schools at Predappio and Faenza; graduated from Normal
School at Forlimpopoli; at 18 and 19, taught in primary school; became
Socialist agitator, editor of Socialist newspapers; led numerous minor up-
risings; in 1914 unexpectedly came out in favor of Italian participation in
World War I; fought at front two years; badly wounded; discharged,
August 1917; returned to publishing political newspapers, shifting from
Socialism to Fascism; dictator of Italy, 1922-.[1, 2, 3]

Sources: [1] B. Mussolini, *Autobiography* (1939).
[2] Various issues of *Chi è?*
[3] *Current Biography,* 1942.

STALIN, JOSEPH

Secretary, Communist Party of USSR, 1922-

Born: 1879[1, 2]

Father: Peasant shoemaker, who occasionally worked in factories; married daughter
of a serf.[1, 2]

Career: Attended theological seminary (curriculum religious in tone and roughly equivalent to that of a Russian high school) in Tiflis to age 19; was then expelled or withdrew from seminary, already one of the most energetic revolutionary organizers of Tiflis; from that time on, engaged continuously in party organization and military activity.[1, 2]

Sources: [1] *Istoriko-revolutionni kalendar* (1941), pp. 695-719.
[2] Boris Souvarine, *Stalin* (1939), *passim*.

STRATUM 6: Landholders and farmers.

	Per cent of the gainfully employed	in USA, about 20; in USSR, about 45
	Per cent of heads of state in this sample whose fathers were in this stratum	0
	Per cent of propaganda ministers in this sample whose fathers were in this stratum	12.5
	Per cent of heads of state plus propaganda ministers whose fathers were in this stratum	6.25

BRACKEN, BRENDAN

British Minister of Information, 21 July 1941-[5]

Born: 1901[1, 4, 6]

Father: Landholder; Irish gentry(?).[7]

Career: Educated at Sydney (Australia)[2, 4, 6] and at Sedbergh (England) (the latter an upper class preparatory school);[1, 4] does not seem to have attended university; "at 24 he started a whole string of financial papers by founding *The Banker* and the *Financial News, Journal of Commerce*, and *Investors Chronicle*";[2] editor of *The Banker*;[6] chairman of *Financial News*, Ltd.;[6] managing director of *The Economist*[2, 3, 6] and owner of 50% of its stock;[2] member of Parliament, 1929-;[1, 4, 6] director of Eyre and Spottiswoode, Ltd. (publishers);[6] close personal associate of Winston Churchill since 1923.[1]

Sources: [1] *Current Biography*, 1941.
[2] *Newsweek*, 28 July 1941.
[3] Cedric Larson, "British Ministry of Information," *Public Opinion Quarterly*, 5:430-31 (Fall 1941).
[4] *Who's Who* (England), 1944.
[5] London *Times*, 21 July 1941.
[6] *Kelly's Handbook of the Titled, Landed and Official Classes* (1940).
[7] Inference from *Current Biography*, 1941; and from an oral statement by a British political scientist who is acquainted with Bracken. The Washington and New York offices of the British Ministry of Information state that they are unable to furnish information on this point.

STRATUM 7: Unskilled laborers, urban and rural.	Per cent of the gainfully employed	35 to 40
	Per cent of heads of state in this sample whose fathers were in this stratum	0
	Per cent of propaganda ministers in this sample whose fathers were in this stratum	0

STRATUM UNKNOWN: No data were available on the occupations of the fathers of three men in the sample (37.5% of the propaganda ministers, or 18.75% of the total sample). These were:

(1) Pierre Maillaud, Free French journalist and broadcaster.
(2) Ramón Serrano Suñer, propaganda specialist of the Spanish Falange. Serrano is described, however, as coming from a "middle class family."
(3) Masayuke Tani, President of the Japanese Cabinet Board of Information. He is said in a Japanese *Who's Who* to be "of a samurai family."

However, information on the careers of the men themselves was available, and is presented below.

MAILLAUD, PIERRE

Founder, Chairman and Managing Editor of Agence Française Indépendante, 1940-44
BBC French political commentator, 1940-44

Born: 1909[1]

Father: No data.[6]

Career: "Ed. Paris;"[1] referred to as "Dr. Maillaud" in review by Varian Fry (*New Republic*, 19 July 1943, p. 84) which gives no other biographical data on him; "Political commentator, *La Journée Industrielle*, 1927-28, *Le Soir*, 1929-30; with Havas Foreign Services, 1931-40, Asst. Man. London 1933-39; Acting Man. 1940; London correspondent *L'Europe Nouvelle*, 1935-39; founded Agence Française Indépendante 1940, now Chairman and Managing Director; BBC French political commentator 1940-; Publications: *Onyx* (poems) 1930; *France* 1931."[1] Also author of *France* (London: Oxford, 1943). Occasional contributor to New York *Times*[2] and London *Spectator*[3]; one of four directors of French Information Agency, 21 Dec. 1943-March 1944;[4] resigned to become war correspondent with French forces, summer 1944.[5]

Sources: [1] *International Who's Who*, 1943-44.
[2] E.g., New York *Times*, 23 Feb. 1941, IV, 5:3; 11 June 1944, VI, 16.
[3] *International Index to Periodicals*, 1940 through 1944.
[4] *France* (Free French newspaper published in London), 21 March 1944, p. 1.
[5] *Pour la Victoire* (Free French newspaper published in New York), 26 August 1944, quoting in French translation an article it says is from the London *Newspaper World* (date not given).
[6] Free French Press and Information Service (New York) states that it cannot furnish information on this point.

NOTE: Although the National Liberation Committee's Commissioner of Information, appointed in June 1943 (New York *Times*, 8 June 1943, p. 1), was Henri Bonnet, he was not selected for purposes of this study. Primarily not a political propaganda specialist but an administrator long identified with League of Nations officialdom, Bonnet appears to have been chosen for the Commissionership, at a time when factions in the Committee could not agree, because he was known as a "non-political" figure. From mid-1940 until that time, Pierre Maillaud had been a central personality in Free French propaganda operations in London.

SERRANO SUÑER, RAMÓN

> Director of Spanish Falange, 1937-Sept. 1942[3]
> Minister of Press and Propaganda, 1939-40[4]

Born: 1901[1, 2, 6]

Father: "Middle class."[6]

Career: Studied law, Universities of Madrid, Rome, and Bologna;[1, 2, 6] had an "obscure" law practice and certain "minor" judicial posts in Saragossa;[1, 2, 6] Catholic Party deputy in Cortes, 1933-36;[1, 4, 6] married sister of Francisco Franco's wife, daughter of a wealthy merchant;[1, 2, 6] received many important posts after Franco's seizure of power (Governor of Valladolid, Minister of Interior, Foreign Minister, etc.);[1, 2, 4, 6] dismissed from positions as Foreign Minister and as head of Falange by Franco, Sept. 1942;[3] member of Falange National Council, 1942-.[4, 5]

Sources: [1] *Current Biography*, 1940.
[2] Johannes Steel, *Men Behind the War* (1943).
[3] New York *Times*, 4 Sept. 1942, p. 1.
[4] *International Who's Who*, 1943-44.
[5] New York *Times*, 24 Nov. 1942, p. 8.
[6] Thomas J. Hamilton, *Appeasement's Child: The Franco Regime in Spain* (1943), p. 117.

TANI, MASAYUKE

> President, Japanese Cabinet Board of Information, 18 Oct. 1941-20 April 1943[4]
> Foreign Minister, 17 Sept. 1942-20 April 1943[4]

Born: 1889[1, 2, 3]

Father: Samurai;[1] probably of lower middle income.[5]

Career: Graduated in political science from Tokyo Imperial University School of Law, 1913;[1, 2] passed diplomatic and consular examinations,[1] and entered Foreign Service, 1914;[1, 2] served in Canton, Hamburg, Holland, 1914;[2] Third Secretary of Embassy, France, 1918, and Second Secretary, 1920;[2] Counselor of Foreign Office, 1923;[1, 2] secretary to Minister of Foreign Affairs, 1923;[1] married Sumiko, sister of Baron Tadamara Shimazu;[1, 2] Chief, First Section of Asiatic Bureau, 1924;[1, 2] First Secretary of Embassy, U.S.A., 1927;[2] later, Counselor of Embassy in Manchukuo, Minister to Austria and Hungary (1936-37);[1, 2, 3] Special Envoy to China, 1937;[3] Vice-Minister of Foreign Affairs, 1939-40.[3]

Sources: [1] *Jinji koshin roku* (Japanese-language *Credit Register*), 1937.
[2] *Who's Who in Japan*, 1939-40.
[3] *International Who's Who*, 1943-44.
[4] *London Times Index.*
[5] Oral statement to the writer by a U.S. journalist who has specialized on Japan for many years and who knows Tani personally.

Table 1 shows that not industrial and commercial management nor economic planning nor manual labor, but political and professional activities, were the principal jobs of the fathers of our group. No less than 7 of the 13 fathers for whom we have data—Churchill, De Gaulle, Franco, Hitler, Pavolini, Tojo, Zhdanov—were in the public official and professional strata. If we consider banking a profession, we may add an eighth, the father of Elmer Davis.

Two fathers—those of Bracken and Roosevelt—were apparently "country squires." The traditional social orientation of the "squire" of course includes a high esteem for the symbols of politics and the professions. Often the "squire" shows a considerable skill in using these symbols, though perhaps with less stamina and perseverance than the full-time public official and professional man.[6]

Next to the public officials and professionals, the most important group is that of the nonfarm manual laborers: the fathers of Goebbels, Mussolini, and Stalin. No manual laborers exclusively employed on the farm appear in our sample, the father of Bracken evidently being not a farm worker but a landlord, and the father of Stalin an artisan and a shoe factory employee as well as a peasant.

The relative contribution of various social strata to the political leadership of Great Power nations appears more clearly if we bear in mind the total distribution of the gainfully employed (some data on this are in Table 1). Less than $\frac{1}{2}$ of 1 per cent of the gainfully employed are in the industrial policy makers and public official strata combined. Only about 4 or 5 per cent of the gainfully employed are professionals. Perhaps 5 or 6 per cent are small and medium business enterprisers in the capitalist countries. Only a fraction of 1 per cent are in the private enterpriser class in the USSR today, if we may judge from official figures. The white collar class as a whole (including big industrial leaders, public officials, professionals, small business, and the clerical groups) comprises only 15 to 25 per cent of the gainfully employed in a Great Power nation. The remaining 75 to

[6] For a description of the preoccupations of Franklin Roosevelt's father, consult Ernest K. Lindley, *Franklin D. Roosevelt* (New York: Blue Ribbon, 1931); also, Rita Halle Kleeman, *Gracious Lady: The Life of Sara Delano Roosevelt*, the President's mother (New York: Appleton-Century, 1935).

85 per cent are "blue collar"—men who work with their hands in commerce, industry and agriculture.

Among the fathers of our heads of state and propaganda specialists, the general ratio between white and blue collar occupations is almost exactly reversed: of the 13 for whom we have data, 10, or 76.2 per cent, were apparently white collar men throughout their careers. Of these all were enterprisers, professionals, squires, or officials; none were clerks. Three others (the fathers of Goebbels, Hitler, and Mussolini) began as manual workers but had risen into the white collar class by middle life. Only the father of Stalin appears to have remained at manual labor.

Thus the clerical workers and the manual workers, whether urban or rural, produced only one-quarter or one-fifth of the number of leaders they would have produced if recruits into positions of top political and propaganda leadership had been drawn proportionately from all the social strata. This finding is consistent with the findings of numerous other studies on the occupations of the fathers of political, literary, scientific, and religious leaders. For example, 76.3 per cent of the Washington correspondents were found by Leo C. Rosten to be children of the "professional, proprietary or clerical groups," while 10.8 per cent were children of urban laborers and 9.4 per cent were children of farmers. Children of professionals constituted 43.3 per cent of the total.[7]

We might infer that having one or more parents in public office or the professions focuses the attention of the child on symbols of social interaction and public responsibility at an early age. This predisposes him to function with relative skill in the arenas of high national politics, where success depends to a great extent on a large vocabulary, on a broad and specific knowledge of social institutions and political techniques, on capacity and leisure for periods of cool calculation and detachment, and on an appearance of understanding problems—especially economic problems—that are supposedly beyond the grasp of the common man.

Public self-dramatization combining earnestness with self-assurance is also an essential. Imitation of the father may ingrain these habits in the son of a professional man or a public official while he is still an infant. Earnestness comes often, but public self-assurance seldom, to those born into the manual laboring groups. "Mr. Willkie, you know I grew up a Georgian peasant. I am unschooled in pretty talk," said shy Joseph Stalin,[8] who seldom makes an unnecessary public appearance.

The disproportionate influence of the nonclerical white collar classes in producing political and propaganda leaders is made still clearer if we look

---

[7] *The Washington Correspondents* (1508), pp. 153, 330. In general, see Pitirim Sorokin, *Social Mobility* (New York: Harpers, 1928).

[8] Wendell L. Willkie, *One World* (1943), Pocket Book edition, p. 71.

at the families of the four men in our sample who alone had fathers who were manual laborers.

(1) In the case of Goebbels, who came from families of manual workers on both sides, there is no evidence of early direct exposure to an environment emphasizing professional or public responsibilities. However, the father apparently rose from factory labor to a foremanship. Perhaps the son's ascent can be traced to the fact that his deformity, stunted physique, and psychopathology made him prefer intellectual, symbolic, and agitational activities to manual or commercial jobs.

(2) In Hitler's case, the father began as a cobbler's apprentice, but by the time of Hitler's birth, the father, then 52 years old, was a public official and held a respected white collar position in his small community. Hitler's mother, a peasant's daughter, appears to have encouraged her son to become an artist—again a white collar aspiration.

(3) A strong white collar influence seems to have come into Mussolini's life through his mother, a schoolteacher who insisted that her son be a teacher and who sent him through normal school. A considerable influence of the same sort appears to have been exerted by his father, who, though not a public officeholder, was a celebrated trade union leader and agitator for reform and enjoyed a large measure of political influence locally. It is also noteworthy that, in the course of his career, the father rose from the blacksmith shop to proprietorship of the local tavern—a white collar enterpriser.

(4) Stalin's mother, although the daughter of a serf, appears to have had intense ambitions for the ascent of her son into the professional classes. She succeeded in keeping him in theological school until he revolted at the age of 19.

Thus, our data, though admittedly based on too small a number of cases to permit a generalization, may lead us to the following hypotheses, which may be tested as further cases accumulate:

(1) A man whose father was a manual laborer has perhaps one-quarter or one-fifth of the chance of the son of a white collar worker to rise to the top of the pyramids of political and propaganda skill in the Great Power nation.

Of course this does not by any means imply that the manual worker's son is not potentially as able, or more able. It does mean that higher income and much greater educational and cultural opportunities would be needed to enable the worker's child to compete successfully with the child of the upper white collar classes. Proof of this is seen in the fact that a two-generation ascent from the manual laboring to the upper white collar brackets is not at all uncommon: the father ascending into a lesser middle class position and the son climbing from that vantage point into a post of high prominence.

(2) If the manual worker's child rises to the top, his ascent may be due in no small measure to the influence of a highly articulate or insistent mother who may have displaced her own frustrated ambitions onto the son, forcing and fostering his development in school and his early assumption of social responsibilities. This hypothesis may be supported by the record of the early assumption of adulthood by Goebbels, Hitler, Mussolini, and Stalin, all of whom had revolted vigorously against their families and (except Hitler) were experienced agitators by the age of eighteen or twenty.

(3) The ascent of a worker's son may also be traced to symbolic compensation for very great physical or psychological handicaps—too great to be overcome within the normal routines of muscular work and plain living that are characteristic of the worker's family. The small, club-footed Goebbels is an extreme case. Hitler was frail and obviously neurotic in childhood, had a severe lung ailment in adolescence, and was badly injured during the first World War. Mussolini seems to have had psychological difficulties throughout his childhood (uncontrollable homicidal rages). In addition, he was severely shocked and wounded in World War I, and hospitalized for a long time. Finally, for the past 20 years he has suffered severely from abdominal ulcers—a physical disorder frequently traceable to childhood emotional disturbances.[9]

Stalin's mother has said: "When [Stalin] entered the theological Seminary he was fifteen and as strong as a lad could be. But overwork up to the age of 19 pulled him down, and the doctors told me that he might develop tuberculosis. So I took him away from school. He did not want to leave. But I took him away. He was my only son."[10] There is, however, no other record of physical disability in Stalin's career.

Small physical stature may also drive a worker's son to seek symbolic compensation. Hitler and Mussolini are of no more than average height for their cultural groups, while Goebbels and Stalin are well below, Stalin being reported as five feet four or five.[11]

(4) The rise of a worker's son to the top is much more probable during a revolutionary period, and in a nation in which the standard of living is felt by a significant section of the middle class to be falling or unsatisfactory. Contrast the Germany of Goebbels' young manhood, the Russia of Stalin's, and the Italy of Mussolini's with the England, United States, France, Japan, and even Spain, of the same period.

[9] See, for a recent report on Mussolini's physical condition, New York *Times*, July 17, 1944, p. 1.

[10] Boris Souvarine, *Stalin* (New York: Alliance, 1939), p. 5.

[11] Willkie, *One World* (1943), Pocket Book edition, p. 68.

Income Origins of Heads of State and Propaganda Ministers

Income, of course, is highly correlated with the strata into which we have classified the population of the Great Power nation. With certain obvious exceptions, the incomes of persons in Stratum 1 are considerably higher than those of Stratum 2, and so on. In the United States, the top incomes, before taxes, are several thousand times the size of the median incomes; after taxes, a wealthy man in the United States may still receive several hundred times as much income as the median family.[12] In Russia, top incomes appear to be about twenty-five or thirty times the pay of the ordinary worker.[13] Other nations are ranged between these two extremes.

A man's father's income, like his father's occupation, will determine his access to education, and also the extent of his ability to get deference and immediate gratification of many of his impulses.

Table 2 presents data on the *probable* income positions of the fathers of our sample of heads of state and propaganda ministers. Naturally, it is impossible to obtain conclusive data on this "delicate" subject at this time. The reader is warned that it has been necessary to impute an income in each case, on the basis of available data on the father's standard of living and on the customary incomes of persons in his occupation. Such imputed data may be of interest if they are not taken for more than they are worth.

The "A, B and C income groups" used in the table are similar to the ones customarily used by professional students of public opinion, such as the *Fortune* poll, the American Institute of Public Opinion, and the National Opinion Research Center.

In common speech, when we speak of the "upper income group," we usually mean the upper 5 per cent or so—those who, in the United States, have an annual family income over three or four thousand dollars.[14] By "middle income group," we usually mean the next 15 or 20 per cent—those from about two to about three or four thousand dollars. And the "C" group are the rest—the bottom 75 to 80 per cent—below about two thousand dollars per year per family.

[12] U.S. National Resources Committee, *Consumer Incomes in the United States* (Washington, D.C.: Government Printing Office, 1938). The median annual family income in the United States in 1935-1936, when the most recent dependable statistics were collected, was about $1,160. *Ibid.*, p. 4. For tables showing net incomes after federal taxes, see New York *Times*, October 5, 1943, p. 14.

[13] Abram Bergson, *The Structure of Soviet Wages: A Study in Socialist Economics* (Harvard Economic Studies, Vol. 76). Cambridge: Harvard University, 1944. *Also*, Socialist Clarity Group, *The USSR* (London, 1942), pp. 32, 46, 48. *Also*, Lewis L. Lorwin and A. Abramson, "The Present Phase of Economic and Social Development in the USSR," *International Labour Review*, 33:5-40 (January, 1936). *Also*, N. S. Timasheff, "Vertical Social Mobility in Communist Society," *American Journal of Sociology*, 50:9-21 (July, 1944).

[14] *Consumer Incomes in the United States*, p. 6 (cited above, note 12).

TABLE 2

ESTIMATED INCOMES OF FATHERS OF HEADS OF STATE, AND FATHERS OF
PROPAGANDA MINISTERS, OF EIGHT GREAT POWER NATIONS

Income group	Per cent of all incomes which are in the group	Per cent of heads of state whose fathers were in the group	Per cent of prop-aganda ministers whose fathers were in the group	Names
A	5	37.5	0 to 25	1. *Heads of State* Churchill Roosevelt Tojo 2. *Propaganda Ministers* Bracken (may have been B) Davis (may have been B)
B	15 to 20	37.5 to 50	50 to 75	1. *Heads of State* De Gaulle Franco Hitler (C in early life, B later) Mussolini (C in early life; may have been B later) 2. *Propaganda Ministers* Goebbels Pavolini Serrano Suñer Zhdanov Bracken (may have been A) Davis (may have been A)
C	75 to 80	25	0	1. *Heads of State* Stalin Mussolini (C in early life; may have been B later) 2. *Propaganda Ministers* None
No data	....	0	25	1. *Heads of State* None 2. *Propaganda Ministers* Maillaud Tani

It is notable that only one or two of the eight heads of state are derived from the bottom 75 to 80 per cent of the national income pyramid, while none of the propaganda ministers appears to have come from that large group. In four countries that have thought themselves in a fortunate economic position for several generations, three of the heads of state (Churchill, Roosevelt, Tojo) are derived from the highest 5 per cent of the national income pyramid, and the fourth (De Gaulle) from a high position in the "B" income group. The propaganda ministers of such countries seem to come from high in the middle income class or the lower portion of the upper class. In "have-not" countries, the heads of state and propaganda ministers alike appear to derive primarily from those whose fathers were in the middle income class.

We may partly explain the predominant role of children of the middle income classes among the political, and especially the propaganda, leaderships of Great Power nations by observing the functions of such leaders in the relations among the high, the middle, and the low income strata.

Members of the "A" income brackets, at least those who have been in those brackets for two or more generations, live in a subjective world that differs greatly from that of the bottom 75 per cent.

With respect to knowledge of the world at large, the horizons of the wealthy are likely to be much broader. They enjoy access to travel, to elaborately financed educational institutions, to private tutors. They can pay for books, magazines, newspapers, and other information services which are beyond the means of the majority. They can afford to spend a large part of their time chatting with equally cultured and well-informed persons. They have funds to spend on serious research if they care to. They can and do hire many others to keep them posted, as is shown by the large number of research agencies, private information services, investment counselors, public relations counsels, law firms, and newsletters that serve a wealthy clientele exclusively. They have freedom from the threatening want that eats away the optimism, the energy, and the zest of many in the "C" income groups. As they are not afraid of losing their jobs and of being blacklisted for future employment because of an indiscreet utterance, they have freedom to think their own thoughts.

Yet this versatility of outlook is offset in part by a certain irresponsibility and obtuseness in human relations which their financial position also makes possible. Their environment narrows their focus of attention until they tend to see only the top 5 per cent of the social pyramid, and tend to speak only its language. The exclusive schools and private universities which they attend are often staffed only with teachers who have refined tastes and discriminating solicitude for the sensibilities of their wealthy charges. Young people under such care develop a taste for literature and fantasy, or for dabbling in genteel fashion in certain of the professions, such as medicine, law, the arts or war (the last far more often in Europe than America). They consort only with one another. They marry only one another. They have no contact whatever with the median man, and have almost no information about him. They are astonished to learn that the median man supports his family on a hundred a month in America, and on an equivalent amount in every other Great Power nation. Eventually their very style of speech becomes unmistakable. They cannot even swear like the median man.[15]

The rich whose foci of attention has thus been narrowed have seldom been able to justify their privileges successfully to the poor. That function is performed in their behalf by communication specialists from the middle income classes: by public relations counsels, attorneys, editors, publicity men, clergymen, journalists, schoolteachers—and notably by politicians.

The middle income classes have sufficient access to education and information to impress the lower with their knowledge. Yet they are obliged to be relatively modest in their mode of life; hence, to appear "democratic." Many of them, in fact, are children or grandchildren of manual workers. They are close enough to the average in culture and outlook to communicate "as man to man." Yet they are far enough above to assume leadership as a matter of course in many situations that baffle the median man. The conditions of their livelihood do not permit the high degree of overt irresponsibility and affectation which, to the lower income classes, is so objectionable a trait of the higher brackets. They please the rich by admiring and imitating their style, but they are able to "turn it off," when advisable, in the presence of the poor. Their eager expectation of climbing into the upper brackets accentuates the earnestness and clarity with which they study and meet the emotional wants of rich and poor. Much more than the wealthy, they have a motive and a knack for giving the public what it thinks it wants. The fact that they are usually unconscious of their own motives and consequences gives added sincerity to their acts.

As our data suggest, in regions and times when populations do not consider themselves prosperous the relative role of the intellectual of middle income origins rises, as compared with the role of the man who is a rich man's son. In such conditions, a danger of mass intolerance may make it inexpedient for the wealthy to appear in public at all. They are then compelled to conduct their public relations entirely through middle class politicians and editors. This is a risky tactic for the rich. If the middle class becomes fully aware of its new power, it may take the profits for itself. Failing this, it may "go left"—at least for long enough to set up a new

---

[15] A careful study of the role of exclusive schools in narrowing the focus of attention of a ruling class is Edward Clarence Mack, *The Public Schools and British Opinion since 1860* (1680).

regime with itself on top. Our fourteen men include a number of cases illustrating this.[16]

Thus far we have spoken only of the *national* income pyramid. Quite often a person having a B or C position in the national pyramid may have an A position in the income pyramid of his local community. In the case of such a person, we might expect that a high expectation of deference, due to his favored income position in the home town, would contrast painfully with the low deference actually commanded by his income if he attempted to play a leading part in the national pyramid. We might expect that such a person would undergo a "crisis of self respect." Some of the pain of this might be reduced by protesting to the family, or even to a public, against the social order, under some such symbol as "human rights *versus* property rights." The hypothesis that early exposure to the social grumblings of middle class parents may have rather powerful effects on later skill with national symbols of politics or revolution may seem to be corroborated by the fact that 5 of the 9 fathers whom we have provisionally classified as B on the national scale were quite clearly A on the local scale: Commandant Franco, Customs Guard Hitler, Professor Pavolini, Squire Bracken, Banker Davis. All of the three others very probably were B on the local scale: Professor de Gaulle, Foreman Goebbels, Business Man Suñer, and Priest (or School Inspector) Zhdanov. The incomes of the 4 of these 9 fathers for whom the writer has acceptable records (Franco, Goebbels, Hitler, and Pavolini) appear to have risen in the course of their careers, suggesting persistence, hardihood, and skill well above the averages of their respective social strata. Their sons, finding these traits impressive against the local community background but small against the national pyramid, may well have striven (consciously or unconsciously) to better their fathers' records.

Authority Symbols in Family Backgrounds of Political and Propaganda Leaders

Certain key symbols, in our society, carry preponderant weight and authority as guides to men's conduct in public, or as justifiers and rationalizers of antisocial behavior. Notable among these are the symbols of the Church, the State, the Law, the Armed Forces and the Schools. We might suppose that a home environment strongly and articulately emphasizing

---

[16] General theories of the processes by which mass political communication specialists of middle income origin may serve or overthrow the upper brackets have been set forth ably by Roberto Michels, *Political Parties* (512a); by Max Nomad, *Rebels and Renegades* (1331b); and by Robert Hunter, *Revolution* (196). That even the leaders of the revolutionary wing of the labor movement tend to be drawn primarily from sons of the middle-income group is shown by the fact that Marx, Engels, Wilhelm Liebknecht, Lenin, and Trotsky all came from families having very comfortable income-positions in the middle classes. In fact, Stalin is almost the only major revolutionary leader of genuinely proletarian origin.

one or more of these symbols would much more strongly predispose a child to public life than one in which these symbols were regarded as secondary or remote. Table 3 seems to bear out this hypothesis rather fully. Every one of the heads of state was directly tied to these authority symbols by the occupation or preoccupation of his family. Every one of the propaganda ministers for whom we have reasonably satisfactory data also had such experience. There is no case running contrary to the present hypothesis unless it is that of Elmer Davis, who seems to have stemmed from a rather nonpolitical, nonpolemical background.

TABLE 3

CHILDHOOD EXPOSURE OF HEADS OF STATE, AND OF PROPAGANDA MINISTERS, OF EIGHT GREAT POWER NATIONS, TO AUTHORITATIVE SYMBOLS OF SOCIETY (THE STATE, THE CHURCH, THE LAW, THE ARMED FORCES, THE SCHOOLS)

Eight Heads of State

Name	Symbols	Manner of exposure
Churchill	State, Army	Father prominent politician, member of Parliament; ancestors famous soldiers; Winston Churchill was educated in military academy.
De Gaulle	Church, Schools, Army, State	Father professor of literature and philosophy in Jesuit universities; Charles de Gaulle received intensive Catholic education, then was sent to military schools and became a professional soldier.
Franco	Navy, State, Church, Army	Father naval commander; mother daughter of naval commander; Franco received intensive Catholic education and graduated from military academy.
Hitler	State	Father civil servant who highly prized his official status, urged his son to follow in his footsteps; but mother encouraged son to become an artist.
Mussolini	State, Schools	Father an active reform politician; mother a schoolteacher who urged Mussolini to become a teacher.
Roosevelt	Army, Navy, State, Law	Father a cousin of Theodore Roosevelt, U.S. President and symbol of U.S. military and naval aspirations. Father mainly business man and gentleman farmer, but mother seems to have encouraged Roosevelt continually to become a political leader. F. D. Roosevelt studied political science and history at Harvard, attended Columbia University Law School, and started career as attorney.

Name	Symbols	Manner of exposure
Stalin	Church	Father apparently not involved with authority symbols; mother very eager for Stalin to become priest. Stalin studied for priesthood until 19.
Tojo	Army, State	Father Lieutenant General, Imperial Japanese Army, and a samurai. Premier Tojo was educated in military academies.

Eight Propa-
ganda Min-
isters

Name	Symbols	Manner of exposure
Bracken	No data	
Davis	No data	Father a banker in a small U.S. city.
Goebbels	Church, Schools	Parents, apparently active Catholics, sent Goebbels to Catholic elementary school; Goebbels attended school on Catholic scholarship; went to six famous German universities and took Ph.D.
Maillaud	No data	
Pavolini	Schools	Father a prominent professor, University of Florence; Pavolini studied law and social sciences.
Serrano Suñer	Church, Law	Evidently had very intense Catholic education. Serrano Suñer took law degree and started career as attorney.
Tani	Army, State, Law	Father a samurai; Tani studied political science and attended law school.
Zhdanov	Schools, Church	Father said to be "priest" and "inspector of public schools."

Table 3 also seems to show that heads of state came rather more often from families preoccupied with the State and the Armed Forces than propaganda ministers. Conversely, the ministers seem to have been much more frequently influenced by intensive exposure to symbols of the School and the Church.

Unfortunately, data are not at hand for tracing exactly the psychological processes by which these authority symbols became integrated into the personalities of these men. Yet it is obvious that this would be necessary if we were to explain them fully. Our data show that a childhood in certain social strata and in families having certain occupations and preoccupations appears to raise the probability that a person will become a political or propaganda leader. What our data do *not* show is why, of all persons who were children of the strata, the occupational or the preoccupational groups in question, these particular men rose to the top. Very probably that could be demonstrated only with psychological data.[17]

[17] When social science finds its feet, a much more refined analysis than we have attempted here can be used to explain men's behavior in relation to political and economic symbols. Study of the

Formal Education of Political and Propaganda Leaders

The informal educational experiences of the home, which almost exclusively dominate and mold the personality during the impressionable years of infancy and early childhood, are supplemented after a time by the more formal educational efforts of the school. While the personality of the child is often already well structured, and may be virtually inalterable, by the time he is old enough to enter the school, his teachers may at least hope to give information and training in those fields in which the child is able to become interested.

Space here forbids a careful analysis of the experiences our sample of men had in the elementary school. However, Table 4 presents in very condensed form a statement of the highest levels of formal education attained by each of them.

TABLE 4

HIGHEST LEVELS OF FORMAL EDUCATION EXPERIENCED BY HEADS OF STATE, AND BY PROPAGANDA MINISTERS, OF EIGHT GREAT POWER NATIONS

Eight Heads of State		*Eight Propaganda Ministers*	
Liberal arts college plus law school	1 Roosevelt	Higher humanistic degree (Ph.D. in literature)	1 Goebbels
Military academy	4 Churchill De Gaulle Franco Tojo	Liberal arts college plus Rhodes scholarship	1 Davis
		Law	3(?) Pavolini(?) Serrano Suñer Tani
Teachers' college (certificate)	1 Mussolini		
Public secondary schools (no college)	2 Hitler Stalin	Public secondary schools plus 1 year agricultural school	1 Zhdanov
		Private preparatory school (apparently no college)	1 Bracken
Elementary schools only	0	Elementary schools only	0
		No data	1 Maillaud

social mobility of grandparents as well as parents casts a great deal of light on this. Far more precise statements on the social mobility of parents and of the subject himself might have been made than are permitted by space in this essay.

Another point to be made on future research method is that psychoanalysis has for two generations called attention to the powerful role of the mother (or mother-substitute) in personality-formation, especially among the political intelligentsia. Despite this, the biographers and journalists continue to report virtually nothing about mothers and nurses. To a psychoanalyst, this omission would suspiciously resemble a further proof of the importance of the maternal factor. Of the mothers of the fourteen men in our sample, only Mrs. Sara Delano Roosevelt has been written up with sufficient clarity to enable us to predict with reasonable probability her son's behavior.

Of our sample of sixteen men, three (Bracken, Hitler, Stalin) seem to have gone no higher than completion of high school, while two others (Mussolini, Zhdanov) seem to have had "advanced" education that is probably no more than the equivalent of graduation from a U.S. high school.

The "practical" and "vocational" emphasis is apparent in the cases of the men who had post-secondary education. Only three of the sixteen (Davis, Goebbels, Roosevelt) appear to have taken the "humanistic" (liberal arts) curriculum. The great majority of the sixteen come from curricula involving neither literary humanism nor emphasis on any form of science. They come from military academies (Churchill, De Gaulle, Franco, Tojo), and from vocational schools for lawyers (Pavolini, Roosevelt, Serrano Suñer, Tani), teachers (Mussolini) and agriculturists (Zhdanov).

But if five of the sample (Bracken, Hitler, Mussolini, Stalin, Zhdanov) did not go beyond secondary school or its equivalent, there is on the other hand no case of a man who stopped after elementary school and did not spend at least a little time at the secondary level.

The data show a total absence of advanced training in the political, economic, and social sciences among the sixteen men. (Roosevelt was an undergraduate major in history and government at Harvard, however, while Pavolini and Tani appear to have taken bachelor's degrees in "law and social sciences," at the Universities of Florence and Tokyo, respectively.)

On the basis of the facts in the table, it might be conjectured that the highest positions in the political pyramid are not for those who have too brief, too long, too humanistic, or too scientific an education.

The modern Great Power nation, with its elaborate division of labor, presents a greater variety of social environments than any previous society. The man with no more than elementary education is not likely to be able to use enough words to gain a following outside his own stratum. No man can speak the diverse languages of the farm, the small town, the factory, the financial center, and the bureaucracy without a fair amount of schooling. On the other hand, the man who is the product of a graduate school (or even of a college of high standing) is likely to speak a jargon which the man in the street will not understand much better than he would a foreign language.

In the United States, a comparatively literate nation, only 4.6 per cent of the adult population are college graduates; about a quarter have graduated from high school; and about 50 per cent have not completed the eighth grade.[18] Numerous studies of reading ability (2022-2102a, *passim*) have shown that a majority of the nation's population are without sufficient vocabulary to do more than make a good guess at the meaning of discussions carried on in the habitual vocabulary of the college graduate. Questions asked by national polling organizations have corroborated this by showing that large percentages of the population do not possess even such information as has been printed repeatedly on the front pages of newspapers they "read regularly."

One of several published studies of topics on which a standard cross-section of the U.S. public is ignorant is by Hadley Cantril, "What We Don't Know Is Likely to Hurt Us," *New York Times Magazine*, May 14, 1944, pp. 9 ff. A national poll showed that 30 per cent of the adult population did not know the Japanese had occupied the Philippines; 60 per cent "had never heard of" the Atlantic Charter; about 95 per cent were "unable to name even one of its provisions." "The facts I have reported and the conclusions they lead to may shock some persons who travel entirely in sophisticated circles without realizing it," says Cantril, Director of the Princeton University Office of Public Opinion Research. "They may embarrass others with a sensitive national pride. They may confirm the cynicism of those with little faith in the common man. But for most people, supporters of democracy, they are a challenge."

These facts mean that the successful propagandist, in order to have enough grasp of social problems to formulate winning policies, must have the equivalent of a secondary education, or perhaps a smattering of college. But in order to keep the knack of "putting himself across" with a broad public, he must have constant contact with "average" and "practical" men. He must avoid becoming overeducated. This is especially essential in the "have not" nations, as the table shows; or in any nation in times of economic depression, crisis, or war.

Our data indicate that if a national leader's education goes beyond the secondary level he usually keeps his mind on practical and vocational matters—preferably military and legal—and avoids too deep a preoccupation with the humanistic approach, whether literary or scientific.

Leadership of the Great Power nation is a specialized career, whose terms compel a man to drive his impulses outward with prodigal vigor. It is a career for extraverts. The life of a leader is a life of high-speed action and ceaseless nervous strain. He must have abundant vitality. He needs every ounce of it to hold his job. Too much of the subjectivism of the literary man and artist would be incompatible with this. Moods and perplexities might undermine the distinctive energies that enable a leader to

[18] U.S. Bureau of the Census, Sixteenth Census (1940), Series P-10, No. 8, "Educational Attainment of the Population 25 Years Old and Over in the United States."

master the administrative crises and beat down the horde of energetic rivals that constantly threaten his position.

In the same way, an extended scientific training might weaken a leader if he took it too seriously, though it might clarify his mind if taken in due proportion. Most of the sixteen men in our sample are famous as omnivorous readers, and many are known to enjoy the company of political scientists, economists, and sociologists. Roosevelt, for example, was once known for his "brain trust." Stalin is said by disinterested reporters to have a wide and exact knowledge of the Marxist scholars. Zhdanov has been described by an associate editor of *Life* magazine as "well educated, cultured, extremely serious," as well as "an inspiring mass speaker."[18a] Mussolini twice acknowledges a debt to the sociologist Pareto.[19] The financial journals controlled by Bracken are staffed with highly trained economists. But the political and propaganda leaders are interested in science mainly for purposes of private self-clarification. Their speeches and writings, unlike those of the scientist, are scarcely designed to present both sides of every controversial issue to the public. In the present stage of popular education, the stock-in-trade of statesmen cannot be confined to policies based only on evidence. Much less can it be hampered by judgments suspended until all the facts are gathered.

Occupational Mobility of Political and Propaganda Leaders

Having acquired the culture of his family and a certain amount of education, a young man begins his career. It is of interest to note the occupational beginnings of the sixteen men in our sample (Table 5). We have seen that in most cases their fathers were men from middle or upper social strata. It is hardly surprising, therefore, that the sons began their careers in white collar work in every case but one. That individual, Adolf Hitler, can scarcely be said to have had an occupation at all during the first decade after "completing" his formal education. Hoping, apparently, to become an artist, he lived in Vienna and Munich, often on relief and occasionally employed as a postcard painter or, reputedly, as a paper hanger.

As for the others, all but three (professional soldiers De Gaulle, Franco, and Tojo) held, as their very first jobs, positions involving the continuous use of highly controversial symbols of public policy. Roosevelt and Serrano Suñer entered on law practices which were interlocked with practical politics. Churchill, though a military officer, was mainly preoccupied with his work as a war correspondent. Bracken, Davis, and Maillaud at once went into journalism, the first working in the highly specialized field of financial reporting and the latter two in broad, general coverage of the news. Tani

---

[18a] Richard E. Lauterbach, *Life*, Jan. 1, 1945, p. 65.
[19] *Autobiography, op. cit.*, pp. 27, 290.

passed his Foreign Service examinations and began his unbroken career in the consular and diplomatic service. The five others (Goebbels, Mussolini, Pavolini, Stalin, Zhdanov) plunged into the thick of "protest politics" as organizers, agitators, and stump speakers, while still in their teens. The data show that an aggressive and continuous preoccupation with politics and journalism, from adolescence onward, is a characteristic of all those who have reached the tops of the political and propaganda pyramids. Such men do not start in other careers and then move into this one.

TABLE 5

SOCIAL STRATA, OCCUPATIONS, AND INCOME-CLASSES OF HEADS OF STATE AND PROPAGANDA MINISTERS OF EIGHT GREAT POWER NATIONS DURING THEIR FIRST DECADE OF EMPLOYMENT*

Eight Heads of State		*Eight Propaganda Ministers*	
2B Professional military officer	4 Churchill (also 4B) De Gaulle Franco Tojo	2B Career diplomat	1 Tani
4A Law practice and politics	1 Roosevelt	4B Lawyer	1 Serrano Suñer
4B Journalist	1 Churchill (also 2B)	4B Journalist	3 Bracken Davis Maillaud
4C Political agitator and organizer	2 Mussolini Stalin	4C Political agitator and organizer	3 Goebbels Pavolini Zhdanov
7C Odd jobs and on relief	1 Hitler		

Income Classes	*Number of Cases*	*Income Classes*	*Number of Cases*
A	1	A	0
B	4	B	5
C	3	C	3

* Numbers represent social strata shown in Table 1. Letters represent the income classes used in Table 2. (A = upper 5%; B = next 15 to 20%; C = bottom 75 to 80% of the income pyramid of a Great Power nation.)

None of these sixteen men except the alleged paper hanger seems to have done more than an aggregate of one year's work as a manual laborer in his entire career. None has been a farmer, though Zhdanov has studied agriculture in a technical institute for a year. No doubt these sixteen men know how to work hard in the field of symbols; but if they have a strong realization of the problems of the bottom 75 or 80 per cent, they must have derived it from sources other than experience of manual work.

The incomes they made in the first jobs they held probably put all of them except Roosevelt into the B or C income classes—evenly divided as between B and C.

Bodily and Emotional Traits
of Heads of State and Propaganda Ministers

It was long ago established by psychologists that a love of symbols and of political activism is likely to stem from sharp deviations from physical and emotional norms.[20] Men decidedly above or below the average in health, endurance, size, physical attractiveness, and emotional stability are to be expected in such a group as we are studying.

We have mentioned the striking physical drawbacks which were overcome by the manual workers' sons in our sample during their rise to power. Similar difficulties were encountered by a number of men in our sample whose fathers had other occupations. Franco is reported as being only five feet three inches in height[21]—not large for a soldier. Serrano Suñer is described by an apparently dependable U.S. journalist as hypertense and "a frail man . . . [whose] bitterness, which was increased by a bad stomach, was shown in his every action and word."[22] De Gaulle was wounded three times during World War I.

Franklin Roosevelt's victorious struggle against infantile paralysis in his forties is well known. No man who has suffered such an illness and has thrown it off can fail to emerge from the ordeal deepened and more detached in his whole attitude to life.

Adding these five to the four manual workers' sons previously mentioned, we find that nine of our sixteen men are known to have overcome serious physical handicaps—and 56.25 per cent is probably considerably higher than the frequency of such handicaps among the general population.

The deviations in the other direction—that of conspicuous health, size, and attractiveness—are also notable, though much less frequent. Bracken, Churchill, Davis, and Roosevelt are certainly well above the average in

[20] Consult, for example, Wilhelm Lange-Eichbaum, *Genie, Irrsinn und Ruhm* (Munich: Reinhardt, second enlarged edition, 1935), and the extensive literature cited therein. Also Ernst Kretschmer, *The Psychology of Men of Genius* (1217a) and Alexander Herzberg, *The Psychology of Philosophers* (1751).

[21] Johannes Steel, *Men Behind the War* (New York: Sheridan House, 1943), p. 258.

[22] Thomas Jefferson Hamilton, *Appeasement's Child: The Franco Régime in Spain* (New York: Knopf, 1943), p. 117.

stature and physical attractiveness. Roosevelt is six feet one and one-half inches tall;[23] De Gaulle, six feet four.[24] Zhdanov has been described by Walter Duranty, the U.S. newspaper correspondent, as "a big, strong-faced man, with black hair and an attractive smile and bright eyes."[25] The vitality of the six men we have just mentioned, like that of Goebbels, Mussolini, Stalin, and Tani, has been reported as overwhelming by many observers, year after year. Repeated physical encounters, assassination attempts and military attacks have shown most of our sixteen men to be more or less indestructible.

It is evident that exceptionally high initial vitality, especially when coupled with the will power and the capacity for solitude that come from successful struggle against disease or physical handicap, is favorable to the growth of elaborate political skill.

Psychological clinics are full of evidence that a struggle against mental or emotional aberration might have the same effect. Unfortunately the ample data available cannot be presented here for the heads of state and propaganda ministers in question.

It may be sufficient for present purposes to remind ourselves that when personality is closely studied by modern psychiatric techniques, many acts that are viewed by laymen as exceptionally splendid and courageous turn out to be based on unconscious destructive impulses: self-destructiveness and other-destructiveness. Such impulses are often linked with unconscious desires to be dramatically attacked by others, and to destroy others along with the self. Drives of this sort are usually rooted in profound frustrations experienced in infancy and early childhood. Often the effects of the early experiences are reinforced by additional frustrations in adolescence and adulthood.

Beneath a heavy veil of repression, such emotional conditioning may cause a talented, articulate, and conscientious individual to become a leader. It literally forces him to find a sanctifying "cause" in the name of which he can arouse himself and others to acts of destruction.[26]

"Any observer of our social scene," says Fromm, "cannot fail to be impressed with the destructiveness to be found everywhere. For the most part

[23] Ernest K. Lindley, *Franklin D. Roosevelt* (New York: Blue Ribbon, 1931), p. 54.

[24] *Time*, May 29, 1944, pp. 33-38; also Noel F. Busch, "De Gaulle, the Prophet," *Life*, Nov. 13, 1944, p. 109.

[25] New York *Times*, March 21, 1939, p. 12.

[26] If the reader can forgive, for the sake of substantial insight, a certain looseness of scholarship, a suggestive interpretation of these factors in a type of personality who frequently becomes one of the supreme leaders of the Great Power nation may be found in L. Pierce Clark's psychoanalytic study, *Napoleon, Self-Destroyed* (New York: Cape and Smith, 1929). The problem has been carefully stated, with special reference to contemporary politics, by the psychoanalyst and social scientist Erich Fromm, *Escape from Freedom* (179), notably pp. 3-23, 179-185. See also Karen Horney, *The Neurotic Personality of Our Time* (New York: Norton, 1937).

it is not conscious as such but is rationalized in various ways. As a matter of fact, there is virtually nothing that is not used as a rationalization for destructiveness. Love, duty, conscience, patriotism have been and are being used as disguises to destroy others or oneself. . . . In most cases the destructive impulses, however, are rationalized in such a way that at least a few other people or a whole social group share the rationalization and thus make it appear to be 'realistic' to the member of such a group."[27]

Eventually the individual with such a drive may achieve the destruction of himself, or of his "cause," along with death or injury for many of those whom he has persuaded to support or attack him. It is not necessary here to recount the numerous occasions on which many of the sixteen men in our sample have, with apparent satisfaction, flung themselves and others into the teeth of needless pain and danger. Ten of the sixteen (Churchill, De Gaulle, Franco, Goebbels, Hitler, Mussolini, Pavolini, Stalin, Tojo, Zhdanov) are well known to have risked their lives voluntarily, time after time. Those in our sample are extraverts, and lovers of life in certain of its forms. But some of them are also devotees of death.

Propaganda Skills of Heads of State and of Propaganda Ministers

As indicated above, there are many books and articles on the "propaganda techniques" that have been found successful in our times. As scores of them are listed among the titles in the bibliography section of this book, no effort will be made to summarize them here.

Not many "propaganda techniques" are peculiar to the twentieth century. On most occasions, the trick can still be turned by means of the rhetoric, the fallacies, and the phraseologies described by Aristotle (138a), Quintus and Marcus Cicero[28] and the medieval and Reformation casuists.

The standard stratagems of a political propaganda campaign as described by modern scientists include the monopolization of propaganda initiatives, the displacement of guilt, the overstressing of the enemy's evil qualities, the presentation of oneself as morally superior, and the coordination of propaganda with violence. These were also well set forth by Shakespeare, about 1593:

[27] *Escape from Freedom*, p. 180.

[28] See Marcus Tullius Cicero, "The Orator," in *Orations*, translated by C. D. Yonge, Vol. 4 (New York and London: Bell, 1894). On the basis of his extensive political experience, Cicero analyzes the skills of "a consummate orator." See also Quintus Tullius Cicero, "On Standing for the Consulship," in Marcus Tullius Cicero, *Treatises*, translated by C. D. Yonge (London: Bohn, 1853). This is one of the most practical campaign handbooks in print. Quintus was his brother Marcus' manager in the campaign in 64 B.C. for the consulship, the highest political office, which they won. Both were professional politicians of upper middle class origin whose careers closely followed the pattern observed among the sons of the upper middle class among the sixteen men in our sample.

GLOUCESTER: I do the wrong, and first begin to brawl.
The secret mischiefs that I set abroach
I lay unto the grievous charge of others.
Clarence, whom I indeed have laid in darkness,
I do beweep to many simple gulls. . . .
Now they believe it; and withal whet me
To be revenged on Rivers, Vaughan, Grey:
But then I sigh; and, with a piece of Scripture
Tell them that God bids us do good for evil:
And thus I clothe my naked villainy
With old odd ends stolen out of holy writ
And seem a saint, when most I play the devil.
(*Enter two Murderers*)
But soft! Here come my executioners.
How now, my hardy stout resolvèd mates! [29]

Nor is the claque at a European *Parteitag* or an American national convention entirely a new conception. Shakespeare described it:

BUCKINGHAM: And when mine orat'ry drew to an end,
I bid them that did love their country's good
Cry "God save Richard, England's royal king!"

GLOUCESTER: Aha! And did they so?

BUCKINGHAM: No, so God help me, they spake not a word;
But like dumb statuës or breathing stones
Gazed on each other and looked deadly pale.
Which when I saw . . . some followers of mine own
At the lower end of the hall hurl'd up their caps
And some ten voices cried "God save King Richard!"
"Thanks, gentle citizens and friends," quoth I,
"This general applause and loving shout
Argues your wisdoms, and your love to Richard."[30]

But if the basic situations of politics and the main techniques of persuasion are centuries old, the modern technology of communication has made for concentrations of propaganda power that are larger, more specialized, and more nearly monopolistic than any that were technically possible before. Today a handful of press agencies, a handful of major newspapers and news magazines, a handful of radio networks, and a handful of motion picture producers control the news and opinion arteries of the world. As Ralph Casey has shown in this book in his essay on communication media, very little competition with existing press associations, newspapers, and

---

[29] *King Richard III*, I, iii, 23-40.   [30] *Ibid.*, III, vii, 21-41.

networks is possible. The cost of setting up new units is prohibitive, and the trained personnel who would be needed have been considerably monopolized by enterprises already in the field.

The total number of agencies, papers, studios, and other mass communication centers is so small that they can very readily be policed and brought under the direct domination of the governmental propaganda chiefs. In a totalitarian propaganda ministry, a few score or a few hundred men can completely monopolize the focus of attention of a nation, except for broadcasts from abroad and news that is smuggled in print or orally.

But control cannot be achieved without the aid of men who know the media. Hence one of the main preoccupations of the mass political propaganda specialist of our time, in contrast to the more individualistic orator and polemicist of earlier days, is administrative in nature. In addition to attracting the support of an interest group and of loyal followers who are personally attached to him, he must obtain and supervise the services of a rather large and complicated group of "experts."

He needs a staff of propagandists and a staff of censors for each of the major channels of communication: the press, the radio, public meetings, the films and, if possible, the schools. If a very sophisticated policy is planned, he may require a staff of specialists in historical and contemporary research. If he is using the full repertory of modern devices for influencing and assessing opinion, he must also have a staff to measure the contents of the channels of communication (radio, newspaper, book, motion picture, and public meeting "monitors"). He needs another staff to observe the responses of his various publics (opinion pollers, psychological observers).

No major government in the period of World War II has been without bureaus performing each of these functions. Each bureau may employ dozens or hundreds of persons. Among the men at the top, a high administrative ability is clearly essential, in addition to the traditional politician's gift of oratory and his skill in "getting out the voters" on election day.

Thus it is not surprising, when we analyze the skills of the men in our sample, that we find a definite difference of aptitudes and division of labor as between the heads of state and the propaganda ministers.

In general, the head of state is both a military figure of some distinction and a vastly effective radio orator—a highly articulate gratifier of his own and the audience's fantasies of mastery, excitement, and adventure. In all ages, of course, the top position in the state has been held more frequently than not by a military commander-in-chief, and very often he has also been an outstanding orator. What the twentieth century has added to the ancient formula is a technological and scientific factor: the techniques of special media—notably radio—and the associated techniques of measuring the predispositions and responses of the vast masses who can now for the first time be reached in a single propaganda campaign. The ancient formula is still acted out by the head of state; the new techniques are managed by the propaganda minister.

In addition to military leadership and to oratory on world networks, the head of the state coordinates the main lines of propaganda policy with the main lines of economic, military, and police policy of his government. Within his directives, the minister takes care of the detail of the propaganda program.

The minister is primarily an organizer and administrator who carries the heavy burden of recruiting and supervising the hundreds or thousands of professionals and skilled workers employed by the ministry. In particular, he devotes a great deal of energy to the timing and coordination of releases through the various media and to the various publics. Since Great Power governments now broadcast and publish in from ten to thirty languages, an enormous technical job is involved in translating and adapting any major propaganda campaign to the vast world audience.

As a result of the complexity and technical novelty of his job, the propaganda minister is likely to be busied with urgent mechanical and administrative problems, to the partial exclusion of considerations of political or social policy. Hence, he is likely to accept the political initiatives of the head of the state, and to innovate only within the limits prescribed by "the Boss."

And should he develop a tendency to innovate to the point of rivalry with his chief, he may be restricted by the fact that he is usually chosen from those who are a half generation or a full generation younger than the head of state, as Table 6 shows. (The men under the propaganda minister are as a rule even younger. The writer has made a study of secondary personnel of leading propaganda ministries, which shows that in most cases they are in their twenties or thirties. A man of 40 is "old" in this occupation.)

TABLE 6

AGES IN 1943 OF HEADS OF STATE, AND OF PROPAGANDA MINISTERS, OF EIGHT GREAT POWER NATIONS

Head of State	Age in 1943	His Propaganda Minister	Age in 1943	Age Difference
Churchill	69	Bracken	42	27
De Gaulle	53	Maillaud	34	19
Franco	51	Serrano Suñer	42	9
Hitler	54	Goebbels	46	8
Mussolini	60	Pavolini	40	20
Roosevelt	61	Davis	53	8
Stalin	64	Zhdanov	47	17
Tojo	59	Tani	54	5

Public Control of the Mass Propaganda Specialist

It is axiomatic in the twentieth century, as earlier, that "Power corrupts; and absolute power corrupts absolutely." In national politics, terrific tension results from the high stakes for which the game is being played. In an age when hemisphere or world political monopolism is technically possible for the first time, it is not merely *great power* but *supreme world power* that is at issue. It would be surprising if this prospect did not bring out the Napoleonic impulses that lurk not far beneath the surface in the sorts of personalities who become the heads and ministers of Great Power nations. For them and for many directly associated with them, reality may seem to confirm the delusions of potential omnipotence that seem, according to the psychoanalysts, to animate so many men of genius and cause their downfall. At any rate, both grandiose and ultra-destructive tendencies are so conspicuous and so well known among the men in our sample that it is unnecessary to recite the numerous data.

Instead, we shall only point out a few of the social implications and inquire into the possibility of social control. It is evident that as long as so much of the world is led by men as brilliant and persuasive, yet unstable and unreasoning, as many of the sixteen in our sample, it will not be too comfortable for ordinary mortals. Thirteen million military deaths, and thirty million deaths among civilians, resulted from the First World War.[31] The probably greater toll of the Second War is not yet counted; nor is the toll of misery exacted by the intervening economic depressions.

If Napoleons and economic bunglers are to yield the stage to humane statesmen who can make the machine age work, there must be control, in all Great Power nations, over the devastating effects of propaganda monopolies that are exercised on behalf of adventurers, bureaucracies, plutocracies and other special interest groups.

An essential safeguard for a humane society is the world-wide breaking of monopolies of every description: monopolies of hereditary privilege, monopolies of money, monopolies of goods and services, monopolies of weapons, monopolies of education, monopolies of access to information, and monopolies in propaganda and communication.[32]

Monopolies are not to be broken by denunciation, and they are not likely to be much affected by public regulatory commissions or by courts. Especially in the field of communication, the most effective approach is probably the establishment and safeguarding of competing enterprises. We have not

[31] Horst Mendershausen, *The Economics of War* (118), p. 307, quoting L. Hersch, "Demographic Effects of Modern Warfare," in *What Would Be the Character of a New War?* (New York: Smith and Haas, 1933).

[32] For a political scientist's analysis of the relations of these types of monopoly to the constitutional structures of nations and to the characteristics of the upper social strata, see Gaetano Mosca, *The Ruling Class* (249).

space here to consider adequately the nature and extent of competition in the major communication channels, but a few remarks may be ventured.

In the *field of radio* the U.S. Federal Communications Commission has gone further than the corresponding agencies in any other country to protect freedom of speech on the air, and to protect the radio audience from one-sided propaganda. As long as such an agency enforces the principle that a person attacked is entitled to as much of a hearing on the air as the attacker, it is not at all probable that this country will fall victim to a mass political propagandist of the European type.

In the *newspaper field*, the second major medium, this country is also relatively free of monopolism. Several agencies with few or no interlocks compete in gathering the news, and a very considerable number of mutually independent papers still exist, despite strong tendencies toward concentration. Other countries have shown signs of a desire to imitate U.S. practice in this regard.

In the *field of motion pictures*, eight giant enterprises in the U.S. dominate production and extend their control into distribution and exhibition. But eight are not one. On certain occasions, a considerable divergence of propaganda "line" has been apparent among them. Control of the industry in other nations is much more concentrated.

The *political party* is another channel. The long evolution of the traditional two-party or multi-party system has given the United States and other English-speaking areas a substantial safeguard in popular sentiment against efforts to monopolize communication in this field. Michels[33] is no doubt perfectly correct in speaking of the "autocratic tendencies of leaders" and the "iron law of oligarchy" that sooner or later pervade any political party, whatever its original idealism. Yet there is also no doubt that the insidious effect of these forces is substantially reduced by a multi-party system. Whether multi-party systems can endure in non-English-speaking areas in our times remains to be seen.

A final channel is the *school*. It is the least monopolized of all the media. With certain very notable exceptions, it is remarkably free in the United States, as compared with other countries, from interlocks with governmental and private pressure groups.

The fact that the school is in most cases a nonprofit institution, even in capitalist countries, may add to its impartiality as a channel for communications concerned with the public welfare. So may the fact that it is low-salaried in every country. Even those school executives who are most subservient to wealthy board members can scarcely hope for incomes that would hold a candle to the salary and dividends of a movie magnate, a network head, the publisher of a newspaper or newsmagazine, or an influ-

[33] Roberto Michels, *Political Parties* (512a).

ential politician. Nor can those who "sell out" expect an appreciable increase in deference from colleagues or the general public.

For these reasons, the personnel of the school are beyond a doubt the most humane and disinterested of all the specialists in mass communication. They share with a handful of highly responsible newspapers, clergymen, politicians, and radio commentators the distinction of speaking most consistently and most impartially on behalf of the general public welfare.

Still another factor contributes to the relative objectivity of the schools. In nearly all countries the educational system, unlike any other communication channel, is generally thought to have a responsibility for taking not *some* but *the whole* of accepted knowledge for its province. It is considered to have a special duty to sift all statements, and to distinguish facts from propaganda. Hence the schools have an opportunity to exert an integrating and clarifying effect on mass communication to a much greater extent than the other media. The latter are generally granted to be relatively shallow because of their hasty deadlines and absence of facilities for research.

Hence it is primarily to the schools, all over the world, that one may look for leadership in establishing certain understandings that are indispensable for the ultimate development of public control of the mass political propagandist.

The "lag" between major political and economic events and the focus of attention of the schools is serious, however—typically a half generation or more—and the personality of the teacher frequently is ineffective outside the classroom. Both of these factors may be altered by curricular changes now under way, and by the gradual introduction of psychiatry into teachers' colleges. However, in the immediate future the schools can scarcely be depended upon to exert short-run correctives upon antisocial propaganda in the other channels.[34] The only sufficiently strong safeguard is the prevention of monopoly and the fostering of free speech in those channels.

Yet as the school draws closer to current events, one of its foremost tasks may be the development of maximum awareness among the population of the nature and power of communication and propaganda. The schools can teach such propositions as the following:

that all parties, all interest groups, all social strata in our times are likely to hire their own propaganda specialists;

that these propagandists will use misrepresentations, fallacies, and psychological devices that can be detected and resisted;

[34] For analysis of the schools by social scientists, consult, among others, Willard Waller, *The Sociology of Education* (New York: 1932); Frances Donovan, *The Schoolma'am* (1741); Logan Wilson, *The Academic Man* (1778); studies by U.S. President's Advisory Committee on Education (1708, 1714, 1715); and Luella Cole, *The Background for College Teaching* (1737).

that spokesmen who live on modest incomes and have no expectation of acquiring vast increments of money or deference are the
most to be trusted;

that the topmost strata of society can afford more numerous and
more skillful spokesmen, whose statements therefore have to be
scrutinized more carefully than what is said by propagandists for
the poor;

that the public would find it easier to know whom to trust if there
were public agencies engaged in the registration, objective analysis, and disclosure of propagandists, so that the exact facts about
contemporary leaders could be kept before the public all the
time;[35]

that ad-less papers and nonprofit radio stations would probably
be more impartial than communication enterprises interlocked
with corporations or run for profit, provided that a broad public
were educated to support them by subscription, and provided that
they were prevented from becoming monopolies themselves;

that the present low level of mass education, even in the United
States, is a chronic threat to the survival of humane values whenever economic depression or other deep misfortune raises the
level of mass insecurity;

that this could be remedied by a relatively modest program of
public financial aid to the millions of able people who cannot now
afford to go to school;[36]

that pending adequate education for the average family, and also
after it has been achieved, much of the meaning of the twentieth
century that is now unknown to ordinary men can be made
available through better facilities for the popularization of
knowledge.[37]

Dealing specifically with the topic of the present essay, it may be taught
that the mass political propagandist who reaches the top in a Great Power
nation is in the last analysis a human being, though he may look like something else. He is, however, a human being of a very exceptional type. As a
personality, and also as a politician attempting to keep himself and his
friends in office, he is potentially dangerous to most other human beings.

[35] I have explored administrative aspects of existing laws on this in "Democratic Control of
Propaganda through Registration and Disclosure" (2529).
[36] For details, see publications of U.S. President's Advisory Committee on Education (1708,
1714, 1715).
[37] See the section in this book on "Outstanding Titles on the Art and Science of Popularization," pp. 122-125.

If viewed objectively, he will often but not quite always be found to have strong militarist tendencies, a fathomless craving for power, an education of dubious scientific value, very little feeling for the everyday problems of the workers and the farmers, a very slight gift for humane social and economic planning, a highly extraverted personality, an unreasoning intolerance of rivals, a gift for organization and management when these are closely related to self-aggrandizement, and powerful destructive compulsions which are likely to make him risk not only his own life but the lives of the people he leads. All these traits he shares with millions, for they are traits of Western Culture as a whole.[38] However, he has them in far higher degree. Therefore he is able to initiate and stimulate their externalization by others.

There are strong countertendencies in the culture, if not in him. If he can be prevented from monopolizing the channels of communication, these countertendencies will be expressed. Consequently, those who plan the promotion of humane tendencies in mass communication might emphasize the urgency of maintaining competition *among* the channels as well as competition *within* them.

If all the parties sold out to "the interests" or fell under the spell of a Bonapartist leader, a free press might still hold out for sanity. If the press were bought or intimidated, free men might still speak over networks not interlocked with papers or with parties. The movies, if still independent, might put on a campaign. So might the schools.

Hence the importance, in an epoch menaced by the technical possibilities of monopolized mass communication, of preventing the formation of interlocks between the government and any channel, between the papers and the networks, the networks and the movies, the parties and the press, and so on through the list of relations that may develop among the media.

The general economic implications, of course, are very great. To some, aware of the massive trends toward concentration of economic and political control in our times, the very mention of the program above may seem like offering advice to an avalanche. To others, less familiar with the facts, it may seem fanciful, or "needlessly complex."

But social science aims to deal with facts and probabilities, unswayed by hopes or fears or wishful thinking. Perhaps we can scarcely expect a world public opinion that did not at once declare war on the Nazi treatment of the Jews, or even on the "peace" of 1919 that ruined the economy and politics of Europe, to find its way to great enlightenment in our times.

[38] For supporting data see Mark A. May and Leonard Doob, *Competition and Cooperation* (235); also *Cooperation and Competition among Primitive Peoples*, edited by Margaret Mead (238); also Ruth Benedict, *Patterns of Culture* (143); Erich Fromm, *Escape from Freedom* (179).

We stand again at a juncture like that of 1919, when John Maynard Keynes wrote that the coming events "will not be shaped by the deliberate acts of statesmen, but by the hidden currents, flowing continually beneath the surface of political history. . . . In one way only can we influence these hidden currents—by setting in motion those forces of instruction and imagination which change *opinion*. The assertion of truth, the unveiling of illusion, the dissipation of hate, the enlargement and instruction of men's hearts and minds, must be the means."[39]

This is a slow process. Perhaps a scientist can only bow to the reproaches (while echoing the hopes) of those who assume that there "must be" easy ways to implement the Four Freedoms. In reality, we still move dimly in the Dawn Age of social integration. We still play Piltdown politics. At any rate, the social sciences can give us this measure of assurance: In so far as freedom from propaganda monopolies can be guaranteed, and mass education can be expanded along such lines as we have indicated, we may have confidence that free men's criticism will outweigh whatever propaganda may be issued by a would-be Bonaparte.

[39] John Maynard Keynes, *The Economic Consequences of the Peace* (New York: Harcourt, Brace and Howe, 1920), p. 296.

DESCRIBING THE
CONTENTS OF COMMUNICATIONS

BY HAROLD D. LASSWELL

THE science of communication may be on the way to providing men with one of the forms of knowledge about themselves—about their ways of acting in concert—without which there can be no dependable basis for congenial relationships. Human beings are now cut off from one another by barriers that prevent sympathetic understanding. Terminological and semantic differences perpetually frustrate well-meaning efforts to build a world in which the dignity of each personality is respected in theory and practice. Unless the stream of mass political communication can be made to provide all the symbols, facts, and interpretations that are needed for rational, concerted, and humane policy, mankind will continue to veer between periods of enormous promise and experiences of crushing catastrophe.

A well developed science of communication would enable us to study the stream of influence that runs from control to content and from content to audience. There is no need of science to forewarn us of the impact of some forms of control on what passes through the media. We have no hesitation in saying that a despotic government is intolerant of criticism, and if we want to confirm this generalization by referring to any given despotism the facts can be gathered by the simple expedient of glancing through the press, listening to broadcasts, and taking a cursory look at films. Adverse news, comment and feature material is "the exception that proves the rule."

Some questions about the effect of control are more complicated. They involve "more or less," not "either-or." Nothing short of systematic, quantitative methods provides us with what we need to know. Suppose we ask whether the tradition of news impartiality is lived up to by the American press when the special interests of the publishers are involved. An opportunity to answer this question arose when the Federal Communications Commission held hearings on the problem of whether local newspaper publishers should be permitted to own local radio stations. It was necessary to proceed by systematic, quantitative methods in comparing the handling of news by a group of station-owning papers and a group of non-station-owners.[1] Two sets of twenty papers each were selected, as alike as possible, except for ownership of radio stations. The forty papers were

---

[1] Milton D. Stewart (forthcoming). Supervised by Paul F. Lazarsfeld, Office of Radio Research.

analyzed for their stories describing the FCC investigation on eleven days spanning three months. The owning group carried twice as many news stories as the nonowning group (3.35 stories per paper, against 1.7 per paper). The station-linked papers played up the witnesses who testified in favor of joint ownership rather than witnesses on the other side. (Fifty-five per cent of the witnesses mentioned by the linked papers were unfavorable to separation; thirty-two per cent of the witnesses referred to in the non-linked papers were in favor of separation.) The station-owning group also selected more quotations in favor of permitting joint ownership than opposing it.

When our problem is to evaluate the impact of content upon audience, rather than the effect of control on content, objective methods are also essential to tested knowledge. A representative problem is to determine the impact of the propaganda emanating from a given source upon all who are exposed to it. We follow the propaganda along its course of dissemination from channel to channel until we come to an audience whose responses can be measured. Often there is some uncertainty about the relationship of a given channel to a known propaganda source. If, however, the parallelisms are high, the probability of affiliation is increased. During World War II it was not difficult to find a known source of Axis propaganda; Axis short-wave radio stations beamed directly toward the United States. The staff of the FCC monitored these broadcasts, and kept a record of the statements made. For convenience, all statements were grouped into broad categories, which were the distinguishing themes of the Axis propaganda line. The theme list was as follows:

1. The United States is internally corrupt. That is to say, there is political and economic injustice, war profiteering, plutocratic exploitation, Communist sedition, Jewish conspiracy, and spiritual decay within the United States.

2. The foreign policies of the United States are morally unjustifiable. That is to say, they are selfish, bullying, imperialistic, hypocritical, and predatory.

3. The President of the United States is reprehensible. That is to say, he is a warmonger and a liar, unscrupulous, responsible for suffering, and a pawn of Jews, Communists, or plutocrats.

4. Great Britain is internally corrupt. That is to say, there is political and economic injustice, war profiteering, plutocratic exploitation, Communist sedition, Jewish conspiracy, and spiritual decay within Great Britain.

5. The foreign policies of Great Britain are morally unjustifiable. That is to say, they are selfish, bullying, imperialistic, hypocritical, and predatory.

6. Prime Minister Churchill is reprehensible. That is to say, he is a war-

monger and a liar, unscrupulous, responsible for suffering, and a pawn of Jews, Communists, or plutocrats.

7. Nazi Germany is just and virtuous. That is to say, its aims are justifiable and noble; it is truthful, considerate, and benevolent.

8. The foreign policies of Japan are morally justifiable. That is to say, Japan had been patient, long suffering; it is not responsible for war.

9. Nazi Germany is powerful. That is to say, Germany has the support of Europe; it possesses the manpower, armaments, materials, and morale essential to victory.

10. Japan is powerful. That is to say, it possesses the manpower, armaments, materials, and morale essential to victory.

11. The United States is weak. That is to say, it lacks the materials, manpower, armaments, and morale essential to victory.

12. Great Britain is weak. That is to say, the British Empire is collapsing; and it lacks the necessary materials, manpower, armaments and morale.

13. The United Nations are disunited. That is to say, they distrust, deceive, envy, and suspect each other.

14. The United States and the world are menaced by Communists, Jews, and plutocrats.

To determine the degree to which certain American magazines coincided with or deviated from the Axis line, the content of the magazines was read and classified according to the degree of consistency or inconsistency with the themes of Axis broadcasts. In one case, the results, compiled from December, 1941, to March, 1942, showed that 1,195 statements were consistent with the Axis line, while only 45 statements contradicted it. The most frequent statements related to theme 11—"The United States is weak"—317 consistent, 5 contradictory. Theme 1—"The United States is internally corrupt"—had 279 consistencies, 26 contradictions. The Nazi "devils"—"Communists," "Jews," "plutocrats"—were said to be world menaces in 156 statements; there was not a single contradiction.[2]

Many "suspect" papers and radio stations were absolved from suspicion by the results obtained when issues and broadcasts were quantitatively analyzed. They were protected from the all too frequent practice of condemning an entire publication on the basis of a few colorful examples of bias in news handling or editorial comment.

It will be noted that care must be taken to distinguish between the description of what is found in the channels of communication, and the inferences about controllers or audience drawn on the basis of content. If confusion is to be avoided, the facts used as indexes of "content" variables

---

[2] Expert testimony by Harold Graves, Jr., and Harold D. Lasswell in U.S. vs. William Dudley Pelley, et al., summarized in opinion of the U.S. Circuit Court of Appeals for the Seventh District, October term and session, 1942.

must be distinct from the indexes of "control" and audience "response." The Stewart study provided data about the publishers and also about content, and inferences based on one about the other were capable of being verified or invalidated.

All sorts of hypotheses are current in scientific and popular writing about the impact of specific kinds of content upon people. One of the most searching sets of suggestions has to do with the effect of optimism and pessimism on conduct. V. L. Parrington remarks that Puritanism "saw too little good in human nature to trust the multitude of the unregenerate; and this lack of faith was to entail grave consequences upon the development of New England."[3]

If hypotheses about the relationship between democracy and a pessimistic view of human nature are to be adequately explored, systematic and quantitative methods must be used to discover the balance of optimism and pessimism in the channels of communication. A step in this direction was taken by Thomas Hamilton in his study of Protestant sermons.[4]

Historians of American Protestantism point out that the pessimistic view of man's nature and earthly estate brought from Europe to the "land of opportunity" by the colonists gradually faded into a more optimistic conception of man's earthly potentialities. More recently, however, the trend appears to have changed. Hamilton examined the sermons published in the monthly magazine called *The Christian Century Pulpit* from October, 1929 to 1940. Each issue contains six or seven sermons delivered by Protestant ministers of various denominations. It is unclear how representative these sermons are of the total flood of sermonizing in the United States. Certainly the selection was influenced by whether the minister was widely known or whether the editors were personally acquainted with him. But in any case, there is no evidence that the selection was biased in any way that would greatly affect expressions of social optimism or pessimism.

The method used was to select one sermon from each issue of the magazine. The order in which the sermons were published was rotated. A sentence classification for social optimism and pessimism was constructed and the frequency of such sentences was counted. Without going into detail, it may in general be said that social optimism sentences were those imputing high value to science and education, holding that the church must be concerned about the "social gospel," and indicating that man is making progress in solving his problems. Social pessimism sentences affirmed man's need for mysticism and ritual, asserted that the sinfulness of man is the root of social problems, and disparaged science and education.

[3] *Main Currents in American Thought* (New York: Harcourt, Brace, 1930), I, p. 11.
[4] Thomas Hamilton, "Social Optimism and Pessimism in American Protestantism," *Public Opinion Quarterly*, 6 (1942): 280-283.

The results disclosed an unmistakable trend toward increasing pessimism. In 1929, 95 per cent of the sentences bearing on the problem were optimistic; only 5 per cent were pessimistic. In 1939-1940, 36 per cent were optimistic and 64 per cent were pessimistic. These provisional results can be checked against similar studies of papers read at ministers' conferences, articles found in professional journals, and theological books most widely preferred by ministers.

Many hypotheses have been put forward about the effect of dramatically presented content upon the attitudes and institutions of society. Content analysis procedures can be applied to films, for the purpose of investigating certain fundamental questions about motion pictures and American culture. What social groups are most frequently brought to the attention of motion picture audiences, thus reflecting and to some extent shaping their interests? What are the values sought by the characters portrayed on the screen? Are these the same values sought by the audience in everyday life, or do they differ profoundly? In the pictures how much success, and how much frustration, are depicted? Can we say, when we have thoroughly explored the significance of the films in the life of middle income Americans (who are known to constitute more of the audience than the highest and lowest income groups), that motion pictures are adaptive or escapist?

One of the few efforts to provide significant data has been made by Dorothy B. Jones.[5] A schedule was worked out with which different observers achieved consistent results when they classified pictures independently. One hundred films released by Hollywood between April, 1941, and February, 1942, were described. No rigid pattern of selection was used. (However, ninety-five per cent of the pictures had been produced by the seven major motion picture producing companies.) It was found that of the 188 major characters, there were twice as many men as women. Does this mean that men's lives are twice as interesting to men and women alike as the lives of women? If we find this ratio changing from year to year or decade to decade, does it mean that the range of women's activities is growing more diversified and exciting?

Three in every five major characters were "independent adults": they were economically established, free of parental control, usually unmarried, and with limited social and economic responsibilities. Although this "social age group" is seldom found in real life, its vigor and freedom from responsibility doubtless make it especially congenial to the free play of audience fantasy.

There was a strong tendency to overemphasize persons from the economic extremes. Two in every five heroes and heroines were definitely

[5] Dorothy B. Jones, "Quantitative Analysis of Motion Picture Content," *Public Opinion Quarterly*, 6 (1942): 411-428.

wealthy and, at the other extreme, two in every five were unmistakably poor or destitute; whereas in real life only about 1 per cent in the United States are definitely wealthy and only about one-third bear the mark of poverty, in the sense in which these terms were used in the study. Many people of high income were presented as living outside the accepted social hierarchy. In relation to social class, they were *déclassé*, usually on account of illegal activities.

What "values" were taken by the screen characters as their goals? Everyone expects that Boy wants Girl, or Girl wants Boy. Content analysis, however, indicates that this by no means exhausts the subject-matter of Hollywood productions. Besides the two-thirds of the 188 major characters who wanted love, one-fourth pursued fame, reputation, prestige. Only one-seventh were concerned with safety as a primary or secondary goal (health, bodily integrity, or survival). Only one-tenth were shown as wanting money or material goods. About the same number were concerned with rightness, that is, with living up to conceptions of duty. (For example, Alvin C. York, in "Sergeant York," who wanted to do his military duty for his country and at the same time maintain religious conviction.) About one-seventh sought a way of life. "Billy The Kid" wanted, among other things, an adventurous life, allowing him to live outside all social groups, with much freedom from responsibility. Harry Pulham, in "H. M. Pulham, Esq.," wanted the traditional way of life of his own circle to such an extent that he was willing to sacrifice his love. In "Underground," three of the main characters were chiefly concerned with the value of democracy as a way of life for the German people.

To what extent were the major characters able to achieve the values sought? To what extent were they frustrated? The balance was heavily on the side of indulgence. Three-fifths of all the major characters were left at the end of the picture with what they wanted. Ten per cent were deprived of everything, while one-seventh were "fifty-fifty." When we consider these results, a number of important questions arise. Is gratification a consequence of what the character does himself, or is it imputed to circumstances outside himself? "Strive and succeed" is one of the principal maxims of a middle class society where each individual is expected to succeed when he has disciplined himself through sacrifice in acquiring some skill, and then in applying himself to a socially respected task. Do motion pictures, by depicting success or failure as a result of nepotism, "pull," or social forces over which we have no control, subtly undermine the expectation that success depends on individual effort? Is romance made into a tool of "getting ahead" by connecting success in love with economic gain? Or do the fantasies offered by the movies provide a form of compensation enabling the audience to live up to the middle class ideal more often than it otherwise would? To learn the answer, further study of the entire process of communication is called for.

So interrelated are the facts of communication with the whole context of life that what appears in the media can be studied with advantage for many other purposes than the scientific explanation or management of communication. On the basis of what appears in press, radio, and film, for example, we may anticipate the moves of the enemy in conducting war. Early in World War II a research group at the British Broadcasting Corporation undertook to forecast the military moves of the Nazis by studying what the Nazis permitted to emerge from the transmitters under their control. The forthcoming thrust toward Norway, for instance, was preceded by statements imputing moves to the British. On the basis of comparisons between broadcasts directed toward the home audience and the foreign audience, forecasts were made about the probability that the British Isles would be invaded by the Nazis in 1940.[6]

Enemy communications are continually used for the purpose of estimating the state of morale among enemy peoples. This is the study of content as a basis of inference about the changing state of attitude toward war, and especially the intensity of the determination to carry on to victory. During World War I a morale chart that became famous was kept in the office of Secretary of War Newton D. Baker.[7]

The preceding examples have indicated how the study of what appears in a channel of communication may contribute to much more than the science of communication itself. Although any fact about what is carried in the media *may* contribute to communication science, the amount may be small. Studies of the act of communication for its own sake may begin at any link in the chain. The terminal point of such an act is response by an audience either immediately on exposure to content or later. Scientific questions are: How does control affect content? How does content affect audience? (If we ask how audiences affect the rest of the process we are posing subquestions already included in the study of control and content.) We always have in mind the eventual task of explaining different effects on the thinking, feeling, and doing of audiences.

What are the kinds of effect in which we are interested? Without going into detail at this point we may classify audience response as follows: (1) attention; (2) comprehension; (3) enjoyment; (4) evaluation; (5) action. It is evident what is involved in "attention" or "comprehen-

[6] Ernst Kris, Hans Speier, and others, *German Radio Propaganda: Report on Home Broadcasts During the War* (New York: Oxford University Press, 1944); also Harwood L. Childs and John B. Whitton, editors, *Propaganda by Short Wave* (Princeton: Princeton University Press, 1942).

[7] Reproduced between pages 192 and 193 in George G. Bruntz, *Allied Propaganda and the Collapse of the German Empire in 1918* (Stanford: Stanford University Press, 1938).

sion." The distinction between "enjoyment" and what is here called "evaluation" is that the former response is to the manner in which the content is presented and the latter to what is referred to by the content. We speak of enjoying a play, speech, or program (including, of course, the negative —not enjoying). We also speak of agreeing, or disagreeing, with a speaker's tribute to Woodrow Wilson or to the ideal of the League of Nations. These are "evaluations." By "actions" we mean buying, giving, volunteering, saving, and similar forms of conduct. The effect of any content on any audience can be studied from all five points of view if an exhaustive appraisal is desired.

It is important to go a little further into the analysis of response before selecting categories of content analysis. Responses are significant because they are interpersonal; they are part of the interaction of members of society. The most fundamental way to examine any response is in terms of values—does it modify or conserve values? By a "value" we mean an object of desire. Representative values are safety, income, power, and respect (the last two are deference values). The act of turning off a radio broadcast is to deny something to those responsible for the program. To comprehend what is being said by a lecturer is at once an indulgence of the listener by himself and of the lecturer (unless the speaker aims at incomprehensibility). The enjoyment of a sermon or an editorial is also a double indulgence. When an institution referred to by an editorial is endorsed, the institution and all who support it have a more favorable relationship to their human environment than before. In overt acts of giving, voting, or buying, the beneficiaries are treated with obvious indulgence.

Any response, then, can be classified according to "orientation" (target), "direction" (if it improves the value position of the target, the direction is "indulgent"; if it diminishes the value position it is "deprivational"), and "intensity."

Before we can be sure of how to classify any given response we need to know (or assume) certain facts about the responder. In particular we need to know where the person draws the line between his "self" and the rest of the world. If a Democrat applauds a Democrat, he is acting indulgently toward part of himself; if he applauds a Republican he is acting indulgently toward objects beyond the boundaries of the "self." Indeed, in an election year the act not only indulges the "nonself"—it actively inflicts a deprivation upon the "self."

The "self" is not to be confused with the "ego"; the "self" of any person includes his ego—the "me," the "I"—and all persons and groups that the ego includes with it. More technically, the "self" is made up of the symbol of the ego and the symbols of all who are recognized as available for full or partial equality of treatment with the ego. Family, friends, neighbors, fellow workers, fellow nationals, and even the members of humanity as a whole, may be incorporated within the structure of the self.[8]

The structure of any personality may be conveniently classified according to "identifications," "demands," and "acceptances." The "identifications" are symbols referring to any person or group: the ego, or others who are parts of the self, or those who are considered to lie beyond the scope of the self. The "demands" are the values sought for the identifications; they are the preferences and determinations. Aspirations for personal achievement, pride of family, love of country, hatred of the enemy, approval of party leaders and persons, are all part of the system of demands within the larger framework of a personality. The "acceptances" are the matter-of-fact assumptions about the shape of events in the past, present, and future. The outlook may be optimistic or pessimistic with reference to the value position of the self in the future (the "expectations").[9]

When we analyze the content of communication we are describing one of the factors affecting response. The identifications, demands, and acceptances of a person are "caused by" (are "functions of") two sets of factors —environment, predisposition. At this point a technical question arises: How do we distinguish the "content of media" from other parts of the environment? We can answer this question when we have a general theory of the process of communication. We say say, for instance, that the channels of communication are parts of the environment specialized for the transmission of signs. What, then, is a sign?

When we look objectively at what appears in print, radio, film, or any other medium, it is obvious that it can be described from two points of view. The captions of a newspaper can be seen as a collection of black marks on white paper, or as a series of references to objects outside the newspaper. We may speak of the physical events as "signs," and the meaning events as "symbols." There are many physical events that are not correlated with symbols and hence are not signs. There are, however, no symbol events in interpersonal communication without signs.[10]

Suppose we examine in more detail the interrelationship of sign with symbol. A convenient starting-point is thinking to oneself, "That is a

[8] American social psychology has been influenced by the accounts of the self given by George Herbert Mead, *Mind, Self and Society* (Chicago: University of Chicago Press, 1934), and Charles Horton Cooley, *Human Nature and the Social Order* (New York: Scribners, 1902).

[9] The present writer made these distinctions in *World Politics and Personal Insecurity* (New York: McGraw-Hill, 1935). Equivalent to "acceptances," as here defined, I have sometimes used "facts" or "expectations."

[10] Charles W. Morris distinguishes between "sign" and "sign vehicle," in "Foundations of the Theory of Signs," *International Encyclopedia of Unified Science*, Vol. I (1938), No. 2, p. 3. In Morris' usage "sign" is equivalent to "symbol" as used here; his "sign vehicle" is equivalent to "sign." The term "symbol" is kept in a central position in the present writer's terminology, following social psychologists like George Herbert Mead and psychopathologists like Sigmund Freud.

broadcast by the President." This moment of judgment may be described as a subjective event in the total stream of subjective events that we recognize as "ourselves thinking and feeling." Suppose we give it a special designation, S^3. S^3 refers to at least two events that occurred before it in the subjective sequence: (1) taking note of the acoustical phenomena emanating from the radio receiving set, and (2) recalling the President's voice. The recognition of the President's voice (event S^2) goes forward so swiftly that S^1 (the noting of the physical stimuli) may not be recognized as a distinct part of the experience. There are certain conditions, however, in which this phase of the sequence stands out. Should the broadcast be somewhat indistinct, the act of perceiving the physical pattern of pitch, intensity and timbre (S^1) would be noted. Only when the sound assumes a pattern that precipitates the recall of "Roosevelt" does the S^2 event take place. Should the reception be so poor that there is nothing but a noise, we would have an example of a physical event lacking correlation with the subjective event of referring. Under these conditions, there would be no symbol, since there is no S^2 or S^3.

An act of communication between two persons is complete when they understand the same sign in the same way. More technically, the sign mediates subjective events that constitute the same references. The recipient of communication assigns his reference (S^3) after exposure to the sign, while the sender of the communication proceeds from his act of reference to the making of a sign, which he then notes and tests (corresponding to a new sequence of S^1, S^2 and S^3 of the type noted above for the receiver).

Our concern is with mass communication, an act of communication in which a great many persons are involved as senders, receivers, or both. (It is a matter of convenience what minimum number of persons must participate before we have an example of mass communication.)

In the light of the distinctions just made, it is evident that we describe symbols when we say, "The headlines are bad news for the Italians today." We speak of signs when we remark, "The ink in the newspaper is poor." Manifestly, the relation between symbol and sign varies through a wide range. The black ink that forms the letters "Italy" in a newspaper headline can be distinguished from most of the blank space between letters, words, and lines. Only the ink and the immediate surrounding space and material are necessary to the reader's recognition of the word. We may use the expression "pure sign" to designate the physical minimum at the focus of attention that is necessary for the discovery of a sign function. All else may be classified as "sign accessory." The language of everyday conversation is composed chiefly of pure signs, since the amount of sound is not appreciably greater than is necessary to maintain intelligibility. One of the most striking examples of a sign accessory is a public monument on which a few words are inscribed. Some signs are recognized as resembling the object to which they refer (the referent) and may be called "icons." A sculptured head is an icon,[11] if it resembles its subject.

How shall we decide what symbols are at the focus of attention of a group? We cannot consider a radio program as entering into the attention of an audience if it is blocked out by static. We can scarcely call it "in the focus of attention" if the vocabulary used is 75 per cent incomprehensible to the audience. A minimum degree of response on the part of an audience must be demonstrated (or assumed) before we are justified in speaking of any content as available to it. In measuring the results of exposure to this content, we call the "effect" the part of the response that is above the minimum necessary to establish a communication-situation.

In examining the effect of any content upon the "identifications" of an audience, we assume that statements about the self probably have some influence. To put this hypothesis to the test, it is necessary to find all the statements in the content that are relevant; i.e., that identify the self of the communicator with the self of the audience, or exclude him from it. "I am an American" is an identification of the self of the speaker or writer, and is classified as a statement of identification with the audience, if the audience is American, or as a statement of exclusion, if the audience is French.

The members of an audience make demands for action, and if we are interested in the effect of a given content upon these demands, we classify the statements of demand, on the testable assumption that these have a direct bearing on the result. "I approve of this bill" is a statement in which the speaker not only refers to an event, which is the consideration of the bill, but simultaneously approves of a certain outcome. He is taking a double degree of responsibility: (1) for the authenticity of the event referred to, and (2) for an attitude on his own part. A statement like "The bill will be passed" does not indicate approval or disapproval, since even those who are opposed to a measure may concede that they are in a minority. We use the term "normative" to refer to all statements of preference (and determination), and the term "non-normative" (or "naturalistic") for all statements that express neither approval nor disapproval.

Many non-normative statements are worth classifying if we want to explain why audiences change their minds about certain statements, after listening to speakers, or fail to do so. A statement like, "The bill will be passed," is neither a demand nor an identification statement. Were it not for the awkwardness of the expression, it might be termed a "nonidentification, nondemand statement" or a "fact statement." For convenience, we can call it an "acceptance statement." When acceptance statements refer to future events, they are "expectations." (It will be noted that an identifica-

[11] Suggested by Morris, as cited, p. 24.

tion statement has the same form as a nondemand statement, and might be classified with acceptances. However, we emphasize the importance of the delimitation of the self by treating identification statements as coordinate with acceptance statements.)

Certain problems arise in classifying normative statements when we contrast such sentences as the following: "I want war," "War is glorious." There is no question about the position of the statement-maker who utters the first sentence, but we can not unequivocally assume that a speaker who uses the second form of statement necessarily takes responsibility for regarding war as "glorious." The maker of such a statement may insist that his remark is to be understood as a naturalistic reference to what other people are believed to think. When the speaker takes full responsibility for approval or disapproval, we may speak of a "normative-demand statement." When the grammatical form is ambiguous, the speaker makes a "normative-ambiguous statement." The normative-ambiguous statement plays a very important part in communication, especially in controversy. The man who says, "The law is so and so" appears to state a norm that transcends his own preferences. If challenged, he may admit that his sentence is to be understood as a forecast about the way certain judges and lawyers would reply to a "poll." He might go on to say that he would not himself join the probable majority.

In defining demand statements, we distinguish between "preference" and "determination." "I am against this bill" falls into the first category. "I am doing everything in my power to support you" is in the second. When he makes a statement of determination the speaker characterizes an event, applies a norm to it, and indicates that he assumes responsibility for acting in such a way as to increase the probability that the approved event will in fact take place.

Not only complete statements, but single words and expressions (unit symbols) may reasonably be expected to exercise some effect upon an audience. The incessant repetition of a common symbol of the self, like "American," may enhance common loyalty and a sense of separation from other countries. Unit symbols may be classified in much the same way as statements. Some refer to persons or groups and may be called identification symbols, examples being "Stalin," "Russians." Some symbols refer to objects of preference or determination, or are utilized in expressing preference or determination (demand symbols). Some symbols (acceptance symbols) are objects of reference in acceptance statements, or are utilized in making the reference. Hence when "national unity" or "social security" are objects of preference or determination, they count as demand symbols; when only acceptance statements are made about them, they are acceptance symbols.

When we classify all statements into identifications, demands and acceptances, we are classifying them according to "purport." The purport of a headline or editorial statement is how it is to be understood. But in content analysis, our task is not done when we have made this preliminary classification of purport. The final classification must be in terms of the way audience values are presented (presentation analysis). Consider the following caption: "United States Victory Inevitable." No one who reads English will have any difficulty understanding the purport of these words, since the vocabulary is well known and the grammar is conventional. If the audience expected to read such a headline is American, the good news is an indulgence of all who want their country to win the war. It is deprivational of a possible audience hostile to the United States.

We may classify references according to direction: "pro," "anti," or "no direction." Alternative terms for pro are "plus" or "positive" or "indulgent"; alternative words for anti are "minus" or "negative" or "deprivational"; and "no direction" may for various purposes be subdivided into "neutral," "indifferent," or "undecided."

Descriptions of content that fall short of presentation analysis may be called "topical." Subject classifications in libraries are topical, in this sense. Or classification of radio programs into "dramatic," "discussion," and the like, are topical; they are incomplete from a scientific point of view, since they are not of equal generality with the categories used in describing response. When we say, for instance, that Luise Rainer starred in a film depicting Chinese, and that audiences, by test, were more friendly to the Chinese after seeing the film, we have an incomplete rendering of the affair from the scientific point of view. The response of the audience is described in general terms of "friendliness," and graded into "more or less." But this content is not described in categories of equal generality, or nuance; we are not using general categories when we say that a *specific individual* is prominent in a certain film. We need to describe the content, independently of the effect, as "friendly (or indulgent)" to a certain degree. Then we can explore hypotheses about the impact of content upon audience response.

Presentation analysis involves more than counting the *number* of statements that "indulge" or "deprive" a given object of reference. Statements are made with varying degrees of *intensity*; and this may affect the intensity of audience response.

Intensity is a matter of "prominence" and "style." No one doubts that the probability of audience response is greater if a statement appears in a front page headline than when it occupies a subordinate position on an inside page. Nor does anyone doubt that some ways of phrasing a statement are more likely than others to affect the audience.

We define prominence as availability to attention. Availability depends upon the arrangement of the components of the stimulus field.[12] We describe such arrangements in terms of "position" and "emphasis"; they vary among audiences according to the predispositions developed through the action of cultural environment upon original nature. Readers accustomed to the English language expect to begin on the left side of the page, while readers of Chinese give priority to the right side. Emphasis devices are fixed within certain limits by the psychophysical characteristics of the stimuli that constitute the pure signs and accessories. Radio broadcasting, for illustration, is restricted to auditory stimuli; yet within this area all sorts of variations in pitch, loudness, and related characteristics are possible.

Several methods have been applied to the problem of describing the prominence of one channel in relation to other channels, and the prominence of one part of a channel relative to all parts. These determinations are made for representative persons in a given society. Subjects are selected because of residence, sex, age, income, official position, or similar criteria, and an analysis made of the way they spend the day.[13] This makes it possible to describe the place in the routine of daily life occupied by radio, print, film, and by theater, meetings, and conversation. Re-surveys show how relations shift among the channels.

More intensive procedures are used to discover the relative prominence of the parts of a given channel. The attention-significance of different positions is often measured by finding how many persons testify to having seen a given article or advertisement. Of those who profess to have read a copy of the issue of a newspaper on a specific day, practically everybody claims to have seen the headline. Only 1 per cent, or less, may recall some positions on inside pages. In research on radio, the attention potential of different hours, stations, and programs is estimated by telephoning to ask whether the radio is tuned in and, if so, to what station. It is also possible to arrive at such estimates by mechanical recording appliances that register the dial movements of receiving sets. Similar methods are used to compare the "attention pull" (or "audience predisposition") of emphasis devices like size of headline, color, and many others.[14]

In arriving at a description of intensity, it is necessary to go beyond prominence, measured by position and emphasis devices, to "symbol style." Prominence relates to signs. But symbol style is a matter of the symbols that compose the statements. "Style," in general, means the pattern in which the elementary units of a whole are arranged. In classifying words

---

[12] The most apt vocabulary for the description of such fields is that of Gestalt psychology as formulated by Max Wertheimer, Wolfgang Köhler, and Kurt Koffka.

[13] See Pitirim A. Sorokin and Clarence Q. Berger, *Time-Budgets of Human Behavior* (Cambridge: Harvard University Press, 1939).

[14] These procedures are conveniently summarized in the standard manuals of advertising and market research.

with respect to intensity—stress toward action—we take note, for instance, of the active verbs, like "do," in relation to inactive verbs. Besides the lexical units (words) are semantic units (meanings), and grammatical units (clauses, phrases, e.g.). Audience predispositions toward action are related to patterns of such symbols, and are open to investigation by the use of methods similar to those appropriate to the study of prominence.

In making cross-channel or intrachannel comparisons, we need a vocabulary to designate patterns of symbol and sign that correspond. At present, there is no universal consensus on the terms to be used in making these distinctions. However, the medium of print (and writing) has fostered a vocabulary in talking about printed matter that is capable of being extended to all other media with a minimum of violence to usage and with few additions. Each channel has its own idiom, yet the fixing of signs in print (and writing), coupled with antiquity, has allowed this channel to exercise a disproportionate influence on the language of all media.

The following twelve terms are useful in the making of cross-channel and intrachannel comparisons: Title, The Issue, An Issue, Edition, Version, Section, Equisection, Item, Marker, Text, Supplementary Sign, Reference.

1. When we classify the output of the channel in terms of symbols, the basic unit is a "title." Books, pamphlets, and other pieces of printed matter usually are given titles, as are plays, films, musical compositions, courses of study, and religious rites. Sometimes the content of a given title varies as when a book passes through many revisions. How are we to identify a title when there is no explicit description appearing on the face of a communication? In the early days of newsletters, a writer often failed to give his product a recurring designation. Under such circumstances, we may lay down the rule that a title includes all serials that emanate from a common source or retain a conspicuous characteristic.

2. During any given period of time the volume of a channel may vary, and major output frequencies may be called "issues." When publications are released at stated intervals, it is customary to speak of quarterly, monthly, weekly, or other "issues." It is also usual to speak of "issuing" a book, pamphlet, poster, map, chart, or picture. When information is given out, releases are said to be "issued." In the same way, feature films are ordinarily said to be "released" or "issued." In our terminology a play is said to be "issued" when it is produced or performed. In the same way, we divide the output of radio into a daily cycle of programs that are "issued" (produced and performed). By extension, we likewise speak of music and dance recitals as "issues."

3. "The issue" designates all units put out in a selected time period. "An issue" is the name for one of these units considered individually. In practice a great many different terms are employed in speaking of such units. Printed matter is issued by "copy," while in other channels equivalent terms are "performance," "observance," or "screening."

4, 5. Issues may be varied in two ways, one involving symbols (expressed in pure signs) and the other sign accessories. When a book is thoroughly revised, we have an example of change in symbols. Without altering the symbols, however, it is possible to print a book on wood-pulp, parchment, cork, or some other accessory. Differences among issues that pertain to symbols are separate "editions," while variations involving only sign accessories are "versions." What we speak of as an edition is called, in the theater, a "production"; manifestly the same play may have several productions and in each of these there may be more or less thorough modifications in actors, properties, and other accessories (versions).

6. We may use the term "section" to name the major parts of an issue as established by pure sign, sign accessory, or a combination of both. This terminology is close to ordinary usage, since books and pamphlets are often subdivided into "sections" or "parts," and newspapers and magazines name their subdivisions "departments" or "sections." The sections of a play are usually called "acts"; the corresponding parts of a musical rendition are "movements."

7. An issue is usually divided by sign accessories into minute parts of approximately equal length. The copy of a printed work is divided into "lines." In music, the "measure" or "bar" is a corresponding component. In films the division is a "foot" or "frame," while in radio it is a time unit like "minute" or "second." We propose to use the term "equisection" as the elementary repetition unit of an issue when it is divided by sign accessories into parts of approximately equal length.

8. The major units of a section that involve changes in pure signs may be called "items." The item in a book is usually a "chapter," while in a newspaper it is a "story," "editorial," or "feature." In a pamphlet the item is often named a "section." The items of a musical movement are usually called "phrases." The items of an act are "scenes," and the corresponding parts of a film are "sequences."

9. Often the item (or any other subdivision of a channel by pure sign) is set off from its surroundings by means of sign accessories. In a book attention is directed to the item (or subdivision) by means of "title page," "front matter," or "heading." In a play such accessories are "curtain," "pause," "prologue," "epilogue." In newsreels the subdivisions are often indicated by the "commentary." In the absence of a current term suitable for cross-channel comparisons, we will use the word "marker" to refer to the part of an item (or channel subdivision by pure sign) that is set off by means of sign accessories. (It is possible that the marker will contain, in addition to sign accessories, pure signs that play a subordinate role.) We may subdivide markers into three categories according to the position they occupy in relation to the item (or subdivision) as a whole. Markers that come at the beginning are "captions"; markers interspersed with the item are "mid-captions"; markers at the end are "closures." In this terminology the heading and the blank space in the chapter of a book is a "caption"; subtitles are "mid-captions"; and the printer's marks at the end, together with the white space, are "closures."

10. The part of an item that is not a marker is a "text." In our vocabulary the caption of a news item is the "marker" and the noncaption part is the "text."

11. In printed matter we find that the prose text may be supplemented by pictures, thus involving a type of sign in contrast with the predominant signs of the item. In picture magazines, on the other hand, words are subordinated to pictures. We may use the term "supplementary sign" when referring to a sign differing from the type of sign predominating in an item. When a picture is used to embellish a news story, it is a "supplementary sign." When words are introduced to embellish a picture, the relationship is reversed and the words are the "supplementary signs." In plays, scenes may be enhanced by means of properties; the latter are supplementary. When the spoken lines in a radio program are supported by musical and sound effects, the latter are supplementary.

12. A "reference" is a single instance of the use of any symbol. It is evident that any symbol may be shown by many different signs, as when an eminent statesman is referred to by the letters of his name or by a photograph, drawing, cartoon, spoken name, or pantomime.

It follows from what has been said that in content analysis we look upon statements and signs as raw material to be summarized in order to bring out either (1) the impact of content upon audience, or (2) the influence of control upon content. An adequate content analysis results in a condensed description of (1) the frequency with which selected symbols have been mentioned, (2) the number of times that the mentioned symbols have been presented favorably, neutrally, or unfavorably, and (3) the number of times the presentations have been made with given degrees of intensity (intensity being measured in terms of prominence—position and emphasis —and dynamic symbol style). In schematic form, we may say:

Content Analysis of a Statement

The final summary of a statement is in "presentation" categories: A statement is indulgent or deprivational of a given symbol (or symbols) to a given audience, with a certain intensity.

Orientation: Name of symbol; list of equivalents.

Direction: Indulgence (improves value position of audience).

Deprivation (impairs value position of audience).

[The value (or values) with respect to which a statement is indulgent or deprivational is a "standard" (or "standards")].

Intensity: Prominence (availability to attention).

Position.

Emphasis Devices (sign accessories guiding attention).

Dynamism of Symbol Style (symbols instigating action).

In comparing frequencies it is necessary to adopt a specified base. Perhaps we are told that a given newspaper refers twice as often to China as to Japan. This statement may be true, and yet leave a misleading impression. Possibly in the course of a year there are only two references to one country and one to the other; or perhaps there were a dozen references to both. We need to express relationships in terms of a whole universe that is held stable. One procedure for establishing this stable base is to add up the frequencies of a selected list of symbols. Our research purposes may be served when we account for the changes in all these symbols as a group, and in relation to one another.

However, this procedure does not take into consideration the total body of symbols that are offered to the audience in a given channel at a selected time. The absolute and relative frequencies of our listed symbols may remain the same but the total number of words in the channel may increase or diminish. May we not, therefore, select as our base of comparison the total number of words in the content described? In selecting a word base, we may or may not assume that there is a constant relationship between the number of words and the magnitude of the universe of meaning that they convey. No data are available at present for examining the validity of this assumption for various communications to various audiences.

Another problem connected with the choice of the word base concerns the relationship of the printed word to pictures, drawings, and other graphic signs. Available experiments provide us with no reliable constants for translating the meaning of 100 printed words into a symbolically equivalent number of graphic, auditory, or other signs.

Since word-counting is slow, it is convenient to determine constant ratios between number of words and equisection units in a given channel. We may count the average number of words printed on a representative page or uttered in a minute of broadcasting time. Constants can be determined for every channel and subchannel, thus allowing for the difference between tabloid and standard newspapers and for variations from discussion programs to dramatic broadcasts. In describing printed matter, space is often used as a measure of content, but the space-words ratio has often been left unstated. Comparisons of spoken and printed media can be made by discovering space-time-words constants. The entire output of a broadcasting station for a twenty-four-hour period may be compared with the successive editions of a newspaper during the same time interval.

A distinction must be made in content analysis, between "weighted" and "unweighted" references. Each appearance of a reference may be counted as 1, as when "Mussolini" is counted twice in the sentence "Mussolini and Hitler meet; Mussolini returns to Rome." This is an unweighted reference. A reference is weighted when additional references (above 1) in a recording unit count for 1. In the previous sentence, "Mussolini" would be counted once under this procedure, although the name occurred twice.

The list of symbols selected for content analysis may vary from the "literal" to the "equivalent." Reader-classifiers may be instructed to count the symbol "liberal" only when it appears literally. In accordance with such rules, even words like "liberalism" are ignored. Since the instructions stick to the lexical form of the word, it is counted even though it appears in a statement that does not refer to politics but to personal generosity. (Some vocabulary tests of school children have been made on this basis; but the word lists so derived are lexical and not semantic units; they could be supplemented by tests of "meaning.")

Categories may allow some degree of discretion to the classifier. As the range of permitted equivalency increases, however, agreement among classifiers may diminish.

The less literal the categories employed, the fuller must be the instructions issued to readers, and the more care must be exercised in choosing and training readers. Experience has shown that high levels of agreement can be obtained even among readers who are not rigidly confined to literal categories.

It must be clear to readers what assumptions are made about the audience. For many purposes this picture may be kept quite simple; special facts do not need to be collected to supplement unchallenged "common knowledge." We do not need special information to tell us that most Americans who are loyal to their country want it to be treated with respect by people of other countries. Moreover, it is not necessary to conduct special inquiries before we accept the view that most loyal Americans will resent statements by foreigners that unsparingly condemn the morals and manners of the country. We may therefore classify statements explicitly criticizing the morality of America as deprivations of this country when they occur in a channel of communication reaching an American audience.[15]

But for many investigations it is important to have rather special information about predispositions of the audience. Only a careful psychological investigation, for instance, can justify us in considering certain "upper class" intonations of voice in a radio program as deprivational of an audience composed, for example, of middlewestern farmers.

When a large volume of content is to be described, operations can be simplified by the use of coding procedures. Each symbol is assigned a number that is recorded every time it occurs. Position on the entry blank shows whether the presentation is indulgent or deprivational. A further condensation is achieved when a number is allocated to the standard according to which the symbol is appraised as indulgent or deprivational.[16] A representative though not exhaustive list of standards is the following:

[15] The scaling techniques of L. L. Thurstone can be used to measure content as well as effect. A "jury" is instructed to sort statements into a definite number of categories. The jury may be chosen from scientists who are also familiar with the usages of a potential audience; or the jury may be representative of the audience. As we have seen, content analysis can also be conducted by means of a logically inclusive scheme that defines and illustrates its categories.

[16] On technical questions see especially the work of N. C. Leites, Ithiel Pool, Irving Janis, Raymond H. Fadner, Abraham Kaplan, Joseph M. Goldsen, Alan Geller, David Kaplan. Although the foregoing exposition has dealt with unit symbols—individual words or phrases—it should be noted that the categories and procedures are also applied in content analysis to complete statements or to groups of statements considered as a whole. In general see Abraham Kaplan, "Content Analysis and the Theory of Signs," *Philosophy of Science*, 10: 230-249 (1943), with comments by Charles Morris. The "recording unit" is the number of words, or word-equivalents, used in reporting symbol counts; the "context unit" is the words that may be examined in making a count. Symbols may thus be recorded "per sentence" or "per hundred words"; in case of doubt, the paragraph or surrounding thousand words may be examined as context.

1. *Expediency* (*Strength*) describes the position of the object of reference in regard to such values as safety, power, goods, respect (power and respect are subcategories of deference).

1a. *Safety*. Refers to physical integrity of persons, groups or things. BRITISH LIVES LOST; BRITISH PILOTS RESCUED; KING ESCAPES BOMBS; AIR MINISTER DIES IN PLANE COLLISION.

1ab. *Efficiency*. Efficiency refers to level of performance of a function. HEALTH OF EVACUATED CHILDREN IMPROVES (biological efficiency); RESISTANCE TO DIPHTHERIA IN DEEP BOMB SHELTERS DECREASES.

1b. *Power*. In the most general sense, power is control over important decisions. It is measured according to the means of decision-making—fighting, diplomacy, voting, for example. GERMANS BREAK THROUGH AT SEDAN; GERMAN PEACE OFFER REBUFFED; LABOR GAINS IN BY-ELECTION; COURT REVOKES LICENSE OF COMMUNIST PERIODICAL.

1bb. *Efficiency*. NEW ANTI-AIRCRAFT DEVICES ARE SUPERIOR; CLEVER AXIS DIPLOMACY WINS AGAIN; PRIME MINISTER SPLITS OPPONENTS AND WINS VOTE OF CONFIDENCE.

1c. *Goods*. This term refers to volume and distribution of goods and services. FOOD RESERVES DOUBLED; SOUTH AMERICAN MARKET PRESERVED.

1cb. *Efficiency*. WAR PLANTS 80 PER CENT EFFICIENT; HIGHLY SKILLED GERMAN OPTICIANS.

1d. *Respect*. BRITISH PRESTIGE SUFFERS; BRITISH RESPECT GERMAN AIRMEN; CAROL BOOED AS HE LEAVES ROUMANIA; SPEAKS CONTEMPTUOUSLY OF ITALIAN ARMY.

1db. *Efficiency*. RIBBENTROP RECEIVED WITH GREAT POMP; EXQUISITE COURTESY OF CHINESE DIPLOMATS EXTOLLED.

2. *Morality*.

2a. *Truth-Falsehood*. GERMAN LIES ARE BOLDER utilizes a moral standard, the obligation to refrain from the deliberate dissemination of falsehood. BBC STICKS TO THE TRUTH.

2b. *Mercy-Atrocity*. ENEMY ATROCITIES MULTIPLY—the term "atrocity" makes use of a moral standard to classify acts, the obligation to refrain from inflicting unnecessary cruelty in the conduct of war. GERMANS RESCUE BRITISH SAILORS.

2c. *Heroism-Cowardice*. The obligation to act courageously; RISKS LIFE TO RESCUE COMRADE; SOLDIER DESERTS WOUNDED COMRADE.

2d. *Loyalty-Disloyalty*. The obligation to serve a common purpose; ALL SECTIONS OF POPULATION PATRIOTIC; FIFTH COLUMN ACTIVE IN NORWAY.

3. *Propriety*. The obligation to learn a conventional code; GERMANS ARE A CRUDE AND BARBAROUS PEOPLE; HIS MANNERS ARE PERFECT. If a code is deliberately violated, we have an example of disrespect (1).

4. *Divinity*. The standard is an obligation to abide by the Will of God; GOD IS ON OUR SIDE; GOD WILL PUNISH OUR ENEMIES.

5. *Legality*. The standard is the obligation to abide by law; JAPANESE GOVERNMENT VIOLATES INTERNATIONAL LAW; COURT UPHOLDS INTERNATIONAL LAW.

6. *Beauty*. The standard is aesthetic; BEAUTIFUL EQUIPMENT DE-SIGNED BY UNITED STATES OF AMERICA; HIDEOUS GERMAN ART ON DISPLAY.

7. *Consistency*. The standards are logical relationships among propositions; HITLER CONTRADICTS SELF; CHURCHILL STATES LOGICAL CASE.

8. *Probability*. Probability of a statement with no imputation of deliberate falsification; EINSTEIN'S THEORY CONFIRMED.

9. *Euphoria-Dysphoria*. The standard is agreeable or disagreeable subjective states; TERROR GRIPS BRUSSELS (terror is dysphoric); FESTIVE SPIRIT IN ROME (festive spirit is euphoric). "Hate" is dysphoric unless explicitly qualified; GLORIOUS HATE SUNG BY POET.

10. *Omnibus*. Statements fusing many standards; THE UNSPEAKABLE TURK.

Our experience of content analysis up to the present time leaves many general and technical questions unresolved. Nevertheless, substantial progress has been made toward the ideal of describing content with categories whose generality is comparable with those long used in studies of effect.[17]

[17] This discussion is a revision of Document 9 issued by the Experimental Division for the Study of Wartime Communication, Library of Congress (1941).

DESCRIBING
THE EFFECTS OF COMMUNICATIONS

BY HAROLD D. LASSWELL

EVERY conceivable method of measuring human activity has been or can be applied to the problem of appraising the impact of content on audience. We have named five kinds of response—or better, five features of any response—that have been the object of special study: attention, comprehension, enjoyment, evaluation, action.

In examining effect upon attention we apply methods that have already been referred to in the review of content analysis. It was pointed out that before anyone is entitled to call any collection of statements a "content" it must be assumed or demonstrated that audience attention reaches a certain minimum level. The part of the response above this level is "effect."

The same considerations apply to comprehension. In describing content it is necessary to assume or demonstrate that the audience has a certain degree of understanding of what is said. All comprehension above this level is effect and is measured by the same methods employed in ascertaining the minimum level.

The very large amount of research that has been done on comprehension shows that much public discourse is carried on in language "over the heads" of the mass audience. Scientific workers in education have undertaken to grade words according to familiarity or "difficulty." In 1932, E. L. Thorndike brought out *A Teachers Word Book of 20,000 Words;* but this was based entirely upon the frequency of the lexical unit without regard to meanings. Semantic counts are now being made by Irving Lorge and others.

Comprehension of printed matter is profoundly affected by the reading skills with which readers approach the page. Slow reading and slow comprehension are related to failure of the eye to focus in the most efficient manner. (Eye movements are studied by special photographic apparatus adapted to the purpose, notably by W. S. Gray.) Comprehension is aided or retarded by the arrangement of signs on a page—type size and design, width of column, and the like. Practice in reading and skillful arrangement of signs do not always improve comprehension; it is limited by the general intelligence and native aptitude of reader or listener, and these predispositions are relatively unchanged through the years.

Scientific research on enjoyment began with an attempt to learn about taste in painting. In the late 'sixties and early 'seventies of the last century Gustav Theodor Fechner took an active part in the controversy over two madonna paintings attributed to Holbein. When the two were exhibited together he placed an album by the pictures and asked visitors to state which was the more beautiful. Actually the experiment was a failure—only 113 opinions being recorded by over 11,000 visitors—and most of the answers had to be rejected for various reasons.[1] However, the fruitfulness of the method caught the imagination of many specialists who utilized it in building up our present knowledge of aesthetic experience and judgment of programs, concerts, exhibits, and other communicated content.

Methods appropriate to the investigation of enjoyment are also applied to studying evaluation, which is unconcerned with the beauty of the "saying" and entirely taken up with the attributes of what is talked about. Oral interviews, direct mail questionnaires, and many other procedures reveal attitude changes on exposure to film, radio, speech, and other channels.

The most crucial inquiries relate to the impact of content on action, the terminal phase of every completed sequence of communication. Representative indexes of such final effect are votes, sales, gifts, enlistments, and attendance. In addition, there is skill acquisition in reading, writing and 'rithmetic—to say nothing of all other acquirable ways of efficient performance. Educational science is largely devoted to the task of measuring and improving the effect of content on skill. In recent times this has meant a high degree of concentration on "visual" content, since film, slide, still picture, chart, table, map, model, and sample, are more abundant than ever. As the operating processes of industry have changed at a more rapid rate, industrial training inside the plant has grown in importance as a field of applied communication. Modern advertising has for years sold itself to business on a basis of its alleged effect on buying habits measured in many ways; and "market research" explores the effect of product design and many other factors on consumer acceptance. The most ancient quantitative index of action is the vote—it may be a "black ball," a brandished spear, a showing of hands, or a button on an electrical voting machine. Literature abounds in many generalizations about the supposed impact of an orator's argument and manner on juries, legislatures, and mass electorates; but only in the last few years have quantitative measures been applied to the "content" dimension of the relationship. Over the centuries the propaganda of the proselyting religions has produced many "practical" textbooks. Quantification, however, has begun but recently.

In the present review of effect analysis, the emphasis will be put upon the different ways that data are gathered. This is justified by the importance of appraising every research report with an eye to the way in which the researcher relates himself to the field of observation. The observer—

[1] Edwin G. Boring, *A History of Experimental Psychology* (New York: Appleton-Century Co., 1929), p. 273.

and every data-gatherer is properly called an observer—has a wide choice of standpoints that he may occupy and an enormous range of possible adaptation of the details of his procedure. This is also true of the investigators of control and content; however, existing methods of describing effect are much further diversified than research on other phases of the total process of communication.

In differentiating observational standpoints several features that affect result must be taken into account. "Duration" is one of these factors. Sometimes the observer rivets his attention upon events during many years in the career-line of a person or in the history of a social situation. At the other extreme the observer sees only one person or situation briefly (as in some quick interviews). Besides duration, another basic factor is "complexity." Complexity or simplicity relates to control over the field of observation or over the recording and processing of data.

There are two ways in which the observer may exercise control over the events that occur in his field of observation: "contact" or "experiment." When the investigator is entirely out of contact with what he describes, there is no possibility that he will influence what goes on there. A modern historian who writes about public opinion in fifth century Athens is a "collector" of records and residues who obviously has no prospect of modifying the events referred to. Even when contact between observer and event is direct, the investigator may have no appreciable effect upon what happens; he is then a "spectator." If the observer takes part in everyday life, he has some influence upon the situation; when the members of the group are unaware of being studied, the researcher is a "participant." Persons may know when they are being observed for scientific or policy purposes; the investigator is then an "interviewer." The observer may go beyond contact to experiment and design his experimental interventions for the purpose of exploring few or many variables.

In "recording" observations the research worker may use procedures that require long training and elaborate instrumentation or techniques of the utmost simplicity. The same is true of "processing" data. For many purposes it is sufficient to "hit the high spots"; at other times painstaking effort must be expended in drawing every shred of meaning out of material.

In general, we may summarize the various standpoints of observation as "intensive" and "extensive." They are intensive when prolonged and complex, extensive when brief and simple. We have noted that complexity is a matter of the degree of control over events in the observational field and of elaborateness in recording and processing data.

Collectors of Tabulated Data

Election returns are useful evidence of effect in all countries where popular government prevails. But we cannot take official figures at face value. The investigator must evaluate the probable honesty of the count, the degree of freedom from intimidation, and the representativeness of results.

In American elections, where honest counting is the rule, conspicuous exceptions are found in counts of the third-party vote and of the vote of the lodging-house areas of large cities, where newcomers from the farm and immigrants from abroad find temporary shelter while they hunt for jobs. Gambling, prostitution, or other illegal operations cluster in such mobile zones, and politics becomes an instrument for protecting the capital invested in property used for illegal purposes. The dominant political group "counts out" the opposition. In both city and country, the officials of the two major parties often agree to assign a nominal figure to the third-party vote, which they do not count at all.

In appraising the significance of election returns, it may be borne in mind that the secret ballot is a comparatively recent innovation. In reading old election returns it is important to remember that the landlord or factory owner was often physically present or represented by agents when his tenants or employees publicly announced their votes. Investigation reveals that in some areas today the poorer members of the community are often doubtful that the secrecy of the ballot is genuinely respected.[2]

How representative are those who go to the polls of those who stay away? This question is difficult to answer because votes are usually recorded by party or by sex, and no subtotals are computed according to age, income, occupation, urban or rural residence, religion, race, nationality of origin, and related characteristics. We know that nonvoters are heavily recruited from those who feel hopeless about the influence of elections, as well as from the complacent, satisfied, and negligent.

In evaluating the representativeness of official election returns, one of the chief obstacles is that election districts do not always coincide with census districts. Census figures may not be reported by city wards or by state congressional or judicial districts. Only in exceptional cases and at great expense have the basic "census tract" data of the United States been made available. The study of electoral districts always reveals some over- or under-representation. The most flagrant examples come about as a result of differential population growth. Since 1928, one-half of the Illinois vote has come from Cook County (Chicago). There has been no redrawing of

[2] Charles E. Merriam and Harold F. Gosnell, *Non-voting: Causes and Methods of Control* (Chicago: University of Chicago Press, 1924).

state, congressional, legislative and judicial districts since 1901; hence down-state Illinois contains nearly two-thirds of the congressional and state senatorial districts and six-sevenths of the judicial districts. Seventy per cent of the down-staters are natives of white parentage; only 34 per cent of Cook County inhabitants are in that category. In the state legislature and in the Illinois delegation in Congress, the native white Protestants are grossly overrepresented in relation to foreign-born and first generation Irish, Polish, and Italian Catholics, and Jews.[3]

In analyzing what an election "means," it is necessary to take into account both the predispositions of the voters before the election and the opportunities available during the election. Before 1928 no major political party in America had nominated a Catholic for President; hence those Catholics who were predisposed to favor a candidate of their own faith had no opportunity to express their choice. The strength of this predisposition in 1928 can be measured by comparing the final vote with the vote in previous years. In Massachusetts, where two-thirds of the church members were Catholic, Alfred E. Smith's vote was 15 per cent higher than "normal expectation," while in Virginia, where 3 per cent of the church members were Catholic, Smith's vote was 20 per cent below "normal."[4]

Some types of election procedure minimize personal and party factors in the result. Referendum elections on school or road bonds are familiar examples. The referendum, however, appears to strengthen the voice of conservative elements in the electorate by providing a means of arousing them to veto legislation alleged to be "put over" by innovative pressure. The initiative procedure, on the other hand, provides means of agitation for active minorities.

In reference to issues that are before the public for some time, it is approximately correct to treat the votes of freely elected officials as representative of the prevailing attitude of their constituents. When this is done, it is possible to gain a great deal of information about the role in national legislation of the opinions of many different kinds of constituents, classified according to social class or type of economic production.[5]

In investigating the vote statistics of private associations, it is necessary to approach them with the same questions in mind as for official figures. Inquiry reveals that dishonesty and intimidation are rife in some so-called business associations or trade unions. Many ex-bootleggers "muscled in"

[3] Albert Lepawsky, *Home Rule for Metropolitan Chicago* (Chicago: University of Chicago Press, 1935), pp. 148-155.

[4] Harold F. Gosnell, *Grass Roots Politics* (American Council on Public Affairs, Washington, D.C., 1942), p. 17.

[5] Arthur N. Holcombe, *Political Parties of Today* (New York: Harpers, 1924); *The Middle Classes in American Politics* (Cambridge: Harvard University Press, 1940); C. O. Paullin, *Atlas of the Historical Geography of the United States*, Carnegie Institution, Washington, D.C. (Publication no. 401, New York, American Geographical Society of New York, 1932).

after the prohibition era on little businessmen engaged in laundering, poultry distribution, and similar enterprises, compelling them to join an association and pay dues for "protection." Racketeering has been particularly noteworthy among trade unions in the building trades and in certain other occupations.

Light is thrown upon the reliability of statistics on the votes of corporation stockholders by examining the relationship between stockholders and boards of directors. When a minority interest collects proxies from voting shareholders who do not attend annual meetings of a corporation, control of the board may be concentrated in a very few hands. There is evidence that many board members do not take their duties seriously, often remaining absent from board meetings and letting control rest in the hands of minorities who represent some special family ownership, bondholding, commercial banking, or active management interest in the corporation. It has often been pointed out that simple ownership is not enough to obtain management control. Effective policy determination, however, is not independent of ownership but is highly focused in the hands of those ownership and management elements that are most strategically situated in the corporate structure.[6]

In addition to regularly collected ballots, students of response data may use "spontaneous" votes, such as letters and telegrams directed to officials and leaders. However, there is no certainty about who follows the admonition to "write your Congressman." During the debate over conscription in World War II, it appears that "pressure," not spontaneity, was involved in stimulating about one-fourth of the letters received by senators. (About one-third of these "pressure" communications were in identical phraseology.) In the controversy just referred to, the largest number per capita of letters originated in cities between 250,000 and 500,000 population. About three-fourths as many came from towns between 2,500 and 10,000. (The open country and hamlets—places under 2,500—were least active; and cities between 2,500 and 5,000 were much below cities between 10,000 and 25,000.) It remains for future researchers to account for the differences observed.[7] We may be sure that the predisposition to write is favored by skill in writing (education) and also the habit of frequent business and personal correspondence. It is also reasonable to suggest that whether letters will be written on controversial issues depends upon the indulgences and deprivations connected with past letter-writing experience. Among the

[6] A. A. Berle, Jr., and Gardiner C. Means, *The Modern Corporation and Private Property* (New York: Macmillan, 1934). The publications of the Temporary National Economic Committee contain a wealth of information on corporation practice.

[7] Rowena Wyant, "Voting Via the Senate Mail Bag (1)," *Public Opinion Quarterly*, 5 (1941): 359-382; Rowena Wyant and Herta Herzog, "Voting Via the Senate Mail Bag (2)," *Public Opinion Quarterly*, 5 (1941): 590-624.

sources of gratification—the indulgences—may be mentioned the deference received from persons who see or hear that one has written to a senator. Besides, acknowledgment may come on the senator's stationery. The act of letter writing may be endorsed by trusted public personages, and one may be on the winning side or the side that puts up a good fight. Among the negative gratifications—or deprivations—are ridicule for writing a letter, lack of acknowledgment, lack of commendation, lack of success in controversy. Writing on a specific issue is doubtless influenced by the degree of personal involvement in the issue.

The same questions that arise in connection with letters to public officials on controversial matters apply to correspondence to editors and contributors to newspapers, magazines, radio programs, and other public media. In some quarters, notably Great Britain, letters published in organs like the *London Times* are treated with respect. In many parts of America, on the other hand, it is suspected that anybody who writes to the papers is a crackpot. These are among the factors that enter into the balance of indulgence and deprivation available to a writer.

In estimating public response, the collector of evidence can rely upon many other kinds of information than official votes and voluntary expressions of opinion. Attitudes can be inferred from the circulation given to different materials. In the Soviet Union posters are issued to workers' clubs, and requests for additional posters are used as an index to the popularity of the individual poster.[8] In general, orders for books, pamphlets and similar matters are looked upon as rough indications of favorable response. Some caution, however, must be used in handling such figures. There are countries where it is not uncommon for publishers to pretend that a book has gone into several editions. Occasionally we find that a book has been ordered by a pressure group in large numbers and circulated broadcast although seldom read.

Many of the sources relied upon by historians and other collectors of opinion evidence involve content analysis and will therefore be referred to only in passing. In World War I, for illustration, the German High Command, in order to study the degree to which the home front was undermined, made a simple content analysis of intercepted letters between soldiers at the front and their families. One indicator of the infectiousness of Allied propaganda was the increasing tendency to use German expressions in the special sense given to them in the Allied propaganda leaflets and whispering campaigns. It was found that the term "Junker" was increasingly employed in the year 1918 in a tendentious sense.[9] Several years ago, Lombroso, the distinguished criminologist, made an ingenious application

---

[8] Direct observation by the writer.
[9] Hans Thimme, *Weltkrieg Ohne Waffen* (Stuttgart and Berlin, Cotta), 1932.

of content analysis procedures to the evaluation of public response toward books. He made a record of the marks left by readers on the margins of copies in public libraries. He did this chiefly for the purpose of comparing the response of the public at large with that of prisoners.[10]

Another ingenious application of content analysis procedures to the evaluation of response was made by the Social Democrats in Germany who organized vigorous counterpropaganda against the Nazis in the State of Baden before the Nazi seizure of power. The socialists invented an emblem for themselves to match the swastika. They engaged in a "chalk war," instructing their supporters to draw three arrows over every Nazi swastika. Counts were made of the number of swastikas found in different places and of the percentage of swastikas that were crossed out by the three arrows. This was a useful measure of the state of Nazi and Social Democratic morale.[11]

Spectators

The collectors of the above sorts of tabulated data on response are out of direct contact with the events they describe. Data can also be assembled by observers on the spot. As a spectator, an observer does not necessarily influence the response that he describes. A true spectator buries himself in the audience and makes records so discreetly that neither actors nor audience are put on their guard.

Psychotechnicians in Moscow have studied the interaction of stage, player, and audience on a scientific basis. Trained observers sit in the theater and unobtrusively follow the script, noting every audience response—applause, boos, leave-taking. It is possible not only to estimate the popularity with various audiences of specific actors and plays, but to ascertain the comparative effectiveness of different parts of every play and of different modes of playing the same role.[12]

Instruments have been devised to aid in estimating such responses as the volume of noise produced by an audience in an auditorium. Recently in the United States party conventions have been entertained by the appearance of large "applausometers" or "noisometers," on which the changing volume of sound is recorded. In this situation the true spectator relationship is disturbed.

Spectators can make valuable observations of public demonstrations, reporting on the number of marchers, the nature of the slogans and floats, and the degree of bystander interest. Among the measures of bystander interest are time consumed in applause, the number who join the proces-

[10] César Lombroso, *Les Palimpsestes des Prisons* (Paris: Masson, 1894).

[11] Sergei Chakhotin, *The Rape of the Masses: The Psychology of Totalitarian Political Propaganda* (New York: Alliance, 1940; London: Routledge, 1940).

[12] Direct observation by the writer.

sion, and the tossing of garlands and confetti. Military officers are trained to observe the demeanor of marching men, noting every evidence of slackness on the part of leaders or rank and file. Years of experience in military inspection produce an eye trained in perceiving the slightest deviation from expected patterns.

Scientific studies of child behavior have relied extensively upon data obtained in a spectator relationship. Children have been allowed to play while observers looked on through one-way glass.[13]

Participant-Observers

The participant-observer resembles the spectator in that he is in direct contact with events that he describes. He differs in that the subjects are aware of his presence even though they remain unaware of the fact that they are being studied. The method of participant-observation is one of the oldest in the history of investigations of collective response. In one of the oldest treatises on East Indian statecraft, it is recommended that attitudes be ascertained by means of agents who start an argument in a public place and induce others to join in.[14]

The chief technical problem confronted by the participant-observer is that of keeping satisfactory records of what has come to his notice. Occasionally it is possible to make records on the spot without arousing any suspicion. A supervisor, for example, may use pencil and paper without appearing to do anything unusual. Very often, of course, the written report of the investigator must be made some time after words have been heard or gestures have been seen. The scientific study of the delayed record-making process has not yet received the attention that its importance justifies.

Participant-observers may remain in prolonged contact with the persons whom they study. According to a recently reported survey of Newbury-port, Massachusetts ("Yankeetown"), Lloyd Warner and his specially trained research workers lived in the community for years, engaging in the ordinary activities of townspeople. Unknown to the individuals observed, they kept track of who invited whom to dinner, who made favorable or unfavorable remarks about whom, who endorsed or condemned national or local policies. Gradually it was possible to build up a picture of the relationships among all the inhabitants of the community. It was possible to discover by whom each person was accepted as an equal, by whom he was regarded as an inferior, and by whom he was accepted as superior. In order to attain the detachment necessary to conduct this research, it was necessary

[13] Methods developed by Arnold Gesell at Yale, John Anderson at the University of Minnesota, and others.
[14] Kautilya, *Arthàsàstra*.

to make use of a staff of highly trained social scientists who had spent many years studying comparative cultures and who had a number of scientific problems in mind calling for the patient collection of day-to-day facts. Those who took part in the research were stimulated by the idea of illuminating Yankee civilization by using the detailed methods of study applied by ethnologists to the description of primitive cultures.[15]

The advantage of data obtained by participant-observers who remain in prolonged contact with a situation is very great. It is possible to obtain systematic insight into the attitudes of individuals who occupy different positions in a given social structure. Generalizations about upper, middle, and lower class attitudes are far more dependable when they rest upon such an intensive basis than when they are the outcome of relatively casual observation.

Interviewers

Since the founding of the *Fortune* poll by Elmo Roper and the establishment by George Gallup of the American Institute of Public Opinion in 1935, polling has become a significant feature of practical politics. There is a long history of tentative groping, theoretical analysis, and partial demonstration behind these enterprises. For at least forty years, and no doubt longer, newspapers have conducted straw ballots in elections and made forecasts.[16]

There are certain obvious advantages connected with a poll of popular opinion. We can be sure that the sample is truly representative; that is, we can know definitely that a certain proportion of people of given age, sex, income, and similar characteristics have been interviewed. We have called attention to the deficiency of official election records from this point of view. Another advantage of the poll is that it can be much more frequently and promptly applied than the public election, the initiative, and the referendum.

That scientific surveys of opinion do not depend upon *how many* people are interviewed but upon the representativeness of the sample was demonstrated to the nation in the sensational failure of the *Literary Digest* poll to predict successfully the outcome of the presidential election of 1936. The *Digest* entered the campaign of that memorable year with high prestige, having foretold with very small error the election of President Roosevelt in 1932. The *Digest* applied the same method in 1936 that had been so successful in 1932. The procedure was to send out hundreds of thousands

---

[15] Lloyd Warner's research is in course of publication by the Yale University Press.

[16] See George Gallup and Saul Forbes Rae, *The Pulse of Democracy* (New York: Simon and Schuster, 1940); Hadley Cantril and associates, *Gauging Public Opinion* (Princeton: Princeton University Press, 1944); Jerome S. Bruner, *Mandate from the People* (New York: Duell, Sloan and Pearce, 1944).

of postal cards at random to persons listed in telephone directories. The error, of course, was in forgetting that only the middle and upper income groups in the U.S. population are rich enough to afford telephones. This had mattered very little in 1932, when discontent was so widespread that middle income groups deserted their former allegiance in large numbers and voted for the Democratic nominee. By 1936 a very large number of the middle income groups were returning to their former Republican allegiance, while the lower income groups remained loyal to the Democratic administration. All during the campaign of 1936, polls constructed on the basis of a more representative income-sample differed drastically from the current results of the *Digest*, and were strikingly vindicated when the final returns came in.

Since polls are conducted by asking people point blank for an expression of opinion on controversial matters, we may ask how trustworthy the results will be. Are some members of the community intimidated by the interviewer to a degree that leads them to conceal or distort their answers? That this factor is important has been suggested by the common tendency of national polls during Presidential elections to underestimate the degree of support for the candidate strongest among the poorer groups. This shows that the polls fail to allow sufficiently for the intimidation factor in interviewing wage earners, Negroes, and other minorities. Daniel Katz conducted an investigation to determine how much the social status of the interviewer and interviewee did in fact affect response.[17] A white collar (or control) staff consisted of college trained interviewers such as are regularly employed by the American Institute of Public Opinion. A working class (or supplemental) staff was made up of wage earners, most of whom had no college training. The two groups of interviewers were sent into the same low rental areas of Pittsburgh with the same instructions and the same ballot or questionnaire. The middle class or white collar interviewers reported a considerably greater incidence of conservative attitudes among low income groups than the working class interviewers. The working class interviewers reported more liberal and radical findings on labor issues than the white collar interviewers. It would, of course, be a mistake to assume from these results that it is always wise to use an interviewer who is a member of the group he is interviewing. It is reasonable to assume that in studies of family problems and sex matters, the housewife may talk more freely to a professional person, such as a nurse or psychiatrist, than to an untrained person from her own social group.

One interesting question is whether some interviewers are much more accurate than others in making estimates of the opinions of interviewees.

[17] Daniel Katz, "Do Interviewers Bias Poll Results?" *Public Opinion Quarterly*, 6 (1942): 248-268.

Robert Travers has experimented with procedures that make it possible to determine the reliability of an individual's judgment of group opinion, and he reports that certain persons are discovered to be remarkably accurate.[18]

Pollers have rightly given a great deal of attention to the phrasing of questions. There are enormous differences in the command of the English language in different parts of the United States. There are seven states in the Union where more than one person in every ten (over ten years of age) is illiterate. About half of the American population have never gone beyond the sixth or seventh year in school. In polling representative Americans, the sentences must be short and use a vocabulary that by test does not exceed the vocabulary of the first few grades of grammar school in complexity. Words must be selected that are free from "loading." A question is loaded in a direction favorable to the President when it reads, "Do you favor the policies of our wartime Commander-in-chief?" rather than, "Do you favor the policies of Franklin D. Roosevelt?" Negative loading of such a question might be, "Do you favor the policies, such as they are, of President Franklin D. Roosevelt?"

In evaluating the results obtained by polls, it is important to give special attention to the *phase* of the total public opinion process that is being reported. Experience has shown that polls conducted during the progress of an electoral campaign validly predict results. There is no difficulty in understanding why the poll should give highly valid results under these conditions. The action alternatives available to the members of the public are limited, and the choices are explicitly defined. The situation is different, however, with polls that are conducted during intercrisis situations, before action alternatives have become clearly outlined to the public at large. If a poll tells us that 60 per cent of the population is in favor of "postwar planning," and the poll is taken early in 1943, are we justified in predicting that those who favor "postwar planning" will endorse economic planning backed by a world police at the end of the war? Can we, as early as 1943, forecast the way in which action alternatives will be presented to the public? No doubt we can assert that "postwar planning" is a "plus phrase"; but in 1943 we cannot say to what policies this vague phrase will be applied. When situations are as yet undefined, polling results are little more than vocabulary tests showing which words are regarded as "plus" words and which are "minus" words.

It should be clear that scientific polling studies justify predictions, not forecasts. That is, they do not say that 61.2 per cent of the vote next week will be for Smith; they say that *under specified conditions* the Smith vote will be 61.2 per cent. It is assumed that future conditions will probably

---

[18] Robert M. W. Travers, "A Study in Judging the Opinions of Groups," *Archives of Psychology*, No. 266, December, 1941.

remain the same as conditions when the sample groups were interviewed, but it is also assumed that a last-minute development may shift the election. A sudden snow storm may keep farmers away from the polls. This may cut down the Smith vote if he is more popular among farmers than among city dwellers. Actually an elaborate set of predictions might be made in every specific election: "If the weather is clear, Smith will probably poll 61.2 per cent of the vote; if the weather is very bad he will probably get 10 per cent less." "If the President endorses Smith in the last week of the campaign, the vote among middle class women will probably increase 5 per cent as shown by the popularity of the President with these women." Forecasts say flatly that such and such an event *will* occur in the future.

The significance of brief answers to questions can be better understood if taken in conjunction with more statements from the interviewee. If a man says that he is in favor of a high protective tariff, he may be asked to explain his reasons. Perhaps he will say that we must keep cheap products out of the country in order to protect the American standard of living; or that a tariff defends the domestic market for his firm's products. We may discern that a given expression of preference depends upon certain general expectations about economic causes and consequences. If we want to preserve the opinion, we will take steps to keep alive the general picture; or if we are opposed to the opinion, we will consider ways and means of altering the general picture of reality thus disclosed. Every detailed opinion is part of a larger "frame of reference" that includes a whole series of demands, factual expectations, and personal or group loyalties. Our possibility of understanding and controlling opinion depends upon our insight into the significant features of this structure.[19]

Some interview procedures have been invented that keep the interviewer and subject in especially prolonged contact with each other and allow for intensive examination of the subject's frames of reference. In many ways the most noteworthy method of this kind is the psychoanalytic interview, in which subject and interviewer may see each other for an hour a day for months or years. The subject is asked to say freely anything that crosses his mind, while the interviewer undertakes to facilitate insight by proposing interpretative hypotheses about the probable causes and consequences of what the subject has to say about his intimate attitudes and activities.[20]

It is possible to combine with the interview the standpoint of a spectator

[19] On the more intensive interviewing methods, see F. J. Roethlisberger and William J. Dickson (with Harold A. Wright), *Management and the Worker, An Account of a Research Program Conducted by the Western Electric Company, Hawthorne Works, Chicago* (Cambridge: Harvard University Press, 1939), Chapter 13, "The Interviewing Method."

[20] Psychoanalytic procedures, even when greatly modified, reveal personality and social types. See Harold D. Lasswell, *Psychopathology and Politics* (Chicago: University of Chicago Press, 1930); John Dollard, *Caste and Class in a Southern Town* (New Haven: Yale University Press, 1937).

and to record unknown to the subject the random movements that he makes. Subjects can be made aware that such reactions are being investigated, although this modifies the interpretation of the results. Much ingenuity has been devoted to the task of devising apparatus capable of measuring involuntary movements of subjects. Starting from the common-sense observation that many people perspire when emotionally aroused, techniques have been invented for recording changes in the conductance of a constant electrical current through the skin. It has been demonstrated that there is a close correspondence between sweat secretion and skin conductivity. Another common-sense starting-point is that when people are excited their pulse rates and blood pressure change. By means of appropriate apparatus it is possible to obtain a continuous record of these reactions. Involuntary grasping movements may also be traced. By the use of these methods the responses of different audiences to plays, films, and other communications have been explored.[21]

How are the data obtained by collectors, spectators, participants, and interviewers brought into proper relation? The question goes beyond the analysis of effect and touches every branch of the study of communication, including content, media, and control analysis. We are brought to the fundamental issue of integrating theory and fact, and integrating both with policy.

Relations among Predisposition, Contents, and Effects

The most serious difficulty to be overcome in the developing science of communication is the fact known to everyone that a word (or gesture) may have so many meanings. This does not sound formidable, yet it puts a far greater stumbling block in the way of the scientist and manager in the social sciences than in many other lines of science and engineering.

A few reminders are enough to establish the importance of this point. Suppose we want to test the hypothesis that theater audiences derive more enjoyment from seeing their superiors insulted than from seeing their equals treated with disrespect. Key words in this hypothesis are "theater audience," "enjoyment," "superiors," "insult." Let us consider the word "insult." Can we write a concise set of instructions in the light of which any competent observer in any part of the world can recognize an instance of insult when he sees it? Obviously it would not be easy to list all the words, intonations, and movements that stand for insulting behavior throughout all social classes in America, Europe, Asia, Africa, and all the islands of the seas. Anthropologists and sociologists have found that it is impossible

---

[21] The techniques applied to the study of deception are more broadly applicable. See the work of John A. Larson and others.

to name one word, or one gesture, that is universally accepted as an "insult."

Contrast this with the procedure available to a physicist or a geological engineer who wants to verify some hypothesis about the distribution of "iron." He can specify exactly what phenomena observers are to call "iron." The eye at the spectroscope is trained to look for a single phenomenon, and when it appears, the observer is entitled to record among his "data statements" that "iron" is present. There is a readily communicable relationship between the "index" used by the data gatherer, and the "concept" (or "variable") term used in phrasing the general hypothesis.

So here we have the root of the difficulties that must be surmounted by analysts and managers of communication: Meanings do not "stay put." There is always a problem in maintaining a clearly understood relationship between "variable" and "index."

Among the most important consequences of this shiftability of meaning is the need of keeping a continuous audit of the varieties and changes of the meanings of particular words (and gestures) in the stream of communication. Suppose that five years ago we chose a scale of words to serve as "indexes" of the term "anger." Today we must be able to demonstrate that the relative significance of the index terms is the same as when we chose them. In short, our procedures must be calibrated through time.

Up to the present our society has made very limited effort to keep abreast of how meanings change. We do have dictionaries. But our dictionaries barely begin to provide us with what is needed for the social understanding or control of communication. Our dictionary makers have never shouldered the burden of reporting on the frequency of use and the variations in meaning found among the major elements in the total population.

We do have census agencies. But they do not consider it within their province to report in detail on reading or listening habits according to age, sex, occupation, income, locality, and other significant categories.

Furthermore, we have social scientists, pure and applied. But it is new for them to re-survey the attitudes of the community, as the Lynds re-surveyed *Middletown*[22] after a ten year interval. However, in connection with modern market, advertising, and opinion research, if not yet among social scientists, important masses of information are available about the trends of meaning.

The technical task of calibrating our methods of observation goes farther than the checking and rechecking of specific procedures in order to be sure that each one gives the same results today that it gave yesterday when applied to the same situation (or, if there is a difference, to determine the

[22] Robert S. Lynd and Helen Merrell Lynd, *Middletown* (New York: Harcourt, Brace, 1929); *Middletown in Transition* (New York: Harcourt, Brace, 1937).

constant that must be introduced as a correction factor). Calibration is also necessary among procedures, since we need to be informed of the degree to which results are affected by the observational method employed in gathering the data.

Let us assume that we have fixed upon a list of terms and definitions to be used in classifying personality according to the nature of fundamental attitudes (1) toward the self and (2) toward others. Suppose that we ask one hundred people to write autobiographies, giving them only a few instructions. Assume further that the same hundred people are directly interviewed by trained psychologists. Will the subjects be classified the same way on the basis of their autobiographies as on the basis of the reports by the psychologists? This question can be determined by proper intercalibration of the two methods.

Thus far we have had relatively few comprehensive studies that have concurrently applied a number of observational standpoints to the same situation or person. An exception is the investigation directed by Henry A. Murray at the Harvard Psychological Clinic, in the course of which nearly every available method of measurement was applied to the same 50 selected college students.[23]

In the field of communication research, it is unusual to find a writer who describes all segments of a process of communication with equal care and intensiveness, and with careful attention to the methods applied. An exception to this general rule is the survey of Erie County, Ohio, during the Presidential campaign of 1940.[24] The predispositions of the county were well known, since many investigations had revealed how the county had voted in local and national elections. In previous Presidential years the community had divided in a pattern that was remarkably close to the vote of the nation at large. In 1940, specialists on content analysis described radio broadcasts, magazines, newspapers, and other mass media to which the local population was exposed. Concurrently, interviewers conducted polls at regular intervals throughout the campaign. One group of potential voters constituted a "panel," who were reinterviewed several times.[25] Non-panel groups served each time as "controls."

Another pioneering study of an integrating type was part of an appraisal of the results of "progressive education." For eight years the read-

---

[23] Henry A. Murray and associates, *Explorations in Personality* (New York and London: Oxford University Press, 1938).

[24] On the poll studies Paul F. Lazarsfeld (assisted by Hazel Gaudet) and Elmo C. Roper collaborated. Bernard Berelson made most of the content analyses, with technical advice from Douglas Waples and Natan C. Leites. Published 1945 as *The People's Choice* (New York: Duell, Sloan and Pearce).

[25] Paul F. Lazarsfeld made the first and most extensive applications of the panel technique, in which the same group is reinterviewed.

ing of a selected group was described in detail and related to all the personality and culture information at hand.[26]

One of the principal consequences of the shiftability of relation between "concept" ("variable") terms and "index" terms is heavy emphasis upon pretesting. Systematic pretests are scientific expansions of the time-honored device of trying out a speech or an article in advance of delivery to the final audience. The public opinion poll, in a sense, is a preview of the final response of the voters, and the results may be used to change the tactics of the candidates. In the final film-editing process, "sneak previews" are frequently run. Drafts of articles, speeches, posters and other communications are often submitted to pretest audiences that are assumed to be representative of the ultimate audience (or familiar with it).

The merit of pretesting is that it can expose in detail and inexpensively the predispositions of a large audience. Ninety or a hundred versions of a tooth paste or a cigarette label may be tried out on very small groups representing the potential market of the world, and as a result the future effect of exposing a total audience to a given set of communications can be foretold. Even though they are correct scientifically, such procedures may not yield infallible results in practice. Just before a new cigarette name is launched, a similar brand name may be unveiled by a competitor, nullifying the effect forecast for a pretested campaign.

Another consequence of the instability of indexes is that laboratory experiments are of seriously limited usefulness for the science of mass communication. The indexes that serve to establish laws in the laboratory cannot always be directly applied to outside contexts. Laboratory experiments consist in the systematic repetition of situations in which the variables measured by selected indexes are systematically changed or held constant. Bound to the tumultuous reality of social life, indexes outside the laboratory may change their interrelationships at rates largely beyond the control of manipulators.

It is no simple matter to extend scientific laws carefully verified in one set-up to another. A striking instance of these difficulties is provided by Clark L. Hull and associates. Their theory of "conditioning" was developed to explain the responses of rats and other animals that were learning to run through mazes. In a maze the problem for the rat is one of economy, of finding the quickest, least "punishing" path that leads to "reward," not "punishment." Rote learning among human subjects differs in certain respects from maze learning among rats. The human subject is typically exposed to a drum on which nonsense syllables are written, and the task is

[26] Douglas Waples supervised the reading studies. He has emphasized the gains of integrated research in *What Reading Does to People* (with Bernard Berelson and Franklyn R. Bradshaw) (University of Chicago Press, 1940).

to learn the order in which the syllables will appear (as shown by correct anticipation). In developing a theory of rote learning, Hull and his associates did not apply their theory of maze learning by rigid extension. Rather they used their knowledge of maze learning to stimulate imagination in inventing hypotheses about what could be found by the direct observation of rote learning. It is significant that this comparatively modest leap from one kind of learning to another called for an elaborate technical treatise.[27] The leap from the laboratory to the multiform processes of mass communication remains to be made.[28]

The postulates and indexes of the experimental situation can be most directly applied to problems of communication whose scope is circumscribed. In general where the time intervals involved are short, and the situation is not complex the transfer is greatest, as in the testing of immediate effect (whether attention, comprehension, enjoyment, evaluation, or action).[29]

The data and postulates of the psychiatric clinic are very helpful in studying contents and responses in communication that takes place in times of crisis. Psychiatric study of people who are under the stress of great internal fear (anxiety) provides many clues to the behavior of people in crowds, mobs, and panics. Notably useful are explanations of how guilt is projected from the self to others (the creation of a scapegoat) and the phenomenon of ambivalence (incompatible emotional attitudes toward the same object, whether self or other). Psychoanalysis provides a set of postulates that construes the activity of a person as the outcome of three major groups of factors: basic drives, unconscious habitual modifications of drives, conscious calculation of available means and ends. Impulse, conscience, and reason are terms that convey approximately the correct meaning. (The technical psychoanalytic terms for the corresponding personality structures are id, superego, and ego.) What people say and how they respond to what is said depend on the relevance and intensity of communications and situations

[27] Clark L. Hull, Carl I. Hovland, Robert T. Ross, Marshall Hall, Donald T. Perkins, Frederic B. Fitch, *Mathematico-Deductive Theory of Rote Learning* (New Haven: Yale University Press, 1940). On the problems involved in rote, problem and insight learning, consult Ernest R. Hilgard and Donald G. Marquis, *Conditioning and Learning* (New York: Appleton-Century, 1940).

[28] We distinguish between full applications of the Clark L. Hull type and suggestive extensions, sometimes only of terminology. A pioneer application of I. P. Pavlov's work on "conditioned reflexes" is by Sergei Chakhotin, *The Rape of the Masses: The Psychology of Totalitarian Political Propaganda* (New York: Alliance, 1940; London: Routledge, 1940). John Dollard has extended both Sigmund Freud and Clark L. Hull to certain societal processes. See Neal E. Miller and John Dollard, *Social Learning and Imitation* (New Haven: Yale University Press, 1941).

[29] Frank N. Stanton and Paul F. Lazarsfeld adapted laboratory instruments to the study of audience response during radio programs, for example.

that appeal to these three levels of personality (the triple-appeal principle).[30]

In analyzing who controls mass communications, we rely mainly upon social historians, political scientists, economists, lawyers, and scientists who specialize on the family, religion, and primitive societies. Every inclusive theory of society provides a body of postulates that bear on the process of communication control. In general, the stream of communication is viewed as an instrument by means of which the powerful protect their value positions (indulgences).[31]

So varied are the specialists whose work has some bearing upon the study of communication that it is usually taken for granted that we are many years from the time when all specialists on the process will share a unified theory. In many ways, however, unity is nearer than we think. Many of the differences that appear to keep laboratory-trained psychologists, clinicians, aptitude testers, social scientists, and others apart from one another have nothing to do with "genuine" differences. They are spurious differences kept alive by the many special vocabularies that so readily convince the layman on first exposure that he has found the modern Tower of Babel.

Fortunately we are able to take a somewhat optimistic view of the future as it relates to the clearing away of difficulties that reside wholly in vocabulary. The ideal of unifying completely the terminology among theorists of communication is likely to prove something of a mirage, but it is well within the range of probability that specialists can learn to translate among the principal vocabularies. We must thank the modern logicians for this possibility. Ever since the time of Charles S. Peirce, the great American pioneer of the last century in this sphere of knowledge, logicians have been busy building methods of relating the languages of science to one another, on the one hand, and to the events that they are supposed to refer to "in reality," on the other. These efforts are variously called "mathematical logic," "symbolic logic," "logical positivism," or "semantics"; and in one form or another they have emerged in all countries where the European intellectual tradition is alive. In some places they have begun to seep into the general media of communication.[32]

[30] Sigmund Freud, *Group Psychology and the Analysis of the Ego* (London, 1922); *Civilization and Its Discontents* (New York, 1930). Among psychoanalytic social psychologists are Ernst Kris, Robert Waelder, and Erich Fromm.

[31] Significant contributors include Jeremy Bentham, Karl Marx, Vilfredo Pareto, Gaetano Mosca, Arnold Toynbee, Pitirim A. Sorokin, Karl Mannheim. Observers who come back from studying a primitive society may be more sensitive to significant features of our own, even as historians absorbed in distant events are often made aware of the special structure of the present. See Margaret Mead, *And Keep Your Powder Dry: An Anthropologist Looks at America* (New York: Morrow, 1942).

[32] Among the manuals see especially *An Introduction to Logic and Scientific Method* by Morris R. Cohen and Ernest Nagel (New York: Harcourt, Brace, 1934). Creative figures in

The modern logics are especially useful in equipping specialists to free themselves from "pseudo" issues that appear when the function of language is not expertly taken into account. One mark of naïveté in this field is to ask, "What *really* is the definition of communication?" Or to say, "These symbols or signs are not given the *true* definition." It is becoming more obvious to all concerned that it is important to refrain from snap judgments about any statement made by a specialist until it is clear how its terms are related to the total system of terms being applied by this specialist.

In fields bordering upon objective analysis of communication there are certain strong biases that must be discounted before an effective job of mutual translation can be done. Some specialists are in favor of "objective" sounding language, and shy away from terms like "conscious," "unconscious," "intention" or "purpose." Others are exasperated by theories that are phrased in words they are inclined to dismiss as "pseudo-objective," such as "conditioning," or "stimulus-response." On careful examination of well-formulated systems of scientific theory, it not infrequently turns out that "subjective" sounding words in one man's discourse are the logical or semantic equivalents of "objective" terms in another man's system, or the reverse.

One source of confusion among specialists has been the use of different ways of grouping the variables in terms of which hypotheses, laws, and principles are stated. Some have made the master grouping a two-term system, while others have preferred a three-term system. An instance of the first is the treatment of any "response" as a function—in the mathematical sense—of "stimuli." This is a logically comprehensive classification, since all pertinent phenomena are response, stimuli, or both. (In the latter case, they interact.) An example of the three-term pattern is the explanation of "responses" as functions of both "environment" and "predisposition." For the sake of brevity we may express these patterns by means of a special notation. The first system treats R (response) as a function of S (stimuli); the second deals with R as a function of E (environment) and P (predisposition).

The two modes of formulation can be translated into one another with little difficulty. Specialists who speak of R as a function of S promptly subclassify S into internal stimuli, arising within the human organism (individual or group), and external stimuli initiated in the surrounding environment. If the internal stimuli are distinguished into a "reaction set" with which the human organism enters a given environment, we have a precise equivalent of what is referred to by P in the other mode of statement.

modern logic include A. N. Whitehead, Bertrand Russell, Hans Reichenbach, C. K. Ogden, I. A. Richards, Rudolf Carnap, and many others.

When we compare the two systems, it is probable that the three-term system holds certain advantages for the general theory of communication. The active propagandist, the immediate controller of content, is accustomed to think in such categories, since he looks upon his practical problem as that of managing the content of communication (part of the environment of the audience) in such a way that the interests and sentiments (the predispositions) of the audience are aroused as he wants them to be (which is the goal response).

From the point of view of an experimentalist these three categories are also convenient. He may design experiments to hold predispositions constant, varying E in order to measure the impact of E (E′, E″, etc.) on R; or he may hold E constant and vary P. When he follows the former plan, he changes the content which is presented to matched audiences; in the latter, he presents matched content to varied audiences.

Experimental and pretesting methods may be used to determine the nature of the predispositions current in an audience. Samples of the audience may be exposed to different combinations of content in order to discover the strength of predispositions to pay attention to different media and symbols, to comprehend various combinations, to enjoy certain patterns, to evaluate various statements, and to act in certain ways after certain presentations.

It is evident that any record of response provides data as to how the audience is disposed to respond to environments in the future. When responses are classified, it is important to distinguish between the *initial* and the *completed* phases of response, since the way in which a response is completed depends partly upon the changes that occur in the environment *after* it has been initiated. The audience may applaud and presently an encore may be delivered (and we may classify this as a "successful" response; the audience is "indulged" by the performer). Or the audience may initiate the same response as before and applaud, but the management may refuse to allow an encore (and we classify this as a "deprivation"). In describing a response (or predisposition) our record is not complete until we have noted whether the final phase is successful or not.

If we allow our imagination enough leeway, we can conceive of a situation in which the responses of great audiences are so intensively and so continuously studied that every new response is promptly classified according to its significance in relation to the predispositions of the audience to respond in the future. Such a program would call for the concurrent use of all observational standpoints, and the exchange of data among scientists whose procedures are properly intercalibrated (i.e., whose theoretical systems have been translated into one another). No doubt this is the "Utopian" dream of skill specialists on this branch of science. But before dismissing it entirely, we may recall that such a dream has been peculiarly successful in enlarging our knowledge of the various physical, chemical, biological, and astronomical patterns of the universe. Laboratories and observatories all over the globe participate in a division of labor that has great forecasting utility and great potential significance for control.

Every well-developed scientific system is aware of the postulates that it utilizes in exploring phenomena. Whenever a postulate or set of postulates leads to no concise results, new postulates or combinations are tried. In research on the process of communication several postulates have been wittingly or unwittingly used by specialists who received their early training in many disciplines. We may state as follows the most general postulate on which practical and scientific work in this field proceeds: *The probability of the occurrence of one response over another varies with the ratio of indulgence to deprivation.* For convenience we call this the postulate of "I-D ratio," the ratio of indulgence to deprivation.[33]

In common with all basic postulates about the nature of human action, this is "truistic." Every propagandist knows that he tries to get a favorable response toward any target by presenting that target in a relatively more favorable light than rival targets, and that success is most likely when the audience is favorably disposed at the start.

The main utility of postulates is to aid the imagination and increase the clarity and consistency of the investigator. In approaching any communications problem we consider the indexes available for describing the variables that we consider to be "indulgent" or "deprivational." This method of analysis is not difficult to apply in general, although many technical perplexities arise in practice.[34] Assume that an audience will be exposed to a motion picture. Assume, further, that we know nothing of the predispositions of the audience (whether they are from Alaska or Panama). Can we justifiably classify various portions of the picture as "indulgent" or "de-

[33] Social psychologists who are close to experimental psychology use the framework of "conditioning" as a guide. The "I-D ratio" postulate, as phrased here, is rather close to their terminology. See, for example, E. L. Thorndike's classical statement of "the law of effect" in *Animal Intelligence* (New York: Macmillan, 1911), p. 244. Under the influence of V. M. Bekhterev's "objective psychology," and similar currents in America, there has been a tendency to purge the vocabulary of psychology of words that in common parlance refer to subjective events exclusively. Instead of a "pleasure-pain" postulate, it is now more common to picture the organism as "abolishing stimuli." Such terms do not need to be restricted to nonsubjective events, and are rarely, if ever, so limited in practice when the discourse is about human relations. See, among others, the publications of Gordon Allport, Herbert Blumer, Hadley Cantril, Leonard Doob, Lawrence K. Frank, Edwin D. Guthrie, Daniel Katz, Frank Klineberg, Arthur W. Kornhauser, Rensis Likert, Mark A. May, Gardner Murphy, Theodore Newcomb, Kimball Young, Goodwin Watson. The field theories of the Gestalt school of Max Wertheimer, Kurt Koffka, Wolfgang Köhler, and Kurt Lewin have influenced the formulation of experimental theory in America, notably by way of Edward C. Tolman. J. F. Brown has applied them to general social psychology.

[34] See, in general, the titles listed in Part 6 of the bibliography section of the present book.

privational"? The answer is "no." In the absence of information about the audience, we may of course keep a quantitative record of symbols exhibited. But these figures are *details*, not *data*. They are potential data, but until they have been explicitly related to the I-D ratio, they are not yet data.

It may be objected that there are some universally valid relations between stimulus (environment) and response. All human beings who are not blind are expected to pay attention to a sudden flash of light in darkness. Yet it is important to recognize that many such "nearly universal" relations hold good only with respect to momentary, unanticipated, and involuntary responses ("the startle responses").[35] Many colors, sounds, and body movements, and most words, call forth no universal attention effects (subject to the limitations just made). Predispositions regarding such stimuli are different from culture to culture, and from situation to situation within each culture. It is commonplace, for instance, that city men do not "hear" forest sounds that are highly differentiated for the woodsman, and *vice versa*. In the realm of words relating to ethics, observations, and expectations, the differential deafness is equally obvious. From the cradle there begins a process of exposure to environments that results in progressive modification of the inherited predispositions.

[35] Carney Landis, William A. Hunt, Hans Strauss, *The Startle Pattern* (New York: Farrar and Rinehart, 1939).

Bibliography

INTRODUCTION TO THE BIBLIOGRAPHY

One Hundred and Fifty Outstanding Titles
on Propaganda, Communication,
and Public Opinion

SINCE the 1935 bibliography listed about 4,500 titles, and the present one almost 3,000, it is felt that the interests of the average reader and the less specialized student of public opinion may be served best by a relatively brief list of major titles. These titles are selected from among the writers of all periods of history and all places who have appeared to be most comprehensive, most meticulous and most free of parochial, nationalistic, racist, or doctrinal prejudice in supplying answers to the question which is central in the minds of scientific students of the communication process: If *who* says *what*, through what *channels* (media) of communication, *to whom*, what will be the *results*? and how can we *measure* what is said and its results?

As in the case of the main bibliography, the goal in selecting the 150 titles has been to choose titles that would represent the whole field of public opinion analysis in due proportions. In a few cases, therefore, it has been necessary to set aside the rule of impartiality, meticulousness and objectivity in order to include a title which appeared to the compilers to be the least unsatisfactory contribution in a particular corner of the field. In other cases, a number of worthy titles have been omitted because other equally worthy ones have appeared to give adequate coverage of some portion of the field.

When the three compilers of this Reference Guide had made their final selection, after studying the contributions of the several thousand contenders, they were interested to find that no fewer than sixty per cent of the 150 "outstanding" titles had appeared since mid-1934, the date when their earlier book went to press. This is taken by them as striking evidence of the rapid growth of scientific interest in the practice and analysis of propaganda and other forms of mass communication. It may also be viewed as further evidence of the need for a reference volume to orient the efforts of the large number of able investigators who have recently come into the field.

Each of the 150 "outstanding" titles has been starred prominently (*) in the text of the bibliography section, and the annotations are somewhat fuller than the annotations given most of the unstarred titles.

The forty per cent of the "outstanding" titles which appeared before

1934 might almost be termed classics, so well known are they to the social scientist if not to the average reader. Hence, it was felt that extended annotation would be unnecessary. Reviews of the earlier works are readily accessible in such sources as the *Encyclopedia of the Social Sciences*; in leading treatises on social theory, such as those of Barnes and Becker, Catlin, Coker, Dunning, Sabine, Sorokin, and others; in book review sections of the social science journals; and in the *Book Review Digest*. There exists as yet, however, no systematic history of the theory of communication.

Outstanding Titles on the Art and Science of Popularization[1]

THE world seems to be getting more complicated faster than its peoples are getting more educated. It is of course a commonplace among educators that the high school graduate of today often has a larger fund of information than the college graduate of a generation or two ago, and that a larger percentage of the population is going to high school and college and graduate school. But this increase in what the younger generation knows is more than offset, it appears, by an increase in what it still has to learn. There has been, and will continue to be, an increase in the complexity of technology, and an increase in the number of people of different cultures and languages who are obliged to work in an economic system, produce for a market, and prepare for a coming world or hemisphere political system that cannot be more than dimly understood without more education than is now possessed by the majority.

Indeed, it may seriously be asked whether an objective, quantitative study would show that even the educated and politically influential classes, taking the world as a whole, possess any significant fraction of the language skill and the political and economic information that would be necessary to govern the new world or hemisphere society without unceasing bloodshed. If this be the case, what of democracy?

A few of the educated and politically influential have already developed an impressive quasi-monopoly of certain forms of knowledge, and this, like mass ignorance, may also bring its dangers. The more one contemplates the potential role of superspecialists and statisticians in the age of mass communication, the more truth may be found among the reasons Lancelot Hogben gives for engaging in his brilliant attempt to democratize and

---

[1] By permission of *The Journalism Quarterly*, much of this passage is adapted from Bruce Lannes Smith, "Scientific and Semi-Scientific Literature on War Information and Censorship," *Journalism Quarterly*, 20:1-20 (March, 1943).

popularize *Mathematics for the Million*: ". . . no society is safe in the hands of its clever people. . . . Today economic tyranny has no more powerful friend than the calculating prodigy."[2]

Confronted with mass ignorance on the one hand and small groups with quasi-monopolized knowledge on the other, democracy may soon discover that it has a difficult course to plot.

Bearing in mind the crucial problems of elite recruitment and adult as well as childhood education, a number of farsighted specialists are becoming interested—belatedly but constructively—in the rules of popularization.

This involves not writing or talking "down" to a public, but the use of simple, meaningful words. Outstanding examples of such work are the well-known Public Affairs Pamphlets—a series of 32-page studies of important public questions, designed by a group of specialists expressly to reach those who have had about nine or ten grades of school (the upper 35 per cent or so of the U.S. population, educationally). *The Peoples Library*, edited by Dr. Lyman Bryson of the Readability Laboratory, Teachers College, is a series of books presenting political and economic problems in the language of these same groups. The National Farm and Home Hour is an example of the same type of responsible popularization of public affairs on the radio.

Many newspapers and magazines make an effort to popularize verified knowledge effectively, not only in their "science pages" but in "backgrounding" their regular coverage of the news. Sidney Kobre (1462)[3] has very thoughtfully explored the possibilities of responsible popularization in newspapers, taking as his examples a variety of stories that have actually appeared in print; but, by and large, the newspapers of larger circulation have neglected to develop this type of service, partly because of the expense of hiring able popularizers and partly because of the lure of higher profits through sensationalism. Conspicuous exceptions are such papers as the London *Times*, the New York *Times* and the *Christian Science Monitor*. For many years these three have deliberately chosen to operate with a relatively small circulation in order to render what they have regarded as a public service. On the whole, their writers appear to be better educated— or at least less irresponsible—than writers for the mass-circulation press; and a higher percentage of their space is given to semipopular versions of technical, scientific, and educational writings.

Perhaps more influential than all three of these newspapers combined, as a channel of mass education and popularization, are the enterprises of

---

[2] Lancelot Hogben, *Mathematics for the Million*, revised and enlarged edition (New York: Norton, 1940), pp. 19, 24.

[3] Numbers in parentheses refer to titles listed in the bibliography section of the present book.

Time, Inc., publishers of *Fortune*, *Time*, and *Life*. Each is pitched for a definite public: *Fortune* for the top 30,000 "key men" in U.S. business; *Time* for some 700,000 readers in the upper and middle cultural strata; and *Life* for a broad public of three million or more in the lower middle class. Yet each maintains a level of vocabulary and information well above the customary level of its particular public. Timeliness, a provocative style, and compelling photos and layouts are counted upon to sugarcoat the relatively heavy dose of fact and analysis.

Outstanding works which point to the technical considerations in the art and science of popularizing are the several vocabulary studies and reader-interest studies by Professor William S. Gray of the Department of Education, University of Chicago (2037, 2087-2089a). Dr. Gray has evolved a "readability formula" which may be used to test the appeal of reading matter in advance of publication. Many advertising firms use similar devices, but over a relatively limited range of topics.

As pointed out by James Clarke, then of the Readability Laboratory of Teachers College, in a report (2303) on the application of Dr. Gray's formula to the production of books for the ordinary man, "It is estimated ... that the average American adult has had about six years' schooling and reads about as well as is expected of a fifth grade child. . . . [But] an adult reacts differently to material in print. His emotional response is more mature, his interest of a different kind, his understanding deepened and also, perhaps, narrowed, by experience."

Two other outstanding works in the field of popularization are *How to Use Pictorial Statistics* (2052), by Dr. Rudolf Modley, head of Pictograph Corporation, who was trained in the social sciences at the University of Vienna; and *International Picture Language: The First Rules of Isotype* (2055), by Dr. Otto Neurath, internationally known semanticist who was founder of the Social and Economic Museum of Vienna.

Since communication, not only to the American people but to all the world, is part of the program of democracy, mention may also be made of *The System of Basic English* (2056) and *The General Basic English Dictionary* (2056). These two important works undertake to select from the scores of thousands of words in the English language about 800 which may be used to express nearly anything that anyone has to say. They may be used either to overcome foreign-language barriers or to simplify, purify, and clarify the wording of something that has been written in complicated English. Along the same lines is Herbert N. Shenton's analysis of *Cosmopolitan Conversation: Language Problems of International Conferences* (2135), a study sponsored by the International Auxiliary Language Association and based on observation of language barriers at a large number of international conferences.

These and other analyses or illustrations of the art and science of popularization, and of the role the scientific popularizer might play in clarifying the new world of high technology, world economics, and world politics have been marked in the text with the sign, **Pop.**

B.L.S.

ORGANIZATION OF BIBLIOGRAPHY

Part 1. Propaganda Strategy and Technique

Part 2. Propaganda Classified by the Name of the Promoting Group

Part 3. Propaganda Classified by the Response to Be Elicited

Part 4. The Symbols and Practices of Which Propaganda Makes Use or to Which It Adapts Itself

Part 5. Channels of Communication

Part 6. Measurement

Part 7. Control and Censorship of Communication

PART 1. PROPAGANDA STRATEGY & TECHNIQUE

A. THEORIES OF PROPAGANDA

Theories of how to conduct successful propaganda have been formulated by public relations counsels, advertisers, political scientists, social psychologists, sociologists, social workers, journalists, publicists, and many others. In this section titles *of the most general interest* are included from the special fields. Less abstract or less important references are listed elsewhere.

1. ALBIG, (JOHN) WILLIAM (D). *Public Opinion.* New York: McGraw-Hill, 1939. 486 pp.

Text by sociologist, University of Illinois. *Contents*: 1. The Nature of Public Opinion. 2. The Development of Public Opinion. 3. Communication. 4. Psychological Processes and Opinion. 5. Language and Public Opinion. 6. The Leader and Personal Symbolism. 7. Legends and Myths. 8. Violence and Public Opinion. 9. Geographic Distribution of Group Opinion. 10. Attitude and Opinion. 11. The Measurement of Opinion. 12. Opinion Measurement: The Attitude Scales. 13. Opinion Change. 14, 15. Censorship. 16. Special Interest Groups. 17. Propaganda. 18. The Art of Propaganda. 19. The Radio. 20. Motion Pictures. 21. The Newspaper. 22. The Graphic Arts and Public Opinion. 23. Public Opinion and Reality. Bibliography in footnotes and pp. 433-64.

2. BARTLETT, FREDERIC CHARLES. *Political Propaganda.* New York: Macmillan, 1940. 158 pp.

British psychologist analyzes its method and effects. Spanish edition: *La propaganda politica*, translated by Francisco Giner de los Ríos (Mexico: Fondo de cultura económica, 1941. 141 pp.).

*2a. BERNAYS, EDWARD L. (CB '42, W). *Crystallizing Public Opinion.* New York: Boni and Liveright, 1923. 218 pp.

A U.S. public relations counsel's early formulation of the techniques of his calling, with some attention to its social consequences.

3. BLANCO WHITE, MRS. AMBER (REEVES). *The New Propaganda.* London: Gollancz, 1939. 383 pp.

Examines from a Freudian point of view the authoritarian propagandas of recent years. Author has been active in British Labour Party politics.

4. BRUNER, JEROME S. "The Dimensions of Propaganda: German Short-Wave Broadcasts to America," *Journal of Abnormal and Social Psychology*, 36: 311-37 (July 1941).

An attempt to work out standard dimensions of propaganda, to make possible quantitative comparative studies. The following nine dimensions are suggested: dissolvent-unifying, negative-positive, temporal, personal-impersonal, stratified-homogeneous, authoritative-casual, colloquiality, immediate-remote, and repetitiousness. Based in part on Ph.D. thesis, social psychology, Harvard.

5. CASEY, RALPH DROZ (D,W). Chapter on "Propaganda and Public Opinion" in Willard Waller (editor), *War in the Modern World* (New York: Random House, 1940).

By U.S. professor of journalism.

*6. CHAKHOTIN, SERGEI. *The Rape of the Masses: The Psychology of Totalitarian Political Propaganda.* New York: Alliance, 1940. London: Routledge, 1940. 317 pp.

By Russian psychologist who has been a leader of European social democracy for many years. Propagandist activity, he says, is of two types: "propaganda by persuasion, mainly for militants, and by suggestion, for the masses. For the former, doctrine is the essential thing, together with technical hints in the maneuvering of the masses. For the latter, the important thing is to find for the doctrine the equivalents of a mysticism—a myth and suggestive expressions, rites, symbols, slogans. . . . This is at present, unfortunately, the monopoly of the dictatorships, and has been the cause for this very reason of their success. It needs studying and putting into practice without loss of time, on behalf of democracy and humanity. . . . In this emotive propaganda, all dishonest forms, all aesthetically and morally debased forms, all crudities that shock the onlooker, must be absolutely avoided." Bibliography, pp. 289-91. French edition: *Le viol des foules par la propagande politique* (Paris: Gallimard, 1939. 270 pp. Bibliography, pp. 265-67).

7. CHILDS, HARWOOD LAWRENCE (D). *Introduction to Public Opinion.* New York: Wiley, 1940. London: Chapman and Hall, 1940. 151 pp.

Lectures before American Council on Public Relations, 1939-40, by Princeton political scientist.

*8. CHILDS, HARWOOD LAWRENCE, editor (D). *Pressure Groups and Propaganda* (Annals of the American Academy of Political Science, vol. 179). Philadelphia, May 1935. 287 pp.

Articles and book reviews by numerous scholars and propagandists.

*9. CHILDS, HARWOOD LAWRENCE, editor (D). *Propaganda and Dictatorship.* Princeton: Princeton University Press, 1936. 153 pp.

Essays by George E. G. Catlin, Harwood L. Childs, Oscar Jaszi (D,W), Harold D. Lasswell (D,W), Fritz Morstein Marx (D), Bertram W. Maxwell, and Arnold J. Zurcher (D,W), with an introduction by DeWitt Clinton Poole (D,W). Bibliographic footnotes.

*10. COMMITTEE FOR NATIONAL MORALE. *German Psychological Warfare: A Critical, Annotated and Comprehensive Survey and Bibliography,* prepared under the direction of Ladislas Farago with the cooperation of Gordon W. Allport (W), E. G. Boring (W), S. S. Stevens and Dr. J. G. Beebe-Center of Harvard University, Kimball Young (D,W) of Queens College, and Floyd Ruch of the University of Southern California. New York, 1941. 144 pp.

"Analytic foreword," 80 pp., outlines theories and practices of German military psychology both inside Germany and abroad. Six hundred titles are listed, with a brief biography of each author and indication of his present status in Germany, where available. Some 200 of the "most significant" titles are abstracted or summarized.

*11. DOOB, LEONARD WILLIAM. *Propaganda: Its Psychology and Technique.* New York: Henry Holt, 1935. 424 pp.

By social psychologist, Yale. The social psychology of suggestion forms the central theme of this book. Consideration is given to the promotional activities of many organizations, such as the Lord's Day Alliance, the Communist and Fascist parties, the munitions makers, and the peace societies. Bibliographic footnotes.

*12. FORD, GUY STANTON, editor (D,W). *Dictatorship in the Modern World,* 2nd (rev.) ed. Minneapolis: University of Minnesota, 1939. 362 pp.

Thoroughgoing revision of a standard work that first appeared in 1935. The six original essays have been rewritten, and nine new ones added, including articles on the economics of fascism (by Calvin B. Hoover) (D,W); women under dictatorships (Mildred Adams); the problem of succession in a dictatorship (Sigmund Neumann) (D); a chronology of dictatorship (Joseph R. Starr) (D); the import and impact of organized propaganda (Peter H. Odegard) (D,W). Contains bibliography.

12a. FRIEDMANN, OTTO. *Broadcasting for Democracy,* introduction by A. D. Lindsay. London: Allen and Unwin, 1942. 62 pp.

Czechoslovak social psychologist compares Nazi and democratic propaganda methods and aims. Pp. 41-61 are a plan for Allied propaganda. Bibliography, p. 62.

*12b. HADAMOVSKY, EUGEN. *Propaganda und Nationale Macht: Die Organisation der öffentlichen Meinung für die nationale Politik.* Oldenburg: Gerhard Stalling, 1933. 153 pp.

Technique of propaganda in behalf of a National Socialist Germany, by Nazi radio chief.

13. HARTSHORNE, EDWARD YARNALL (D). "Reactions to the Nazi Threat: A Study of Propaganda and Culture Conflict," *Public Opinion Quarterly*, 5: 625-39 (Winter 1941).

Harvard sociologist's analysis of resistances and receptivities met by propaganda, with special reference to Nazi propaganda in the U.S.

13a. HERNÁNDEZ, JOSÉ M.; and GALANG, RICARDO C. *What Every Filipino Should Know About Propaganda: What It Is; Where It Comes From; How To Detect It; How To Fight It; How To Have Our Own Propaganda*, preface by Dr. Camilo Osias, 1941. Manila: Office of Publicity and Propaganda, Civilian Emergency Administration, 1941. 56 pp.

A nontechnical presentation, relying largely on the work of the Institute for Propaganda Analysis, but using examples familiar to Filipinos. Major Hernández is Professor of Languages and Social Arts, Philippine Military Academy; Lt. Galang is Assistant Professor in the same department. Dr. Osias is Director of Publicity and Propaganda of the Civilian Emergency Administration. Bibliography, p. 56.

*14. INSTITUTE FOR PROPAGANDA ANALYSIS, INC. *Propaganda Analysis: A Monthly Letter to Help the Intelligent Citizen Detect and Analyze Propaganda.* New York, October 1937–December 1941.

This Institute, staffed by a Board of some fifteen well-known educators and social scientists, was "a non-profit corporation organized for scientific research in methods used by propagandists in influencing public opinion. It [was to] conduct a continuous survey and analysis of propagandas." It also supplied study courses for use at the secondary school level. For the first year, it operated under a grant of $10,000 donated by the late Edward A. Filene. With the coming of World War II, it voluntarily dissolved, stating that it could not hope to publish objective analyses in a country at war.

*14a. LASSWELL, HAROLD DWIGHT (D,W). *Propaganda Technique in the World War.* New York: Knopf, 1927.

London: Kegan Paul, Trench and Trubner, 1927. New York: Peter Smith, 1938. 233 pp.

U.S. political scientist discusses propaganda organization, war guilt and war aims, satanization and demoralization of the enemy, maintenance of the illusion that "we" are winning, preservation of "friendship" with allies and neutrals, and means of assessing results of propaganda. Bibliography, pp. 223-29.

15. LASSWELL, HAROLD DWIGHT (D,W); and BLUMENSTOCK, DOROTHY. *World Revolutionary Propaganda: A Chicago Study.* New York and London: Knopf, 1939. 393 pp.

By two political scientists formerly at University of Chicago. This volume is of high methodological interest because it represents the first attempt to take measurements of the volume and effects of every medium of propaganda in the Communist revolutionary movement of a large city. Bibliographic footnotes.

*15a. LENIN, VLADIMIR ILYICH (ESS). *Agitation und Propaganda: Ein Sammelband.* Vienna: Verlag für Literatur und Politik, 1929. 250 pp.

"Einzige autorisierte Ausgabe." Propaganda spreads belief; agitation exploits the passing emotional opportunity, according to the definitions employed in this relatively systematic treatise on world revolutionary propaganda by a Russian theorist, administrator and politician.

15b. LUTOSLAWSKI, A. T. *O Propagandzie.* London: A. R. Foster (76 Prince's Gate Mews, S.W. 7), 1942. 116 pp.

General treatise "About Propaganda." Title page describes the author as Licencié en droit (Paris), and Diplomé de l'École Libre des sciences politiques. Bibliography, pp. 112-16, cites writers in English, French, German, Polish—most of them relatively nontechnical.

15c. MUENSTER, HANS AMANDUS. *Publizistik: Menschen, Mittel, Methoden* (Meyers kleine Handbuecher, no. 17). Leipzig: Bibliographisches Institut, 1939. 167 pp.

"[Political] Publicity: People, Media, Methods." By Director of Institut für Zeitungswissenschaft, University of Leipzig. Bibliography, pp. 165-67.

*16. Münzenberg, Willi. *Propaganda als Waffe*. Paris: Carrefour, 1937. 281 pp.

By a leader of the German Communist Party youth movement.

17. Parsons, Talcott (D). "Propaganda and Social Control," *Psychiatry*, 5: 551-72 (November 1942).

By Harvard sociologist (Ph.D. Heidelberg).

18. Pintschovius, Karl. *Die Seelische Widerstandskraft im Modernen Krieg*. Oldenburg and Berlin: Stalling, 1936. 192 pp.

Study of emotional factors which, according to this German social psychologist, would begin to move in a revolutionary direction inside Germany in the event of a long-drawn-out war. Bibliography, pp. 177-86.

19. Ranulf, Svend. "Propaganda," *Theoria*, 3: 240-56 (1936).

Critical appraisal of recent literature by a Danish sociologist.

*20. Research Project on Totalitarian Communication. [Directors: Drs. Ernst Kris and Hans Speier (D).] A joint inquiry conducted by various scientists under the auspices of the New School for Social Research, New York City.

Mimeographed *Research Papers*: 1. German Radio Bulletins. 83 pp.; 2. A Study of War Communiqués: Methods and Results. 137 pp.; 3. German Freedom Stations Broadcasting to Britain. 177 pp.; 4. (Has not yet appeared.) 5. Data on a German Defeat Situation. 82 pp.; 6. Topics of the Day: A German Radio Program. 125 pp. *Forthcoming*: 1. A Statistical Analysis of Stereotypes in German Broadcasts; 2. German Front Reports during the Russian Campaign; 3. Predictions in German Propaganda.

*21. Rogerson, Sidney. *Propaganda in the Next War*. London: Bles, 1938. 188 pp.

One volume in a series on "The Next War," edited by B. H. Liddell Hart (CB '40), of which other volumes deal with sea power, air power, and tanks. This volume contains advice for British propagandists whose task it will be to get the U.S. into the war on their side. "The American is the great champion of the oppressed—and frequently of the *soi-disant* oppressed. . . . They are more susceptible than most people to mass suggestion. . . . They are at this moment the battleground of an active propaganda of labels. . . . It will be difficult to get the United States to participate in a war. . . . It will need a definite threat to America which will have to be brought home by propaganda to every citizen." There are detailed suggestions for this campaign and also for campaigns to demoralize the Germans and to maintain British morale. The author is a captain in the British army.

*21a. Schönemann, Friedrich. *Die Kunst der Massenbeeinflussung in den Vereinigten Staaten von Amerika*. Stuttgart: Deutsche Verlagsanstalt, 1924. 212 pp.

Analysis of U.S. domestic propaganda during World War I is used by this German specialist on U.S. history and psychology, as the basis of a general treatise on "The Art of Influencing the Masses in the United States."

22. Smith, Bruce Lannes (D). "Literature on [War] Propaganda Technique and Public Opinion," *Psychological Bulletin*, 38: 469-83 (June 1941).

General bibliographic essay by U.S. political scientist.

23. Smith, Bruce Lannes (D). "Scientific and Semi-Scientific Literature on War Information and Censorship," *Journalism Quarterly*, 20: 1-20 (March 1943).

Critical bibliographic essay on major books and articles of recent years.

24. Sonnabend, H. "Sociological Implications of Propaganda," *Proceedings and Transactions of Rhodesia Scientific Association* (Salisbury, South Africa), 37: 67-79 (1939).

Lucid general statement of social functions of propaganda by social scientist, Witwatersrand University. Bibliography, pp. 78-79.

25. Speier, Hans (D). Chapter on "Morale and War Propaganda" in Hans Speier and Alfred Kähler (editors), *War* *in Our Time* (New York: Norton, 1939).

By ex-German social scientist, on staff of New School for Social Research.

26. SPEIER, HANS (D). "The Radio Communication of War News in Germany," *Social Research*, 8: 399-418 (November 1941).

Social scientist's analysis of contents of German war news broadcasts, based on the BBC listening post's *Daily Digest of Foreign Broadcasts*. Factors which determine form and content of war news include: the social type of war; the technological character of warfare; the certainty or uncertainty of victory; the available techniques of communication; the political and military ideology and psychological doctrines of the propagandists and makers of news policy; and the intelligence and predisposition of the audience to be reached.

27. STURMINGER, ALFRED. *Politische Propaganda in der Weltgeschichte: Beispiele vom Altertum bis in die Gegenwart.* Salzburg: Bergland, 1938. 320 pp.

World history of propaganda, by German scholar. Bibliography, pp. 315-20.

28. TAYLOR, EDMOND (LAPIERRE) (W). *The Strategy of Terror.* Boston: Houghton Mifflin, 1940. 278 pp.

Paris correspondent of Chicago *Tribune* reports on morale-breaking devices employed during the current war by the British, the French, and the Germans. Among the devices are whispering campaigns, employment of professional defeatists, persons clothed in heavy mourning, persons who start controversies over the authority of religion, the state, and the police. Included also is a first-hand appraisal of strategic and psychological factors that are believed to have influenced the French government at Munich. For biographical sketch of the author, see Frank Cleary Hanighen, *Nothing But Danger* (New York, 1939), p. 50.

*28a. THIMME, HANS. *Weltkrieg ohne Waffen: Die Propaganda der Westmächte gegen Deutschland, ihre Wirkung und ihre Abwehr.* Stuttgart: Cotta, 1932. 294 pp.

Propaganda of World War I described by German historian. Based on German archival material. Main emphasis is laid on Entente propaganda against Germany, particularly the pamphlet war on the troops.

28b. THOMAS, IVOR. *Warfare by Words.* Middlesex and New York: Penguin Books, 1942. 96 pp.

General theory of propaganda technique and organization. By a British Labour M.P., graduate of Oxford, who has been employed in the Ministry of Information. Bibliographic footnotes.

29. WANDERSCHECK, HERMANN. *Weltkrieg und Propaganda.* Berlin: Mittler, 1936. 260 pp.

Gives especial attention to the British campaign against Germany.

30. WILSON, CHARLES H. "Hitler, Goebbels and the Ministry for Propaganda," *Political Quarterly*, 10: 83-99 (January-March 1939).

Summarizes the propaganda theories of Hitler and Goebbels and describes the administrative organization of Nazi propaganda agencies.

B. THEORIES OF CLOSELY RELATED METHODS OF COLLECTIVE MANAGEMENT

Propaganda is only one of the principal methods of controlling collective responses. Successful social and political management often depends upon a proper coordination of propaganda with coercion, violent or nonviolent; economic inducement (including bribery); diplomatic negotiation; and other techniques. *The entries in this section, devoted to methods marginal to the propaganda field, are very severely limited to suggestive and representative titles.*

I. VIOLENCE
INCLUDES ESPIONAGE, INTELLIGENCE, CIVILIAN DEFENSE

31. "Air Power," March 1941 issue of *Fortune.*

Issue devoted to "air power as world power." "Its underlying theme is that air power may become the decisive element in world power; and the method of presenting the articles therefore reflects the two inseparable aspects of that power: the military and the commercial."

32. *The* [Army] *Officer's Guide,* 9th ed. Harrisburg, Pa.: Military Service Publishing Co., 1942. 492 pp.

The question of censoring soldiers' mail has been handled in this edition, as have the duties of the Instructor and of the Public Relations Officer.

33. BALDWIN, HANSON WEIGHTMAN (CB '42,W). *Strategy For Victory.* New York: Norton, 1941. 172 pp.

Analysis of strategy that would be needed to defeat the dictators. By an Annapolis graduate and former naval officer, now military and naval specialist of New York *Times.*

34. BALDWIN, HANSON WEIGHTMAN (CB '42,W). *United We Stand! Defense of the Western Hemisphere.* New York: McGraw-Hill, 1941. 364 pp.

Bibliography, pp. 347-48.

35. BALDWIN, HANSON WEIGHTMAN (CB '42,W). *What Every Citizen Should Know About the Navy.* New York: Norton, 1941. 219 pp.

Outlines the training and the tasks of enlisted men and officers. Sketches their daily life, describes their quarters, notes their disciplines. Different types of naval vessels are described and sketched, as are the types and tasks of fighting planes, equipment, communications and bases. A final chapter on naval strategy is illustrated with charts. A glossary of naval terms precedes an appendix of naval statistics.

36. BANSE, EWALD. *Germany Prepares for War* (rev.). New York: Harcourt, Brace, 1941. 370 pp.

New edition of this book which outlined the basic Nazi war plan in 1932. The author is a German geographer, appointed by the Nazis as Professor of Military Science at Brunswick Technical College, and generally regarded as a leading exponent of Nazi military ideas. Includes lengthy passages on war

psychology, together with careful analysis of the military geography of each of the European nations.

37. BERCHIN, MICHEL; and BENHORIN, ELIAHU. *The Red Army.* New York: Norton, 1942. 277 pp.

By two Russian émigré journalists.

38. BIENSTOCK, GREGORY. *The Struggle for the Pacific.* New York: Macmillan, 1937. 299 pp.

Heavily documented economic and strategic analysis by a German economist. Bibliography, pp. 271-79 and ends of chapters.

39. BRODIE, BERNARD. *Sea Power in the Machine Age.* Princeton: Princeton University, 1941. 466 pp.

Treatise on development of sea war since the 18th century. Bibliographic footnotes.

40. CHASE, STUART (CB '40, W); and TYLER, MARIAN. *The New Western Front.* New York: Harpers, 1939. 196 pp.

Two U.S. popularizers of economic and social problems examine vested and emotional interests that favor U.S. intervention in Europe and Asia, and find on the basis of economic analysis that confining U.S. interests to the Western Hemisphere would be more profitable. Bibliography, pp. 191-92.

41. CLIVE, LEWIS. *The People's Army,* with an introduction by Major Clement R. Attlee (New Fabian Research Bureau publication). London: Gollancz, 1938. 288 pp.

Outlines a Labour Party policy of reforms to make the British Army serve as a "defender of democracy."

*42. COMMITTEE FOR NATIONAL MORALE. *The Axis Grand Strategy: Blueprints for Total War,* compiled and edited by Ladislas Farago. New York: Farrar and Rinehart, 1942. 614 pp.

A book of readings from authoritative Axis sources.

43. DAVIS, GEORGE THURMAN (D). *A Navy Second to None: The Development of Modern American Naval Policy.* New York: Harcourt,

Brace, for Yale University Institute of International Studies, 1940. 508 pp.

Comprehensive study of the development of American naval policy. "The United States occupies the most impregnable position in the world. . . . The American people live in the safest country on the face of the earth. By what nation or nations could this country be assailed? . . . let us bear in mind that the present American fleet and the additions previously authorized . . . provide sea power adequate to guard the New World and to make any threat to our island empire a risk which no country could assume. Let us not squander the wealth of our people upon needless armament which may jeopardize the stability of our institutions or tempt us to pursue the will-o'-the-wisp of economic ambitions or power politics in distant parts of the world." By a U.S. historian, research associate, Yale University Institute of International Studies. Bibliography, pp. 485-98.

44. DENLINGER, SUTHERLAND; and GARY, CHARLES BINFORD. *War in the Pacific: A Study of Navies, Peoples, and Battle Problems.* London: Williams and Norgate, 1937. New York: McBride, 1936. 348 pp.

45. DUPUY, RICHARD ERNEST (W); and CARTER, HODDING R. *Civilian Defense in the United States.* New York: Farrar and Rinehart, 1942. 296 pp.

In this war the American civilian is subject to three methods of attack: military attack or invasion from the air or from the sea; psychological attack by propaganda; sabotage. The authors, two U.S. army officers, offer suggestions on all three. Bibliography, pp. 277-85.

46. ELIOT, GEORGE FIELDING (CB '40,W). *The Ramparts We Watch.* New York: Reynal and Hitchcock, 1938. 370 pp.

Analysis of the military and naval strategy of keeping the U.S. free of invaders. The author is a former major, Military Intelligence Reserve, U.S. Army, and a widely recognized authority on military and naval subjects. Illustrates with extreme clarity the position of the U.S. in the world balance of power, and the drastic—perhaps permanent—loss of liberty and democracy which might menace this country in the event of a long war. Bibliography, pp. 361-62.

47. FOERTSCH, HERMANN. *Kriegskunst von Heute und Morgen.* Berlin: Andermann, 1939. 258 pp. English edition: *The Art of War*, foreword by George Fielding Eliot (CB '40,W). New York: Veritas, 1940. 273 pp.

High German General Staff officer assigns to psychological forces an equal, if not greater role than military forces.

48. FULLER, MAJOR GENERAL J. F. C. *Decisive Battles: Their Influence Upon History and Civilization.* New York: Scribner's, 1940. 1060 pp.

By well known British military historian.

49. GALTIER-BOISSIÈRE, JEAN. *Les mystères de la police secrète.* Paris: Le Crapouillot, 1936. 2 vols.

Volume 1: from Lieutenant-General La Reynie to Fouché. Volume 2: from the *provocateur* Delaveau to Chiappe, contemporary prefect of Paris police.

50. GLOVER, CHARLES WILLIAM. *Civil Defense: A Manual Presenting with Working Drawings the Methods Required for Adequate Protection against Aerial Attack*, third edition, enlarged and revised. Brooklyn, N.Y.: Chemical Publishing Company, 1941. 794 pp.

Comprehensive. Based on British experience. Profusely illustrated. Bibliography, pp. 766-73.

51. GRIFFIN, LIEUT. COLONEL ROBERT ALLEN, editor; and SHAW, LIEUT. COLONEL RONALD M., assistant editor. *School of the Citizen Soldier: Adapted from the Educational Program of the Second Army, Lieut. Gen. Ben Lear, Commanding.* New York: Appleton-Century, 1942. 558 pp.

Text of 37 lectures which comprise a part of the Second Army's unique educational program. This program was launched in January 1942 with the announced purpose of filling in gaps left by the educational system. Sections dealing with world trade and strategic raw materials are by Professor William G. Fletcher. Nearly half the book is a summary of American historical and constitutional development by Ralph Henry Gabriel (D,W), Professor of History at Yale. A board of Second Army officers, headed by Lieut. Col. Griffin, compiled the remainder—an outline of the world crisis, some chapters on the American, Japanese and Nazi armies, and on the technique of employing and resisting propaganda. Bibliography, pp. 533-37 and ends of chapters.

*52. *Handbuch der neuzeitlichen Wehrwissenschaften*, edited by Major General Hermann Franke. Berlin: De Gruyter, 1936-39. 5 vols.

Standard reference manual for German Army. General Franke and Dr. Friedrich Bertkau have articles on "Psychological Warfare" (geistiger Krieg), vol. 1, pp. 105-09; "Propaganda," pp. 555-56; "Military Propaganda" (Wehrpropaganda), pp. 710-12. See also "Military Psychology" (Wehrpsychologie), p. 712, by Dr. Max Simoneit.

53. Harris, Joseph Pratt (D,W). "Training Administrators for the Government of Occupied Territories," *Public Management*, 24: 354-57 (December 1942).

U.S. Army program of training for military government is described by one of its administrators, a U.S. political scientist.

54. Hart, Basil Henry Liddell (CB '40). *The War in Outline, 1914-1918*. New York: Modern Library, 1939. 285 pp.

New edition of a standard work by London *Times* military specialist.

55. Haushofer, Karl (CB '42). *Geopolitik des Pazifischen Ozeans: Studien über die Wechselbeziehungen zwischen Geographie und Geschichte*, 3rd ed. Heidelberg and Berlin: Vowinckel, 1938. 338 pp.

Elaborate analysis of armaments and resources, actual and potential, by well-known German geographer and political theorist. Many maps and sketches. Bibliography, pp. 287-312.

56. Herring, Edward Pendleton (D). *The Impact of War: Our American Democracy Under Arms*. New York: Farrar and Rinehart, 1941. 306 pp.

Historical analysis of effects of U.S. wars on U.S. social policies, by Harvard political scientist. Annotated bibliography, pp. 285-94.

57. Ishimaru, Tota. *The Next World War*. London: Hurst and Blackett, 1937. 352 pp.

Japanese lieutenant-commander analyzes many possible war combinations of fighting forces as of 1939-40, when, he says, "the dividing line between peace and catastrophe" will have been reached.

58. Knight, Bruce Winton (D, W). *How to Run a War*. New York: Knopf, 1936. 243 pp.

Authoritative though ironic handbook on the conduct of a war, addressed to the moneyed classes by a Dartmouth professor of economics. Includes valuable suggestions on details of the mobilization of industry, the control of opinion, and the management of inflated currency.

59. League of Nations. *Armaments Yearbook*. Geneva, 1924–.

60. League of Nations. *Statistical Yearbook of the Trade in Arms and Ammunition*. Geneva, 1924–.

61. Levinson, Edward. *I Break Strikes: The Technique of Pearl L. Bergoff*. New York: McBride, 1935. 314 pp.

Study of an organization of strike-breakers. Bibliography, pp. 308-12.

62. McKinley, Silas Bent. *Democracy and Military Power*, new and enlarged edition, introduction by Charles Austin Beard (D,W). New York: Vanguard, 1941. 350 pp.

Well-known U.S. historian surveys relation between military technology and democracy from Greek and Roman days to the present. Conclusion: Democracy has been possible only in periods when mass infantry has been the dominant military form. The trend in our time, he finds, is toward planes, tanks and tyranny. First edition, 1934. Bibliography, pp. 345-50.

63. Miksche, Ferdinand Otto. *Attack: A Study of Blitzkrieg Tactics*, translated from the Czech, with an introduction, by Tom Wintringham. New York: Random House, 1942. 267 pp.

64. MUSTE, ABRAHAM JOHN. *Nonviolence in an Aggressive World*. New York: Harpers, 1940. 211 pp.

Well-known U.S. church and labor leader marshals the arguments for nonviolence as a constructive method of creating a peaceful world, and suggests a political program. Chapter 2, "Pacifism as Revolutionary Strategy," states: "It is now generally recognized that the balance of power in deciding whether a people shall turn toward reaction or toward social progress rests with certain sections of the middle class—farmers, the better paid workers, technicians, small business people, professional people. . . . If the workers and left-wing intellectuals renounce the democratic process, for whatever reason . . . the reactionaries and Fascists are given the opportunity which they covet to pose as the defenders of order and national integrity . . . multitudes of these middle class elements will choose a Fascist dictatorship. . . ." Bibliography, pp. 204-05.

65. *The Naval Officer's Guide*, by Arthur A. Ageton. New York: Whittlesey House, 1943. 514 pp.

Commander Ageton is an Annapolis graduate with 20 years' experience in the U.S. Navy. Bibliography, p. 503.

66. NICKERSON, HOFFMAN (W). *The Armed Horde, 1793-1939: A Study of the Rise, Survival and Decline of the Mass Army*. New York: Putnam's Sons, 1941. 427 pp.

By a U.S. author who has specialized in military history. Analytical outline of military history and technique, emphasizing dependence of military doctrines and forms upon social ideologies. Views the conscripted mass army as "the chief symptom of governmental despotism," and "a potential revolution." Asserts that mechanization of war may lead to return of professional military classes, less bloodthirsty and destructive than "the armed horde." Bibliography, pp. 401-18.

67. PIERCE, W. O'D. *Air War: Its Psychological, Technical and Social Implications*. New York: Modern Age, 1939. 224 pp.

By an Irish scientist. Includes passages from the author's *Air War: Its Technical and Social Aspects* (London: Watts, 1937). Devotes 55 pages to "Morale in the Air" and 60 to "Morale and the Home Front." Bibliography, pp. 217-19.

68. PRATT, FLETCHER (CB '42, W). *Sea Power and Today's War*. New York: Harrison-Hilton, 1939. 237 pp.

A technical study of the strength of the sea powers and an analysis of their strategy in time of war, by a U.S. free lance magazine writer, author of a number of military and naval histories.

69. PULESTON, WILLIAM DILWORTH (W). *The Armed Forces of the Pacific: A Comparison of the Military and Naval Power of the United States and Japan*. New Haven: Yale University, 1941. 273 pp.

Captain Puleston, U.S.N., retired, is a graduate of Naval War College, and was for several years director of the Office of Naval Intelligence in the Navy Department. His view: "Whatever temporary successes Japan might have in the western Pacific, her final defeat would be inevitable" (p. 260).

70. RANKIN, ROBERT STANLEY (D, W). *When Civil Law Fails: Martial Law and Its Legal Basis in the United States*. Durham: Duke University, 1939. 225 pp.

Duke University political scientist analyzes conditions under which martial law has taken the place of civil law in U.S. history, from the Battle of New Orleans to the present day. Bibliography, pp. 206-16.

71. ROSINSKI, HERBERT. *The German Army*. New York: Harcourt, Brace, 1940. 267 pp.

General treatise. Dr. Rosinski (Ph.D. Berlin) was formerly lecturer at the German War Office, at the German Military Academy and at the University of Berlin; is now a writer for New York *Times*.

*72. ROWAN, RICHARD WILMER (W). *The Story of Secret Service*. Garden City: Doubleday, 1937. 732 pp.

Authoritative and comprehensive treatise on secret agents from the time of Moses to the present; about a third of the book deals with World War I. The author has published several other books on espionage, counterespionage, sabotage and propaganda, including

Terror in Our Time (New York: Longmans, Green, 1940. 438 pp.).

73. SCHWEDER, ALFRED. *Politische Polizei*. Berlin: Heymann, 1937. 192 pp.

74. SEVERSKY, ALEXANDER P. DE (CB '41). *Victory through Air Power*. New York: Simon and Schuster, 1942. 354 pp.

Well-known Russian-American aeronautical engineer develops a totalistic theory of global air strategy, without which, he feels, the United Nations cannot win the war.

75. SHRIDHARANI, KRISHNALAL JETHALAL (CB '42). *War Without Violence: A Study of Gandhi's Method and Its Accomplishments*. New York: Harcourt, Brace, 1939. 351 pp.

Pointing to passive resistance as "a surer way to peace" than Western pacifism, this author, a disciple of Gandhi, discusses means of organizing it on many fronts: the general strike, the boycott, the nonpayment of taxes, social ostracism, civil disobedience. Bibliography, pp. 325-32.

76. SOCIAL SCIENCE RESEARCH COUNCIL. COMMITTEE ON PUBLIC ADMINISTRATION. *Civil-Military Relations: Bibliographical Notes on Administrative Problems of Civilian Mobilization*. Chicago: Public Administration Service, 1940. 77 pp.

Annotates over 450 government documents (hearings, reports, etc.), memoirs and biographies, journals and periodical articles, accounts by participants and by scholars. Covers American, British, Canadian, German, and French materials from 1914 to the present. Interpretive analyses for each country on planning, coordination, personnel, budgeting, procurement and priorities, reporting and accountability, consultation and decentralization. Prepared under the direction of Professor Edward Pendleton Herring (D) of Harvard University.

77. SPEIER, HANS (D). "Class Structure and 'Total War,'" *American Sociological Review*, 4: 370-80 (June 1939).

Specialist in sociology of war, New School for Social Research, analyzes the Great Power state to determine the role of each class during total mobilization.

*78. SPEIER, HANS (D); and KÄHLER, ALFRED, editors. *War in Our Time*. New York: Norton, 1939. 362 pp.

Symposium by graduate faculty of New School for Social Research, dealing with economic, political, and social bases of war. Hans Speier has a chapter on "Morale and Propaganda." Bibliographic footnotes.

79. SPROUT, HAROLD HANCE (D); and SPROUT, MARGARET TUTTLE (D). *Toward a New Order of Sea Power: American Naval Policy and the World Scene, 1918-1922*. Princeton: Princeton University, 1940. 332 pp.

By Princeton political scientist and his wife. Companion piece to *The Rise of American Naval Power* (Princeton: Princeton University, 1939. 398 pp.), which covered the development of U.S. naval power and policy, 1776-1918. The present book deals primarily with the Washington Naval Conference of 1921-22. A third book, now in preparation, is intended to bring the record up to date. Bibliographic footnotes.

80. SPYKMAN, NICHOLAS JOHN (D, W). *America's Strategy in World Politics: The United States and The Balance of Power* (Institute of International Studies, Yale University). New York: Harcourt, Brace, 1942. 500 pp.

Professor Spykman, late director of the Yale Institute of International Studies, was born in the Netherlands and spent several years in the Middle and Far East and Australasia before coming to the United States. He believes that the balance of power must continue to be the way of the future as it has been the way of the past. Peace-making would be directed toward balancing the "strength between members of regional groups." Bibliography, pp. 473-80.

81. STEVENS, WILLIAM OLIVER (W); and WESTCOTT, ALLAN FERGUSON (D,W). *A History of Sea Power*, rev. ed. Garden City: Doubleday, Doran, 1937. 434 pp.

Standard text by two professors of the U.S. Naval Academy. Bibliography at ends of chapters.

82. STRAUSZ-HUPÉ, ROBERT. *Geopolitics: The Struggle for Space and Power.* New York: Putnam's Sons, 1942. 274 pp.

By a Viennese who has lived in the U.S. for nearly 20 years and has long been a citizen. He has been an associate editor of *Current History* and a special lecturer in the Department of Political Science, University of Pennsylvania.

83. THOMAS, SHIPLEY. *S-2 in Action.* Harrisburg: Military Service Publishing Co., 1940. 128 pp.

Technique of espionage in wartime.

84. THOMPSON, JAMES WESTFALL (CB '41,W); and PADOVER, SAUL K. (W). *Secret Diplomacy; A Record of Espionage and Double-Dealing, 1500-1815.* London: Jarrolds, 1937. 286 pp.

By two well-known U.S. historians. Cryptography, pp. 253-63. Bibliography, pp. 265-78.

85. THOMSON, SIR BASIL HOME. *The Scene Changes.* Garden City: Doubleday, Doran, 1937. 455 pp.

Autobiography of the World War I head of Scotland Yard's Current Intelligence Division, who is the author of several other works dealing with secret service and espionage systems.

*86. VAGTS, ALFRED HERMANN FRIEDRICH (D). *The History of Militarism: Romance and Realities of a Profession.* New York: Norton, 1937. 510 pp.

The administration of armies and their influence upon civilization, from the Middle Ages to the present day. The author is an ex-German social scientist, now in the U.S. Part 3, "The Military and Politics," pp. 317-91, illustrates the skills of the military men in public speaking, journalism and other symbolic activities, and their psychology in dealing with political-economic problems. Bibliography, pp. 489-510.

*87. WALLER, WILLARD WALTER (D), editor. *War in the Modern World.* New York: Random House, 1940. 572 pp.

Symposium by a dozen social scientists and journalists. Contains a chapter on "Propaganda and Public Opinion," by Ralph D. Casey (D,W). In "The Prospects of Western Civilization," Ralph Linton (D,W), U.S. anthropologist, also discusses current and emerging opinions.

88. "The War Department," *Fortune,* January 1941.

89. WERNER, MAX, pseud. *Battle for the World: The Strategy and Diplomacy of the Second World War,* translated by Heinz and Ruth Norden. New York: Modern Age, 1941. 403 pp.

By ex-German military theorist who correctly predicted (1) the outcome of the Battle of France and (2) the Russian resistance. Extensively documented from European sources. Bibliography, pp. 385-92. See also the author's *The Military Strength of the Powers* (New York: Modern Age, 1939. 376 pp.), and his *The Great Offensive: The Strategy of Coalition Warfare,* translated by Heinz and Ruth Norden (New York: Viking, 1942. 360 pp. Bibliography, pp. 347-51).

90. WINTRINGHAM, TOM. *New Ways of War.* New York: Penguin Books, 1940. 128 pp.

Tactics of a "People's War" of defense against an invader using the most modern techniques of planes and tanks. The author is a British military theorist, author of several books, who served in the B.E.F. (1914-18), commanded the British Battalion of the International Brigade in Spain, and became director of the Local Defense Volunteers (England).

91. WINTRINGHAM, TOM. *The Story of Weapons and Tactics: From Troy to Stalingrad.* Boston: Houghton Mifflin, 1943. 230 pp.

Survey of the history of warfare. The appropriate tactics for a prodemocratic army, he says, are those of a "People's War": trained popular armies, operating on guerrilla principles. Defense should be a "web" or network, which can be penetrated but not broken; offense a mass uprising, "more like an explosion than a campaign." In the background must stand the disciplined industry of a Great Power nation, to supply the equipment.

92. WOLLENBERG, ERICH. *The Red Army.* London: Secker and Warburg, 1938. 283 pp.

Analysis of the political organization of the

Red Army; reveals but little about its fighting effectiveness. The author served in the Red Army 1921-36. Bibliography, pp. 273-76.

*93. WRIGHT, QUINCY (D,W). *A Study of War.* Chicago: University of Chicago, 1942. 1,533 pp.

Professor of international law and relations, University of Chicago, summarizes the findings of a great number of research workers on the causes of war, including the 66 extended studies, of which nearly a score have been published, composing the University of Chicago's "Causes of War" series. Concludes that a whole civilization may be destroyed by war and that the balance of power—a very old device in power politics—is unlikely to prevent this. Therefore (and this conclusion is reinforced by the economic and technological parts of the study) the main hope of the world, if any, is the establishment of a world authority, a reorganized League of Nations. Heavily documented.

II. MANAGEMENT OF GOODS AND SERVICES

*94. BRADY, ROBERT ALEXANDER. *Business as a System of Power.* New York: Columbia University, 1943. 340 pp.

Comparative analysis of political consequences of the "bureaucratic centralism" brought about by commercial enterprises of Germany, Italy, Japan, France, Great Britain and United States. Discusses the methods of propaganda, coercion and political manipulation by means of which the ascendancy of such enterprises is maintained. By well-known U.S. economist. Bibliography, pp. 321-30.

95. BRADY, ROBERT ALEXANDER. "Policies of National Manufacturing Spitzenverbände," *Political Science Quarterly,* 56: 199-225, 379-91, 515-44 (June, September, December 1941).

Compares central trade associations, such as National Association of Manufacturers; Federation of British Industries; Confédération Générale du Patronat Français; the Japanese House of Mitsui; the Reichsverband der Deutschen Industrie and its successor (after the Nazi coup), the Reichsgruppe Industrie. Stress is placed on the view that these organizations have more similarities than differences, and that in all cases they tend to become the Gov-

ernment, following a period of "liberal" reformism and experiment with antitrust laws.

96. CLARK, COLIN. *The Conditions of Economic Progress.* New York: Macmillan, 1940. 504 pp.

A comparative study of the investigations into national income which have been made in all the principal countries. By Oxford economist. Bibliographic footnotes.

97. CLARK, HAROLD FLORIAN (D, W); and others. *Life Earnings in Selected Occupations in the United States.* New York: Harpers, 1937. 408 pp.

Economist, Teachers' College (Columbia), writes of income situations in the main branches of the professions, clerical occupations, skilled and unskilled labor, and farming, up to 1936. Bibliography, pp. 403-06.

98. CHERNE, LEO M. (CB '40). *Your Business Goes to War.* Boston: Houghton Mifflin, 1942. 496 pp.

"The blueprints of economic mobilization," drawn by executive secretary, Tax Research Institute of America.

99. DAVIES, ERNEST. "*National Capitalism*": The Government's Record as Protector of Private Monopoly. London: Gollancz, 1939. 320 pp.

Monopolistic tendencies in England since the Conservative government came into power in 1931. Bibliography in text.

100. DOUGLAS, WILLIAM ORVILLE (CB '41,W). *Democracy and Finance: The Addresses and Public Statements of William O. Douglas as Member and Chairman of the Securities and Exchange Commission,* edited, with introduction and notes, by James Allen. New Haven: Yale University, 1940. 301 pp.

101. EMENY, BROOKS. *The Strategy of Raw Materials: A Study of America in Peace and War* (from a Ph.D. thesis, Yale University). New York: Macmillan, for Bureau of International Research, Harvard University and Radcliffe College, 1934. 202 pp.

Bibliography, pp. 189-95.

102. EZEKIEL, MORDECAI (D,W). *Jobs For All, through Industrial Expansion.* New York: Knopf, 1939. 331 pp.

Continues the line of thought first developed by Dr. Ezekiel, a prominent New Deal economist, in his *$2,500 a Year* (New York, 1936). Proposes to rescue business and democracy through an Industrial Expansion Administration primarily dedicated to increasing production. In a manner similar to the revised AAA, this body would guarantee the public purchase, at an agreed discount, of the unsalable surplus commodities produced by certain key industries. The expansion plan would be restricted to a small number of major industries, and would be drawn up by them, subject to approval by the Expansion Administration. In competitive lines of business, competition would be vigorously preserved. In monopolistic lines, the price at which the Administration would buy its share of the product would be determined in terms of the public interest. The immediate objectives would be jobs for all, and a national income of at least $100,-000,000,000 a year. Full democratic procedure—notice, hearing, full discussion, and freedom of speech—would be insisted upon.

103. GALLOWAY, GEORGE BARNES (D). *Postwar Planning in the United States.* New York: Twentieth Century Fund, 1942. 158 pp.

A listing, with explanation, of the organizations and agencies concerned with problems of postwar planning. Bibliography, pp. 129-58.

104. (Pop.) GOSLIN, RYLLIS ALEXANDER; and GOSLIN, OMAR PANCOAST. *Don't Kill the Goose.* New York: Harpers, 1939. 169 pp.

A sequel to the popular volume of pictorial economics by the same authors, entitled *Rich Man, Poor Man* (Harpers, 1935). Tells how purchasing power is distributed, why failure to utilize productive capacity occurs and how individual incomes and the standard of living might be improved. Includes programs for national housing and youth problems.

105. (Pop.) GOSLIN, RYLLIS ALEXANDER; and GOSLIN, OMAR PANCOAST. *Our Town's Business.* New York: Funk and Wagnalls, 1939. 355 pp.

In 1937-38 hundreds of women's clubs throughout the country participated in a program of what may be called civic education, sponsored by the National Federation of Business and Professional Women and built on the theme of "Our Town's Business." Omar and Ryllis Goslin, authors of *Rich Man, Poor Man,* took part in the preparation of study materials for this program, and it was from that work that the idea of the present book grew. It follows "lines of the utmost simplification," in text and pictorial chart, seeking to clarify basic economic facts.

106. HANSEN, ALVIN HARVEY (D, W). *Fiscal Policy and Business Cycles.* New York: Norton, 1941. 462 pp.

Problems which the depression, partial recovery and war have presented, as they relate to American fiscal policy and the business cycle. By Harvard professor of economics, an adviser of the F. D. Roosevelt Administration. Bibliographic footnotes.

107. HARDY, CHARLES OSCAR (D, W). *Wartime Control of Prices.* Washington, D.C.: Brookings Institution, 1940. 216 pp.

Brookings economist analyzes measures U.S. might adopt to prevent runaway prices during the war boom.

108. HARRIS, SEYMOUR EDWIN (D). *The Economics of American Defense.* New York: Norton, 1941. 350 pp.

General treatise by Harvard economist. Bibliographic footnotes.

109. HESSEL, MARY STANLEY; MURPHY, W. J.; and HESSEL, F. A. *Strategic Materials in Hemisphere Defense.* New York: Hastings House, 1942. 235 pp.

A discussion of sources and uses of the fourteen strategic and critical materials. Bibliography, pp. 225-35.

110. HICKS, JOHN RICHARD; HICKS, URSULA KATHLEEN; and ROSTÁS, LÁSZLÓ. *The Taxation of War Wealth.* New York: Oxford University, 1941. 304 pp.

Analysis of excess profits taxes and war levies of the leading capitalist countries, by British economists.

111. KEY, VALDIMER ORLANDO, JR. (D). *The Techniques of Political*

Graft in the United States (part of Ph.D. thesis on this subject, Political Science, University of Chicago). Chicago: University of Chicago Libraries, 1936. 75 pp.

Bibliographic footnotes.

112. LEAGUE OF NATIONS. ECONOMIC INTELLIGENCE SERVICE. *Europe's Trade: A Study of the Trade of European Countries with Each Other and with the Rest of the World* (League of Nations Publication 1941.II.A.I). Princeton, 1941. 116 pp.

The first comprehensive study of Europe's trade.

113. LEAGUE OF NATIONS. ECONOMIC INTELLIGENCE SERVICE. *Raw Materials and Foodstuffs—Production by Countries, 1935 and 1938* (1939. II.A.24). Geneva, 1940.

Brings together in a handy form information which previously could be obtained only by much research. Information is given for some 200 different commodities and nearly 140 countries or areas, and the tables are so compiled that the complete production of any country can be seen by a glance at a single page.

113a. LEAGUE OF NATIONS. ECONOMIC INTELLIGENCE SERVICE. *The Network of World Trade* (L. of N. 1942. II. A. 3). New York: Columbia University Press, 1942. 171 pp.

A companion volume to *Europe's Trade* (L. of N. 1941. II. A.I), a comprehensive statistical analysis of the economic networks of the European continent.

114. LEAGUE OF NATIONS. ECONOMIC INTELLIGENCE SERVICE. *World Economic Survey*. Geneva, annually, 1932–. New York: Columbia University, 1939–.

115. LEWIS, CLEONA (D); and MCCLELLAND, JOHN C. *Nazi Europe and World Trade*. Washington, D.C.: Brookings Institution, 1941. 200 pp.

Statistical analysis of the degree of economic self-sufficiency achieved by Nazi-con-

trolled Europe. By two U.S. economists. Bibliographic footnotes.

116. LORWIN, LEWIS LEVITZKI (D, W). *Economic Consequences of the Second World War*. New York: Random House, 1942. 510 pp.

By well-known U.S. economist. Regarded by most reviewers as one of the most comprehensive and reasonable of the books forecasting the postwar world.

117. MACDONALD, DWIGHT. "The Monopoly Committee: A Study in Frustration," *American Scholar*, 8: 295-308 (Summer 1939).

Editor of *Partisan Review* places Temporary National Economic Committee in historical perspective, analyzing motives of the Federal Trade Commission, the New Dealers, and the monopolists.

118. MENDERSHAUSEN, HORST. *The Economics of War*, rev. ed. New York: Prentice-Hall, 1943. 390 pp.

Survey of the problems confronting the economic system of a country preparing for, fighting, and emerging from a war, "for undergraduate courses." First edition, 1940. Dr. Mendershausen, formerly of the University of Geneva, became a professor at Bennington College, and economist with the National Bureau of Economic Research. Includes elaborate tables on strategic materials.

119. MICHELS, ROBERTO. *Il Boicottagio: Saggio su un aspetto delle crisi.* Turin: Einaudi, 1934. 136 pp.

Economic and political aspects of the boycott, especially Indian boycotts of British goods and German boycotts of the Jews. By a Swiss-Italian social scientist.

120. RATNER, SIDNEY. *American Taxation: Its History as a Social Force in Democracy*. New York: Norton, 1942. 561 pp.

The history of American taxation viewed as a product of the contending segments of American life and as a factor in shaping American democracy. Bibliography, pp. 515-27.

121. ROUSH, GAR A. (W). *Strategic Mineral Supplies*. New York: McGraw-Hill, 1939. 485 pp.

Standard survey of the more important strategic mineral commodities by well-known U.S. metallurgist, editor of *The Mineral Industry* and a major, Staff Specialist Reserve, U.S. Army. Bibliography, pp. 11-14.

122. RYAN, JOHN AUGUSTINE (D, W). *Distributive Justice: The Right and Wrong of Our Present Distribution of Wealth,* 3rd ed., rev. New York: Macmillan, 1942. 357 pp.

Complete revision of standard work on Catholic conceptions of reasonable profits, wages and economic practices and of "monopolistic injustices." By Director, Department of Social Action, National Catholic Welfare Conference. Bibliography at end of each section.

123. SIMPSON, KEMPER (W). *Big Business, Efficiency and Fascism: An Appraisal of the Efficiency of Large Corporations and of Their Threat to Democracy.* New York: Harpers, 1941. 203 pp.

A study recently prepared for the Federal Trade Commission compares the efficiency of business operation among monopolistic, large, medium-sized and small companies in America's major industries. Contrary to common belief, and claims of big business, the colossal corporations, in virtually every case, are operating at higher unit costs and with less efficiency than medium-sized and smaller corporations. The Commission's findings, here presented in popular form, reinforce the author's argument that full employment and a higher standard of living can only be achieved under a return to competitive economy. This survey covers such basic industries as steel, cement, farm machinery, flour, sugar, milk products, automobiles, chemicals, rayon, etc. Documentation in text.

124. STALEY, (ALVAH) EUGENE (D). *Raw Materials in Peace and War.* New York: Council on Foreign Relations, 1937. 326 pp.

Comprehensive factual data about the present uses and control of raw materials throughout the world, and a theory of "the various degrees of monopoly power which may be exercised with relation to specific commodities." By an economist, Fletcher School of Law and Diplomacy, Tufts College. Illustrates comprehensively the major material controls and limits in world and national economic development. Bibliographic footnotes.

125. STALEY, (ALVAH) EUGENE (D). *War and the Private Investor: A Study in the Relations of International Politics and International Private Investment* (University of Chicago "Causes of War" studies), foreword by Quincy Wright, introduction by Sir Arthur Salter. New York: Doubleday, Doran, 1935. 562 pp.

After examining all of the cases since about 1880 in which there is any reason for believing private investments have been a factor in international political disputes, the author finds that very frequently it was governments, not private investors, that first advocated economic activity or war in the areas in question. As a remedy for war, he suggests "denationalization of investments" and world-wide supervision through a World Investment Commission, a World Commercial Court, international incorporation laws, a World Investment Bank, and a World Consular Service.

126. STEAD, WILLIAM HENRY (D, W). *Democracy against Unemployment: An Analysis of the Major Problem of Post-war Planning.* New York: Harpers, 1942. 280 pp.

The author is Dean, School of Business and Public Administration, Washington University, and was formerly Chief Executive Officer, U.S. Employment Service. Bibliography, pp. 263-72.

127. STEINER, GEORGE A. *Economic Problems of War.* New York: John Wiley, 1942. 692 pp.

By a U.S. economist. After two preliminary chapters, one a generalized statement of the total problem and the other a survey of American resources, there follows a description of the economic war organizations of England, Germany, and Japan. Nothing is said about Russia. The next two parts of the book are devoted to a close examination of the economic difficulties which confront the U.S. in waging global war. A separate chapter is devoted to each problem—money, finance, credit, prices, raw materials, production, labor, agriculture, transportation, housing, and others. Each is analyzed against its historical background, reference is made to what was done during the first World War, and a description is given of the current measures. Finally, the book deals with postwar readjustment. Bibliography, pp. 671-75.

128. Sweezy, Maxine Bernard (Yaple). *The Structure of the Nazi Economy* (Harvard Studies in Monopoly and Competition, no. 4). Cambridge: Harvard University, 1941. 255 pp.

Extensive analysis by U.S. economist based on current German sources. Bibliography, pp. 241-46.

129. Twentieth Century Fund. Special Committee on Taxation. *Facing the Tax Problem* (606 pp.) and *Studies in Current Tax Problems* (303 pp.). New York, 1937.

Comprehensive survey of the Federal and state taxation systems of the United States. The first volume offers the Committee's analysis and recommendations; the second contains supporting research memoranda.

130. U.S. National Resources Committee. *Consumer Incomes in the United States: Their Distribution in 1935-36.* Washington, D.C.: Government Printing Office, 1938. 104 pp.

Based on a canvass of over 300,000 families, this is the most exact analysis ever made of U.S. consumer incomes, and the first one to appear since the estimates for 1929 in the Brookings Institution's *America's Capacity to Consume* (Washington, D.C.: 1934). Illustrates authoritatively the shape and size of the income pyramid in a country subject to monopolistic competition. Can be read to advantage in connection with the Twentieth Century Fund's *Facing the Tax Problem* (New York: 1937), a comprehensive survey of the Federal and state taxation systems of the U.S.

*131. U.S. National Resources Committee. *The Structure of the American Economy: Part 1, Basic Characteristics.* Washington, D.C.: Government Printing Office, 1939. 396 pp.

Comprehensive analysis by a group of social scientists. Lists the 200 largest U.S. nonfinancial corporations and the 50 largest financial

institutions; analyzes their interlocking relationships and their techniques of social control. Divides U.S. big business into eight monopolistic "community-of-interest groups," each centered upon a nucleus of financial and industrial firms; together these eight interest groups are said to control assets of about 61 billion dollars, fairly evenly distributed among industrials, rails, utilities, and banks. Also discusses business, labor, and farm organizations. Includes numerous charts, graphs, maps.

132. U.S. National Resources Committee. Sub-committee on Technology. *Technological Trends and National Policy, including the Social Implications of New Inventions.* Washington, D.C.: Government Printing Office, 1937. 388 pp.

Pp. 39-67, by Bernhard J. Stern (D), deal with psychological and socio-economic "Resistances to the Adoption of Technological Innovations." Pp. 210-49, by T. A. M. Craven (W), and a committee of the Engineering Department of the FCC, and by A. E. Giegengack (W), Public Printer, are on the technology of communications.

*133. U.S. Temporary National Economic Committee. *Hearings* pursuant to Public Resolution no. 113, 75th Congress, "authorizing and directing a Select Committee to make a full and complete study and investigation with respect to the concentration of economic power in, and financial control over, production and distribution of goods and services." Washington, D.C.: Government Printing Office, 1939-41. 30 vols.

These 30 volumes, together with the 43 volumes of supplementary monographs, the *Final Report and Recommendations of the Committee* (783 pp.) and the *Final Report of the Executive Secretary of the Committee* (435 pp.), constitute the most thorough inventory available on monopolistic tendencies in U.S. industry and distribution. They should be read in conjunction with the monograph series of the National Bureau of Economic Research (about 40 volumes) and the comparable monographs of the Brookings Institution and the Twentieth Century Fund.

C. THEORIES OF THE GENERAL PATTERNS
OF COLLECTIVE RESPONSE

No theory of propaganda is adequate unless it has been formulated with reference to the main body of psychological, social-psychological, and general social scientific theory. The titles in this section sample the principal trends of theory and methods in these several fields. Definitions of concepts like *crowd, public, opinion, suggestion, stimuli, response, collective representations, imitation,* and *myth* are included here, together with attempts to state general "laws of collective behavior."

134. ALEXANDER, FRANZ (CB '42). *Our Age of Unreason: A Study of Irrational Forces in Social Life.* Philadelphia: Lippincott, 1942. 371 pp.

Restatement of psychoanalytic theory, indicating certain points of departure for problems of social theory. By Director of Chicago Institute for Psychoanalysis. Bibliography, pp. 342-59.

135. ALLPORT, FLOYD HENRY (D, W). "Toward a Science of Public Opinion," *Public Opinion Quarterly,* 1 no. 1: 7-23 (January 1937).

Highly generalized essay by social psychologist, Syracuse University.

136. ALLPORT, GORDON WILLARD (W). *Personality: A Psychological Interpretation.* New York: Holt, 1937. 588 pp.

General treatise by Harvard psychologist. Bibliography in text and footnotes.

137. ALLPORT, GORDON WILLARD (W). *The Use of Personal Documents in Psychological Science* (Social Science Research Council Bulletin 49). New York: Social Science Research Council, 1942. 210 pp.

A study prepared for the Council's Committee on Appraisal of Research. Bibliography, pp. 192-201.

138. AMERICAN PSYCHIATRIC ASSOCIATION. MILITARY MOBILIZATION COMMITTEE. *Psychiatric Aspects of Civilian Morale.* New York: Family Welfare Association of America, 1942. 62 pp.

A pamphlet presenting the experience of the civilians in wartime in other countries and discussing anxiety, morale, and fatigue and their control.

*138a. ARISTOTLE (ESS). *Politics; Rhetoric.* Athens, *ca.* 340 B.C.

General theory of the techniques of the advocate, the politician, and the propagandist under conditions of constitutional government and revolutionary change. By Athenian political scientist, tutor of Alexander the Great and other political figures.

*139. ARNOLD, THURMAN WESLEY (CB '40, D,W). *The Folklore of Capitalism.* New Haven: Yale University, 1937. 400 pp.

Influential treatise by Yale professor of law, subsequently Assistant Attorney-General of the United States. Continuing the line of analysis he began in *Symbols of Government* (New Haven: Yale University, 1935. 278 pp.), he emphasizes the need for careful selection and dissemination of symbols by principal administrators of the Federal Government. Chapter 14, "Some Principles of Political Dynamics," formulates 14 provocative generalizations on the psychology of public affairs, which may be regarded as a pungent summary of Mr. Arnold's views.

140. ASCOLI, MAX; and LEHMANN, FRITZ. *Political and Economic Democracy,* foreword by Alvin Johnson. New York: Norton, 1937. 336 pp.

Twenty-one essays by the Graduate Faculty of Political and Social Science at the New School for Social Research. An essay by Emil Lederer deals especially with public opinion and "the values of democracy."

141. BARNES, HARRY ELMER (D, W); BECKER, HOWARD (D,W); and BECKER, FRANCES BENNETT, editors. *Contemporary Social Theory.* New York: Appleton-Century, 1940. 947 pp.

College text, including contributions by the editors and by various other social scientists. Note sections on "Psychological Studies of Social Processes," by Kimball Young (D,W) and Douglas W. Oberdorfer; "Contributions of Psychoanalysis to the Interpretation of Social Facts," by Alexander Goldenweiser (W), etc. Bibliography, classified and annotated, in footnotes, ends of chapters, and pp. 889-912.

142. BARNES, HARRY ELMER (D, W); and BECKER, HOWARD (D,W). *Social Thought from Lore to Science.* Boston: Heath, 1938. 2 vols. (1178 pp.)

Two U.S. social scientists trace history of social thought from preliterate peoples to the present day. Volume 2 surveys intensively the development of sociology as a specialized science during the nineteenth and twentieth centuries in each of the major language areas of the world. Using the point of view of the German *Wissensoziologische* school, the authors have attempted to place each major social theory in its cultural context. Bibliography, vol. 1, pp. iii-lix; vol. 2, pp. iii-li.

***142a.** BAUER, WILHELM. *Die öffentliche Meinung in der Weltgeschichte.* Wildpark-Potsdam: Athenaion, 1930. 403 pp.

Lavishly illustrated. Standard treatise on history of public opinion by a professor of modern history in the University of Vienna. Bibliography, pp. 396-98.

143. BENEDICT, RUTH FULTON (CB '41, D). *Patterns of Culture.* Boston and New York: Houghton Mifflin, 1934. 291 pp.

Columbia University anthropologist's analysis of Western culture through comparisons with the cultures of the Pueblos, Dobu, and the Northwest Coast of America. Bibliography, pp. 279-86.

144. BERNARD, LUTHER LEE (D, W). *Social Control in its Sociological Aspects.* New York: Macmillan, 1939. 711 pp.

College text by U.S. social psychologist. Includes passages on public opinion, propaganda, and advertising. Bibliography in footnotes and ends of chapters.

145. BIRD, CHARLES (W). *Social Psychology.* New York: Appleton-Century, 1940. 564 pp.

College text by Professor of Psychology, University of Minnesota. Bibliography at ends of chapters.

146. BIRD, CHARLES (W). "Suggestion and Suggestibility: A Bibliography," *Psychological Bulletin,* 36: 264-83 (April 1939).

Indexed list of 233 titles. "An attempt has been made to include all pertinent references published in English."

147. BLATZ, WILLIAM EMMET. *Hostages to Peace: Parents and the Children of Democracy.* New York: Morrow, 1940. 208 pp.

The home is "the nursery of Mars," breeding war in every generation. But child guidance, nursery practices, and parental counseling may be used as means of eliminating some of the terrors of childhood and thereby promoting a rational, peaceful, democratic adult life in future generations. By well-known psychiatrist, Professor of Child Psychology, University of Toronto.

148. BLAU, ALBR. *Geistige Kriegführung.* Potsdam: Voggenreiter, 1938. 80 pp.

Standard text on psychological warfare. Dr. Blau is a leading figure in the German Army's psychological general staff.

149. BOAS, FRANZ (CB '40, CB '43, D,W). *The Mind of Primitive Man,* rev. ed. New York: Macmillan, 1938. 285 pp.

Revision of a famous anthropological treatise which first appeared in 1911. Chapter 12 is on "The Emotional Associations of Primitives."

150. BOGARDUS, EMORY STEPHEN (D,W). *Fundamentals of Social Psychology,* 3rd ed., rev. New York: Appleton-Century, 1942. 538 pp.

By U.S. sociologist. Bibliography at end of each chapter and pp. 525-26.

151. BOURNE, GEOFFREY. *War, Politics and Emotion,* introduction by Dorothy Canfield Fisher. New York: Liveright, 1941. 110 pp.

"Politics must become a science, and politicians must become qualified in it." By a physician on the staff of St. Bartholomew's Hospital, England.

152. BRIQUET, RAUL. *Psicologia Social.* Rio de Janeiro: Livraria Francisco Alves, 1935. 267 pp.

In addition to standard theoretical material, there is treatment of such themes as leadership, public opinion, crowds, and revolution. The bibliography alludes to books not well known in the United States, as well as to major social psychologists of Europe and America.

153. BROWN, JUNIUS FLAGG. *Psychology and the Social Order: An Introduction to the Dynamic Study of Social Fields.* New York: McGraw-Hill, 1936. 529 pp.

Systematic Gestaltist analysis by University of Kansas professor of psychology. An effort to unify the social sciences, this volume contains a "Methodological Section," a "Sociological Section," a "Psychological Section," and a "Political Science Section." The author's views are conveniently summarized in a "Résumé of the Argument," pp. 462-68. Bibliography, pp. 503-17.

154. BROWN, JUNIUS FLAGG; and MENNINGER, KARL AUGUSTUS (W). *The Psychodynamics of Abnormal Behavior.* New York: McGraw-Hill, 1940. 484 pp.

Comprehensive intermediate textbook written from the standpoints of psychoanalysis and Gestalt psychology, by two specialists of the Menninger Clinic. Bibliography, pp. 453-70.

155. BURNHAM, JAMES (CB '41). *The Managerial Revolution: What is Happening in the World.* New York: John Day, 1941. 285 pp.

Revision of Marxist theory by New York University professor of philosophy, who asserts that the beneficiaries of the two "world revolutions" of recent years—the Communist and the Nazi—are not the proletarians nor the Germans but the skilled workers of the newer managerial class in every large nation.

156. BURTT, HAROLD ERNEST (W). *Principles of Employment Psychology,* new ed. New York: Harpers, 1942. 568 pp.

By professor of psychology, Ohio State University. Cites most of the standard aptitude tests and the simpler personality inventories. Bibliography at ends of chapters.

157. CANTRIL, HADLEY; GAUDET, HAZEL; and HERZOG, HERTA. *The Invasion from Mars,* with the broadcast script of *War of the Worlds.* Princeton: Princeton University, 1940. 228 pp.

Princeton social psychologists conducted interviews with many persons who were frightened by a famous 1938 radio presentation featuring Orson Welles. Psychological reasons for panic and suggestibility were formulated, as were some of the implications for mass thinking in a democracy.

*158. CANTRIL, HADLEY. *The Psychology of Social Movements.* New York: John Wiley, 1941. 274 pp.

By Princeton social psychologist. Part I extends concepts of social psychology to account for the concrete situations analyzed in Part II—namely, the lynching mob, the Kingdom of Father Divine, the Oxford Group, the Townsend Plan and the Nazi Party. Undertakes to state conditions of suggestibility in critical situations. Bibliographic footnotes.

159. CARNAP, RUDOLF (D). *Introduction to Semantics* (Studies in Semantics, volume 1). Cambridge: Harvard, 1942. 263 pp.

Analysis of "the signifying function of language," by University of Chicago professor of philosophy. Bibliography, pp. 255-56.

160. CATTELL, RAYMOND BERNARD; COHEN, J.; and TRAVERS, R. M. W., editors. *Human Affairs: An Exposition of What Science Can Do For Man.* New York and London: Macmillan, 1938. 360 pp.

"The 1938 official manifesto of Scientific Humanism." This collection of papers deals with such topics as "Psychological Needs," by David Katz; "Psychology in the Industrial Life of the Nation," by E. Chambers; "Neurosis and Civilization," by Emanuel Miller. Of special interest for the analysis of public opinion is "Present Trends in the Building of Society," by Karl Mannheim, who deals explicitly with conditions and techniques of mass management under the circumstances he has observed on the Continent and in England. Appendix includes brief biographies of the contributors.

161. CHAPIN, FRANCIS STUART (D, W). *Contemporary American Institutions: A Sociological Analysis.* New York and London: Harpers, 1935. 423 pp.

Systematic treatise by U.S. sociologist. Bibliography at ends of chapters.

162. CHASE, STUART (CB '40,W). *The Tyranny of Words.* New York: Harcourt, Brace, 1938. 396 pp.

A primer on semantics. U.S. journalist and economist discusses confusions that arise from emotional connotations of everyday language. Based on the logic and semantics of such writers as Count Alfred Korzybski, C. K. Ogden and I. A. Richards, and P. W. Bridgman. Bibliography, pp. 385-86.

163. COMMITTEE FOR NATIONAL MORALE. *Research Memoranda.*

The Committee has prepared some two dozen *Memoranda* dealing with morale factors in various countries (China, France, Germany, Hungary, Italy, Spain, United States); and with the roles of propaganda and psychiatry in specific morale situations in industry, combat zones, the family, etc.

*164. "Communications," special issue of *Studies in Philosophy and Social Science,* 9 no. 1 (May 1941).

Symposium on problems of modern mass communication. "It is the outcome of collaboration between the Institute of Social Research and Columbia University's Office of Radio Research." Paul Felix Lazarsfeld (D), in "Remarks on Administrative and Critical Communications Research," undertakes to place the field in perspective, drawing distinctions between "administrative research"—that which "is carried through in the service of some kind of administrative agency," public or private—and "critical research"—that which develops a general theory of social trends. T. W. Adorno writes "On Popular Music" and its social consequences; Charles A. Siepmann on "Radio and Education"; Herta Herzog "On Borrowed Experience: An Analysis of Listening to Daytime Sketches"; William Dieterle (W) on "Hollywood and the European Crisis." Harold D. Lasswell (D,W) sets forth a number of recommendations on the use of "Radio as an Instrument of Reducing Personal Insecurity," drawing illustrations from his own experience as co-producer of the "Human Nature in Action" series over NBC. Included also in this issue are reviews of a number of

major books on propaganda and public opinion.

165. COTTRELL, LEONARD SLATER, JR. (D); and GALLAGHER, RUTH. *Developments in Social Psychology,* 1930-40 (Sociometry Monograph no. 1). New York: Beacon House, 1941. 58 pp.

By U.S. social scientists.

166. DENNIS, LAWRENCE (CB '41, W). *The Coming American Fascism.* New York: Harpers, 1936. 333 pp.

The author, an investment counsel who is a leading U.S. political theorist, asserts that a "disciplined party of the élite" will seize power in the United States in order to guarantee private ownership for small enterprisers and establish a planned economy, equalized incomes, group representation, regionalism adapted to administrative efficiency, and strict government control of education.

*167. DENNIS, LAWRENCE (CB '41, W). *The Dynamics of War and Revolution.* New York: Harpers, 1940. 259 pp.

Analyzes the future of U.S. foreign and domestic policy in terms of world trends toward collectivism. "The fact is that democracy worked only while an aristocracy ruled. . . . The world is getting back to aristocratic rule by new élites. . . . As the plan of the War and Navy Departments to replace the traditional American system with a totalitarian dictatorship by the Chief Executive in the exercise of his war powers is both legal and highly patriotic, I cannot possibly be prosecuted, investigated or even criticized for applauding . . . the new order which this plan and its governmental agents are eminently well suited to initiate under the smoke screen of a war to preserve the American system and check the march of dictatorship abroad. . . . At some stage of the game it will be the task of a new élite to take over the new revolution made by the President as a war dictator. . . . Order and action versus anarchy and stagnation are the issues, not democracy and liberty versus dictatorship and regimentation."

*167a. DICEY, ALBERT VENN (ESS). *Lectures on the Relation between Law and Public Opinion in England in the Nineteenth Century.* London and New York: Macmillan, 1905 (Reprinted 1914, 1924). 503 pp.

By Oxford University professor of law and political science, who was for a time a practicing attorney. This volume traces the influence of early 19th century individualistic sentiment on legislation and court decisions of that period and on the subsequent collectivist trends in opinion and law.

168. DOLLARD, JOHN (ADRIAN) (D). *Criteria for the Life History, with Analyses of Six Notable Documents.* New Haven: Yale University Institute of Human Relations, 1935. 288 pp.

Research Associate, Yale University Institute of Human Relations, presents seven criteria for dealing with the life history of the individual and applies these criteria to famous life history documents by Freud, Taft, Adler, Clifford R. Shaw, Thomas and Znaniecki, and H. G. Wells.

169. (Pop.) DOLLARD, JOHN (ADRIAN) (D). *Victory Over Fear.* New York: Reynal and Hitchcock, 1942. 215 pp.

Psychoanalytically trained social scientist, on staff of Yale Institute of Human Relations, describes sources of fear and ways of overcoming it.

170. DOOB, LEONARD WILLIAM. *The Plans of Men.* New Haven: Yale University, 1940. 411 pp.

Social psychologist, Yale, analyzes the social and other sciences for what they have contributed or failed to contribute to guiding society. Proposes more active social planning, beginning provisionally with regionalism. Bibliography, pp. 386-96.

171. DUBLIN, LOUIS ISRAEL (CB '42, D,W); and BUNZEL, BESSIE. *To Be or Not To Be: A Study of Suicide.* New York: Harrison Smith and Robert Haas, 1933. 443 pp.

A comprehensive study by two statisticians of Metropolitan Life Insurance Company. The section on "The Psychology of Suicide" uses psychoanalytic concepts. Bibliography, pp. 415-28. See also Cavan, Ruth Shonle (D): *Suicide* (Chicago: University of Chicago, 1928).

172. DURBIN, EVAN FRANK MOTTRAM; and others. *War and Democracy: Essays on the Causes and Preven-*

tion of War. London: Kegan Paul, 1938. 360 pp.

Symposium by British intellectuals. Pp. 1-150 are an essay by Mr. Durbin and John Bowlby, "Personal Aggressiveness and War: An Examination of the Psychological and Anthropological Evidence." These British social scientists approach the subject from a psychoanalytic angle, quoting such writers as Susan Isaacs and Edward Glover. Conclusion: Adolf Hitler is right in saying (*My Struggle*, English edition, p. 70) that "Men do not die for business—but for ideals." "The desire to destroy those upon whom they have projected all their own wicked impulses" is believed by the English writers "to play as large a part in civilized communities as it does in primitive. . . . In leaders this need is more pressing and vocal, but it is impossible to account for the hatred which can so easily be stimulated in ordinary citizens in certain circumstances without supposing that there is this need latent in everyone" (pp. 149-50). A program of childhood training is suggested. The adult societal contexts that determine whether repressed aggressions in civilized communities shall be discharged or inhibited are implied but not stated. The psychological propositions, however, are developed at length and with clarity. Bibliographic footnotes.

173. EELLS, RICHARD S. F. "Public Opinion in American Statecraft," *Public Opinion Quarterly*, 6: 391-410 (Fall 1942).

Mr. Eells, a graduate student in the department of politics, Princeton, considers the views on public opinion held by the Founding Fathers; the influence of social and technological changes since 1787 upon the role of U.S. public opinion; and the role of public opinion today in the light of these changes.

174. ELIASBERG, WLADIMIR. "German Philosophy and German Psychological Warfare," *Journal of Psychology*, 14: 197-216 (October 1942).

By German psychiatrist and psychologist now in U.S., who is author of technical articles on criminology and social psychology.

175. FREEMAN, ELLIS. *Conquering the Man in the Street: A Psychological Analysis of Propaganda in War, Fascism, and Politics.* New York: Vanguard, 1940. 356 pp.

Semipopular exploration of the psychology of dictatorship. Dr. Freeman is the author of two texts, *Social Psychology* and *General Psychology*. Bibliographic notes, pp. 337-43.

*176. FREUD, SIGMUND. *The Basic Writings of Sigmund Freud*, translated and edited, with an introduction, by Dr. Abraham Arden Brill. New York: Modern Library, 1938. 1001 pp.

By Viennese physician who was the founder of psychoanalysis. *Contents*: Psychopathology of Everyday Life. Interpretation of Dreams. Three Contributions to the Theory of Sex. Wit and the Unconscious. Totem and Taboo. History of the Psychoanalytic Movement. See also the same author's *Group Psychology and the Analysis of the Ego*, translated from the German by James Strachey (London: International Psychoanalytical Press, 1922. 134 pp.), which sets forth the theory that groups form through "identification" in relation to a leader, and the unconscious psychodynamics of the identification process. Valuable also is his *Civilization and Its Discontents*, translated by Joan Riviere (New York: Jonathan Cape and Harrison Smith, 1930. 144 pp.), a succinct formulation of the psychological aspects of some of the insecurities which underlie the mass-suicidal reactions that are a characteristic feature of Western civilization.

177. FREUD, SIGMUND. "An Outline of Psychoanalysis," *International Journal of Psychoanalysis*, vol. 21, no. 1: 27-84 (January 1940).

Freud's own summary of his work, written just before his death. A succinct statement of the hypotheses he took to be established facts, the hypotheses he took to be probable, and the hypotheses he took to be doubtful, in the science he founded.

178. FRIEDRICH, CARL JOACHIM (D); and MASON, EDWARD S. (D,W), editors. *Public Policy, Yearbook of the Graduate School of Public Administration of Harvard University*, vol. 3. Cambridge, Mass.: Graduate School of Public Administration, 1942. 275 pp.

"Almost half the volume deals with 'War Morale and Civil Liberties'; the other half is about equally divided between 'Labor and the War' and 'Some Problems of War Finance and Government.' . . . Gordon Allport (W) points out that we have better facilities for measuring morale than we have had previously, and

that significant conclusions can be drawn from such measurement; Edward L. Bernays (CB '41,W) presents a hortative discourse on 'The Integration of Morale'; David Riesman offers a long, well-documented, penetrating, but somewhat academic exposition of the legal status of civil liberties in a period of transition, and points the way to the development of more satisfactory criteria for the definition and evaluation of civil liberties; Alan Burr Overstreet (D,W) summarizes administrative plans for the control of civil liberties as of the time the article was written."—Harvey Pinney, *Annals*, 225: 242-43 (January 1943).

*179. FROMM, ERICH. *Escape from Freedom.* New York: Farrar and Rinehart, 1941. 305 pp.

By psychoanalytically trained sociologist, associated with Society for Advancement of Psychoanalysis. "In modern individualistic civilization . . . the individual is indeed 'free' in a sense, but he is thrown upon his own, placed in a position of great insecurity and confronted with problems and responsibilities in the face of which he feels inadequate, helpless and lost. The result is various movements or gropings in the direction of escape. Three mechanisms of escape are discussed at length—authoritarianism, destructiveness, and automaton conformity."—Frank Hyneman Knight (D,W), *American Journal of Sociology*, 48: 299 (September 1942). Bibliographic footnotes. English edition: *The Fear of Freedom* (International Library of Sociology and Social Reconstruction, edited by Dr. Karl Mannheim. London: K. Paul, Trench, Trubner, 1942. 257 pp.).

180. FRY, CLEMENTS COLLARD; and ROSTOW, EDNA G., collaborator. *Mental Health in College.* New York: Commonwealth Fund, 1942. 365 pp.

A study of emotional problems presented by students who consulted the division of college mental hygiene in the Department of University Health at Yale University. Includes case histories illustrating what is referred to as "the Graduate School syndrome," which may be of interest to self-critical social scientists.

181. GALLUP, GEORGE HORACE (CB '40,W). "We, the People Are Like This: A Report on How and What We Think," *New York Times Magazine*, June 8, 1941, pp. 3 ff.

General conclusions drawn from five years of interviews by the American Institute of Public Opinion.

182. GILLESPIE, ROBERT DICK. *Psychological Effects of War on Citizen and Soldier.* New York: Norton, 1942. 251 pp.

English psychiatrist's observations. Bibliography, pp. 245-50.

183. GINS, GEORGII CONSTANTINO-VICH. *Ocherki sotsialnoi psikologie: Vedeniye v izucheniye prava i nravstvennosti.* Harbin: Russko-ma'nczurskaja knigotorogovlja, 1936. 263 pp.

General treatise on contemporary politics and social psychology by professor in University of Harbin, formerly at St. Petersburg.

184. (Pop.) GRABBE, PAUL; with MURPHY, GARDNER (W). *We Call It Human Nature.* New York: Harpers, 1940. 120 pp.

Pictorial popularization of basic principles of psychology, using the most advanced visual techniques. Bibliography, p. 117.

185. GRATTAN, CLINTON HARTLEY (W). *Preface to Chaos: War in the Making.* New York: Dodge, 1936. 341 pp.

Marxist analysis of "certain traditional economic and political forms" which, according to this U.S. political journalist, are leading to a World War followed by a series of revolutions. Much reference is made to the role of propaganda and opinion. Bibliography in text, footnotes, and index.

186. GRAVES, ALONZO. *The Eclipse of a Mind.* New York: Medical Journal Press, 1942. 722 pp.

An extensive account in autobiographical form of the life and experience of a manic-depressive psychotic. A case history which is a vivid supplement to the theoretical treatises cited in the present bibliography.

187. GRAY, LOUIS HERBERT (D, W). *Foundations of Language.* New York: Macmillan, 1939. 530 pp.

"The aim has been to present, so far as our present state of knowledge permits, an encyclopaedic compendium of linguistics in a single volume; and, since Indo-European is the branch most studied, to give, at the same time, an introduction to Indo-European linguistics as a whole, for which no up-to-date manual in English exists."—Preface. Author is Professor of Comparative Linguistics, Columbia. Chapter 13, "History of the Study of Language," is a bibliographic essay.

188. HARDING, D. W. "General Conceptions in the Study of the Press and Public Opinion," *Sociological Review*, 29: 370-90 (October 1937).

Discusses the meaning of "propaganda," "permissible opinion," "ruling opinion," "collective judgment," and the analysis of newspapers.

189. HARRISSON, THOMAS HARTNETT. "What is Public Opinion?" *Political Quarterly*, 11:368-83 (October 1940).

By a leader of the Mass-Observation movement.

190. HAYAKAWA, SAMUEL ICHIYÉ (D). "General Semantics and Propaganda," *Public Opinion Quarterly*, 3: 197-208 (April 1939).

Dr. Hayakawa (Ph.D. Wisconsin 1935), born in Canada of Japanese parents, is a professor of English who has been influential in the popularization of general semantics. This popular article discusses a few aspects of the general problem of mass education in the elements of semantics.

191. HAYAKAWA, SAMUEL ICHIYÉ (D). *Language in Action: A Guide to Accurate Thinking, Reading, and Writing.* New York: Harcourt, Brace, 1941. 243 pp.

Guide to semantics.

192. HELLPACH, WILLY HUGO. *Geopsyche: Die Menschenseele unterm Einfluss von Wetter und Klima, Boden und Landschaft*, 5th ed. Leipzig: W. Engelman, 1939. 341 pp.

"The Collective Mind as Influenced by Weather, Climate, Soil and Topography." By German social psychologist. Bibliography, pp. 271-322.

193. HOOK, SIDNEY (D,W). *Reason, Social Myths and Democracy.* New York: John Day, 1940. 302 pp.

Studies in contemporary political thought,

by New York University professor of philosophy.

*194. Horkheimer, Max, ed. (D). *Autorität und Familie* (Research reports of the International Institute of Social Research, vol. 5). Paris: Alcan, 1936. 947 pp.

Three ex-German social scientists, Max Horkheimer, Erich Fromm, and Herbert Marcuse, examine Western European patterns of family and authority in sociological, psychoanalytic, and historical terms. These three essays are followed by data collected from an extensive series of questionnaires. Following this are 386 pages of summaries of monographs of other writers on the subject. This is capped by abstracts of the entire work in French and in English (pp. 861-935). There are also many bibliographic footnotes.

195. Horney, Karen (CB '41). *The Neurotic Personality of Our Time.* New York: Norton, 1937. 299 pp.

Psychoanalyst, associated with Society for Advancement of Psychoanalysis, states in fairly simple language a theory of certain personality-reactions that she believes to be characteristic of our times.

*196. Hunter, (Wiles) Robert (W). *Revolution: Why, How, When?* New York: Harpers, 1940. 385 pp.

By veteran U.S. Socialist scholar, leader, and teacher (University of California). Surveys world revolutionary history and concludes that revolution depends on four factors: a governmental system discredited by defeat in war or economic collapse or both; a ruined monetary system; an exhausted populace; an active insurgent minority composed of "embittered aggressive sections of leaders of the middle classes" operating with the support of a rebellious military. It is not the populace that makes revolutions but the middle class, or what would correspond to the middle class in other times than ours. Revolutions are not made by mass misery, but by structural collapse. Poverty much more often induces apathy than militant despair. Defeat and inflation basically explain Lenin, Mussolini, Hitler. Revolutionary technique, as practiced by these three men, is described in a few swift pages. Bibliographic footnotes.

*197. Jones, Alfred Winslow. *Life, Liberty and Property: A Story of Conflict and a Measurement of Conflicting Rights.* Philadelphia: Lippincott, 1941. 397 pp.

Akron, Ohio, was chosen under the auspices of the Institute for Applied Social Analysis for a test study of opinion centering upon attitudes toward corporate wealth. A representative sample of Akron's population, plus that of outlying communities on a small scale, was obtained. Each individual in the sample was then given the facts concerning seven specific economic situations: coal "bootlegging" in Pennsylvania, a stay-in strike in a Michigan power house, a threat made by an Akron rubber company to move its plant, a farm mortgage foreclosure averted by mob threat, use of tear gas to drive strikers out of a plant, the migration of a dress concern in breach of a union contract, mob action to prevent dispossession of a tenement family. An eighth question required the person interviewed to indicate the order in which he would assign the net profits of a corporation to the stockholders, bankers, employees, etc., under ten categories. The replies were believed to indicate the attitudes of those questioned toward "corporate property," as distinguished from other kinds of property. This study was reported in abridged form in *Fortune*, February 1941.

198. Jones, F. Elwyn. *The Defence of Democracy.* New York: Dutton, 1938. 352 pp.

Deals with prodemocratic and profascist propagandas in all the Western countries, including Germany and Italy. The author is a young British labor attorney, who wrote the best seller, *Hitler's Drive to the East* (1937).

199. *Journal of the History of Ideas.* Lancaster, Pa., quarterly, January 1940–.

"A journal which will emphasize the interrelations of studies in the fields of history of philosophy, of literature and the arts, of the natural and social sciences, of religion, and of political and social movements." Editor: Arthur O. Lovejoy (D,W) of Johns Hopkins University; managing editor: Philip P. Wiener (D), College of the City of New York.

200. *Journal of Politics.* Gainesville, Fla., quarterly, 1939–.

New journal published by Southern Political Science Association in cooperation with University of Florida.

201. JOUSSAIN, ANDRÉ. "Le Change-ment temporaire du sens des mots dans les crises sociales," *Revue internationale de sociologie*, 44: 637-62 (November-December 1936).

202. KATZ, DANIEL; and SCHANCK, RICHARD LOUIS. *Social Psychology*. New York: John Wiley, 1938. 700 pp.

College text by two U.S. social psycholo-gists. Bibliography at ends of chapters.

203. KLINEBERG, OTTO. *Social Psy-chology*. New York: Holt, 1940. 570 pp.

By Columbia University psychologist. Bib-liography at ends of chapters.

204. KORZYBSKI, ALFRED (W). *Science and Sanity: An Introduction to Non-Aristotelian Systems and General Semantics*, 2nd ed., with supplementary introduction and bibliography. Lancaster, Pa.: Science Press for the International Non-Aristotelian Library Publishing Co., 1941. 806 pp.

Standard treatise by internationally famous Polish-American semanticist. Bibliography, pp. li-lv, 767-81.

205. KROUT, MAURICE HAIM. *In-troduction to Social Psychology*. New York: Harpers, 1942. 823 pp.

College text. Bibliography, pp. 748-803.

206. LANDIS, CARNEY (W); and PAGE, JAMES DANIEL. *Modern Society and Mental Disease*. New York: Farrar and Rinehart, 1938. 190 pp.

"Their facts indicate that mental disease varies by age, sex, educational status, economic status, nativity, race, urban and rural areas, and other such conditions. They steadfastly explain these away and arrive at the conclusion that social factors are of little significance in the etiology of mental diseases. The arguments used might furnish model horrible examples for textbooks in . . . statistics. An additional fault is that some of the strongest contrary evidence, though known to the authors, is ig-nored." Robert E. L. Faris (D), in *American Journal of Sociology*, 44: 769-70 (March 1939). Bibliography, pp. 175-85.

207. LA PIERE, RICHARD TRACY. *Collective Behavior*. New York: Mc-Graw-Hill, 1938. 577 pp.

General treatise by Stanford University so-ciologist. Bibliography at ends of chapters.

208. LA PIERE, RICHARD TRACY; and FARNSWORTH, PAUL RANDOLPH (D). *Social Psychology*. New York: Mc-Graw-Hill, 1936. 504 pp.

A standard text. The authors are a sociol-ogist and a psychologist, respectively, at Stan-ford University. Bibliographies at ends of chapters.

209. LASSWELL, HAROLD DWIGHT (D,W). "Chinese Resistance to Jap-anese Invasion: The Predictive Value of Pre-Crisis Symbols," *American Journal of Sociology*, 43: 704-16 (March 1938).

"The Chinese responded to local Japanese encroachments in 1931 by submission, and in 1932 by partial resistance. Why did they move from partial to total resistance in the crisis of July-August, 1937?" A general theory is sug-gested.

210. LASSWELL, HAROLD DWIGHT (D,W). "The Contribution of Freud's Insight Interview to the Social Sciences," *American Journal of Sociology*, 45: 375-90 (November 1939).

211. LASSWELL, HAROLD DWIGHT (D,W). "The Garrison State," *Amer-ican Journal of Sociology*, 46: 455-68 (January 1941).

"The garrison state is a 'developmental con-struct' about the future course of world-poli-tics, whose function is to stimulate the indi-vidual specialist to clarify for himself his expectations about the future as a guide to the timing of scientific work. The trend of the time is away from the dominance of the spe-cialist on bargaining, who is the businessman, and toward the supremacy of the specialist on violence, the soldier. . . . It is probable that the ruling élite of the garrison state will acquire most of the skills that we have come to accept as part of modern civilian manage-ment. Particularly prominent will be skill in the manipulation of symbols in the interest of morale and public relations."

212. LASSWELL, HAROLD DWIGHT (D,W). "Person, Personality, Group, Culture," *Psychiatry*, 2: 533-61 (November 1939).

"The four terms which figure in the title of this article are among the cardinal terms in [psychiatry,] the science of interpersonal relations. The purpose of this discussion is to clarify the method by which the meaning of these terms may be made explicit. The terminology owes something to the Cambridge logical school, and especially Whitehead."

213. LASSWELL, HAROLD DWIGHT (D,W). *Politics: Who Gets What, When, How.* New York and London: McGraw-Hill, 1936.

A brief version of the system of social analysis set forth by this U.S. political scientist in his *World Politics and Personal Insecurity: A Contribution to Political Psychiatry* (New York: McGraw-Hill, 1935. 307 pp.), in which he states and applies the configurative method of analysis, developing implications of his *Psychopathology and Politics* (Chicago: University of Chicago, 1930). Annotated bibliography, pp. 251-59.

214. LASSWELL, HAROLD DWIGHT (D,W). "The Propaganda Technique of the Pamphlet on 'Continental Security' (Political Symbol series, number 1)," *Psychiatry*, 1: 441-47 (August 1938).

This magazine had a department on propaganda, with a twofold purpose: (1) "it will publish pamphlets which give clear, and possibly vivid, expression to programs of political action in America"; (2) it will "cultivate the analysis of influential political symbols with special reference to their use in propaganda. Whenever a pamphlet is presented in this department, it will invariably be accompanied by an objective analysis of its propaganda technique." The first pamphlet is reproduced in full in the magazine, together with analysis of its techniques.

215. LASSWELL, HAROLD DWIGHT (D,W). "The Propaganda Technique of Recent Proposals for the Foreign Policy of the U.S.A." *Psychiatry*, 2: 281-87 (May 1939).

216. LASSWELL, HAROLD DWIGHT (D,W). "The Relation of Ideological Intelligence to Public Policy," *Ethics*, 53: 25-34 (October 1942).

An effort to clarify the possible contributions of systematic thinkers to policymakers. "The intelligence operation constantly asks for new specifications of objectives. . . . We still hear of 'victory' as a goal; but 'victory for what?' is not made manifest. The crux of the matter is that deep timidities complicate the task of translating democratic aspirations into compelling institutional terms. Slogans like the 'Four Freedoms' are not enough unless they are completed by slogans that point to the operating rules of a society that puts freedom into practice. We are in a war of ideas, but we have not found our ideas. It is essential to face our timidities without fear and to deal with them directly."

217. LASSWELL, HAROLD DWIGHT (D,W). "The Relation of Skill Politics to Class Politics and National Politics," *Chinese Social and Political Science Review*, 30: 298-311 (1937).

218. LAVINE, HAROLD; and WECHSLER, JAMES. *War Propaganda and the United States.* New Haven: Yale University, 1940. 363 pp.

Describes both foreign and domestic efforts to control U.S. opinion; analyzes social forces that produce receptivity and resistance to various propaganda appeals; discusses organization and importance of propaganda bureaus, war correspondents, British lecturers, German postcards, U.S. "benefit" social functions. Mr. Lavine has been a staff writer of Institute for Propaganda Analysis; Mr. Wechsler a New York journalist. See pp. 153-96.

219. LAWLEY, F. E. *The Growth of Collective Economy.* London: P. S. King, 1938. 2 vols.

Analyzes collectivist tendencies in all parts of the world, showing that collectivism has been hastened by trade associations, monopolies, cartels, and business collusion as well as by government regulation and government corporations. Surveys also the immediate prospects of world economic controls. Vol. 1: "The Growth of National Collective Economy." Vol. 2: "The Growth of International Collective Economy." By a journalist and former official of the International Labor Office. Extensive bibliography in text and appendices.

220. LAY, W. A. *Experimental Pedagogy*, translated by Adolf Weil and E. K. Schwartz, with an introduction by Paul Rankov Radosavljevich. New York: Prentice-Hall, 1936. 371 pp.

First English translation of an influential treatise, stressing "bio-communal" aspects of "world-wide" education (*Weltpädagogik*). The 125-page introductory essay evaluates numerous American, Asiatic, and European contributions to experimental pedagogy.

221. LERNER, MAX (CB '42, D, W). *Ideas Are Weapons: The History and Uses of Ideas*. New York: Viking, 1939. 553 pp.

Essays by Williams College political scientist. An essay on "Freedom in the Opinion Industries" advocates that Congress pass a "Truth in Opinion Act" establishing a body of administrators to "regulate anti-social propaganda." In his opinion, this would aid the development of "democratic collectivism."

222. LEWIN, KURT (W). *The Conceptual Representation and the Measurement of Psychological Forces* (Contributions to Psychological Theory, no. 4). Durham: Duke University, 1939. 247 pp.

Aims to define and characterize a set of concepts that will facilitate investigations of the dynamics of behavior; "it is concerned less with developing specific theories than with providing a conceptually strict language which can be used by many psychological theories." The utility of the language is demonstrated by applications to experimental work. The author is a well-known psychologist, now at University of Iowa. Bibliography, pp. 229-33.

223. LIN, MOUSHENG HSITIEN. *Anti-Statism: Essay in Its Psychiatric and Cultural Analysis* (Ph.D. thesis, political science, Chicago). Washington, D.C.: William Alanson White Psychiatric Foundation, 1939. 87 pp.

Psychiatrically trained political scientist investigates social and psychological conditions under which theorists develop opposition to symbols of the state. Taoist, Cynic-Stoic, Liberal, Communist, and Anarchist theories of the "stateless society" are examined, and the theorists' personality structures are related to their theories. Conclusions: Anti-statism generally emerges from a rising social class that is frustrated; anti-statist theorists are generally individuals whose self-esteem has been wounded through deprivations and discriminations, and who discharge their energies in ways that are familiar to the psychiatrist. Dr. Lin is on the staff of China Institute in America. Bibliography, pp. 84-87.

224. LINTON, RALPH (D,W). *The Study of Man: An Introduction*. New York and London: Appleton-Century, 1936. 503 pp.

By U.S. anthropologist. Bibliography, pp. 491-97. Spanish edition: *Estudio del hombre* (Mexico City: Fondo de cultura económica, 1942. 562 pp.).

*224a. LIPPMANN, WALTER (CB '40, W). *Public Opinion*. New York: Harcourt, Brace, 1922. 427 pp.

The now popular concept *stereotype* was first presented in this treatise on news handling and mass communication by a U.S. journalist.

*224b. LOWELL, A(BBOTT) LAWRENCE (CB '43, D,W). *Public Opinion in War and Peace*. Cambridge, Mass.: Harvard University, 1923. 302 pp.

General treatise, very influential in its day, by a U.S. political scientist, president of Harvard University.

*224c. LUKÁCS, GEORG. *Geschichte und Klassenbewusstsein: Studien über Marxistische Dialektik*. Berlin: Malik-Verlag, 1923. 342 pp.

By Hungarian Marxist sociologist. See the last chapter, "Methodisches zur Organizationsfrage," for a dialectical analysis of propaganda and allied tactical questions.

*225. LYND, ROBERT STAUGHTON (D,W); and LYND, HELEN MERRELL. *Middletown in Transition: A Study in Cultural Conflicts*. New York: Harcourt, Brace, 1937. 622 pp.

U.S. sociologists reexamine the social structure of a "representative American community" (Muncie, Indiana). Attitudes, reading habits, and other factors in the opinion patterns are reported in detail. See especially Chapter 12, "The Middletown Spirit." Bibliographic footnotes.

226. MACKENZIE, FINDLAY, editor (D). *Planned Society Yesterday, Today, Tomorrow: A Symposium by Thirty-Five Economists, Sociologists, and Statesmen*, with a foreword by Lewis Mumford (CB '40). New York: Prentice-Hall, 1937. 989 pp.

Chapter 17, pp. 629-41, by Harold D. Lasswell (D,W), is on "Propaganda in a Planned Society." Pp. 921-39 contain brief biographical sketches of the authors. Bibliography, pp. 939-79.

227. MALZBERG, BENJAMIN (W). *Social and Biological Aspects of Mental Disease*. Utica, New York: State Hospitals Press, 1940. 360 pp.

"If present trends continue, mental disease will soon become our foremost health problem." This is an exhaustive statistical analysis of relations of mental disorder to such factors as age, urbanism, marital status, nativity, race, birth order, economic factors, literacy. Dr. Malzberg is statistician of New York State Department of Mental Hygiene. Bibliography, pp. 354-57.

*228. MANNHEIM, KARL. *Ideology and Utopia: An Introduction to the Sociology of Knowledge*, with an introduction by Louis Wirth (D,W), translated from the German by Louis Wirth and Edward A. Shils (International Library of Psychology, Philosophy, and Scientific Method). New York: Harcourt, Brace, 1936. 318 pp.

Ex-German sociologist's influential treatise on the social role of fictions in the organization and disruption of Western culture. Systematic development of a sociology based upon Marx, Engels, Sorel, Pareto, and Max Weber. Revolutionary and counterrevolutionary propagandas are discussed at length. Bibliography, pp. 281-304.

229. MANNHEIM, KARL. *Man and Society in an Age of Reconstruction*, translated by Edward A. Shils. New York: Harcourt, Brace, 1940. 469 pp.

Based upon the author's *Mensch und Gesellschaft im Zeitalter des Umbaus* (Leiden, Holland: Sitjhoff, 1935. 207 pp.), one of the outstanding treatises of contemporary social science. Essays a comprehensive developmental theory of social control. Analyzes the role of intellectuals in conceiving "methods by which the modern state can adapt itself to social interdependence." Elaborately classified bibliography, pp. 383-455. The first two parts of this study have appeared in substance in English as *Rational and Irrational Elements in Contemporary Society* (Hobhouse Memorial Lecture. London: Oxford, 1934. 36 pp.) and "The Crisis of Culture in the Era of Mass-Democracies and Autarchies," *Sociological Review*, 26: 105-29 (April 1934).

230. MARR, HEINZ. *Die Massenwelt im Kampf um ihre Form: Zur Soziologie der deutschen Gegenwart*. Hamburg: Hanseatische Verlagsanstalt, 1934. 578 pp.

231. MARSHALL, JAMES (W). *Swords and Symbols: The Technique of Sovereignty*. New York: Oxford University, 1939. 168 pp.

Takes the view that words are "merely symbols and in political life they are built up to imitate the words of philosophy and religion and give to political issues a greatness which they rarely possess." Redefines in operational terms a number of current symbols and ideologies, such as "democracy," "the withering of the state," etc. The author, President of the Board of Education of the City of New York, has for a number of years actively practiced law and politics as well as political science. Contains bibliography.

232. MARSHALL, T. H. "Authority and the Family," *Sociological Review* (London), 29: 1-19 (January 1937).

Review of *Autorität und Familie*, by Max Horkheimer (D), Erich Fromm, and Herbert Marcuse (D), cited above. Pp. 17-19 contribute an especially concise formulation of the problem of stating and testing hypotheses on relations among (a) family constellations, (b) economic roles, and (c) the receptivity of individuals and groups to leadership in the name of authoritative symbols of conservatism or revolution.

233. MASLOW, ABRAHAM HAROLD; and MITTELMANN, BELA. *Principles of Abnormal Psychology: The Dynamics of Psychic Illness*. New York: Harpers, 1941. 638 pp.

Bibliography, pp. 547-95.

234. May, Mark Arthur (W). *Education in a World of Fear.* Cambridge: Harvard University, 1941. 64 pp.

U.S. psychologist, Director of Yale Institute of Human Relations, analyzes the "national anxiety" of the U.S., and suggests educational procedures looking toward a fuller use of mental hygiene principles.

234a. May, Mark Arthur (W). *A Social Psychology of War and Peace.* New Haven: Yale University, 1943. 284 pp.

Director of the Institute of Human Relations in Yale University vigorously challenges the popular conception that the underlying causes of war are found in man's "fighting instincts." He holds that human nature is neither belligerent nor peaceful, but neutral, and that specific attitudes are caused by particular social environments. Bibliographic footnotes.

235. May, Mark Arthur (W); and Doob, Leonard William. *Competition and Cooperation* (Report of the Social Science Research Council's Committee on Personality and Culture, Subcommittee on Competitive-Cooperative Habits; Social Science Research Council Bulletin no. 25). New York, April 1937. 191 pp.

A "tentative orienting theory of cooperation and competition," a statement of existing knowledge on the subject, and a selection of "a few promising research problems." Bibliography, pp. 175-86. Abstracted by Mark A. May in *American Journal of Sociology*, 42: 887-92 (May 1937).

236. Mead, George Herbert. *Mind, Self and Society from the Standpoint of a Social Behaviorist*, edited, with introduction, by Charles William Morris (D). Chicago: University of Chicago, 1934. 400 pp.

Influential treatise on social psychology by U.S. professor of philosophy. Bibliography, pp. 390-92.

237. Mead, Margaret (CB '40, D,W). "Public Opinion Mechanisms among Primitive Peoples," *Public Opinion Quarterly*, 1 no. 3: 5-16 (July 1937).

Well-known anthropologist (Ph.D. Columbia 1928) describes opinion formation among the Arapesh, the Iatmul and the Balinese.

238. Mead, Margaret, editor (CB '40, D,W). *Cooperation and Competition Among Primitive Peoples.* New York: McGraw-Hill, 1937. 531 pp.

Thirteen articles by a group of U.S. anthropologists who spent a year organizing field notes and published sources. "Interpretive statement" by Margaret Mead, pp. 458-511. Bibliography, pp. 513-15 and ends of chapters.

*239. *Mental Health* (Occasional Publications of the American Association for the Advancement of Science, no. 9), edited by Forest Ray Moulton (D,W). Lancaster, Pa.: Science Press, 1939. 470 pp.

Symposium of a score of specialists in psychiatric, medical, and social research. See Part 4, "Economic Aspects of Mental Health." Note especially Part 5, "Physical and Cultural Environment," with contributions by Ruth Benedict (CB '41, D), Lawrence K. Frank (D,W), Harold D. Lasswell (D,W), Edward Sapir, Harry Stack Sullivan (CB '42), Gregory Zilboorg (CB '41, W), and others. Also Part 6, "Mental Health Administration"; and Part 7, "Professional and Technical Education in Relation to Mental Health." Bibliography at ends of contributions.

240. *Mental Hygiene*, quarterly magazine of the National Committee for Mental Hygiene, 1937–.

Contains articles, especially book reviews, which will enable those interested in the social studies to keep abreast of the expanding mental hygiene movement and aware of new discoveries about personality.

241. Merriam, Charles Edward (D,W). *The New Democracy and the New Despotism.* New York: McGraw-Hill, 1939. 278 pp.

General observations on contemporary politics by veteran U.S. political scientist.

242. Michels, Roberto. "Le Métabolisme social en général et celui de l'après guerre en particulier," in *Archives de Sociologie*, Sér.B, 5-6, pp. 27-44. Rome: International Institute of Sociology, Italian Committee for the Study of Problems of Population, 1935.

Well-known German-Swiss-Italian sociologist, author of half a dozen influential political treatises, brings together the essential conclusions of several recent studies of European elites, indicating the contemporary shift from moral and intellectual and wealth criteria to technical and particularly political skill in recruiting leaders.

243. MICHELS, ROBERTO. *Nuovi studi sulla classe politica: Saggio sugli spostamente sociali ed intellettuali nel dopoguerra.* Milan: Dante Alighieri, 1936. 188 pp.

Treatise on European elite recruitment written immediately before the author's death. Deals especially with Germany and Italy.

244. MICHELS, ROBERTO. *Umschichtungen in den herrschenden Klassen nach dem Kriege.* Stuttgart and Berlin: W. Kohlhammer, 1934. 133 pp.

Changes among the ruling classes since the World War. Bibliography, pp. 121-29.

*245. "Military Psychology," special issue of *Psychological Bulletin* (June 1941).

Fourteen critical bibliographic essays prepared by 27 scholars at the request of the Emergency Committee in Psychology appointed by the Division of Anthropology and Psychology of the National Research Council, and edited by Carroll C. Pratt (D), professor of psychology, Rutgers University. This is an attempt to summarize and indicate the sources of psychological knowledge having to do with human engineering in times of national crisis. "German Military Psychology" is covered by H. L. Ansbacher; "Morale" by Irvin L. Child; "[War] Propaganda Technique and Public Opinion" by Bruce Lannes Smith (D); "War Neuroses" by William H. Dunn.

246. MILLER, NEAL ELGAR; and DOLLARD, JOHN (ADRIAN) (D). *Social Learning and Imitation.* New Haven: Yale University Press for the Institute of Human Relations, 1941. 341 pp.

Theory of the nature of imitative behavior, based in part on experiments with children. By two social psychologists, Yale Institute of Human Relations. Bibliography, pp. 327-34.

*247. MORRIS, CHARLES WILLIAM (D). *Foundations of the Theory of Signs* (International Encyclopedia of Unified Science, vol. 1, no. 2). Chicago: University of Chicago, 1938. 59 pp.

Introductory technical study in semantics by University of Chicago professor of philosophy, editor of the works of George Herbert Mead. Reflects Dr. Morris's close working relations with the scientific empiricists such as Rudolf Carnap. Bibliography, p. 59.

248. MORSTEIN MARX, FRITZ (D), editor. *Public Management in the New Democracy.* New York: Harpers, 1940. 266 pp.

Discussion by public administration experts. Bibliography, pp. 253-57.

*249. MOSCA, GAETANO (CB '42). *The Ruling Class,* translated by Hannah D. Kahn, edited and revised, with an introduction, by Arthur Livingston (D, W). New York and London: McGraw-Hill, 1939. 514 pp.

Translation of widely known treatise, *Elementi di scienza politica,* by emeritus professor of political science, University of Rome. Chapters 7 and 8 of special interest to students of propaganda.

*250. MURPHY, GARDNER (W); MURPHY, LOIS BARCLAY; and NEWCOMB, THEODORE MEAD (D). *Experimental Social Psychology: An Interpretation of Research upon the Socialization of the Individual,* rev. ed. New York and London: Harpers, 1937. 1121 pp.

Revision of a manual by three well-known U.S. social psychologists which has been generally accepted as standard since its first appearance in 1931. Covers all the usual methods of psychological measurement. Bibliography, pp. 1057-1103.

*251. MURPHY, GARDNER (W); and LIKERT, RENSIS (D). *Public Opinion and the Individual: A Psychological Study of Student Attitudes on Public Questions, with a Retest Five Years Later.* New York and London: Harpers, 1938. 316 pp.

Having correlated attitudes with many other personal characteristics over a period of several years, these psychologists at Columbia University conclude that, "Most of the more easily described objective factors commonly quoted as causes of radical or conservative tendencies did not seem to be very important, while certain very personal factors, such as the personalities of the parents and the individual student's reading habits, seemed to be important. . . . Despite the quantitative emphasis of the study as a whole, quantitative methods were not ready when it became apparent to us that the most important variables to be followed up were of this rather intangible or personal sort. . . . It is believed that the next steps in attitude research may well be taken in the direction of gathering better diary, interview, and other biographical material, developing safeguards against error, and methods of formulating more penetrating and revealing questions. . . . The cooperation of sociologists, child psychologists, psychiatrists, and historians will be needed in the development of a technique really adequate for the study of the genesis of personal attitudes on public issues" (pp. 263-64). Bibliography, pp. 309-10.

252. MURRAY, HENRY ALEXANDER; and others. *Explorations in Personality: A Clinical and Experimental Study of Fifty Men of College Age by the Workers at the Harvard Psychological Clinic.* New York and London: Oxford University, 1938. 761 pp.

Of high methodological interest because of the elaborate battery of investigational techniques and the multiple-variable form of analysis.

253. MURRAY, HENRY ALEXANDER. "Psychology and the University," *Archives of Neurology and Psychiatry,* 34: 803-17 (October 1935).

Utility of a psychiatric clinic to a university is discussed by Director of Harvard Psychological Clinic.

254. "National Morale," November 1941 issue of *American Journal of Sociology.*

Includes "Psychiatric Aspects of Morale," by Harry Stack Sullivan (CB '42), psychiatrist, William Alanson White Psychiatric Foundation, and consultant, Selective Service System; "Military Morale," by Brig. Gen. James A. Ulio (W), U.S.A.; "Propaganda and Morale," by George Creel (W), formerly

chairman, Committee on Public Information; "Radio and Morale," by James Rowland Angell (CB '40,W), psychologist and consultant of NBC; "A Note on Governmental Research on Attitudes and Morale," by Edward A. Shils, social scientist, University of Chicago; and many other contributions.

254a. (Pop.) NATIONAL RESEARCH COUNCIL, in collaboration with SCIENCE SERVICE. *Psychology for the Fighting Man: Prepared for the Fighting Man Himself.* Washington, D.C. and New York: *Infantry Journal* and Penguin Books, 1943. 456 pp.

By about 60 U.S. psychologists, psychiatrists, and other specialists convened by the National Research Council and Science Service. Written in a language believed to be adapted to the needs of a large percentage of the U.S. forces. "This book tells all about military psychology. It is prepared from manuscripts written by experts, but it has been rewritten in popular form without sacrifice of its scientific accuracy. What it says is as true as scientists can make it today. . . . This book starts in with the psychology of the proper uses of your sense organs in war—your eyes, your ears, your nose, your organs of balance. It tells about the aptitude and abilities of soldiers for the many jobs to which the Army may assign them, and how soldiers actually are assigned to different jobs. It discusses efficiency, both physical and psychological. It tells about morale and emotion, about the effects and control of fear and anger, about how men's motives help them or hurt them as soldiers. It discusses leadership, panic, rumor, propaganda, psychological warfare."—Preface.

255. NEUMANN, SIGMUND (D). *Permanent Revolution: The Total State in a World at War.* New York: Harpers, 1942. 388 pp.

Careful analysis of political leaders, political lieutenants, the masses, the material environment, and the symbolic environment. By Wesleyan University political scientist. Bibliography, pp. 311-75.

*255a. OGDEN, CHARLES KAY; and RICHARDS, IVOR ARMSTRONG (W). *The Meaning of Meaning: A Study of the Influence of Language upon Thought and of the Science of Symbolism,* 4th ed. rev., with supplementary essays by Bronislaw Malinowski and Francis Graham Crookshank (International Library of Psychology, Philosophy, and Scientific Method). New York: Harcourt, Brace. London: Kegan Paul, Trench, and Trubner, 1936. 363 pp.

An influential semantic analysis of the variable meaning of words, by two Cambridge University philosophers.

256. OSBORN, REUBEN. *Freud and Marx: A Dialectical Study*, introduction by John Strachey (W). New York: Equinox, 1937. 285 pp.

Dialectical materialist's comparative study of two influential analysts of ideology. Chapter 12 makes suggestions as to the "effect which a knowledge of psychoanalytic theory might be expected to have upon Marxists' political work." Bibliographic footnotes.

257. PALMER, PAUL ARTHUR (D). "The Concept of Public Opinion in Political Theory," in *Essays in History and Political Theory in Honor of Charles Howard McIlwain* (Cambridge, Mass., 1936), pp. 230-57.

By a U.S. political scientist.

258. PALMER, PAUL ARTHUR (D). "Ferdinand Tönnies's Theory of Public Opinion," *Public Opinion Quarterly*, 2: 584-95 (October 1938).

Since Tönnies's *Kritik der öffentlichen Meinung* (Berlin 1922) "remains the most comprehensive analysis of public opinion phenomena which has appeared in any language, a brief critical summary may be of some value."

***259**. PARETO, VILFREDO. *The Mind and Society (Trattato di sociologia generale)*, edited by Arthur Livingston (D, W); translated by Andrew Bongiorno (D) and Arthur Livingston, with the advice and active cooperation of James Harvey Rogers. New York: Harcourt, Brace, 1935. 4 vols.

One of the major treatises of European social science of recent decades, by Italian political sociologist who was first trained as an engineer. Proposes a systematic sociology of politics and stresses the role of social myths and suggestibility, and the relations between elites and masses. Bibliography, vol. 1, p. xviii, and vol. 4, pp. 1931-2033.

260. PEEL, ROY VICTOR (D); and ROUCEK, JOSEPH SLABEY (D), editors. *Introduction to Politics*. New York: Crowell, 1941. 587 pp.

Introductory college text on political science by a score of U.S. professors. Unusual among U.S. texts in that it seeks to indicate "the place of politics in the social sciences and emphasizes the dynamic factors of folklore, symbols, attitudes, opinions and ideologies." "Political Ideas and Folklore" are discussed by Elizabeth A. Weber; "Influence of Symbols on Politics" by Karl Loewenstein (D); "Leaders and Followers" by Sigmund Neumann (D); pressure groups and legislation by John W. Manning (D); "Politics and Education" by K. C. Leebrick (D,W). Bibliography at end of each chapter.

261. PEMBERTON, H. EARL. "The Spatial Order of Cultural Diffusion," *Sociology and Social Research*, 22: 246-51 (January 1938).

Suggests hypotheses on rates of diffusion; presents as indices three maps, showing diffusion of (1) Cooperative credit societies in the U.S., 1910-29; (2) Postage-stamp usage in Europe, 1840-63; (3) Public junior colleges in the U.S., 1910-28. This technique of analysis would be applicable in constructing "weather-maps of public opinion."

262. PENNINGTON, LEON ALFRED; HOUGH, ROMEYN B., JR.; and CASE, H. W. *Psychology of Military Leadership*, foreword by Brigadier General Wilton B. Persons. New York: Prentice-Hall, 1943. 288 pp.

Considers the military officer as instructor, learner, leader, disciplinarian, personnel technician. Discusses adjustment of officers and men to military service and to battle. Chapter 10 is on "Army Morale." Dr. Pennington is Assistant Professor of Psychology, University of Illinois; Lt. Col. Hough, retired librarian of Army War College; Mr. Case, a personnel manager of a large U.S. aircraft corporation. Bibliography at ends of chapters.

263. *Pesquisa* (Research). Rio de Janeiro, quarterly, 1941–.

Scientific journal published by The Instituto de Altos Estudos em Ciencias Economicas, Politicas e Sociais, Brazil's first institution for graduate work in the social sciences.

*263a. PLATO (ESS). *The Republic.* Athens, *ca.* 400 B.C.

Celebrated speculative treatise on the illusions and mythology that appeal to the mass mind; on elite recruitment; on educational theory; and on techniques of persuasion. By Athenian philosopher who for a time was a public administrator.

264. POLLOCK, HORATIO MILO (W). *Mental Disease and Social Welfare.* Utica, N.Y.: State Hospitals Press, 1941. 237 pp.

Statistical studies based on population of New York State hospitals. In the U.S. now, "one person in every ten may expect to be seriously afflicted with a mental disease in the course of his lifetime." The annual economic loss due to mental disease is, in the United States, over three-quarters of a billion dollars. Dr. Pollock has been Director of the Statistical Bureau, New York State Department of Mental Hospitals, for 30 years.

265. POVIÑA, ALFREDO. *Historia de la sociología latino-americana*, preface by José Medina Echevarría. Mexico City: Fondo de Cultura Económica, 1941. 236 pp.

Historical survey of Latin American sociology, by professor in the University of Córdoba (Argentina). Includes annotated bibliography of leading writers, pp. 141-65, 221-26.

266. *Psychiatry: Journal of the Biology and the Pathology of Interpersonal Relations.* Washington, D.C.: William Alanson White Psychiatric Foundation, February 1938–.

Quarterly under the joint editorship of psychiatrists and social scientists. "The journal is purposed to present authoritative but relatively non-technical treatises, reports, surveys, reviews, and abstracts pertaining to psychiatry as a basic oriented discipline having relations to all significant phases and problems of human life and to all human relations; this must include relevant biological and social science contributions, and occasional philosophical presentations."

267. "Psychoanalysis as Seen by Analysed Psychologists," *Journal of Abnormal and Social Psychology*, 35: 3-55, 139-255 (January, April 1940).

Papers by Edwin G. Boring (W), Carney Landis (W), Junius Flagg Brown, Raymond R. Willoughby, Percival M. Symonds (W), Else Frenkel-Brunswik, David Shakow, Donald V. McGranahan. Comment by Franz Alexander (CB '42) and Hanns Sachs, psychoanalysts. *Conclusion*, according to Alexander: "The verdict has been returned: the majority has acquitted the defendant. . . . It will not be long before the traditional tendency of psychoanalysis for isolation and the refutation of the need for experimental findings will cede to a demand for greater conceptual clarity, for quantitative methods, the introduction of experimental procedures, and the co-ordination of psychoanalytic findings with physiology and the social sciences."

268. *Psychometrika: A Journal Devoted to the Development of Psychology as a Quantitative Rational Science.* Colorado Springs, Colorado, quarterly, 1936–.

Official journal of the Psychometric Society.

269. *Public Opinion Quarterly*, January 1937–.

Aims to supply comprehensive impartial analysis of all major efforts to control public opinion and collective emotions. Published by School of Public and International Affairs, Princeton University.

270. QUEEN, STUART ALFRED (D, W); and THOMAS, LEWIS FRANCIS (D). *The City: A Study of Urbanism in the United States.* New York: McGraw-Hill, 1939. 500 pp.

By two U.S. sociologists. Bibliography at ends of chapters.

*271. RANULF, SVEND. *Moral Indignation and Middle Class Psychology: A Sociological Study.* Copenhagen: Levin and Munksgaard, 1938. 205 pp.

The phenomena of moral indignation and the "disinterested tendency to inflict punishment" are examined by Danish sociologist as they have appeared among the Nazis, the Protestants, the Puritans, the Aristocrats, the Catholics, the Teutons, the Hindus, the Chinese, the Israelites, the Bolsheviks, and certain primitive peoples. These attitudes are found to be "a distinctive characteristic of the lower middle class," arising from "a feeling of fear and weakness such as is inseparable from the

forced self-control of the small bourgeoisie."
Bibliographic footnotes.

272. REDL, FRITZ. "Group Emotion and Leadership," *Psychiatry*, 5: 573-96 (November 1942).

Psychoanalyst and educator (Ph.D. Vienna) redefines, elaborates and tests basic hypotheses advanced in Freud's *Group Psychology and the Analysis of the Ego* (1921).

273. ROBINSON, THOMAS HOBEN (D); and others. *Men, Groups and the Community: A Survey in the Social Sciences.* New York: Harpers, 1940. 965 pp.

College text on general social science by Colgate University professors. Includes chapters on "Communications" (pp. 80-103), and "Propaganda" (pp. 104-44). Bibliography at ends of chapters.

274. ROETHLISBERGER, FRITZ JULES (D). *Management and Morale,* foreword by Elton Mayo. Cambridge: Harvard University, 1941. 194 pp.

The basic assumption of this book, as stated in the foreword by Elton Mayo, is that there has been a progressive deterioration in the capacity of men to work together. Throughout the world, "the capacity for spontaneous effective cooperation with other people has disappeared." There is increasing recognition that workers' demands for increased wages may represent merely a way of expressing fundamental dissatisfaction with the failure of the industrial organization to satisfy the desire for social approval and recognition, for security, for self-expression, and other deep-seated wants.

These conclusions are derived, in the main, from observations in an experimental relay-assembly room at the Hawthorne Works of the Western Electric Company, supplemented by extended interviews with workers in the plant.

275. ROSANOFF, AARON J. (CB '43). *Manual of Psychiatry and Mental Hygiene,* 7th ed. New York: Wiley, 1938. 1091 pp.

Revision of a standard work by U.S. psychiatrist, enlarged by some 400 pages since the last edition. The author's earlier classifications of mental disorder have been extensively modified. Freudian contributions are stressed, while those of Adler, Jung, Eugen Kahn and even Kretschmer are ignored or omitted. The many case descriptions are of value to students of public opinion who have not yet familiarized themselves with the insights of the guidance clinic and the mental hospital.

276. ROSTEN, LEO CALVIN (CB '42, W). "Men Like War," *Harpers,* 171:189-97 (July 1935).

A U.S. political scientist uses psychoanalytic tools to probe the hidden causes of war.

277. RUSSELL, BERTRAND (CB '40, W). *Power: A New Social Analysis.* New York: Norton, 1938. 305 pp.

Taking power as a fundamental concept in social analysis, as energy is fundamental in physics, Russell analyzes its transformations through the forms of wealth, armed authority, civil authority, and skill in propaganda. Foreseeing the march of western civilization toward the possibility of "a new tyranny . . . more drastic and more terrible than any previously known," he advocates further analysis of "collective excitement." "To admire collective enthusiasm is reckless and irresponsible," he holds, "for its fruits are fierceness, war, death, and slavery."

278. SCHILDER, PAUL (CB '41,W). *Goals and Desires of Man: A Psychological Survey of Life.* New York: Columbia University, 1942. 305 pp.

General theory of personality based on the author's large psychiatric and psychoanalytic experience in private practice, in the university clinic of Vienna, and in Bellevue Hospital, New York City. Bibliography, pp. 285-92.

278a. SCHUMPETER, JOSEPH ALOIS. *Capitalism, Socialism and Democracy.* New York: Harpers, 1942. 381 pp.

Analysis of the relation between democracy and capitalism, and of the practicability of socialism, by Harvard economist, who predicts the growth, all over the world, of a kind of "militarist socialism" with certain "fascist features." Pp. 146-55 are on the sociology of the intellectuals. Bibliographic footnotes.

279. SHELDON, WILLIAM HERBERT (W); and STEVENS, S. S., collaborator. *The Varieties of Temperament: A Psychology of Constitutional Differences.* New York: Harpers, 1942. 520 pp.

Study by two Harvard medical psychologists on the relation between physical characteristics and psychological features of personality. Based on detailed analysis of 200 cases. Bibliographic footnotes.

280. SHERIF, MUZAFER. *Psychology of Social Norms*, introduction by Gardner Murphy (W). New York: Harpers, 1936. 209 pp.

General social psychology, by psychologist trained at Columbia.

281. SHERIF, MUZAFER. *A Study of Some Social Factors in Perception* (Ph.D. thesis; Archives of Psychology, no. 187). 1935. 60 pp.

Bibliography, pp. 53-54.

282. SHRODES, CAROLINE; VAN GUNDY, JUSTINE; and HUSBAND, RICHARD W., editors. *Psychology through Literature: An Anthology*. New York: Oxford University, 1943. 389 pp.

Selections from literary classics, to be used as supplementary reading in an introductory course in social psychology or mental hygiene. Includes sections on the neuroses and psychoses as well as the "normal." Annotated bibliography, pp. 369-85, lists a number of other sources of such material.

*283. SIMONEIT, MAX. *Wehrpsychologie: Ein Abriss ihrer Probleme und praktische Folgerungen*. Berlin: Bernard and Graefe, 1935. 161 pp.

The basic German textbook of military psychology. Dr. Simoneit is scientific director of the High Command's Central Psychological Laboratory, and editor of *Soldatentum*, bimonthly technical journal on military psychology. Bibliographic footnotes.

284. SMITH, BRUCE LANNES (D). "Propaganda Analysis and the Science of Democracy," *Public Opinion Quarterly*, 5: 250-59 (June 1941).

Present methods of teaching propaganda analysis often produce destructive cynicism in students. The remedy suggested is a "Science of Democracy," some elements of which are outlined here. Article includes a chart of U.S. social strata, their incomes, and some of their national pressure organizations.

285. SMITH, CHARLES W., JR. (D). "The Intelligence Factor in Public Opinion: A Comment on Some Recent Pub-

lications," *Journal of Politics*, 1: 301-11 (August 1939).

Rapid review of a dozen major books of recent years, by University of Alabama political scientist.

286. SMITH, CHARLES W., JR. (D). *Public Opinion in a Democracy: A Study in American Politics*. New York: Prentice-Hall, 1939. 598 pp.

Analyzes prospects for re-creating a public opinion capable of sustaining U.S. democracy. Bibliography, pp. 567-85.

287. SMITH, (JAMES) MAPHEUS (D,W). "Leadership: The Management of Social Differentials," *Journal of Abnormal and Social Psychology*, 30: 348-58 (October 1935).

By U.S. sociologist.

288. SOCIAL SCIENCE RESEARCH COUNCIL. COMMITTEE ON PERSONALITY AND CULTURE. SUB-COMMITTEE ON COMPETITION AND COOPERATION. *Memorandum on Research in Competition and Cooperation*, by Mark Arthur May (W), Gordon Allport (W), Gardner Murphy (W), and others. New York, April 1937. *Ca.* 400 pp., mimeo.

Interpretative summaries of existing publications on the subject.

*289. SOCIETY FOR THE PSYCHOLOGICAL STUDY OF SOCIAL ISSUES. *Industrial Conflict: A Psychological Interpretation* (First *Yearbook* of the Society), edited by George Wilfried Hartmann and Theodore Mead Newcomb (D). New York: Cordon, 1939. 583 pp.

First publication of this group of "militantly progressive" scientists and social leaders, organized to promote psychological wisdom on crucial topics. Contains contributions by a variety of writers, including economists, personnel managers, lawyers, sociologists, educational philosophers, historians, political scientists, business leaders, labor leaders, psychiatrists, and psychologists. Among other papers are: "Objectivity in the Social Sciences," by Hadley Cantril and Daniel Katz; "Social Psychology and Public Policy," by Ernest L. Hilgard; "The Johnstown Strike of 1937: A

Case Study of Large-Scale Conflict," by Keith Sward; "An Employer and an Organizer View the Same Series of Conflicts," by the editors; "Analysis of 'Class' Structure of Contemporary American Society: Psychological Bases of Class Divisions," by Arthur W. Kornhauser; "Labor Unions as Seen by Their Members: An Attempt to Measure Attitudes," by Theodore Mead Newcomb (D); "Psychology of Conciliation and Arbitration Procedures," by Samuel Perkins Hayes, Jr.; "Propaganda and Symbol Manipulation," by Selden Cowles Menefee (D); "The Problem of Teaching Realistically the Psychology of Industrial Conflict," by Ellis Freeman. Contains extensive bibliography.

290. SOCIETY FOR THE PSYCHOLOGICAL STUDY OF SOCIAL ISSUES. *Civilian Morale* (Second *Yearbook* of the Society), edited by Goodwin Barbour Watson (D,W). Cornwall, N.Y.: Cornwall Press, 1942. 463 pp.

A collection of articles by U.S. psychologists, organized under the following heads: "Theory of Morale," "How Morale Develops," "The State of American Morale," "Morale in Industry," and "Recommendations." Bibliography, pp. 437-47.

291. SOCIETY FOR PSYCHOLOGICAL STUDY OF SOCIAL ISSUES. COMMITTEE ON LEADERSHIP AND MORALE. *Newsletter.* Irregularly, June 15, 1942–.

Includes brief outlines of current research in leadership and morale. "Sent to Committee members only." Thirty social scientists and psychologists are listed as Committee members in the first issue.

292. *Sociometry: A Journal of Interpersonal Relations.* Beacon, New York, quarterly, July 1937–.

A technical journal looking toward integration of the social sciences through exact analysis of interpersonal demands and responses, as these are viewed by many types of specialists.

293. SOCIETY OF SOCIOLOGY AND THE SOCIAL SCIENCES. *Sociological Prolegomena.* Belgrade, Yugoslavia, 1938. 438 pp.

First part of the volume deals with the relation of sociology to political history, philosophy, biology, psychology, history, ethnology, statistics, economics, law, and social action;

second part appraises the state of sociology and the other social sciences in the U.S., France, Rumania, and Yugoslavia.

*294. SOROKIN, PITIRIM ALEXANDROVITCH (CB '42, D,W). *Social and Cultural Dynamics.* Volume 1, *Fluctuations of Forms of Art.* Volume 2, *Fluctuations of Systems of Truth, Ethics, and Law.* Volume 3, *Fluctuations of Social Relationships, War, and Revolution.* Volume 4, *Basic Problems, Principles and Methods.* New York: American Book Company, 1937-41. 4 vols.

Harvard sociologist's philosophy of history. Includes bibliography. See also his well-known *Sociology of Revolution* (1925) and *Social Mobility* (1928).

295. SOULE, GEORGE HENRY, JR. (W). *The Strength of Nations: A Study in Social Theory.* New York: Macmillan, 1942. 268 pp.

Editor of *New Republic* deals with ills of the nation from the standpoint of recent advances in psychoanalytic and psychiatric knowledge. Bibliography, pp. 259-62.

296. STAGNER, ROSS; and KROUT, MAURICE HAIM. "Correlational Study of Personality Development and Structure," *Journal of Abnormal and Social Psychology,* 35: 339-55 (July 1940).

Methodological study by two U.S. social psychologists.

297. STARCH, DANIEL (W); STANTON, HAZEL MARTHA (D); and KOERTH, WILHELMINE. *Psychology in Education.* New York: Appleton-Century, 1941. 722 pp.

Textbook for prospective teachers. Dr. Starch is director of research, American Association of Advertising Agencies, and was 20 years a psychology professor. Bibliography at ends of chapters.

298. SULLIVAN, HARRY STACK (CB '42). "Conceptions of Modern Psychiatry," *Psychiatry,* 3: 1-117 (February 1940).

By well-known U.S. psychiatrist, a trustee of William Alanson White Psychiatric Foundation and a pioneer in exploring relations between psychiatry and the other social sciences.

299. SULLIVAN, HARRY STACK (CB '42). "Psychiatry in the Emergency: Its Task in a Changing Social Order and in National Defense," *Mental Hygiene*, 25: 5-10 (January 1941).

300. THORNDIKE, EDWARD LEE (CB '41, D,W); and others. *Adult Interests* (Institute of Educational Research Studies in Adult Education). New York: Macmillan, 1935. 265 pp.

Columbia University psychologist, an exponent of "scientific pedagogy," offers the results of research on the interests of adults as shown by their willingness and ability to memorize different classes of subject matter, including nonsense.

301. THORNDIKE, EDWARD LEE (CB '41, D,W). *Human Nature and the Social Order*. New York: Macmillan, 1940. 1019 pp.

Facts and principles of psychology for students of the social sciences. Bibliography, pp. 988-99.

302. THORNDIKE, EDWARD LEE (CB '41, D,W); and others. *The Psychology of Wants, Interests, and Attitudes*. New York and London: Appleton-Century, 1935. 301 pp.

Like *Adult Interests* (1935), this volume is the result of a three-year study of interests and motives in relation to learning. Bibliography, pp. 289-92.

303. THURSTONE, LOUIS LEON (W). *Primary Mental Abilities* (Psychometric Monographs, no. 1). Chicago: University of Chicago, 1938. 121 pp.

Applies the multiple-factor analysis which the author, a well-known U.S. psychologist and statistician, developed in his *Vectors of Mind* (1935). Fifty-six tests were given to 240 volunteers, and "mental profiles" were statistically derived.

304. THURSTONE, LOUIS LEON (W); and THURSTONE, THELMA GWINN. *Factorial Studies of Intelligence* (Psychometric Monographs, no. 2).

Chicago: University of Chicago, 1941. 94 pp.

305. TIFFIN, JOSEPH HAROLD. *Industrial Psychology*. New York: Prentice-Hall, 1942. 386 pp.

By a U.S. psychologist. Bibliographic footnotes.

*305a. TÖNNIES, FERDINAND. *Kritik der öffentlichen Meinung*. Berlin: Springer, 1922. 583 pp.

Standard history and analysis of theories of public opinion, by German sociologist. For a brief critical summary, see Paul A. Palmer, "Ferdinand Tönnies's Theory of Public Opinion" (cited above, item 258).

306. TOYNBEE, ARNOLD JOSEPH. *A Study of History*. London: Oxford University, 1934-39. 6 vols.

Philosophy of world history, by well-known British historian and political publicist, long a leading figure in the Royal Institute of International Affairs and in the University of London. Includes bibliography.

307. URBAN, WILBUR MARSHALL (W). *Language and Reality: The Philosophy of Language and The Principles of Symbolism* (Library of Philosophy). New York: Macmillan, 1939. 755 pp.

Idealist philosopher's theory of signs and symbols. Postulates a "mutuality of mind" or "transcendental self" common to all who seek to communicate. Bibliographic footnotes.

308. WAELDER, ROBERT (D). *Psychological Aspects of War and Peace* (Geneva Research Center publication). New York: Columbia University, 1939. 56 pp.

Ex-Viennese psychoanalyst, now on staff of Boston Psychoanalytic Institute, presents a brief outline of major problems of mass psychology, with suggestions for further research.

*309. WAPLES, DOUGLAS (D,W), editor. *Print, Radio and Film in a Democracy: Ten Papers on the Administration of Mass Communications in the Public Interest—Read before the Sixth Annual Institute of the Graduate Li-*

brary School, the University of Chicago —August 4-9, 1941. Chicago: University of Chicago, 1942. 197 pp.

Some aspects of governmental policies are discussed by Harold L. Elsten, then Research Analyst, Special War Policies Unit, U.S. Department of Justice, in "Mass Communication and American Democracy"; and by Ernst Kris, Co-director, Research Project on Totalitarian Communication, New School for Social Research, in "Mass Communication under Totalitarian Governments." Bernard Berelson, Special Analyst, Federal Communications Commission, Paul Felix Lazarsfeld (D), Associate Professor of Sociology, Columbia University, and Donald Slesinger (W), Executive Director, American Film Center, analyze effects of press, radio and films on public opinion. "Communications Research and Politics," by Harold D. Lasswell (D,W), Director of War Communications Research, Library of Congress, deals with the role of systematic symbol analysis in the formation of democratic public policy. "The Improvement of Present Public Opinion Analysis" is considered by Harold Foote Gosnell, Associate Professor of Political Science, University of Chicago. Samuel A. Stouffer (D), Professor of Sociology, University of Chicago, relates how "A Sociologist Looks at Communications Research." "Implications of Communications Research for the Public Schools" are taken up by Ralph W. Tyler (D,W), Chairman of Department of Education, University of Chicago; and "Implications of Communications Research for the Public Library," by Ralph A. Beals, Assistant Librarian, District of Columbia Public Library. Reading list, pp. 185-89.

310. WARNOTTE, DANIEL. "Les Vertus bourgeoises, leur origine, leur signification," *Revue de l'Institut de Sociologie,* 19: 1-14 (1939).

Belgian sociologist reviews the recent work of Svend Ranulf, Danish scholar, whose leading concept is "moral indignation," and who finds that this "disinterested tendency to inflict punishment" exists only in societies where there is a lower middle class. Substituting intense morality for the gratifications of the wealthy and for the submissive enjoyments of the laborer, this class finds rationalizations for its sadistic impulses in our times which perhaps it could not find before the breakdown of plutocracy and plutocratic traditions.

311. WATKINS, GORDON S. (D, W); and DODD, PAUL A. (D). *The Management of Labor Relations.* New York: McGraw-Hill, 1938. 780 pp.

By two University of California economists. Chapters 1-5 review the history of labor relations from ancient times, indicating the emerging self-consciousness of specialists in personnel problems. Chapter 21 is on "The Education and Training of Employees," and chapter 23 on "The Employee Magazine." Three chapters deal with "Joint Relations and Collective Bargaining." Bibliography, pp. 741-54.

312. WEBER, ALFRED. *Kulturgeschichte als Kultursoziologie.* Leiden: Sijthoff, 1935. 424 pp.

A sociological analysis of the data of world history from primitive times to the present. By Heidelberg sociologist. Spanish edition: *Historia de la cultura* (Mexico: Fondo de cultura económica, 1941. 469 pp.).

***312a.** WEBER, MAX (ESS). *Wirtschaft und Gesellschaft (Grundriss der Sozialökonomik,* III Abteilung), 2nd ed. Tübingen: Mohr, 1925. 840 pp.

Economic and social analysis of Western civilization by celebrated German sociologist, jurist, and political economist. See also the author's *Politik als Beruf* ("Politics as a Career") in his *Gesammelte politische Schriften,* pp. 396-451 (Munich: Drei Masken, 1921), a sociological analysis of the politician and the public administrator.

313. WERTHAM, FREDERIC (W), *Dark Legend: A Study in Murder.* New York: Duell, Sloan and Pearce, 1941. 270 pp.

This analysis of a case of matricide, by Senior Psychiatrist, Department of Hospitals, New York City, may serve as a somewhat representative case history on the psychology of murder.

314. WHITE, LEONARD DUPEE (D, W), editor. *The Future of Government in the United States.* Chicago: University of Chicago, 1942. 274 pp.

Essays in political science, presented in honor of Charles Edward Merriam (D,W), University of Chicago political scientist, by a dozen of his students. Dr. Merriam contributes an autobiography. Harold D. Lasswell (D,W) writes on "The Developing Science of Democracy"; Leo C. Rosten (CB '42, W) on "Political Leadership and the Press"; Harold Foote Gosnell on "The Future of the American Party System"; Louise Overacker (D) on "Trends in Party Campaign Funds"; and various other writers consider urbanism, governmental planning, public administration, the theory of sovereignty, and world politics. Bibliography of Charles E. Merriam, pp. 269-74.

315. WILSON, FRANCIS G. (D). *"The Federalist* on Public Opinion," *Public Opinion Quarterly*, 6: 563-75 (Winter 1942).

By U.S. professor of political theory.

316. WILSON, FRANCIS G. (D). "James Bryce on Public Opinion: Fifty Years Later," *Public Opinion Quarterly*, 3: 420-35 (July 1939).

317. WIRTH, LOUIS (D,W), editor. *Eleven Twenty-Six: A Decade of Social Science Research.* Chicago: University of Chicago, 1940. 498 pp.

Proceedings of conference commemorating the tenth anniversary of the opening of the Social Science Research Building at the University of Chicago. Includes a paper on "Factor Analysis . . . of Human Traits," by Louis Leon Thurstone (W), with discussion by William Line and Edward Lee Thorndike (CB '41, D,W). Also reports of various round tables on social science methodology. Bibliography, pp. 296-486, lists all social science publications of the "Chicago school" since 1929.

318. WOOLF, LEONARD SIDNEY. *After the Deluge* (vol. 2): *A Study of Communal Psychology.* New York: Harcourt, Brace, 1940. 317 pp.

By British political publicist.

★318a. WRIGHT, QUINCY (D,W), editor. *Public Opinion and World Politics.* Chicago: University of Chicago, 1933. 237 pp.

Lectures by John W. Dafoe, Jules Auguste Sauerwein, Edgar Stern-Rubarth, Ralph Haswell Lutz (D,W) and Harold Dwight Lasswell (D,W), sponsored by the Norman Wait Harris Foundation at the University of Chicago.

319. *The Yenching Journal of Social Studies*, Peiping, China, 1938–.

New magazine published in English by Yenching University, covering social research and theory.

320. YODER, DALE (D,W). *Personnel Management and Industrial Relations.* New York: Prentice-Hall, 1942. 848 pp.

Revision of a rather technical college text formerly entitled *Personnel and Labor Relations* (1938), by University of Minnesota Professor of Business Administration. Bibliographic footnotes.

321. ZAWADSKI, BOHAN; and LAZARSFELD, PAUL FELIX (D). "Psychological Consequences of Unemployment," *Journal of Social Psychology*, 6: 224-51 (May 1935).

PART 2. PROPAGANDA CLASSIFIED BY THE NAME OF THE PROMOTING GROUP

A. NATIONAL GOVERNMENTS AND OFFICIAL INTERNATIONAL AGENCIES

322. AIKMAN, DUNCAN. "The Machinery for Hemisphere Cooperation," *Public Opinion Quarterly*, 6: 549-62 (Winter 1942).

Office of Coordinator of Inter-American Affairs is discussed by a U.S. journalist on its staff.

323. AKZIN, BENJAMIN. *Propaganda by Diplomats* (International Law and Relations, vol. 5, no. 7). Washington, D.C.: Digest Press, American University Graduate School, 1936. 22 pp., photolithographed.

323a. *Anuário da prensa brasileira*, ediçao do Departamento de Imprensa e Propaganda. Rio de Janeiro, 1941–.

"Annual of the Brazilian Press," issued by the Brazilian Government's Department of Press and Propaganda (D. I. P.). Edition of 1941 includes a lengthy history of legislation on the press from the colonial days of Brazil to the regime of Vargas. Cites the laws in detail and outlines the duties of each division of D. I. P. Includes official lists of registered journalists, publications and radio stations. Contains an "Introduction to the History of Caricature in Brazil," studies of radio and motion pictures in Brazil, and an "Historical Sketch of Brazilian Commercial Publicity." Describes the present and former departments of official propaganda of the national government and of the various states. Contains a directory of Brazilian publications (papers, magazines, almanacs, etc.) and publishers. Describes the officially sanctioned organizations, Associaçao Brasileira de Imprensa and Sindicato dos Jornalistas Profissionais.

323b. ARGENTINE CHAMBER OF DEPUTIES. COMISIÓN INVESTIGADORA DE ACTIVIDADES ANTI-ARGENTINAS. *Informes* (Reports), August 1941–.

Reports of legislative committee investigating foreign propaganda and other foreign activities in Argentina.

324. BAKER, GLADYS. *The County Agent*. Chicago: University of Chicago, 1939. 225 pp.

Story of the rise of the county agent from itinerant teacher of better farming to his present position as local representative and administrator of a vast federal adjustment program. Discusses his role in conducting educational activities, elections, referenda, and enforcement campaigns. By political scientist trained at University of Chicago. Bibliography, pp. 214-15.

325. BANE, SUDA LORENA; and LUTZ, RALPH HASWELL, editors. *The Blockade of Germany after the Armistice, 1918-1919: Selected Documents of the Supreme Economic Council, Superior Blockade Council, American Relief Administration, and Other Wartime Organizations* (Hoover Library on War, Revolution and Peace, publication no. 16). Stanford University: Stanford University, 1942. 874 pp.

Includes extensive treatment of propaganda, and a chapter, pp. 573-625, on "American and Allied Policies on Censorship, 1918-19."

326. BELL, ULRIC. "The Democratic Diplomacy of Secretary Hull," *Public Opinion Quarterly*, 2: 36-47 (January 1938).

By a U.S. newspaper man who has served as press adviser to Secretary of State Cordell Hull. Describes the Secretary's press conferences and his theory and technique of public relations.

327. BELLQUIST, ERIC CYRIL. "Maintaining Morale in Sweden," *Pub-*

lic Opinion Quarterly, 5: 432-47 (Fall 1941).

Sweden's program for building morale during the present emergency and the activities of the State Information Agency are described by U.S. political scientist who spent 1939 in northern Europe.

328. BENDINER, ROBERT. *The Riddle of the State Department.* New York: Farrar and Rinehart, 1942. 231 pp.

By managing editor of *The Nation.* Reviews U.S. foreign policy since 1933; discusses leading State Department figures and the structure and powers of the Department.

329. BISCHOFF, RALPH FREDERIC. *Nazi Conquest through German Culture* (Harvard Political Studies). Cambridge: Harvard University, 1942. 198 pp.

Contents: The Nationalism of the Nazi. Nazi Nationalism in Retrospect. German Culture Organizes. The Power of German Culture in Czechoslovakia. German-American or American-German? Bibliographic footnotes.

330. BOTTAI, GIUSEPPE. *Politica fascista delle arti* (Problemi della scuola e della vita). Roma: Signorelli, 1940. 386 pp.

Use of the arts in Fascist politics and propaganda, by former Minister of Education under Mussolini.

331. BOURGIN, SIMON. "Public Relations of Naval Expansion," *Public Opinion Quarterly*, 3: 113-17 (January 1939).

Roosevelt Administration's handling of its naval expansion program in 1937-38 is described by an observer who was then in the Washington Office of Foreign Policy Association.

332. BREYCHA-VAUTHIER, ARTHUR CARL DE. *Sources of Information: A Handbook on the Publications of the League of Nations*, preface by James T. Shotwell. New York: Columbia University, 1939. 118 pp.

Standard work which has appeared in German and French in its earlier editions.

332a. "The [British] Ministry of Information: Its Functions and Or-

ganisation," *War-Time Trading Bulletin*, 4: no. 26: 722-51 (1942).

"This is the first time the activities of this Ministry have been published in such detail."—Foreword. Includes functional chart and description of work of each Division; names and pictures of Division heads; no financial data.

333. BROOKINGS INSTITUTION. *Report on Governmental Activities in Library, Information, and Statistical Services* (report to U.S. Senate Select Committee to Investigate the Executive Agencies of the Government, pursuant to S.R. 217, 74th Congress). Washington, D.C.: Government Printing Office, June 1937. 31 pp.

*334. BRUNTZ, GEORGE G. *Allied Propaganda and the Collapse of the German Empire in 1918* (Hoover War Library Publications, no. 13), foreword by Harold D. Lasswell. Stanford University, 1938. 246 pp.

Systematic analysis of propaganda organization, methods and tactics, symbols and appeals, selected determinants in the material environment, and means of measuring the effects. By U.S. historian. Bibliography, pp. 223-32.

335. BURTON, MARGARET ERNESTINE. *The Assembly of the League of Nations* (Ph.D. thesis, Columbia University). Chicago: University of Chicago, 1941. 441 pp.

Chapter 7 is on "The Assembly as an Opinion-Forming and Policy-Making Body." Bibliography, pp. 419-21.

336. CARSTENSEN, RICHARD. *Der Einfluss der französischen Kulturpropaganda auf das Geistesleben Dänemarks.* Berlin-Leipzig: Nibelungen-verlag, 1941. 77 pp.

"Influence of French cultural propaganda on the spiritual life of Denmark." Bibliography, pp. 76-77.

337. CHERRINGTON, BEN MARK. "The [State Department's] Division of Cultural Relations," *Public Opinion Quarterly*, 3: 136-38 (January 1939).

By Chief of the Division, a well-known specialist in adult education.

338. CHILDS, HARWOOD LAWRENCE. "The American Government in War-Time: Public Information and Opinion," *American Political Science Review*, 37: 56-68 (February 1943).

Year-end summary of developments. By Princeton political scientist.

*339. CHILDS, HARWOOD LAWRENCE (D); and WHITTON, JOHN BOARDMAN (D,W), editors. *Propaganda by Short Wave*. Princeton: Princeton University, 1942. 355 pp.

Summarizes the Princeton Listening Center's pioneering studies of foreign short-wave broadcasts. Systematic monitoring of the short-wave propaganda of the more important belligerent countries was commenced in November 1939, and continued until June 1941, when the work was taken over by a federal agency—the Monitoring Service of the Federal Communications Commission. An introductory chapter traces the development of the use of radio as a technique in international politics and shows how the totalitarian states launched a "war of words" long before the League of Nations or the democracies. Separate chapters by different investigators analyze the broadcasts of Germany (by Philip E. Jacob), Britain (Daniel Katz), Italy (Bruno Foa) and France (Arturo Mathieu). Jacob also discusses "Atrocity Propaganda," and Edrita Fried, Viennese psychologist, writes on "Techniques of Persuasion." Dr. Childs summarizes available data on "America's Short Wave Audience." Bibliographic footnotes.

340. CIVIL SERVICE ASSEMBLY OF THE UNITED STATES AND CANADA. *Public Relations of Public Personnel Agencies*. Chicago: Public Administration Service, 1941. 259 pp.

Report submitted to Civil Service Assembly by a committee of political scientists and other authorities on public administration, under the chairmanship of William E. Mosher. Includes a scale which rates the "diagnostic value" of a public report (i.e., shows whether the report contains "valid and significant indices" of the skill with which an agency is performing its function). Also includes samples of scales for measuring (1) public response to an agency's public relations and (2) public attitude on

various other questions of interest to administrators. Bibliographic footnotes.

341. COGGESHALL, REGINALD. "Peace Conference Publicity: Lessons of 1919," *Journalism Quarterly*, 19: 1-11 (March 1942).

Staff member of Boston *Globe* explores pitfalls which trapped negotiators at Paris and suggests a press-diplomatic program for the next peace conference.

342. COLE, TAYLOR. "The Italian Ministry of Popular Culture," *Public Opinion Quarterly*, 2: 425-34 (July 1938).

By U.S. political scientist.

343. "Correspondence with the Public," *Public Administration*, 14: 276-300 (July 1936).

Three articles on correspondence as an aspect of a public relations policy: "By a Railroad," by Ashton Davies; "By the Post Office," by W. D. Sharp; "By a Tax Department," by M. Kliman.

*343a. CREEL, GEORGE (W). *How We Advertised America: The First Telling of the Amazing Story of the Committee on Public Information That Carried the Gospel of Americanism to Every Corner of the Globe*. New York and London: Harpers, 1920. 466 pp.

By the head of the Committee on Public Information, the organization that directed the United States government news and publicity campaign during World War I. See also his *Complete Report of the Chairman of the Committee on Public Information, 1917, 1918, 1919* (Washington, D.C.: Government Printing Office, 1920. 290 pp.).

344. "Culture's Weak Case: Can't Show Much on Propaganda," *Variety*, May 25, 1938, pp. 27 ff.

Lengthy story on U.S. Senate hearings concerning bills to create a government-operated radio station "with which to combat foreign radio propaganda flooding South America." Story avers that witnesses favoring the station were unable to produce evidence that European propaganda in South America has an appreciable effect on U.S. interests.

345. CUSHMAN, ROBERT EUGENE. *The Independent Regulatory Commissions.* New York: Oxford University, 1941. 780 pp.

History, analysis, and appraisal of such agencies as Federal Reserve Board, FTC, FPC, FCC, SEC, NLRB, CAA, with discussion of problems of structure and personnel. An outgrowth of work done for President's Committee on Administrative Management by Dr. Cushman, a Cornell University political scientist. Bibliographic footnotes.

346. DAUGHERTY, WILLIAM E. "China's Official Publicity in the United States," *Public Opinion Quarterly*, 6: 70-86 (Spring 1942).

By U.S. political scientist who has spent three years in China.

347. DE LOS RIOS, FERNANDO. "Nazi Infiltration in Ibero-America," *Social Research*, 7: 389-409 (November 1940).

By Spanish political scientist, former cabinet member in Spanish Republican Government, on staff of New School for Social Research since 1939.

348. DOBIE, R. M. "U.S. Travel Campaign Cancelled by Washington," *Editor and Publisher*, June 28, 1941, p. 7.

Account of U.S. efforts to subsidize the South American press through "tourist advertising," under auspices of State Department and Office of Coordinator of Inter-American Affairs.

349. "Donovan Strategy: Counterpropaganda," *Newsweek*, 18: 21 (November 17, 1941).

Propaganda efforts of the Office of the Coordinator of Information, U.S. Government agency [later named Office of Strategic Services] under Col. [later General] William Joseph Donovan. A staff of geographers, historians, psychologists and journalists "winnow the day's diplomatic dispatches" and other news and "plan an appropriate shortwave news menu": a 10,000 word daily report which is telegraphed to eleven shortwave stations.

350. DURANT, HENRY; and DURANT, RUTH. "Lord Haw-Haw of Hamburg: His British Audience," *Public Opinion Quarterly*, 4: 443-50 (September 1940).

The Director of the British Institute of Public Opinion and his wife describe the size and characteristics of Lord Haw-Haw's British radio audience and analyze the impact of his propaganda up to August 1, 1940.

350a. DUTCH EAST INDIES GOVERNMENT. *Ten Years of Japanese Burrowing in the Netherlands East Indies: Official Report of the Netherlands East Indies Government on Japanese Subversive Activities in the Archipelago during the Last Decade.* New York: Netherlands Information Bureau, 1942. 132 pp.

Also available in Spanish.

350b. "Enlargement and Reorganization of the [Japanese] Government Agency for Information," *Tokyo Gazette*, 4 no. 7: 292-94 (January 1941).

Official announcement of concentration of propaganda and censorship functions of Japanese Government in the hands of the Cabinet Board of Information. Describes, in "officialese," the structure and functions of the Board.

351. ERIKSON, ERIK HOMBURGER. "Hitler's Imagery and German Youth," *Psychiatry*, 5: 475-93 (November 1942).

Psychoanalyst's interpretation of Hitler's motives and of the appeal of his symbols.

352. FELLGIEBEL, GENERAL. "Aufklärung und Propaganda durch Nachrichtenmittel," *Militärwissenschaftliche Rundschau* (published by German Ministry of War), 1: 493-510 (1936).

German general's views on "propaganda through the news channels."

353. FERNANDEZ ARTUCIO, HUGO. *The Nazi Underground in South America.* New York: Farrar and Rinehart, 1942. 311 pp.

By well-known Uruguayan anti-Axis publicist, Professor of Philosophy in the University of Montevideo.

354. "Fiftieth Anniversary of Pan-American Union," commemorative issue of *Pan-American Union Bulletin*, 74: 189-360 (June 1940).

Includes a history of the Union, 1890-1940, and special articles on problems of inter-American trade, agriculture, communications, intellectual cooperation and public health.

355. FOSTER, HARRY SCHUYLER, JR. "The Official Propaganda of Great Britain," *Public Opinion Quarterly*, 3: 263-71 (April 1939).

By U.S. political scientist. Based on his research on this subject as a Social Science Research Council Fellow in England, 1937-38.

356. GAUS, JOHN MERRIMAN; and WOLCOTT, LEON O. *Public Administration and the United States Department of Agriculture*. Chicago: Public Administration Service, 1941. 542 pp.

By two U.S. political scientists, under auspices of Social Science Research Council's Committee on Public Administration. "Afforded unusual opportunities for observation within the Department both in Washington and the field, the authors have written the first over-all account of its growth . . . [and of] the impact of the Department's work on state and local governments, and its relations to Land Grant Colleges and the [State] Extension Service."

357. *Germany Speaks*, "by 21 leading members of party and state." London: Butterworth, 1938. 407 pp.

Twenty-one essays on objectives of National Socialism, including one on "The Essence of Propaganda in Germany" by Dr. G. Kurt Johannsen, Managing Director of the Hanse Press, and one on "The Press and World Politics" by Dr. Otto Dietrich, Secretary of State, Reich Chief of Press.

358. GIBBERD, KATHLEEN. *I. L. O.: The Unregarded Revolution*. London: Dent, 1937. 152 pp.

Brief but apparently authoritative introduction to the work of the International Labor Office, by a British trade unionist who has been associated with the I.L.O. in both Geneva and London.

359. GIUDICI, ERNESTO. *Hitler con-quista América*. Buenos Aires: Editorial Acento, 1938. 305 pp.

German propaganda in Latin America. Bibliographic footnotes.

360. GORDON, LINCOLN. *The Public Corporation in Great Britain*. New York: Oxford University, 1938. 351 pp.

Port of London Authority, Central Electricity Board, British Broadcasting Corporation, London Passenger Transport Board; based on three years' study in England by Harvard instructor in government.

361. GORDON, MATTHEW. *News is a Weapon*, introduction by Elmer Davis. New York: Knopf, 1942. 267 pp.

Impressionistic discussion of Axis news policy by Chief, Foreign Service Division, U.S. Office of War Information, a U.S. newspaperman. Discusses various channels.

362. GRADY, JAMES FRANCIS; and HALL, MILTON. "When Government Writes to Its Citizens," *Public Opinion Quarterly*, 3: 463-68 (July 1939).

363. GRADY, JAMES FRANCIS; and HALL, MILTON. *Writing Effective Government Letters*. Washington, D.C.: Employee Training Publications, 1939. 109 pp.

Two U.S. government public relations men compile a manual on standards of clearness, vocabulary, "correct" usage for government correspondence. Has been very favorably received by high officials of U.S. Civil Service Commission. Chapter 9 is on "Training and Supervision of Letter Writers." Annotated bibliography, pp. 101-09.

364. GRAVES, HAROLD NATHAN, JR. "Lord Haw-Haw of Hamburg: The Campaign Against Britain," *Public Opinion Quarterly*, 4: 429-42 (September 1940).

The Director of Princeton's short-wave Listening Center describes techniques of Lord Haw-Haw's radio campaign to undermine British morale, quoting extensively from his broadcasts.

365. GRAVES, HAROLD NATHAN, JR. "Propaganda by Short Wave: Berlin Calling America," *Public Opinion Quarterly*, 4: 601-19 (December 1940).

German short-wave broadcasts to the United States.

366. GRAVES, HAROLD NATHAN, JR. "Propaganda by Short Wave: London Calling America," *Public Opinion Quarterly*, 5: 38-51 (March 1941).

367. GUTHEIM, FREDERICK A. "Federal Participation in Two World's Fairs," *Public Opinion Quarterly*, 3: 608-22 (October 1939).

U.S. government information specialist describes federal participation in the New York and San Francisco fairs, 1939.

368. HARDING, T. SWANN. "Informational Techniques of the Department of Agriculture," *Public Opinion Quarterly*, 1 no. 1: 83-96 (January 1937).

For many years the author has been editor of scientific publications for the U.S. Department of Agriculture.

369. HARGRAVE, JOHN. *Words Win Wars: Propaganda the Mightiest Weapon of All.* London: W. Gardner, Darton, 1940. 227 pp.

An expostulation against the alleged lethargy of the British Ministry of Information.

370. HERRING, HUBERT CLINTON. *And So To War.* New Haven: Yale University, 1938. 172 pp.

U.S. Congregational minister, a specialist in international relations, avers in substance that President F. D. Roosevelt and Secretary Cordell Hull conducted after July 1937 a "campaign of education" to bring U.S. public opinion into line with British policy. Analyzes the channels employed, and the 45 "lessons" which the American people are said to have been "taught" up to March 1938.

371. HIGH, STANLEY HOFLUND. *Roosevelt—And Then?* New York: Harpers, 1937. 326 pp.

"Inside stuff" about personalities and events in Washington by a journalist and commentator who has handled some of the New Deal's publicity. Contains material on the government's propaganda expenditures and on use of publicity experts.

372. HITLER, ADOLF. *Mein Kampf.*

Various editions are currently available: Unabridged German edition (Munich: Eher, 1939. 781 pp.); "Unexpurgated" English edition, translated and annotated by James Murphy (London: Hurst and Blackett, 1939. 566 pp.); "Complete and unabridged, fully annotated" U.S. edition (New York: Reynal and Hitchcock, 1939. 1000 pp.).

373. HULEN, BERTRAM D. *Inside the Department of State.* New York: McGraw-Hill, 1939. 328 pp.

Detailed study of daily routine, of personnel, and of the handling of "incidents," by New York *Times* correspondent who has covered Washington for many years. Chapter on "The Press Conference System" views the conference as "a well-established government institution," "an effective substitute for the system of interpellation of Cabinet ministers."

374. HULTEN, CHARLES M. "How the OWI Operates Its Overseas Propaganda Machine," *Journalism Quarterly*, 19: 349-55 (December 1942).

"Professor Hulten, of the staff of the School of Journalism, University of Oregon, is on leave for public relations work with the unified war information service, Bureau of the Budget, Washington."

375. "Information Please," *Life*, July 27, 1942, pp. 37-39.

Pictures and comment on activities of Office of War Information and other federal government public relations agencies.

376. "Information Worse Confounded," *Time*, 38: 18 (October 20, 1941).

Survey of set-up of U.S. information agencies, on occasion of founding of Office of Facts and Figures.

377. "The Japanese Empire," *Fortune*, 14: no. 3 (September 1936).

This entire issue of the magazine is devoted to Japan. A section on "The Science of Thought Control" discusses official propaganda and censorship.

378. JOESTEN, JOACHIM. *Rats in the Larder: The Story of Nazi Influence in*

Denmark. New York: Putnam's Sons, 1939. 260 pp.

By ex-German journalist.

379. KANE, R. KEITH. "The Office of Facts and Figures," *Public Opinion Quarterly*, 6: 204-20 (Summer 1942).

R. Keith Kane, New York attorney, was director of the Bureau of Intelligence, one of the four major branches of the Office, which was organized in the Office of War Information to coordinate the various research and investigation activities carried on by the government and allied organizations.

380. KIRKPATRICK, CLIFFORD. *Nazi Germany: Its Women and Family Life*. Indianapolis: Bobbs-Merrill, 1938. 353 pp.

Includes material on propaganda for an increased birth rate and for other Nazi policies. By U.S. sociologist. Bibliography, pp. 300-33.

381. KRIS, ERNST. "German Propaganda Instructions of 1933," *Social Research*, 9: 46-81 (February 1942).

Study of alleged Nazi instructions to party agents abroad. By psychoanalyst on staff of New School for Social Research.

382. LARSON, CEDRIC. "How Much Federal Publicity Is There?" *Public Opinion Quarterly*, 2: 636-44 (October 1938).

Survey of available data by U.S. historian. Comment on this article was contributed by James L. McCamy, political scientist, in *Public Opinion Quarterly*, 3: 473-75 (July 1939).

383. LARSON, CEDRIC. "The British Ministry of Information," *Public Opinion Quarterly*, 5: 412-31 (Fall 1941).

By a member of the Morale Division of the U.S. War Department, co-author of *Words that Won the War* (1939).

384. LASKER, BRUNO; and ROMAN, AGNES. *Propaganda from China and Japan: A Case Study in Propaganda Analysis* (Studies of the Press and Public Opinion in Pacific Countries). New York: American Council, Institute of Pacific Relations, 1938. 120 pp.

Examines "a sample of the printed propaganda that reached the United States from China and Japan between July and December 1937." By staff members of the Institute of Pacific Relations. Bibliographic footnotes.

385. LAWFORD, STEPHEN. *Sowing Justice: Or, the Romance of the International Labour Office*. London: Nicholson and Watson, 1939. 150 pp.

386. LEHMANN, ERNST HERBERT. *Wie sie lügen: Beweise feindlicher Hetzpropaganda*. Berlin: Niebelungen-verlag, 1939-40. 40 pp.

German attack on the alleged lies in the propaganda of Germany's enemies.

387. LEONHARDT, HANS LEO. *Nazi Conquest of Danzig* (Ph.D. thesis, international relations, Chicago). Chicago: University of Chicago, 1942. 363 pp.

A detailed and well-documented account of the Nazi movement in Danzig from the beginning of agitation to the eventual political control. The author was legal consultant to the democratic opposition. Bibliography, pp. 343-49.

388. LOWE, BOUTELLE ELLSWORTH. *The International Protection of Labor: International Labor Organization, History, and Law*, new ed., revised and enlarged. New York: Macmillan, 1935. 594 pp.

By a U.S. historian and social scientist. Contains résumés of proceedings of eighteen I.L.O. annual conferences and a chronological account of the movement for international labor legislation since 1818. Bibliography, pp. 331-87.

389. LUCATELLO, GUIDO. "La fonction de la propagande politique dans l'état totalitaire et son organisation dans les états italien et allemand," *Revue de droit internationale*, 17: 251-59, 18: 144-59 (1939).

390. LYDDON, W. G. *British War Missions to the United States, 1914-1918*. New York: Oxford University, 1938. 245 pp.

Analyzes activities of the 500 officials and 10,000 assistants who managed British commercial and informational activities in the U.S.

*391. McCamy, James Lucian (D). *Government Publicity: Its Practice in Federal Administration* (Ph.D. thesis, political science. Chicago). Chicago: University of Chicago, 1939. 275 pp.

Analyzes recent U.S. government publicity by subject, volume, cost, media. Summarizes the law regulating it. Deals briefly with personnel and organization. By a Bennington College political scientist, who has served as Assistant to the Secretary of Agriculture. Bibliographic footnotes.

392. McCamy, James Lucian. "Variety in the Growth of Federal Publicity," *Public Opinion Quarterly*, 3: 285-92 (April 1939).

393. McKenzie, Vernon. *Here Lies Goebbels!* London: Michael Joseph, 1940. 319 pp.

Study of Europe's current propaganda wars by Canadian-American journalist and professor of journalism. Packed with suggestions for improving British propaganda technique, both in Europe and America.

394. McKenzie, Vernon. "United Nations Propaganda in the United States," *Public Opinion Quarterly*, 6: 351-66 (Fall 1942).

More than forty "Free" movements and allied members of the United Nations are now competing for the attention and support of public opinion in the United States. To what extent, and *how*, should these propaganda activities be controlled? "Professor McKenzie has just returned to his post as Director of the School of Journalism, University of Washington, after serving in an advisory capacity with the British Information Services in London and New York."

395. McMillan, George E. "Government Publicity and the Impact of War," *Public Opinion Quarterly*, 5: 383-98 (Fall 1941).

A U.S. government information specialist reviews some of the more important developments in government publicity since the outbreak of the Second World War.

396. Martin, Kingsley. "The Ministry of Information [of Great Britain]," *Political Quarterly*, 10: 502-16 (October 1939).

396a. Mass-Observation. *Home Propaganda: A Report Prepared by Mass-Observation for the Advertising Service Guild.* London: Advertising Service Guild, 1941. 78 pp.

A study of the extent and impact of British official home front propaganda, with discussion of reasons for success of certain campaigns and failure of others.

397. Mercey, Arch A. "Modernizing Federal Publicity," *Public Opinion Quarterly*, 1 no. 3: 87-94 (July 1937).

By a U.S. government information specialist.

398. Miller, J. C. "Japan Turns Back the Clock," *Amerasia*, 2: 396-404 (October 1938).

On the New People's Association, an organization for "intellectual mobilization" in China.

399. Mock, James R.; and Larson, Cedric. "Public Relations of the U.S. Army," *Public Opinion Quarterly*, 5: 275-82 (June 1941).

By two U.S. government officials.

*400. Mock, James R.; and Larson, Cedric. *Words That Won the War: The Story of the Committee on Public Information, 1917-1919.* Princeton: Princeton University, 1939. 372 pp.

Based on files of the Committee, "an historical source of the first importance." George Creel, Committee head, newspaper crusader and Wilsonian idealist, emerges as a "remarkable man, who in spite of having more than a fair share of mercurial temperament, carried his liberalism through the hatred and hysteria of war." Personnel, activities, and expenditures of each of the Committee's score of special divisions are traced in detail. Proposed blueprints for "Tomorrow's Committee" are reviewed. "If the record of the last war is to be taken, American resistance to repressive measures may not be great. The question arises whether, in the event of a new war, America would feel like indulging in the luxury of some 'Creel Committee' to stand as a buffer between military dictatorship and civil life."

Dr. Mock, seven years a Findlay College history professor, is on the staff of the National Archives. Mr. Larson has served in several federal agencies. Bibliographic notes, pp. 349-56.

401. MOTTA LIMA, PEDRO; and BARBOZA MELLO, JOSÉ. *El nazismo en el Brasil: Proceso del estado corporativo.* Buenos Aires: Claridad, 1938. 221 pp.

402. MULLEN, J. "Goebbels's Guiding Hand," *Nation*, 145: 179 (August 14, 1937).

Goebbels's orders to traveling German correspondents who covered the Paris Exposition.

403. NATIONAL SOCIALIST PARTY OF GERMANY. REICHSPROPAGANDA-LEITUNG. *Propagandaschriften der Nationalsozialistischen deutschen Arbeiterpartei.* Munich and Berlin, 1932–.

A file of these propaganda documents is available in the New York Public Library.

404. *The Nazi Conspiracy in Spain,* by the editor of *The Brown Book of the Hitler Terror,* translated from the German manuscript by Emile Burns. London: Gollancz, 1937. 256 pp.

Study of Nazi propaganda in Spain, by the editor of *The Brown Book of the Hitler Terror.* Spanish edition: *La Conspiración Nazi en España,* por el editor de *The Brown Book of the Hitler Terror,* traducido del manuscrito alemán por Emilio Burns, versión española de Ricardo J. Zevada, prólogo de Clementina B. de Bassols. Mexico City: Editorial revolucionaria, 1938. 300 pp.

405. *The Nazi International* (Friends of Europe Publications, no. 69). London, 1938. 32 pp.

Anonymous account of alleged Nazi propaganda throughout the world. Though brief, the part on the U.S. appears to be accurate. Also published in *Quarterly Review,* vol. 271 (October 1938).

406. "Nazi Soft Pedal in Latin America: Nazi Propaganda to be Disseminated by Spanish Falangist Agencies," *Living Age,* 360: 139-42 (April 1941).

407. NEUBURGER, OTTO. *Official Publications of Present-Day Germany:* *Government, Corporate Organizations and National Socialist Party, with an Outline of the Governmental Structure of Germany.* Washington, D.C.: Government Printing Office, 1942. 130 pp.

By a member of the Division of Documents, Library of Congress.

408. "Newsman's Soldier," *Time,* August 18, 1941, p. 42.

On Brigadier General Alexander Day Surles, head of U.S. Army's press section, 1935-39, just reappointed head of U.S. Army public relations. "Instead of his old staff of two well-meaning assistants, he found, going at *Panzer* tilt, eight big departments, manned by a dozen lieutenant colonels, 15 majors, ten captains, 25 lieutenants, 20 civilian writers, picture and radio editors, assorted experts of all shades, plus more than 150 clerks, typists, stenographers, mimeograph operators, etc. . . . [The section] now has [a staff of] 61. . . . Under Major Earle Looker, ex-adman and Roosevelt biographer, the Department of Intelligence and Analysis . . . digests spot news, reviews periodicals and newsreels once a week, monitors and records all radio commentators, playing them back on portable machines to all officers interested."

409. ODEGARD, PETER H.; and BARTH, ALAN. "Millions for Defense," *Public Opinion Quarterly,* 5: 399-411 (Fall 1941).

An account of the purposes, theory, organization, and promotional activities of the U.S. Treasury's bond sales program, by two of the campaign's organizers.

410. "Office of War Information," special issue of *Public Opinion Quarterly,* 7: 1-138 (Spring 1943), edited by Harwood L. Childs.

Symposium by 15 specialists. Elmer Davis, the OWI Director, writes on its goals and costs. Lester G. Hawkins, Jr., and George S. Pettee, members of the Sources Division, outline the organization as of February 1943 and identify the key personnel. Joseph Barnes, Alan Barth, Leonard Carlton and A. H. Feller, all of OWI, discuss various branches of the agency. Notable are the remarks on abolition of the Bureau of Intelligence, a branch intended to place the findings of social science and current investigations at the disposal of OWI policymakers in a unified way. Loss of this bureau leaves OWI policy substantially in the hands of newspaper, radio, literary and business personnel, without the services of statistical and scientific specialists on social trends. "It is inconceivable," says the editor's note, "that governments in wartime, or at any other time, can function effectively without the kind of intelligence this bureau assembled." Carl J. Friedrich, Harvard political scientist, writes on "Principles of Informational Strategy." David Nelson Rowe, Princeton historian and lecturer on Far Eastern affairs, offers proposals as to symbolic objectives and administrative framework of "OWI's Far Eastern Outposts." Robert J. Landry, radio editor of *Variety*, discusses OWI from the point of view of the radio industry; Walter Wanger, Hollywood producer, from that of the movie industry; and Paul Scott Mowrer, editor of Chicago *Daily News*, from the angle of the newspapermen who receive its output. Matthew Gordon, Chief, Foreign Service Division of OWI, asserts, without presenting data, that OWI "has not made the Axis any happier." Jerome S. Bruner, social psychologist of the Princeton Office of Public Opinion Research, presents carefully reasoned data on OWI's effects on the U.S. public, including poll results that seem to show that OWI has not made the U.S. public much wiser. Millions, his data show, are untouched, confused, suspicious, uninformed, misinformed. "Most of OWI's job still lies ahead," he asserts.

411. PADOVER, SAUL K. "How the Nazis Picture America," *Public Opinion Quarterly*, 3: 663-69 (October 1939).

By a U.S. historian (Ph.D. Chicago), who has served since 1938 as assistant to Secretary of the Interior Harold L. Ickes.

412. PETERSON, HORACE CORNELIUS. *Propaganda for War: The Campaign Against American Neutrality, 1914-1917.* Norman, Oklahoma: University of Oklahoma, 1939. 357 pp.

Fairly exhaustive study of the means employed by British propagandists to defeat competing propagandists from the Central Powers. Stresses class and regional differences in American public opinion: plutocratic and upper-middle classes were the earliest to support the war; the East was more easily converted to the Allied cause than the West and Middle West; but West and Middle West had higher voluntary enlistment rates after they had been won over by the propaganda. Like previous studies, this volume calls attention to the dependence of the U.S. press upon British-controlled cables for war news, and the effect of

this in building up an unneutral attitude. Author is a University of Oklahoma historian. Bibliography, pp. 343-52.

413. PFIFFNER, JOHN McDONALD. *Research Methods in Public Administration*, New York: Ronald, 1940. 447 pp.

General text by public administration professor, University of Southern California. Includes chapters on "Preparing the Report" and on "Dissemination and Adoption of Research Results." Bibliography at ends of chapters.

414. POKORNÝ, JIŘÍ. *S Druhého Břehu.* Prague: Svaz Narodního Osvobození, 1938. 113 pp.

German propaganda in Russia, 1917.

415. POLLACK, J. H. "Public Relations Problems of Alien Registration," *Public Opinion Quarterly*, 6: 622-27 (Winter 1942).

How U.S. Department of Justice handled registration of aliens of enemy nationality early in 1942.

416. POSSONY, STEFAN T. "Needed —a New Propaganda Approach to Germany," *Public Opinion Quarterly*, 6: 335-50 (Fall 1942).

Dr. Possony, Ph.D. Vienna, was Editor of the Free Austrian broadcasts of the French Ministry of Information 1939-40 and later a member of the Princeton Institute for Advanced Study. Since January, 1942, he has served as German News Editor for Columbia Broadcasting System's short-wave broadcasts to the enemy.

417. POTTER, PITMAN BENJAMIN. "League [of Nations] Publicity: Cause or Effect of League Failure?" *Public Opinion Quarterly*, 2: 399-412 (July 1938).

Dr. Potter (Ph.D. Harvard 1918) was Professor of International Organization at the Graduate Institute of International Studies, Geneva, 1930-41.

418. PUTNEY, BRYANT. "Federal Publicity," *Editorial Research Reports*, March 18, 1940, pp. 203-19.

General survey, citing figures on the volume of federal publicity and quoting extensively from James L. McCamy's and Pendleton

Herring's views on its place in a democratic social system.

*419. READ, JAMES MORGAN (D). *Atrocity Propaganda, 1914-1919.* New Haven: Yale University for University of Louisville, 1941. 319 pp.

By University of Louisville historian. Heavily documented. Bibliography, pp. 297-310.

420. REYNOLDS, MARY T. "The [U.S.] General Staff as a Propaganda Agency, 1908-1914," *Public Opinion Quarterly*, 3: 391-408 (July 1939).

Mrs. Reynolds (Ph.D. Columbia 1939) has been an assistant in government at Harvard.

421. RILEY, NORMAN. *999 and All That.* London: Gollancz, 1940. 223 pp.

British newspaperman's account of his dealings with the bureaucracy of the British Ministry of Information and with British censors.

422. ROLLINS, RICHARD. *I Find Treason: The Story of an American Anti-Nazi Agent.* New York: Morrow, 1941. 291 pp.

By a Columbia graduate student in sociology who has spent a number of years investigating fascist activities in U.S. Includes a lengthy dossier of facsimiles of alleged propaganda materials.

423. ROWE, DAVID NELSON. "Japanese Propaganda in North China, 1937-1938," *Public Opinion Quarterly*, 3: 564-80 (October 1939).

Eyewitness account. Dr. Rowe (Ph.D. Chicago 1935) is a professor of Far Eastern history, who was born in Nanking and lived in China during his youth.

424. ROWE, DAVID NELSON. "The T'ai Chi Symbol in Japanese War Propaganda," *Public Opinion Quarterly*, 5: 532-47 (Winter 1941).

Psychological analysis of Japanese Army's use of classical Chinese and Korean symbol of harmonious interaction (also known as Yin and Yang), on flags and in propaganda of puppet governments in occupied areas.

425. SALVEMINI, GAETANO. *Italian Fascist Activities in the United States*, introduction by William Yandell Elliott.

Washington, D.C.: American Council on Public Affairs, 1941. 24 pp.

By well-known professor of Italian history, now at Harvard, who has recently made special studies of Fascist propaganda in the U.S.

426. SAUNDERS, DERO AMES. "The Failure of Propaganda and What to Do About It," *Harpers*, 183: 648-54 (November 1941).

By speakers' director of the Institute for Propaganda Analysis and Council for Democracy, who has been executive secretary of League for Fair Play (a nonprofit speakers' bureau). Asserts that morale of the democracies is low and cannot be raised until a sincere propagandist brings forth a vision of a "Brave New World." Of the Roosevelt-Churchill Eight-Point "program," he says: "True [it] has done no harm—unless it discourages others from trying to shape democracy's vision."

427. SCHMECKEBIER, LAURENCE FREDERICK. *Government Publications and Their Use*, 2nd. rev. ed. Washington, D.C.: Brookings Institution, 1939. 479 pp.

A guide to catalogs, indexes, bibliographies and other aids that may help in finding public documents. Author is a member of the Institute of Government Research of the Brookings Institution.

428. SCHMECKEBIER, LAURENCE FREDERICK. *International Organizations in which the United States Participates* (Institute for Government Research, Studies in Administration, no. 30). Washington, D.C.: Brookings Institution, 1935. 370 pp.

A reference work, with lengthy bibliographies on each organization.

428a. SCHMIDT, ALFRED. *Publizistik im Dorf* (Leipziger Beitraege zur Erforschung der Publizistik). Dresden: Dittert, 1939. 195 pp.

"[Political] Publicity in the Village." How the State may influence rural populations.

429. SCHMIDT, WOLFGANG. "Methoden der britischen Propaganda," *Zeitschrift für neusprächlichen Unterricht*, 38: 305-15 (1939).

430. SCHUMAN, FREDERICK LEW-IS. *The Nazi Dictatorship: A Study in Social Pathology and the Politics of Fascism*, 3rd ed. New York: Knopf, 1936. 516 pp.

A comprehensive analysis of German National Socialism, largely in terms of a psychological political science. By a U.S. political scientist.

431. SCURLA, HERBERT. *Die dritte Front: Geistige Grundlagen des Propagandakrieges der Westmächte*, 2nd ed. (Schriftenreihe des Deutschen akademischen Austauschdienstes, hrsg. von Karl Schwarz. Bd. 4). Berlin: H. Stubenrauch, 1940. 92 pp.

British and French propaganda in World War II. Bibliography, pp. 89-92.

432. SEOANE, MANUEL ALEJANDRO. "If I Were Nelson Rockefeller," *Harpers*, 186: 312-18 (February 1943).

Editor of the Chilean news-weekly *Ercilla* tells what he thinks of the work of the Office of Coordinator of Inter-American Affairs. "If I were Nelson Rockefeller," he says, "I would not be completely satisfied with . . . the Coordinator's Press, Radio and Motion Picture Divisions. . . . There are over eight hundred persons employed in the Coordinator's Office and of these only some seventeen are Latin Americans. . . . And sixteen of these occupy obscure positions as translators. . . . *En Guardia* (OCIAA magazine) publishes 80,000 copies monthly . . . but so far as I know this is a waste of paper, time and money, for it is not read by the people who feel themselves closest to the United States in aims. It is circulated among Latin American government officials and foreign embassies. It is a magazine read by diplomats and conservatives. The people do not read it; the few who manage to see it are infuriated." Suggestions are given for U.S. subsidy of the Latin American press, for more meaningful press, movie, and radio material, and for increasing inter-American travel.

433. SERENO, RENZO. "Italian War Propaganda at Home," *Public Opinion Quarterly*, 3: 468-72 (July 1939).

By ex-Italian political scientist who has continued his work in the U.S.

434. SHARP, WALTER RICE. "Methods of Opinion Control in Present-Day Brazil," *Public Opinion Quarterly*, 5: 3-16 (March 1941).

Based on this U.S. political scientist's observations on a trip to Brazil.

434a. SINGTON, DERRICK; and WEIDENFELD, ARTHUR. *The Goebbels Experiment: A Study of the Nazi Propaganda Machine*. New Haven: Yale University, 1943. 274 pp.

General survey of activities of NSDAP through the Party Propaganda Department, Ministry of Public Enlightenment and Propaganda, Reich Chambers of Culture, Press, Broadcasting, and Films, and other Nazi-controlled channels. Includes organization charts of these agencies. Based largely "upon broadcasts by the German radio during the war, upon the German press from 1933 to 1942, and on German publications of many kinds which have reached England up to June 1942." By two members of the BBC monitoring service. Bibliography, pp. 262-66.

435. "Slant-eyed Haw-Haw," *Newsweek*, 19: 36 ff. (February 9, 1942).

Broadcasts by American-born Japanese Lord Haw-Haw, one Charles Yoshii, a University of Oregon alumnus.

436. SOUTHWORTH, H. RUTLEDGE. "Spanish Phalanx and Latin America," *Foreign Affairs*, 10: 148-52 (October 1939).

A study of the early history of the Falange, its ideology and its place in the alleged Axis plan of world domination. By a U.S. magazine writer.

437. SPEIER, HANS. "Magic Geography," *Social Research*, 8: 310-30 (September 1941).

Social scientist's analysis of German technique of employing maps for war propaganda. Maps "put into clear focus the hazy impressions gained by laymen from communiqués and newspaper dispatches."

438. SPIVAK, JOHN LOUIS. *Secret Armies: The New Technique of Nazi Warfare*. New York: Modern Age, 1939. 160 pp.

Nazi propaganda in the U.S., described by a U.S. journalist.

439. SQUIRES, JAMES DUANE. *British Propaganda at Home and in the United States from 1914 to 1917* (Harvard Historical Monographs, no. 6). Cambridge: Harvard University, 1935. 124 pp.

Check list of British propaganda sent to the United States between 1914 and 1917, pp. 86-104. By U.S. historian. Bibliography, pp. 105-08.

440. STANKOVITCH, MIHAÏLO. *Les services de presse des gouvernements et de la Société des Nations* (thesis, University of Paris). Paris: Librairie sociale et économique, 1939. 225 pp.

Comprehensive treatise on history of governmental press services of leading countries and of the League of Nations. Bibliography, pp. 211-25.

441. STRAUSZ-HUPÉ, ROBERT. *Axis America: Hitler Plans Our Future.* New York: Putnam's Sons, 1941. 274 pp.

Describes Nazi propaganda in Western Hemisphere. Includes a chapter on "Offensive by Radio," by Charles J. Rolo.

442. TAKEUCHI, TATSUJI. *War and Diplomacy in the Japanese Empire* (University of Chicago Causes of War Studies), introduction by Quincy Wright. Garden City: Doubleday, Doran, 1935. 524 pp.

Contains hitherto inaccessible material on opinions of governing officials at crisis points in the history of Japanese foreign policy. Dr. Takeuchi (Ph.D. Chicago) became Professor of International Relations, Kwansei Gakuin University. Bibliography, pp. 485-89.

443. TALLENTS, STEPHEN. "British Broadcasting and the War," *Atlantic,* 165: 361-68 (March 1940).

BBC official's version of BBC activities.

444. TAYLOR, EDMOND (LAPIERRE). "Hitler's 'Frightful Weapon': Propaganda," *New York Times Magazine,* June 1, 1941, pp. 3 ff.

U.S. journalist reviews a few of the more than 700 books and articles that German writers have published on this aspect of modern warfare during the last twenty years. "Hit-ler's theories were taken up and expanded by hundreds of trained propaganda technicians, among whom General Fellgiebel, General Hermann Franke, Colonel Blau, Eugen Hadamovsky, Ewald Banse, Karl Pintschovius and Leonhard Stark are the most important, though little known, names."

445. TAYLOR, EDMOND (LAPIERRE). "How America Can Take the [Propaganda] Offensive," *Fortune* (May 1941).

U.S. journalist suggests that U.S. launch a "political super-Blitzkrieg against Hitler" by (1) government radio stations; (2) government subsidy for noncommercial propaganda films; (3) "morale ambassadors" abroad; (4) use of Fort Knox gold to "encourage" foreign politicians who "believe in the democratic ideals of the U.S."; (5) stamping propaganda messages on U.S. gifts to distressed areas abroad.

446. TEJERA, ADOLFO. *Penetración nazi en América latina,* preface by Dr. Juan Andrés Ramírez. Montevideo: Editorial Nueva América, 1938. 149 pp.

By Uruguayan journalist.

446a. THIERFELDER, FRANZ. *Englischer Kulturimperialismus: Der British Council als Werkzeug der geistigen Einkreisung Deutschlands* (Schriften des deutschen Instituts für aussenpolitische Forschung und des Hamburger Instituts für auswärtige Politik, Heft 26). Berlin: Junker und Dünnhaupt, 1940. 67 pp.

"British Cultural Imperialism: The British Council as an Instrument for the Spiritual Encirclement of Germany."

447. THOMSON, CHARLES A. H. "Public Relations of the 1940 Census," *Public Opinion Quarterly,* 4: 311-18 (June 1940).

By a Brookings Institution Fellow.

448. U. S. DEPARTMENT OF STATE. *National Socialism: Basic Principles, Their Application by the Nazi Party's Foreign Organization, and the Use of Germans Abroad for Nazi Aims.* Washington, D.C.: Government Printing Office, 1943. 510 pp.

Prepared in the Special Unit of the Division

of European Affairs by Raymond E. Murphy, Francis B. Stevens, Howard Trivers and Joseph M. Roland. Based on studies of German literature and philosophy; German statutes, decrees, and other official records; authoritative writings and statements of German leaders under the National Socialist regime; and confidential reports and information obtained over a period of years by representatives of the Department of State. Bibliographic footnotes.

448a. U.S. DEPARTMENT OF STATE. *Program of the Department of State in Cultural Relations.* Washington, D.C.: Government Printing Office, 1941. 16 pp.

Reprint from Department of State Appropriation Hearings for 1942 (77th Congress, first session), outlining the Department's expenditures and activities.

449. U.S. NATIONAL ARCHIVES. *Guide to the Material in the National Archives.* Washington, D.C.: Government Printing Office, 1940. 303 pp.

Catalogues much material on propaganda campaigns of public agencies. Note especially such establishments as Committee on Public Information, Federal Council of Citizenship Training, Advisory Committee on Education by Radio, etc. Note also the collection of "Gift Motion Pictures and Sound Recordings."

450. "The U.S. Short Wave," *Time*, November 3, 1941, pp. 54-56.

Survey of activities of the Office of the Coordinator of Information ("Donovan Committee") and the networks. "Programs for Europe and Latin America have taken a terrific spurt during the last few months. . . . Broadcasters know that the only programs Europeans care to take risks for are news and factual programs."

*450a. VIERECK, GEORGE SYLVESTER (CB '40). *Spreading Germs of Hate*, foreword by Colonel Edward M. House. New York: Liveright, 1930. 327 pp.

Autobiographical material on activities of a German-American journalist engaged in pro-German propaganda during World War I.

451. WALEY, H. D. "British Documentaries and the War Effort," *Public Opinion Quarterly*, 6: 604-09 (Winter 1942).

British Ministry of Information has released one "short" per week in England for two years. It has also exported films to dominions and colonies, and has begun regular importation and distribution of Russian movies. The author is on staff of National Film Library, official repository.

452. WANDERSCHECK, HERMANN, compiler. *Bibliographie zur englischen Propaganda im Weltkrieg* (Bibliographische Vierteljahrshefte der Weltkriegsbücherei, Heft 7). Stuttgart: Weltkriegsbücherei, 1935. 69 pp.

A classified, annotated bibliography of about 1000 titles, covering both treatises and source materials in the extensive collection of the Weltkriegsbücherei.

453. WANDERSCHECK, HERMANN. *Die englische Lügenpropaganda im Weltkrieg und Heute* (Schriften des deutschen Instituts für aussenpolitische Forschung und des Hamburger Instituts für auswärtige Politik, hrsg. in Gemeinschaft mit den Deutschen auslandswissenschaftlichen Institut, heft 38). Berlin: Junker und Dünnhaupt, 1940. 70 pp.

"Lying English Propaganda in the World War and Today."

454. WARE, HENRY. "Soviet Advertising," *American Quarterly on the Soviet Union*, January 1939, pp. 66-72.

455. WESTBROOK, LAWRENCE. "Error and Remedy in WPA Publicity," *Public Opinion Quarterly*, 1 no. 3: 94-98 (July 1937).

By a WPA administrator.

456. WILCOX, FRANCIS ORLANDO. "The Use of Atrocity Stories in War," *American Political Science Review*, 34: 1167-77 (December 1940).

Study of Italy's use of atrocity stories in the Ethiopian campaign, by University of Louisville political scientist. *Conclusion*: the stories may have influenced opinion inside Italy, but they seem to have been ignored in the world press. They "created not the slightest ripple in a country [U.S.] where German atrocities had been so gullibly devoured some two decades earlier."

457. WILLIAMS, MARGARET HICKS. " 'The President's' Office of Government Reports," *Public Opinion Quarterly*, 5: 548-62 (Winter 1941).

By a staff member of this federal agency.

458. WILSON, MILBURN LINCOLN. "Rural America Discusses Democracy," *Public Opinion Quarterly*, 5: 288-94 (June 1941).

A veteran administrator of U.S. Department of Agriculture describes the prodemocratic activities of the Department's Extension Division.

459. WRIGHT, ALMON R. "Records of the Food Administration: New Field for Research," *Public Opinion Quarterly*, 3: 278-84 (April 1939).

Opportunity for research in propaganda and censorship of World War I is pointed out by staff member of National Archives.

B. POLITICAL PARTIES

For Communist parties in particular countries, see this section. For Communism throughout the world, see Part 3 A.

For Fascist parties, see this section and also Part 2 A.

461. ARNESON, BEN ALBERT. "Workers Parties Show Gains in Sweden and Norway," *American Political Science Review*, 31: 96-100 (February 1937).

By U.S. political scientist.

462. ATTLEE, CLEMENT RICHARD. *The Labour Party in Perspective.* London: Gollancz, 1937. 287 pp.

Survey of Labour Party by Opposition leader in Parliament.

463. BAYER, ERNST. *Sport, Politik und Presse: Der Sport als Mittel des politischen Kampfes und der parteipolitischen Propaganda in der Zeit des Weimarer Systems, 1919-1933* (inaugural dissertation, Heidelberg). Heidelberg: Meister, 1936. 63 pp.

Sport used as means of party propaganda by the party press; the commercial press declared the political neutrality of sport, thus "fostering attitudes of liberal internationalism." The Nazi state uses sport as an instrument of national power. Bibliography, pp. 59-62.

464. BELL, TOM. *The British Communist Party: A Short History.* London: Lawrence and Wishart, 1937. 201 pp.

465. BERDAHL, CLARENCE ARTHUR. "The American Government in War-Time: Political Parties and Elections," *American Political Science Review*, 37: 68-80 (February 1943).

Year-end summary of developments. By University of Illinois political scientist.

466. BERDAHL, CLARENCE ARTHUR. "Party Membership in the U.S.," *American Political Science Review*, 36: 16-50, 241-62 (February, April 1942).

Study of those who work within the party organization, and prevailing customs as to rules of membership and exclusion.

467. BIGELOW, BURTON. "The Machinery Behind Political Pamphleteering," *Journalism Quarterly*, 14: 7-17 (March 1937).

Report on volume, distribution, and symbolism of Republican campaign pamphlets. By a Buffalo, N.Y., advertising specialist who served as director of the Correspondence and Distribution Division of the Republican National Committee in the 1936 campaign.

468. BLACK, THEODORE MILTON. *Democratic Party Publicity in the 1940 Campaign.* New York: Plymouth Publishing Company, 1941. 169 pp.

The author was an employee of the Democratic National Committee's Publicity Division during the Presidential campaign. Bibliography, pp. 159-69.

469. BONE, HUGH ALVIN. *Smear Politics: An Analysis of 1940 Cam-*

paign Literature, introduction by Senator Guy M. Gillette. Washington, D.C.: American Council on Public Affairs, 1941. 49 pp.

Study of "smear campaigns" conducted by Republicans, New Dealers, and "non-political" groups in the 1940 elections. By U.S. political scientist. Says Senator Gillette, chairman of the U.S. Senate Special Committee on Campaign Expenditures: "The . . . Committee . . . investigating campaign practices was astounded at the revelation of the extent to which the circulation of scurrilous, obscene, vicious, subversive, and destructive campaign literature was used in the 1940 contest. It also was disturbing to the Committee to learn that one-half of this volume of literature was entirely unsigned or only partially identified. One-third was wholly anonymous, and this included the most virulent, dishonest, and defamatory portion of the material. It was evident to the members of the Committee and to the students of the problem who have examined the report that the nation should no longer delay the enactment of legislation to prevent, if possible, carefully planned and often highly financed efforts to control the American electorate at the polls, whether such attempts emanate from foreign sources or originate within our own borders."

470. BRADERMAN, EUGENE MAUR. *A Study of Political Parties and Politics in Mexico since 1890* (Ph.D. thesis, University of Illinois, 1938).

471. BRASILLACH, ROBERT. *Léon Degrelle et l'avenir de "Rex."* Paris: Plon, 1936. 85 pp.

On Degrelle, leader of Rexism, a Belgian Fascist movement.

472. BRIDGES, RONALD. "The Republican Program Committee," *Public Opinion Quarterly*, 3: 299-306 (April 1939).

Managing editor of *Young Republican*, national magazine of the Young Republicans, describes work of Republican Program Committee, a body of 280 party members who frame a suggested party program.

473. BURDETTE, FRANKLIN L. *Filibustering in the Senate*. Princeton: Princeton University, 1940. 252 pp.

Comprehensive account of U.S. Senate fili-

busters from John Randolph to Huey Long and after. By U.S. political scientist. Bibliographic footnotes.

474. BURTON, RALPH. "The French Chamber of Deputies: Party Attitudes," *American Political Science Review*, 30: 549-56 (June 1936).

475. CAMPBELL, JOHN C. "Political Extremes in South America," *Foreign Affairs*, 20: 516-34 (April 1942).

Political parties and shirted movements are described by a Rockefeller Fellow on staff of Council on Foreign Relations.

476. CASEY, RALPH DROZ. "The National Publicity Bureau and British Party Propaganda," *Public Opinion Quarterly*, 3: 623-34 (October 1939).

Based on material gathered by this U.S. political scientist on a Guggenheim fellowship in England, 1937-38. The National Publicity Bureau "carried through the first modern, large-scale propaganda campaign on a national basis in the history of British politics, yet it worked so unobtrusively and anonymously that few outside the ranks of professional politicians and organization men had any appreciation of its potency. Its major point of policy is to remain discreetly in the background." Yet "it created striking innovations in the use of propaganda media . . . , retained some of the best brains in the commercial public relations field in London, and helped the National Government win its spectacular victory over the Labour and Liberal Parties."

477. CASEY, RALPH DROZ. "Republican Propaganda in the 1936 Campaign," *Public Opinion Quarterly*, 1 no. 2: 27-44 (April 1937).

478. CASEY, RALPH DROZ. "The Republican Rural Press Campaign," *Public Opinion Quarterly*, 5: 130-32 (March 1941).

Techniques used by rural press section of Republican Party in the 1940 campaign.

479. CHRISTENSEN, ASHER NORMAN; and KIRKPATRICK, EVRON MAURICE. *The People, Politics and the Politicians: Readings in American Government*. New York: Henry Holt, 1941. 1001 pp.

Compiled by two University of Minnesota political scientists. Section on public opinion and propaganda includes selections by Max Lerner, George Gallup and the Institute for Propaganda Analysis. There are several sections on the political party. Pressure groups and lobbying are covered by George H. Sabine, Henry A. Bellows, Belle Zeller and Edwin E. Witte.

480. COLE, GEORGE DOUGLAS HOWARD. *The People's Front.* London: Gollancz, 1937. 366 pp.

Analysis of the position of the British Labour Party from the standpoint of a well-known member who dissents from its Executive Committee's decision to withhold support from People's Front groups.

481. COMMUNIST PARTY OF THE SOVIET UNION. *History of the Communist Party of the Soviet Union (Bolsheviks),* authorized by the Central Committee of the CPSU (B). New York: International Publishers, 1939. 364 pp.

Official history. Bibliography in text.

482. COUSENS, THEODORE WELLS. *Politics and Political Organizations in America.* New York: Macmillan, 1943. 617 pp.

Text by Lafayette College political scientist. Includes complete tabular records of the electoral and popular vote in all presidential elections from 1788 through 1940; tables showing the party lines in every Congress, and the growth of minor parties; full statistical data on campaign expenditures, including those of the 1940 election; and a tabular comparison of the Democratic and Republican campaign literature in 1940. Bibliography at ends of chapters and pp. 541-62.

483. DANGERFIELD, ROYDEN J.; and FLYNN, RICHARD H. "Voter Motivation in the 1936 Oklahoma Democratic Primary," *Southwestern Social Science Quarterly,* 17: 97-105 (September 1936).

Statistical and descriptive study of a campaign. "It is evident that in the first primary election, personality and speaking ability were more important than economic issues. This was even more true in the second primary. . . .

The Oklahoma voter was converted—not convinced."

484. DEGEN, MARIE LOUISE. *The History of the Woman's Peace Party.* Baltimore: Johns Hopkins, 1939. 266 pp.

Bibliography, pp. 253-56.

485. "Democratic Party," *Fortune* (October 1939).

486. DONNELLY, THOMAS CLAUDE, editor. *Rocky Mountain Politics,* foreword by Arthur Norman Holcombe. Albuquerque: University of New Mexico, 1940. 304 pp.

Study of the political, economic and social forces that determine voting behavior in the Rocky Mountain region, by a group of Rocky Mountain political scientists. Pressure groups, press and public opinion in each state are among the topics covered. Bibliography, pp. 292-95.

487. EHRICH, EMIL WILLI HEINRICH. *Die Auslandsorganisation der NSDAP* (Schriften der Deutschen Hochschule für Politik). Berlin: Junker und Dünnhaupt, 1937. 32 pp.

Foreign office of the Nazi Party.

488. EWING, CORTEZ A. M. *Presidential Elections, from Abraham Lincoln to Franklin D. Roosevelt.* Norman: University of Oklahoma Press, 1940. 226 pp.

By University of Oklahoma political scientist. "Mr. Ewing's study is an addition to the growing and rich field of statistical electoral analysis. His purpose is 'to attempt an interpretation of the more fundamental development of theories which have lain behind and beneath American politics' and 'to follow the popular decision, as far as possible, through the votes in presidential elections.' He develops these aims specifically about three main problems, the roles of sections, minor parties, and the electoral college. It is unfortunate that he confined his topics. If he had used census and other data he could have sampled for voting patterns on basic factors like income and occupation, national origin and race, rural and urban, and religion.

"The approach is that of the Turner school, historical-sectional, with a bias for midwestern agrarian democracy. But the history is often glib generality and warped by his bias and details are often clichés and misstatements of fact. The sectional treatment, though an important contribution, is hampered by a dubious statistical base—specifically in grouping Oklahoma with the South and in too broad a Western section.

"Ewing's interpretation of our political system is orthodox and sound. He believes it to be a two-party system responsive to public opinion which, in turn, is shaped by historical currents. The function of third parties is, not to win elections, but to introduce new ideas and educate voters to accept them. In his view, this system would work best in a Jeffersonian agrarian economy rather than in our industrialized economy. The statistical work reveals three significant facts: The South is largely outside the national democratic political system and the whole country suffers for it. The electoral college is a vestigial remain which ought to be dispensed with. And since 1896 there has been a tendency toward landslide elections, though he does not explain it."—Irving Bernstein in *Public Opinion Quarterly*, 5:502 (Fall 1941).

489. FARLEY, JAMES ALOYSIUS. *Behind the Ballots.* New York: Harcourt, Brace, 1938. 392 pp.
Disarmingly frank autobiography of F. D. Roosevelt's Postmaster General, full of details about Democratic Party personalities, organization, conflicts.

490. "Fascism Holds Its First Open Meeting in Canada," *Life*, July 18, 1938, pp. 9-11.
Meeting of Adrien Arcand's National Unity Party. See also *Time*, July 18, 1938, p. 9.

491. FISCHER, LUDWIG; and HAIDN, CARL, editors. *Das Recht der NSDAP: Vorschriften-sammlung mit Anmerkungen, Verweisungen und Sachregister herausgegeben von Reichsamtsleiter, Amtsgerichtsrat Dr. C. Haidn und Hauptamtsleiter Dr. Ludwig Fischer*, foreword by Reichsminister Dr. Frank . . . , 3rd ed. Munich: Eher, 1938. 783 pp.
Regulations of the Nazi Party.

492. FOSTER, WILLIAM ZEBULON; and others. *Party Building and Political Leadership.* New York: Workers Library, 1937. 127 pp.
By U.S. Communist leaders.

493. GERTH, HANS (HEINRICH). "The Nazi Party: Its Leadership and Composition," *American Journal of Sociology*, 45:517-41 (January 1940).
Careful study by ex-German sociologist. Includes hitherto unavailable data on party composition.

493a. GOSNELL, HAROLD FOOTE. *Grass Roots Politics: National Voting Behavior of Typical States.* Washington, D.C.: American Council on Public Affairs, 1942. 195 pp.
Comparison of national vote in recent elections with the votes of six states ("Industrial" Pennsylvania, "Progressive" Wisconsin, "Farm Belt" Iowa, "Utopian" California, Illinois [scene of "rural-urban" conflict], Long's Louisiana), which, taken together, may be regarded as an indicator of "the main outlines of the pattern of national politics." Concludes with an essay on "The Future of the American Party System." Bibliographic notes, pp. 159-86.

494. GOSNELL, HAROLD FOOTE. *Machine Politics: Chicago Model*, foreword by William Fielding Ogburn. Chicago: University of Chicago, 1937. 249 pp.
Treatise based on many years of observation and experiment by a University of Chicago political scientist. Bibliography, pp. 214-19.

495. HERRING, E(DWARD) PENDLETON. *The Politics of Democracy: American Parties in Action.* New York: Norton, 1940. 468 pp.
Historical analysis of the American party system by Harvard political scientist. Bibliography, pp. 437-54.

496. "His Excellency's Loyal Opposition," *Fortune*, February 1937.
Republican Party.

497. ICKES, HAROLD LeCLAIR. "Who Killed the Progressive Party [1916]?" *American Historical Review*, 46: 306-37 (January 1941).

498. Kane, Harnett Thomas. *Louisiana Hayride: The American Rehearsal for Dictatorship, 1928-40.* New York: Morrow, 1941. 471 pp.

Detailed account of the career of Huey Long; by a young newspaper man who had a ringside seat for many of the more sensational incidents of the Long regime. Bibliography, pp. 457-58.

499. "The Kelly-Nash Political Machine," *Fortune*, 14: 47-52, 114-30 (August 1936).

One wing of the Democratic organization in Chicago. "Since the Kelly machine occupies a crucial position in a crucial state in this crucial year, it is perhaps the most instructive example to be found on the American horizon."

500. Ketchum, Carlton G. "Political Financing, 1937 Model," *Public Opinion Quarterly*, 2: 135-40 (January 1938).

Efforts of Republican Party to tap the lower-income groups. By head of Finance Division of Republican National Committee.

*501. Key, Valdimer Orlando, Jr. (D). *Politics, Parties and Pressure Groups.* New York: Crowell, 1942. 814 pp.

Textbook by Johns Hopkins political scientist. "All the customary data . . . are included, but there has been added an extensive treatment of pressure groups, as well as a discussion of violence, bribery and education as political techniques, matters not usually dealt with in the texts."—Preface. Chapter 19 undertakes to "summarize and synthesize the numerous quantitative studies of electoral behavior." Bibliographic footnotes.

502. Knoles, George Harmon. *The Presidential Campaign and Election of 1892* (Stanford University Publications. University Series. History, Economics, and Political Science. Vol. 5, no. 1). Stanford University: Stanford University, 1942. London: Oxford University, 1942. 268 pp.

Bibliography, pp. 248-52.

503. Laidler, Harry Wellington. *American Socialism: Its Aims and Practical Program*, 2nd ed. New York: Harpers, 1937. 330 pp.

Dr. Laidler (Ph.D. Columbia) is a U.S. Socialist publicist, executive secretary of League for Industrial Democracy. Bibliography, pp. 300-05.

504. Laidler, Harry Wellington. *Toward a Farmer-Labor Party.* New York: League for Industrial Democracy, 1938. 55 pp.

505. "The Landon Boom," *Fortune*, 13: 76-79 (March 1936).

506. Lawrence, David. *Who Were the Eleven Million?* New York: Appleton-Century, 1937. 79 pp.

Political journalist analyzes President F. D. Roosevelt's popular majority of 11,000,000 in the 1936 election, and outlines a plan for defeating him through a campaign directed toward 7,000,000 independent voters who favored Roosevelt. The sole slogan suggested for this campaign is "preservation of the independence of the judicial and legislative departments of the Government." Mr. Lawrence does not allude to possible material change in employment, social security, control of monopolism, or the allocation of income.

507. Litchfield, Edward H. "A Case Study of Negro Political Behavior in Detroit," *Public Opinion Quarterly*, 5: 267-74 (June 1941).

U.S. political scientist analyzes three aspects of Negro political behavior: voting participation, major party affiliation, and third party voting.

508. Logan, Edward Bates, editor. *The American Political Scene.* New York: Harpers, 1936. 264 pp.

By six political scientists. *Contents*: "Present Day Characteristics of American Political Parties," by Arthur Norman Holcombe; "Party Organization in the United States," by Edward B. Logan; "The Politician and the Voter," by John Thomas Salter; "Presidential Campaigns," by Harold Rozelle Bruce; "The Use of Money in Elections," by James Kerr Pollock; "Pressure Groups and Propaganda," by Harwood Lawrence Childs.

509. McHenry, Dean Eugene. *His Majesty's Opposition: Structure and Problems of the British Labour Party,*

1931-1938. Berkeley: University of California, 1941. 320 pp.

By U.S. political scientist. Bibliography at ends of chapters.

510. McKean, Dayton David. *The Boss: The [Frank] Hague Machine in Action.* Boston: Houghton Mifflin, 1940. 285 pp.

Private and public life and opinions of a well-known Democratic Party boss. By U.S. political scientist.

511. Mader, Joseph H. "The North Dakota Press and the Non-Partisan League," *Journalism Quarterly,* 14: 321-32 (December 1937).

512. Merriam, Charles Edward; and Gosnell, Harold Foote. *The American Party System,* 3rd ed. New York: Macmillan, 1940. 476 pp.

Standard text by two U.S. political scientists. Bibliographic footnotes.

*512a. Michels, Roberto. *Political Parties: A Study of the Oligarchical Tendencies of Modern Democracy,* translated by Eden and Cedar Paul. New York: Hearst's International Library Company, 1915. 416 pp.

German-Swiss-Italian political scientist's influential analysis of oligarchical tendencies of political parties. German edition: *Zur Soziologie des Parteiwesens in der modernen Demokratie: Untersuchungen über die oligarchischen Tendenzen des Gruppenlebens,* 2nd ed. Leipzig: A Kröner, 1925. 528 pp. See also his treatise on patriotism: *Der Patriotismus: Prolegomena zu seiner soziologischen Analyse* (Munich and Leipzig: Duncker und Humblot, 1929. 269 pp.).

513. "Mr. Roosevelt's Party," *Fortune,* June 1938.

Democratic Party.

514. National Socialist Party of Germany. *Organisationsbuch der NSDAP.* Munich: Eher, at intervals. About 550 pp.

515. National Socialist Party of Germany. *Party Yearbooks,* issued annually on Parteitage (party convention days), contain speeches, annual reports, statistics.

*516. Odegard, Peter H. (D,W); and Helms, E. Allen (D). *American Politics: A Study in Political Dynamics.* New York and London: Harpers, 1938. 882 pp.

Two U.S. political science professors produce a textbook on political parties with much more emphasis upon attitudes than their predecessors. Students of propaganda will be especially interested in chapters 17 and 18 on "The Engineering of Consent." Bibliographic footnotes.

*516a. Ostrogorsky, Moisei Yakovlevitch (ESS). *Democracy and the Organization of Political Parties,* translated from the French by Frederick Clarke, preface by James Bryce. New York: Macmillan, 1902. 2 vols.

Russian political scientist's quasi-realistic analysis of modification of legal institutions by extralegal and informal means, such as propaganda, bribery and violence.

517. Overacker, Louise. "Campaign Funds in the Presidential Election of 1936," *American Political Science Review,* 31: 473-98 (June 1937).

By a political scientist who is the author of a treatise on *Money in Elections* (1928) and of "Campaign Funds in a Depression Year," *American Political Science Review,* 27: 776-8 (October 1933). Gives details of receipts and expenditures of Democratic and Republican party and nonparty organizations, with analysis of the economic interests represented and lists of individuals and families who made large contributions.

518. Overacker, Louise. "Labor's Political Contributions," *Political Science Quarterly,* 54: 56-68 (March 1939).

By Wellesley political scientist who specializes in analyzing campaign funds.

*518a. Overacker, Louise. *Money in Elections,* largely from material collected by Victor J. West. New York: Macmillan, 1932. 476 pp.

U.S. political scientist presents data on the use of money in elections in U.S. and abroad.

Discusses disclosure of campaign expenditures as a possible means of social control. Bibliography, pp. 419-59.

519. PEEL, ROY VICTOR; and DONNELLY, THOMAS CLAUDE. *The 1932 Campaign: An Analysis.* New York: Farrar and Rinehart, 1935. 250 pp.

These two U.S. political scientists are already well known for *The 1928 Campaign* (New York: R. R. Smith, 1931. 183 pp.).

520. PEEL, ROY VICTOR; with SNOWDEN, GEORGE. "From Four Years of Politics the Candidates Emerge," *Public Opinion Quarterly*, 4: 451-64 (September 1940).

Preconvention campaigns in U.S., 1936-40, described by two U.S. political scientists.

521. "Political Campaign Funds," *Fortune* (July 1940).

It takes about $25,000,000 to elect a U.S. President. Article, based on work of political scientists, tells where the money comes from and how it is spent.

522. *Politics and Political Parties in Roumania.* London: International Reference Library Publishing Company, 1936. 560 pp.

Reference work, including statements on history and platforms of parties; on the election laws; and on foreign policy. Pp. 349-85 contain material on the political press. Pp. 385-557 contain a *Who's Who* of Rumanian political figures, including the royal family.

523. POLLOCK, JAMES KERR. "The British Party Conference," *American Political Science Review*, 32: 525-36 (June 1938).

"That the task of developing party machinery for adequate discussion of public questions is not an impossible one is demonstrated by British party experience. Since the World War, and even before, British parties have held regular annual conferences in which delegates and Government ministers discuss the important issues of the day . . . and pass resolutions; [but] they do not nominate candidates for public office."

524. POLLOCK, JAMES KERR. "Campaign Funds and their Regulation in

1936," *American Political Science Review*, 30: 507-12 (June 1936).

525. POPOV, NIKOLAI NIKOLAEVITCH. *Outline History of the Communist Party of the Soviet Union.* New York: International Publishers, 1935. 2 vols.

Translation of the sixteenth edition of a standard Russian history of the party. Bibliographic notes, pp. 439-60.

526. "The Republican Party, Up From the Grave," *Fortune* (August 1939).

527. SAIT, EDWARD MCCHESNEY. *American Parties and Elections*, rev. ed. New York: Appleton-Century, 1939. 790 pp.

Standard treatise by Pomona College political scientist.

528. SCHATTSCHNEIDER, ELMER ERIC. *Party Government.* New York: Farrar and Rinehart, 1942. 219 pp.

By U.S. political scientist. Bibliography, pp. 211-14.

529. SCHMECKEBIER, LAURENCE FREDERICK. *Congressional Apportionment.* Washington, D.C.: Brookings Institution, 1941. 233 pp.

History of traditional methods, with description and discussion of "the five modern workable methods," compiled in anticipation of the 1941 reapportionment by a Brookings Institution scholar. Bibliographic footnotes.

530. SHANNON, JASPER BERRY. "Presidential Politics in the South: 1938, I, II," *Journal of Politics*, 1: 129-45, 278-300 (May, August 1939).

531. SINCLAIR, THORNTON. "The Nazi Party Rally at Nuremberg," *Public Opinion Quarterly*, 2: 570-83 (October 1938).

By U.S. political scientist who has observed Nazi technique in Germany over a period of years.

532. SIX, FRANZ ALFRED. *Die politische Propaganda der NSDAP im*

Kampf um die Macht (inaugural dissertation, Heidelberg). H e i d e l b e r g : Winter, 1936. 76 pp.

"Political Propaganda of National Socialist Party in the Struggle for Power." Bibliography, pp. 73-74.

533. STADERMAN, RICHARD A. "How a Research Bureau Works for the Democratic Party," *Public Opinion Quarterly,* 1 no. 4: 107-08 (October 1937).

Discussion of Democratic National Research League by its president. The League furnishes "quotations, arguments, anecdotes, statistics, 'literature,' and ideas on campaign tactics and strategy, at the request of [Democratic] candidates for the U.S. Senate, House of Representatives, State Legislatures, and local offices."

534. STARR, JOSEPH RANKIN. "Labor and Farmer Groups and the Three-Party System," *Southwestern Social Science Quarterly,* 17: 6-19 (June 1936).

Movements and attitudes, mainly during 1935. By U.S. political scientist.

535. (Pop.) STARR, JOSEPH RANKIN. "Political Parties and Public Opinion," *Public Opinion Quarterly,* 3: 436-48 (July 1939).

Discusses potentialities of various methods of developing "a specialized adult education designed to help voters to comprehend matters of state." Takes the view that political parties might well develop agencies for research and popularization, as is done in England.

536. STARR, JOSEPH RANKIN. "Research Activities of British Political Parties," *Public Opinion Quarterly,* 1 no. 4: 99-107 (October 1937).

Use of social science by political parties. Based on research conducted in Great Britain.

537. (Pop.) STARR, JOSEPH RANKIN. "The Summer Schools and Other Educational Activities of the British Liberal Party," *American Political Science Review,* 31: 703-20 (August 1937).

538. (Pop.) STARR, JOSEPH RANKIN. "The Summer Schools and Other Educational Activities of British Socialist Groups," *American Political Science Review,* 30: 956-74 (October 1936).

Training of propagandists for the Socialist movement, introduced by the Fabian Society and adapted by other groups.

539. STEIN, GUENTHER. "Social Unrest in Japan: The Social Mass Party," *Asia,* 37: 606-09 (September 1937).

540. STEVENSON, JOHN REESE. *The Chilean Popular Front,* foreword by Dana Gardner Munro. Philadelphia: University of Pennsylvania, 1942. London: Oxford University, 1942. 155 pp.

Based on observation, and interviews with many leaders, in Chile. Bibliography, pp. 148-55.

541. STOKE, HAROLD WALTER. "Propaganda Activities of British Political Parties," *American Political Science Review,* 30: 121-25 (February 1936).

542. STRAUSS, PATRICIA. *Bevin and Co.: The Leaders of British Labour.* New York: Putnam's Sons, 1941. 246 pp.

Account of the activities of top Labour Party officials in Britain's war effort.

543. THOMSON, CHARLES A. H. "Research and the Republican Party," *Public Opinion Quarterly,* 3: 306-13 (April 1939).

Mr. Thomson was on the staff of the Research Division of the Republican National Committee, May-September 1938.

544. THYSSEN, FRITZ. *I Paid Hitler.* New York: Farrar and Rinehart, 1941. 320 pp.

By German Catholic capitalist who contributed to Nazi party campaign funds because he believed that they were the people who could save his country from Bolshevism.

545. U.S. CIVIL SERVICE COMMISSION. *Political Activity and Political*

Assessments of Federal Office-holders and Employees. Washington, D.C.: Government Printing Office, 1943. 28 pp.

Regulations drawn up by Commission under Corrupt Practices Acts.

546. U.S. Senate. Special Committee to Investigate Expenditures of Presidential, Vice-Presidential, and Senatorial Candidates in 1936. *Investigation of Campaign Expenditures in 1936: Report* (75th Congress, 1st session, Senate Report 151). Washington, D.C.: Government Printing Office, March 4, 1937. 139 pp.

The "Lonergan report."

547. Walsh, William J. "How to Use a Speakers Bureau in a Political Campaign," *Public Opinion Quarterly,* 3: 92-106 (January 1939).

"Taylorism" applied to propaganda organization. By a Democratic Party political organizer in New York.

548. Wengert, E. S. "TVA Enlists Local Cooperation," *Public Opinion Quarterly,* 1 no. 2: 97-101 (April 1937).

Public relations of Tennessee Valley Authority, described by U.S. political scientist.

549. Zink, Harold. "A Case Study of a Political Boss," *Psychiatry,* 1: 527-33 (November 1938).

Psychiatric study of David Curtis Stephenson, political boss of Indiana during the years 1922-25. "Besides heading the most powerful political machine ever organized in Indiana, he had charge of the Ku Klux Klan in seventeen states of the Middle West." Dr. Zink is Professor of Political Science, DePauw.

C. FUNCTIONAL GROUPS: ADVERTISING AND OTHER BUSINESS GROUPS, FARMERS' GROUPS, ORGANIZED LABOR AND PROFESSIONALS, RELIGIOUS GROUPS, WOMEN'S GROUPS, YOUTH GROUPS, ETC.

I. GENERAL

550. *Directory of International Organizations in the Field of Public Administration,* Chicago: Public Administration Service, at intervals, 1936–.

Covers 200 or more organizations; information concerning membership, finances, secretariat, activities, library, publications, and affiliations.

551. Ewing, Cortez A. M. "Lobbying in Nebraska's Legislature," *Public Opinion Quarterly,* 1 no. 3: 102-04 (July 1937).

In Nebraska's unicameral legislature, 43 seats on the floor are reserved for legislators, 60 for lobbyists. University of Oklahoma political scientist discusses possible effects of this.

551a. Harvey, Ray Forrest, editor. *The Politics of This War.* New York: Harpers, 1943. 328 pp.

Political aspects of World War II are discussed by U.S. journalists under editorship of New York University political scientist. Harold M. Fleming, Wall Street correspondent of *Christian Science Monitor,* writes on "The Politics of Profits"; Ralph Hendershot, financial editor of New York *World-Telegram,* on "The Politics of Big Business"; William J. Enright, assistant business editor of New York *Times,* on "The Politics of Small Business"; Wesley McCune, of *Newsweek's* Washington Bureau, on labor; Alfred D. Stedman, editorial board member of *United States News* and former assistant administrator (1933-39) of AAA, on farmers' groups. Dr. Harvey writes on "The Politics of the Armed Forces," and synthesizes the findings of the book in a concluding chapter.

552. Heckscher, Gunnar. "Group Organization in Sweden," *Public Opinion Quarterly,* 3: 130-35 (January 1939).

Swedish economist discusses farmer, labor and cooperative pressure groups.

553. HERRING, E(DWARD) PEND-LETON. *Public Administration and the Public Interest.* New York and London: McGraw-Hill, 1936. 416 pp.

First-hand studies of relations between special-interest agencies and administrative bodies by a Harvard professor of government. Especial attention is given to trade associations. There are chapters on each of the leading Federal commissions and on interest-representation for consumers, farmers, laborers, businessmen, and scientists. Pp. 362-77 are on "Publicizing Administrative Activities." Bibliographic footnotes.

554. McKEAN, DAYTON DAVID. *Pressures on the Legislature of New Jersey* (Studies in History, Economics, and Public Law, no. 440). New York: Columbia University, 1938. 251 pp.

Study of pressure groups by a political scientist and public administrator who was a member of the New Jersey Assembly, 1934-35. He detected 164 active groups, of which he selected 7 for detailed analysis. Conclusion: "techniques have changed somewhat with improvements in facilities for communication. There are still traces of corrupt practices, but the lobby of the last generation is gone, and with it most of the social lobby. Today, groups are coming more and more to understand and to use as a basis for all their other work, the techniques of propaganda perfected at the time of the World War."

555. McKINNEY, MADGE MAUDE. "Constitutional Amendment in New York State," *Public Opinion Quarterly*, 3: 635-45 (October 1939).

Influence of church, labor and rural groups in New York political campaigns, described by a Hunter College political scientist.

556. MARSHALL, C. B. "Organized Groups," *Public Opinion Quarterly*, 4: 151-61 (March 1940).

Reports on the legislative programs of major organized peace, farm, labor and women's groups, and of American Legion, in current session of Congress. By a Harvard student of political science.

557. MILLER, CLYDE RAYMOND. "For the Analysis of Propaganda," *Public Opinion Quarterly*, 2: 133-34 (January 1938).

Formation of Institute for Propaganda Analysis is announced by its secretary. Includes list of officers.

557a. *Public Administration Organizations: A Directory of Unofficial Organizations in the Field of Public Administration in the United States and Canada, 1932–.* Chicago: Public Administration Clearing House, 1932–.

A standard compilation issued annually. Gives the addresses of about 2000 associations and the names of directors, and—for each of about 560 *national* organizations—data on membership, finances, secretariat, activities, affiliations, and publications.

558. U.S. DEPARTMENT OF COMMERCE. BUREAU OF FOREIGN AND DOMESTIC COMMERCE. *Trade and Professional Associations of the United States.* Washington, D.C.: Government Printing Office, 1942. 324 pp.

Names, addresses, leaders, size of staff, size of membership, year of establishment and main activities of over 3000 organizations with a gross membership of 40,000,000 persons: 1100 associations of manufacturers; 560 of finance, service, transportation; 540 of agriculture, labor, consumer, military, foreign trade; 500 professional men and women; 400 wholesale and retail. National and regional associations in 300 cities are cited. Contains section on federal agencies serving associations. Bibliography, pp. 299-305.

559. WHITEMAN, LUTHER; and LEWIS, SAMUEL L. *Glory Roads: The Psychological State of California.* New York: Crowell, 1936. 267 pp.

California's experiences with recent crusades: Technocracy; the Utopian Society; Townsend's Old Age Revolving Pensions; Rochedale Co-operatives; Tradex; Upton Sinclair's EPIC. Leadership, programs, techniques, and membership are analyzed, with considerable documentation. Mr. Whiteman is a founder and Secretary of the Social Credit Association. Mr. Lewis has been associated with the Progressive Movement and the Townsend campaign.

560. ZELLER, BELLE. *Pressure Politics in New York: A Study of Group Representation before the Legislature.*

New York: Prentice-Hall, 1937. 310 pp.

Chapters 8 and 9 summarize pressure techniques and estimate their effectiveness. The author is Assistant Professor of Government, Brooklyn College, New York. Extensive bibliographic footnotes.

II. ADVERTISING AND OTHER BUSINESS GROUPS

561. *Advertising and Publishing Production Yearbook: The Reference Manual of the Graphic Arts.* New York: Colton Press, 1934–.

A compilation of information for those engaged in advertising production.

562. AGNEW, HUGH ELMER. *Outdoor Advertising.* New York: McGraw-Hill, 1938. 310 pp.

By a New York University professor of marketing.

563. AGNEW, HUGH ELMER; and DYGERT, WARREN B. *Advertising Media.* New York: McGraw-Hill, 1938. 465 pp.

By two New York University professors of marketing.

564. AINSWORTH, GARDNER. "The New York Fair: Adventure in Promotion," *Public Opinion Quarterly*, 3: 694-704 (October 1939).

By a Princeton senior.

565. AMERICAN BANKERS ASSOCIATION. RESEARCH COUNCIL. *Public Relations for Banks.* New York, 1937. 4 parts.

Study No. 1: "Banking and Public Opinion"; Study No. 2: "How Some Banks Have Dealt With Their Public Relations Problems"; Study No. 3: "News About Your Bank"; Study No. 4: "What Your Community Thinks About Its Banks."

566. APPEL, JOSEPH HERBERT. *Growing Up With Advertising.* New York: Business Bourse, 80 West Fortieth Street, 1940. 301 pp.

History and analysis of U.S. advertising practice, based on the author's career in department store advertising, 1899-1936. For a quarter of a century Mr. Appel was also a leader in the truth-in-advertising movement.

567. BALDWIN, WILLIAM H. "Pressure Politics and Consumer Interests: The Sugar Issue," *Public Opinion Quarterly*, 5: 102-10 (March 1941).

Mr. Baldwin has worked in the interest of, among others, the American Bottlers of Carbonated Beverages and the Hershey Corporation, an American company producing and refining cane sugar in Cuba. He has been a member of the Cuban Committee of the National Foreign Trade Council.

568. BALDWIN, WILLIAM H.; and BEACH, BREWSTER S. "McKesson & Robbins: A Study in Confidence," *Public Opinion Quarterly*, 4: 305-10 (June 1940).

Public relations counsels describe their handling of the sensational bankruptcy of a large corporation.

569. BATCHELOR, BRONSON. *Profitable Public Relations.* New York and London: Harpers, 1938. 252 pp.

A general text, written from a businessman's point of view.

570. BAUS, HERBERT M. *Publicity: How to Plan, Produce and Place It.* New York: Harpers, 1942. 252 pp.

By Publicity Director of Los Angeles Chamber of Commerce, a Lecturer in Publicity, University of Southern California.

571. BEDELL, CLYDE. *How to Write Advertising That Sells.* New York: McGraw-Hill, 1940. 524 pp.

Text by Lecturer, Northwestern University School of Commerce, who has been advertising manager of a number of large firms.

572. BELDEN, CLARK. "Community Relations of 263 Manufacturers," *Public Opinion Quarterly*, 2: 665-71 (October 1938).

Public relations campaigns of New England Council (manufacturers' association) are described by Executive Secretary of New England Gas Association.

573. BELDEN, CLARK. "What We Are Doing About Public Relations,"

New England Gas News (July 1937), pp. 24-34.

Numerous practical suggestions by the Executive Secretary of the New England Gas Association. His paper entitled "Research in Public Relations," in *New England Gas News* for June 1936, furnishes a check list of 46 specific public relations ideas for utilities.

574. BERNAYS, EDWARD L. "Recent Trends in Public Relations Activities [of large corporations and trade associations]," *Public Opinion Quarterly*, 1 no. 1: 147-51 (January 1937).

By a U.S. public relations counsel.

575. BERTHAULT, ANNE. *La publicité des sociétés de commerce avant et après le décret du 30 octobre* 1935 (thesis, University of Paris). Paris: Les Presses modernes, 1936. 126 pp.

Public relations of French trade associations under the Popular Front government.

576. BIGELOW, BURTON. "Should Business Decentralize Its Counter-Propaganda?" *Public Opinion Quarterly*, 2: 321-24 (April 1938).

Mr. Bigelow was head of the literature-distribution division of the Republican National Committee in 1936.

577. BLUMENTHAL, FRANK H. "Anti-Union Publicity in the Johnstown 'Little Steel' Strike of 1937," *Public Opinion Quarterly*, 3: 676-82 (October 1939).

By a Princeton graduate student in political science.

*578. BORDEN, NEIL HOPPER. *The Economic Effects of Advertising*. Chicago: Richard D. Irwin, 1942. 988 pp.

Treatise by Professor of Advertising, Harvard Graduate School of Business Administration. Bibliographic footnotes.

579. BORDEN, NEIL HOPPER. *Problems in Advertising*, 3rd ed. New York: McGraw-Hill, 1937. 698 pp.

Presentation of a wide variety of advertising problems and cases gathered by the Harvard Business School with the assistance of a group of advertising agencies and publishers. Bibliography, pp. 677-92.

580. BRATTER, HERBERT MAX. "Committee for the Nation: A Case History in Monetary Propaganda," *Journal of Political Economy*, 49: 531-53 (August 1941).

Scholarly study of propaganda for monetary change, issued 1932-35 by a group of nationally prominent businessmen who were alleged by Secretary of Agriculture Wallace and Secretary of the Treasury Morgenthau to be speculators. "Paid secretary of the committee and public relations expert was Dr. Edward A. Rumely, a former physician and newspaperman," who has subsequently served as public relations counsel for other enterprises, including the National Committee to Uphold Constitutional Government.

581. BREWSTER, ARTHUR JUDSON; and PALMER, HERBERT HALL. *Introduction to Advertising*, 4th ed. rev. New York: McGraw-Hill, 1941. 524 pp.

Standard text by two professors of business, Syracuse University.

582. BRISCO, NORRIS ARTHUR. *Telephone Selling*. New York: Prentice-Hall, 1940. 351 pp.

Discussion of this type of salesmanship, by Dean, School of Retailing, New York University.

582a. BURNETT, VERNE EDWIN. *You and Your Public: A Guide Book to the New Career—Public Relations*. New York: Harpers, 1943. 194 pp.

By vice-president in charge of public relations, General Foods, Inc. Completely nontechnical.

583. BURTT, HAROLD ERNEST. *Psychology of Advertising*. Boston: Houghton Mifflin, 1938. 473 pp.

Heavily documented college text, by Ohio State University psychologist. "Supplements two of the author's previous works, *Principles of Employment Psychology* and *Psychology and Industrial Efficiency*, in rounding out the field of business psychology."—Preface. Bibliographic footnotes.

584. CAPLES, JOHN. *Advertising for Immediate Sales*. New York: Harpers, 1936. 281 pp.

585. CLARK, SAMUEL DELBERT. *The Canadian Manufacturers' Association: A Study in Collective Bargaining and Political Pressure* (Toronto University History and Economics series, vol. 7). Toronto: University of Toronto, 1939. 107 pp.

586. COLE, REMSEN J. "A Survey of Employee Attitudes," *Public Opinion Quarterly*, 4: 497-506 (September 1940).

Mr. Cole, a Philadelphia public relations counsel, conducted an elaborate poll of the attitudes of Philadelphia workers toward their jobs, their employers, and company policies. He shows how such surveys may be made the basis for an employee relations program.

587. CRAWFORD, HENRY PAINE. "New Status of Chambers of Commerce in Mexico," *George Washington Law Review*, 10: 261-71 (January 1942).

"Whether Mexico proposes to nationalize its commerce and industry is a question which suggests itself automatically after reading the text of the newly enacted Law of Chambers of Commerce and Industry," says specialist in Latin American law, U.S. Department of Commerce. Membership in quasi-official chambers of commerce is compulsory for "all taxpayers who derive their incomes from commerce and industry."

588. CRIPPEN, JOHN K. *Successful Direct Mail Methods*. New York: McGraw-Hill, 1936. 336 pp.

589. DAHL, JOSEPH OLIVER. *Advertising and Promotion for Hotels and Restaurants: A Reference Book for Hotel and Restaurant Executives, Sales Managers, Advertising and Publicity Directors, etc.* Stamford, Connecticut: The Dahls, 1939. 242 pp.

By a prolific writer on hotel and restaurant management and advertising. Bibliography, pp. 232-34.

590. DALTON, JOHN EDWARD. *Sugar: A Case Study of Government Control*. New York: Macmillan, 1937. 311 pp.

Analyzes activities of the sugar bloc in the United States Congress, which has successfully promoted a Federal control system that adds to tariff protection a system of guaranteed profits for beet and cane growers, at a cost to American consumers of about $2 per person per year. The author is ex-chief of the Sugar Section of the Agricultural Adjustment Administration, and is on the faculty of the Harvard Graduate School of Business Administration. Bibliographic footnotes.

591. DANIELIAN, NOOBAR RETHEOS. *A. T. and T.: The Story of Industrial Conquest*. New York: Vanguard, 1939. 460 pp.

Public relations of American Telephone and Telegraph Company are dealt with in chapters 12, 13, and 14 of this comprehensive survey of the corporation by a New Deal economist. The exhaustively documented data are based on Federal Communications Commission's "Telephone Investigation." Bibliography, pp. 423-43.

592. DAUGHTERS, CHARLES G. *Wells of Discontent: A Study of the Economic, Social, and Political Aspects of the Chain Store*, with an introduction by Representatives Wright Patman, John F. Dockweiler, and Gerald J. Boileau, members of the Congressional Committee of Investigation of Trade Practices of Big-Scale Buying and Selling. New York and Chicago: Published by Charles G. Daughters and distributed by Newson and Company, 1937. 370 pp.

A study by a U.S. lobbyist for small business, based on the Congressional investigations which led to the Robinson-Patman Act. Chapters 2 and 3, respectively, are entitled "Chain Store Propaganda Methods," and "Chain Store Lobbying Practices." Chapter 13, "The Decline of the Middle Classes," analyzes the U.S. political scene as a whole in terms of a theory of middle-class politics. This volume may be supplemented by reference to HOUSE OF REPRESENTATIVES SELECT COMMITTEE TO INVESTIGATE THE AMERICAN RETAIL FEDERATION. *Investigation of the Trade Practices of Big-Scale Retail and Wholesale Buying and Selling Organizations*, hearings June 5, 1935-March 17, 1936 (74th Congress, 1st session). Washington, D.C.: Government Printing Office, 1936. 4 vols.

593. DAVIS, RALPH CURRIER. *Industrial Organization and Management.* New York: Harpers, 1940. 660 pp.

Standard treatise on management practices. Chapters 23-28 deal with personnel management, including procurement, supervision, morale, employee education, and objectified personnel research. By Professor of Business Organization, Ohio State University. Bibliography, pp. 623-26.

594. DUFFY, BEN. *Advertising Media and Markets.* New York: Prentice-Hall, 1939. 437 pp.

595. DUTTON, WILLIAM SHERMAN. *Du Pont: One Hundred and Forty Years.* New York: Scribner's, 1942. 396 pp.

A history of the Du Pont industries. "More than fifty executives of the company, including members of the Du Pont family, have contributed in the form of suggestions. The result is the Du Pont Company as seen by Du Pont men."—Preface. Bibliography in text. May be supplemented with *The Du Pont Dynasty* (New York, 1935) by John K. Winkler, U.S. journalist.

596. EDWARDS, GURDEN. "Banking and Public Opinion," *Public Opinion Quarterly*, 1 no. 2: 5-26 (April 1937).

By director of public relations, American Bankers Association.

597. ELIASBERG, WLADIMIR. *Reklamewissenschaften: Ein Lehrbuch auf soziologischer, volkswirtschaftlicher und psychologischer Grundlage.* Vienna: Rohrer, 1936.

Scientific advertising, its sociological, economic, and psychological foundations. By Viennese psychologist.

598. FINE, BENJAMIN. "New York Course on Public Relations," *Public Opinion Quarterly*, 5: 111-13 (March 1941).

Meetings of American Council on Public Relations are described by New York *Times* specialist on education.

599. GARCEAU, OLIVER. "Can Little Business Organize?" *Public Opinion Quarterly*, 2: 469-73 (July 1938).

By Harvard instructor in government.

600. "General Motors," series of four articles in *Fortune*, December 1938 through March 1939.

Includes extensive treatment of public relations activities carried on through the Customer Research and other divisions as well as through the Public Relations office.

601. GIBSON, W. B., compiler. *The Annual Report: A Study of Over 500 Reports of Leading American Business Institutions, Showing the Present Style Trend and Important Physical Characteristics.* New York: Marketing Research Division, Mead Sales Co., 1939. 33 pp.

Careful study by market research experts of a paper manufacturer. Contains bibliography.

602. GOODE, KENNETH MACKARNESS. *Advertising.* New York: Greenberg, 1941. 497 pp.

"Published originally under the title, 'Manual of Modern Advertising'. . . . Revised and reissued in 1937 under the title, 'Modern Advertising.' The present enlarged and completely revised edition, under its new title (the book's seventh printing), was issued in 1941."

603. GOODE, KENNETH MACKARNESS; and KAUFMAN, MAX ZENN. *Showmanship in Business.* New York and London: Harpers, 1936. 218 pp.

Salesmanship and advertising.

604. GOTT, PHILIP P. "Trade Promotion by Trade Associations," *Public Opinion Quarterly*, 1 no. 1: 126-30 (January 1937).

By a staff member of Chamber of Commerce of the U.S.

605. GREEN, THOMAS S., JR. "Mr. [William John] Cameron and the Ford Hour," *Public Opinion Quarterly*, 3: 669-75 (October 1939).

Symbols used by a big business, analyzed by a staff member of Council of State Governments.

606. GRISWOLD, GLENN. "Humanized Employee Relations: Studebaker an Example," *Public Opinion Quarterly*, 4: 487-96 (September 1940).

Public relations counsel for the Studebaker Corporation describes an example of "humanized" employee relations.

607. GRISWOLD, GLENN. "The McGraw-Hill Public Relations Forums," *Public Opinion Quarterly*, 3: 704-09 (October 1939).

The author organized and directed this series of businessmen's forums on problems of public relations.

608. HAASE, ALBERT E. "First Agency Census: Important Government Report Shows that 44% of Advertising Billings Originate in 15 Companies," *Printers' Ink*, April 1, 1937, pp. 32 ff.

Monopolistic tendencies in advertising are shown in this analysis of the first Federal census of the advertising agency business, covering operations for the year 1935.

609. HALL, ROBERT C. "Representation of Big Business in the House of Commons," *Public Opinion Quarterly*, 2: 473-77 (July 1938).

By a U.S. student of economics (A.B. Harvard; Dip. Ec. Oxon.). "As of January 1, 1937, almost all of the important national business associations were represented in the present House of Commons by an officer, a director, or a leading member of the association. . . . In the present House, 761 companies were represented by 806 directors. Of course in many instances one man may be a director of a number of companies. . . . Thus 109 Members of Parliament are directors of two or more corporations, while 16 of their number hold a total of 282 directorships and 72 chairmanships. . . . In Britain, economic legislation is introduced, debated and enacted by leaders in the business world. . . ."

610. HARLOW, REX FRANCIS. "The American Council on Public Relations," *Public Opinion Quarterly*, 4: 324-26 (June 1940).

By Stanford University Lecturer in Education and Political Science, president of this nonprofit corporation carrying on instruction and research in public relations. Mimeographed transactions of the Council are available.

611. HARLOW, REX FRANCIS. *Public Relations in War and Peace*. New York: Harpers, 1942. 220 pp.

612. HARTWELL, DICKSON. "Current Problems in Public Relations," *Public Opinion Quarterly*, 6: 236-47 (Summer 1942).

"An experiment designed to provide readers with practical, helpful information on public relations techniques and procedures. To secure material for the article the *Quarterly* invited a group of public relations executives to discuss two current . . . public relations problems. . . . Mr. Hartwell (a public relations counsel) prepared statements of the problems, directed the discussion, and summarizes herewith some of the observations of the members of the group."

613. HARTWELL, DICKSON. "Telling the Employees," *Public Opinion Quarterly*, 5: 93-101 (March 1941).

Public relations counsel discusses opportunities for management to build employee good will and reduce costly ignorance by telling workers about business affairs. Cites reporting practices of many large firms.

614. HEPNER, HARRY WALKER. *Effective Advertising*. New York: McGraw-Hill, 1941. 584 pp.

"Text for the first-year course in advertising. The author, who is associate professor of psychology at the College of Business Administration, Syracuse University, has selected those subjects which are readily teachable. . . . Professor Hepner has developed an interesting *Teacher's Manual* to accompany the textbook. In addition he has made available a series of teaching film strips with instructions for use in an inexpensive projector for visualization of subjects outlined in his text. There is a *Student's Workbook* for instructors. . . ."—Howard T. Hovde, in *Annals*, November 1941, p. 235.

615. HERON, ALEXANDER R. *Sharing Information with Employees*. Stanford: Stanford University, 1942. 204 pp.

A nontechnical discussion of how to get the desired information to the employee and establish understanding, by a U.S. industrial relations manager.

616. HEYEL, CARL. *Human-Relations Manual for Executives*. New York: McGraw-Hill, 1939. 253 pp.

Practical suggestions by Manager, Conference Planning Division, American Management Association. *Contents*: I. Getting Along with People. II. Developing the Working Force. III. Developing First-line Supervision. IV. Stimulating Best Performance. V. Making Work Easier. VI. Making Work Safer. VII. Paying People. VIII. Dismissing People. IX. Improving Management-employee Understanding. Bibliography in text.

616a. HOTCHKISS, GEORGE BURTON. *Advertising Copy* (rev. ed.). New York and London: Harpers, 1936. 432 pp.

617. HOTCHKISS, GEORGE BURTON. *An Outline of Advertising: Its Philosophy, Science, Art and Strategy*, rev. ed. New York: Macmillan, 1940. 631 pp.

Standard text. Bibliography at ends of chapters.

618. HOWARD, KENNETH S. *How to Write Advertisements* (McGraw-Hill Practical Business Manuals). New York: McGraw-Hill, 1937. 257 pp.

619. HOWER, RALPH MERLE. *The History of an Advertising Agency* (Harvard Studies in Business History, no. 5). Cambridge: Harvard University, 1939. 652 pp.

The seventy-year history (to 1930) of N. W. Ayer and Son, Philadelphia agency which ranks among the 5 or 10 largest in the U.S. By assistant professor in Harvard Graduate School of Business Administration. Bibliographic footnotes.

620. HUSE, ROBERT. "Regional Development and the New England Council," *Public Opinion Quarterly*, 2: 413-24 (July 1938).

For several years the author was a member of the staff of the Council, a regional trade association.

621. ILG, RAY A. *Public Relations for Banks*, foreword by Tom K. Smith. New York and London: Harpers, 1937. 235 pp.

622. KENNER, H. J. *The Fight for Truth in Advertising: A Story of What Business Has Done and Is Doing to Establish and Maintain Accuracy and Fair Play in Advertising and Selling for the Public's Protection.* New York: Round Table Press, 1936. 298 pp.

Account of Better Business Bureaus in the United States; sponsored by the Advertising Federation of America.

623. KLEPPNER, OTTO. *Advertising Procedure*, 3rd ed., rev. New York: Prentice-Hall, 1941. 705 pp.

Standard text, by head of a New York agency. Bibliography, pp. 610-21.

624. LARRABEE, CARROLL BURTON; and MARKS, HENRY WILLIAM. *Check Lists of Advertising, Selling, and Merchandising Essentials.* New York and London: McGraw-Hill, 1937. 396 pp.

Itemized reminders, compiled for the use of advertisers and merchandisers by two of the editors of Printers' Ink Publications. Pp. 377-93 offer suggestions for "Good Business Conventions."

625. LARRABEE, CARROLL BURTON; and MARKS, HENRY WILLIAM, editors. *Tested Selling Ideas from the Files of "Printers' Ink" and "Printers' Ink Monthly."* New York and London: McGraw-Hill, 1936. 368 pp.

626. LARSON, HENRIETTA MELIA. *Jay Cooke: Private Banker* (Harvard Studies in Business History). Cambridge: Harvard University, 1936. 512 pp.

Lays stress on Cooke's methods of marketing securities among the small investors by means of trained salesmen, "campaigns of education" in the press, and carefully cultivated relations with legislators. Bibliography, pp. 435-98.

627. LEBENSBURGER, MYRON M. *Selling Men's Apparel Through Advertising.* New York: McGraw-Hill, 1939. 310 pp.

628. LEIGHTON, GEORGE R. "Cassandra, Inc.," *New Yorker*, October 5, 1940, pp. 23-34.

"The Research Institute of America, a thriving business run by a young lawyer from the Bronx named Leo M. Cherne, and a young Bible salesman from Emporia, Kansas, named Carl Hovgard . . ." specializes in interpreting governmental policy to businessmen by means of news-letters, legal analyses, and books.

629. Lichtenberg, Bernard. "Business Backs the New York World Fair to Meet New Deal Propaganda," *Public Opinion Quarterly*, 2: 314-20 (April 1938).

By a U.S. public relations man.

630. Long, Norton E. "Public Relations Policies of the Bell System," *Public Opinion Quarterly*, 1 no. 4: 5-22 (October 1937).

By a Harvard instructor in government (Harvard A.B. '32, Ph.D. '37).

631. Madden, Clarence. *The Advertising of Hotels: An Inquiry and Some Suggestive Considerations Written for the Hotel Executive Who Needs Well-Founded Opinions About the Profit-Possibilities of Advertising in His Own Operation.* Chicago: *Hotel Monthly* Press, 1935. 136 pp.

632. *Market Research Sources, 1940: A Guide to Information on Domestic Marketing* (U.S. Bureau of Foreign and Domestic Commerce Series, no. 110). Washington, D.C.: Government Printing Office, 1940. 236 pp.

Supplement to a series published by this Bureau, 1926–.

632a. Mickelson, Siegfried. "Promotional Activities of the Northern Pacific's Land Department," *Journalism Quarterly*, 17: 324-34 (December 1940).

Advertising and promotional campaign by Northern Pacific Railway's Land Department, 1896-1902, aided in sale of more than 17,-000,000 acres.

633. *Modern Publicity: The Annual of "Art and Industry."* New York and London: The Studio Publications, 1924–.

Annual collection of commercial art.

634. Moore, Herbert. *Psychology for Business and Industry.* New York: McGraw-Hill, 1939. 527 pp.

Text by psychologist, Mount Holyoke College, dealing with job hunting, personnel problems, advertising and marketing. Bibliography at ends of chapters.

635. "Most Efficient, Glamorous Bank," *Fortune*, January 1941.

First National Bank in Palm Beach, Florida, an example of ingenious public relations policies.

636. Nathan, Theodore R. *Hotel Promotion.* New York: Harpers, 1941. 268 pp.

637. Nixon, H. K. *Principles of Selling*, 2nd ed., rev. New York: McGraw-Hill, 1942. 361 pp.

638. O'Leary, John W. "The 'What Helps Business' Campaign," *Public Opinion Quarterly*, 2: 645-50 (October 1938).

U.S. Chamber of Commerce publicity campaign described by chairman of the Chamber's executive committee.

639. Parry, Thomas W., Jr. "Public Relations for a Railroad," *Public Opinion Quarterly*, 3: 154-61 (January 1939).

Public relations counsel for a U.S. railway gives a case-history of his campaign on behalf of this client.

640. Pearce, Charles Albert. *Trade Association Survey* (Temporary National Economic Committee, Investigation of Concentration of Economic Power, Monograph no. 18). Washington, D.C.: Government Printing Office, 1941. 501 pp.

641. Powel, Harford. "What the War Has Done to Advertising," *Public Opinion Quarterly*, 6: 195-203 (Summer 1942).

The author is an advertising man with years of experience on prominent magazines and with a famous agency.

*641a. Presbrey, Frank Spencer. *The History and Development of Advertising.* Garden City: Doubleday, Doran, 1929. 642 pp.

History of advertising since ancient Babylon. Includes hundreds of illustrations. The author (1855-1936) was a U.S. journalist and editor, founder of the Frank Presbrey Company, a well-known advertising firm.

642. PRESCOTT, H. M. "Toward a More Pleasing Service," *Bell Telephone Quarterly*, 19: 87-96 (April 1940).

Suggestions for improving the public relations of the telephone company.

643. PRESTON, HAROLD P. *Successful Mail Selling.* New York: Ronald Press, 1941. 228 pp.

Manual for advertising men. Bibliography, pp. 222-24.

644. "Propaganda Purge," *Time*, July 10, 1939, p. 42.

Advertising Federation of America's campaign against a social studies text (*An Introduction to Problems of American Culture*) by Professor Harold Rugg of Teachers College, Columbia University.

645. RAMSAY, MARION LIVINGSTON. *Pyramids of Power: The Story of Roosevelt, Insull, and the Utility Wars.* Indianapolis: Bobbs-Merrill, 1937. 342 pp.

The author was a Washington correspondent for more than ten years, and later an official of the Rural Electrification Administration. Bibliography, pp. 319-26.

646. REDLICH, FRITZ. *Reklame: Begriff, Geschichte, Theorie.* Stuttgart: Enke, 1935. 272 pp.

An historical survey of advertising, drawing upon a wide range of literature. Bibliography, pp. 265-72.

647. REED, VERGIL DANIEL. *Advertising and Selling Industrial Goods.* New York: Ronald Press, 1936. 287 pp.

Bibliography, pp. 271-81.

648. REIS, BERNARD J. *False Security: The Betrayal of the American Investor*, introduction by John Thomas Flynn. New York: Equinox, 1937. 362 pp.

Inside stories of manipulated investment losses in the field of so-called "safe" investments over the past two decades. Based on

court cases and official reports. The author discusses SEC and other proposed remedies, and concludes that none will be effective except a "nationwide non-profit investors' organization." Bibliography, pp. 339-47.

649. RIDGEWAY, GEORGE L. *Merchants of Peace: Twenty Years of Business Diplomacy through the International Chamber of Commerce, 1919-1938.* New York: Columbia University, 1938. 419 pp.

By Associate Professor of History, Wells College. Bibliographic footnotes.

650. RUSSELL, OLAND D. *The House of Mitsui.* Boston: Little, Brown, 1939. 328 pp.

A dominant family in Japanese shipping, heavy industry, munitions, mining and banking. The author, a U.S. journalist, was formerly Tokyo correspondent of New York World.

651. SANDAGE, CHARLES HAROLD. *Advertising Theory and Practice*, rev. ed. Chicago: Business Publications, 1939. 747 pp.

Standard text. Bibliography at ends of chapters.

652. SCHATTSCHNEIDER, ELMER ERIC. *Politics, Pressures, and the Tariff: A Study of Free Private Enterprise in Pressure Politics, as Shown in the 1929-1930 Revision of the Tariff* (Ph.D. thesis, Columbia, 1935). New York: Prentice-Hall, 1935. 301 pp.

This study by a U.S. political scientist, based on the 20,000 pages of testimony on the Smoot-Hawley bill before the House and Senate committees during 1929 and 1930, is the first detailed treatment of tariff-making from the political angle.

653. SCROGGS, WILLIAM OSCAR. "The American and British Munitions Investigations," *Foreign Affairs*, 15: 320-29 (January 1937).

Congressional and Parliamentary investigations of munitions industry.

654. "Self-Evident Subtlety," *Time*, August 1, 1938, p. 22.

U.S. Senate Civil Liberties Committee's investigation of promotional activities conducted by American Iron and Steel Institute through a publicity firm and a lecturer "sponsored" by "neutral" groups.

655. SILVERBERG, LOUIS G. "Citizens' Committees: Their Role in Industrial Conflict," *Public Opinion Quarterly*, 5: 17-37 (March 1941).

By NLRB information officer.

656. STANLEY, THOMAS BLAINE. *The Technique of Advertising Production*. New York: Prentice-Hall. 214 pp.

A study of layout, planning, illustration, technical processes, etc., by New York University professor of marketing.

657. STEPHENSON, H. E.; and MC-NAUGHT, CARLTON. *The Story of Advertising in Canada: A Chronicle of Fifty Years*. Toronto: Ryerson, 1940. 364 pp.

By two veteran Canadian agencymen.

658. STRATTON, SAMUEL S. "Public Relations in Steel," *Public Opinion Quarterly*, 1 no. 2: 107-11 (April 1937).

Activities of American Iron and Steel Institute.

659. STRONG, EDWARD KELLOGG, JR. *Psychological Aspects of Business*. New York: McGraw-Hill, 1938. 629 pp.

Chapters on rating-scales, measurement of attitudes, employer-employee relations, etc., have been added to this revision of *The Psychology of Selling and Advertising* (1925), by psychology professor, Graduate School of Business, Stanford. Bibliographic footnotes.

660. "Technical Publicity Association Marks 35th Anniversary: Oldest Organized Group of Industrial Advertising and Marketing Men Celebrates with All-Day Seminar," *Industrial Marketing*, June 1940, pp. 23-32.

661. U.S. BUREAU OF THE CENSUS. CENSUS OF BUSINESS: 1935. *Advertising Agencies*. Washington, D.C.: Government Printing Office, March 1937. 10 pp.

Number of agencies, total revenue receipts of agencies, employment, pay rolls, total operating expenses, and total billings to clients. 85 firms omitted to report, but gave no explanations; 47 refused to report.

662. U.S. BUREAU OF FOREIGN AND DOMESTIC COMMERCE. *Advertising Methods in Argentina*, by R. F. Woodward (Trade Information Bulletin no. 828). Washington, D.C.: Government Printing Office, 1935. 24 pp.

663. U.S. BUREAU OF FOREIGN AND DOMESTIC COMMERCE. *Advertising in Brazil* (Trade Information Bulletin no. 838). Washington, D.C.: Government Printing Office, 1937. 32 pp.

664. U.S. BUREAU OF FOREIGN AND DOMESTIC COMMERCE. *Advertising in South Africa*, by E. B. Lawson ('Trade Information Bulletin no. 829). Washington, D.C.: Government Printing Office, 1936. 48 pp.

665. U.S. FEDERAL TRADE COMMISSION. *Utility Corporations: Summary Report to the Senate of the United States, pursuant to S.R. No. 83, 70th Congress, 1st Session, on Efforts by Associations and Agencies of Electric and Gas Utilities to Influence Public Opinion, 1934* (Senate Document 92, part 71-A). Washington, D.C.: Government Printing Office, 1934. 486 pp.

666. U.S. HOUSE OF REPRESENTATIVES. COMMITTEE ON INTERSTATE AND FOREIGN COMMERCE. *Drugs and Cosmetics* (hearings before a subcommittee, July 22-August 12, 1935, on H. R. 6906, H. R. 8805, H. R. 8941 and S. 5, 74th Congress, 1st session, to regulate foods, drugs, and cosmetics). Washington, D.C.: Government Printing Office, 1936. 774 pp.

667. U.S. SECURITIES AND EXCHANGE COMMISSION. *Report of Study and Investigation of Work, Activities, Personnel, and Functions of Protective and Reorganization Committees* (pursuant to sec. 211 of the Securities Exchange Act of 1934). Washington, D.C.: Government Printing Office, 1937. Five parts to August 1937.

Part 1 (916 pp.) is on strategy and techniques of protective and reorganization committees. Part 5 (833 pp.) analyzes agencies promoting interests of holders of defaulted foreign governmental bonds.

668. U.S. SENATE COMMITTEE ON EDUCATION AND LABOR. *Violations of Free Speech and Rights of Labor: Employers' Associations and Collective Bargaining in California* (Report No. 1150, 77th Congress, 2nd session, pursuant to Senate Res. 266 [74th Congress], a Resolution to Investigate Violations of the Right of Free Speech and Assembly . . .). Washington, D.C.: Government Printing Office, 1942. In 2 parts, total 152 pp.

Based on La Follette Committee hearings on the West Coast. Stresses role of Associated Farmers.

669. U.S. SENATE. SPECIAL COMMITTEE TO INVESTIGATE LOBBYING ACTIVITIES. *Hearings*, pursuant to S. Res. 165 and S. Res. 184, resolutions providing for an investigation of lobbying activities in connection with the so-called Holding Company Bill (S. 2976), 74th Congress, 2nd session. Washington, D.C.: Government Printing Office, 1935-36. 2095 pp. to April 17, 1936.

Hearings on the Rayburn-Wheeler anti-holding company bill, containing testimony on propaganda for and against the Tennessee Valley Authority.

669a. U.S. SENATE. SPECIAL COMMITTEE TO STUDY PROBLEMS OF AMERICAN SMALL BUSINESS. *The Fate of Small Business in Nazi Germany* (Senate Committee Print no. 14, 78th Congress, 1st session). Washington, D.C.: Government Printing Office, 1943. 152 pp.

Careful statistical study of the liquidation of German small business by big business in combination with the Nazi Party, with allusion to the parallel situation developing at present in the U.S. Prepared under the direction of

Bertram M. Gross by Drs. A. R. L. Gurland, Otto Kirchheimer and Franz Leopold Neumann of the Institute of Social Research, Columbia University, under a grant from the Carnegie Corporation of New York. Bibliographic footnotes.

670. U.S. SENATE. SPECIAL COMMITTEE INVESTIGATING MUNITIONS INDUSTRY. *Hearings* (74th Congress, 2nd session, pursuant to S. Res. 206 [73rd Congress], to make certain investigations concerning manufacture and sale of arms and other war munitions). Washington, D.C.: Government Printing Office, 1937. 37 parts to June 1937.

The "Nye Committee's" investigation of alleged arms profiteers.

671. U.S. SENATE. SPECIAL COMMITTEE TO INVESTIGATE THE MUNITIONS INDUSTRY. *International Regulation of the Trade in and Manufacture of Arms and Ammunition*, by Manley O. Hudson (73rd Congress, 2nd session, Senate Committee Print no. 1). Washington, D.C.: Government Printing Office, 1935. 104 pp.

672. UNIVERSITY OF CHICAGO. SOCIAL SCIENCE RESEARCH COMMITTEE. *Rotary? A University Group Looks at the Rotary Club of Chicago: At the Instance of the Oldest Club in Rotary, a Committee of Social Scientists from the University of Chicago Reports Herewith an Inquiry into the History, Achievement and Possibilities of that Club.* Chicago: University of Chicago, 1934. 293 pp.

673. WALKER, STROTHER HOLLAND; and SKLAR, PAUL. *Business Finds Its Voice.* New York: Harpers, 1938. 93 pp.

Slightly revised reissue of three articles from *Harpers Magazine*, January, February, March 1938.

First-hand account of techniques employed by big business, 1935-37 inclusive. The first article deals especially with paid advertising campaigns and radio facilities; the second with motion pictures and talking slide films as used by big business; the third with coordinating bodies and committees, and with the case histories of two famous campaigns: manufacturers *vs.* auto strikers (1934) and chain stores *vs.* California chain store tax (1935). The authors, both of whom have had experience in advertising, were formerly associate editors of *Tide,* a fortnightly magazine of the advertising trade.

674. WEBER, ARNOLD. *Reklame und Propaganda im kapitalistischen und im kollektivistischen Wirtschaftssystem* (part of Ph.D. thesis, Basel). Basel: Haupt, 1936. 52 pp.

Bibliography, pp. 50-51.

675. WEISS, EDWARD BENJAMIN; and others. *The Handbook of Advertising.* New York: McGraw-Hill, 1938. 530 pp.

Symposium by leading authorities in the various branches.

676. WELD, LOUIS DWIGHT HARVELL. "It's Really Scientific: Why *Printers' Ink Index* is the Only Accurate Measure of Advertising Changes," *Printers' Ink,* May 14, 1936, p. 7.

A monthly index of advertising activity.

677. WELD, LOUIS DWIGHT HARVELL. Series of statistical and research reports on advertising activity, in *Printers' Ink Monthly,* January 1935 to date.

Representative titles are the following: "Advertising Activity and the Stock Market" (October 1935, pp. 55 ff.). "Advertising, Retail Food Prices, and the Cost of Living: Advertising Activity and Food Prices Follow Each Other Closely" (January 1936, pp. 46 ff.). "Advertising Developments During 1935: Increase of 6% Over 1934; Radio Gained on Other Media" (March 1936, pp. 48 ff.). "Linage, Newsprint, and Circulation" (May 1936, pp. 47-48). "Advertising and Corporation Profits" (June 1936, pp. 46 ff.). "Advertising and National Income" (July 1936, pp. 46 ff.). The author of this series is Director of Research for the advertising firm of McCann-Erickson, Inc.

678. WELD, LOUIS DWIGHT HARVELL. Series of articles comparing German, French, English, and U.S. advertising, *Printers' Ink,* November and December 1937, January and February 1938.

679. WILK, KURT. "International Organization and the International Chamber of Commerce," *Political Science Quarterly,* 55: 231-48 (June 1940).

By an ex-German professor of public law and political science, in U.S. since 1936.

680. WISEMAN, MARK. *The Anatomy of Advertising: An Analytical Approach to Campaign Planning and Advertising Making* (Volume 1, *Campaign Planning;* Volume 2, *Advertising Making*). New York: Harpers, 1942. 2 vols.

By New York advertising man.

681. WOODS, HENRY FITZWILLIAM, JR. *Profitable Publicity: How to Do It, How to Get It.* New York: Dorset House, 1941. 208 pp.

Basic factors of publicity work, by publicity director of a large U.S. advertising agency. Pp. 199-202 provide a list of U.S. news and feature syndicates.

682. WRIGHT, MILTON. *Public Relations for Business.* New York: McGraw-Hill, 1939. 346 pp.

Based upon experiences of firms which, according to the author, a public relations counsel, have been successful in their campaigns.

683. YOUNG, JAMES WEBB "Recent Trends in Advertising," *Public Opinion Quarterly,* 1 no. 2: 135-38 (April 1937).

By a U.S. advertising executive who has also been a professor of business history, University of Chicago.

III. FARMERS' GROUPS

*684. BAKER, OLIVER EDWIN (D,W); BORSODI, RALPH; and WILSON, MILBURN LINCOLN (D,W). *Agriculture in Modern Life.* New York: Harpers, 1939. 303 pp.

Part 1, "Our Rural People," by Dr. Baker, Senior Agricultural Economist, U.S. Department of Agriculture, deals with the impacts upon agriculture of inventions, mechanization, low incomes, migrations, declining birth rates. Part 2, "A Plan for Rural Life," by Mr. Borsodi, author of many books on farm economics and founder of various self-sustaining home projects, explores conflicts between traditional and modern concepts of agriculture. In Part 3, "Science and Folk-lore in Rural Life," a careful study of culture patterns and folklore is presented by Dr. Wilson, Undersecretary of Agriculture, who also submits a plan for rural reeducation. In Part 4, "A Dialogue: The Future of Rural Life," the three authors attempt in informal fashion to integrate their several points of view. See especially pp. 228-46, "Folklore Farming and Scientific, Commercial Agriculture."

685. COLLINS, HENRY HILL, JR. *America's Own Refugees: Our 4,000,-000 Homeless Migrants.* Princeton: Princeton University, 1941. 323 pp.

Based mainly on testimony before the Tolan Committee of the House of Representatives Investigating the Interstate Migration of Destitute Citizens, 1940-41.

686. FRIEDRICH, CARL JOACHIM. "The Agricultural Basis of Emotional Nationalism," *Public Opinion Quarterly*, 1 no. 2: 50-61 (April 1937).

Agricultural regions are the most nationalistic, in Germany as elsewhere, according to this study of election returns by a Harvard political scientist. "Wherever we have democracy, the rule of the people in foreign affairs, we must reckon with this powerful constituent element. Cut off from much experience with the outside world, the agricultural population will tend to carry its attachment to the paternal soil into the field of foreign relations, supporting irrational emotional appeals, no matter how extreme."

687. McDERMOTT, WILLIAM F. "Rebirth of the Barefoot Boy—and Girl," *Rotarian*, 51: 26-30 (November 1937).

How the National 4-H movement began; its early leadership; how it is financed; what the 1,145,000 young members are doing; by a Chicago journalist.

688. McWILLIAMS, CAREY. *Ill Fares the Land: Migrants and Migratory Labor in the United States.* Boston: Little, Brown, 1942. 419 pp.

Finds that corporations and banks increasingly control U.S. agrarian enterprise. The small farmer—the yeoman of history—is by way of disappearing, and his hired man and independent field hands are supplanted by migrant workers, poor, exploited, hopeless and almost helpless. This analysis by a U.S. rural relief administrator is based on his own observations, the reports of Congressional committees, and studies by economists and sociologists. Bibliography, pp. 391-411.

689. MANNICHE, PETER. *Denmark: A Social Laboratory.* New York: Oxford University, 1939. 216 pp.

Introduction to Danish farm life, cooperatives, folk high schools, and social legislation. The author is Principal, International People's College, Elsinore, Denmark. Bibliography, pp. 214-15.

690. SCHMIDT, CARL THEODORE. *American Farmers in the World Crisis.* New York: Oxford University, 1941. 345 pp.

Discussion of the American farmer's predicament and the effort of the government to alleviate it, by U.S. economist. Includes a section on farm pressure groups. Bibliography, pp. 333-34.

690a. U.S. DEPARTMENT OF AGRICULTURE. *Yearbook of Agriculture.* Washington, D.C.: U.S. Government Printing Office, 1894-.

Standard reference work containing articles on all aspects of agriculture by widely recognized specialists. Some issues include material on social consequences of federal farm programs and on opinions and attitudes of the U.S. rural population.

IV. ORGANIZED LABOR AND PROFESSIONALS

For skill groups and professionals employed primarily in the channels of mass communication (press, radio, motion pictures, educational system), see Part 5.

For skill groups and professionals employed primarily in governments and political parties, see also Parts 2 A and 2 B, respectively, and 5 A. For Communist parties, see 2 B and 3 A.

691. *The American Labor Press: An Annotated Directory*, introduction by John Rogers Commons. Washington,

D.C.: American Council on Public Affairs, 1940. 120 pp.

Detailed information about each of the 677 papers and magazines in the labor field issued by the American Federation of Labor, the Congress of Industrial Organizations, independent unions, miscellaneous labor agencies, etc. Compiled by University of Wisconsin WPA Project.

692. "American Medical Association," *Fortune* (November 1938).

693. ARIMA, SEIHO. "A National Labour Movement," *Contemporary Japan*, 5: 599-604 (March 1937).

About the Union of Patriotic Labourers, and Farmers, an anti-Marxist organization in Japan, said to have 60,000 members.

694. BERNSTEIN, IRVING. "John L. Lewis and the Voting Behavior of the C.I.O.," *Public Opinion Quarterly*, 5: 233-49 (June 1941).

The reaction of C.I.O. officials and editors to Lewis's endorsement of Willkie is described by a Brookings Institution Fellow, and the vote of the rank and file analyzed in selected localities.

695. BRAMELD, THEODORE, editor. *Workers' Education in the United States* (Fifth Yearbook of the John Dewey Society). New York: Harpers, 1941. 338 pp.

Essays by a dozen specialists, including George Sylvester Counts, J. B. S. Hardman, Mark Starr. Bibliography, pp. 303-15.

696. BRAND, CARL FREMONT. *British Labour's Rise to Power: Eight Studies* (Hoover Library on War, Revolution and Peace, publication no. 17). Stanford University: Stanford University, 1941. 305 pp.

Scholarly history of British Labour Party from its inception to mid-1939. Bibliographic footnotes.

697. BROCKWAY, (ARCHIBALD) FENNER. *The Workers' Front*. London: Secker and Warburg, 1938. 254 pp.

By a leader of the Independent Labour Party of Great Britain.

698. BROOKS, ROBERT ROMANO RAVI. *As Steel Goes . . .: Unionism in a Basic Industry*. New Haven: Yale University, 1940. 275 pp.

The C.I.O. and trade unionism in steel. By Williams College economist. Bibliographic notes, pp. 261-68.

699. BROOKS, ROBERT ROMANO RAVI. *Unions of Their Own Choosing: An Account of the National Labor Relations Board and Its Work*. New Haven: Yale University, 1939. 296 pp.

Shows that public opinion concerning the Board has been formed in large part by newspapers' disproportionate emphasis upon cases in which it has met opposition. Bibliography, pp. 258-74.

700. BROOKS, ROBERT ROMANO RAVI. *When Labor Organizes*. New Haven: Yale University, 1937. 361 pp.

"A guide book to the facts behind the La Follette committee investigations, Harlan County and Remington Rand, and the split between A.F. of L. and C.I.O." Bibliography, pp. 345-54.

701. BROWN, ESTHER LUCILE. *Lawyers and the Promotion of Justice*. New York: Russell Sage Foundation, 1938. 302 pp.

Fifth volume in this author's series on the professions. Contains material on lawyers' associations, incomes, functions. Other volumes deal with nurses (1936, 1940), engineers (1936), social workers (1935, 1942), physicians (1937). Together these books constitute a survey of the living conditions of an important segment of the middle-income skill groups.

702. CARSEL, WILFRED. *A History of the Chicago Ladies' Garment Workers' Union*, introduction by Paul H. Douglas. Chicago: Normandie House, 1940. 323 pp.

Prepared at request of Chicago Joint Board, International Ladies' Garment Workers' Union, and "written primarily with the purpose of presenting an historical interpretation of the union to its membership." Bibliography, pp. 287-316.

703. CAYTON, HORACE R.; and MITCHELL, GEORGE SINCLAIR. *Black*

Workers and the New Unions. Chapel Hill: University of North Carolina, 1939. 473 pp.

History of the Negro in three U.S. industries (iron and steel, meat-packing, railroad car shops) and his relationship to unions. Includes a sociological analysis of the Birmingham area. Mr. Cayton is a sociologist trained at University of Chicago; Mr. Mitchell a Farm Security administrator. Bibliography, pp. 458-67.

704. COLE, GEORGE DOUGLAS HOWARD. *British Working Class Politics, 1832-1914*. London: George Routledge, 1941. 320 pp.

By a British historian and economist influential in labor politics. Bibliography, pp. 307-09.

705. COLE, GEORGE DOUGLAS HOWARD; and others. *British Trade Unionism Today: A Survey, with the Collaboration of Thirty Trade Union Leaders and Other Experts*. London: Gollancz, 1939. 501 pp.

History and survey, said by the editor to be the most comprehensive since the work of Sidney and Beatrice Webb (*History of Trade Unionism*, 1894; *Industrial Democracy*, 1897).

706. COLE, GEORGE DOUGLAS HOWARD; and POSTGATE, RAYMOND WILLIAM. *The British Common People, 1746-1938*. New York: Knopf, 1939. 588 pp.

707. COMMITTEE FOR INDUSTRIAL ORGANIZATION. *The C.I.O.: What It Is and How It Came To Be*. Washington, D.C., reissued at intervals since 1937. Pamphlet.

The C.I.O. also publishes a weekly newspaper, *C.I.O. News*, and a monthly magazine, *Economic Outlook*.

*707a. CROOK, WILFRID HARRIS (D). *The General Strike: A Study of Labor's Tragic Weapon in Theory and Practice*. Chapel Hill: University of North Carolina, 1931. 649 pp.

Comprehensive history by a U.S. sociologist. Bibliography, pp. 625-36.

708. CROSSER, PAUL K. *Ideologies and American Labor* (based on Ph.D. thesis, Columbia). New York: Oxford University, 1941. 221 pp.

Traces the historic and philosophic roots of paternalistic unionism, liberalistic unionism, revolutionary unionism in U.S. Bibliography, pp. 197-212.

709. DAVID, HENRY. *The History of the Haymarket Affair: A Study in American Social Revolutionary and Labor Movements*. New York: Farrar and Rinehart, 1936. 579 pp.

By a U.S. scholar. Bibliography, pp. 545-61 and ends of chapters.

710. FRANKLIN, CHARLES LIONEL. *The Negro Labor Unionist of New York: Problems and Conditions among Negroes in the Labor Unions in Manhattan, With Special Reference to the N.R.A. and Post-N.R.A. Situations* (Columbia University Studies in History, Economics, and Public Law, no. 420). New York: Columbia University, 1936. 415 pp.

Bibliography, pp. 398-402.

711. GARCEAU, OLIVER. "Organized Medicine Enforces Its 'Party Line,'" *Public Opinion Quarterly*, 4: 408-28 (September 1940).

By a Harvard instructor in government. Through the medical press, group sanctions, expulsion, boycott, and its politicians, the American Medical Association molds the opinions of the nation's doctors. Article contains a personality sketch of Dr. Morris Fishbein, the Association's chief promoter.

712. GARCEAU, OLIVER. *The Political Life of the American Medical Association*. Cambridge: Harvard University, 1941. 186 pp.

American Medical Association is studied as a political institution, with emphasis upon its organizational structure and its internal politics. Relations of organized medicine to the state and to other groups receive only incidental attention and have been treated more fully by the author in "Organized Medicine Enforces Its Party Line," cited above. Bibliography, pp. 179-82.

713. U.S. Bureau of Labor Statistics. *Handbook of American Trade Unions* (U.S. Bureau of Labor Statistics, Bulletin 618). Washington, D.C.: Government Printing Office, 1936. 340 pp.

714. Harris, Herbert. *Labor's Civil War.* New York: Knopf, 1940. 298 pp.

Contemporary history of U.S. labor movement, by well-known U.S. journalist. Stresses A.F. of L.-C.I.O. controversies.

715. Henig, Harry. *The Brotherhood of Railway Clerks* (Ph.D. thesis, Columbia). New York: Columbia University, 1937. 300 pp.

Historical and descriptive study of one of the strong units in the U.S. railway industry. Bibliography, pp. 293-96.

716. Hutt, Allen. *The Post-War History of the British Working Class.* London: Gollancz, 1937. 320 pp.

By a British trades-unionist writer. Bibliography in text.

*716a. Inter - Church World Movement, Commission of Inquiry. *Public Opinion and the Steel Strike,* supplementary report of the investigators to the Commission of Inquiry, with the technical assistance of the Bureau of Industrial Research, New York. New York: Harcourt, Brace, 1921. 341 pp.

Opinion as influenced by press, civil government, actions of workers, reports of spies, and conceptions or misconceptions of foreign-language communities, during one of the largest U.S. larbor upheavals, immediately after World War I.

717. Kohno, Mitsu. "Japan's Proletarian Movement," *Contemporary Japan,* 5: 577-85 (March 1937).

Surveys activities and social composition of Japan Labour Union Council and of the Social Mass Party (Socialist). The writer, a Social Mass Party M. P., represented Japan's labor at the 1936 I.L.O. conference. 400,000 (6 per cent) of Japan's laborers are said to be organized.

718. Labor Research Association. *Labor Fact Book.* New York: International Publishers, at intervals, 1931–.

Summarizes data on "Labor and Progressive Political Movements," "Legislation," "The Struggle for Civil Rights," "Trade Union Trends," etc. Includes bibliographies.

719. Lang, Harry. *"62": Biography of a Union.* New York: Undergarment and Negligee Workers Union, I.L.G.W.U., Local 62, 1940. 222 pp.

The author, a New York labor journalist, was for five years an organizer and business agent of the Union. Bibliography, p. 222.

720. Latham, Earl G. "The Case of the Taunton Moulders: A Study of Lobbying Technique," *Public Opinion Quarterly,* 2: 115-20 (January 1938).

A spectacular campaign to secure favorable legislative action on workmen's compensation is described by a Harvard instructor in government.

721. Lefranc, E.; and Lefranc, G. "The General Confederation of Labour and Workers' Education in France," *International Labour Review,* 37: 618-43 (May 1938).

A "Workers' Institute," established in 1932, has played a dynamic part in workers' education.

722. Levinson, Edward. *Labor on the March.* New York: Harpers, 1938. 335 pp.

Current activities in the U.S. labor movement, described by a writer well-known for many magazine articles on the subject. Bibliography, pp. 300-05.

723. Lieberman, Elias. *The Collective Labor Agreement.* New York: Harpers, 1939. 233 pp.

Manual for labor leaders and business executives, describing history, legal status, and methods of labor negotiations. The author has been counsel for International Ladies' Garment Workers Union for some 25 years.

724. McDonald, David John; and Lynch, Edward A. *Coal and Unionism: A History of the American Coal Miners' Unions.* Silver Spring, Maryland: Lynald Books, 1940. 226 pp.

Deals mainly with history of United Mine Workers; written by two of their officials on the Union's 50th anniversary. Bibliography, p. 227.

*725. Marquand, Hilary Adair, editor. *Organized Labour in Four Continents, 1920-1937.* New York and London: Longmans, Green, 1939. 518 pp.

Text in 11 chapters by well-known scholars, on organized labor in Australia (by Lloyd Ross); Canada (Leo Warshaw); France (André Philip); Germany (Erich Roll); Great Britain (H. A. Marquand); Italy (J. P. Van Aartsen); Japan (I. F. Ayusawa); Mexico (William E. Zeuch); Russia (Maurice Dobb); Scandinavia (Halvard M. Lange); U.S.A. (Selig Perlman) (D,W). Bibliographic footnotes.

726. Marshall, T. H. "The Recent History of Professionalism in Relation to Social Structure and Social Policy," *Canadian Journal of Economics and Political Science*, 5: 325-40 (1939).

Organization in free professions is characterized by three factors: (1) the association guarantees the technical efficiency of its members by testing their ability before they are admitted to practice; (2) it imposes a code of ethics; and (3) it does what it can to protect the field from invasion by the unqualified. There is a real problem as to whether or not the professional codes are arbitrary fabrications of the professional mind or whether they reflect some real characteristics which distinguish the professions from the trades. There appears to be a trend toward the transfer of individual competitiveness from the economic to the educational world. This is typified in the many semiprofessions of the business and administrative world.

727. Martin, Edward M. *The Role of the Bar in Electing the Bench in Chicago* (Ph.D. thesis). Chicago: University of Chicago, 1936. 365 pp.

The Secretary of the Committee on Judicial Selection of the National Municipal League and the American Judicature Society tells the story of the struggle of the organized bar "to prevent the degradation of the Bench" at the hands of political bosses.

728. Mills, Alden B. *Hospital Public Relations.* Chicago: Physicians' Record Company, 1939. 361 pp.

Managing Editor of *The Modern Hospital* sets forth a carefully formulated policy of public relations which could well be adopted by other public and private administrative units.

729. Morgan, William Gerry. *The American College of Physicians: Its First Quarter Century.* Philadelphia, 1940. 275 pp.

An official history containing the constitution, by-laws, list of publications, requirements of admission, etc.

730. Nockels, Edward N. "Labor's Experience in Radio," *American Federationist*, 44: 276-81 (March 1937).

Address by Secretary of the Chicago Federation of Labor before the First National Conference on Educational Broadcasting (December 1936). Describes educational broadcasts of WCFL and W9XAA (Chicago), the American Federation of Labor's pioneer radio station.

731. Perlman, Selig; and Taft, Philip. *Labor Movements (History of Labor in the United States,* by John R. Commons and associates, vol. 4). New York: Macmillan, 1935. 683 pp.

The concluding volume of the monumental history, the first two volumes of which were published by Professor Commons in 1920.

732. Pleysier, A. "Workers' Education and Broadcasting," *American Federationist*, 43: 1056-63 (October 1936).

Report to the International Conference on Workers' Education, London, July 1936, by the Secretary of the Labor Radio International.

733. Radin, Max. "The Achievements of the American Bar Association," series in *American Bar Association Journal*, November 1939-April 1940.

History of the Association from its beginnings, by University of California professor of legal history.

734. Ram, Vangala Shiva. *The State in Relation to Labour in India.* Delhi: University of Delhi, 1940. 175 pp.

Ten lectures, delivered at the University of Delhi in 1938, by a professor of Lucknow University who has served on the Secretariat of the League of Nations. A concise survey of labor legislation and labor conditions in India.

735. REICH, NATHAN. *Labour Relations in Republican Germany: An Experiment in Industrial Democracy, 1918-1933.* New York: Oxford University, 1938. 293 pp.

By a social scientist at Hunter College. Bibliography, pp. 285-88.

736. ROSENFARB, JOSEPH. *The National Labor Policy and How it Works.* New York: Harpers, 1940. 732 pp.

Heavily documented analysis of the working of the National Labor Relations Act, by an NLRB attorney. Propaganda and censorship of various kinds are included among the "unfair" practices forbidden by the Act, and receive extensive treatment in this book. Bibliographic footnotes.

737. SEIDMAN, JOEL. *The Needle Trades* (Labor in Twentieth Century series, vol. 1). New York: Farrar and Rinehart, 1942. 356 pp.

Scholarly historical study by an economist of League for Industrial Democracy. Bibliography, pp. 321-32.

738. SEIDMAN, JOEL. "Organized Labor in Political Campaigns," *Public Opinion Quarterly*, 3: 646-54 (October 1939).

*738a. SOREL, GEORGES (ESS). *Reflections on Violence*, authorized translation by Thomas Ernest Hulme. New York: Huebsch, 1912. New York: Peter Smith, 1941. 299 pp.

Theory of the role of trade unions and unorganized workers in revolutionary situations, by French engineer, political commentator, and social theorist. Stresses the importance of "myth" (overoptimism) in stimulating mass action. French edition: *Réflexions sur la violence* (Paris: Rivière, 1912. 440 pp.). Bibliographic footnotes.

739. STARR, MARK. "A Trade Union Pioneers in Education: The Educational Program and Activities of the In-

ternational Ladies' Garment Workers' Union," *American Federationist*, 43: 54-60 (January 1936).

By this union's educational director.

740. STOLBERG, BENJAMIN. *The Story of the C.I.O.* New York: Viking, 1938. 294 pp.

Free-lance writer's account, containing much material on factionalism within the C.I.O.

741. STRACHEY, JOHN. *What Are We To Do?* New York: Random House, 1938. 398 pp.

British Marxist's analysis of British and American labor movements. Bibliography, pp. 387-88.

742. U.S. NATIONAL LABOR RELATIONS BOARD. *Collective Bargaining in the Newspaper Industry* (NLRB Bulletin, no. 3). Washington, D.C.: Government Printing Office, 1939. 194 pp.

743. WAGNER, AUGUSTA. *Labor Legislation in China.* Peking: Yenching University, 1939. 301 pp.

Examines the rise, extent (less than one-fifth of one per cent of the total population, 1937), and condition of China's industrial labor, against a background of general labor conditions. Although ambitious laws were passed during this period, "the gap between legal standards and current conditions has been nearly maximal." Includes bibliography which has been reviewed as "well-grounded in Chinese-language sources."

744. WALSH, J(OHN) RAYMOND. *C.I.O.: Industrial Unionism in Action.* New York: Norton, 1937. 293 pp.

History, aims, and leadership of the C.I.O. By U.S. economist. Bibliography, pp. 283-87.

745. WARBASSE, JAMES PETER. *The Doctor and the Public: A Study of the Sociology, Economics, Ethics, and Philosophy of Medicine, Based on Medical History.* New York: Hoeber, 1935. 572 pp.

By a U.S. physician, nationally known as a leading promoter of the cooperative movement. Bibliography, pp. 555-56.

746. Young, Dallas M. *A History of the Progressive Miners of America, 1932-1940* (Ph.D. thesis, University of Illinois, 1940).

747. Ziskind, David. *One Thousand Strikes of Government Employees.* New York: Columbia University, 1940. 279 pp.

Scholarly study of labor tactics. Bibliography, pp. 261-68.

V. RELIGIOUS GROUPS

748. Algermissen, Konrad. *Die Gottlosenbewegung der Gegenwart und ihre Überwindung.* Hanover: Giesel, 1933. 358 pp.

"The Present-day Atheist Movement and How to Overcome It."

749. Algermissen, Konrad. *Konfessionskunde,* fifth edition. Hanover, Giesel, 1939. 890 pp.

Comparative study of creeds and diffusion of Catholicism, Protestantism and Near Eastern Christian denominations. Bibliography at beginnings of chapters.

750. Bates, Ernest Sutherland. *American Faith: Its Religious, Political and Economic Foundations.* New York: Norton, 1940. 479 pp.

From the Colonies to about 1850. Holds that Protestantism began as a radical lower-class movement, social and economic as well as theological, which was ultimately taken over by the rising bourgeoisie under Luther, Calvin, and others. Both in the Old World and the New the struggle for religious freedom was part of a broader struggle for social, economic, and political advancement. Before his death in 1939, Dr. Bates was a well-known U.S. professor and critic of literature.

751. Boucher, André. *Petit atlas des missions catholiques,* 2nd ed., rev. Paris: A. Hatier, 1933. 244 pp.

752. Brown, Stephen James Meredith. *Catholic Juvenile Literature: A Classified List,* compiled and edited with an introduction by Stephen J. Brown, with the assistance of Dermot J. Dargan (Catholic Bibliographical Series, no. 5). London: Burns, Oates, and Washbourne, 1935. 70 pp.

753. Cantril, Hadley; and Sherif, Muzafer. "The Kingdom of Father Divine," *Journal of Abnormal and Social Psychology,* 33: 147-67 (April 1938).

Studies the cult world (the "microcosm") of a Negro leader and his followers. Reasons for existence: provides more meaningful environment, higher status, escape from material hardship.

754. Code, Joseph Bernard. *Dictionary of the American Hierarchy.* New York: Longmans, Green, 1940. 425 pp.

Biographies of more than 500 Roman Catholic prelates who have occupied American sees or Americans who have been raised to the episcopate.

755. *Comment propager nos idées, par la presse, par le tract et l'affiche, par le livre, par les conférences, par le théâtre, par le cinéma, par la radiodiffusion, par le phonographe, par la chanson: Manuel practique à l'usage des hommes d'action.* Paris: Bloud et Gay, 1932. 487 pp.

How to use modern publicity techniques in the service of Catholicism.

756. Dexter, Lewis Anthony. "Administration of the Social Gospel," *Public Opinion Quarterly,* 2: 294-99 (April 1938).

Efforts of church lobbies and pressure groups, described by a U.S. student of social science.

757. Gissen, Max. "Clerical Fascism in Latin America." *New Republic,* 106: 232 ff. (February 16, 1942).

Political Catholicism and its exploitation by the Falange in the latter's attempts to dominate Latin America.

758. Gorce, Matthieu Maxime. *La politique de l'Eternel: sociologie, philosophie, ecclésiologie, avec les grandes encycliques de Léon XIII et de Pie XI.*

Paris: Presses universitaires de France, 1941. 311 pp.

History of the social politics of the Roman Catholic Church.

759. HARNEY, MARTIN PATRICK. *The Jesuits in History: The Society of Jesus through Four Centuries.* New York: America Press, 1941. 513 pp.

The author, himself a Jesuit, is Professor of the History of the Reformation, Boston College. Bibliography, pp. 469-77.

760. HOEY, ALLAN SPENCER. *The Official Religion of the Roman Imperial Army* (Ph.D. thesis, Yale, 1940). 210 pp.

Religion in a garrison state.

761. HOPKINS, CHARLES HOWARD. *The Rise of the Social Gospel in American Protestantism, 1865-1915* (Ph.D. thesis, Yale; Yale Studies in Religious Education, no. 14). New Haven: Yale University, 1940. 352 pp.

Heavily documented. Bibliographic footnotes.

762. HUTCHISON, JOHN A. *We Are Not Divided: A Critical and Historical Study of the Federal Council of the Churches of Christ in America.* New York: Round Table Press, 1941. 336 pp.

Bibliography, pp. 317-26.

763. (Pop.) INSTITUTE FOR PROPAGANDA ANALYSIS. *The Fine Art of Propaganda: A Study of Father [Charles E.] Coughlin's Speeches,* edited by Alfred McClung Lee and Elizabeth Briant Lee. New York: Harcourt, Brace, 1939. 140 pp.

Analysis in terms of the Institute's "Seven Common Propaganda Devices." Visual symbols for each "Device" are interpolated in the text of the speeches, together with comment. Annotated bibliography of some leading works on propaganda, pp. 135-40.

764. INTERNATIONAL MISSIONARY COUNCIL. *Directory of Foreign Missions: Mission Boards, Societies, Colleges,* *Co-operative Councils and Other Agencies of the Protestant Churches of the World.* New York, at intervals, 1933–.

See also the numerous monographs published by the Council.

765. INTERNATIONAL MISSIONARY COUNCIL. *Interpretative Statistical Survey of the World Mission of the Christian Church: Summary and Detailed Statistics of Churches and Missionary Societies, Interpretative Articles, and Indices,* edited by Joseph I. Parker. New York and London, 1938. 323 pp.

766. MAYNARD, THEODORE. *The Story of American Catholicism.* New York: Macmillan, 1941. 694 pp.

Semipopular history by Catholic historian. Bibliography, pp. 649-75.

767. MORGAN, THOMAS B. *A Reporter at the Papal Court: A Narrative of the Reign of Pope Pius XI.* New York: Longmans, Green, 1937. 302 pp.

Reminiscences of reporter who covered the Vatican for some 15 years.

768. MOTT, JOHN RALEIGH. *Five Decades and a Forward View.* New York: Harpers, 1939. 139 pp.

An account of the missionary movement of the past fifty years, by one of its leading figures.

769. MURRAY, ROBERT HENRY. *Group Movements throughout the Ages.* New York: Harpers, 1936. 377 pp.

Brief accounts of the promotional activities and social origins of eight Christian groups: Montanists, Franciscans, Friends of God, Port Royalists, Methodists, Evangelicals, Tractarians, and the Oxford Group or Buchmanites. The author is Supervisor of Historical Studies in Oxford University and has written a number of volumes in social, political, and religious history.

770. NATIONAL SPIRITUAL ASSEMBLY OF THE BAHÁ'ÍS OF THE UNITED STATES AND CANADA. *The Bahá'í World: A Biennial International Record,* vol. 8. Wilmette, Ill.: Bahá'í Publishing Committee, 1942. 1039 pp.

Comprehensive and profusely illustrated survey of the world-wide activities of this religious group. Includes extensive bibliography.

771. "Ninth Inning Rally," *Time*, April 4, 1938, pp. 10-11.

How one speech by the Rev. Charles E. Coughlin apparently evoked more than 100,000 telegrams urging Senators to oppose the Reorganization Bill. This almost repeated the feat of 1935 when, after a speech by Coughlin, over 200,000 persons wired Congress about their opposition to the World Court.

772. Russell, Elbert. *The History of Quakerism*. New York: Macmillan, 1942. 586 pp.

By the Dean Emeritus of the Divinity School, and Professor of Biblical Interpretation, Duke University. Bibliography, pp. 547-59.

773. Sencourt, Robert (pseud. of Robert Esmonde Gordon George). *The Genius of the Vatican.* London: Cape, 1935. 315 pp.

A general survey of the history of the Papacy. Bibliography, pp. 293-307.

774. Spivak, John Louis. *Shrine of the Silver Dollar.* New York: Modern Age, 1940. 180 pp.

Father Charles E. Coughlin's objectives and methods, described by U.S. journalist.

775. Sullivan, John Francis. *The Externals of the Catholic Church: Her Government, Ceremonies, Festivals, Sacraments, and Devotions,* 5th ed. revised to conform to the new code of canon law. New York: P. J. Kenedy, 1942. 385 pp.

Bibliography in preface.

776. "The Vatican," *Fortune* (September 1939).

777. Williams, John Paul. *Social Adjustment in Methodism: The Adjustment of the Methodist Episcopal Church to the Changing Needs of Its Constituency* (Teachers College Contributions to Education, no. 765). New York: Teachers College, Columbia University, 1938. 131 pp.

Attitudes of present-day Methodists were secured through 189 interviews and 347 responses to questionnaires from various official and lay groups in and around Springfield, Massachusetts. Dr. Williams (B.D. Garrett Biblical Institute; Ph.D. Columbia) has been a professor of the history of religion in Massachusetts State College (1929-39) and Mount Holyoke College (1939-).

778. Williams, Michael. "Views and Reviews: Pro-Deo Organization in its Struggle against Nazism," *Commonweal*, 35: 92, 120-21 (November 14 and 21, 1941).

"The work of the reorganized international Center of Information Pro-Deo has been set up in Lisbon, Portugal, according to a bulletin recently issued by a branch established in [New York City]. What is supremely important in the statement made by the American branch of the Pro-Deo movement—which for so long has taken a foremost place in the international Catholic struggle against communism—is its declaration of the fundamental conclusions reached by the Pro-Deo leaders as a result of its intimate and expert studies of both communism and nazism. First, so it puts the matter: 'nazism is much more dangerous for the normal classes of society than communism.' "

VI. WOMEN'S GROUPS, YOUTH GROUPS, GROUPS FOR THE AGED

779. Chambers, Merritt Madison, editor. *Youth-Serving Organizations,* 2nd ed. Washington, D.C.: American Youth Commission of the National Council on Education, 1941. 237 pp.

A directory of more than 300 national nongovernmental organizations that have youth serving programs or youth memberships. Contains bibliography.

780. Ellenwood, James Lee. *Look at the "Y"!* New York: Association Press, 1941. 155 pp.

Account of YMCA work by a "Y" official.

781. Fiske, Frances. *So You're Publicity Chairman.* New York: McGraw-Hill, 1940. 189 pp.

For leaders of women's clubs.

782. Fudge, Helen Gilchrist. *Girls' Clubs of National Organization in the United States—Their Development and Present Status* (Ph.D. thesis). Philadelphia, Pa.: Westminster Press, 1940. 349 pp.

783. Gould, Leslie A. *American Youth Today*, foreword by Eleanor Roosevelt. New York: Random House, 1940. 307 pp.

An officer of the American Youth Congress examines the problem of youth today and discusses the organization and aims of the Youth Congress. Includes its Creed and Constitution. Bibliography, pp. 287-88.

784. Harcourt, Robert, Comte d'. *L'Évangile de la force: Le visage de la jeunesse du troisième reich.* Paris: Plon, 1936. 249 pp.

Use of propaganda in Nazi youth organizations.

785. Hill, Frank Ernest. *The American Legion Auxiliary: A History, 1924-1934.* Indianapolis: American Legion Auxiliary, 1935. 286 pp.

Continues an official history compiled by the Auxiliary's historian, Vye Smeigh (Mrs. Joseph H.) Thompson, *History, National American Legion Auxiliary* (Pittsburgh: Jackson-Remlinger Publishing Company, 1921-22-23-24-26).

786. Lash, Joseph P.; and Wechsler, James A. *War Our Heritage.* New York: International Publishers, 1936. 159 pp.

The peace movement among American students is described by Lash, executive secretary of American Student Union, and Wechsler, editor of the *Student Advocate*, author of *Revolt on the Campus*, and former editor of the *Columbia Spectator*.

787. Library of Congress. Division of Bibliography. *Youth Movements in the United States and Foreign Countries, Including a Section on the National Youth Administration.* June 12, 1936. 46 pp., mimeo.

788. Mendenhall, Paul. *Bibliography of Studies on Scouting.* New York: Research Service, Boy Scouts of America, December 1938. 25 pp., mimeo.

About 110 titles of research materials on the Boy Scout movement, mostly published since 1927.

789. Menefee, Louise A.; and Chambers, Merritt Madison. *American Youth: An Annotated Bibliography.* Washington, D.C.: American Youth Commission of the American Council on Education, 1938. 500 pp.

Definitive bibliography of some 2500 items. Of especial interest to specialists in public opinion are the chapters on "Attitudes of Youth," "Education," and "Social Organizations."

790. Murray, William D. *History of the Boy Scouts of America.* New York: Boy Scouts of America, 1937. 574 pp.

Bibliography, pp. 391-416.

791. Neuberger, Richard Lewis; and Loe, Kelley. *An Army of the Aged: A History and Analysis of the Townsend Old Age Pension Plan*, introduction by Bruce Bliven. Caldwell, Indiana: Caxton Printers, 1936. 329 pp.

By two U.S. journalists.

792. Nicholson, Edwin. *Education and the Boy Scout Movement in America* (Teachers College Contributions to Education, no. 826). New York: Teachers College, Columbia University, 1941. 117 pp.

Bibliography, pp. 113-17.

793. Ostryakov, S. *20 let V.L.K.-S.M. istoricheskaya spravka.* Moscow: Molodaya Gvardia, 1938. 126 pp.

"Twenty years of the Young Communist League of the U.S.S.R."

794. Schirach, Baldur von. *Die Hitler-Jugend: Idee und Gestalt.* Berlin: Zeitgeschichte, 1934. 220 pp.

By leader of Hitler-youth movement.

795. Sims, Mary Sophia Stevens. *The YWCA: The Natural History of a*

Social Institution. New York: Woman's Press, 1936. 251 pp.

796. STRACK, CELESTE. "The Student Movement in the United States," *Communist,* 16: 142-60 (February 1937).

By Director of the High School Division, American Student Union.

797. SVEISTRUP, HANS; and VON ZAHN-HARNACK, AGNES. *Die Frauenfrage in Deutschland: Strömungen und Gegenströmungen, 1790-1930.* Burg: August Hopfer, 1934. 800 pp.

A classified and indexed bibliography which comes close to presenting an exhaustive list of publications on the woman question in Germany.

798. TAYLOR, JOHN WILKINSON. *Youth Welfare in Germany: A Study of Governmental Action Relative to the Care of Normal German Youth* (Ph.D. thesis, Teachers College, Columbia University). Nashville, Tennessee: Baird-Ward, 1936. 259 pp.

U.S. professor of education describes the activities, organization, and social composition of the several youth organizations permitted or encouraged in Germany, as well as the many government services for youth. Bibliography, pp. 251-57.

799. U.S. HOUSE OF REPRESENTATIVES. SELECT COMMITTEE TO INVESTIGATE OLD AGE PENSION PLANS AND ORGANIZATIONS. *Old-Age Pension Plans and Organizations* (hearings, 74th Congress, 2nd session, pursuant to H. R. 443). Consolidated print, with corrections. Washington: Government Printing Office, 1937. 2 vols.

800. U.S. SENATE. COMMITTEE ON EDUCATION AND LABOR. *American Youth Act* (hearings on S. 3658, a bill to provide vocational training and employment for youth between the ages of sixteen and twenty-five; to provide for full educational opportunities for high school, college, and post-graduate students, and for other purposes; 74th Con-

gress, 2nd session). Washington, D.C.: Government Printing Office, 1936. 279 pp.

Includes testimony of representatives of many youth groups.

801. WALDO, EDNA LA MOORE. *Leadership for Today's Clubwoman,* introduction by Anne Steese Richardson. New York: Rugby House, 1939. 339 pp.

How to participate in the activities of a woman's club. Chapter 15 is on "How to Raise Money"; chapters 16 and 17 are on publicity; chapter 19 on "Conventions and their Management." In America, clubwomen now number some 12,000,000, according to the introduction. Bibliography, pp. 321-24.

802. WORLD YOUTH CONGRESS, GENEVA, 1936. *Youth Plans a New World, Being the Official Record of the First World Youth Congress, Organized by the International Federation of League of Nations Societies.* Geneva, 1937. 208 pp.

"35 countries were represented, some ten international youth organizations gave . . . valuable collaboration, especially the protestant ones, and there were present over 700 delegates or observers."—Preface.

803. WORLD YOUTH CONGRESS, VASSAR COLLEGE, 1938. *Youth Demands a Peaceful World: Report of the Second World Youth Congress.* New York: World Youth Congress, 1938. 52 pp.

Official report of conference of more than 600 delegates and observers from 54 countries who met at Vassar College in August 1938 to discuss problems of peace and world social security.

VII. OTHER GROUPS
CULTURAL MINORITIES, IMMIGRANTS, INTOLERANCE MOVEMENTS, PATRIOTIC SOCIETIES, ETC.

[See also Part 3, B, III below.]

804. *American Jewish Yearbook 5699* (September 26, 1938-September 13, 1939), edited by Harry Schneiderman for the American Jewish Committee. Philadelphia: Jewish Publication Society of America, 1938. 771 pp.

This issue contains 64 pages of "Statistics of Jews and Jewish Organizations in the United States: A Historical Review of Censuses, 1850-1937," by Harry Sebee Linfield. Also includes an index of the 40 volumes of the *Yearbook*.

805. BRITT, STEUART HENDERSON; and MENEFEE, SELDEN COWLES. "Did the Publicity of the Dies Committee in 1938 Influence Public Opinion?" *Public Opinion Quarterly*, 3: 449-57 (July 1939).

Experimental study by two social psychologists.

806. BROWN, FRANCIS J.; and ROUCEK, JOSEPH SLABEY, editors. *Our Racial and National Minorities: Their History, Contributions, and Present Problems*. New York: Prentice-Hall, 1937. 877 pp.

Contributions by a score of writers, many of them social scientists. Includes chapters on "The Immigrant Press" (Mark Villchur), "The School and the Immigrant" (E. George Payne), "The Immigrant in Politics" (Wallace S. Sayre). Bibliography, pp. 781-847.

*807. CHICAGO COMMISSION ON RACE RELATIONS. *The Negro in Chicago: A Study of Race Relations and a Race Riot*. Chicago: University of Chicago, 1922. 672 pp.

Race relations in a U.S. metropolis analyzed by a State commission, on the occasion of the riots after World War I. Chapters 9 and 10 are on public opinion in race relations; chapter 9 on current beliefs regarding Negroes on the part of white citizens, and opinions of Negroes on racial problems; chapter 10, on "Instruments of Opinion Making": the press, Negro and white; pressure groups and propaganda for and against the Negro.

808. CHILD, CLIFTON JAMES. *The German-Americans in Politics, 1914-1917*. Madison, Wis.: University of Wisconsin, 1939. 193 pp.

Scholarly study of purposes and activities of the National German-American Alliance and other German-American groups, by Englishman who wrote the book while at University of Wisconsin as a Commonwealth Fund fellow. Bibliography, pp. 181-85.

809. CRENSHAW, OLLINGER. "Knights of the Golden Circle: Secret Southern Military Organization Aiming to Annex Mexico," *American Historical Review*, 47: 23-50 (October 1941).

810. CULP, DOROTHY. *The American Legion: A Study in Pressure Politics* (Ph.D. thesis, University of Chicago, 1939).

811. DOBYNS, FLETCHER. *The Amazing Story of Repeal: An Exposé of the Power of Propaganda*. Chicago: Willett, Clark, 1940. 457 pp.

Story of Association against the Prohibition Amendment. Bibliography at ends of chapters.

812. ELDREDGE, HANFORD WENTWORTH. "Enemy Aliens: New Haven Germans during the World War," *Studies in the Science of Society*, George Peter Murdock, editor (Yale University, 1937), pp. 201-24.

Based on Ph.D. thesis, sociology, Yale University, 1935. Bibliographic footnotes.

813. GELLERMAN, WILLIAM. *The American Legion as Educator* (Teachers College Contributions to Education, no. 743). New York: Teachers College, Columbia University, 1938. 280 pp.

Extensively documented analysis of the Legion by a Northwestern University professor who is himself a Legionnaire. Bibliography, pp. 274-80.

814. GRAEBER, ISACQUE; and BRITT, STEUART HENDERSON (D), editors. *Jews in a Gentile World: The Problem of Anti-Semitism*. New York: Macmillan, 1942. 436 pp.

Articles by 18 different authors prominent in their respective fields. After an introduction by Carl Joachim Friedrich, the following main aspects of the problem are considered: "The Problem of Race," by Carleton S. Coon and M. Jacobs; "The History and Sociology of Anti-Semitism," by J. O. Hertzler and Talcott Parsons; "The Psychology of Anti-Semitism," by J. F. Brown and Ellis Freeman; "The

American Scene," by Leonard Bloom and Samuel Koenig; "Anonymous," by Jessie Bernard; "The Rhythm of the Two Worlds," by Everett V. Stonequist, Carl Mayer and Joseph W. Cohen; "The Mirage of the Economic Jew," by Miriam Beard and Jacob Lestchinsky; and "The Perspective of the Future," by Raymond Kennedy.

814a. Jack, Robert L. *History of the National Association for the Advancement of Colored People.* Boston: Meador, 1943. 110 pp.

The work, function and ideology of the largest Negro organization in America, described by a member of the Department of Social Sciences, Morgan State College (Maryland). Bibliography, pp. 102-06.

815. *Jewish Social Studies.* New York, quarterly, January 1939–.

Sponsored by Conference on Jewish Relations.

817. Karpf, Maurice Joseph. *Jewish Community Organization in the United States.* New York: Bloch, 1938. 234 pp.

Extensively documented sociology of problems faced by U.S. Jews and of institutions they have developed to cope with them. Dr. Karpf, President of the Faculty and Director of the Graduate School for Jewish Social Work, New York City, is a well-known specialist in this field. Bibliography, pp. 203-23.

818. Kienle, Edward C. "Press Relations and a Wedding," *Public Opinion Quarterly,* 1 no. 4: 136-38 (October 1937).

The author was one of the public relations counsels retained to grapple with the many delicate public relations problems of the Franklin D. Roosevelt, Jr.-Ethel du Pont wedding.

819. Leach, Kent Watson. *Sociology of the D. A. R.'s* (M.A. thesis, sociology, Oberlin, 1938).

820. Loucks, Emerson Hunsberger. *The Ku Klux Klan in Pennsylvania: A Study in Nativism* (Ph.D. thesis, Columbia). Harrisburg, Penn.: Telegraph Press, 1936. 221 pp.

"Nativism" is defined as protection of "the recognized" culture against "alien influences."

This is a field study of the Pennsylvania Realm of the Klan, based on the author's personal contacts. Bibliographic essay, pp. 200-09.

821. Mecklin, John Moffatt. *Le Ku Klux Klan,* translated from the English by A. and H. Collin Delavaud. Paris: Payot, 1934. 223 pp.

By U.S. sociologist. A new chapter covering the decade since this book was first published has been added to the French translation.

823. Pitcairn, Raymond. "The Pink-Slip Strike," *Saturday Evening Post* (June 8, 1935).

One of the leaders of the movement tells how protest against publicity of income-tax returns was organized by the Sentinels of the Republic.

824. Ross, Colin. *Unser Amerika: Der deutsche Anteil an den Vereinigten Staaten.* Leipzig: Brockhaus, 1936. 317 pp.

Views of Nazi publicist on the German language minority in the U.S.

825. Saunders, Dero Ames. "The Dies Committee: First Phase," *Public Opinion Quarterly,* 3: 223-38 (April 1939).

By executive secretary (A.B. Dartmouth; M.A. Columbia) of the League for Fair Play, a nonprofit lecture and program bureau in New York.

826. Strong, Donald Stuart. *Organized Anti-Semitism in America: The Rise of Group Prejudice during the Decade 1930-40* (Ph.D. thesis, political science, Chicago). Washington, D.C.: American Council on Public Affairs, 1941. 191 pp.

Activities of 121 anti-Semitic organizations that arose between 1933 and 1940 are discussed, eleven of them in considerable detail: the German-American Bund, Silver Shirts, National Union for Social Justice, Defenders of the Christian Faith, Edmondson Economic Service, American Vigilant Intelligence Federation, Industrial Defense Association, James True Associates, American Christian Defenders, Order of '76, and Paul Reveres. Detailed information is given on such topics as leadership, membership, meetings, funds, and propaganda. Includes bibliography.

827. TOZIER, ROY. *America's Little Hitlers: Who's Who and What's Up in U. S. Fascism* (Little Blue Books, no. 1761). Girard, Kansas: Haldeman-Julius Publications, 1940. 64 pp.

By research director of Friends of Democracy.

829. U.S. HOUSE OF REPRESENTATIVES. SPECIAL COMMITTEE ON UN-AMERICAN ACTIVITIES. *Investigation of Nazi Propaganda Activities and Investigation of Certain Other Propaganda Activities* (hearings, 73rd Congress, 2nd session). Washington, D.C.: Government Printing Office, 1934–.

The "Dickstein Committee," which was empowered to investigate both radical and hyper-patriotic pressure groups. This committee also released a *Public Statement* in New York City, November 24, 1934 (Washington, D.C.: Government Printing Office, 1934. 12 pp.), and a *Report* (74th Congress, 1st session, House Report 153. Washington, D.C.: Government Printing Office, 1935. 24 pp.).

830. U.S. HOUSE OF REPRESENTATIVES. SPECIAL COMMITTEE ON UN-AMERICAN ACTIVITIES. *Investigation of Un-American Activities and Propaganda* (Reports and hearings on H.R. 282, 75th Congress, 3rd session, *et seq.*). Washington, D.C.: Government Printing Office, 1938–.

The "Dies Committee" hearings on U.S. Fascist and Communist activities.

831. (Pop.) WISE, JAMES WATERMAN; and LEVINGER, LEE JOSEPH. *Mr. Smith, Meet Mr. Cohen.* New York: Reynal and Hitchcock, 1940. 182 pp.

An attempt to interpret U.S. Jews factually to average Americans. Indicates why they came here, what they are most interested in, what they do best, what organizations they join, what they teach their children, etc. Mr. Wise is a New York public relations man, Dr. Levinger a Cleveland historian, civic leader and research worker. Bibliography, pp. 179-82.

PART 3. PROPAGANDA CLASSIFIED BY THE RESPONSE TO BE ELICITED

A. RESPONSE TOWARD SYMBOLS OF WORLD POLITICAL GOALS (INTERNATIONALISM; INDEPENDENCE NATIONALISM; PAN-NATIONALISM; IMPERIALISM; INTERNATIONAL REVOLUTION AND COUNTERREVOLUTION)

Studies that emphasize the goal sought by the propagandist are listed here.

832. ANTONIUS, GEORGE. *The Arab Awakening: The Story of the Arab Nationalist Movement.* Philadelphia: Lippincott, 1939. 471 pp.

Arab politician and diplomat recounts historical bases of the movement and states the arguments favoring Arab—as opposed to Jewish—control of Palestine.

833. ARMSTRONG, ELIZABETH H. *The Crisis of Quebec, 1914-1918.* New York: Columbia University, 1937. 270 pp.

Carefully documented study of French-Canadian separatist movement. Bibliography, pp. 251-58.

834. BAILEY, STANLEY HARTNOLL. *International Studies in Modern Education.* London and New York: Oxford University, 1938. 309 pp.

A study of educational and research institutions and curricula for the teaching of international law and relations, issued under auspices of Royal Institute of International Affairs. French edition: *Les études internationales dans l'enseignement contemporain* (Paris: International Institute of Intellectual Cooperation, 1938. 234 pp.).

835. BICKERTON, MAX. "The Revolutionary Movement in Japan," *Political Quarterly*, 6: 81-89 (January 1935).

835a. BOEHRINGER, RUDOLF. *Die Propaganda Thomas Paines während des amerikanischen Unabhängigkeitskampfes.* Berlin: Junker und Dünnhaupt, 1938. 105 pp.

"Thomas Paine's Propaganda during the American Struggle for Independence." Bibliography, pp. 102-05.

*836. BORKENAU, FRANZ. *World Communism: A History of the Communist International.* New York: Norton, 1939. 442 pp.

Dr. Borkenau was a member of the German Communist Party 1921-29, and a research worker for the Comintern. After extensive analysis of effects of the Comintern on opinion, he concludes: "As long as the Comintern exists the average citizen and even the average politician in the West will judge Russia more after the revolution of 1917 than after the execution of Sinovjev and Bukharin. It would therefore be in the interest of Russia itself to dissolve the Comintern and to prove, by scrupulous abstention from interference abroad, that it can be treated on an equal footing with those democratic powers whose ideals it professes to share. Closer cooperation between the great democratic powers and Russia would become a practical proposition as a result, and the mere possibility of such closer cooperation would be a powerful contribution to the maintenance of peace and the prevention of aggression" (p. 428). Bibliographic notes, pp. 430-36.

837. BROWDER, EARL R. *The People's Front.* New York: International Publishers, 1938. 354 pp.

Executive secretary of U.S. Communist Party defines his party's aims.

838. BUTHMAN, WILLIAM CURT. *The Rise of Integral Nationalism in France, with Special Reference to the Ideas and Activities of Charles Maurras* (Ph.D. thesis; Columbia Studies in History, Economics and Public Law, no.

455). New York: Columbia University, 1939. 355 pp.

Bibliography, pp. 335-50.

839. CHAMBERLIN, WILLIAM HENRY. *History of the Russian Revolution, 1917-1921.* New York: Macmillan, 1935. 2 vols.

An account of the Revolution to the New Economic Policy, heavily documented. By U.S. journalist who lived for some years in Russia. Documents, vol. 1, pp. 429-511; vol. 2, pp. 465-503. Bibliography, vol. 2, pp. 505-24.

840. DEWEY, JOHN; and others. *Not Guilty.* New York: Harpers, 1938. 422 pp.

Final report of the Commission that went to Mexico to hear evidence on the charges made against Leon Trotsky in the Moscow propaganda trials.

841. DUTT, R(AJANI) PALME. *World Politics, 1918-1936.* New York: Random House, 1936. 389 pp.

A Marxist interpretation.

842. ENGELBRECHT, HELMUTH CARL. *The Revolt against War*, foreword by Robert Staughton Lynd. New York: Dodd, Mead, 1937. 367 pp.

General treatise on contemporary war psychology and war propaganda, from the point of view of a promoter of peace. Bibliography, pp. 337-53.

843. FAINSOD, MERLE. *International Socialism and the World War* (Harvard Political Studies). Cambridge: Harvard University, 1935. 238 pp.

A survey of the period from August, 1914, to the creation of the Communist International at Moscow in 1919. By Harvard historian. Bibliography, pp. 225-32.

844. FISCHER, JOSEF; PATZAK, VACLAV; and PERTH, VICENC. *Ihr Kampf: Die wahren Ziele der sudeten deutschen Partei.* Karlsbad: Graphia, 1937. 141 pp.

Describes development of the Konrad Henlein movement among the Sudeten Germans of Czechoslovakia since the World War. First appeared in Czech in May 1937.

845. FORTES, M.; and EVANS-PRITCHARD, E. E., editors. *African Political Systems.* New York: Oxford University for International Institute of African Languages and Cultures, 1940. 301 pp.

A pioneer study of native and colonial political practices, by a group of British, German and American social scientists. Bibliographic footnotes.

846. FULLER, JOHN DOUGLAS PITTS. *The Movement for the Acquisition of All Mexico, 1846-48* (Ph.D. thesis, Johns Hopkins University). Baltimore: Johns Hopkins University, 1935. 174 pp.

By professor of history, Virginia Military Institute. Traces the emergence, growth, and decline of an annexationist movement. The data are drawn largely from a study of newspapers. Bibliography, pp. 165-68.

847. GANKIN, OLGA HESS; and FISHER, HAROLD HENRY. *The Bolsheviks and the World War: The Origins of the Third International* (Hoover Library on War, Revolution, and Peace, Publication no. 15). Stanford University: Stanford University, 1940. 856 pp.

A collection of documents selected from the mass of material dealing with the international socialist movement of 1914-18, with special emphasis on the part played by the Bolshevik faction of the Russian Social Democratic Labor party, precursor of the present Communist Party of the U.S.S.R. Contains chronology, biographical notes which provide much information not easily obtainable from other sources. The story told in the present volume ends in the middle of 1918 and the next installment is promised in *The Bolsheviks and World Revolution: The Founding of the Third International*. Annotated bibliography, pp. 729-70.

848. GREAT BRITAIN. PALESTINE ROYAL COMMISSION. *Report of the Palestine Royal Commission*, presented to Parliament by the Secretary of State for the Colonies. Geneva, 1937. 505 pp. London: H. M. Stationery Office, 1937. 404 pp.

849. HAILEY, MALCOLM HAILEY, BARON, editor. *An African Survey.* New

York and London: Oxford University for Royal Institute of International Affairs, 1938. 1837 pp.

Comprehensive political, economic, geographic, and anthropological study of all Africa south of the Sahara, developed over a period of several years by a group of Institute specialists.

850. HEALD, STEPHEN A., compiler. *A Directory of Societies and Organizations in Great Britain Concerned with the Study of International Affairs*, introduction by Sir William H. Beveridge. London: Royal Institute of International Affairs, 1929. 64 pp.

*851. HOBSON, JOHN ATKINSON (CB '40). *Imperialism: A Study*, "third entirely revised edition." London: Allen and Unwin, 1938. 386 pp.

Reissue of a standard work that first appeared in 1902, by an English economist.

852. HOLTOM, DANIEL CLARENCE. *Modern Japan and Shinto Nationalism: A Study of Present-day Trends in Japanese Religions* (The Haskell Lectures in Comparative Religion). Chicago: University of Chicago, 1943. 178 pp.

The author, a professor of church history (Ph.D. Chicago 1919), has lived and taught in Japan more than 30 years. Bibliography at ends of chapters.

853. INTERNATIONAL LABOUR OFFICE. *Yearbook*. Geneva, 1931–.

854. *International Sanctions: A Report of a Group of Members of the Royal Institute of International Affairs*. New York and London: Oxford University, 1938. 247 pp.

General study of available procedures for preparing in time of peace for the uniform and simultaneous application of sanctions. A chapter on "The Attitude of the United States of America" reviews attempts to appraise U.S. public opinion, and concludes that U.S. wealth and the strength of isolationist sentiment places this nation "clearly in a position, if it chooses, to render ineffective many of the forms of pressure which might be employed to compel observance of international law."

855. INTERNATIONAL STUDIES CONFERENCE (11th, Prague, 1938). *University Teaching of International Relations*, edited by Sir Alfred Zimmern. Paris: International Institute of Intellectual Cooperation, 1939. New York: Columbia University, 1939. 353 pp.

"If this was not the first international conference as yet held on this subject, it was certainly the first to be held under official auspices and probably the most representative and the most frank and outspoken."—Preface. Reports were received from more than a dozen countries.

856. JAMES, C. L. R. *World Revolution, 1917-36: The Rise and Fall of the Communist International*. London: Secker and Warburg, 1937. 429 pp.

Anti-Stalinist analysis of world politics, containing material on slogans and activities of the Fourth (Trotskyist) International. Bibliography in text and footnotes.

*856a. KEHR, ECKART. *Schlachtflottenbau und Parteipolitik, 1894-1901: Versuch eines Querschnitts durch die innenpolitischen, sozialen, und ideologischen Voraussetzungen des deutschen Imperialismus*. Berlin: Ebering, 1930. 464 pp.

German Navy League propaganda viewed as an example of the role of big business and governmental interests in the promotion of war and imperialism. By a German historian.

857. KNAPLUND, PAUL. *The British Empire, 1815-1939*. New York: Harpers, 1941. 850 pp.

By professor of history, University of Wisconsin. Appendix lists British Imperial officials, 1801-1940. Bibliography, pp. 803-27.

857a. LEAGUE OF NATIONS. *Handbook of International Organisations: Associations, Bureaux, Committees, etc.* (League of Nations XII. B. International Bureaux. 1937. XII. B. 4). Geneva, 1938. 491 pp.

Directory of several hundred public and private associations in many fields of activity. *Data given*: Address; Year of establishment; Membership; Object; Mode of government; Finances; Activities; History; Publications. Has geographic and subject indexes.

858. LEAGUE OF NATIONS. *Statistical Yearbook of the League of Nations, 1926–*. Geneva: The League Secretariat, 1927–. New York: Columbia University, 1939–.

859. LEAGUE OF NATIONS. COUNCIL. *Report on the Work of the League, 1920–*. Geneva, annually, 1920–. New York: Columbia University, 1939–.

860. LEAGUE OF NATIONS. INTERNATIONAL INSTITUTE OF INTELLECTUAL CO-OPERATION. *Recueil des accords intellectuels*. Paris, 1938. 232 pp.

Annotated collection of international agreements relating to intellectual cooperation, artistic, literary, and scientific.

861. LENIN, VLADIMIR ILYITCH. *The Communist International* (Selected Works, vol. 10). New York: International Publishers, 1938. 334 pp.

862. LENIN, VLADIMIR ILYITCH. *The Theoretical Principles of Marxism* (Selected Works, vol. 11). New York: International Publishers, 1939. 772 pp.

863. LEVENSOHN, LOTTA. *Outline of Zionist History*, foreword by Chaim Weizmann. New York: Scopus, 1941. 157 pp.

Sponsored by Jewish National Fund and Palestine Foundation Fund.

864. LIEPMAN, HEINZ. *Fires Underground*. Philadelphia: Lippincott, 1936. 300 pp.

Dramatic first-hand account of Socialist and Communist underground organizations in Germany, February 1930—June 1933.

865. "Literature on the Chinese Soviet Movement," *Pacific Affairs*, 9: 421-35 (September 1936).

Bibliographic essay prepared by staff of the American Council, Institute of Pacific Relations.

866. MACMILLAN, WILLIAM MILLER. *Africa Emergent: A Survey of Social, Political, and Economic Trends in British Africa*. London: Faber, 1938. 414 pp.

African holdings and policies of British Empire described by late Professor of History, University of the Witwatersrand, author of several other treatises on African social problems.

867. MADDOX, WILLIAM PERCY. *European Plans for World Order* (James-Rowe-Patten Pamphlet series, no. 8). Philadelphia: American Academy of Political and Social Science, 1940. 44 pp.

Includes "Official Peace Aim Declarations" of Britain, Germany, the Vatican; "Minority [i.e., British Labour] Party Peace Proposals"; various plans for "Reorganizing the League of Nations," for an "International Police Force," and for three types of "Federal Unions" and "Regional Federations." Dr. Maddox is a University of Pennsylvania political scientist.

868. MAUNIER, RENÉ. *Sociologie coloniale: Vol. 1, Introduction à l'étude du contact des races; Vol. 2, Psychologie des expansions*. Paris: Domat-Montchrestien, 1936. 2 vols.

Interracial contacts and the psychology of imperialism and expansionism. By a well-known sociologist (University of Paris). Bibliography, vol. 1, pp. 195-205; vol. 2, pp. 421-24.

869. MAZOUR, ANATOLE G. *The First Russian Revolution, 1825: The Decembrist Movement, Its Origins, Development, and Significance*. Berkeley: University of California, 1937. 324 pp.

Stresses the point that these revolutionists had little faith in the masses and omitted to foster mass support for their revolt. Personalities of leaders are traced from their early lives to their exile in Siberia. Dr. Mazour is Research Assistant in History, University of California. Bibliography, pp. 293-318, cites mostly Russian sources.

870. PALMER, GERALD EUSTACE HOWELL, compiler. *Consultation and Coöperation in the British Commonwealth: A Handbook on the Methods and Practice of Communication and Consultation between the Members of the British Commonwealth of Nations,* introduction by Professor Arthur Berriedale Keith. London: Oxford, 1934. 264 pp.

"Issued under the joint auspices of the Royal Institute of International Affairs and the Canadian Institute of International Affairs, on behalf of the first unofficial Conference on British Commonwealth Relations." Bibliography, pp. 244-56.

871. PAN-AMERICAN UNION. COLUMBUS MEMORIAL LIBRARY. *Theses on Pan-American Topics Prepared by Candidates for Degrees in Universities and Colleges in the United States.* Washington, D.C.: Columbus Memorial Library of the Pan-American Union, 1941. 170 pp.

872. PINSON, KOPPEL SHUB. *A Bibliographical Introduction to Nationalism.* New York: Columbia University, 1935. 70 pp.

A comprehensive, classified, and annotated bibliography, compiled by a U.S. professor of modern European history.

873. PRATT, JULIUS WILLIAM. *Expansionists of 1898: The Acquisition of Hawaii and the Spanish Islands* (The Albert Shaw Lectures on Diplomatic History, 1936). Baltimore: Johns Hopkins University, 1936. 393 pp.

Heavily documented study challenging widely held opinions as to the order in which supporters of the expansionist movement began their efforts to mold American opinion. By a U.S. professor of history. Bibliography, pp. 361-76.

874. REIMANN, GÜNTHER. *Germany: World Empire or World Revolution.* London: Secker and Warburg, 1938. 319 pp.

Thoroughgoing social-economic study by a social analyst attached to the Communist International. Contains much material on the psychology of leaders and masses of middle-class origin. Bibliographic footnotes.

875. RICHES, CROMWELL ADAMS. *Majority Rule in International Organization: A Study of the Trend from Unanimity to Majority Decision.* Baltimore:

Johns Hopkins University, 1940. 322 pp.

Study in international law and practice by Goucher College political scientist. Bibliography, pp. 307-14.

876. ROSENBERG, ARTHUR. *A History of Bolshevism: From Marx to the First Five Years' Plan,* translated by Ian F. D. Morrow. London: Oxford University, 1939. 250 pp.

By well-known ex-German historian. Bibliography, pp. 241-46.

877. ROYAL INSTITUTE OF INTERNATIONAL AFFAIRS. *The British Empire: A Report on Its Structure and Problems, by a Study Group of Members of the Royal Institute of International Affairs,* 2nd ed. London and New York: Oxford University, 1938. 342 pp.

Bibliographic footnotes.

878. ROYAL INSTITUTE OF INTERNATIONAL AFFAIRS. *The Colonial Problem: A Report by a Study Group of Members of the Royal Institute of International Affairs.* New York and London: Oxford University, 1937. 448 pp.

Bibliographic footnotes.

879. ROYAL INSTITUTE OF INTERNATIONAL AFFAIRS. *Nationalism.* London: Oxford, 1939. 360 pp.

Report by a study group, dealing with bases of nationalism in various countries and among various sections of the population. Bibliographic footnotes.

880. SAVORD, RUTH. *American Agencies Interested in International Affairs.* New York: Council on Foreign Relations, 1942. 200 pp.

Directory of almost 500 organizations, with subject and personnel indices, compiled by librarian of Council on Foreign Relations.

881. SCHUMACHER, HANS HEINRICH. *Kulturpropaganda in der französische Tagespresse.* Hamburg, 1939. 123 pp.

882. SMITH, WILLIAM ROY. *Nationalism and Reform in India.* New

Haven: Yale University, 1938. 485 pp.

Indian politics and social movements in the twentieth century, described by a U.S. historian. Bibliography, pp. 450-56.

882a. STALIN, JOSEPH. *Problems of Leninism.* Moscow: Foreign Languages Publishing House, 1940. 667 pp.

Translation of 11th Russian edition of *Problems of Leninism.* Includes selected theoretical speeches of Stalin since 1924, and full texts of his *Reports* to the 17th (1934) and 18th (1939) Congresses of the Communist Party of the Soviet Union. Pp. 647-67 are on "Measures to Improve the Composition of the Party," "Selection, Promotion and Allocation of Cadres," and "Party Propaganda"—its practice and theory.

883. STREIT, CLARENCE KIRSHMAN. *Union Now: A Proposal for a Federal Union of the Democracies of the North Atlantic.* New York: Harpers, 1939. 344 pp.

Plan of an organization called "Union Now" for a federal union of the democracies, to replace the League of Nations. By leader of the group, a U.S. correspondent who has had 20 years' experience in Europe—the last nine of them covering Geneva for the New York *Times.*

884. THWAITE, DANIEL. *The Seething African Pot: Black Nationalism, 1882-1935.* London: Constable, 1936. 258 pp.

885. TIMS, RICHARD W. *Germanizing Prussian Poland: The H-K-T Society and the Struggle for the Eastern Marches in the German Empire, 1894-1919* (Studies in History, Economics and Public Law, no. 487; Ph.D. thesis, Columbia). New York: Columbia University, 1941. 312 pp.

Material gained from newspapers, German and Polish language publications, and similar sources, enables the author to give an account of the German Eastern Marches Association (or H-K-T Society, from the initials of the three founders' names), a nationalistic pressure group and propaganda organization which tried to influence German public opinion and policies concerning the Ostmarken. Bibliography, pp. 289-308.

886. TROTSKY, LEON. *The Revolution Betrayed: What Is the Soviet Union and Where Is It Going?,* translated by Max Eastman. New York: Doubleday, Doran, 1937. 308 pp.

Trotsky's reply to the Soviet propaganda trials. Trotsky takes the view that "imperialism will sweep away the régime which issued from the October revolution" unless propaganda and direct action succeed in strengthening the position of proletarian and colonial forces throughout the world.

887. TROTSKY, LEON. *The Third International After Lenin,* translated by John G. Wright. New York: Pioneer Publishers, 1936. 357 pp.

888. U.S.S.R. PEOPLES' COMMISSARIAT OF JUSTICE. *The Case of the Anti-Soviet Trotskyite Center.* New York: Bookniga, 1937. 580 pp.

Official Soviet government report on famous propaganda trial in U.S.S.R.

889. VALOIS, GEORGES. *Technique de la révolution syndicale.* Paris: Liberté, 1935. 320 pp.

890. WEINBERG, ALBERT KATZ. *Manifest Destiny: A Study of Nationalist Expansionism in American History.* Baltimore: Johns Hopkins University, 1935. 559 pp.

By a U.S. historian (Ph.D. Johns Hopkins). Attitudes toward 15 symbols, such as "Natural Right," "Geographical Predestination," "the White Man's Burden," and "Self-Defense" are subjected to analysis. Bibliographic notes, pp. 487-542.

891. WERNER, LOTHAR. *Der Alldeutsche Verband, 1890-1918: Ein Beitrag zur Geschichte der öffentliche Meinung in Deutschland in den Jahren vor und während des Weltkrieges.* Berlin: Ebering, 1935. 294 pp.

The Pan-German League from 1890 to 1918. Bibliography, pp. 288-94.

892. WORLD CITIZENS ASSOCIA-

TION. *The World's Destiny and the United States: A Conference of Experts on International Relations, Convened by the World Citizens Association in 1941.*

Chicago, 84 East Randolph Street, 1941. 309 pp.

Includes a statement of the Association's by-laws and platform.

B. RESPONSE TOWARD GOAL-SYMBOLS OF NATIONAL, STATE, AND LOCAL GROUPS

I. NATIONAL, STATE, AND LOCAL GOVERNMENT POLICY

893. BENSON, GEORGE CHARLES SUMNER. "Interstate Cooperation," *Public Opinion Quarterly*, 1 no. 1: 123-26 (January 1937).

Campaigns of Council of State Governments are described by a U.S. political scientist.

894. CIVIL SERVICE ASSEMBLY OF THE UNITED STATES AND CANADA. *Employee Training in the Public Service.* Chicago: Public Administration Service, 1941. 172 pp.

Analysis of opportunities and facilities for employee training, and of methods of evaluating results, by a committee of the Civil Service Assembly. Bibliography, pp. 169-72.

895. CLARK, W. C. "Municipal Reports or Museum Pieces?" *Public Opinion Quarterly*, 3: 292-98 (April 1939).

By U.S. political scientist. A survey of distribution of reports in cities listed in *Municipal Year Book, 1938*, as publishing annual reports.

896. FOX, WILLIAM T(HORNTON) R(ICKERT). "Will the Public Support a Merit System?—A Pennsylvania Experiment," *Public Opinion Quarterly*, 3: 117-23 (January 1939).

Political scientist describes public relations of a group of promoters of the merit system.

897. GRAVES, WILLIAM BROOKE. "Public Reporting in the American States," *Public Opinion Quarterly*, 2: 211-28 (April 1938).

By U.S. political scientist.

898. HAZELRIGG, HAL. "Has the City Lost Its Voice?" *Public Opinion Quarterly*, 2: 457-65 (July 1938).

Public relations of city government are discussed by a staff member of Public Administration Clearing House.

899. HILL, L. "Advertising Local Government in England," *Public Opinion Quarterly*, 1 no. 2: 62-72 (April 1937).

"For 28 years, as general secretary of the National Association of Local Government Officers, Mr. Hill had an unusual opportunity to study the evolution of English public opinion in regard to public administration. Mr. Hill holds a M.A. degree from Liverpool University, and is a Commander of the British Empire."

900. HOLWAY, CHRISTIE P. "How a State Publicity Campaign Popularized Conservation," *Public Opinion Quarterly*, 1 no. 4: 140-43 (October 1937).

The author directed the Wisconsin publicity campaign he describes.

901. NATIONAL ASSOCIATION OF HOUSING OFFICIALS. *Public Relations of Local Housing Authorities: A Committee Report on a Vital Function of Local Public Housing Agencies.* Chicago, 1939. 38 pp.

Includes bibliography.

902. OLANDER, OSCAR GUSTAV. *Police Courtesy.* Lansing, Mich.: Franklin De Kleine Co., 1937. 48 pp.

Pocket manual of public relations for policemen, by Commissioner of Michigan State Police.

903. PFIFFNER, JOHN McDONALD. *Public Administration.* New York: Ronald Press, 1935. 525 pp.

Standard text by a U.S. political scientist. Part V is on "Public Relations." Bibliographies at ends of chapters and in footnotes.

904. PRICE, DON K. "The Promotion of the City Manager Plan," *Public Opinion Quarterly*, 5: 563-78 (Winter 1941).

Assistant Director of Public Administration Clearing House tells why the use of publicity symbols and techniques in promoting the city manager plan has spread less rapidly in recent years.

905. RIDLEY, CLARENCE EUGENE; and SIMON, HERBERT A. *Specifications for the Annual Municipal Report.* Chicago: International City Managers' Association, 1939. 59 pp.

By two officials of International City Managers' Association. Supplemented by *A Checklist of 266 Suggested Items for the Annual Municipal Report.* Chicago: International City Managers' Association, 1940. 18 pp.

906. ROGERS, NORMAN H. "Public Well-being," *Local Government Service*, 17: 167-72 (July 1937).

NALGO, the British National Association of Local Government Officials, organized a "Coronation Essay Competition" open to every citizen for the twelve best suggestions on: "How best to make known to the community during Coronation Year, the debt in public well-being which any given city, town, or village owes to local government." This article is the essay which was awarded first prize. The twelve suggestions constitute a national program of public relations for local governments. See also the editorial on this subject, same issue, p. 181.

907. SIMON, HERBERT A.; and RIDLEY, CLARENCE EUGENE. "Trends in Municipal Reporting," *Public Opinion Quarterly*, 2: 465-68 (July 1938).

By two officials of International City Managers' Association.

908. SLY, JOHN FAIRFIELD; and ROBBINS, JAMES JACOB. "Popularizing the Results of Government Research," *Public Opinion Quarterly*, 2: 7-23 (January 1938).

The Princeton School of Public Affairs in 1935 began a continuing survey of local government in New Jersey, hoping to improve governmental standards, and to make the program clear to the people of the state. In this article, the executive secretary of the survey, Dr. Sly (Ph.D. Harvard 1926), and his collaborator, Dr. Robbins (A.M. Harvard 1927; Ph.D. Princeton 1939) discuss the lines of thought which guided the publicity campaign.

909. TOMLIN, MAURICE. *Police and Public.* London: Longmans, Green, 1936. 286 pp.

A study of British policing by a former assistant commissioner of the London Metropolitan Police. Stresses attitudes of police and public toward one another. Contains a brief chapter on "Police in Fiction."

910. U.S. NATIONAL RESOURCES PLANNING BOARD. *The Future of State Planning.* Washington, D.C.: Government Printing Office, March 1938. 117 pp.

Report by a special review group on "what state planning boards might become," and a discussion of methods for their advancement. Includes a directory of members of all state planning boards and a bibliography of each board's reports.

911. VAN LOON, JANET. "Radio and Better City Government," *Public Opinion Quarterly*, 2: 100-04 (January 1938).

Author of a series of scripts on city government describes their contents and effects.

912. WILSON, LOGAN. "Public Opinion and the Individualized Treatment of Criminals," *Journal of Criminal Law*, 28: 674-83 (January 1938).

913. WOOLPERT, ELTON D. Series of articles in *Public Management*, January through July, 1940, outlining an elaborate public relations program for city governments.

914. WOOLPERT, ELTON D. *Municipal Public Relations.* St. Paul, Minn.: International City Managers' Association, 1940. 50 pp.

II. HOUSING, HUMANITARIANISM, SOCIAL SECURITY

915. ARONOVICI, CAROL. *Housing the Masses.* New York: Wiley, 1939. London: Chapman and Hall, 1939. 291 pp.

Comprehensive study of U.S. housing problems and housing education by a well-known U.S. specialist. Chapter 9 is on "Housing Education." Pp. 277-86 are a bibliographic essay on "Housing Literature."

916. ASCHER, CHARLES STERN. "Federal Housing Symbols Are Tiresome," *Public Opinion Quarterly*, 1 no. 1: 110-12 (January 1937).

By a specialist in public administration who was the first director of National Association of Housing Officials (1934).

916a. BROWN, JOHN CROSBY. "Public Relations in the Philanthropic Field," *Public Opinion Quarterly*, 1 no. 2: 138-43 (April 1937).

By president of a fund-raising firm.

917. CLAPPER, RAYMOND. "Social Work and the Press," *Survey Midmonthly*, 75: 365-66 (December 1939).

Well-known Washington correspondent tells social workers' conference that (1) social workers might learn from politicians never to be too busy to spend a few minutes with a reporter; (2) successful press agents "must be as intimately associated with the whole operation of the agency as anyone in the set-up . . . almost an alter-ego for the top executive . . . give the reporter access to firsthand sources, making it very clear what cannot be published and why. Leave no room for doubt or confusion on that point and 99 per cent of your trouble will be eliminated"; (3) social workers ought to be technical in their work, but never in the way they talk about it. "I have never liked the terms 'cases' and 'clients' "; (4) social workers can make news by calling in reporters to cover cases that are bound to arouse wide public sympathy and by stressing the speed and efficiency with which the agency leaps at the opportunity to render aid.

918. COMMONS, JOHN ROGERS; and ANDREWS, JOHN BERTRAM. *Principles of Labor Legislation*, 4th rev. ed. New York: Harpers, 1936. 606 pp.

First published in 1916, this well-known treatise concisely describes nearly every type of labor legislation that has been put into effect in the United States, and gives references to what has been done abroad. The revision brings the data up to September 1936. Bibliography, pp. 535-84.

919. *Directory of Psychiatric Clinics in the United States*, compiled and edited by the Division on Community Clinics of the National Committee for Mental Hygiene. New York: Commonwealth Fund, at intervals, 1925-.

For locating the services available in your community or near by. Contains addresses, names of staff members, office hours, numbers of cases examined during the preceding year, etc.

920. GERLINGER, IRENE HAZARD. *Money Raising: How To Do It*. New York: Suttonhouse, 1938. 311 pp.

Surveys problems of financing educational and social agencies: community chests, churches, hospitals, colleges, clubs, museums, orchestras, little theaters, libraries. Chapter 2 is on wartime publicity and campaign methods, chapter 12 on "the new profession of fund-raising counsel." The author is vice-president of Pacific College, Newberg, Oregon. Bibliography, pp. 277-95.

921. HULETT, J. E., JR. "Propaganda and the Proposed Child Labor Amendment," *Public Opinion Quarterly*, 2: 105-15 (January 1938).

Careful study of work of National Child Labor Committee, by social psychologist trained at University of Wisconsin.

921a. JONES, JOHN PRICE. *The Technique to Win in Fund Raising*. New York: Inter-river Press, 1934. 230 pp.

By president of a corporation which specializes in fund raising.

922. LATIMER, HENRY RANDOLPH. *The Conquest of Blindness: An Autobiographical Review*. New York: American Foundation for the Blind, 1938. 363 pp.

Through an autobiography recounting his lifetime of work for the blind, the author gives a running history of campaigns against blindness over the last half century, in the United Kingdom as well as in the U.S.

923. LENDE, HELGA, editor. *What of the Blind?* New York: American Foundation for the Blind, 1938. 214 pp.

Surveys the development and present scope of campaigns for aid to the blind. Bibliographic essay, pp. 206-09.

923a. LEVY, HAROLD P. *A Study in Public Relations: A Case History of the Relations Maintained between a Department of Public Assistance and the People of a State*, introduction by Mary Swain Routzahn. New York: Russell Sage Foundation, 1943. 165 pp.

How the Pennsylvania Department of Public Assistance takes care of its public relations problems. By a research associate of the Foundation.

923b. NATIONAL ASSOCIATION OF HOUSING OFFICIALS. *Housing Officials' Yearbook, 1935–.* Chicago, 1935–.

Contains materials on the public relations of housing officials.

924. NATIONAL COMMITTEE FOR MENTAL HYGIENE, 50 West 50th Street, New York City.

Can supply the latest bibliography, and much inexpensive pamphlet material, on such topics as: "Behavior Problems of School Children," "Mental Hygiene in the Training of Teachers," etc. Also publishes *Understanding the Child: A Magazine for Teachers* (50c per year), and *Mental Hygiene* (quarterly journal).

925. NATIONAL EDUCATION ASSOCIATION. EDUCATIONAL POLICIES COMMISSION. *Social Services and the Schools.* Washington, D.C., 1939. 147 pp.

"A systematic analysis of co-operative relationships between public schools and public health, welfare, and recreational agencies and public libraries. Although many controversial questions were encountered, a framework of policy has been developed."—Foreword. May indicate rising social consciousness among the middle-income skill groups. Bibliography, pp. 142-44.

926. PALMER, HAROLD D.; and HARPER, EDWARD O. "College Mental Hygiene Methods," *Mental Hygiene*, 21: 397-415 (July 1937).

Describes the exceptionally well-developed program in effect at the University of Pennsylvania in 1936-37. Reproduces (pp. 404-07) the forms on which records of the students'

emotional-bodily development are kept. Teachers and administrators will find this article full of practical suggestions.

927. PARKER, J. S. "Explaining Social Security Legislation to Wisconsin Business Men," *Journal of National Education Association*, 26: 89-90 (March 1937).

"It is not enough merely to pass social security legislation. That legislation must also be explained to the general public. In particular, it must be 'sold' to the responsible business executives." The author reports his experiences in this task while engaged in "a program of adult education sponsored jointly by the extension division of the University of Wisconsin and by the vocational schools of the state."

927a. PIERCE, LYMAN L. "Philanthropy—A Major Big Business," *Public Opinion Quarterly*, 2: 140-45 (January 1938).

By president of a U.S. fund-raising corporation.

928. POST, LANGDON W. *The Challenge of Housing.* New York: Farrar and Rinehart, 1938. 309 pp.

By a U.S. public administrator who has gained a national reputation in the housing field. Includes the story of his campaigns to make housing front-page news (chapter 5, "Meeting the Opposition," and other passages).

929. ROUTZAHN, MARY SWAIN; and ROUTZAHN, EVART GRANT. *Publicity for Social Work.* New York: Russell Sage Foundation, 1936. 392 pp.

New edition of a standard treatise. The authors have published a number of other books and articles in this field.

930. SCHNAPPER, M. B. *Public Housing in America* (Reference Shelf, vol. 13, no. 5). New York: H. W. Wilson, 1939. 369 pp.

Debate manual. Bibliography, pp. 353-69.

931. *Social Work Yearbook: A Description of Organized Activities in Social Work and in Related Fields, 1929–.* New York: Russell Sage Foundation, 1930–.

Encyclopedia-like articles on all phases of social work, and a directory of agencies. See Index for such topics as "Publicity in social work," "Trade unionism in social work," etc.

932. U.S. HOUSE OF REPRESENTATIVES. WAYS AND MEANS COMMITTEE. *Social Security, Hearings Relative to Social Security Act Amendments of 1939, 76th Congress, 1st Session.* Washington, D.C.: Government Printing Office, 1939. 3 vols. (2612 pp.)

III. PEACE, DEMOCRACY, TOLERANCE

[See also Part 2, C, VII above.]

933. ATWATER, ELTON. "Organizing American Public Opinion for Peace," *Public Opinion Quarterly,* 1 no. 2: 112-21 (April 1937).

General survey of peace organizations.

934. BERNAYS, EDWARD L. *Speak Up for Democracy: What You Can Do—A Practical Plan of Action for Every American Citizen.* New York: Viking Press, 1940. 127 pp.

Noted public relations counsel urges all U.S. citizens to "speak up for democracy" through every available channel of communication. He outlines "twenty common charges against democracy," and answers them. He maps out a complete public relations program, utilizing the "group leadership approach," and a multitude of channels such as holiday celebrations, press conferences, direct-mail, forums, radio, movies, youth groups. Symbols involved include celebrated American documents (emphasis on Bill of Rights), patriotic ceremonies, birthdays of famous Americans, and lists of appeals to special interest groups. Includes extensive bibliography on democratic practice, dictatorships, U.S. customs, leadership techniques, and public opinion.

935. BURDETTE, FRANKLIN L. "Education for Citizenship," *Public Opinion Quarterly,* 6: 269-79 (Summer 1942).

In the United States literally hundreds of group agencies outside the formal educational system seek in their own way to promote educational ideals. Dr. Burdette presents a comprehensive picture of their objectives, activities, and techniques. The author (Ph.D. Princeton 1938) is Executive Secretary of the National Foundation for Education in American Citizenship.

936. CLARKE, WILLIAM FRANCIS. *The Folly of Bigotry: An Analysis of Intolerance.* Chicago: Non-Sectarian League for Americanism, 1940. 137 pp.

A series of addresses on causes and possible cures of U.S. and foreign intolerance movements, by vice-president of Non-Sectarian League for Americanism.

937. COMMISSION ON INTERRACIAL COOPERATION, INC. *Democratic Processes at Work in the South: Report of the Commission, 1939-41.* Atlanta, Georgia, 1941. 21 pp.

By Jessie Daniel Ames, secretary of the Commission.

938. CONGRESO CONTRA EL RACISMO Y EL ANTISEMITISMO. *Actas del primer congreso.* Buenos Aires: Comité contra el racismo y el antisemitismo de la Argentina, 1938. 270 pp.

Transactions of first Congress Against Racism and Anti-Semitism.

939. COUNCIL AGAINST INTOLERANCE IN AMERICA. *An American Answer to Intolerance: Experimental Form, 1939* (Teacher's Manual No. 1, Junior and Senior High Schools). New York: Council Against Intolerance in America, 1939. 116 pp.

Manual for teachers, dealing with "Recognition of Prejudice," "Study of Propaganda Devices," "Reaffirmation of American Ideals," and "Accurate Knowledge in Propaganda Domains" (i.e., scientific data on topics that are frequently misrepresented by propagandists). Includes a 15-page bibliography.

940. COUNCIL AGAINST INTOLERANCE IN AMERICA. *We're All Americans* (Teacher's Manual No. 2, Elementary Schools). New York City, 1941. 92 pp.

Bibliography, pp. 82-91.

941. COUNCIL FOR DEMOCRACY. *Action: A Newsletter on the Defense of American Democracy.* New York (285 Madison Ave.), 1941-.

A periodical supplement to the Council's community guidebook, *Defense on Main Street.*

942. CURTI, MERLE EUGENE. *Peace or War: The American Struggle, 1636-1936.* New York: Norton, 1936. 374 pp.

A compact history of the American peace movements by a well-known U.S. historian, a specialist in this field. Bibliographic notes, pp. 313-58.

943. DONINGTON, ROBERT; and DONINGTON, BARBARA. *The Citizen Faces War,* introduction by Sir Norman Angell. London: Gollancz, 1936. 286 pp.

History and analysis of British conscientious objection in World War I, and a plea for "collective security."

944. JONES, MARY HOXIE. *Swords Into Ploughshares: An Account of the American Friends' Service Committee, 1917-1937.* New York: Macmillan, 1937. 374 pp.

History of the American Friends' Service Committee's campaign for peace and public service from 1917 to 1937.

945. LARSON, CEDRIC. "The Council for Democracy," *Public Opinion Quarterly,* 6: 284-90 (Summer 1942).

By a U.S. Federal administrator.

946. LIGT, BARTHÉLEMY DE. *La Paix créatrice: Histoire des principes et des tactiques de l'action directe contre la guerre.* Paris: Rivière, 1934. 536 pp.

A pacifist scholar accumulates comprehensive information on numerous groups and theories which have resisted war with symbols of "moral force," "enlightenment," and "religious revolt." Bibliography, pp. 515-26.

947. LIGT, BARTHÉLEMY DE. *The Conquest of Violence: An Essay on War and Revolution,* introduction by Aldous Huxley. New York: Dutton, 1938. 317 pp.

Well-known pacifist social theorist outlines a "Plan of Campaign Against All War and All Preparation for War," calling upon war-resisters to refuse *in time of peace* to make war materials or to pay taxes for war-producing purposes. Bibliography, pp. 289-96.

948. LINN, WALTER ARMIN. *False Prophets of Peace.* Harrisburg, Pennsylvania: Military Service Publishing Company, 1939. 367 pp.

A study of pacifist movements since the War of 1812 and their effect upon war. Bibliography, pp. 366-67.

949. MATTHEWS, MARY ALICE, compiler. *The Peace Movement: Select List of References on the Work of National and International Organizations for the Advancement of Peace.* Washington, D.C.: Carnegie Endowment for International Peace Library, 700 Jackson Place, 1940. 67 pp.

Select list of references, with special attention to the movement in the U.S.

950. *Peace Year Book.* London: National Peace Council, 1910–.

Some issues are entitled "*International Peace Year Book.*"

951. TATE, MERZE. *The Disarmament Illusion: The Movement for a Limitation of Armaments to 1907* (Ph.D. thesis, Harvard). New York: The Macmillan Company for Bureau of International Research, Harvard University and Radcliffe College, 1942. 398 pp.

An historical and analytical study of the disarmament movement down to 1907. Bibliography, pp. 365-78.

952. SAVARY, PETER. "Men Against War," *Christian Science Monitor Magazine,* November 10, 1937, p. 4.

On War Resisters' International.

953. STERNBERGER, ESTELLE MILLER. *The Supreme Cause: A Practical Book About Peace.* New York: Dodd, Mead, 1936. 218 pp.

Presents the views of many American authorities on the programs of the various peace movements. By Executive Director of the Emergency Peace Campaign. Bibliography, pp. 203-18.

IV. HEALTH AND MENTAL HYGIENE

954. ACHILLES, PAUL STRONG. *The Effectiveness of Certain Social Hygiene Literature* (Ph.D. thesis, Columbia, 1923). New York, 1923. 117 pp.

Study made under auspices of American Social Hygiene Committee.

955. BAILEY, STANLEY HARTNOLL. *The Anti-Drug Campaign: An Experiment in International Control.* London: King, 1936. 264 pp.

Survey of the international drive against drug addiction from 1909 to the time of writing, stressing the details of the work of the League of Nations.

956. BAUER, WILLIAM WALDO; and EDGLEY, LESLIE. *Your Health Dramatized.* New York: Dutton, 1939. 528 pp.

Radio plays adapted from the radio health dramatizations broadcast during 1937-38 by American Medical Association and NBC especially for junior and senior high schools. Bibliography, pp. 524-28.

957. BAUER, WILLIAM WALDO; and HULL, THOMAS GORDON. *Health Education of the Public: A Practical Manual of Technic.* Philadelphia: W. B. Saunders, 1937. 227 pp.

Manual on community health campaigns. Explains objectives of various public health programs, and use of radio, films, speeches, public meetings, etc., in promoting them. Bibliography, pp. 215-17.

958. BENJAMIN, HAZEL C. "Lobbying for Birth Control," *Public Opinion Quarterly*, 2: 48-60 (January 1938).

From 1934 to 1937 Miss Benjamin (M.A., political science, Chicago) was in charge of the records of the National Committee on Federal Legislation for Birth Control.

959. BRITISH SOCIAL HYGIENE COUNCIL, INC. *Empire Social Hygiene Yearbook, 1934–.* London: Allen and Unwin.

The term "social hygiene" refers to "all the various efforts which are now being made, and the others which remain to be made, in order to combat the incidence of venereal disease." Lists voluntary organizations in social hygiene throughout the world. Includes bibliographies.

959a. BROWN, MARTIN WALSMAN; CLARK, KATHERINE G.; and TAYLOR, PERRY R. *How to Organize Group Health Plans.* Camden, N.J.: Joint Committee of Twentieth Century Fund and Good Will Fund and Medical Administration Service, Inc., 1942. 72 pp.

A manual of rather specific information concerning the promotional, legal, and financial problems involved in organizing group health plans.

960. CABOT, HUGH. *The Patient's Dilemma: The Quest for Medical Security in America.* New York: Reynal and Hitchcock, 1940. 284 pp.

Well-known U.S. surgeon argues that the U.S. ought to be dotted with medical centers where rich and poor alike may be examined and treated not by one doctor but by half a dozen specialists who have every essential laboratory and therapeutic facility at their disposal. "Private practice is no longer good enough." Briefly suggests a possible propaganda campaign.

961. CACHUAT, MAURICE. *Le Mouvement du "birth control" dans les pays anglo-saxons, avec un appendice sur la stérilisation et le contrôle des naissances en Allemagne* (Bibliothèque de l'Institut de Droit Comparé de Lyon, sér. centrale, vol. 32). Paris: Giard, 1934. 553 pp.

Bibliography, pp. xxxi-lxxx and 541-47.

962. DAVIS, MICHAEL MARKS. *America Organizes Medicine.* New York: Harpers, 1941. 335 pp.

Growing out of the work of the Committee on Research in Medical Economics (a nonprofit organization supported by a grant from the Julius Rosenwald Fund), of which Dr. Davis is Chairman, this study presents an analysis of contemporary medical care problems, with a suggested program for America. Dr. Davis was one of the organizers of the Committee on the Costs of Medical Care which conducted nationwide studies from 1927 to 1932; has been a consultant on health studies for the government since 1934. Bibliography, pp. 302-20.

963. DE KRUIF, PAUL HENRY. *Health is Wealth.* New York: Harcourt, Brace, 1940. 246 pp.

By well-known popularizer of biology and the medical sciences, who pleads the cause of the millions who cannot afford to pay a physician. Includes "Fundamental Principles of a Non-Controversial National Health Program," as drawn up by a nationally known group of physicians.

964. FREEDMAN, HARRY L. "Role of the Mental Hygiene Clinic in a Military Training Center," *Mental Hygiene,* 27: 83-121 (January 1943).

By director of a U.S. Army mental hygiene unit.

965. GEBHARD, BRUNO. "Mass Education by Health Exhibits," *Quarterly Review of New York City Cancer Committee,* 4: 80-83 (January 1940).

"Success of the traveling exhibits on tuberculosis in this country is well known. The medium has also been used in the cancer field but usually on a small scale." Details of the management of traveling exhibits are given. Dr. Gebhard is technical consultant, American Museum of Health, Inc.

966. GALL, ALICE CREW. *In Peace and War: A Story of Human Service.* New York: Crowell, 1941. 278 pp.

History of Red Cross. Bibliography included in preface.

967. (Pop.) GRUENBERG, BENJAMIN CHARLES. *Science and the Public Mind,* foreword by John C. Merriam. New York and London: McGraw-Hill, 1935. 196 pp.

Evaluates the views of scientists and popularizers on the strategy of the diffusion of knowledge. The social sciences are not included in the category "science." The Appendix lists current agencies of adult education. The study was undertaken at the invitation of the American Association for Adult Education.

968. GUMPERT, MARTIN. *Dunant: The Story of the Red Cross.* New York: Oxford University, 1938. 323 pp.

Henri Dunant, a young Swiss banker, was so overcome by his visit to a battlefield that he gave up his banking career to organize the first promotional campaign for the International Red Cross. Years later, a forgotten man in a village poorhouse, he was awarded the first Nobel Peace Prize. The author is a physician and historian who formerly lived in Germany. Bibliography, pp. 319-23.

969. HISCOCK, IRA V.; and others. *Ways to Community Health Education.* New York: Commonwealth Fund, 1939. 306 pp.

970. *The Health Status and Health Education of Negroes in the United States* (Yearbook No. 6; *Journal of Negro Education,* 6: 261-587, July 1937).

Part III is on health education campaigns among Negroes.

971. HIMES, NORMAN EDWIN. *The Medical History of Contraception.* Baltimore: Williams and Wilkins, 1936. 553 pp.

By Colgate University sociologist. Chapter 5 contains materials on the birth control movement, its publicity, famous trials, and writers. Bibliography, pp. 425-90.

972. HOFFMAN, PAUL GRAY; in collaboration with Neil M. Clark. *Seven Roads to Safety.* New York: Harpers, 1939. 87 pp.

President of Automotive Safety Foundation (and also of Studebaker Corporation) states the Foundation's achievements and explains its seven-point program: promotion of Legislation, Motor Vehicle Administration, Enforcement, Engineering, Education, Technical Personnel Training, and Research to bring about safety on U.S. roads.

973. JOHNSEN, JULIA EMILY, compiler. *Socialization of Medicine* (The Reference Shelf, vol. 10, no. 5). New York: H. W. Wilson, 1936. 335 pp.

Selected arguments and bibliography.

974. KINGSBURY, JOHN ADAMS. *Health in Handcuffs.* New York: Modern Age, 1939. 210 pp.

U.S. movement for cooperative medicine, described by a U.S. authority on public health problems. Data are based on findings of National Health Conference, July 1938.

975. LAWTON, ANNE M. "Telling Our Story Through Radio: Types of Radio Programs Used by Nursing Agencies," *Public Health Nursing*, 32: 484-87 (August 1940).

976. *The Mental Hygiene Movement from the Philanthropic Standpoint.* New York: Department of Philanthropic Information, Central Hanover Bank and Trust Company, 1939. 73 pp.

Brief and lucid summary of the achievements and possible future contributions of the U.S. mental hygiene movement. Available, for 25 cents, from National Committee for Mental Hygiene, 50 West 50th St., New York City. Bibliographic footnotes.

977. MILLS, ALDEN B. *Hospital Public Relations.* Chicago: Physicians' Record Company, 1939. 361 pp.

General treatise by managing editor of *Modern Hospital*, who was formerly executive secretary of research staff of Committee on Costs of Medical Care. "The entire personnel—from floor maid, orderly, engineer, mechanic, clerk, telephone operator, hostess, admitting officer, technician and therapist to dietitian, social worker, nurse, physician and administrator—has an important role to perform in the development of public relations." Principles of public relations are developed which may be applied to other objectives. Bibliography at ends of chapters.

978. MYRDAL, ALVA REIMER. *Nation and Family: The Swedish Experiment in Democratic Family and Population Policy.* New York: Harpers, 1941. 441 pp.

Carefully documented analysis of the setting and accomplishments of contemporary movements supporting birth control, sex education, and a conscious population policy in Sweden. Bibliography, pp. 427-36.

979. NATIONAL EDUCATION ASSOCIATION. *Safety and Safety Education.* Washington, January 1939. 64 pp.

Some 1400 briefly annotated references, in two groups: (1) books, pamphlets, bulletins; (2) magazine articles, 1936-39.

980. NELSON, NELS ALBIN; and CRAIN, GLADYS L. *Syphilis, Gonorrhea and the Public Health.* New York: Macmillan, 1938. 359 pp.

Social diseases and the development of public educational programs, by two workers in the Massachusetts Department of Public Health. Bibliography at ends of chapters.

981. PARRAN, THOMAS. *Shadow on the Land: Syphilis.* New York: Reynal and Hitchcock, 1937. 309 pp.

Surveys social hygiene problems in the United States and abroad, and describes the vigorous campaign of public education being waged currently by the author, the Surgeon General of the United States Public Health Service.

982. PATRY, FREDERICK L. "A State Wide Mental Hygiene Program for the Elementary School," *Journal of Abnormal and Social Psychology*, 32: 74-99 (April-June 1937).

Concise but comprehensive statement of the philosophy, organization, and supervision of a state-wide program, by psychiatrist of the New York State Education Department. Contains charts and extensive selected bibliography.

983. PRITCHARD, E. G. "Motion Picture Films for Health and Safety Education, Available from Five State Agencies," *Health Officer*, 4: 300-12 (December 1939).

984. *Researches in Parent Education* (University of Iowa Studies in Child Welfare). Iowa City: University of Iowa, 1932-39. 4 vols.

A group of studies covering such topics as (1) "A Home Program for Mothers in Sex Education" (Ph.D. thesis of Katharine W. Hattendorf); (2) "A Standard for Estimating the Validity of Child Developmental Principles," by R. H. Ojemann; (3) "An Experimental Investigation of Methods in Parent Education," by Hazel S. Schaus; (4) "Handicaps of School Entrants," by Laura L. Remer; (5) "A Study of Fifty Home Libraries with Special Reference to their Function in Child Development," by Gertrude H. Nystrom; (6) "A Device for Measurement of Parent Attitudes and Practices," by Lois M. Jack (the complete questionnaire and scoring method of the attitude indicator is reproduced).

985. RESNICK, DAVID. "Social Hygiene and the Public Mind," *Journal of Social Hygiene*, 23: 333-42 (October 1937).

Publicity manager's account of a social hygiene campaign, with suggestions for a practical community promotional program focusing on Social Hygiene Day.

986. RORTY, JAMES. *American Medicine Mobilizes*. New York: Norton, 1939. 358 pp.

Pressures for and against group medicine and other public health measures described by a U.S. journalist. Stresses role of American Medical Association.

987. STERN, BERNHARD JOSEPH. *Society and Medical Progress*. Princeton: Princeton University, 1941. 264 pp.

Analysis of social factors affecting the diffusion and utilization of medical science. By U.S. sociologist whose Ph.D. thesis (Columbia 1927) was on *Social Factors in Medical Progress*. Bibliography, pp. 223-47.

988. STEVENSON, GEORGE SALVADORE. "Ways of Developing and Utilizing Psychiatry in Community Health and Welfare Programs," *Mental Hygiene*, 24: 353-65 (July 1940).

By Medical Director, National Committee for Mental Hygiene.

989. STEVENSON, GEORGE SALVADORE; and SMITH, GEDDES. *Child Guidance Clinics: A Quarter Century of Development*. New York: Commonwealth Fund, 1936. 186 pp.

The standard history of the child guidance movement in the United States, supplying figures and analysis. The movement has grown from one clinic in 1909 to over 200 in 1935.

990. STOWELL, T. C. "Social Hygiene on the Air," *Journal of Social Hygiene*, 22: 165-72 (April 1936).

991. WITMER, HELEN LELAND. *Psychiatric Clinics for Children, with Special Reference to State Programs*. New York: The Commonwealth Fund, 1940. 437 pp.

Faculty member of Smith College School of Social Work, who is Research Associate of National Committee for Mental Hygiene, surveys against a background of psychiatric and sociological knowledge the theoretical and historical basis of clinical child psychiatry; the status of state-financed clinics in the U.S.; and plans for effective psychiatric service in the future. Bibliographic footnotes.

V. COOPERATIVES AND CONSUMER EDUCATION

992. CAMPBELL, PERSIA CRAWFORD. *Consumer Representation in the New Deal* (Ph.D. thesis; Studies in History, Economics and Public Law, no. 477). New York: Columbia University. London: P. S. King, 1940. 298 pp.

By Australian-American economist who was executive secretary of Consumers National Federation, 1937-40. Bibliographic footnotes.

993. CARR-SAUNDERS, ALEXANDER MORRIS; FLORENCE, P. SARGANT; PEERS, ROBERT; and others. *Consumers' Coöperation in Great Britain: An Examination of the British Coöperative Movement*. London: Allen and Unwin, 1938. 566 pp.

First comprehensive study since Beatrice Potter Webb's *The Cooperative Movement in Great Britain* (first edition 1922, tenth edition 1930). Bibliography, pp. 541-46.

994. *Consumers Co-operation* (Annals of the American Academy of Political and Social Science, vol. 191), edited by John Grist Brainerd. May 1937. 292 pp.

995. DANIELS, JOHN. *Co-operation: An American Way*. New York: Covici, Friede, 1938. 399 pp.

U.S. cooperative movement, its accomplishments and prospects, described by a U.S. freelance writer.

996. EDWARD A. FILENE GOOD WILL FUND. *Consumer Cooperative Leadership: Organizing and Running Consumer Cooperatives*. Boston, 1942. 173 pp.

A manual for those who wish to start cooperatives. Annotated bibliography, pp. 164-68.

997. EDWARDS, ALICE L. "Consumer Interest Groups," *Public Opinion Quarterly*, 1 no. 3: 104-11 (July 1937).

By a former executive secretary of American Home Economics Association.

998. HALL, ROBERT C. "British Cooperatives in Politics," *Public Opinion Quarterly*, 3: 124-30 (January 1939).

Based on the author's studies in England as a graduate student in economics.

999. KRESS, ANDREW JOHN, editor. *Introduction to the Coöperative Movement.* New York: Harpers, 1941. 370 pp.

Anthology of over 300 selected readings on the consumer cooperative movement from Robert Owen to the present.

1000. NATIONAL CONFERENCE ON CONSUMER EDUCATION. *Making Consumer Education Effective.* Columbia, Mo.: Institute for Consumer Education, Stephens College, 1940. 253 pp.

Proceedings of the Second National Conference on Consumer Education, held at Stephens College, April 1-3, 1940. Addresses are grouped under the following heads: "Special Approaches to Consumer Education" (i.e., Better Business Bureaus and Cooperatives); "What Should Be Taught About Advertising in a Consumer Course?"; "Vitalizing Economic Education"; and "Current Economic Issues of Interest to Consumers." Summarizes the discussions of 18 round table groups.

1001. *Report of the Inquiry on Coöperative Enterprise in Europe, 1937,* Jacob Baker, chairman. Washington, D.C.: Government Printing Office, 1937. 321 pp.

Survey of the European cooperative movement, with comment on the applicability of European methods to problems in the U.S., by a commission of inquiry sent to Europe by President F. D. Roosevelt.

1002. TERESHTENKO, VALERY J.; and research staff of the Cooperative Project. *Cooperative Education: Bibliographical Review of Literature on Coöperative Education.* New York: Federal Works Agency, Work Projects Administration, 1941. 363 pp.

Education for, in, and by cooperative societies. Annotations of 567 titles. Thoroughly indexed. Includes a list of 213 student cooperatives in the U.S.

1002a. WALES, NYM (pseud. of HELEN FOSTER [MRS. EDGAR] SNOW). *China Builds for Democracy: A Story of Cooperative Industry.* New York: Modern Age, 1942. 310 pp.

First-hand account of Indusco, the industrial cooperative movement in China. Bibliography, pp. 308-10.

1003. WARBASSE, JAMES PETER. *Cooperative Democracy through Voluntary Association of the People as Consumers,* 4th ed., rev. New York: Harpers, 1942. 285 pp.

Standard treatise by president emeritus of Cooperative League of the United States. Bibliography, pp. 271-73.

PART 4. THE SYMBOLS AND PRACTICES OF WHICH PROPAGANDA MAKES USE OR TO WHICH IT ADAPTS ITSELF

A propagandist is both helped and handicapped by the symbols and practices of his publics. His skill consists in maneuvering successfully within the limits imposed by current vocabularies, preferences, and practices.

This section includes:

1. A limited number of historical and genetic studies of collective attitudes toward persons, groups, policies, doctrines, institutions, and practices.

2. A limited number of general social and cultural histories of such large social aggregates as:
  (a) races
  (b) broad social strata
  (c) the following Great Power nations and areas:
China, England (for British Empire as a whole see 3 A [Imperialism]), France, Germany, Italy, Japan, Latin America (as a whole), Russia, and U.S.

1004. ABEL, THEODORE F. (D). *Why Hitler Came Into Power.* New York: Prentice-Hall, 1938. 301 pp.

Six hundred of Hitler's followers submitted their life-histories to this Columbia University sociologist. Placing these intimate documents in the perspective of European history since the turn of the century, he concludes that the success of the National Socialist Party may be attributed to widespread social discontent, which created receptivity for "the particular ideology and program for social transformation adopted by the Nazis"—a receptivity that was clinched by "the National Socialist organizational and promotional technique" and by "charismatic leadership."

1005. ABEND, HALLETT EDWARD (CB '42, W). *Ramparts of the Pacific.* New York: Doubleday, Doran, 1942. 332 pp.

Discussion of Far Eastern problems by New York *Times* correspondent who has spent some fifteen years in China.

1005a. AMERICAN YOUTH COMMISSION. *Youth and the Future: The General Report of the American Youth Commission.* Washington, D.C.: American Council on Education, 1942. 296 pp.

Outcome of six years' research and deliberation by a nationally prominent group of men and women. Includes outlines of a postwar plan for dealing with the expected mass unemployment.

1006. ANDERSON, EUGENE NEWTON (D). "Meinecke's *Ideengeschichte* and the Crisis in Historical Thinking," in *Medieval and Historiographical Essays in Honor of James Westfall Thompson* (Chicago: University of Chicago, 1938), pp. 361-96.

1007. ANDERSON, PAULINE RELYEA. *The Background of Anti-English Feeling in Germany, 1890-1902* (Ph.D. thesis, Bryn Mawr). Washington, D.C.: American University, 1939. 382 pp.

Bibliographic footnotes.

1008. ANGUS, HENRY F(ORBES) (D), editor. *Canada and Her Great Neighbor: Sociological Surveys of Opinions and Attitudes in Canada Concerning the United States.* New Haven: Yale University for Carnegie Endowment for International Peace, 1938. 451 pp.

Professor Angus is head of the Department of Economics, Political Science and Sociology, University of British Columbia.

1009. AUXIER, GEORGE WASHINGTON. *The Cuban Question as Reflected in the Editorial Columns of*

Middle Western Newspapers, 1895-1898 (Ph.D. thesis, Ohio State University, 1938). 328 pp.

Bibliography, pp. 322-27.

1009a. BABCOCK, FRANKLIN LAWRENCE. *The U.S. College Graduate.* New York: Time, Inc., 1941. 112 pp.

Statistical report, based on research conducted by *Time* magazine, of the "status" of living graduates of 1048 U.S. colleges—that is, "who they are, how and where they live, what they earn and at what they work."

1010. BARNES, HARRY ELMER (D,W). *Society in Transition: Problems of a Changing Age.* New York: Prentice-Hall, 1939. 1034 pp.

General survey of recent and current social conditions by well-known U.S. sociologist. Scientific propaganda is dealt with in chapter 14, mental hygiene in chapters 10 and 19. Bibliography, pp. 970-99.

1011. BAUERMANN, WERNER. *Die Times und die Abwendung Englands von Deutschland um 1900* (inaugural dissertation, Cologne). Köln: Orthen, 1939. 78 pp.

Deals with the years 1899-1901. Continues Karl Otto Herkenberg's *The Times und das deutsch-englische Verhältnis im Jahre 1898* (Berlin, 1925), which dealt only with 1898. Bibliography, p. 5.

1012. BEARD, CHARLES AUSTIN (CB '41, D,W); and BEARD, MARY RITTER (CB '41, W). *The American Spirit: A Study of the Idea of Civilization in the United States.* New York: Macmillan, 1942. 696 pp.

Volume IV of *The Rise of American Civilization*, a standard history by these two well-known U.S. historians.

*1013. BEARD, MIRIAM. *A History of the Business Man.* New York: Macmillan, 1938. 779 pp.

As Alfred Vagts (D), cited above (no. 86), traces the history of the military man as a social type through many centuries, so this book by his wife, a U.S. social scientist, traces the business man, beginning with the ancient Mediterranean civilizations. Illustrates the psychology of a social type which has always been present in the Western world, and which has competed successfully with the military man, on many occasions, for the last word in deciding social policies. Bibliography, pp. 767-72.

1014. BEERS, HENRY PUTNEY (D). *Bibliographies in American History: A Guide to Materials for Research.* New York: H. W. Wilson, 1938. 339 pp.

A general bibliographic guide for research in American history, compiled by a U.S. historian. See such sections as: Public Opinion, Negro and Slavery, Social Reform, and Religious History.

1015. (Pop.) BELL, HOWARD M. *Youth Tell Their Story: A Study of the Conditions and Attitudes of Young People in Maryland.* Washington, D.C.: American Youth Commission of the American Council on Education, 1938. 275 pp.

One of a series of regional studies written by social scientists for the Commission. 13,500 young people aged 16-24 were interviewed with respect to their employment prospects, their home lives, and their attitudes toward such topics as war, relief, marriage, government, unions, etc.

1016. BERGER, IDA. *La description du prolétariat dans le roman naturaliste allemand* (thesis, University of Paris). Paris: Imprimerie centrale, 1935. 119 pp.

Bibliography, pp. 118-19.

1017. BERREY, LESTER V.; and VAN DEN BARK, MELVIN. *The American Thesaurus of Slang*, foreword by Louise Pound (D,W). New York: Crowell, 1940. 1174 pp.

"In these 1174 pages the amazing mass of American substandard speech—over 100,000 terms—has been defined and grouped in the time-tested arrangement, by ideas, of *Roget's Thesaurus*. In addition there are some 400 pages of special slang: motion picture, radio, hobo slang, journalism, sport, literary, Army, Navy, and several other categories. The whole work is exhaustively cross-indexed. . . ."

1018. BINGHAM, ALFRED MITCHELL. *Insurgent America: The Re-*

volt of the Middle Classes. New York: Harpers, 1935. 260 pp.

In the expectation that American politics in the proximate future will disclose the functional and psychological dominance of the middle class, the author, a U.S. political journalist, editor of *Common Sense*, foresees a successful "radical" or "commonwealth" party, organized in the name of symbols derived from the Populist and Technocratic traditions. Bibliographic footnotes.

1019. BISSON, THOMAS ARTHUR (W). *Japan in China.* New York: Macmillan, 1938. 417 pp.

Social, economic, political study by staff member of Foreign Policy Association.

1020. BOGGS, RALPH STEELE (D). *Bibliography of Latin American Folklore* (Inter-American Bibliographical and Library Association Publications, ser. 1, vol. 5). New York: H. W. Wilson, 1940. 109 pp.

A selection of some six or seven hundred titles from the author's collection of some 8000 accumulated over a period of about 15 years. Dr. Boggs is professor of Spanish, University of North Carolina.

1021. BÖMER, KARL. *Das dritte Reich im Spiegel der Weltpresse: Historische Dokumente über den Kampf des Nationalsozialismus gegen die ausländische Lügenhetze.* Leipzig: Armanen-Verlag, 1934. 173 pp.

"The Third Reich as Mirrored in the World Press." By well-known German professor of journalism.

1022. BORGESE, GIUSEPPE ANTONIO (D,W). *Goliath: The March of Fascism.* New York: Viking, 1937. 483 pp.

History of Italian culture and politics from Dante to Mussolini, portraying the background and rise of modern Fascism. By an Italian professor of literary criticism, exiled for his beliefs.

1023. BORKENAU, FRANZ. *The Spanish Cockpit: An Eye-Witness Account of the Political and Social Conflicts of the Spanish Civil War.* London: Faber and Faber, 1937. 303 pp.

By a Marxist scholar (see title 836, above).

1024. BOWMAN, CLAUDE CHARLTON (D). *The College Professor in America: An Analysis of Articles Published in the General Magazines, 1890-1938* (Ph.D. thesis, sociology, University of Pennsylvania). Harrisburg, Pa.: Central Publishing Company, 1938. 196 pp.

Tabulation and analysis of magazine references to such symbols as "The Academic Personality," "The Academic Salary," "The Academic Life," "Teaching and Research," "Professors in Political Affairs," "Academic Freedom in War Time," "The New Deal and the Brain Trust," etc. Bibliography, pp. 190-94.

1025. BRADY, ROBERT ALEXANDER. *The Spirit and Structure of German Fascism*, foreword by Harold J. Laski (CB '41, W). New York: Viking, 1937. 401 pp.

Viewing the National Socialist state as "monopoly capitalism at its zenith," this U.S. economist carefully analyzes the position of labor, management, bureaucracy, and profit-takers. Indicates the contributions to National Socialist propaganda made by the National Federation of German Employers' Associations, the National Federation of German Industry, the National Chamber of [German] Industry and Commerce, and the Herrenklub, and describes the "coordination of the spirit" under the new educational system. Bibliography, pp. 405-13.

1026. BRIEFS, GOETZ ANTONY (D,W). *Le Prolétariat industriel*, translated from the German by Yves Simon (D), preface by Jacques Maritain (CB '42, D). Paris: Desclée de Brouwer, 1936. 302 pp.

General theory of the proletariat, by a former professor at the Technische Hochschule, Berlin, who came to the United States. First appeared in 1926 in vol. 9 of *Grundriss der Sozialökonomik.* Bibliography, pp. 7-10.

1027. BROWN, MAYNARD W. *American Public Opinion and European Armaments, 1912-1914* (Ph.D. thesis, political science, University of Wisconsin, 1936).

1028. BRUNNER, EDMUND DE SCHWEINITZ (D,W); and LORGE, IRVING. *Rural Trends in Depression Years: A Survey of Village-Centered Agricultural Communities, 1930-1936.* New York: Columbia University, 1937. 387 pp.

Two U.S. social psychologists trace another stage in the histories of 140 village-centered communities which were studied in 1923-24 and in 1929-30 under the direction of Dr. Brunner. Contains materials on rural attitudes, schools, adult education, and religion.

1029. (Pop.) BRYSON, LYMAN (CB '40, W). *Which Way America?: Communism, Fascism, Democracy* (The People's Library series). New York: Macmillan, 1939. 113 pp.

Comparison of rival political symbols by a Teachers College professor of adult education. The People's Library series is intended to present weighty topics in words based on the findings of the "Readability Laboratory" at Teachers College.

1030. BURKE, WILLIAM JEREMIAH. *The Literature of Slang: A Bibliography,* introductory note by Eric Partridge. New York: New York Public Library, 1939. 180 pp.

1031. BYAS, HUGH (CB '43). *Government by Assassination.* New York: Knopf, 1942. 369 pp.

Analysis of Japanese government and economics by New York *Times* correspondent who has specialized on Japan for some 25 years.

1031a. *Cambridge Bibliography of English Literature,* edited by Frederick Wilse Bateson. Cambridge: Cambridge University, 1941. 4 vols.

"The first attempt since 1824 to bring the whole of English literature within the bounds of a single work of reference." Volume 1: A.D. 600-1660; volume 2: 1660-1800; volume 3: 1800-1900; volume 4: copious Index. Each volume contains bibliography on the educational system; the development of science and pseudo-science; and the technology of public communication (see Index under "Books," "Education," "Schools," "Science," etc.). There are about 178 pages of data by H. Graham Pollard, lecturer in the history of newspapers, University of London, on the history of newspapers and magazines of the United Kingdom (1: 736-63; 2: 656-738; 3: 779-846).

1032. CANTRIL, HADLEY. "Educational and Economic Composition of Religious Groups: An Analysis of Poll Data," *American Journal of Sociology,* 48: 574-79 (March 1943).

Intercorrelation of economic status, education, and religious affiliations of about 14,000 persons is analyzed by Director of Princeton Office of Public Opinion Research, using data from Gallup polls and from polls conducted by the OPOR, 1939-40.

*1032a. CARROLL, EBER MALCOLM (D,W). *French Public Opinion and Foreign Affairs, 1870-1914.* New York: Century, 1931. 356 pp.

A detailed study of public opinion and its currents, based on newspapers, documents, and magazine writings. By a diplomatic historian at Duke University.

1033. CARROLL, EBER MALCOLM (D,W). *Germany and the Great Powers, 1866-1914: A Study in Public Opinion and Foreign Policy.* New York: Prentice-Hall, 1938. 852 pp.

Exhaustively documented.

1034. CASE, LYNN MARSHALL (D), compiler and editor. *French Opinion on the United States and Mexico, 1860-67: Extracts from the Reports of the Procureurs Généraux.* New York: Appleton-Century, 1936. 452 pp.

How Napoleon III used the quarterly reports of provincial law officers as a means of opinion measurement when censorship had closed ordinary channels of expression. By a U.S. diplomatic historian (Ph.D. Pennsylvania 1931).

1035. CHAMBERLIN, WILLIAM HENRY (W). *Japan Over Asia,* revised and enlarged edition. Boston: Little, Brown, 1939. 463 pp.

Standard work by well-known U.S. journalist.

1036. CHAMBERLIN, WILLIAM HENRY (W). *The World's Iron Age.*

New York: Macmillan, 1941. 402 pp.

Analysis of current world politics.

1037. CHARLESWORTH, MARTIN PERCIVAL. "The Virtues of a Roman Emperor: Propaganda and the Creation of Belief," British Academy, London, *Proceedings*, 1937, 23: 105-33.

Creating mass approval of a dictator. Bibliography, pp. 128-33.

1038. CHASE, STUART (CB '40, W). *The Road We Are Traveling, 1914-1942: Guide Lines to America's Future.* New York: Twentieth Century Fund, 1942. 106 pp.

The first of six books by Mr. Chase being published by the Twentieth Century Fund under the heading, "When the War Ends." Discusses the pattern of change and basic trends, 1914-42, and outlines a postwar economy.

1039. CLOUGH, SHEPARD BANCROFT (D). *France: A History of National Economics, 1789-1939.* New York: Scribner's, 1939. 498 pp.

By Columbia University historian who has written a number of books dealing with public opinion and civic training. Bibliography, pp. 369-487.

1040. COAN, OTIS W.; and LILLARD, RICHARD G. *America in Fiction: An Annotated List of Novels That Interpret Aspects of Life in the United States.* Stanford University: Stanford University, 1941. 180 pp.

Main classifications: Pioneering; Farm and Village Life; Industrial America; Politics; Religion; The Southern Tradition; Minority Ethnic Groups. Bibliography, pp. 168-171.

1041. COHN, DAVID LEWIS. *The Good Old Days*, introduction by Sinclair Lewis (W). New York: Simon and Schuster, 1940. 597 pp.

History of American morals and manners as seen through the Sears, Roebuck catalogs, 1905-1940, by ex-department store man, now turned author.

1041a. COLE, GEORGE DOUGLAS HOWARD. *Europe, Russia and the Future.* New York: Macmillan, 1942. 233 pp.

By a leader of the British Labour Party, who is director of Nuffield College of Social Reconstruction and lecturer on Economics at Oxford University. Voices an appeal to progressives in every country, and particularly to Socialists, to formulate their plans now for postwar reconstruction of Europe, and to "face the fact" that this must be done in cooperation with the Soviet Union. "Soviets will be, all over Nazi-occupied Europe, indispensable instruments of the coming revolution. But it does not follow that these Soviets must everywhere turn into instruments of totalitarian socialism after the Russian model. Far from it. . . . The Soviets can become the instruments of a new and reinvigorated parliamentarism, of a 'liberal' socialism, and of a policy of tolerant democracy. . . ."

1042. COREY, LEWIS. *The Crisis of the Middle Class.* New York: Covici, Friede, 1935. 379 pp.

This U.S. trade union economist examines reasons for expecting that the white-collar nonpropertied middle class will join the proletarians in a united front against fascism. Bibliography, pp. 367-79.

1043. CORWIN, EDWARD SAMUEL (D,W). *The President: Office and Powers: History and Analysis of Practice and Opinion.* New York: New York University, 1940. 476 pp.

By Princeton political scientist.

1044. COSTRELL, EDWIN. *How Maine Viewed the War, 1914-1917* (University of Maine Studies, 2nd series, no. 49). Orono, Maine, February 1940. 101 pp.

Carefully documented M.A. thesis (Maine) on World War I propaganda as it affected Maine. "Proceeding as it does on the assumption that the newspapers of a state reflect roughly the views of its inhabitants, this paper has been based primarily on newspaper research." Bibliography, pp. 93-95.

1045. CROTHERS, GEORGE DUNLAP. *The German Elections of 1907* (Studies in History, Economics and Public Law, no. 479). New York: Columbia University, 1941. 277 pp.

Study of changes in public sentiment with regard to national policies. Bibliography, pp. 254-65.

1046. Curti, Merle Eugene (D,W). "Public Opinion and the Study of History," *Public Opinion Quarterly*, 1 no. 2: 84-87 (April 1937).

U.S. historian describes a few examples of current historical research on propaganda and public opinion.

1047. Davidson, Philip Grant, Jr. (D). *Propaganda and the American Revolution, 1763-1783.* Chapel Hill: University of North Carolina, 1941. 460 pp.

By a U.S. historian (Ph.D. Chicago 1929). Bibliography, pp. 411-42.

1048. Davies, Joseph E. (CB '42, W). *Mission to Moscow.* New York: Simon and Schuster, 1941. 659 pp.

Record of confidential dispatches to the State Department, official and personal correspondence, current diary and journal entries, up to October, 1941. Mr. Davies was Ambassador to the Soviet Union from 1936 to 1938 and subsequently served in the same capacity in Belgium.

*1049. Davis, Allison (D); and Dollard, John Adrian (D). *Children of Bondage.* Washington, D.C.: American Youth Commission, 1940. 327 pp.

Personality development of Negro youth in two cities of the Deep South, Natchez and New Orleans. Though the background material was supplied by interviews with over 200 Negro adolescents, this is not a statistical survey. Instead the authors have concentrated their attention on eight individual case histories. Dr. Dollard is Research Associate, Yale Institute of Human Relations; Dr. Davis is head of the division of social studies, Dillard University.

1050. Davis, Allison (D); Gardner, Burleigh B.; and Gardner, Mary R. *Deep South: A Social Anthropological Study of Caste and Class.* Chicago: University of Chicago, 1941. 558 pp.

Analysis directed by W. Lloyd Warner (D), University of Chicago sociologist.

1051. Daykin, Walter L. "Negro Types in American White Fiction," *Sociology and Social Research*, 22: 45-52 (September 1937).

General survey of literary works.

1051a. Deuel, Wallace Rankin. *People Under Hitler.* New York: Harcourt, Brace, 1942. 392 pp.

General description of social life in Nazi Germany. Author was instructor in political science, American University, Beirut, 1926-29; since 1929, *Chicago Daily News* correspondent in Washington, Rome, Berlin. Bibliography, pp. 379-80.

1052. Deutsche Hochschule für Politik. *Jahrbuch,* 1938, edited by Paul Meier-Benneckenstein. Berlin, 1939.

First issue of a new political annual reflecting Nazi views. Since 1934, the Hochschule has published some 50 monographs, an authoritative series expressing Nazi policies.

*1052a. Dibelius, Wilhelm. *England: Its Character and Genius*, translated from the German by Mary Agnes Hamilton, introduction by A. D. Lindsay, Master of Balliol College, Oxford. New York and London: Harpers, 1930. 569 pp.

General historical analysis of England, with much emphasis on its literature and its educational system, by professor of English, University of Berlin. Bibliography, pp. 525-43.

1053. Dietz, Heinrich. *Agitation und Massenhysterie in England: Propagandamethoden historisch gesehen.* Essen: Essenerverlagsanstalt, 1941. 192 pp.

"Agitation and Mass-Hysteria in England: Propaganda Methods Viewed Historically."

1054. Dodd, William Edward Jr.; and Dodd, Martha, editors. *Ambassador [William E.] Dodd's* (CB '40) *Diary, 1933-1938*, introduction by Charles Austin Beard (CB '41, D,W). New York: Harcourt, Brace, 1941. 464 pp.

Memoirs of U.S. Ambassador to Nazi Germany.

1055. Dulles, Foster Rhea (D,W). *America Learns to Play: A*

History of Popular Recreation, 1607-1940. New York: Appleton-Century, 1940. 441 pp.

By U.S. historian. Well documented, with many illustrations. Bibliography, pp. 375-423.

1056. DURANT, HENRY W. *The Problem of Leisure.* London: Routledge, 1938. 276 pp.

Based on careful studies of problems of leisure that confronted different classes in English society: the aristocracy, the middle classes, the working class, and the unemployed. Includes sections on cinema, radio, and other communication channels. Bibliography, pp. 265-71.

1057. EMBREE, JOHN FEE (D). *Suye Mura: A Japanese Village,* introduction by A. R. Radcliffe-Brown. Chicago: University of Chicago, 1939. 354 pp.

First comprehensive social analysis of a Japanese village. Emphasizes transition toward Western culture patterns. By anthropologist trained at University of Chicago. Bibliography, pp. 327-29.

1058. EVANS, KENNETH. *The Changing Occupational Distribution and the Rise of Professional Services in the South* (Ph.D. thesis, sociology, North Carolina 1938).

1059. FAULKNER, HAROLD UNDERWOOD (D,W). *American Political and Social History,* 2nd ed. New York: Crofts, 1941. 804 pp.

By a Smith College professor of history. Bibliography, pp. 735-82 and ends of chapters.

1060. FERRÉ, LOUISE MARIE. *Les Classes sociales dans la France contemporaine* (thesis, University of Paris). Seine-et-Oise: the author, 1936 (?). 267 pp.

Bibliography, pp. 231-62.

1060a. FLEISHER, WILFRID. *Volcanic Isle.* London: Cape, 1942. 256 pp. New York: Doubleday, Doran, 1941. 345 pp.

Study of political, economic and psychological forces in Japan since 1868. Chapter 9 is on

"Press and Censorship." For more than 20 years the author, a U.S. journalist, has specialized in Japanese affairs (was on Tokyo staff of *Japan Advertiser* 1918-19, 1923-25, 1929-40; also wrote for New York *Times* and New York *Herald Tribune*).

1061. FLORINSKY, MICHAEL T. (CB '41, D,W). *Toward an Understanding of the U.S.S.R.: A Study in Government, Politics, and Economic Planning.* New York: Macmillan, 1939. 245 pp.

Columbia scholar's analysis of two decades in U.S.S.R., "based almost exclusively on official Russian sources." Bibliography, pp. 233-37.

1062. FODOR, MARCEL WILLIAM (W). *The Revolution is On,* introduction by Dorothy Thompson (CB '40, W). Boston: Houghton Mifflin, 1940. 239 pp.

Well-known European correspondent emphasizes the "socialist" side of the "National Socialist" revolutions of Germany, Russia, Japan and Italy, and suggests that similar trends may develop, though more gradually, in the U.S.

1063. FRANK, JEROME N. (CB '41, W). *Save America First.* New York: Harpers, 1938. 432 pp.

Well-known New Deal attorney analyzes U.S. economic relations, internal and external, and offers a plan of social control. Contains much material on the historical background of various typical American opinions concerning economic policy.

1064. FRAZIER, EDWARD FRANKLIN (CB '40, D,W). *The Negro Family in the United States.* Chicago: University of Chicago, 1939. 686 pp.

Thoroughgoing history and analysis by Professor of Sociology, Howard University. Bibliography, pp. 641-69.

1065. FROELICH, WALTER (D). "European Experiments in Protecting Small Competitors," *Harvard Business Review,* 17: 442-52 (Summer 1939).

Small competitors flocked to Fascism, hoping for protection against monopolistic giants. The party accepted their support, then crushed them in the interest of wartime efficiency and administrative simplicity.

1066. GABRIEL, RALPH HENRY (D,W). *The Course of American Democratic Thought: An Intellectual History since 1815.* New York: Ronald Press, 1940. 452 pp.

By Yale professor of American history. Chapter 30, "The New American Symbolism," emphasizes the tendency of Americans to "worship" the memory of Abraham Lincoln. Bibliography, pp. 419-34.

1067. GARRETT, MITCHELL BENNETT (D,W). *The Estates General of 1789: The Problems of Composition and Organization.* New York: Appleton-Century, 1936. 268 pp.

U.S. historian fully classifies for the first time the hundreds of pamphlets growing out of the controversies of the period. Bibliography, pp. 222-64.

1068. GERTH, HANS HEINRICH (D); and MILLS, C(HARLES) WRIGHT. "A Marx for the Managers," *Ethics,* 52: 200-15 (January 1942).

Review of James Burnham's (CB '41) *The Managerial Revolution,* by two social scientists. Includes perspective discussion of the role of intellectual and managerial skills in the Great Power state. "The crucial fact in Germany concerning these skilled personnels in their relation to power is that their very indispensability and scarcity value for a war economy insures their loss of income and personal freedom, and provides a decade of overwork. The close supervision over them partakes of army discipline. Not power but subjugation to martial law is their lot. They are as enslaved as any wage worker. . . . As experts they give advice, but they receive orders. . . . [Abroad], witness the army purges and [in the U.S.] the shuffling of the 'self-confident young men' of the New Deal. It is not irrelevant to contrast the insecurity of tenure of the expert with the legally guaranteed inheritance of private owners. In totalitarian régimes the personal insecurity of experts increases proportionately to the influence of their advice."

1069. GILLETTE, JOHN MORRIS (D,W). *Rural Sociology,* 3rd ed. New York: Macmillan, 1936. 778 pp.

This veteran University of North Dakota sociologist has practically rewritten the third edition of his standard treatise. There are sections on such channels of opinion as rural schools and churches, on communications, on attitudes, and on the "mental capacity" of rural-urban migrants. Many statistics are included; bibliography cites 600 writers.

1070. (Pop.) GOULD, KENNETH MILLER. *Windows on the World.* New York: Stackpole, 1938. 421 pp.

An introduction to world affairs (big business, the New Deal, democracy, cooperatives, socialism, communism, fascism, social security, etc.) for young people in their teens. The author is managing editor of *Scholastic,* the U.S. high school weekly, and has had extensive experience writing for this age level. Book includes charts, illustrations, bibliography.

1071. GRAY, LOUIS HERBERT (D,W), editor. *The Mythology of All Races.* Boston: Marshall Jones, 1916-32. 13 vols.

By a score of scholars. Volume 1, Greek and Roman; 2, Eddic; 3, Celtic and Slavic; 4, Finno-Ugric and Siberian; 5, Semitic; 6, Indian and Iranian; 7, Armenian and African; 8, Chinese and Japanese; 9, Oceanic; 10, North American; 11, Latin-American; 12, Egyptian and Indo-Chinese; 13, Complete index. Bibliography at end of each volume.

1071a. GRIERSON, PHILIP. *Books on Soviet Russia, 1917-42: A Bibliography and a Guide to Reading.* London: Methuen, 1943. 354 pp.

Comprehensive bibliography by a Cambridge University Fellow. Copiously annotated. Covers most aspects of Russian social life.

1072. GRZESINSKI, ALBERT C. *Inside Germany.* New York: Dutton, 1939. 374 pp.

Autobiography of German labor leader who rose to an important post in the Prussian Ministry of the Interior under the Weimar Republic. Stresses in a relatively objective tone the many psychological errors of the regime, including its "lack of experience in the revolutionary process, where it is always necessary to be vigorously dogmatic, to man offices with trusted comrades, and to reform ideologies with an emotional tonic." Indicates the failure of the "representatives and spokesmen of the democratic regime" to appreciate the magnitude of their propaganda task, and to protect the new state against "slanderous attacks upon its symbols and institutions." See also review of this book by Paul F. Douglass (W) in *Annals of American Academy of Political and Social Science*, 203: 210-11 (May 1939).

1073. GURVITCH, GEORGES. "Social Structure of Pre-War France," *American Journal of Sociology*, 48: 535-54 (March 1943).

Careful sociopolitical analysis. Formerly a professor of sociology, University of Strasbourg, Dr. Gurvitch is now the director of the Institute of Sociology at Ecole Libre des Hautes Etudes, New York. Article includes material on the numerous French fascist organizations and their leaders.

1074. HAAN, HUGO VON. "International Aspects of the Terminology and Ideology of Management," *International Labour Review*, 37: 421-39 (April 1938).

Note the definitions of "Management," "Organisation," and "Rationalisation."

1075. HACKER, LOUIS MORTON (D,W); and KENDRICK, BENJAMIN BURKS (D,W). *The United States since 1865*, rev. ed. New York: F. S. Crofts, 1934. 833 pp.

By two U.S. historians. The story is organized about the growth of monopoly and finance capitalism, the expansion and decline of American agriculture, and the impact of these processes upon American politics and culture. Bibliography, pp. 791-835.

*1076. HALE, ORON JAMES (D). *Publicity and Diplomacy, with Special Reference to England and Germany, 1890-1914* (University of Virginia Institute for Research in the Social Sciences, monograph no. 27). New York: Appleton-Century, 1940. 486 pp.

By U.S. historian.

1077. HAMILTON, THOMAS J. *Appeasement's Child: The Franco Regime In Spain*. New York: Alfred A. Knopf, 1943. 327 pp.

Study of the rise of Falangism (Fascism) in Spain, by U.S. journalist who has been foreign correspondent for Associated Press and New York *Times*. Bibliography, pp. 324-27,

cites biographies of Falange leaders and titles on Franco's political theories and educational system.

1078. *Handbook of Latin American Studies: A Selective Guide to the Material Published . . . on Anthropology, Archives, Art, Education, Folklore, Geography, Government, History, International Relations, Labor and Social Welfare, Language and Literature, Law, Libraries, Music, and Philosophy*, edited by Lewis Hanke and others for the Joint Committee on Latin American Studies of the National Research Council, the American Council of Learned Societies, and the Social Science Research Council. Cambridge: Harvard University Press, annually, 1936–.

Copiously annotated bibliography, with introductory essays.

1079. HAYCRAFT, HOWARD (CB '41). *Murder for Pleasure: The Life and Times of the Detective Story*. New York: Appleton-Century, 1941. 409 pp.

The detective story comprises at present one-fourth of the output of English-language fiction. This is an historical treatment, from "the world's first detective story" (Poe's *Murders in the Rue Morgue*) to the present. Includes a chapter on detective story markets.

1080. HEIDEN, KONRAD. *A History of National Socialism*. London: Methuen, 1934. New York: Knopf, 1935. 430 pp.

An abridged translation of a thoughtful treatise by a well-known ex-German journalist.

1081. HEINDEL, RICHARD HEATHCOTE (D). *The American Impact on Great Britain, 1898-1914: A Study of the United States in World History* (Ph.D. thesis, Pennsylvania). Philadelphia: University of Pennsylvania, 1940. 439 pp.

Heavily documented study of the influence of the United States upon Great Britain's industrial, social, and literary development, by University of Pennsylvania historian. Bibliography at ends of chapters.

1082. HERRING, HUBERT CLINTON. *Good Neighbors, Argentina, Brazil, Chile: An Introduction to the A B C Powers and Seventeen Other Latin-American Countries*. New Haven: Yale University, 1941. 381 pp.

By secretary of Committee on Cultural Relations with Latin America. Discusses Nazi, Italian and U.S. propaganda. Bibliography, pp. 353-60.

1083. HOAG, C(HARLES) LEONARD. *Preface to Disarmament: The Washington Disarmament Conference and Public Opinion*, introduction by Admiral Harry Ervin Yarnell (W). Washington, D.C.: American Council on Public Affairs, 1941. 205 pp.

Comprehensive study of influence of public opinion, pressure groups and the press on the Disarmament Conference, by Professor of History and Government, Springfield College, Mass. Bibliography at ends of chapters.

1084. HOLCOMBE, ARTHUR NORMAN (D,W). *The Middle Classes in American Politics*. Cambridge: Harvard University, 1940. 304 pp.

Historical studies by Harvard political scientist. Bibliography, pp. 289-99.

1085. HOOVER, CALVIN BRYCE (D,W). *Dictators and Democracies*. New York: Macmillan, 1937. 110 pp.

Professor of Economics at Duke University surveys the prospects of dictatorships. He is the author of two comprehensive economic studies, *The Economic Life of Soviet Russia* (1931) and *Germany Enters the Third Reich* (1933). Chapter II, "Twenty Years of a Totalitarian State: Terror as a Social Institution," deals with opinion-management.

1086. HUGHES, ERNEST RICHARD. *The Invasion of China by the Western World* (Pioneer Histories series). New York: Macmillan, 1938. 324 pp.

Analysis of the slow diffusion of Western cultural patterns into China. Discusses the role of militarists, missionaries, and secular intellectuals, the preexisting receptivities and resistances of the Chinese culture, and the current mass movements involving westernization. The author is Reader in Chinese Religion, Oxford. Bibliography, pp. 303-09.

1087. HUTCHINSON, WILLIAM THOMAS (D), editor. *The Marcus W. Jernegan Essays in American Historiography*. Chicago: University of Chicago, 1937. 417 pp.

Appraisals of the work of twenty-one widely recognized U.S. historians who have written about the U.S. Vernon Louis Parrington is discussed by William Thomas Utter (D).

1088. INMAN, SAMUEL GUY (D,W). *Latin America: Its Place in World Life*, rev. ed. New York: Harcourt, Brace, 1942. 462 pp.

Standard treatise by U.S. specialist in this field. Bibliography, pp. 437-44.

1089. *In Re: Germany: A Critical Bibliography of Books and Magazine Articles on Germany*. New York: Research and Information Service of American Friends of German Freedom (342 Madison Ave.), February 1941–.

Monthly containing annotated bibliography of material appearing during the preceding month.

1090. JAFFE, ABE J. "Social Trends in the Soviet Union," *American Journal of Sociology*, 42: 383-87 (November 1936).

A set of charts on economic, educational, and social trends, similar to the types of data in *Recent Social Trends* (1933), report of President Hoover's Committee on Recent Social Trends in the United States.

1091. JAFFE, A. J.; and SHANAS, ETHEL. "Economic Differentials in the Probability of Insanity," *American Journal of Sociology*, 44: 534-39 (January 1939).

"Data for the city of Chicago were analyzed in an attempt to discover the possible relationship between economic status and the prevalence of insanity. A higher incidence of insanity was found among the poorer populations than among the richer. Approximately the same differentials were found for each sex and nativity or racial group. . . . A white male residing in an area in Chicago where the median rental is under $50 has about 1 chance in 18 of being admitted to a mental hospital at some time during his life. One in a richer area has only about 1 chance in 21."

Among the white females, the poor have 1 chance in 20, the richer 1 chance in 22.

1092. JOHNSON, CHARLES SPURGEON (D,W). *The Negro College and Professional Graduate*. Chapel Hill: University of North Carolina, 1937. 475 pp.

Study of all Negroes who have received American academic degrees; major attention is given to the location, occupations, and social-economic backgrounds of living graduates. The survey considers more than 43,000 college and professional graduates up to 1936. The author is Director of the Department of Social Sciences, Fisk University.

1093. JOHNSON, CHARLES SPURGEON (D,W). *Patterns of Negro Segregation*. New York: Harpers, 1943. 332 pp.

The extent and character of discrimination against the U.S. Negro. Bibliographic footnotes.

1094. JOHNSON, CHARLES SPURGEON (D,W). *Statistical Atlas of Southern Counties: Listing and Analysis of Socio-Economic Indices of 1104 Southern Counties*. Chapel Hill: University of North Carolina, 1941. 355 pp.

Compiled for use of Julius Rosenwald Fund's Council on Rural Education, as a guide to educational policy. Bibliography, pp. 310-55, cites many theses on education and social structure produced by Southern scholars over the last 30 years.

1095. JOSEPHSON, MATTHEW (W). *The President Makers: The Culture of Politics and Leadership in an Age of Enlightenment, 1896-1919*. New York: Harcourt, Brace, 1940. 584 pp.

Sequel to this author's two previous U.S. histories, *The Robber Barons: The Great American Capitalists, 1861-1901* (1934) and *The Politicos, 1865-1896* (1938). Bibliography, pp. 567-71.

1096. KAISER, HANS. " 'Die Vereinigten Staaten von Europa' in der englischen Kriegszielpropaganda," *Monatshefte für auswärtige Politik*, 7: 671 ff. (1940).

" 'The United States of Europe' in English War-Aims Propaganda."

1097. KIPLINGER, WILLARD MONROE (CB '43, W). *Washington Is Like That*. New York: Harpers, 1942. 522 pp.

The personnel, working habits, and social organization of the nation's capital, described in semi-popular style by editor of well-known newsletter.

1098. KIRK, BETTY. *Covering the Mexican Front: The Battle of Europe vs. America*. Norman: University of Oklahoma, 1942. 367 pp.

By a U.S. newspaper correspondent who has lived in Mexico City since 1936. Includes material on Stalinist, Trotskyite, Sinarchist and Falange political efforts in Mexico. Undocumented.

1099. KIRKPATRICK, FREDERICK ALEXANDER. *Latin America: A Brief History* (Cambridge Historical Series). New York: Macmillan, 1939. 456 pp.

By a well-known British historian.

1100. KOHN-BRAMSTEDT, ERNST. *Aristocracy and the Middle Class in Germany: Social Types in German Literature, 1830-1900*, foreword by George Peabody Gooch. London: P. S. King, 1937. 362 pp.

Bibliography, pp. 341-52.

1101. KRAUS, MICHAEL (D). *A History of American History*. New York: Farrar and Rinehart, 1937. 607 pp.

Survey of American historians of America, comparable in some respects with Vernon Louis Parrington's *Main Currents in American Thought*, which surveyed U.S. literature to 1920. The present work, which includes current writers, contains appraisals of all the widely recognized historians and many lesser figures. By assistant professor of history, College of the City of New York. Contains bibliography.

1102. LAHR, OTTMAR EUGEN. *Französische Kriegszielpropaganda am Ende des Weltkrieges*. Essen: Essener Verlagsanstalt, 1941. 178 pp.

"French Propaganda on War Aims at the End of the World War."

1103. Lajos, Ivan. *Germany's War Chances as Pictured in German Official Literature.* London: Gollancz, 1939. 160 pp.

By Hungarian professor of constitutional law. "Essential portions of this book are derived from Fritz Sternberg's *Germany and a Lightning War*" (London: Faber and Faber, 1938).

1104. Lasswell, Harold Dwight (D,W). "Public Opinion and British-American Unity," in *Conference on North Atlantic Relations, Data Papers.* Princeton: American Committee for International Studies, 1941.

1105. Lederer, Emil; and Lederer-Seidler, Emy. *Japan in Transition.* New Haven: Yale University, 1938. 260 pp.

Economic, social, and psychological analysis of the Japanese people, by two ex-German social scientists.

1106. Lerner, Max (CB '42, D,W). *It Is Later Than You Think: The Need for a Militant Democracy.* New York: Viking, 1938. 260 pp.

Williams College political scientist finds that, since complete capitalist collapse in the U.S. will be followed by Fascism, the preservation of democracy requires the bolstering of capitalism by a central planning board which will simultaneously increase production in twenty or thirty basic industries, meanwhile guaranteeing profits to private owners. Deals but little with the propaganda strategy which would be involved.

1107. Lin, Mousheng Hsitien. *Men and Ideas: An Informal History of Chinese Political Thought*, introduction by Pearl S. Buck. New York: John Day, 1942. 256 pp.

The work of leading Chinese political thinkers of the past three thousand years is surveyed by a psychoanalytically trained political scientist (Ph.D. Chicago) in the service of the official Chinese news agency in the U.S. Bibliography, pp. 241-44.

1108. Lin Yu-Tang (CB '40, W). *My Country and My People.* New York: Reynal and Hitchcock, 1935. 382 pp.

One of the best received books on the character and philosophy of the Chinese, by a Chinese philosopher.

1109. Linebarger, Paul Myron Anthony (D). *The China of Chiang K'ai-shek: A Political Study.* Boston: World Peace Foundation, 1941. 449 pp.

By Duke University political scientist. Includes chapters and leading documents on Chinese government and party politics, including Kuomintang and Chinese Communist Party. Bibliographic footnotes.

1110. Lively, James K. "Propaganda Techniques of Civil War Cartoonists," *Public Opinion Quarterly*, 6: 99-106 (Spring 1942).

1110a. Lochner, Louis Paul. *What About Germany?* New York: Dodd, Mead, 1942. 395 pp.

Analysis of Nazi movement with emphasis on censorship and propaganda. Author was for some 25 years a U.S. correspondent in Europe (head of Berlin Bureau of Associated Press, 1928-41).

1111. Loewenstein, Karl (D). *Brazil Under Vargas.* New York: Macmillan, 1942. 381 pp.

An account of President Getulio Vargas' rise and his administration, by Amherst College political scientist. Three chapters are on "Public Opinion Management and the Dynamics of Social Life under Vargas." Bibliographic footnotes.

1112. Lovenstein, Meno. *American Opinion of Soviet Russia* [1917-33], introduction by Broadus Mitchell (D). Washington, D.C.: American Council on Public Affairs, 1941. 210 pp.

Dr. Lovenstein gathered material from a sample of magazines, books, newspapers, Congressional hearings, and government pronouncements. British books and magazines and those published in foreign languages were excluded, even though they contributed to American opinion. The opinion of the "extreme left" was omitted not only because, the author says, "its content is obvious, but also because it represents so small a part of total American opinion." Conclusion: The only sources of opinion which thoroughly and truthfully reported Russia were the liberal weeklies—the *Nation* and the *New Republic*. Business magazines and the professional journals of economists were "most disappointing," from the standpoint of thoroughness and truthfulness. As for the newspapers: "in most cases there was a great show of common sense and a practical appreciation of day-by-day adjustments." Bibliography, pp. 167-210.

*1113. LUNDBERG, FERDINAND. *America's Sixty Families*. Garden City, N.Y.: Halcyon House, 1939. 544 pp.

Analysis of who owns and controls the largest U.S. fortunes and how they are used. Chapters 7 and 8 are on the control of sections of the press. Chapter 9 is on foundations and endowments. Chapter 10 is on the educational system. By a U.S. journalist. Bibliography, pp. 547-53.

1114. McCULLY, BRUCE TIEBOUT. *English Education and the Origins of Indian Nationalism* (Studies in History, Economics, and Public Law, no. 473). New York: Columbia University, 1941. 418 pp.

Bibliography, pp. 397-408.

1115. McGILL, NETTIE PAULINE; and MATTHEWS, ELLEN NATHALIE. *The Youth of New York City*. New York: Macmillan, 1940. 420 pp.

Socio-economic study for the Research Bureau of the Welfare Council of New York City, by two of its staff members. Includes material on time-budgets, reading habits, radio and movie preferences, etc., based on interviews with thousands of young people.

1116. MASON, MARY GERTRUDE. *Western Concepts of China and the Chinese, 1840-1876*. Durham, N.C.: Seeman Printery, 1939. 288 pp.

Scholarly study based on a mass of books and magazines, *Hansard's Parliamentary Debates, Journals of the California Legislature*, etc. Newspapers were not sampled. Extensive bibliography, pp. 20-63 and in text.

1117. MEIERS, MILDRED; and KNAPP, JACK. *Thesaurus of Humor*, 2nd ed. New York: Crown Publishers, 1940. 605 pp.

Humor of the world arranged and clas for ready reference.

1118. MERTL, JAN. *Byrokr* Prague: Orbis, 1937. 265 pp.

History and analysis of the Czechos civil service in terms of the bureaucratic t tions of England, the United States, France. By a Czechoslovak social scic Contains extensive bibliography.

1119. METZGER, CHARLES HE (D). "Propaganda in the Amer Revolution," *Mid-America*, n.s. 243-61 (1940).

By U.S. historian.

1120. MILIUKOV, PAUL. *Out of Russian Culture*, edited by Mic Karpovich (D), translated from I sian by Valentine Ughet and Ele Davis. Philadelphia: University of P sylvania, 1942. 3 volumes.

Standard treatise by well-known Ru historian. Part I, *Religion and the Chu* Part II, *Literature*; Part III, *Architec Painting and Music*. Bibliography at en chapters.

1121. MODERN HUMANITIES SEARCH ASSOCIATION (London). *W in Progress*, 1938–. Guildford Esher: Billing and Sons, 1938–.

Annual listing of studies being made b search workers in the humanities throug the world. Among the thousands of st here listed are many that will interest dents of public opinion. Examples: "Poli Slang," and "A Vocabulary Study of the gressional Record since 1900."

1122. MOORE, FREDERICK. *W Japan's Leaders: An Intimate Re of Fourteen Years as Counsellor to Japanese Government, Ending Dec ber 7, 1941*. New York: Scribn 1942. 365 pp.

Account of Japanese diplomacy of r years, by a former adviser and public tions counsel of the Japanese government

1123. MORISON, SAMUEL EL (D,W); and COMMAGER, HE STEELE (D,W). *The Growth of*

American Republic, 3rd ed., rev. New York: Oxford University, 1942. 2 vols.

Standard treatise. Dr. Morison is a Harvard historian, Dr. Commager an historian at Columbia. Includes extensive bibliography.

1124. MUNRO, DANA GARDNER (D,W). *The Latin American Republics: A History*. New York: Appleton-Century, 1942. 650 pp.

From the beginning to the present, including inter-American relations in the present war. By Princeton historian. Bibliography, pp. 619-33.

*1125. NEUMANN, FRANZ LEOPOLD (D). *Behemoth: The Structure and Practice of National Socialism*. New York: Oxford University, 1942. 532 pp.

Based on original German sources, this is a scholarly analysis of forces underlying the National Socialist movement. Deals with the social, political, and economic structure of the totalitarian state, with special attention to the relation of the party to the state. Contains one of the few exact, thorough and documented analyses in English of the new ruling class of Germany. Proposes a program of psychological warfare against National Socialism. Dr. Neumann, an ex-German trade union economist and attorney, is a member of the Institute of Social Research, Columbia University. Bibliography, pp. 477-518.

1126. (Pop.) NEURATH, OTTO. *Modern Man in the Making*. New York: Knopf, 1939. 159 pp.

History of mankind from the earliest world empires (Rome and China) to the present, presented mainly in the "Isotype" (pictorial statistics) language of which Dr. Neurath was the originator. His theme is "the growing unification of world civilization," as illustrated by a great number of social indices. Bibliographic notes, pp. 135-58.

1127. NEVINS, ALLAN (D,W). *The Gateway to History*. New York: Appleton-Century, 1938. 412 pp.

Well-known U.S. historian shows, by means of several hundred illustrations, how historical myths and fallacies have been propagated, intentionally and unintentionally, by members of his profession. Bibliography, pp. 385-402.

1128. NICOLSON, HAROLD. "British Public Opinion and Foreign Policy,"

Public Opinion Quarterly, 1 no. 1: 53-63 (January 1937).

General essay by British diplomatist, M.P., and historian. Takes as illustrations the Peace Ballot of 1934, the "Abyssinian episode" of 1935, and the Spanish Civil War of 1936.

1129. NOBLE, GEORGE BERNARD (D). *Policies and Opinions at Paris, 1919: Wilsonian Diplomacy, the Versailles Peace, and French Public Opinion* (Ph.D. thesis, Columbia, 1935). New York: Macmillan, 1935. 475 pp.

Reed College political scientist emphasizes the bearing of public opinion on the work of the negotiators. In an introductory chapter, Professor Noble analyzes and classifies the Parisian and provincial press, as well as the political parties and 46 "non-political associations," as exponents of public opinion. Bibliography, pp. 429-39.

1130. NORDSKOG, JOHN ERIC. *Social Reform in Norway: A Study of Nationalism and Social Democracy* (Social Science series, no. 12). Los Angeles: University of Southern California, 1935. 184 pp.

Based on Norwegian sources. Evaluates the effect of Russian propaganda in stimulating social reform in Norway in the name of national social solidarity. Bibliography, pp. 161-77.

1131. OBRDLÍK, ANTONÍN. *Povolání a Veřejné Blaho*. Prague: Orbis, 1937. 263 pp.

"Occupations and Public Welfare." Sociologist at Masaryk University summarizes replies to 900 questionnaires on attitudes of Czech citizens toward various occupations, and formulates reasons for the preferences expressed. *Most deference went to*: peasants, teachers, workers, artisans, physicians. *Medium deference went to*: engineers, merchants, industrialists. *"Negative deference" went to*: soldiers, politicians, priests, lawyers. The volume contains an English summary.

1132. ODUM, HOWARD WASHINGTON (D,W); and MOORE, HARRY ESTILL (D). *American Regionalism: A Cultural-Historical Approach to National Integration*. New York: Holt, 1938. 693 pp.

Standard analysis, by two U.S. sociologists. Bibliography, pp. 643-75 and footnotes.

1133. OGDEN, MARY ELAINE. *The Social Orientation of the Society Girl* (M.A. thesis, sociology, Chicago, 1938).

1134. PADOVER, SAUL KUSSIEL (W). "Kautsky and the Materialist Interpretation of History," in *Medieval and Historiographical Essays in Honor of James Westfall Thompson* (Chicago: University of Chicago, 1938), pp. 439-64.

The bibliography of this exhaustively documented biographical sketch by a U.S. historian (Ph.D. Chicago) might well serve most investigators as an authoritative guide to the literature of the principal Marxian controversies.

1135. PALM, FRANKLIN CHARLES (D,W). *The Middle Classes, Then and Now.* New York: Macmillan, 1936. 421 pp.

"An historical introduction to the study of the middle classes, . . . giving a brief, simple, factual account from the earliest times to the present."—Preface. By a professor of history, University of California. Bibliography in text.

1136. PARKES, HENRY BAMFORD (D,W). *Marxism: An Autopsy.* Boston: Houghton Mifflin, 1939. 300 pp.

Scholarly reconsideration of Marxist premises by New York University historian. Includes an economic and political analysis of current events in U.S., and "An American Program" based on the work of John Maynard Keynes (CB '41, W), Gardiner C. Means (W), and Alvin Harvey Hansen (D,W). Bibliographic notes, pp. 261-90.

*1137. PARRINGTON, VERNON LOUIS. *Main Currents in American Thought: An Interpretation of American Literature From the Beginnings to 1920,* one-volume edition. New York: Harcourt, Brace, 1939. 3 vols. in one.

Reprint of a standard work in the social interpretation of U.S. literature, by famous U.S. literary historian. Heavily documented.

1138. PARTRIDGE, ERIC HONEYWOOD. *Dictionary of Clichés.* New York: Macmillan, 1940. 259 pp.

The author has compiled many dictionaries.

1139. PARTRIDGE, ERIC HONEYWOOD. *Dictionary of Slang and Unconventional English: Slang, Including the Language of the Underworld, Colloquialisms and Catch-Phrases, Solecisms and Catachreses, Nicknames, Vulgarisms and Such Americanisms as Have Been Naturalized,* 2nd ed. revised and enlarged. London: Routledge, 1938. 1051 pp.

A scholarly volume.

1140. PATUTSCHNICK, KARL HELMUT. "Über den politischen Wert der in den letzten Jahren erschienenen Doktordissertationen," *Nazionalsozialistische Bibliographie,* Jahrg. 1, Heft 6, pp. xvii-xxxii (1938).

"Political value of the doctoral dissertations of recent years," as viewed by Nazi writer.

1141. PAXSON, FREDERIC LOGAN (D,W). *America at War, 1917-1918.* Boston: Houghton Mifflin, 1939. 465 pp.

Volume 2 of *American Democracy and the World War,* by professor of history, University of California. Bibliography in text.

1142. PERLMAN, LOUIS. *Russian Literature and the Business Man* (Ph.D. thesis, Columbia). New York: Columbia University, 1937. 207 pp.

Descriptions of the businessman as he appears in Russian literature down to the present time. The author received his primary and secondary education in Russian schools. Bibliography, pp. 203-07.

1143. PHILLIPS, JAMES EMERSON, JR. *The State in Shakespeare's Greek and Roman Plays* (Columbia University Studies in English and Comparative Literature, no. 149). New York: Columbia University, 1940. 230 pp.

Bibliography, pp. 209-20.

1144. POSTGATE, RAYMOND; and VALLANCE, AYLMER. *England Goes to Press.* Indianapolis: Bobbs-Merrill, 1937. 295 pp.

American edition of *Those Foreigners: The English People's Opinion on Foreign Affairs as Reflected in their Newspapers since Water-*

loo (London: Harrap, 1937). Contains extensive excerpts from newspapers and much comment on the role of propaganda.

1145. POWDERMAKER, HORTENSE (D). *After Freedom: A Cultural Study in the Deep South.* New York: Viking, 1939. 408 pp.

U.S. social scientist's analysis of culture-patterns (including opinion-patterns) in a Mississippi county during the post-Emancipation period. Trained at Columbia and University of London, Dr. Powdermaker is the author of several other anthropological studies. Bibliography, pp. 377-80.

1146. (Pop.) RADIN, MAX (D, W). *The Law and Mr. Smith.* Indianapolis: Bobbs-Merrill, 1938. 333 pp.

A concise history, for laymen, of the role of law in various stages of western civilization, the technique of judicial interpretation, and certain fundamental legal categories. Dr. Radin is professor of law, University of California.

*1147. RAPER, ARTHUR FRANKLIN (W). *The Tragedy of Lynching* (University of North Carolina Social Study series). Chapel Hill: University of North Carolina, 1933. 499 pp.

Careful study by U.S. social scientist.

1148. READ, JAMES MORGAN (D). "Atrocity Propaganda and the Irish Rebellion," *Public Opinion Quarterly*, 2: 229-44 (April 1938).

Atrocity propaganda in the 17th century, described by University of Louisville historian.

*1149. *Recent Social Trends in the United States* (Report of President Hoover's Committee on Recent Social Trends). New York: McGraw-Hill, 1933. 1568 pp.

Standard source book for quantified data on population, resources, economic organization, education, age and sex groups, functional groups, taxation, health, governmental services, etc. Note especially "Changing Attitudes and Interests" (pp. 382-443), by Hornell Norris Hart (D,W), sociologist, a study of contents of newspapers and other periodicals in the U.S., 1905-32. A supplement to *Recent Social Trends* appeared as vol. 47 no. 6 of *American Journal of Sociology* (May, 1942).

In the supplement, note especially pp. 907-17, "Communications," by Douglas Waples (D,W).

1150. REDDICK, LAWRENCE DUNBAR (D). *The Negro in the New Orleans Press, 1850-1860: A Study in Attitudes and Propaganda* (Ph.D. thesis, University of Chicago, 1939).

1151. *Refugees: Showing the Causes, the Facts, the Administrative and Economic Difficulties, the Human Adjustments, and the Efforts at Solution, of Forced Migration* (Annals of the American Academy of Political and Social Science, vol. 203, May 1939, edited by Francis J. Brown). 271 pp.

See especially article on "Exiles and Refugees in American History," by Frances L. Reinhold, Swarthmore political scientist, dealing with "specific historical attitudes of various arms of government."

1152. RIESMAN, DAVID. "The Politics of Persecution," *Public Opinion Quarterly*, 6: 41-56 (Spring 1942).

Psychology of anti-Semitism is discussed by University of Buffalo professor of law, a consultant of Council for Democracy.

1153. ROBERTS, STEPHEN H. *The House That Hitler Built.* London: Methuen, 1937. 380 pp.

Full length study of the National Socialist movement and its consequences in world politics. By professor of modern history, University of Sydney, Australia.

1154. ROYAL INSTITUTE OF INTERNATIONAL AFFAIRS. *Political and Strategic Interests of the United Kingdom.* London: Oxford University, 1939. 304 pp.

1155. SAVETH, EDWARD NORMAN. "Race and Nationalism in American Historiography: The Late Nineteenth Century," *Political Science Quarterly*, 54: 421-41 (September 1939).

1156. SCHMAUCH, WALTER W. *Christmas Literature through the Cen-*

turies. Chicago: Walter M. Hill, 1938. 418 pp.

Extensively documented narrative on Christmas broadsides, pamphlets, poems, stories, hymns and other symbols, from Elizabethan days to the 20th century. Bibliography in text and pp. 391-405.

1157. SCHMITT, BERNADOTTE EVERLY (CB '42, D,W), editor. *Some Historians of Modern Europe: Essays in Historiography by Former Students of the Department of History of the University of Chicago.* Chicago: University of Chicago, 1942. 533 pp.

Life and works of 22 celebrated historians whose work has been done in the last two generations. Bibliography at ends of chapters.

1158. SCHÖNEMANN, FRIEDRICH. "Deutschland in der öffentlichen Meinung Amerikas," *Zeitschrift für neusprachlichen Unterricht,* 36: 193-214 (1937).

Germany in U.S. public opinion. Dr. Schönemann, a prominent German publicist, is known for his treatise on "The Art of Influencing Mass Opinion in the U.S." (in German, 1924).

1159. SCHURZ, WILLIAM LYTLE. *Latin America: A Descriptive Survey.* New York: Dutton, 1941. 378 pp.

Having lived for many years in South America and the countries bordering the Caribbean, Mr. Schurz, a U.S. government official, is able to give a first-hand account of the land, its people, government, economy, and international relations. Bibliographic footnotes.

1160. SEEBER, EDWARD DERBYSHIRE (D). *Anti-Slavery Opinion in France during the Second Half of the Eighteenth Century* (Johns Hopkins Studies in Romance Literatures and Languages, extra volume no. 10). Baltimore: Johns Hopkins University, 1937. 238 pp.

By a U.S. historian. Bibliography, pp. 201-29.

1161. SIBLEY, ELBRIDGE (D). "Some Demographic Clues to Stratifi-

cation," *American Sociological R.* 7: 322-30 (June 1942).

Bowdoin College sociologist points o dwindling educational and social opport of the lower and middle income classes U.S.

1162. SIMPSON, GEORGE E (D). *The Negro in the Philad Press.* Philadelphia: University of sylvania, 1936. 158 pp.

By U.S. sociologist (Ph.D. Pennsylv Based on space-measurement and attitud ysis of four Philadelphia newspapers, 32. Bibliography summarizes some lished theses.

1163. SNOW, EDGAR PARKS '41, W). *Battle for Asia.* New Random House, 1941. 431 pp.

Analysis of the Oriental crisis, with reference to the role of the U.S., by the of *Red Star Over China* (1937), a U.S nalist who has spent a number of years Orient.

*1163a. SOMBART, WERNER. *Bourgeois: Zur Geistesgeschicht modernen Wirtschaftsmenschen,* ed. Munich and Leipzig: Duncke Humblot, 1920. 540 pp.

Treatise by German historian and theorist. Bibliography, pp. 465-526. A lier edition was translated by M. Eps *The Quintessence of Capitalism: A St the History and Psychology of the M Business Man* (London: Unwin, 191 York: Dutton, 1915. 400 pp.). See a author's *Proletarische Sozialismus* (Jer cher, 1924. 2 vols. Bibliography, vol. 424-77), a history of the doctrine a movements of Socialism.

1164. *The Soviet Comes of A* "28 of the foremost citizens o U.S.S.R.," foreword by Sidney and trice Webb (CB '43). London: F 1938. 337 pp.

Symposium covering numerous asp Soviet life, including press, communi theatre and motion pictures.

1165. STEARNS, HAROLD ED (W), editor. *America Now: A quiry into Civilization in the U*

States, by thirty-three American men and women, a Chinese, a Mexican, and an Englishman. New York: Scribner's, 1938. 606 pp.

Contains essays on "Public Opinion" [Bruce Bliven (CB '41, W)]; "Advertising" [Roy Sarles Durstine (W)]; "Literature" [John (Rensselaer) Chamberlain (CB '40, W)]; "Education" [Christian Gauss (D,W)]. Also on channels of propaganda ("Radio and Movies," "The Theater," "Magazines," "Newspapers"); on symbols ["Economics" by Walton Hale Hamilton (D,W), "The Law" by Zechariah Chafee Jr. (CB '42, D,W), "Psychiatry" by Karl Augustus Menninger (W), "Radicalism," "The Intellectual Life," "Race Prejudice"]; and on special-interest groups ["Business" by John Thomas Flynn (W), "The New Labor Movement" by Louis Stark, "Communist Mentalities," "The Negro," "Protestant Faiths," "Catholicism," "Industry"].

1166. STEIN, GUENTHER. "Through the Eyes of a Japanese Newspaper Reader," *Pacific Affairs*, 9: 177-90 (June 1936).

Translations from typical issues of two leading Japanese newspapers, with comment on the symbolism in terms of which the Japanese public appears to think.

1167. STELLE, CHARLES C. "Ideologies of the T'ai P'ing Insurrection," *Chinese Social and Political Science Review*, 20: 140-49 (April 1936).

1168. TANSILL, CHARLES CALLAN (D,W). *America Goes to War*. Boston: Little, Brown, 1938. 731 pp.

Motives of America's entrance into World War I are re-examined by U.S. historian in the light of a considerable amount of new source material, including some of the J.P. Morgan files collected by the Nye Committee. Bibliography, pp. 664-79.

1169. TARACOUZIO, TIMOTHY ANDREW (W). *War and Peace in Soviet Diplomacy*. New York: Macmillan, for Bureau of International Research of Harvard University and Radcliffe College, 1941. 354 pp.

Analysis of Marxist conceptions of war and peace and of the international relations of U.S.S.R., based primarily on Russian sources.

By Harvard historian. Bibliography, pp. 301-11.

1170. TAYLOR, WALTER FULLER (D). *The Economic Novel in America*. Chapel Hill, N.C.: University of North Carolina, 1942. 378 pp.

Analysis of "socially conscious" U.S. writers of the period from 1870 to 1900 when many of the great fortunes were built and monopolies founded. By a U.S. professor of American literature. Bibliography, pp. 341-65.

1171. "The Thirty Thousand Managers," *Fortune* (February 1940).

Study of some of the personal characteristics of the 30,000-odd managers of the largest U.S. corporations. *Fortune* sampled 100 corporation presidents in a list composed as follows: "The first ten railroads and utilities in point of assets; the first five companies in the oil, steel, chain-store, and mining groups; and the first sixty other industrials."

*1171a. THOMPSON, GEORGE CARSLAKE. *Public Opinion and Lord Beaconsfield, 1875-1880*. London: Macmillan, 1886. 2 vols.

By a barrister of the Inner Temple. Disraeli's political technique is analyzed in terms of an elaborate conception of public opinion. Distinguishes *opinion* which is "predominant" from that which is "public"; defines *biases, notions, policies, views*.

1172. THOMPSON, JAMES WESTFALL (CB '41, W); with HOLM, BERNARD J. *A History of Historical Writing*. New York: Macmillan, 1942. 2 vols.

1173. TOMASIĆ, DINKO. "Peasants and Propaganda in Croatia," *Public Opinion Quarterly*, 1 no. 3: 68-74 (July 1937).

Croatian political scientist, now in U.S., states some principles of propaganda among a largely agrarian population.

*1173a. TROTSKY, LEON (CB '40). *The History of the Russian Revolution*, translated from the Russian by Max Eastman. New York: Simon and Schuster, 1932. 3 vols.

Relatively objective report by one of the revolution's outstanding leaders. The author was exceptionally sensitive to the interplay of psychological and material factors.

1174. TUPPER, ELEANOR; and McREYNOLDS, GEORGE E. *Japan in American Public Opinion*, introduction by George Hubbard Blakeslee (D,W). New York: Macmillan, 1937. 448 pp.

Editorials, Congressional debates, public documents, and publications of pressure groups are used to shed light on attitudes of the American people toward Japan, 1905-36. The authors are American historians. Bibliography, pp. 449-59.

1175. TURNER, EWART EDMUND. "German Influence in South Brazil," *Public Opinion Quarterly*, 6: 57-69 (Spring 1942).

Mr. Turner collected the material for this article during the course of two visits to Brazil in 1940 and 1941. From 1927 to 1937 he was a pastor of the American Church in Berlin, studied at the University of Berlin, and served as correspondent for several religious publications in the United States.

1176. UNGER, ERICH. *Das Schrifttum zum Aufbau des neuen Reiches, 1919 - 1. 1. 34.* Berlin: Junker und Dünnhaupt, 1934. 187 pp.

"Literature on the Building of the New Germany." Bibliography of some 3000 titles.

1177. VAGTS, ALFRED HERMANN FRIEDRICH (D). *Deutschland und die Vereinigten Staaten in der Weltpolitik.* New York: Macmillan, 1935. 2030 pp.

Well-known ex-German historian analyzes the period between 1890 and 1906. Draws extensively upon economic data and diplomatic documents, with occasional passages on the development of public opinion. Bibliography in text.

1178. WARD, HARRY FREDERICK (W). *Democracy and Social Change.* New York: Norton, 1940. 293 pp.

Professor in Union Theological Seminary analyzes U.S. social conditions; concludes that "because of the strength of American capitalism, our habit of direct action, and the social ignorance of the upper-income section of our population, the fiercest struggle between democratic forces and the fascist state will take place on our own soil."

1179. WARNER, W(ILLIAM) LLOYD (D); and LUNT, PAUL S. *The Social Life of a Modern Community* (Yankee City series, vol. 1). New Haven: Yale University, 1941. 460 pp.

First of a series of reports constituting an anthropological study of Newburyport, Mass., by a group of U.S. social scientists. Bibliographic footnotes.

*1180. WEBB, SIDNEY; and WEBB, BEATRICE (CB '43). *Soviet Communism: A New Civilisation?* London: Longmans, Green, 1935. 2 vols.

Comprehensive study of Soviet politics, economics, and culture by two experienced English social scientists.

1181. WEBSTER, DONALD EVERETT. *The Turkey of Atatürk: Social Process in the Turkish Reformation.* Philadelphia: American Academy of Political and Social Science, 1939. 337 pp.

Thoroughgoing analysis of Turkey by U.S. sociologist. Chapter 9, "Leadership," emphasizes the role of the new middle-income skill groups, telling of the work of typical public administrators, teachers, and social workers. Chapters are also given to "Propaganda," "Press," "Education," "Rural Uplift," etc. Bibliography, pp. 323-26, cites titles in various languages. Appendix includes glossary, Constitution of Turkey, and Program of People's Party of Turkey (1935)—the latter valuable to students of the unifying symbols of the one-party state.

1182. WECTER, DIXON (D,W). *The Hero in America: A Chronicle of Hero Worship.* New York: Scribner's, 1941. 530 pp.

Study of U.S. heroes from Captain John Smith to F. D. Roosevelt, with a summarizing chapter entitled, "How Americans Choose Their Heroes." By University of California professor of English. Bibliography, pp. 493-513.

1183. WECTER, DIXON (D,W). *The Saga of American Society: A Record of Social Aspiration, 1607-1937.* New York: Scribner's, 1937. 504 pp.

Study of the "social sets" in the United States, including chapters on books of etiquette, gentlemen's clubs, women in Society, the Society page, the pursuit of foreign titles, Society and sport, and Society's philanthropies. Bibliography, pp. 485-93.

1184. WERTENBAKER, CHARLES CHRISTIAN (W). *A New Doctrine for the Americas.* New York: Viking, 1941. 211 pp.

Analysis of Hemisphere politics by an editor of *Time* magazine. Bibliography, pp. 209-11.

1185. WEYER, MARY E. *The Decline of French Democracy: The Beginning of National Disintegration,* introduction by André Maurois (W). Washington, D.C.: American Council on Public Affairs, 1941. 73 pp.

Scholarly study of the *union sacrée* [political party truce] of 1914. Chapter 5 is on "Military Events, Censorship, and the Press." Bibliography, pp. 72-73.

1186. WHEELER-BENNETT, JOHN WHEELER. *Hindenburg, The Wooden Titan.* New York: Morrow, 1936. 490 pp.

Analysis of the creation and maintenance of attitudes toward General-President von Hindenburg over the preceding twenty years. By deputy chairman of the Information Committee, Royal Institute of International Affairs.

1187. WHITAKER, ARTHUR PRESTON (D,W), editor. *Mexico Today* (Annals of the American Academy of Political and Social Science, vol. 208). Philadelphia, March 1940. 252 pp.

Includes articles on "Political Leadership in Mexico" [Henry Bamford Parkes (D,W)]; "The Labor Movement" [Vicente Lombardo Toledano (CB'40)]; and "Commercial and Cultural Broadcasting" (Philip L. Barbour, official of International Division of N.B.C.).

1188. *Who Was Who in America: A Companion Volume to Who's Who in America.* Chicago: Marquis, 1942. 1396 pp.

"The 25,000 biographies removed because of deaths of biographees, from the 21 volumes of *Who's Who in America* published since its founding in 1897, until—and including—the 1940-41 biennial volume."

1189. WIGMORE, JOHN HENRY (D,W). *Panorama of the World's Legal Systems,* new ed. Washington, D.C.: Washington Law Book Company, 1936. 1400 pp.

First revision in some years of this massive, copiously illustrated compendium on legal practices by Dean of Northwestern University Law School.

1190. WISAN, JOSEPH EZRA (D). *The Cuban Crisis as Reflected in the New York Press, 1895-1898* (Columbia University Studies in History, Economics, and Public Law, no. 403). New York: Columbia University, 1934. 477 pp.

By historian, College of the City of New York. Bibliography, pp. 461-66.

1191. WITTKE, CARL FREDERICK (D,W). *German-Americans and the World War, with Special Emphasis on Ohio's German-Language Press.* Columbus: Ohio State Archaeological and Historical Society, 1936. 223 pp.

Based almost exclusively on study of the German-language press, particularly in Ohio, in World War I. By Professor of History, Ohio State University. Bibliographic footnotes.

1192. WORKS, GEORGE ALAN (W); and LESSER, SIMON O. *Rural America Today: Its Schools and Community Life.* Chicago: University of Chicago, 1942. 450 pp.

School problems receive intensive consideration, but in addition there are chapters on such related subjects as rural health, recreation, and social welfare, the problems of rural youth, rural Negroes, and community planning. Dr. Works is Professor of Education, University of Chicago; Mr. Lesser is a freelance writer on social problems. Bibliography at ends of chapters.

1193. WOYTINSKY, WLADIMIR S. (D). *Labor in the United States.* New York: Social Science Research Council, 1938. 333 pp.

Well-known social statistician reclassifies existing census data on occupations, to bring out distribution of the population by class of work and by skills. Also discusses employment statistics and figures on occupational mobility.

1194. YAKHONTOFF, VICTOR ALEX-ANDROVICH. *Eyes on Japan.* London: Williams and Norgate, 1936. New York: Coward McCann, 1936. 343 pp.

General survey of Japanese social life and foreign policy by an Imperial Russian general who was formerly military attaché at Tokyo. Bibliography, pp. 313-18.

PART 5. CHANNELS OF COMMUNICATION

A. COMMUNICATION SPECIALISTS

I. BUSINESS SPECIALISTS

ADVERTISING MEN, INDUSTRIAL RELATIONS
EXPERTS, PRESS AGENTS, PUBLICITY MEN,
PUBLIC RELATIONS COUNSELS, ETC.

1195. BALDWIN, WILLIAM H. "Association of Publicity Directors," *Public Opinion Quarterly*, 1 no. 4: 139-40 (October 1937).

On National Association of Accredited Publicity Directors, Inc., of New York City. By a New York publicity man.

1196. CLAIR, BLANCHE; and DIGNAM, DOROTHY, editors. *Advertising Careers for Women.* New York: Harpers, 1939. 268 pp.

Twenty-two lectures on advertising vocations presented by the Philadelphia Club of Advertising Women. Contains much practical advice by women specialists in agency work and in retail, cosmetics, food, home equipment, industrial, insurance, publication, and radio advertising.

1197. HEGGIE, B. A.; and O'MALLEY, J. J. "Fifty Per Cent," *New Yorker*, January 25, 1941.

Profile of William Colston Leigh, head of the lecture bureau, W. Colston Leigh, Inc., which handles many famous speakers.

1198. HICKS, CLARENCE JOHN. *My Life in Industrial Relations: Fifty Years in the Growth of a Profession.* New York: Harpers, 1941. 180 pp.

By chairman of the board of trustees, Industrial Relations Counselors, Inc., a nonprofit organization created for the purpose of giving advice, based on research, to large enterprises.

1199. MERCEY, ARCH A. "School for Federal Publicity Men at American University," *Public Opinion Quarterly*, 2: 324-28 (April 1938).

A curriculum for the training of symbol specialists is described by a Federal government publicity man who helped to organize it.

1200. *New York Times* obituaries on such persons as Ivy Lee (November 10, 1934) and Paul D. Cravath (July 2, 1940).

Times obituaries are an excellent source on big business promoters, whose activities are usually not fully described by the U.S. press while they are alive. Lee was a celebrated public relations counsel of big business, known especially for his handling of the Rockefeller interests; Cravath was a celebrated big business lawyer. See also *Times* story on Lee's connection with German Dye Trust, July 12, 1934.

1201. O'DEA, MARK. *Advertising as a Career: A Vocational Guide for Youth*, 2nd ed. New York: The Author, 1939. 128 pp.

1202. "Portrait of a Press Agent," *Time*, January 8, 1940, pp. 44-45.

On Broadway press agents in general and Richard Maney in particular. "Broadway's press agents (officially known as press representatives) number some 50 (a few of them women). About 15 really count. . . . They earn a minimum salary of $150 a week."

1203. THRUELSEN, RICHARD. "Men at Work: Advertising Agency Executive," *Saturday Evening Post*, 213: 22-23 (May 24, 1941).

Brief description of the life-experiences of a representative young account executive in a well-known New York agency.

1204. *Who's Who in Advertising, 1931*, edited by John L. Rogers. New York: Harpers, 1931. 284 pp.

Lists about 5000 names. Introduction describes these as "the top one-third of America's advertising personnel," and gives a few statistical tables derived from the data.

1205. WILLIAMS, WYTHE. "This Man Leads Small Business," *Commentator*, 3 no. 5: 3-7 (June 1938).

On Dewitt M. Emery of Akron, Ohio;

chairman of National Small Business Men's Association. By a U.S. political journalist.

II. PROFESSIONALS AND SEMIPROFESSIONALS

CIVIL SERVANTS, CLERGYMEN, "INTELLECTUALS," LAWYERS, PHYSICIANS, POPULARIZERS, PSYCHIATRISTS, SOCIAL WORKERS, WELFARE ADMINISTRATORS, ETC.

For educators, see Part 5 B.

1205a. ALLPORT, GORDON WILLARD; and VELTFORT, HELENE R. "Social Psychology and the Civilian War Effort," *Journal of Social Psychology,* 18: 165-233 (1943).

Detailed survey of war-connected activities and publications of social psychologists and related scientists since 1940, by two Harvard psychologists. Bibliography cites 306 items.

1206. AMERICAN BAR ASSOCIATION. SPECIAL COMMITTEE ON THE ECONOMIC CONDITION OF THE BAR. *The Economics of the Legal Profession: A Manual Designed Primarily for the Use of State, Local and Junior Bar Associations, Describing the Results of the Bar Surveys Which Have Been Made To Date: The Chief Proposals Which Have Been Advanced for Improving the Economic Condition of the Profession and Increasing Its Capacity for Usefulness; and the Methods and Forms Which Were Used in the Several Surveys.* Chicago: American Bar Association, 1938. 230 pp.

On the basis of surveys made in Connecticut, Wisconsin, Missouri, New York County, and California, the Committee concludes that "the public relations of the bar are defective" (p. 11), and recommends among other measures, "experiments in the way of setting up legal service bureaus under bar association auspices to render low-cost, efficient, specialized service to the low income groups," together with "experiments in organized bar association advertising" and public relations. Bibliographic footnotes.

1207. BLÁHA, IN. ARNOŠT. "Le Problème de l'intellectuel," *Revue internationale de sociologie,* 44: 361-72 (July-August 1936).

The intellectual as a social type.

1208. BLÁHA, IN. ARNOŠT. *Sociologie Inteligence.* Prague: Orbis, 1937. 397 pp.

"Sociology of the Intelligentsia." Social composition and functions of the intelligentsia are statistically and critically analyzed by the head of the department of sociology at Masaryk University. The volume contains an English summary.

1209. BORKENAU, FRANZ. *Pareto.* New York: Wiley, 1936. 219 pp.

Study of celebrated Italian sociologist. By a European scholar well versed in Marxism. Spanish edition *Pareto,* versión española de Nicolás Dorantes (Mexico: Fondo de cultura económica, 1941. 180 pp.).

1210. BRIN, HEINRICH (HENNOCH). *Zur Akademiker- und Intellektuellenfragen in der Arbeiterbewegung* (Dissertation, Basel). Strasbourg, 1928. 155 pp.

Role of intellectuals in the labor movement. By a student of Roberto Michels. Bibliography, pp. 149-55.

1211. BROWN, ALEC. *The Fate of the Middle Classes.* London: Gollancz, 1936. 288 pp.

A Marxist analysis of the role of middle-class intellectuals, by one of them. Bibliography is occasionally cited in the text.

1212. CLARK, CECIL. "Fascism and the Intellectuals," *Contemporary Review,* 148: 585-90 (November 1935).

1213. DALE, HAROLD EDWARD. *The Higher Civil Service of Great Britain.* New York: Oxford University, 1941. 232 pp.

A partially quantified description of this profession and the life of its members as of 1939. The author was formerly Principal Assistant Secretary, British Ministry of Agriculture and Fisheries. Chapter 7, pp. 178-91, is on "Relations with the Public and the Press." Bibliographic footnotes.

1214. HAYS, ARTHUR GARFIELD. *City Lawyer: The Autobiography of a Law Practice.* New York: Simon and Schuster, 1942. 482 pp.

By attorney of American Civil Liberties Union.

1215. HELLMAN, GEORGE SIDNEY. *Benjamin N. Cardozo: American Judge.* New York: Whittlesey House, 1940. 339 pp.

By a personal friend of long standing, with access to family archives and letters.

1216. HERRING, E(DWARD) PENDLETON. *Federal Commissioners: A Study of Their Careers and Qualifications* (Harvard Political Studies). Cambridge: Harvard University, 1936. 151 pp.

By Harvard political scientist. Includes FCC members. Bibliography, pp. 146-47 and in footnotes. See also title 1220, below.

1216a. HYNEMAN, CHARLES S. "The Political Scientist and National Service in Wartime," *American Political Science Review,* 36: 931-45 (October 1942).

Report of the Committee on Wartime Services of the American Political Science Association.

1217. JONES, ERNEST. "Sigmund Freud, 1856-1939," *International Journal of Psychoanalysis,* vol. 21 no. 1: 2-26 (January 1940).

Obituary by a fellow analyst, founder of the International Journal of Psychoanalysis.

*1217a. KRETSCHMER, ERNST. *Psychology of Genius,* translated, with an introduction, by Raymond Bernard Cattell (International Library of Psychology, Philosophy and Scientific Method). London: Kegan Paul, Trench and Trubner, 1931. 256 pp.

Case histories and general analysis by well-known German psychiatrist.

1218. LASSWELL, HAROLD DWIGHT; and McDOUGAL, MYRES S. "Legal Education and Public Policy: Professional Training in the Public Interest," *Yale Law Journal,* 52: 203-95 (March 1943).

A program for the education of lawyers, designed by two professors in the Yale Law School, who say, "The war period is a propitious moment to retool our system of legal education. America's huge plants for the fabrication of lawyers are practically closed for the duration; yet if the end of the present war in any way resembles the termination of World War I, their doors will swing wide to admit a dammed-up stream of returning soldiers who want legal training. In the rush of conversion from war to peace the archaic conventions and confusions of the past may win out over the vital needs of our civilization and the doors may open to admit the unwary members of an entire generation into a reguilded vacuum." Heavily documented with references to existing writings on legal education and to recommended curricular material.

1219. LIN, MOUSHENG HSITIEN. Review of Edgar Snow's *Red Star Over China* (London: Gollancz, 1937), *China Institute Bulletin* (119 West 57th Street, New York City), 2 no. 7: 123-25 (April 1938).

Chinese political scientist finds evidence in Edgar Snow's book and elsewhere that both the Communist and Kuomintang parties in China consist mostly of workers led by intellectuals of middle-class origin. This review lends support to the increasingly accepted interpretation of the current series of world crises as a suicidal and fratricidal propaganda battle between "leftist" and "rightist" intellectuals of essentially similar social origins—both of these groups exploiting in some degree the nonrational hopes of the less-informed masses.

1220. MACMAHON, ARTHUR WHITTIER; and MILLETT, JOHN D. *Federal Administrators: A Biographical Approach to the Problem of Departmental Management.* New York: Columbia University, 1939. 524 pp.

Life-history data on high federal administrators, collected by two Columbia political scientists. Comparable in some ways with E. Pendleton Herring's *Federal Commissioners: A Study of Their Careers and Qualifications* (1936), cited above.

1221. MARCUSE, LUDWIG. *Soldier of the Church: The Life of Ignatius Loyola,* translated from the German by Christopher Lazare. New York: Simon and Schuster, 1940. 352 pp.

Dr. Marcuse (Ph.D. Berlin 1917) is a scholar in the field of the history of philosophy.

1222. MAY, MARK ARTHUR; and others. *The Education of American*

Ministers. New York: Institute of Social and Religious Research, 1934. 4 vols.

Many U.S. ministers do not have a theological training or equivalent. Most of those who teach Christian sociology have no background in systematic sociology or social research, according to this study of ministers and the institutions that train them. Dr. May is a well-known U.S. social psychologist. Bibliography, pp. 275-80.

1223. MENNINGER, FLO V. *My Life*. New York: Richard R. Smith, 1939. 310 pp.

Autobiography of one of the early women settlers of Kansas, the mother of the famous psychiatrists, Karl and William Menninger.

1223a. MILLS, C(HARLES) WRIGHT. *A Sociological Account of Pragmatism* (Ph.D. thesis, sociology, Wisconsin 1942). 455 pp.

Empirical analysis of the social origins and roles of pragmatist philosophers and their publics, and of the central conceptions of pragmatism. Includes biographies of John Dewey, William James and Charles Peirce. Bibliographic notes, pp. 416-55.

1224. MIRSKY, DMITRI S. (pseudonym of DMITRI PETROVICH SVYATO-POLK-MIRSKY). *The Intelligentsia of Great Britain*, translated by Alec Brown. London: Gollancz, 1935. 237 pp.

A leftist's evaluation of the activities of contemporary British writers and thinkers.

1225. MORSTEIN MARX, FRITZ. "The Bureaucratic State: Some Remarks on Mosca's *Ruling Class*," *Review of Politics*, 1: 457-72 (October 1939).

By political scientist, Queens College, New York.

1226. NELLES, WALTER. *The Education of Albert De Silver*, edited by Lewis Gannett, introduction by Roger Baldwin. New York: Norton, 1941. 221 pp.

Life and philosophy of Albert De Silver, associate director of American Civil Liberties Union during and after the World War. By counsel for the Union.

1227. NEW JERSEY STATE BAR ASSOCIATION. COMMITTEE ON W.P.A. *Survey of the Economic Status of the Legal Profession in New Jersey, with Tables, Statistics and Conclusions: 1941 Report to the New Jersey State Bar Association*. Newark, N.J., 1941. 80 pp.

Based on questionnaires filled out by 2353 of the approximately 7000 lawyers in the state. Tabulations and text concerning years of schooling, age, national origins, etc., and their relation to income. Also data on kinds of practice, fees, distribution of lawyers, etc.

1228. SHANNON, J. R.; and SHAW, MAXINE. "Education of Business and Professional Leaders," *American Sociological Review*, 5: 381-83 (June 1940).

Data from *Who's Who in America*, 1938-39, show amount of formal schooling undergone by U.S. leaders.

1229. STONE, IRVING. *Clarence Darrow for the Defence: A Biography*. New York: Doubleday, Doran, 1941. 570 pp.

Biography of celebrated Chicago attorney. Bibliography, pp. 545-48.

1230. STREET, ELWOOD. *The Public Welfare Administrator*. New York: McGraw-Hill, 1940. 422 pp.

By welfare professor and executive. Topics include local agency and institutional work, legal phases, statistics, records, personnel, procedure, etc. Chapter 9 is on "Staff Discipline and Morale"; chapter 18, "The World Outside the Agency," is on public relations. Bibliography at ends of chapters and pp. 406-07.

1231. SULLIVAN, HARRY STACK. "A Year of Selective Service Psychiatry," *Mental Hygiene*, 26: 7-15 (January 1942).

Review of the accomplishments of the Selective Service System in 1941 by one of its principal psychiatric consultants. "The need that cries from every side, the need that reaches above all others, is the urgent necessity for indoctrinating medical men with the simple fundamentals of psychiatry. Careful search fails to reveal over 3500 well-trained male psychiatrists in these United States. With the work of mobilization, with the work of Navy recruiting, with the maintenance of troops, with the care of the inevitable mental casualties in troops, with the demands, the inescapable demands, of civilian care, institutional and otherwise, and with the presently to become staggering problems of technical aid in the maintenance of civilian morale and solidarity, 3500 psychiatrists cannot possibly do all the psychiatric work . . . as a preliminary to the stresses, strains, disasters, bad news and all the deprivations that the American people are about to experience. . . ."

1231a. TAYLOR, MARTHA BARRIS. *History of the Federal Civil Service: 1789 to the Present.* Washington, D.C.: Government Printing Office, 1941. 162 pp.

"Prepared in the Information and Recruiting Division of the U.S. Civil Service Commission," this is an historical guide to U.S. civil service traditions and aspirations. Bibliography, pp. 151-54.

1231b. *Twentieth Century Authors: A Biographical Dictionary of Modern Literature,* edited by Sidney Jasspon Kunitz and Howard Haycraft. New York: H. W. Wilson, 1942. 1577 pp.

"Primary emphasis has been on professional men and women of letters whose vocation is the writing of books of fiction, poetry, history, biography, criticism, etc. . . . writers of this century, of all nations, whose books are familiar to readers of English. . . . The sketches range, in assigned length, from 300 to 1500 words, roughly in proportion to the importance of the subject, but frequently influenced by extraneous considerations, such as . . . amount of available data. . . . Sketches of others of the same generation who flourished earlier may be found in two biographical dictionaries by the same editors: *British Authors of the Nineteenth Century* (1936) and *American Authors: 1600-1900* (1938). . . . The names of such authors have been entered in the present alphabet, with cross-references to the pertinent volume. . . . Every living author in this volume who could be reached was invited to write his own sketch. . . . [Other data have been added by the editors.—BLS.] Each biographical sketch is followed by a list of the principal works of the author in question, with original dates of publication. A list of biographical and critical sources about each author is also given. . . ." Included are 1850 biographies and 1700 portraits; many are scholars, social theorists, journalists, political propagandists, educators.

1232. WARNOTTE, DANIEL. "Bureaucratie et fonctionnairisme," *Revue de l'Institut de Sociologie,* 17: 219-60 (1937).

Consequences of increased importance of bureaucrats in the larger countries are described by Belgian sociologist. "Inevitably the clerks who handle the details are in a position to give their own interpretations to rules and laws, and to serve the interests of the political party in power or even their own interests rather than those of the people. The prestige of being a government employee and the attendant security and special privileges have attracted an overabundance of young workers. The feeling of self-importance which is derived from the individual's personal identification with the power of the state, and absorption in a narrowly circumscribed job where formal rules and precedents are all important, sets the functionary off from his former fellows. But, in spite of the shortcomings of the bureaucratic system, it has served to transmit civilization and to meet the needs that are demanded of the state, guaranteeing a minimum existence without too heavily constraining the governed." —Summary in *American Journal of Sociology,* 44: 1023 (May 1939).

1233. WELLMAN, FRANCIS L., editor. *Success in Court.* New York: Macmillan, 1941. 404 pp.

Skills of the lawyer are discussed by ten experienced attorneys.

1234. WHITE, WILLIAM ALANSON. *The Autobiography of a Purpose.* New York: Doubleday, Doran, 1938. 293 pp.

Dr. White was for 30 years principal administrator of St. Elizabeth's Hospital, Washington, D.C. One of the nation's outstanding psychiatrists, he blended in his long career a broad and deep understanding of the problems of personality; a distinguished administrative ability; and exceptional skill in public relations.

1234a. WOODWORTH, ROBERT SESSIONS. *The Columbia University Psychological Laboratory: A Fifty-Year Retrospect.* New York: Published by the author, Columbia University, 1942. 23 pp.

History of Columbia's psychology department, with data on careers of its 278 Ph.D. graduates, by one of its senior professors.

1235. WOOLSTON, HOWARD BROWN. "American Intellectuals and Social Reform," *American Sociological Review*, 1: 363-73 (June 1936).

Questionnaire analysis of attitudes of Pacific Coast social scientists, Chamber of Commerce secretaries, labor union secretaries, and state senators, toward NRA and toward social activism on the part of professors. By University of Washington professor of sociology.

III. POLITICAL SPECIALISTS

AGITATORS, GOVERNMENTAL PUBLICITY MEN, LABOR LEADERS, LOBBYISTS, POLITICIANS, PROPHETS, ETC.

1236. AMERINGER, OSCAR. *If You Don't Weaken.* New York: Holt, 1940. 476 pp.

Autobiography of Socialist editor of Oklahoma City *American Guardian.*

1237. ANDERSON, H. DEWEY. "The Educational and Occupational Attainments of Our National Rulers," *Scientific Monthly*, 40: 511-18 (June 1935).

1238. ANTONGINI, TOMMASO. *D'Annunzio.* Boston: Little, Brown, 1938. 583 pp.

The author of this biography was d'Annunzio's private secretary from 1908 onward. Students of the type of personality which is capable of developing great skill in political agitation will find many unvarnished data here. Arthur Livingston, well-known American Italianist, places d'Annunzio in social perspective in a review of this book, *New York Times Book Review*, June 12, 1938, pp. 1 ff.

1239. ARNETT, ALEX MATHEWS. *Claude Kitchin and the Wilson War Policies.* Boston: Little, Brown, 1937. 341 pp.

Biography of a Democratic leader of the House who led a campaign against the war policies of Woodrow Wilson and was caught in a cross fire of opposing propagandas. By professor of history, University of North Carolina. Bibliography, pp. 301-37.

1240. ARRARÁS, JOAQUÍN. *Francisco Franco: The Times and the Man*, translated by J. Manuel Espinosa. Milwaukee: Bruce Publishing Company, 1938. 210 pp.

"Official biography," by a Spanish journalist and historian. Bibliography, pp. 209-10. "Authorized" South American edition (in Spanish), Buenos Aires, 1937.

1241. BADE, WILFRED. *Joseph Goebbels* (Colemans kleine Biographien). Lübeck: Coleman, 1938. 82 pp.

1242. BALABANOFF, ANGELICA. *My Life as a Rebel.* New York: Harpers, 1938. 358 pp.

Autobiography of Russian girl who left her middle-class home at 17, rose through the revolutionary movement to become first secretary of the Third International.

1243. BARRÈS, PHILIPPE. *Charles De Gaulle.* New York: Doubleday, Doran, 1941. 260 pp.

Leader of the Free French forces.

1244. BATE, DON. *Wang Ching-Wei: Puppet or Patriot.* Chicago: Ralph Fletcher Seymour (410 S. Michigan Ave.), 1941. 187 pp.

Biographical and political study of the Chinese head of the Nanking ("Japanese puppet") Government.

1245. BEALS, CARLETON. *The Story of Huey P. Long.* Philadelphia: Lippincott, 1935. 414 pp.

By U.S. journalist.

1246. BEIN, ALEX. *Theodore Herzl: A Biography.* Philadelphia: Jewish Publication Society of America, 1941. 545 pp.

Life of the Zionist leader. Translated from the German. Bibliography, pp. 523-30.

1247. BENGALEE, SUFI MUTIUR RHAMAN. *The Life of Muhammad.* Chicago: Moslem Sunrise Press, 1941. 286 pp.

His life, character, and teachings described for the Western world by a Mohammedan writer. Bibliography, pp. 281-82.

1248. BERKOV, ROBERT. *Strong Man of China: The Story of Chiang*

Kai-shek. Boston: Houghton Mifflin, 1938. 288 pp.

Analysis of the personality and policies of Generalissimo Chiang Kai-shek, by manager of Shanghai bureau of United Press. Bibliography, pp. 285-88.

1249. BLOOR, ELLA REEVE. *We Are Many: An Autobiography*. New York: International, 1940. 319 pp.

A veteran labor leader and a D.A.R., this daughter of a New York Presbyterian business man is now the "grand old woman" of the U.S. Communist Party.

1250. BRINTON, CRANE. *The Lives of Talleyrand*. New York: Norton, 1936. 315 pp.

By Harvard historian. Bibliography, pp. 301-11.

1251. BROCK, HENRY IRVING. "Army's Morale Builder," *New York Times Magazine* (September 7, 1941).

Brigadier-General Frederick Henry Osborn, head of the Morale Branch (later known as Special Services Branch) of the United States Army, is a "Hudson River squire" who "has been a civilian all his life." A director in numerous corporations, he is also a trustee of numerous philanthropies. By New York *Times* feature writer.

1252. BROCKWAY, MARIAN L. *A Study of the Geographical, Occupational, and Political Characteristics of Congressmen, 1800-1919* (M.A. thesis, sociology, Kansas 1938).

1253. CARNES, CECIL. *John L. Lewis: Leader of Labor*. New York: Robert Speller, 1937. 331 pp.

Biography of leader of the Committee for Industrial Organization, by a U.S. newspaper reporter.

1254. CARR, EDWARD HALLETT. *Michael Bakunin*. New York and London: Macmillan, 1937. 501 pp.

By Professor of International Politics, University College of Wales, a specialist in Russian revolutionary history. Bibliography, pp. 489-91.

1255. CARTER, JOHN FRANKLIN (pseud.: UNOFFICIAL OBSERVER).

American Messiahs. New York: Simon and Schuster, 1935. 238 pp.

U.S. journalist's study of prominent contemporary U.S. politicians who have espoused the underdog: Huey Long, Charles E. Coughlin, Upton Sinclair, Dr. Francis E. Townsend, Floyd B. Olson, Philip and Robert La Follette, Burton K. Wheeler, Norman Thomas, and others.

1256. CARTER, JOHN FRANKLIN (pseud.: JAY FRANKLIN). *LaGuardia*. New York: Modern Age, 1937. 176 pp.

Biography of Mayor Fiorello H. LaGuardia of New York City.

1257. CARTER, JOHN FRANKLIN (pseud.: JAY FRANKLIN). *The New Dealers*. New York: Simon and Schuster, 1934. 414 pp.

Biographical sketches of the early New Dealers.

1258. CECIL, EDGAR ALGERNON ROBERT GASCOYNE-CECIL, VISCOUNT. *A Great Experiment: An Autobiography*, preface by Nicholas Murray Butler. New York: Oxford University, 1941. 390 pp.

English Conservative statesman, prominent in League of Nations diplomacy.

1259. CLARK, DELBERT. "Steve Takes Care Of It," *New York Times Magazine*, July 27, 1941, pp. 11 ff.

Sketch of Stephen Tyree Early, press relations officer of F. D. Roosevelt.

1260. "A Congress to Win the War," *New Republic*, 106: 683-712 (May 18, 1942).

Special supplement to *New Republic*, giving brief life histories and records of Congressmen considered antidemocratic by Union for Democratic Action.

★1261. CRAWFORD, KENNETH GALE (W). *The Pressure Boys: The Inside Story of Lobbying in America*. New York: Messner, 1939. 308 pp.

Lobbyists, especially those of the private property interests, are described by Washington correspondent of the New York *Post* and the *Nation*.

1262. *Current Biography*, monthly, New York, January 1940–.

Published by H. W. Wilson Company. Consists of brief biographies of persons prominent in the news of the day, with bibliography of source materials on their careers.

1263. DANIELS, JOSEPHUS. *Editor in Politics*. Chapel Hill: University of North Carolina, 1941. 644 pp.

Second volume of memoirs of well-known North Carolina journalist, diplomat and politician, covering the period from Cleveland to Wilson. The first, entitled *Tar Heel Editor* (1940), covered his career from 1862 to about 1893.

1264. DAVIS, FORREST. *Huey Long: A Candid Biography*. New York: Dodge Publishing Co., 1935. 312 pp.

By U.S. journalist.

1265. DE LA MORA, CONSTANCIA. *In Place of Splendor*. New York: Harcourt, Brace, 1939. 433 pp.

Autobiography of Spanish aristocrat who became head of the Loyalist foreign press service of Spain during the Franco revolution. Touches upon many aspects of Spanish history during the eight years of the Republic.

1266. DENNISON, ELEANOR E. *The Senate Foreign Relations Committee*. Stanford University: Stanford University, 1942. 201 pp.

Its organization, personnel, and procedure and its influence on the history of American foreign relations. Bibliography, pp. 148-54. See companion piece on *House Committee on Foreign Affairs* by Westphal, title 1378, below.

1267. *Deutsche Führerlexikon, 1934-35*. Berlin: Stollberg, 1934. 709 pp.

Who's Who of Nazi leaders. Includes references to their social origins, and organization-tables for party, state and movement.

1268. DU BOIS, WILLIAM EDWARD BURGHARDT. *Dusk of Dawn: An Essay Toward an Autobiography of a Race Concept*. New York: Harcourt, Brace, 1940. 334 pp.

Autobiography of Director of Publications and Research, National Association for the Advancement of Colored People.

1269. DUTCH, OSWALD (pseud.). *Hitler's Twelve Apostles*. London: E. Arnold, 1939. 271 pp. New York: McBride, 1940. 249 pp.

Brauchitsch, Frick, Funk, Goebbels, Goering, Hess, Himmler, Ley, Ribbentrop, Alfred Rosenberg, Schirach and Streicher, described by an apparently well-informed writer.

1270. ELLIS, ELMER. *Henry Moore Teller, Defender of the West*. Caldwell, Idaho: The Caxton Printers, 1941. 409 pp.

Biography of the late Senator from Colorado, by University of Missouri historian. Bibliography, pp. 393-401.

1271. ERGANG, ROBERT REINHOLD. *The Potsdam Fuehrer: Frederick William I, Father of Prussian Militarism*. New York: Columbia University, 1941. 290 pp.

By historian, New York University. Bibliography, pp. 255-70.

1272. ESSARY, J. FREDERICK. "Lobbyists Must Live," *American Mercury*, 47: 325-29 (July 1939).

Well-known Washington correspondent reports: "The old button-holing, money-passing methods of promoting legislation or executive action have gone. The lobby has reformed. It has become more scientific, more refined, better directed, and less suspiciously clothed. . . . Relatively few organizations concentrate upon Congress. Most of them do business with some agency of the executive department. . . ."

1273. ESTORICK, ERIC. *Stafford Cripps: Prophetic Rebel*. New York: John Day, 1941. 285 pp.

By U.S. publicist.

1274. FRASER, GEOFFREY; and NATANSON, THADEE. *Léon Blum: Man and Statesman*. Philadelphia: Lippincott, 1937. London: Gollancz, 1937. 320 pp.

1275. FROEMBGEN, HANNS. *Kemal Atatürk: A Biography*, translated from the German by Kenneth Kirkness. London: Jarrolds, 1937. 285 pp.

A partly fictionized biography.

1276. GALLACHER, WILLIAM. *Revolt on the Clyde.* New York: International Publishers, 1936. London: Lawrence and Wishart, 1936. 301 pp.

Autobiography of a Communist member of Parliament.

1277. GITLOW, BENJAMIN. *I Confess: The Truth about American Communism*, introduction by Max Eastman. New York: Dutton, 1940. 611 pp.

Communist Party of U.S., described over the entire course of its history in autobiography of one of its founders, who rose to be its candidate for Vice Presidency of U.S. in 1924 and 1928, and who was a member of Third International's Executive Committee and Praesidium. Asserts that neither Stalinites, Trotskyites nor Lovestonites have "anything to offer the dispossessed of America." They have, the author asserts, neglected to develop an American vocabulary and symbolism, and have therefore "continued to stew in the embalming fluid of the mummified Lenin."

1278. GITTLER, LEWIS FREDERICK. "France Finds a Huey Long," *Current History*, April 1937, pp. 60-63.

Jacques Doriot of the French Popular Party, described by U.S. journalist.

1279. GOEBBELS, PAUL JOSEPH. *My Part in Germany's Fight*, translated by Dr. Kurt Fiedler. London: Hurst and Blackett, 1935. 288 pp.

German edition: *Vom Kaiserhof zur Reichskanzlei: Eine historische Darstellung in Tagebuchblättern, vom 1. januar 1932 bis zum 1. mai 1933*. Munich: Eher, 1934. 308 pp. Collections of selected public addresses of Dr. Goebbels have also been published in German.

*1280. GOSNELL, HAROLD FOOTE (D). *Negro Politicians: The Rise of Negro Politics in Chicago*. Chicago: University of Chicago, 1935. 404 pp.

University of Chicago political scientist's intensive study of the role and tactics of Negroes in Chicago. A full-length objective analysis of Negro political leadership. Bibliography, pp. 380-87.

1281. GRITZBACH, ERICH. *Hermann Goering: The Man and His Work*. London: Hurst and Blackett, 1939. 256 pp.

German edition: *Hermann Goering, Werk und Mensch* (Munich: Eher, 1938. 345 pp.) has run through some 20 editions.

1282. GUEDALLA, PHILIP. *Mr. [Winston S.] Churchill*. New York: Reynal and Hitchcock, 1942. 346 pp.

Biography of British Prime Minister by British historian. Bibliography, pp. 327-38.

1283. HAHN, EMILY. *The Soong Sisters*. New York: Doubleday, Doran, 1941. 349 pp.

Descendants of a family represented in Chinese official life for 16 generations, the three Soong sisters became the wives, respectively, of Revolutionary Sun Yat Sen, Generalissimo Chiang Kai-shek, and Finance Minister H. H. Kung, at the same time exerting wide social influence through their own activities.

1284. HARRIMAN, MARGARET CASE. "The Candor Kid," *New Yorker*, January 4 and 11, 1940.

Profile of Clare Boothe Brokaw Luce, journalist-playwright-politician and wife of Henry R. Luce, publisher, of Time, Inc.

1285. HARRISON, CARTER HENRY, II. *Stormy Years*. Indianapolis: Bobbs-Merrill, 1935. 351 pp.

The author of this autobiography was five times Mayor of Chicago between 1897 and 1913, and his father, Carter Henry Harrison I, was also Mayor for five terms in the 80's and early 90's.

1286. HARTMANN, GEORGE WILFRIED. "Homogeneity of Opinion among Liberal Leaders," *Public Opinion Quarterly*, 1 no. 3: 75-78 (July 1937).

Ten U.S. leftist leaders exhibit a high degree of inner consistency in their social attitudes, as measured by a "fairly exhaustive" questionnaire administered by a Teachers College social psychologist.

1287. HAXEY, SIMON (pseud.). *England's Money Lords: Tory M.P.* New York: Harrison-Hilton, 1939. 263 pp.

Survey of interlocking family relationships and interlocking directorates of conservative British M.P.'s, believed to have been written by a leftist group under a collective pseudonym.

1288. Hedin, Sven Anders. *Chiang Kai-shek, Marshal of China*, translated from the Swedish by Bernard Norbelie. New York: John Day, 1940. 290 pp.

By a noted explorer, well acquainted with China.

1289. Heiden, Konrad. *Ein Mann gegen Europa*. Munich: Europa Verlag, 1937. 390 pp.

Continues the author's best-selling biography of Hitler, bringing the data on the Führer and his country up to the early months of 1937. Contains an index to both volumes.

*1290. Heiden, Konrad. *Der Führer: Hitler's Rise to Power*, translated by Ralph Manheim and Norbert Guterman. Boston: Houghton Mifflin, 1944. 788 pp.

Extensive revision of standard biography of Adolf Hitler (*Hitler: A Biography*. New York: Knopf, 1936. 415 pp.). The data in the revised book cover the period to mid-1934. The author, for many years Munich correspondent of the *Frankfurter Zeitung*, observed the tactics of the Nazi movement at close range. He is also well known for his *History of National Socialism* (New York: Knopf, 1935. 430 pp.).

1291. Heinberg, John G. "The Personnel Structure of French Cabinets," *American Political Science Review*, 33: 267-78 (April 1939).

Continues the author's "Personnel of French Cabinets," *American Political Science Review*, 25: 389-96 (May 1931). Finds that 41 men "may be said to constitute the personnel structure of cabinets under the Third Republic," from March 1879 to March 1938, having "held the premiership and the important ministries of foreign affairs and finance for two-thirds of the entire period; the ministries of war and marine for half the period; the interior portfolio for almost half; and other ministries for considerable tenures." Table shows their various tenures. Ten of the 41 are selected for rather detailed career analysis. This reveals that prerequisites have been (1) long service on legislative commissions that gave access to specialized knowledge; (2) continuous local political success. But "none of the ten, and very few of their biographers, describe their local relationships or their campaign strategy and technique. Living French politicians tell no tales, and deceased ones leave

no written tales behind them." The author is a University of Missouri political scientist.

1292. Heuss, Theodor. *Friedrich Naumann: Der Mann, Das Werk, Die Zeit*. Stuttgart: Deutsche Verlagsanstalt, 1937. 751 pp.

Biography of an influential "progressive nationalist" social theorist (1860-1919), author of *Mitteleuropa*, a volume pleading for cooperation of all countries in Central Europe under German economic leadership. Dr. Heuss, also a political theorist, was a close friend and collaborator of Naumann's for many years.

1293. Hinton, Harold Boaz. *Cordell Hull: A Biography*, foreword by Sumner Welles. New York: Doubleday, Doran, 1942. 377 pp.

On U.S. Secretary of State.

1294. Hollis, Christopher. *Lenin* (Science and Culture series). Milwaukee: Bruce, 1938. 277 pp.

A Catholic's interpretation of the life of Lenin. Bibliography at ends of chapters.

1295. Hombourger, René. *Goebbels*. Paris: Sorlot, 1939. 320 pp.

1296. Hotaling, Burton L. "Huey Pierce Long as Journalist and Propagandist," *Journalism Quarterly*, 20: 21-29 (March 1943).

By a member of the Department of Journalism, Tulane University. Material was gathered from persons closely connected with Long, who, for the most part, had never before been interviewed on the subject.

1297. Johnson, Gerald White. *Roosevelt: Dictator or Democrat?* New York: Harpers, 1941. 303 pp.

Study of President F. D. Roosevelt and his reputation by Baltimore *Sun* editorial writer.

1298. Jones, Jack. *Unfinished Journey*, preface by David Lloyd George. London: Hamilton, 1937. New York: Oxford University, 1937. 303 pp.

Autobiography of a Welsh coal miner who became a professional politician and served at one time or another in the Socialist, Communist, Lloyd George, Mosley, and finally Baldwin, movements. Reveals with candor the motives of the politician of working-class origin in England at the present stage.

1299. JOSEPHSON, MATTHEW. *The Politicos: 1865-1896.* New York: Harcourt, Brace, 1938. 760 pp.

Study of U.S. national political figures whose careers paralleled those of the monopoly capitalists described by the author in a previous volume, *The Robber Barons* (New York: Harcourt, Brace, 1934. 474 pp.).

1300. JUNGNICKEL, MAX. *Goebbels.* Leipzig: Kittler, 1933. 92 pp.

1301. KERZHENTSEV, PLATON MIKHAILOVITCH. *The Life of Lenin.* New York: International Publishers, 1938. 336 pp.

An "official" Stalinist biography. Bibliography, pp. 330-36. French edition: *Vie de Lénine,* translated from the Russian by Jeanne Toscane (Paris: Éditions sociales internationales, 1937. 272 pp.).

1302. KLAUSNER, JOSEPH. *Menahem Ussishkin: His Life and Work,* translated from the Hebrew by I. M. Lask. New York: Scopus Publishing Co., 1942. 158 pp.

Biography of the late chairman of the World Zionist Action Committee and world president of the Jewish National Fund. Dr. Klausner is a professor in the Hebrew University, Jerusalem.

1303. KOENIG, SAMUEL. "Social Attitudes and Backgrounds of Labor Leaders, with Special Reference to New Haven and New Britain, Connecticut," *Sociology and Social Research,* 25: 264-65 (January-February 1941).

One of the rare sociological studies of U.S. labor leaders, this is a U.S. social scientist's report of interviews with 44 leaders in both A.F. of L. and C.I.O.—"about 95% of the more important ones and approximately 70% of the total in the two cities. The Italians, Jews, Irish, and Poles make up about two-thirds of the total leadership. . . . Of the 44 labor leaders, 25 were . . . with A.F. of L. and 19 with C.I.O. unions. Close to two-thirds . . . are American born, and all, except two, come from the working class. The bulk . . . had an elementary school education, but a considerable number were either graduated from or attended high school. Only three . . . received a college education. The majority . . . , since the bulk of the population adheres to that faith, are Catholics, while Protestants and Jews are about evenly divided. . . . No essential differences seem to exist with regard to nativity, economic background, education, and religion between the A.F. of L. and C.I.O. labor union leaders. As the two cities covered are among the six largest in the state, it may be safely assumed that the leaders in the rest of the state share essentially the same characteristics." The only attitude data presented are on church and synagogue attendance. About one-third said they attended regularly; one-third, irregularly; one-third, that they never attended.

1304. KOEVES, TIBOR. *Satan in Top Hat: The Biography of Franz von Papen.* New York: Alliance, 1941. 359 pp.

Nazi diplomat. By a journalist with many years of experience in Europe.

1305. KORNGOLD, RALPH. *Robespierre and the Fourth Estate,* introduction by Crane Brinton. New York: Modern Age, 1941. 417 pp.

Reissue of the author's *Robespierre, First Modern Dictator* (1937). Views Robespierre as a great class leader, a representative of the proletariat who fought savagely to emancipate the common people. Bibliography, pp. 395-403.

1306. KORNIS, JULES. *L'Homme d'état: Analyse de l'ésprit politique.* Paris: Alcan, 1938. 576 pp.

Theory of types of national leaders, by professor in the University of Budapest. Emphasizes skills, psychological traits, social-class origins, and nationality.

1307. KORSCH, KARL. *Karl Marx* (Modern Sociologists series). New York: Wiley, 1938. 247 pp.

Bibliography, pp. 237-44.

1308. KRAUSE, WILLI. *Reichsminister Dr. Goebbels.* Berlin-Schöneberg: Deutsche Kultur-Wacht, 1934. 62 pp.

1309. "The Labor Governors," *Fortune,* June 1937.

Frank Murphy of Michigan and George H. Earle of Pennsylvania.

1310. Lasswell, Harold Dwight. "The Propagandist Bids for Power," *American Scholar*, 8: 350-57 (Summer 1939).

Surveys Europe's experiences in recent years with propagandists. "That sector of the propaganda group that stayed in the pay of business (and continued to be in business for itself) lost out. It lost to that fraction of the propaganda group that played active politics. And it ultimately lost to that minority of propagandists who combined propaganda with mass organization and with mass violence. . . . After this glance at the general trend of world affairs, we bring our eyes back to America with renewed interest."

1311. Lasswell, Harold Dwight. "The Relation of Skill Politics to Class Politics and National Politics," *Chinese Social and Political Science Review*, 21: 298-313 (October-December 1937).

Defines conception of a "skill commonwealth." Refers to role of men with propaganda skill in recent world politics.

1312. Leopold, Richard William. *Robert Dale Owen: A Biography.* Cambridge: Harvard University, 1940. 470 pp.

Biography of a U.S. politician and reformer, son of Robert Owen, the celebrated British philosopher of "Universal Reform." By Harvard historian. Bibliography, pp. 417-40.

1313. Lief, Alfred. *Democracy's Norris: The Biography of a Lonely Crusade.* New York: Stackpole, 1939. 546 pp.

Senator George William Norris of Nebraska. Bibliography, pp. 529-38.

1314. Lipson, Leslie. *The American Governor: From Figurehead to Leader.* Chicago: University of Chicago, 1939. 282 pp.

By professor of political science, Victoria University College, New Zealand. Bibliography, pp. 269-75.

1315. Loth, David Goldsmith. *Woodrow Wilson: The Fifteenth Point.* Philadelphia: Lippincott, 1941. 365 pp.

Biography.

1316. Lutz, Alma. *Created Equal: A Biography of Elizabeth Cady Stanton, 1815-1902.* New York: John Day, 1940. 345 pp.

Bibliography, pp. 327-30.

1317. McCamy, James Lucian. "F. D. R. in Review," *Public Opinion Quarterly*, 6: 134-39 (Spring 1942).

U.S. political scientist's review of personality of President F. D. Roosevelt as shown by his *Public Papers and Addresses, 1937-40* (New York: Macmillan, 1941. 4 vols.).

1318. McKinney, Madge Maude. "The Personnel of the Seventy-seventh Congress," *American Political Science Review*, 36: 67-75 (February 1942).

Hunter College political scientist presents data on age, place of birth, religion, education, political experience, economic affiliations, father's occupation, and military service of members of the current Congress.

1319. Mangam, William D. *The Clarks: An American Phenomenon.* New York: Silver Bow, 1941. 257 pp.

Biographies of Senator William Andrews Clark of Montana and his children give an external, undocumented story of circumstances attending the accumulation and dissipation of the fortune of a copper magnate and politician. The author was for thirty years the general business agent of one of the Senator's sons.

1320. Mason, Alpheus Thomas. "Brandeis: Moulder of Social Insurance Opinion," *Public Opinion Quarterly*, 2: 533-56 (October 1938).

By Princeton professor of politics, author of *Brandeis: Lawyer and Judge in the Modern State* (1933) and *The Brandeis Way: A Case Study in the Workings of Democracy* (1938).

1321. Mason, John Brown. "Lawyers in the 71st to 75th Congresses: Their Legal Education and Experience," *Rocky Mountain Law Review* (December 1937).

By U.S. political scientist.

1322. Maurer, James Hudson. *It Can Be Done.* New York: Rand School, 1938. 374 pp.

Autobiography of a veteran U.S. labor leader, Socialist candidate for the Vice-Presidency in 1928 and 1932.

1323. MAYER, GUSTAV. *Friedrich Engels: A Biography*. New York: Knopf, 1936. 332 pp.

The first substantial biography of Engels to appear in English. Translated from a condensation of the author's *Friedrich Engels* (Berlin: Springer, 1920. 2 vols.).

1324. MEHRING, FRANZ. *Karl Marx: The Story of His Life*, translated by Edward Fitzgerald. New York: Covici, Friede, 1935. 608 pp.

By a well-known historian of socialism. Bibliographic notes, pp. 557-63. Bibliography, pp. 585-99.

1325. MILLER, JOHN CHESTER. *Sam Adams, Pioneer in Propaganda*. Boston: Little, Brown, 1936. 437 pp.

Biography stressing propaganda techniques of an agitator who helped to organize Boston for the American Revolution. Bibliographic footnotes.

1326. MILLIN, SARAH GERTRUDE. *General [Jan] Smuts*. Boston: Little, Brown, 1936. London: Faber and Faber, 1936. 2 vols.

By a South African novelist. Contains extensive bibliography.

1327. MINTON, BRUCE; and STUART, JOHN. *Men Who Lead Labor*. New York: Modern Age, 1937. 270 pp.

Biographies of U.S. labor leaders William Green, William Hutcheson, Edward F. McGrady, John L. Lewis, Heywood Broun, A. Philip Randolph, Harry Bridges, and others. By two U.S. journalists. Bibliography, pp. 250-64.

1328. MYERS, HENRY LEE. *The United States Senate: What Kind of Body?* Philadelphia: Dorrance, 1939. 125 pp.

The period covering the two administrations of Woodrow Wilson and the World War, described by a former U.S. Senator from Montana.

1329. NEHRU, JAWAHARLAL. *Toward Freedom: The Autobiography of Jawaharlal Nehru*. New York: John Day, 1941. 445 pp.

Indian Nationalist leader. English edition: London: John Lane, 1939. 618 pp.

1330. NEUBERGER, RICHARD LEWIS; and KAHN, STEPHEN B. *Integrity: the Life of George W. Norris*. New York: Vanguard, 1937. 401 pp.

Bibliography, pp. 385-89.

1331. NICOLAIEVSKY, BORIS; and MAENCHEN-HELFEN, OTTO. *Karl Marx: Man and Fighter*. Philadelphia: Lippincott, 1936. 391 pp.

"The book is distinguished by such firm grasp of the data, and by such power of interpretation, that it will long stand as the commanding work in its field."—Harold D. Lasswell in *Public Opinion Quarterly*, 1 no. 4, p. 149 (October 1937). Nicolaevsky, head of the Russian Historical-Revolutionary Records Office in Moscow, 1919-21, is the author of more than a hundred historical articles and the editor of six volumes on the history of the Russian social Democratic movement. Maenchen-Helfen, at one time a lecturer in the University of Berlin, has traveled in Asia on ethnological expeditions and has spent two years at the Marx-Engels Institute, Moscow.

1331a. NOMAD, MAX (pseud.). *Apostles of Revolution*. Boston: Little, Brown, 1939. 467 pp.

The history of revolution in the last century is analyzed through biographies of significant personalities such as Blanqui, Marx, Bakunin, S. G. Nechayef, Stalin. By a Polish-American Marxist scholar deeply influenced by Waclaw Machajski. Bibliography, pp. 441-47.

*1331b. NOMAD, MAX (pseud.). *Rebels and Renegades*. New York: Macmillan, 1932. 430 pp.

Historical analysis of the role of the intellectual in social movements, by a Polish-American political analyst. Through biographies of outstanding labor and political leaders of the preceding and current generations (Aristide Briand, William Zebulon Foster, James Ramsay MacDonald, Errico Malatesta, Benito Mussolini, Joseph Pilsudski, Philipp Scheidemann, Leon Trotsky), it discusses competition of the intellectuals with manual workers, plutocracy, and aristocracy. Bibliography, pp. 407-16.

1332. Olden, Rudolf. *Hitler*, translated by Walter Ettinghausen. New York: Covici, Friede, 1936. 394 pp.

The author was formerly a political commentator on the *Berliner Tageblatt*. Bibliography, pp. 375-77.

1333. Omura, Bunji. *The Last Genro: Prince Saionji, the Man Who Westernized Japan*. Philadelphia: Lippincott, 1938. 442 pp.

Life of Prince Saionji, 87 years old in 1937, and the last of the group of Japanese elder statesmen known as the Genro.

1334. Pankhurst, Estelle Sylvia. *The Life of Emmeline Pankhurst: The Suffragette Struggle for Women's Citizenship*. Boston: Houghton Mifflin, 1936. 179 pp.

By the suffragette leader's daughter. See also Emmeline Pankhurst's *My Own Story* (New York: Hearst's, 1914, 364 pp.).

1335. Pinchon, Edgcumb. *Zapata: The Unconquerable*. New York: Doubleday, Doran, 1941. 332 pp.

Fictionized biography of Emiliano Zapata (*ca.* 1879-1919), the Mexican peasant general and revolutionary.

1336. Playne, Caroline Elisabeth. *Bertha von Suttner and the Struggle to Avert the World War*. London: Allen and Unwin, 1936. 248 pp.

History of European peace movements, through biography of a leading peace promoter. By British historian.

1337. Powderly, Terence Vincent. *The Path I Trod: The Autobiography of Terence Vincent Powderly* (Columbia Studies in American Culture, no. 6). New York: Columbia University, 1940. 460 pp.

Leader of Knights of Labor.

1338. Preston, Wheeler. *American Biographies*. New York: Harpers, 1940. 1147 pp.

"Who's Who" of notable Americans from Colonial times. Does not include living persons. Bibliography at end of each biography.

1339. Pringle, Henry Fowles. *The Life and Times of William Howard Taft*. New York: Farrar and Rinehart, 1939. 2 vols.

Based on letters to which the author, a U.S. journalist, was given access by Taft's family. Bibliography, pp. 1083-87.

1340. Rauschning, Hermann. *Men of Chaos*. New York: Putnam's Sons, 1942. 341 pp.

Portraits of a dozen major Nazi leaders, by an exiled Nazi and Junker, formerly president of the Danzig senate.

1341. Roper, Daniel Calhoun. *Fifty Years of Public Life*. Durham: Duke University, 1941. 422 pp.

Autobiography of U.S. Democratic politician, diplomat, and Cabinet member.

1341a. Ross, James Frederick Stanley. *Parliamentary Representation*. London: Eyre and Spottiswoode, 1943. 245 pp.

Quantitative and qualitative analysis of the ages, educations, occupations, hereditary titles and party ties of the 1823 members who sat in the House of Commons, 1918-36. Discussion of the historical background and contemporary forces which have brought about the social composition of this body. Bibliography in footnotes and p. 235.

1342. Ross, Malcolm. *Death of a Yale Man*. New York: Farrar and Rinehart, 1939. 385 pp.

Autobiography of a Yale-graduated ex-bond salesman, ex-manual laborer, ex-journalist who became public relations director for the National Labor Relations Board.

1343. Roucek, Joseph Slabey. "The Sociology of the Diplomat," *Social Science*, 14: 370-74 (October 1939).

1344. Ryan, Msgr. John Augustine. *Social Doctrine in Action: A Personal History*. New York: Harpers, 1941. 297 pp.

Autobiography of professor at Catholic University and Director of the Department of Social Action, National Catholic Welfare Conference.

1345. SADLER, ARTHUR LINDSAY. *The Maker of Modern Japan: The Life of Tokugawa Ieyasu.* London: Allen and Unwin, 1936. 429 pp.

Sixteenth century Japanese statesman. "Not only did Tokugawa Ieyasu found a dynasty of rulers and organize a system of government, but he rounded off his achievement by contriving before his death to arrange for his deification afterwards, and to set in train the reorientation of the religion of the country so that he would take the premier place in it." By Professor of Oriental Studies, University of Sydney. Bibliography, pp. 411-12, cites mostly Japanese sources.

1346. SALTER, JOHN THOMAS. "Sol Levitan: A Case Study in Political Technique," *Public Opinion Quarterly,* 2: 181-96 (April 1938).

Wisconsin politician described by U.S. political scientist.

1347. SANGER, MARGARET (HIGGINS). *An Autobiography.* New York: Norton, 1938. 504 pp.

Leader of U.S. birth control movement and other reforms.

1347a. SCHMIDT-PAULI, EDGAR VON. *Die Männer um Hitler.* Berlin: Verlag für Kulturpolitik, 1932. 189 pp.

A brief description of the Nazi organization, with biographies, averaging about 4 or 5 pages in length, of about 25 Nazi leaders (including early ones like Gregor Strasser and Gottfried Feder). Undocumented.

1348. SCHNEIDER, JOSEPH. "The Definition of Eminence and the Social Origins of Famous English Men of Genius," *American Sociological Review,* 3: 834-49 (December 1938).

13,551 biographies in the English *Dictionary of National Biography,* 1400-1850, were analyzed to determine relationships between the social origin of the subject and his fame.

1349. SCHRIFTGIESSER, KARL. *The Amazing Roosevelt Family, 1613-1942.* New York: Wilfred Funk, 1942. 367 pp.

The last two-fifths of the narrative center upon the lives of Theodore and Franklin D. Roosevelt and their families. Bibliography, pp. 355-58.

1350. SELVER, PAUL. [*Thomas Garrigue*] *Masaryk,* introduction by Jan Masaryk. London: Michael Joseph, 1940. 326 pp.

Scholarly biography. The author has for years been a friend of the family.

1351. SENDER, TONI. *Toni Sender: The Autobiography of a German Rebel.* New York: Vanguard, 1939. 319 pp.

Toni Sender, Socialist, pacifist, labor leader of upper middle class origins, was a woman member of the German Reichstag through the thirteen years before Hitler came into power.

1352. SILONE, IGNAZIO. *The School for Dictators.* New York: Harpers, 1938. 336 pp.

Exiled Italian novelist ironically gives advice to an American who wishes to become a fascist dictator. Based on the author's personal observations of the required techniques of propaganda and violence, as these were applied in Italy.

1353. SINGH, ANUP. *Nehru: The Rising Star of India,* introduction by Lin Yutang. New York: John Day, 1939. 168 pp.

Jawaharlal Nehru, Indian Nationalist leader. Dr. Singh, born in the Punjab, received his Ph.D. in political science at Harvard and has lectured widely in U.S. and Canada.

1354. SMITH, RIXEY; and BEASLEY, NORMAN. *Carter Glass: A Biography,* introduction by Senator Harry Flood Byrd and preface by Douglas Southall Freeman. New York: Longmans, Green, 1939. 519 pp.

Rixey Smith has been secretary to Senator Glass for many years.

1355. SMITH, SAMUEL DENNY. *The Negro in Congress, 1870-1901.* Chapel Hill: University of North Carolina, 1940. 160 pp.

Survey of the careers of the 22 Negroes who served in Congress during that period. Dr. Smith is Associate Professor of Social Studies, Mississippi State College for Women. Bibliography, pp. 145-51.

1356. SOULE, GEORGE HENRY. *Sidney Hillman: Labor Statesman*. New York: Macmillan, 1939. 237 pp.

U.S. journalist's biography of labor leader who has been president of the Amalgamated Clothing Workers since 1914, an adviser of the President of the United States, the second in command of the CIO, and a prime mover of Labor's Non-Partisan League.

1357. SOUVARINE, BORIS. *Stalin: A Critical Survey of Bolshevism*, translated by Cyril Lionel Robert James. New York: Alliance Book Corp., 1939. 690 pp.

The author was a founder of the French Communist Party and a former member of the Executive Council of the Communist International. French edition: *Staline: Aperçu historique du bolchévisme* (Paris: Plon, 1935. 574 pp. Bibliography, pp. 545-70).

1358. *State Legislators* (Annals of the American Academy of Political and Social Science, vol. 195, January 1938), edited by William Brooke Graves. 252 pp.

"In contradistinction to the studies of the mechanics of organization and procedure, this volume is focused upon the legislator himself. Some of the points covered are: average caliber, functions, education, occupations, length of legislative experience, salaries and compensation; factors of influence—character of districts represented, the governor, the lobby (discussed by a political scientist, a lobbyist, and a legislator); the extent to which state legislators enter other fields of public service; . . . the Nebraska one-house legislature."

1358a. STEEL, JOHANNES (pseud.). *Men Behind the War: A 'Who's Who' of Our Time*. New York: Sheridan House, 1943. 488 pp.

German-born U.S. journalist's account of lives and influence of famous contemporary military and political leaders all over the world.

1359. STEELE, ZULMA. *Angel in Top Hat*. New York: Harpers, 1942. 319 pp.

Biography of Henry Bergh, founder of the American Society for the Prevention of Cruelty to Animals. Bibliography, pp. 303-09.

1360. STEVENS, WILLIAM BERTRAND. *Editor's Quest*. New York: Morehouse, Gorham, 1940. 240 pp.

Memoir of Frederick Cook Morehouse, editor of *The Living Church*, 1900-32.

1361. STEWART, WATT; and PETERSON, HAROLD F. *Builders of Latin America*. New York: Harpers, 1942. 343 pp.

Biographies of Latin American leaders, from the Incas to the present, written for high school students by two historians in New York state teachers' colleges. Bibliography, pp. 310-12.

1362. STIRN, ERNEST W. *An Annotated Bibliography of Robert M. LaFollette [Sr.]: The Man and His Work*. Chicago: University of Chicago, 1937. 571 pp.

1363. STOKES, RICHARD LEROY. *Léon Blum: Poet to Premier*. New York: Coward-McCann, 1937. 276 pp.

Biography of the French Socialist Premier; includes description of "le New Deal français." By U.S. music and drama critic, playwright, and newspaper correspondent. Bibliographic footnotes.

1364. STONER, JOHN EDGAR. *Salmon O. Levinson and the Pact of Paris: A Study in the Techniques of Influence*, forewords by John Dewey and Quincy Wright. Chicago: University of Chicago, 1943. 367 pp.

Biography of U.S. philanthropist and peace promoter, by University of Indiana political scientist. Bibliographic footnotes.

1365. STRASSER, OTTO. *Hitler and I*, translated by Gwenda David and Eric Mosbacher. Boston: Houghton Mifflin, 1940. 249 pp.

In the early days of the Nazi movement from 1920 onward, Strasser was a member of the party hierarchy. In 1933 he fled from Germany. His brother, Gregor, stayed behind, only to be riddled with bullets in 1934. Otto Strasser became conspicuous as the self-appointed leader of the "Freedom Front," a band of exiles hoping to destroy Hitler as a "betrayer" of the German Revolution.

1366. STRAUSS, PATRICIA. *Bevin &
Co.: The Leaders of British Labor.* New
York: Putnam's Sons, 1941. 246 pp.

By wife of a Labour M. P., George Russell
Strauss.

1367. SWING, RAYMOND GRAM.
Forerunners of American Fascism. New
York: Julian Messner, 1935. 168 pp.

Essays on Father Charles E. Coughlin, Huey
Long, Theodore G. Bilbo, Francis E. Townsend, William Randolph Hearst, and the effect of economic depression upon the lower
middle classes, by a U.S. journalist.

1368. TARBELL, IDA MINERVA. *All
in the Day's Work: An Autobiography.*
New York: Norton, 1939. 412 pp.

Autobiography of the well-known biographer of Standard Oil Company, of Judge
Gary, and of Abraham Lincoln.

1368a. THOMAS, ELBERT DUNCAN.
Thomas Jefferson, World Citizen. New
York: Modern Age, 1942. 280 pp.

A portrait, based chiefly on Jefferson's words
on democracy, liberty, religion, agriculture,
and foreign affairs. By U.S. Senator from
Utah (Ph.D. California 1924), a former professor of political science in University of
Utah. Bibliography, pp. 272-74.

1369. THOREZ, MAURICE. *Son of
the People,* translated by Douglas Gar-
man. New York: International Publishers, 1938. 237 pp.

Autobiography of leader of Communist Party of France. French edition: *Fils du peuple*
(Paris: Editions sociales internationales, 1937.
219 pp.).

1370. TORRES, HENRY. *Pierre Laval,* translated by Norbert Guterman.
New York: Oxford, 1941. 266 pp.

Denunciatory biography of French politician
by a one-time friend and associate now living
in America—an attorney, author, editor, and
former vice chairman of the Foreign Affairs
Committee of the French Parliament. Stresses
the informal alliance between politicians and
wealthy families for control over press, radio
and public opinion. French edition: *Pierre
Laval: La France Trahie* (New York: Brentano's, 1941).

1371. TIMPERLEY, H. J. "Makers
of Public Opinion About the Far East,"
Pacific Affairs, 9: 221-30 (June 1936).

By an Australian journalist, a specialist on
the Far East.

1372. UTLEY, FREDA. *The Dream
We Lost: Soviet Russia Then and Now.*
New York: John Day, 1940. 371 pp.

Study of USSR and world politics. Includes
autobiography of this British-born leftist politician and journalist.

1373. VALTIN, JAN (pseud.). *Out
of the Night.* New York: Alliance, 1941.
841 pp.

Autobiography of a German Communist who
was for some years an organizer of International of Seamen and Harbor Workers. Tor-
tured by the Nazis, he escaped to the U.S. by
pretending to be a Gestapo agent. The book
contains a series of stirring eye-witness accounts of the last years of the Weimar Republic, and of Communist-led waterfront organizations in a dozen countries.

1374. VAN GELDER, ROBERT. "An
Interview With Archibald MacLeish,"
New York Times Magazine, May 10,
1942, p. 2.

U.S. poet, Director of the Library of Congress and head of the Office of Facts and Figures, discusses his life and earlier aims.

1375. VERMEIL, EDMOND. *Doctri-
naires de la révolution allemande, 1918-
1938,* 2nd ed. Paris: Dorlot, 1939. 387
pp.

Well-known French historian discusses contemporary ideological leaders of Germany, including such Nazi leaders as Darré, Goebbels,
Hitler, Ley, Alfred Rosenberg. Bibliography,
pp. 371-82.

1376. WALLIS, JAMES HAROLD.
*The Politician: His Habits, Outcries, and
Protective Coloring: A Textbook for
Office Seekers (and for Enlightened
Voters) Setting Forth Infallible Guides
to Political Success, Illustrated and En-
riched with Many Examples from the
Careers of Contemporary American Pol-
iticians, Complete with an Appendix, a
Comprehensive and Intelligible Index,*

and Other Accessories Proper to a Textbook. New York: Stokes, 1935. 333 pp.

1377. "Washington Correspondents Name Ablest Members of Congress in *Life* Poll," *Life*, March 20, 1939, pp. 13-17.

"*Life* believes that the ranking members of the Washington press corps, as shrewd, experienced, objective first-hand observers, are uniquely equipped to assay the worth of the people's representatives in Congress." Each correspondent was asked to list those whom he considered the ten ablest members of each house of Congress, to give each one a numerical rating on integrity, intelligence, industry, and influence, and to write a thumbnail sketch of each one's "political credo, practices, or personality." "The results of the poll . . . would be interesting to alert citizens at any time. In confused and troubled 1939 they constitute a noteworthy public record." Article quotes and tabulates the opinions.

1378. WESTPHAL, ALBERT CHARLES FREDERICK. *The House Committee on Foreign Affairs* (Studies in History, Economics, and Public Law, no. 493). New York: Columbia University, 1942. 268 pp.

An analytical study of the committee and its work, by historian, College of the City of New York. Bibliography in footnotes.

1379. "Who is Frank Knox?" *Fortune* (November 1935).

Publisher of Chicago *Daily News*; Secretary of Navy under F. D. Roosevelt; Republican Party politician.

1380. "Who's Who in Government Publicity," *Public Opinion Quarterly*, 4: 168-70, 318-23 (March, June 1940).

Covers publicity staffs of five federal departments: *Agriculture*: Milton S. Eisenhower, Morse Salisbury, Samuel B. Bledsoe, Wallace L. Kadderly, Keith Himebaugh, Gove Hambidge, Fred W. Henshaw, Elmer M. Rowalt, Russell Smith, Ruth Van Deman, Frank L. Teuton, Lester A. Schlup, James B. Hasselman, Marvin M. Sandstrom, Ruth de Forest Lamb, John L. Stewart, Dana Parkinson, Dallas S. Burch, L. S. Richardson, Ernest G. Moore, Edwy B. Reid, Wayne H. Darrow, George A. Barnes, Marion Livingston Ram-

say, John Fischer, John A. Bird; *Commerce*: Victor Sholis, Frederick N. Polangin, L. W. Cain, Allan Miller, J. T. Mooney, Alfred O'Leary, William Tate; *Interior*: Michael W. Straus, Walton Onslow, Harry B. Gauss, Daisy D. Reck, Shannon Allen; *Labor*: James Fitz-Gerald, Harold D. Jacobs, Elizabeth Enochs, Mary V. Robinson; *State*: Michael J. McDermott, Sheldon Thomas.

1381. WILLIAMS, BLANCHE COLTON. *Clara Barton: Daughter of Destiny*. Philadelphia: Lippincott, 1941. 468 pp.

Heavily documented biography of founder and promoter of U.S. Red Cross. By a Hunter College professor of English literature.

1382. WILLIAMS, WAYNE CULLEN. *William Jennings Bryan*. New York: Putnam's Sons, 1936. 516 pp.

By a lawyer who knew Bryan personally. Social and economic forces receive less emphasis than Bryan's personal qualities and avowed policies.

1383. WILSON, FORREST. *Crusader in Crinoline: The Life of Harriet Beecher Stowe*. Philadelphia: Lippincott, 1941. 706 pp.

Bibliography, pp. 643-57.

1384. WINSTON, SANFORD. "Studies in Negro Leadership: Age and Occupational Distribution of 1,608 Negro Leaders," *American Journal of Sociology*, 37: 595-602 (January 1932).

By sociologist, State College of North Carolina.

1385. WOODWARD, COMER VANN. *Tom Watson: Agrarian Rebel*. New York: Macmillan, 1938. 518 pp.

Thomas E. Watson, leader of Georgia dirt-farmers, Populist candidate for President in the late Reconstruction period, made use of many rabble-rousing techniques which are almost identical with those in use today. This biography stresses Watson's propaganda techniques and his incoherent personality-structure. The author is a University of Florida social scientist. Bibliography, pp. 487-501.

1386. ZAUSNER, PHILIP. *Unvarnished: The Autobiography of a Union Leader*, introduction by L. P. Lindelof. New York: Brotherhood Publishers, 1941. 381 pp.

By a veteran leader of Brotherhood of Painters, Decorators and Paperhangers of America.

B. CHANNELS OF COMMUNICATION

I. GENERAL

1386a. BURKE, WILLIAM JEREMIAH; and HOWE, WILL D. *American Authors and Books, 1640-1940.* New York: Gramercy Publishing Co., 1943. 858 pp.

A reference book listing biographical data on U.S. authors and editors, descriptions of publishing houses, magazines and newspapers, libraries, literary clubs, and societies, etc. Includes copious bibliography.

1387. GLOVER, JOHN GEORGE; and CORNELL, WILLIAM BOUCK, editors. *The Development of American Industries: Their Economic Significance,* rev. ed. New York: Prentice-Hall, 1941. 1005 pp.

Includes a chapter on "The Book Publishing Industry," by S. P. Hunnewell (pp. 159-69), and a chapter on "The Radio Industry," by the editors (pp. 821-63).

1388. HINKEL, HANS, editor. *Handbuch der Reichskulturkammer,* edited by Gerichtsassessor Guenther Gentz. Berlin: Deutscher Verlag für Politik und Wirtschaft, 1937. 351 pp.

Apparently a thorough study of state control of channels of communication in Germany. Contains detailed and specific sections on the Reichspressekammer, Reichskammer der bildenden Künste, Reichsmusikkammer, Reichsschrifttumskammer, Reichstheaterkammer, Reichsfilmkammer, Reichsrundfunkkammer.

1389. LARSON, CEDRIC. "The Cultural Projects of the WPA," *Public Opinion Quarterly,* 3: 491-96 (July 1939).

"The Federal Writers Project, the Federal Historical Records Survey, the Federal Theater Project, the Federal Arts Project, and the Federal Music Project all have their national headquarters in Washington, and the writer has kept in constant touch with them over a period of more than two years."

*1390. LAZARSFELD, PAUL FELIX. *Radio and the Printed Page: An Introduction to the Study of Radio and its Role in the Communication of Ideas.* New York: Duell, Sloan and Pearce, 1940. 354 pp.

Office of Radio Research, a foundation-supported organization directed by Dr. Paul Felix Lazarsfeld, has conducted unusually detailed and controlled interviews (based upon standardized samples of the U.S. population) to determine value of radio and newspaper stimuli in changes of attitude. This is perhaps the most complete study available on techniques of measuring the contents of U.S. radio programs and the characteristics and preferences of radio audiences, and on relations of press coverage to radio coverage.

1390a. *Leipziger Beiträge zur Erforschung der Publizistik* series, edited by Dr. Hans Amandus Münster, Direktor of the Institut für Zeitungswissenschaft of the University of Leipzig. Dresden: Dittert, *ca.* 1939–.

A series of monographs on radio, press and movies, with special emphasis on their political potentialities.

1391. LIEBERT, HERMAN. "International Communications," *Public Opinion Quarterly,* 5: 295-98 (June 1941).

Survey of the quarter's developments, by U.S. journalist.

1392. McSPADDEN, JOSEPH WALKER. *How They Sent the News.* London: Harrap, 1937. 219 pp.

Story of communication media through the centuries: drums, smoke signals, heliographs, semaphores, telephones, radio, television, cables, etc.

1393. RIEGEL, OSCAR WETHERHOLD. "Press, Radio and the Spanish Civil War," *Public Opinion Quarterly,* 1 no. 1: 131-36 (January 1937).

By Professor of Journalism, Washington and Lee University.

1394. RIEGEL, OSCAR WETHER-HOLD; and others. "Press, Radio, Films," *Public Opinion Quarterly*, 4: 136-50, 285-96, 507-22, 674-86 (March, June, September, December 1940) and 5: 114-29, 298-307 (March, June 1941).

Quarterly surveys of significant developments relating to press, radio, films, by specialists in each channel.

1395. STARR, MARK. *The Eye Route: Visual Aids—Means and Agencies—For Workers' Education.* New York: Educational Department of International Ladies' Garment Workers' Union, 1938. 22 pp.

Lists and comments on the available pictorial books, pamphlets, magazines, posters, maps, charts, film strips, projectors, and their dealers. Bibliography, p. 22. List of dealers and sources, pp. 19-21.

1396. WAPLES, DOUGLAS. "Communications," *American Journal of Sociology*, 47: 907-17 (May 1942).

Data and comment intended to bring up to date the information presented on this subject in *Recent Social Trends* (1933), report of President Hoover's Committee on Recent Social Trends.

1397. WEARIN, OTHA D.; and KIRCHHOFER, ALFRED H. "Joint Ownership of Newspapers and Radio Stations," *Public Opinion Quarterly*, 2: 300-08 (April 1938).

Opposing views of Mr. Wearin, a Democratic Representative in Congress from Iowa, and Mr. Kirchhofer, president of American Society of Newspaper Editors.

*1397a. WILLEY, MALCOLM MAC-DONALD (D,W); and RICE, STUART ARTHUR (D,W). *Communication Agencies and Social Life.* New York and London: McGraw-Hill, 1933. 229 pp.

Survey prepared, under the direction of a group of sociologists, for President Hoover's Committee on Recent Social Trends.

*1398. WILSON, LOUIS ROUND (D,W). *The Geography of Reading: A Study of the Distribution and Status of Libraries in the United States.* Chi-cago: American Library Association and University of Chicago, 1938. 481 pp.

Traces the sociology of reading not only in libraries but in connection with other channels of communication, such as magazines, newspapers, schools, and adult educational facilities. Contains 117 tables, 173 charts. The author is Dean of the Graduate Library School, University of Chicago. Bibliography, pp. 445-62. See Chapter 11, "Public Schools," for data on distribution of schools, educational levels, literacy levels, school expenditures, salaries of teachers and principals, etc.

II. NEWSPAPERS AND MAGAZINES

1. CONTROL, ORGANIZATION, EQUIPMENT

1399. "Advertisers' Advertiser," *Time*, August 1, 1938, p. 20.

Summary history of *Printers' Ink*, on the occasion of its 50th anniversary.

1400. ALLEN, JOHN EDWARD. *The Modern Newspaper: Its Typography and Methods of News Presentation.* New York: Harpers, 1940. 234 pp.

Attempts at modernization of the American daily newspaper; a sequel to the author's *Newspaper Make-Up*. By editor of *Linotype News*.

1401. ALLPORT, GORDON WILLARD; and FADEN, JANET M. "The Psychology of Newspapers: Five Tentative Laws," *Public Opinion Quarterly*, 4: 687-703 (December 1940).

Boston newspapers' treatment of Neutrality Act is discussed by Dr. Allport, Harvard social psychologist, and Miss Faden, a Radcliffe psychology student.

1402. AMERICAN NEWSPAPER PUBLISHERS' ASSOCIATION. BUREAU OF ADVERTISING. *The Newspaper as an Advertising Medium.* New York, 1940. 170 pp.

A presentation of the advantages newspapers can offer to advertisers. Includes much statistical material on the press. Bibliography and source list, pp. 161-63.

1403. ARCINIEGAS, GERMÁN. "Journalism in Colombia," *Quarterly Journal* *of Inter-American Relations*, 1: 89-95 (July 1939).

By Colombian magazine editor (*Revista de las Indias*).

1404. BARNHART, THOMAS FREDERICK. *Newspaper Sales Promotion: The Fields, the Media, the Methods.* Minneapolis: Burgess, 1939. 243 pp.

Practical manual by University of Minnesota professor of journalism. Bibliography, pp. 227-37.

1405. BARNHART, THOMAS FREDERICK. *The Weekly Newspaper: A Bibliography, 1925-41.* Minneapolis: Burgess, 1941. 107 pp.

*1406. BARNHART, THOMAS FREDERICK (D). *Weekly Newspaper Management.* New York: Appleton-Century, 1936. 444 pp.

Includes a chapter on "Newspaper Promotion."

1407. BARNS, MARGARITA. *The Indian Press: A History of the Growth of Public Opinion in India.* New York: Macmillan, 1940. 491 pp.

Comprehensive analysis by British journalist. Carefully documented. Bibliography, pp. 476-79.

1408. BESSIE, SIMON MICHAEL. *Jazz Journalism: The Story of the Tabloid Newspapers.* New York: Dutton, 1938. 247 pp.

Several illustrations of tabloid make-up. Breezily written.

1408a. *Bibliographie zur Geschichte des schweizerischen Zeitungswesens*, compiled under the direction of Professor Werner Naef by Fritz Blaser. Basel: Birkhäuser, 1940. 86 pp.

Standard bibliography of Swiss journalism. Published under the sponsorship of the Swiss Historical Society as part of the project of the Commission on the History of the Press, of the International Committee of Historical Sciences. Dr. Blaser (Ph.D. Neuchâtel) is compiler of the current bibliography on the same subject published annually in the *Schweizerisches Gutenbergmuseum*, a journal of the history of publishing and journalism.

1409. *Bibliography of Foreign-Language Newspapers and Periodicals Published in Chicago.* Chicago: Work Projects Administration, Chicago Public Library Omnibus Project, 1942. 150 pp., mimeo.

Names, addresses, how often published, names of editors, political affiliations, dates of establishment and expiration, and other data on Chicago foreign-language periodicals of the last 100 years.

1410. "Bibliography of the History of the Canadian Press," *Canadian Historical Review*, 12: 416-33 (1941).

Compiled by A. J. E. Lunn for the National Committee for Canada of the International Committee of Historical Sciences.

1411. BIBLIOTHÈQUE POLONAISE DE PRESSE. Series of 11 volumes, each published in French and Polish by École Supérieure de Journalisme de Varsovie, 1921–.

These cover many phases of the history of Polish journalism and politics.

1412. BIRD, GEORGE LLOYD; and MERWIN FREDERIC E., editors. *The Newspaper and Society: A Book of Readings.* New York: Prentice-Hall, 1942. 627 pp.

Readings for college courses, arranged by two U.S. professors of journalism. Bibliography at ends of chapters.

1412a. BJURMAN, GUNNAR ABRAHAM. *Tredje statsmakten: Tidningspressens utreckling och nutida ställning.* Stockholm: Bonnier, 1935. 300 pp.

"The Third Power." A survey of the press of all times and places, by well-known Swedish journalist. Includes one of the few over-all accounts of the contemporary Swedish press. Bibliography, pp. 293-300.

1412b. BRAUKSIEPE, WERNER. "Das holländische Schrifttum zum Zeitungswesen," *Zeitungswissenschaft*, 15: 386-405 (August 1940).

Bibliographic essay citing and describing 319 Dutch contributions to the study of journalism. This is the standard bibliography on the Netherlands press.

1413. BRENNECKE, ERNEST, JR.; and CLARK, DONALD LEMEN. *Magazine Article Writing*, new edition, rewritten and enlarged. New York: Macmillan, 1942. 486 pp.

College text by two Columbia University professors of English.

1414. BROWN, STEPHEN JAMES MEREDITH. *The Press in Ireland: A Survey and a Guide.* Dublin and London: Browne, 1937. 304 pp.

About half of this book is devoted to an historical survey and half to a description of contemporary publications.

1415. BRUCKER, HERBERT. *The Changing American Newspaper.* New York: Columbia University, 1937. 111 pp.

Current trends in typography, make-up, and the treatment of news. Develops the idea that "instead of using page one to tell only some of the more spectacular news, it could be used to tell all the news in adequate summary." By assistant to the Dean, Graduate School of Journalism, Columbia University.

1415a. *Bulletin of International Committee of Historical Sciences.* Paris, 1928–.

A special commission of this Committee was established in 1929 to create and maintain an "International Bibliography of the Press." A series of "preliminary studies" have been published in the *Bulletin,* among them: G. Bourgin, "Bibliographie et Archives: France," 6: 26-70 (1934); A. Silander, "Le developpement de la presse finlandaise," 6: 78-84 (1934); Marc Jaryc, "Essai d'une bibliographie de l'histoire de la presse espagnole," 6: 84-100 (1934); Edward G. Hawke, "A Brief History of the British Newspaper Press," 7: 223-41 (1937); T. Barath, "Histoire de la presse hongroise," 7: 243-66 (1937); K. Baschwitz, "History of the Daily Press in the Netherlands," 10: 96-113 (1938).

Projected also is a handbook on the history of the press in all countries. For an account of the project, see Marc Jaryc, "Studies of 1935-42 on the History of the Periodical Press," cited below, No. 1459b.

1416. BUSH, CHILTON ROWLETTE. *Newspaper Reporting of Public Affairs: An Advanced Course in Newspaper Reporting and a Manual for Professional Newspaper Men,* enlarged edition. New York: Appleton-Century, 1940. 455 pp.

Revision of text which appeared in 1929. Gives especially ample coverage (some 300 pages) on technique of court reporting and handling news of administrative agencies. About 100 pages are given to the remainder of the book, e.g., the reporting of politics, business, finance, and labor. The author is head of the Department of Journalism, Stanford. Bibliography, pp. 435-43, cites few books written since 1930.

1417. CAMPBELL, WALTER STANLEY (pseud. of STANLEY VESTAL). *Writing Magazine Fiction.* New York: Doubleday, Doran, 1940. 292 pp.

Practical rules, and some model stories for study. The author is Director of Courses in Professional Writing, University of Oklahoma. Bibliography, pp. 291-92.

1418. CARRINGTON, EVELYN M. "American Magazines Today," *Educational Forum,* 5: 87-97 (November 1940).

Surveys circulation and characteristics of well-known U.S. magazines.

1419. CARSWELL, HOWARD J. "Business News Coverage," *Public Opinion Quarterly,* 2: 613-21 (October 1938).

By a U.S. newspaper man who has specialized on business and financial reporting. Favors popularization of the technical matter, indices, etc., that usually appear in the business sections of U.S. papers.

1420. CHARNLEY, MITCHELL VAUGHN; and CONVERSE, BLAIR. *Magazine Writing and Editing.* New York: Cordon, 1938. 352 pp.

By two U.S. professors of journalism. For some seven years Professor Charnley was an editor of *American Boy* magazine, and has been managing editor of *Journalism Quarterly* and *The Quill.* Bibliography at ends of some chapters.

1421. "Chicago *Sun*," *Fortune,* February 1942.

New daily founded by Marshall Field III, U.S. millionaire.

1421a. CHILDS, MARQUIS WILLIAM. *I Write from Washington.* New York: Harpers, 1942. 331 pp.

Essays on newspaper activity in Washington, D.C.—especially in the New Deal period. Based on about 20 years' experience as correspondent of *St. Louis Post-Dispatch.*

1422. "Chinese Current Periodicals," *China Institute Bulletin,* 3 no. 3: 87-96 (December 1938).

A list supplementary to *A Guide to Leading Chinese Periodicals,* published by the China Institute in 1936. Indicates that "a new crop of popular magazines and bulletins . . . express the spirit, sentiments, and ideas of the Chinese people under the present state of storm and stress."

1423. COOPER, KENT. *Barriers Down: The Story of the News Agency Epoch.* New York: Farrar and Rinehart, 1942. 324 pp.

General manager of Associated Press tells the story of a two-decade attempt to free the U.S. press from the monopolistic controls and barriers created by the established European news agencies: Reuters, Havas, Wolff, and others. Strongly advocates the gathering and forwarding of news on a mutualized, non-profit basis.

1424. COSTELLO, HELEN MURCHIE. "Col. [Robert R.] McCormick's [Chicago] *Tribune,* 1910-41," *New Republic,* 105: 724-27 (December 1, 1941).

By U.S. journalist.

1424a. CUTTEN, THEO E. G. *History of the Press in South Africa* (abridgment of M.A. thesis). Capetown: National Union of South African Students, 1935. 160 pp.

1425. "The Daily Press in Denmark," *Danish Foreign Office Journal—Commercial and General Review,* no. 202, pp. 121-33 (November 1937).

1426. "Debate on Reuters," *Time,* November 3, 1941, p. 62.

House of Commons debate on sale of potentially controlling stock of Reuters, Britain's greatest press association, to Newspaper Proprietors' Association, a group of London publishers. Later on, ownership embraced the Press Association, the organization of non-London provincial publishers.

1427. DEMAREE, ALBERT LOWTHER. *The American Agricultural Press, 1819-1860* (Columbia Studies in the History of American Agriculture, no. 8). New York: Columbia University, 1941. 430 pp.

Study of the farm journals of the first half of the 19th century. Bibliography, pp. 391-408.

*1428. DESMOND, ROBERT WILLIAM (D,W). *The Press and World Affairs,* introduction by Harold J. Laski (Ph.D. thesis, London School of Economics and Political Science). New York: Appleton-Century, 1937. 421 pp.

Comprehensive treatise covering the press in a score of countries, and the main news arteries of the world. The author is a U.S. reporter, teacher, correspondent, and editor. Analyzes the conditions under which foreign correspondents and news agencies do their daily work, and the propaganda power which may be wielded by those who control them. Bibliography, pp. 379-91.

1429. DRESLER, ADOLF. *Geschichte der italienischen Presse* (3rd vol.). Munich: Oldenbourg, 1943. 183 pp.

Volumes 1 and 2, previously published, covered the periods from the beginning to 1815, and from 1815 to the prewar period, respectively. This concluding volume brings the history well into the period of Fascism.

1430. DRESLER, ADOLF. *Geschichte des* Völkischen Beobachters *und des Zentralverlages der NSDAP Franz Eher Nachfolger.* Munich: Zentralverlag der NSDAP, 1937.

The 50-year history of Hitler's official organ and the 35-year history of the publishing house of Franz Eher, today the official Nazi publisher. The author is known for many publications on the history of journalism.

1431. DYAR, RALPH E. *Newspaper Promotion and Research.* New York: Harpers, 1942. 270 pp.

Elements of newspaper promotional work. The author is Director of Promotion and Research, Spokane *Spokesman-Review*.

1432. Eliasberg, Wladimir. "La Marché des annonces des journaux allemands depuis 1933," *Revue de l'Institut de Sociologie*, 17: 522-26 (1937).

"The Market for Advertisements in German Newspapers since 1933." There has been a great decrease in number of newspapers and in volume of advertising.

1433. Eulau, Heinz H. F. "Six Great Newspapers of South America," *Journalism Quarterly*, 19: 287-93 (September 1942).

By a political scientist trained at University of California.

1433a. Fairfax, John Fitz-Gerald. *The Story of John Fairfax, Commemorating the Centenary of the Fairfax Proprietary of the Sydney* Morning Herald, *1841-1941*. Sydney: J. Fairfax and Sons, 1941. 169 pp.

Biographical sketch of founder of the Sydney *Morning Herald*, oldest newspaper of the southern hemisphere. Supplements the centennial volume published in 1931: *A Century of Journalism: The Sydney* Morning Herald *and its Record of Australian Life* (Sydney: J. Fairfax and Sons. 805 pp.).

1434. Ford, Arthur R. "Canadian Press [news agency], 1903 to the Present," *Canadian Historical Review*, 23: 241-46 (September 1942).

1434a. Franzmeyer, Fritz. *Presse-Dissertationen an deutschen Hochschulen, 1885-1938*, herausgegeben von Walther Heide. Leipzig: Börsenverein der deutschen Buchhändler, 1940. 167 pp.

Indexed list of 1353 German, Austrian, and Bohemian theses, more than 300 of them published since 1935, dealing with the press. A large number of the theses are regional and local histories or histories of individual journalists and newspapers. "Ludwig Solomon's *Geschichte des deutschen Zeitungswesens* (Oldenburg, 1906) remains to this day the only full-length study of the evolution of German journalism."—Marc Jaryc, *Journal of Modern History*, 15: 130 (June 1943).

1434b. *Freedom of the Press: What It Is, How It Was Obtained, How It Can Be Retained.* New York: Newspaper-Radio Committee, 1942. 105 pp.

Testimony of six witnesses (Ernest Angell, Ralph Droz Casey, Arthur Garfield Hays, Frank Luther Mott, Roscoe Pound, Frederick Seaton Siebert) called by the Newspaper-Radio Committee in the hearings held by FCC to determine whether the Commission should bar newspapers from owning radio stations. The Committee was formed to present the cases of papers that owned stations, and stations that owned papers. Testimony included summaries of data and opinions on problems of communications control, the development of the concept of freedom of the press, the history of the press and the associations, and the recent relations of the newspapers and radio.

1435. Fyfe, (Henry) Hamilton. *Press Parade: Behind the Scenes of the Newspaper Racket and the Millionaires' Attempt at Dictatorship* (The Changing World Library). London: Watts, 1936. 154 pp.

General considerations on effects of newspaper amalgamations and interlocking ownership of newspapers in England, by a veteran British journalist.

1436. Garnett, Burt P. (i.e., Garnett, Burrett Parkell). "New Experiments in Newspaper-Making," *Editorial Research Reports*, May 1, 1940, pp. 331-47.

New papers with new methods: their investments, circulation, advertising, innovations; their effect on newspaper employees and readers. By a U.S. journalist, one of the founders of Editorial Research Reports.

1437. (Pop.) Garst, Robert Edward; and Bernstein, Theodore Menline. *Headlines and Deadlines: A Manual for Copyeditors*, 2nd ed. New York: Columbia University, 1940. 217 pp.

Includes a "headline vocabulary" (pp. 159-98) and a glossary of newspaper terms (pp. 199-207). By two New York City newspaper men.

1437a. German periodicals. *Zeitungswissenschaft*, vol. 11, no. 5 (May 1936).

Special issue, edited by Ernst Herbert Lehmann, on history of German periodicals in the fields of philosophy, history, German philology, theater, motion pictures, military affairs, agriculture, sports, and labor groups. The essays are by students in Dr. Lehmann's seminar in the Institut für Zeitungswissenschaft in the University of Berlin.

1438. *Gestalten und Erscheinungen der politischen Publizistik* series. Leipzig: Noske, 1934–.

New York Public Library has several volumes of this series on political journalism and propaganda, written by scholars now inside Germany. Series editor: Hans Amandus Münster.

1439. GOLENKINA, VERA ALEKSANDROVNA. *The Soviet Press.* Moscow: Foreign Languages Publishing House, 1939. 32 pp.

1440. GOSSIN, ALBERT. *La presse suisse* (thesis, Neuchâtel). Neuchâtel: Delachaux and Niestlé, 1936. 124 pp.

Bibliography, pp. 123-24.

1441. GRAMLING, OLIVER. *AP: The Story of News.* New York: Farrar and Rinehart, 1940. 506 pp.

History of Associated Press by director of AP's membership department, assisted by William A. Kinney of the Washington Bureau.

1442. "Green Felt and Gold C," *Time*, October 16, 1939, p. 58.

British War Office authorized 12 U.S. correspondents at the front, 17 British, 3 Australian, 1 South African, 1 Canadian. Officers' uniforms with green and gold insignia were prescribed. Article lists authorized U.S. correspondents.

1442a. GREENFIELD, KENT ROBERTS. *Economics and Liberalism in the Risorgimento: A Study of Nationalism in Lombardy, 1814-48* (Johns Hopkins Historical Publications). Baltimore: Johns Hopkins, 1934. 365 pp.

By Johns Hopkins professor of modern history. Part I surveys Lombardian agriculture, commerce and industry. Part II, "Journalism," is an account of the influence of liberalism and economic change on the Italian press, and the efforts of journalists to promote industrialization as a means to nationalist ends. Bibliography, p. 329.

1443. GREGORY, WINIFRED, compiler. *American Newspapers 1821-1936: A Union List of Files Available in the U.S. and Canada.* New York: H. W. Wilson, 1937. 791 pp.

For the first time, a union list of newspaper files is available to researchers.

***1443a.** GROTH, OTTO. *Die Zeitung: Ein System der Zeitungskunde.* Mannheim: J. Bensheimer, 1928-30. 4 vols.

Treatise on the science of journalism. The author was for many years on the staff of *Frankfurter Zeitung.* Bibliography, vol. 4, pp. 445-549.

1444. GRUENBECK, MAX. *Die Presse Grossbritanniens: ihr geistiger und wirtschaftlicher Aufbau* (Wesen und Wirkungen der Publizistik, vols. 5-6). Leipzig: Noske, 1936. 2 vols.

Cultural and economic structure of the British press. Bibliography, pp. 267-74.

1445. GUTHRIE, JOHN ALEXANDER. *The Newsprint Paper Industry: An Economic Analysis* (Harvard Economic Studies, vol. 48). Cambridge: Harvard University, 1941. 274 pp.

Based on Ph.D. thesis, Harvard. Bibliography, pp. 253-65.

1446. HANFORD, MABEL POTTER. *Advertising and Selling Through Business Publications*, foreword by Roy S. Durstine. New York and London: Harpers, 1938. 190 pp.

The use of trade papers. Bibliography, pp. 182-90.

1447. HARLOW, REX FRANCIS. *The Daily Newspaper and Higher Education: A Report on Certain Findings and Inferences of the Stanford School-Press Relations Investigation.* Stanford University: Stanford University, 1938. 44 pp.

After studying what 44 West Coast daily newspapers published about 33 colleges and universities, and after interviewing editors and college presidents, Dr. Harlow finds that if the newspapers control college news, it will be personal, incorrect, and insignificant; controlled by the colleges, it will be incorrect and unreadable.

1447a. HARRIS, (HENRY) WILSON. *The Daily Press* (Current Problems series, no. 18). Cambridge: Cambridge University Press, 1943. 146 pp.

General essay by editor of *The Spectator* on origins and functions of the press, the journalist, the editor and the publisher. Bibliographic footnotes.

1448. HAUSER, ERNEST O. "News of the Far East in U.S. Dailies," *Public Opinion Quarterly*, 2: 651-58 (October 1938).

Based on a study made by Dr. Hauser for Institute of Pacific Relations.

1449. HEIDE, WALTHER; and LEHMANN, ERNST HERBERT, editors. *Handbuch der Zeitungswissenschaft*. Leipzig: Hiersemann, 1940–.

Alphabetical encyclopedia on all subjects relating to the press, edited by two well-known German professors of journalism. The first two issues (out of a projected nine) contain biographies of famous journalists and publishers, and articles on such topics as "Advertising," "Bibliography of the Press," and the press in various geographical areas. Plan of the *Handbuch* is outlined by Dr. Lehmann in *Zeitungswissenschaft*, 12: 290-96 (May 1937).

1450. HERRMANN, WILHELM. *Die Geschichte der ALA: Eine Zeitungswissenschaftliche Studie* (inaugural dissertation, Berlin). Limburg an der Lahn: Limburger Vereinsdruckerei, 1938. 152 pp.

History of Allgemeine Anzeigen-gesellschaft m. b. h. (the Alfred Hugenberg interests), German press syndicate. Bibliography, pp. 151-52.

1451. HERSEY, HAROLD BRAINERD. *Pulpwood Editor: The Fabulous World of the Thriller Magazines Revealed by a Veteran Editor and Publisher*. New York: Stokes, 1937. 301 pp.

Gives details of the functions, management, contents, and personnel of the pulpwood magazines, drawn from the writer's twenty-five years of experience in this field.

1451a. HINDLE, WILFRED HOPE. *The London Morning Post, 1772-1937: A Portrait of a Newspaper*. London: Routledge, 1937. 260 pp.

A history written by a British journalist after the merger of this once highly influential paper with the *Daily Telegraph*. From 1849 to 1867 the *Post* was Lord Palmerston's mouthpiece. Bibliography, p. 246.

*1451b. *History of the London Times*. London: The *Times*, 1935–.

A scholarly and profusely illustrated anonymous work by "a group of past and present members of the staff." Volume 1 covers the period to 1841; volume 2, to 1884; a third volume has been promised. Bibliography, vol. 1, pp. 468-502; vol. 2, pp. 538-601.

1451c. HOENIG, HANS OTTO. *Das Aktuelle in der deutschen Presse: Ein Beitrag zur Erforschung der politischen Publizistik der Gegenwart* (Dissertation, 1938, Leipzig; Leipziger Beitraege zur Erforschung der Publizistik). Dresden: Dittert, 1938. 65 pp.

"Current Actuality in the German Press."

1452. HOOD, PETER. *Ourselves and the Press: A Social Study on News, Advertising and Propaganda*. London: Lane, 1939. 287 pp.

General discussion of the British press and its propaganda activities.

1453. HOWE, QUINCY. *The News and How to Understand It*. New York: Simon and Schuster, 1940. 250 pp.

How to understand the news "in spite of the newspapers, in spite of the magazines, in spite of the radio." By well-known U.S. editor and radio commentator. Describes the syndicates, the columnists, the publishers, the commentators, and briefly characterizes their financial and social affiliations.

1454. HUGHES, HELEN MacGILL. "Human Interest Stories and Democracy," *Public Opinion Quarterly*, 1 no. 2: 73-83 (April 1937).

"Paradoxically, it is not the political news that informs people about one another. It is the revelations of private life and those inconsequential items that in the newspaper office are known as human interest stories."

1455. HUGHES, HELEN MACGILL. *News and the Human Interest Story,* introduction by Robert Ezra Park. Chicago: University of Chicago, 1939. 313 pp.

Study of transition of newspapers from political reporting services to entertainment and advertising media for "men who do not want to read." By sociologist trained at University of Chicago. Bibliography, pp. 292-303.

1456. HYDE, GRANT MILNOR. *Newspaper Handbook,* third edition revised of the author's *Handbook for Newspaper Workers.* New York: Appleton-Century, 1941. 337 pp.

By Director, School of Journalism, University of Wisconsin. Covers grammar, punctuation, typography, headlines, proofreading, illustrations, newspaper ethics, libel, story patterns, etc. Bibliography, pp. 303-16.

1457. ICKES, HAROLD LE CLAIR. *America's House of Lords: An Inquiry into the Freedom of the Press.* New York: Harcourt, Brace, 1939. 214 pp.

Comments on U.S. publishers by U.S. Secretary of the Interior.

1458. ICKES, HAROLD LE CLAIR, editor. *Freedom of the Press Today: A Clinical Examination by Twenty-eight Specialists.* New York: Vanguard, 1941. 308 pp.

"A veteran publisher, Frank B. Noyes, pronounces the American press free and uncontrolled. Edward Keating of Labor finds it free but controlled, Kenneth Crawford follows the 'half-slave, half-free' argument, while Herbert Agar sees the press losing a freedom which it does not deserve. . . . Another Louisville editor, Tom Wallace, holds the press free but not faultless. . . . Frank Knox contributes . . . the thought that the press is free 'because it is a privately owned public utility.' . . . Bruce Bliven of *The New Republic* and Arthur Robb of *Editor and Publisher* both see improvement in the press, Mr. Bliven declaring that the American people get the newspapers they deserve, a thought capable of moving in either direction. Manchester Boddy echoes Mr. Bliven with the thought that the press is 'no better than the people it serves . . . and very much like them.' Freda Kirchwey sees no change in the press until the economic system is changed. William L. Chenery says that readers determine the success of a publication and that without them a publication soon dies. Ralph Ingersoll says that if *PM* lives, other papers will copy and lose their chains. . . . J. B. S. Hardman would license newspapers under a Free Press Authority. . . . Harold Lasswell sets up four standards for a more intelligent press. . . . Raymond Clapper believes criticism a healthful thing for newspapers, then points out that the daily press is belabored for intolerance by liberal weeklies which fail to give the other side a break. Louis Stark contributes a chapter on labor reporting. . . . Some contributors, notably Richard J. Finnegan, stress human failings rather than devilish purpose in newspapers. Their faults, he says, are not want of truth, integrity or fairness, but lack of understanding."—S. T. Williamson in *New York Times Book Review,* April 20, 1941, p. 20.

1459. IRWIN, WILL. *Propaganda and the News: Or What Makes You Think So?* New York: McGraw-Hill, 1936. 325 pp.

A veteran newspaper writer skims through the history of journalism from ancient Rome to the postwar dictatorships. Attention is given to press agents, to presidential campaigns (especially 1928), and to the training of propagandists. Scholars will use this material with considerable caution.

1459a. JARKOWSKI, STANISLAW "Die polnische Presse in Vergangenheit und Gegenwart," *Zeitungswissenschaft,* 13: 505-612 (1937).

Historical-analytic study of the Polish press, past and contemporary. Professor Jarkowski, a specialist in the history of the press of his country, was director of the Warsaw High School for Journalism at the time this was written. Bibliography, pp. 604-12.

1459b. JARYC, MARC. "Studies of 1935-42 on the History of the Periodical Press: Bibliographical Article," *Journal of Modern History,* 15: 127-41 (June 1943).

By late secretary of International Committee of Historical Sciences, an authority on the history of the press. Critically reviews about 150 contributions of recent years, dealing with the history of the press in all quarters of the world.

1459c. JOHNSON, GERALD WHITE; KENT, FRANK RICHARDSON; MENCKEN, HENRY LOUIS; and OWENS, HAMILTON. *The Sunpapers of Baltimore: 1837-1937.* New York: Knopf, 1937. 446 pp.

By four famous members of the staffs of the *Baltimore Sun* and *Baltimore Evening Sun.* Bibliographic footnotes.

1460. JOHNSON, STANLEY; and HARRISS, JULIAN. *The Complete Reporter: A General Text in News Writing and Editing, Complete with Exercises.* New York: Macmillan, 1942. 424 pp.

By two University of Tennessee professors. Bibliography, pp. 413-16.

1461. *Journalism.* For detailed bibliography on journalism, see the extensive annotated lists in each issue of *Journalism Quarterly* and *Zeitungswissenschaft.* For annotated, but less extensive and less specialized lists, see each issue of *Public Opinion Quarterly.*

*1462. (Pop.) KOBRE, SIDNEY. *Backgrounding the News: The Newspaper and the Social Sciences.* Baltimore, Md.: Twentieth Century Press, 1939. 271 pp.

"The purpose of this book . . . is to explore the possibilities of welding the rapidly developing social sciences to the newspaper." Blueprints are drawn up for "a more socially adequate newspaper." Bibliography, pp. 263-66. Mr. Kobre is an experienced newspaper man, trained in the social sciences.

1462a. KOBRE, SIDNEY. "The Revolutionary Colonial Press: A Social Interpretation," *Journalism Quarterly* 20: 193-204 (September 1943).

Influence on the Colonial newspapers of growth of trade and commerce, population increase, urbanization, cultural changes and other factors.

1463. LARSON, CEDRIC. "The German Press Chamber," *Public Opinion Quarterly,* 1 no. 4: 53-70 (October 1937).

How the Nazis organized their press control.

1464. LASKY, JOSEPH. *Proofreading and Copy Preparation: A Textbook for the Graphic Arts.* New York: Mentor Press, 1941. 656 pp.

By a U.S. specialist in this craft. Bibliography at ends of chapters and pp. 613-21.

1465. LAWRENCE, RAYMOND D. "Haldeman-Julius Has Made Propaganda Profitable," *Public Opinion Quarterly,* 3: 79-91 (January 1939).

U.S. professor of journalism discusses the Little Blue Books series and *American Freeman,* a "personal journal," both published by E. Haldeman-Julius of Girard, Kansas. Data given: (1) quantity of propaganda disseminated; (2) ideas and symbols used; (3) personality traits of the propagandist; (4) media; (5) techniques.

*1466. LEE, ALFRED McCLUNG (W). *The Daily Newspaper in America: The Evolution of a Social Instrument.* New York: Macmillan, 1937. 797 pp.

Two centuries of press influence on American social life, analyzed by a U.S. sociologist and professor of journalism. Pp. 705-53 present elaborate statistical tables on development of U.S. press since 1790. Bibliography at ends of chapters and pp. 754-65.

1467. LEE, ALFRED McCLUNG. "Recent Developments in the Newspaper Industry," *Public Opinion Quarterly,* 2: 126-33 (January 1938).

Discusses trends toward further financial concentration and local monopolism in control of the U.S. press. Data presented in this paper were continued in the author's "Trends Affecting the Daily Newspaper," *Public Opinion Quarterly,* 3: 497-502 (July 1939).

1467a. LESSER, JUANA. *Die argentinische Presse: Ihr Einfluss in der Entwicklung und dem Fortschritt des Landes (El periodismo argentino: Su influencia en la evolución y en el progreso* *del país*), preface by Walther Heide. Berlin: De Gruyter, 1938. 268 pp.

Traces the evolution of Argentine journalism since 1764 (the date of the earliest existing written news bulletins). About half the book deals with the Argentine press of today. Set in double column (German and Spanish). Bibliography in text.

1468. LIN MOUSHENG HSITIEN. *A Guide to Leading Chinese Periodicals.* New York: China Institute in America, 1936. 34 pp.

Annotated bibliography of 157 periodicals, which are classified under the four headings: (1) bibliography and library; (2) the humanities; (3) the social sciences; (4) the natural sciences and technology.

1469. LIN SHU-SHEN. *Histoire du journalisme en Chine* (Ph.D. thesis, University of Lille). Avesnes-sur-Helpe: L'Observateur, 1937. 164 pp.

Chinese journalism, from the earliest days to the present. The authoress, a graduate of the National Normal University, Peking, has been an official in the Chinese National Government's Department of Education. Bibliography, pp. 159-62, cites Chinese, French, and English-language sources.

1470. LIN YU-TANG. *A History of the Press and Public Opinion in China.* Shanghai: Kelly and Walsh, 1936. 179 pp.

By a well-known Chinese scholar. Published for the China Institute of Pacific Relations.

1470a. LORENZ, ERICH. *Die Entwicklung des deutschen Zeitschriftenwesens: Eine statistische Untersuchung* (Beiträge zur Erforschung der deutschen Zeitschrift, vol. 1; inaugural dissertation, Berlin). Charlottenburg: R. Lorenz, 1937. 76 pp.

Historical study of the development of German periodicals. Bibliography, pp. 74-76.

1471. LÖWENTHAL, RUDOLF. "The Russian Daily Press in China," *Chinese Social and Political Science Review*, 21: 330-40 (October-December 1937).

Place and circulation data.

1472. LÖWENTHAL, RUDOLF. "Western Literature on Chinese Journalism: A Bibliography," *Nankai Social and Economic Quarterly*, 9: 1007-66 (January 1937).

Of the 681 titles, 609 are in English.

1473. LUNDBERG, FERDINAND. "News-Letters: A Revolution in Journalism," *Harpers*, 180: 463-73 (April 1940).

By a well-known U.S. journalist. "These three letter agencies—Whalen-Eaton (estimated circulation 6,000-7,000), Kiplinger (estimated 30,000-40,000), and Research Institute (20,000) and their subdivisions—probably have 90 per cent of the commercial newsletters. Others include *Congressional Intelligence, Manufacturers' News Letter,* Chester Wright's *Labor Letter,* a new weekly letter by David Lawrence, a Babson *Letter* included with the Babson financial service, and Franklin Roudybush's *Week by Week,* staffed by diplomatic, army, and naval experts, containing as a rule devastatingly shrewd forecasts in foreign affairs. Lawrence Dennis, former investment banker and dabbler in Fascist theories, sells for $24 a year the *Weekly Foreign Letter,* which, like these others, contains much information and many views not found—until later—in the newspapers. Less well-established is *The Insider,* published by Johannes Steel and Charles Hedges.

". . . the most successful of these letters without apology examine all events from the point of view of intensely class-conscious business men, because, as one editor explains, business men are the only ones willing and able as a group to pay the relatively high price."

A number of U.S. and foreign news-letters which promote other causes are also listed and described. "All in all, there appear to be hundreds of news-letters of all types in Europe and the U.S."

1474. MacDougALL, CURTIS DANIEL. *Newsroom Problems and Policies.* New York: Macmillan, 1941. 592 pp.

Textbook for seniors or graduate students in journalism, by Professorial Lecturer in Journalism, Northwestern University.

1475. McNAUGHT, CARLTON. *Canada Gets the News.* Toronto: Ryerson Press, 1940. 271 pp.

A report in the International Research Series of the Institute of Pacific Relations. Describes the machinery for bringing foreign news to the Canadian press. Includes a survey of space devoted to various types of news and features in a sample of Canadian papers. Bibliography in text.

1476. MACNEIL, NEIL. *Without Fear or Favor.* New York: Harcourt, Brace, 1940. 414 pp.

Activities of metropolitan newspapers are described by assistant managing editor of New York *Times.*

1477. Magazines. *Scribner's* series of articles on five types: Uzzell, Thomas H. "The Love Pulps," 103: 36 ff. (April 1938); Edwards, Jackson. "One Every Minute," 103: 17 ff. (May 1938); Pringle, Henry Fowles. "High Hat," 103: 17 ff. (July 1938) (see title 1503, below); Manchester, Harland. "True Stories," 103: 25 ff. (August 1938) and "Farm Magazines," 103: 25 ff. (October 1938).

1478. MANSFIELD, F. J. *The Complete Journalist: A Study of the Principles and Practice of Newspaper Making,* foreword by the Rt. Hon. David Lloyd George. London: Sir I. Pitman, 1935. 389 pp.

A comprehensive treatise. The author served for 20 years on the staff of the London *Times* and taught journalism for a decade in the University of London.

1479. MATHEWS, JOSEPH JAMES. "Death of Press Reform in France," *Public Opinion Quarterly,* 3: 409-19 (July 1939).

Efforts of the Popular Front under Léon Blum to remedy the "corruption" of the French press are described by a U.S. historian.

1480. MERRIMAN, LEE M. *Between Deadlines: A Realistic Study of Journalism.* Chicago: Sanborn, 1941. 347 pp.

Textbook for a course in journalism, by News Editor of Pasadena, California, *Star-News* and *Post.*

1481. MILLARD, OSCAR E. *Uncensored! The True Story of the Clandestine Newspaper* La libre Belgique *Published in Brussels During the German Occupation.* London: Hale, 1937. 287 pp.

1482. MINSKY, LOUIS. "Propaganda Bureaus as 'News Services,'" *Public Opinion Quarterly,* 2: 677-79 (October 1938).

In the eyes of editors who receive countless "news services," "the camouflage is no disguise at all," says the editor of Religious News Service, New York City.

1482a. MISCHKE, ALFRED. "Die Besitzverhältnisse in der englischen Tages- und Sonntagspresse," *Zeitungswissenschaft,* 12: 678-94 (October 1937).

German professor sets forth and discusses several large charts showing interlocking investment interests and monopolistic tendencies among the wealthy families who own the press of England.

1483. MOTT, FRANK LUTHER. *American Journalism: A History of Newspapers in the United States Through 250 Years: 1690 to 1940.* New York: Macmillan, 1941. 772 pp.

Scholarly history by director of the School of Journalism, University of Iowa. Bibliography at ends of sections.

*1484. MOTT, FRANK LUTHER (D,W). *History of American Magazines,* vols. 2 and 3. Cambridge, Massachusetts: Harvard University, 1938. 608 and 649 pp.

Volume 2, 1850-65; Volume 3, 1865-85. Continuation of a standard work.

1484a. MOTT, FRANK LUTHER. *Jefferson and the Press.* Baton Rouge: Louisiana State University Press, 1943. 65 pp.

University of Missouri Dean of Journalism analyzes Jefferson's frequent references to the press and the apparent inconsistencies between his early philosophical statements and his later fulminations against the newspapers of his day. Copious bibliography in footnotes.

1485. MOTT, FRANK LUTHER, compiler. "A List of Unpublished Theses in the Field of Journalism on File in the

Libraries of American Universities," *Journalism Quarterly*, 13: 329-55 (September 1936).

*1486. Mott, Frank Luther (CB '41, D,W); and Casey, Ralph Droz (D,W), editors. *Interpretations of Journalism: A Book of Readings.* New York: Crofts, 1937. 534 pp.

"The purpose of this book is to make the chief utterances of the past three hundred years on the subject of newspapers and the press easily accessible."—Introduction. The compilers are U.S. professors of journalism.

1487. Mott, George Fox, editor. *An Outline Survey of Journalism*, rev. ed. (College Outline Series). New York: Barnes and Noble, 1940. 381 pp.

Revision of standard text. Contains bibliography.

1488. Movius, Gerald W. "Comic Strip Propaganda," *Scribner's Commentator*, 11: 17-20 (November 1941).

By secretary of Senator Gerald P. Nye. "Almost without exception comic strip propaganda is designed to give [the impression that] the U.S. is in hideous peril, for it is literally swarming with alien agents, all of Prussian or Japanese cast, [while] organized government is practically helpless . . . and its very existence depends on the assistance of weird individuals" who are above the law.

1488a. Muenster, Hans Amandus. *Jugend und Zeitung* (Zeitung und Zeit, vol. 4). Berlin: Duncker, 1932. 155 pp.

"Youth and the Newspaper." By well-known German professor of journalism. Bibliography, pp. 152-55.

1489. Nafziger, Ralph Otto. *The American Press and Public Opinion during the World War, 1914-17* (Ph.D. thesis, political science, Wisconsin, 1936). 503 pp.

Analyzes newsgathering problems faced by U.S. to April 1917. Includes qualitative analysis of war news in 15 leading U.S. dailies, geographically distributed. Concludes that papers reflected rather than led opinion, and "tended to trail behind the government in the development of policy." Bibliography, pp. 472-503.

1490. Nafziger, Ralph Otto. *Foreign News Sources and the Foreign Press: A Bibliography.* Minneapolis: Burgess Publishing Company, 1937. 124 pp.

A preliminary edition of title 1491, below.

1491. Nafziger, Ralph Otto. *International News and the Press: An Annotated Bibliography*, with historical-analytic essay by the editor and foreword by Ralph Droz Casey. New York: Wilson, 1940. 193 pp.

Covers channels of news communication, organization of news-gathering, role of the press in international affairs, and role of the press in foreign countries, since about 1900. By University of Minnesota professor of journalism. "Represents an attempt to bring together some of the titles of books, pamphlets, and magazine articles which deal with the broad subject of world-wide news-gathering and the foreign press. No attempt has been made to assemble titles which are not likely to be found in American libraries, nor has an effort been made to include citations in such bibliographies as Lasswell, Casey, and Smith's *Propaganda and Promotional Activities*, Karl Bömer's *Handbuch der Weltpresse*, and Rudolf Löwenthal's *Western Literature on Chinese Journalism*."

1492. Nash, Vernon; and Loewenthal, Rudolf. "Responsible Factors in Chinese Newspapers," *Chinese Social and Political Science Review*, 20: 420-26 (October 1936).

General article on social factors affecting Chinese press.

1493. "New Organization and Functions of Havas News Agency," *China Weekly Review*, 95: 285 (January 1941).

1494. "News for the East: The Story of Reuters [News Agency]," *Great Britain and the East*, 57: 10-11 (November 29, 1941).

1495. Nobbe, George. *The North Briton: A Study in Political Propaganda.* New York: Columbia University, 1939. 274 pp.

Eighteenth century British political newspaper. The author is Associate in English, Columbia. Bibliographic footnotes.

1496. OZAWA, MASAMOTO. "Printed Food for the Millions," *Contemporary Japan*, 6: 60-68 (June 1937).

Survey of leading Japanese magazines and newspapers by a former *Asahi* editorialist.

1497. PAN AMERICAN UNION. DIVISION OF INTELLECTUAL COOPERATION. *A Selective List of Periodicals of General Interest Published in Latin America.* Washington, D.C.: Pan American Union, 1940. 28 pp., mimeo.

Extensively annotated.

1498. PAN AMERICAN UNION. DIVISION OF INTELLECTUAL COOPERATION. *Latin American Journals Dealing with the Social Sciences and Auxiliary Disciplines.* Washington, D.C., 1941. 74 pp., mimeo.

Annotated. Lists 192 journals. Similar directories now in preparation: *Latin American Scientific Journals; Latin American Legal Journals; Latin American University Periodicals.*

1499. PANTENBURG, JOSEF WILHELM. *Die Entwicklung des Anzeigenwesens der Berliner Presse von der Aufhebung des Intelligenzzwanges bis zu den Generalanzeigern* (inaugural dissertation, Berlin). Berlin: Triltsch und Huther, 1938. 79 pp.

Bibliography, pp. 75-76.

1500. PATTERSON, HELEN MARGUERITE. *Writing and Selling Special Feature Articles*, introduction by Grant Milnor Hyde. New York: Prentice-Hall, 1939. 578 pp.

College text by assistant professor of journalism, Wisconsin. Bibliography, pp. 551-58.

1500a. *Pechat strany sotsializma.* Moscow: Vsesoiuzny nauchnoizdatelsky institut, 1939. 80 pp.

"The Press of the Land of Socialism." Study of number and geographic distribution of Soviet newspapers, magazines, libraries, printing presses, etc. Includes data on distribution of

writings of individual authors. The whole is presented as a series of striking pictorial statistics, in eight colors. Bibliography, pp. 78-79.

1500b. PEÑA, ENRIQUE A. *Estudio de los periódicos existentes en la "Biblioteca Enrique Peña."* Buenos Aires: Amorrortu, 1935. 632 pp.

A very detailed and richly illustrated catalog of a great collection of Argentine periodicals that have appeared since 1822. Bibliography in text.

*1501. POLITICAL AND ECONOMIC PLANNING GROUP (P E P). *Report on the British Press.* London, 1938. 333 pp.

Comprehensive and carefully quantified analysis by a nonpartisan group of British businessmen, economists, administrators, journalists and others. Includes quantitative analysis of newspaper contents and readership. *Findings*: a large number of independent papers are being supplanted by a small number of mass-circulation journals; number of separate newspaper proprietors of importance is decreasing; there is little likelihood of competition from new entrants; rise of national advertising expands the feature and entertainment side in relation to news and comment; being a business concern, the giant paper pursues maximum revenue through nonjournalistic types of enterprise such as free reader insurance. "Any realistic attempt to recommend improvements in the British Press must clearly grasp the fact that progress depends far more upon such intangibles as better education and a heightened sense of responsibility than upon any structural or mechanical changes which can be given effect either by national legislation or by administrative measures of the professional bodies and managements concerned."—Page 206 of the *Report*. *Suggestions*: a Press Institute and a Press Tribunal, to study the press and adjust grievances; newspapers cooperatively owned by subscribers and staff; restriction of nonjournalistic enterprises of newspapers; improved public relations activity on the part of the government.

1501a. POLLARD, JAMES EDWARD. *Principles of Newspaper Management.* New York: McGraw-Hill, 1937. 462 pp.

College text by Ohio State University professor of journalism. Bibliography, pp. 437-39.

1501b. POPOFF, EMIL ZWETANOFF. *Entwicklung und Charakter des bulgarischen Zeitungswesens* (dissertation, Berlin, 1937). Limburg a. d. Lahn, 1937.

By a Bulgarian student in a German university. Seems to be the only extended study published in recent years and not in Bulgarian.

1501c. PORTER, PHILIP WILEY; and LUXON, NORVAL NEIL. *The Reporter and the News.* New York and London: Appleton-Century, 1935. 560 pp.

College text on journalism. Mr. Porter is a staff member of Cleveland *Plain Dealer;* Mr. Luxon, an Ohio State University professor of journalism. Bibliography, pp. 532-41.

*1502. *The Press in the Contemporary Scene* (Annals of American Academy of Political and Social Science, vol. 219, January 1942), edited by Malcolm M. Willey (D,W) and Ralph D. Casey (D,W).

Articles by a score of specialists, including the following journalists: Burrett Parkell Garnett (W), Nelson P. Poynter, Watson Davis (W), Louis Stark, Charles Merz (W), J. Donald Adams (D,W), Raymond D. Lawrence, Richard J. Finnegan (W), and Arthur T. Robb.

1503. PRINGLE, HENRY FOWLES. "High Hat: The Luxury Group: *Vogue, Harper's Bazaar, Town and Country, Country Life and the Sportsman, Spur*," *Scribner's,* 104: 17-21 (July 1938).

Well-known U.S. magazine and newspaper writer analyzes the appeal of this group of magazines, and the preferences of those to whom they appeal.

1503a. RAICHLE, WALTHER. *Das ungarische Zeitungswesen: Seine Entwicklung bis zum Jahre 1938* (Ungarische Bibliothek, vol. 1, no. 22); inaugural dissertation, Berlin). Berlin: de Gruyter, 1939. 151 pp.

"The Press in Hungary to 1938." Bibliography, pp. 148-51.

1504. "Reader's Digest," *Fortune,* November 1936.

A magazine of reprints that accepts no advertising.

*1504a. RIEGEL, O(SCAR) W(ETHERHOLD) (W). *Mobilizing for Chaos: The Story of the New Propaganda.* New Haven: Yale University, 1934. 231 pp.

Analyzes the main newspaper, cable, and radio arteries of the world, tracing the effects of the enchainment of news sources through the power of large business interests and monopolistic news systems, and especially through the influence of hyper-nationalistic political pressures and government censorship. By an experienced U.S. correspondent, later Professor of Journalism, Washington and Lee University. Bibliography, pp. 215-22.

1505. ROGERS, LINDSAY. "President Roosevelt's Press Conferences," *Political Quarterly,* 9: 360-72 (July 1938).

By Columbia University political scientist.

1506. ROSELIUS, ERNST. *Amerikanische Jugend schreibt Zeitungen: Mittel der Erziehung zum Gemeinschaftsgeist in den Vereinigten Staaten* (Wesen und Wirkungen der Publizistik, vol. 3). Leipzig: Universitätsverlag, 1936. 152 pp.

Doctoral dissertation on American high school and college publications by a German scholar who has been employed by a large U.S. advertising firm. Contains an historical-analytic essay on U.S. public opinion. Bibliography, pp. 124-30.

*1506a. ROSEWATER, VICTOR (W). *History of Co-operative Newsgathering in the United States.* New York and London: Appleton-Century, 1930. 430 pp.

A history of Associated Press, with chapters on United Press and International News Service. By a U.S. journalist (Ph.D. Columbia 1893), on the staff of Omaha *Bee* for some thirty years. Bibliography, pp. 411-16 and in footnotes. May be supplemented with *Fortune's* articles, "Associated Press" (February 1937) and "United Press" (May 1933).

1507. Ross, ISHBEL. "Geography, Inc.," *Scribner's,* 130 no. 6: 23-27 ff.

New York journalist's study of *National Geographic Magazine.*

*1508. Rosten, Leo Calvin (CB '42, W). *The Washington Correspondents.* (Ph.D. thesis, Chicago). New York: Harcourt, Brace, 1937. 436 pp.

The Washington correspondents of U.S. newspapers were investigated intensively by this U.S. political scientist over a period of 16 months. Social composition, reading preferences, attitudes, salaries, and other data are presented in detail. Bibliography, pp. 371-421.

*1508a. Salmon, Lucy Maynard. *The Newspaper and the Historian.* New York: Oxford University, 1923. 566 pp.

Vassar historian presents an extensive study of reliability of the newspaper as historical source material. Discusses news-collecting and news-distributing procedures and organizations, and the roles of war correspondents, general correspondents, interviewers and publishers. Reviews the history of reporting, caricature, cartoons and illustrations during World War I. Bibliography, pp. 493-566. See also *The Newspaper and Authority*, by the same author (New York: Oxford University, 1923. 505 pp.), a scholarly examination of newspaper "trustworthiness."

1509. Schramm, J. R. "Cost Analysis of Scholarly Periodical Printing," *Proceedings of American Philosophical Society*, 80 no. 1: 1-24 (February 1939).

1510. "Section XII," *Time*, 30: 42 (December 20, 1937).

How the New York *Herald Tribune* sold the Cuban government and business interests, for $32,000, a 40-page section, not labeled "Advertising," in its issue of November 21, 1937; how the U.S. liberal press reacted; and how the Cuban government bestowed medals on Mrs. Ogden Reid of the *Herald Tribune* and on the press agent who negotiated the deal.

1511. Shaw, Archer Hayes. *The Plain Dealer: One Hundred Years in Cleveland, 1842-1942.* New York: Knopf, 1942. 402 pp.

Mr. Shaw has been chief editorial writer of the *Plain Dealer* for some 30 years.

1511a. *Sifri o pechati SSSR.* Moscow: Vsesoiuzny knizhnaya palata, 1939. 52 pp.

"Figures on the Press of the Soviet Union." Statistical tables on production of books, magazines, newspapers, and on circulation of works of particular authors.

1512. Sontheimer, Morton. *Newspaper Man: A Book About the Business.* New York: McGraw-Hill, 1941. 336 pp.

Reminiscences and information, based on the author's "19 years in the newspaper business."

1512a. Starzynski, Roman. *Dzieje, stan obecny i znaczenie agencyj informacyjnych.* Warsaw, 1935.

"History, Present Condition and Nature of the Information Agencies." "To find in one place information concerning the early history of the great news agencies like Havas, Reuter, and Wolff, one has to turn to a small book in the Polish language, R. Starzynski's *Agencje informacyjne.*"—Marc Jaryc, *Journal of Modern History*, 15: 129 (June 1943). Before his death in 1938, Starzynski was an influential Polish government propagandist: Director of the Polish Radio (governmental) and of the official Polish Telegraph Agency.

1513. Steed, Henry Wickham. *The Press.* New York: Penguin Books, 1939. 250 pp.

By veteran British journalist.

1514. Stiewe, Willy. *Das Pressephoto als publizistisches Mittel* (Wesen und Wirkungen der Publizistik, vol. 2). Leipzig: Noske, 1936. 129 pp.

Press photos as propaganda media. Bibliography, p. vi.

1515. Stolberg, Benjamin. "Muddled Millions: Capitalist Angels of Left-Wing Propaganda," *Saturday Evening Post*, February 15, 1941.

U.S. journalist says that "during the last two decades rich Americans have supported Communist and fellow-traveling journalism and other propaganda in print to the tune of more than $3,000,000. During the 1930's the non-Communist left-wing press, liberal or radical, got thousands where the Communist-dominated press got hundreds of thousands."

1516. Straumann, Heinrich. *Newspaper Headlines: A Study in Linguistic Method.* London: Allen and Unwin, 1935. 263 pp.

Bibliography, pp. 259-63.

1517. Thayer, Frank. *Newspaper Management*, revised edition. New York: Appleton-Century, 1938. 465 pp.

Revised edition of a 1926 text for college students, by University of Wisconsin professor of journalism.

1518. Torres, Teodoro. *Periodismo.* Mexico City: Botas, 1937. 272 pp.

History of Mexican journalism from 1828 to the present by a prominent Mexican editor. Contains a 62-page bibliography of newspapers founded in Mexico, 1830-1934.

1518a. Traub, Hans Karl Theodor. *Grundbegriffe des Zeitungswesens: Kritische Einfuehrung in die Methode der Zeitungswissenschaft.* Stuttgart: Poeschel, 1933. 184 pp.

"Basic Conceptions of Journalism: A Critical Introduction to the Methods of Journalistic Science." Bibliographic footnotes.

1519. U.S. Work Projects Administration of California. *History of San Francisco Journalism, 1870-1938.* San Francisco, Calif., 1939-40. 4 vols.

1519a. Ullstein, Hermann. *The Rise and Fall of the House of Ullstein.* New York: Simon and Schuster, 1943. 308 pp.

This powerful German publishing house, which owned a group of newspapers, illustrated weeklies and other media, was dispossessed by the Nazis. Book illustrates failure of the democratic press of the Republican era of Germany to organize against Nazism. Author, one of several brothers who managed the firm, escaped to U.S.

1520. University of Berlin. Deutsches Institut für Zeitungswissenschaft. *Handbuch der deutschen Tagespresse*, 6th ed. Leipzig: Armanen, 1937. 477 pp.

*1521. University of Berlin. Deutsches Institut für Zeitungswissenschaft. *Handbuch der Weltpresse: Eine Darstellung des Zeitungswesens aller Länder*, edited by Dr. Karl Bömer, 3rd rev. ed. Leipzig and Frankfort: Armanen, 1937. 632 pp.

Aims to describe briefly the leading newspapers and news agencies of all countries. Includes photographs and brief word pictures of 150 well-known newspapermen.

1521a. Valle, Rafael Heliodoro. "Bibliografía del periodismo de la América española," in *Handbook of Latin American Studies*, 7: 559-91 (1941).

Annotated bibliography (in Spanish) on journalism in Latin America, compiled with a prefatory essay by well-known Latin American journalist.

1522. Vitray, Laura; Mills, John, Jr.; and Ellard, Roscoe. *Pictorial Journalism.* New York: McGraw-Hill, 1939. 437 pp.

Techniques of graphic design, photography, photo editing. The first two authors are U.S. journalists, the third, a U.S. professor of journalism.

1523. Watson, Elmo Scott. *A History of Newspaper Syndicates in the United States, 1865-1935* (revision of M. Sc. thesis, journalism, Northwestern University). Chicago: Western Newspaper Union, 1936. 98 pp.

Compact chronological account of syndicates. Bibliography, pp. 86-89. Directory of newspaper syndicates in the U.S., pp. 90-94.

1523a. Weill, Georges Jacques. *El Diario: Historia y función de la prensa periódica, versión española de Paolino Masip, con un apéndice sobre periodismo y periodistas en Hispano-América por J. A. Fernández de Castro y Andrés Henestrosa.* Mexico: Fondo de cultura económica, 1941. 441 pp.

Translation of *Le journal* (Paris: La Renaissance du livre, 1934. 450 pp.), celebrated general history of the press in all countries by University of Caen historian. Two Latin-

American scholars have added a 100-page Appendix on "Journalism and Journalists in Hispanic America." Bibliography, pp. 397-408. Bibliography to Appendix, pp. 409-12.

1524. WOLSELEY, ROLAND EDGAR. *The Journalist's Bookshelf*, 2nd ed. Minneapolis: Burgess, 1939. 66 pp.

Bibliography of U.S. journalism compiled by Northwestern University journalism professor. First appeared January 1939; second edition, October 1939, includes 100 more titles, with the addition of a section on radio journalism.

1525. YALMAN, AHMET EMIN. "The Inter-Balkanic Press League," *Public Opinion Quarterly*, 3: 688-93 (October 1939).

By a Turkish journalist and editor, author of several historical works.

1526. YAZAKI, DAN. "The Wartime Publishing Industry in Japan," *Contemporary Japan*, 9: 595-605 (May 1940).

2. PERSONNEL

1527. BARRETT, JAMES WYMAN. *Joseph Pulitzer and his World*. New York: Vanguard, 1941. 449 pp.

The author was the last city editor of the New York *World*.

1528. BARTLETT, VERNON. *Intermission in Europe: The Life of a Journalist and Broadcaster*. New York: Oxford University, 1938. 296 pp.

Autobiography of a British journalist and broadcaster, editor of *World Review*.

1529. BARLOW, REUEL R. "French and British Schools of Journalism: A Comparative Analysis," *Journalism Quarterly*, 13: 157-69 (June 1936).

Comparative education of newspaper personnel.

1530. BARLOW, REUEL R. "Journalistic Education Under the Third Reich," *Journalism Quarterly*, 12: 357-66 (December 1935).

1531. BEALS, CARLETON. *Glass Houses: Ten Years of Free-Lancing*. Philadelphia: Lippincott, 1938. 413 pp.

Reminiscences of a widely traveled U.S. journalist.

1532. BENT, SILAS. *Newspaper Crusaders: A Neglected Story*. New York: McGraw-Hill, 1939. 313 pp.

U.S. newspaperman's story of editors, publishers and reporters who have sought to promote "social justice," from colonial times to the present. Bibliography, pp. 297-98.

1533. BILKEY, PAUL ERNEST. *Persons, Papers, and Things: Being the Casual Recollections of a Journalist*. Toronto: Ryerson Press, 1940. Boston: Bruce Humphries, 1941. 235 pp.

Autobiography of editor-in-chief of *Montreal Gazette*.

1534. BOLLES, JOSHUA K., JR. *Father Was an Editor*. New York: Arthur D. Fuller, 1940. 284 pp.

Portrait of Joshua K. Bolles, Sr., who was one of the town's leading citizens as editor of *The New Milford* [Conn.] *Gazette* at the end of the 19th century.

1535. BONSAL, STEPHEN. *Heyday in a Vanished World*. New York: Norton, 1937. 445 pp.

Reminiscences of New York *Herald Tribune* correspondent who covered the Balkans at the turn of the century.

1536. BOOKER, EDNA LEE. *News Is My Job: A Reporter in War-torn China*. New York: Macmillan, 1939. 375 pp.

Eyewitness tale of the war in China by an INS newspaper correspondent who has lived there 17 years.

1537. BRITT, GEORGE. *Forty Years —Forty Millions: The Career of Frank A. Munsey*. New York: Farrar and Rinehart, 1935. 309 pp.

Career of U.S. publisher. By U.S. journalist, for some 15 years a reporter on leading New York dailies.

1538. BROCK, HENRY IRVING. "Thomas Nast, Symbol-Maker," *New York Times Magazine*, September 22, 1940, pp. 6 ff.

Biographical sketch commemorating 100th

anniversary of birth of American political cartoonist, inventor of Democratic donkey and Republican elephant. By New York *Times* staff writer.

1539. Brown, Sevellon. "[American] Society of Newspaper Editors," *Public Opinion Quarterly*, 1 no. 4: 114-20 (October 1937).

By one of the directors of this group. Includes a reprint of the Society's ethical code, "Canons of Journalism."

1540. Carlson, Oliver. [*Arthur*] *Brisbane: A Candid Biography*. New York: Stackpole, 1937. 373 pp.

By U.S. journalist. Bibliography, pp. 354-58.

1541. Carlson, Oliver. *The Man Who Made News: James Gordon Bennett*. New York: Duell, Sloan and Pearce, 1942. 440 pp.

Biography of James Gordon Bennett, Sr., 1795-1872. Bibliography, pp. 423-28.

1542. Carlson, Oliver; and Bates, Ernest Sutherland. *Hearst, Lord of San Simeon: An Unauthorized Biography*. New York: Viking, 1936. 332 pp.

Bibliography, pp. 315-18.

1543. Carter, John Franklin. *The Rectory Family*. New York: Coward, McCann, 1937. 275 pp.

Autobiographical picture of the New England family of a well-known contemporary political commentator (pseudonym: Jay Franklin).

1544. Chamberlin, William Henry. *The Confessions of an Individualist*. New York: Macmillan, 1940. 320 pp.

Autobiography of well-known correspondent of the *Christian Science Monitor*.

1545. Clough, Frank C. *William Allen White of Emporia*. New York: Whittlesey House, 1941. 265 pp.

Study of editor of Emporia *Gazette* by managing editor of the Emporia *Gazette*.

1546. Colquhoun, A. H. U. *Press, Politics, and People: The Life and Letters of John Willison, Journalist and Correspondent of "The Times."* London: Macmillan, 1936. 306 pp.

The subject of this biography was for many years a well-known Canadian editor, and correspondent of the London *Times*.

*1546a. *Conditions of Life and Work of Journalists* (International Labour Office, Studies and Reports, Series L, no. 2). Geneva, 1928. 219 pp.

Analysis of working conditions in various countries. Includes a study of trade union organizations of journalists, and associations of mutual welfare. Bibliographic footnotes.

1546b. Copeland, Fayette. *Kendall of the* Picayune: *Being His Adventures in New Orleans, on the Texan Santa Fe Expedition, in the Mexican War, and in the Colonization of the Texas Frontier*. Norman: University of Oklahoma Press, 1943. 351 pp.

Biography of one of the founders of the New Orleans *Picayune*, an important early American war correspondent and pioneer Texan. The author had access to a collection of the notes and diaries in the possession of the Kendall family. Bibliography, pp. 321-33.

1547. Dennis, Charles Henry. *Victor Lawson: His Time and Work*. Chicago: University of Chicago, 1935. 471 pp.

Lawson was owner-publisher of the Chicago *Daily News* for 49 years.

1548. Ellis, Elmer. *Mr. Dooley's America: A Life of Finley Peter Dunne*. New York: Knopf, 1941. 310 pp.

Biography of U.S. humorist and journalist, by U.S. historian. Bibliographic footnotes.

1549. Filler, Louis. *Crusaders for American Liberalism*. New York: Harcourt, Brace, 1939. 422 pp.

History of the "muckrakers," from about 1900 until the World War. Bibliography, pp. 403-07.

1550. Fischer, Louis. *Men and Politics: An Autobiography*. New York: Duell, Sloan and Pearce, 1941. 672 pp.

U.S. journalist chronicles his two decades of experience in Europe as a free-lance correspondent.

1551. FYFE, (HENRY) HAMILTON. *My Seven Selves.* London: Allen and Unwin, 1935. 320 pp.

The author of these reminiscences was long affiliated with the Northcliffe press as manager, star reporter, and propagandist.

1552. GAUVREAU, EMILE. *My Last Million Readers.* New York: Dutton, 1941. 488 pp.

Autobiography of editor of celebrated New York tabloids, exponent of the hardest-boiled type of journalism.

1553. GIBBS, WOLCOTT. "A Very Active Type Man," *New Yorker*, May 2 and 9, 1942.

Profile of Ralph McAllister Ingersoll, editor of the newspaper *PM.*

1554. HANSON, ELISHA. "The American Newspaper Publishers Association," *Public Opinion Quarterly*, 2: 121-26 (January 1938).

By general counsel of the Association.

1555. HEATH, S. BURTON. *Yankee Reporter.* New York: Wilfred Funk, 1940. 391 pp.

Autobiography of a Pulitzer Prize winner.

1555a. HEIDE, WALTHER. *Wie studiere ich Zeitungswissenschaft?* Essen: Essener Verlagsanstalt, 1938. 52 pp.

By president of the *Deutsche Zeitungswissenschaftliche Verband* (DZV), organization which coordinates the study of journalism in Germany. Lists the various schools, departments and institutes, explains the curricula and degrees, and itemizes library materials and other facilities in each school. Describes procedures for official admission to this highly restricted profession.

1556. HOUGH, HENRY BEETLE. *Country Editor.* New York: Doubleday, Doran, 1940. 325 pp.

Autobiography of editor of *Martha's Vineyard Gazette.*

1557. HUNT, FRAZIER. *One American and His Attempt at Education.* New York: Simon and Schuster, 1937. 400 pp.

Reminiscences of U.S. foreign correspondent.

1557a. IRWIN, WILL(IAM) HENRY. *The Making of a Reporter.* New York: Putnam's Sons, 1942. 440 pp.

Autobiography of famous U.S. journalist.

1558. JOHNSTON, ALVA. "The Great Macfadden," *Saturday Evening Post* (June 21 and 28, 1941).

Bernarr Macfadden, publisher of many U.S. mass-circulation magazines. By a U.S. journalist.

1559. KELLY, FLORENCE FINCH. *Flowing Stream: The Story of Fifty-six Years in American Newspaper Life.* New York: Dutton, 1939. 570 pp.

Newspaperwoman's reminiscences.

1560. KISCH, EGON ERWIN. *Sensation Fair*, translated by Guy Endore. New York: Modern Age, 1941. 376 pp.

Record of the first 30 years of the life of this Czech journalist, poet, and novelist.

1561. "Knight in White Armor: Lowell Mellett Heads the Office of Government Reports," *Nation's Business*, 29: 29-30 ff. (June 1941).

Sketches personality and career of one of President F. D. Roosevelt's six secretaries, a Scripps-Howard editor who became chief of the Office of Government Reports.

1562. KOENIGSBERG, MOSES. *King News: An Autobiography.* New York: Stokes, 1941. 511 pp.

By former president and general manager of International News Service and of King Features Syndicate.

1563. LANIA, LEO (pseud. of HERRMANN, LAZAR). *Today We Are Brothers: The Biography of a Generation*, translated from German by Ralph Marlowe. Boston: Houghton Mifflin, 1942. 344 pp.

Experiences of a Viennese journalist, novelist, playwright, and motion-picture producer.

1563a. Lawrence, Raymond D. "Kansas Publishers: A Professional Analysis," *Journalism Quarterly*, 15: 337-8 (December 1938).

An application to Kansas publishers of the social and cultural analysis utilized by Leo C. Rosten in *The Washington Correspondents*.

1564. Liebling, Abbott Joseph. "The Boy in the Pistachio Shirt," *New Yorker*, August 2 and 9, 1941.

Profile of Roy Wilson Howard, of Scripps-Howard papers.

1565. Lundberg, Ferdinand. *Imperial Hearst: A Social Biography*, with a preface by Charles Austin Beard. New York: Equinox, 1936. 406 pp.

Bibliography, pp. 382-90.

1566. Lunn, Arnold Henry Moore. *Come What May: An Autobiography*. Boston: Little, Brown, 1941. 348 pp.

Autobiography of English journalist.

1567. McKenzie, Vernon. *Through Turbulent Years*. New York: McBride, 1938. 304 pp.

Reminiscences of a journalist and political writer, professor in the School of Journalism, University of Washington.

1568. "Men of War," *Time*, June 3, 1940, p. 58.

On Germany's official *Pressekompanie*, war correspondents who are trained to fight as soldiers and report their battles to the German press.

1569. Mencken, Henry Louis. *Newspaper Days: 1899-1906*. New York: Knopf, 1941. 313 pp.

Autobiography of Baltimore journalist.

1570. Mowrer, Lilian T. *Journalist's Wife*. New York: Morrow, 1937. 414 pp.

Wife of Edgar Ansel Mowrer, celebrated U.S. foreign correspondent, tells of 20 years of experience in Europe.

1570a. Nixon, Raymond Blalock. *Henry W. Grady: Spokesman of the New South*. New York: Knopf, 1943. 360 pp.

Definitive life of famous Southern journalist and post-bellum advocate of economic and spiritual union of the reconstructed South with the Union. Grady was director of the news and editorial policies of the Atlanta *Constitution*, with the South's largest circulation, and was Southern correspondent for various important Northern journals including the New York *Herald*. First written as a Ph.D. dissertation. By Chairman of Department of Journalism, Emory University, who had access to the Grady family papers. Bibliography, pp. 351-60.

1571. Noyes, Alexander Dana. *The Market Place: Reminiscences of a Financial Editor*. Boston: Little, Brown, 1938. 384 pp.

By financial editor of the New York *Times*. Based on some 50 years of day-to-day handling of financial news.

1571a. O'Dell, De Forest. *History of Journalism Education in the United States* (Ph.D. thesis; Teachers College Contributions to Education, no. 653). New York: Columbia University, 1935. 116 pp.

Bibliography, pp. 113-16.

1572. Older, Cora Miranda Baggerly. *William Randolph Hearst, American*. New York and London: Appleton-Century, 1936. 581 pp.

The author, Mrs. Fremont Older, was a star reporter on Hearst newspapers, and remained a personal friend of Mr. Hearst until her recent death.

1573. O'Malley, Charles J. *It Was News to Me*. Boston: Bruce Humphries, 1939. 409 pp.

Autobiography of Irish-American journalist.

1573a. Prugger, Francis V. "Social Composition and Training of Milwaukee *Journal* News Staff," *Journalism Quarterly*, 18: 231-44 (September 1941).

An application to the editorial and news men of a daily newspaper staff of the social and cultural analysis utilized by Leo C. Rosten in *The Washington Correspondents*.

1574. Rand, Clayton. *Ink on my Hands*, preface by William Allen White. New York: Carrick and Evans, 1941. 348 pp.

Autobiography of editor of Philadelphia, Mississippi, *Neshoba Democrat*.

1575. Redmond, Pauline; and Redmond, Wilfred. *Business Paper Writing: A Career*. New York: Pitman, 1939. 194 pp.

A study of opportunities in this field of journalism.

1576. Rich, Everett. *William Allen White: The Man From Emporia*. New York: Farrar and Rinehart, 1941. 374 pp.

Bibliography, pp. 347-61.

1577. Riegel, Oscar Wetherhold. "Hispanic-American Press Conference," *Public Opinion Quarterly*, 1 no. 2: 133-34 (April 1937).

Reports one of a series of attempts—abortive thus far—to organize Western Hemisphere journalists.

1578. Rogers, Charles Elkins. *Journalistic Vocations*, 2nd ed. New York: Appleton-Century, 1937. 354 pp.

Revision of a standard treatise on editorial, reportorial, circulation, and other career opportunities for journalists. Includes data on positions obtained by recent graduates of journalism schools, and their reported earnings. Contains new sections on American Newspaper Guild and on radio in journalism.

1579. Seldes, George. "Roy Howard," *New Republic*, 95: 322-25 (July 27, 1938).

Free-lance journalist's analysis of alleged conservative trend in the policy of the 24 Scripps-Howard papers since the death of Robert Paine Scripps in 1938.

1580. Shirer, William Lawrence. *Berlin Diary: Journal of a Foreign Correspondent, 1934-41*. New York: Knopf, 1941. 605 pp.

By well-known U.S. journalist. Includes accounts of his many altercations with the German propaganda ministry and censors.

1581. Shuler, Marjorie Knight, Ruth Adams; and Fuller, Muriel. *Lady Editor: Careers for Women in Publishing*. New York: Dutton, 1941. 288 pp.

Requirements for success in journalism, book publishing, and magazine writing.

1582. Smallzried, Kathleen Ann. *Press Pass: A Woman Reporter's Story*. New York: Dutton, 1940. 340 pp.

Autobiography of a U.S. woman journalist (South Bend, Indiana, *News-Times*).

1583. Stoddart, Dayton. *Lord Broadway*, *Variety's* Sime. New York: Wilfred Funk, 1941. 385 pp.

Biography of Simon J. ("Sime") Silverman, founder of *Variety*, inimitable trade organ of the entertainment industry.

1584. Stokes, Thomas L. *Chip Off My Shoulder*. Princeton: Princeton University, 1940. 561 pp.

Autobiography of a Washington correspondent, 1939 Pulitzer prize winner.

1585. Tabouis, Geneviève R. *They Called Me Cassandra*, introduction by Edgar Ansel Mowrer. New York: Scribner's, 1942. 436 pp.

Memoirs of a French journalist.

1586. Van Gelder, Robert. "An Interview With Captain Hartzell Spence," *New York Times Book Review*, August 16, 1942, pp. 2 ff.

On the Executive Editor of *Yank*, the weekly newspaper for soldiers.

1587. Vaughn, Miles W. *Covering the Far East*. New York: Covici Friede, 1936. 408 pp.

Reminiscences of an American correspondent with 10 years of experience in the Orient.

1588. Villard, Oswald Garrison. *Fighting Years*. New York: Harcourt, Brace, 1939. 543 pp.

Autobiography of a noted U.S. liberal journalist, stressing especially the years 1898-1928.

1589. Wharton, Don. "Julius David Stern," *Scribner's,* 100: 45-49 ff. (December 1936).

Publisher of an aggressive chain of newspapers on the U.S. Eastern seaboard.

1590. Woodhead, H. G. W. *Adventures in Far Eastern Journalism.* Tokyo: Hokuseido Press, 1935. 280 pp.

By a prominent China journalist, editor of the *China Yearbook.*

1591. Woolf, Samuel Johnson. *Here Am I.* New York: Random House, 1941. 374 pp.

Reminiscences of U.S. artist and journalist, long connected with New York *Times.*

1592. Ybarra, Thomas Russell. *Young Man of Caracas* (1941; 324 pp.), foreword by Elmer Davis; and *Young Man of the World* (1942; 316 pp.). New York: Ives Washburn.

Autobiography of the first 30 years of this New York *Times* specialist on Latin America, whose father was a Venezuelan general and whose mother was a Bostonian and a daughter of General Grant's Minister to Venezuela.

1593. Young, Art. *Art Young: His Life and Times,* edited by John Nicholas Beffel. New York: Sheridan House, 1939. 467 pp.

Autobiography of a U.S. leftist cartoonist.

3. QUANTITATIVE STUDIES OF AUDIENCES, COVERAGE AND EFFECTS
[See also Part 6.]

1594. "The Abuse of Power," *Fortune* (January 1936).

A survey of public opinion on "abusers of power" revealed considerable distrust of the American press.

1595. Bush, Chilton Rowlette. "Notes on a New Method for Determining 'Newspaper Audience,'" *Journalism Quarterly,* 19: 371-74 (December 1942).

"This new method consists in measuring the number of 'impressions' of the specific media rather than the units purchased (circulation). The lead in this technique has been taken by *Life* magazine to measure 'magazine audiences' and by Columbia Broadcasting System to measure 'new effective program audience.'" Dr. Bush is Director of the Division of Journalism, Stanford University.

1596. Crosley, Archibald M. "Reading Habits: Their Influence on the Choice of Media for Industrial Advertising," *Industrial Marketing,* 22 no. 12, pp. 31-32 (November 1937).

1500 industrial executives and engineers were interviewed in their offices in an effort to learn what they regularly read.

1597. Ferguson, L. W. "Preferred Position of Advertisements in the *Saturday Evening Post,*" *Journal of Applied Psychology,* 18: 749-56 (December 1934).

1598. Gallup, George Horace. "I Asked 100,000 People What They Read in Newspapers," *Advertising and Selling,* 31 no. 1: 41-43 (January 1938).

Detailed classification of reading interests of men and women as shown by a specially devised interviewing technique.

1599. Gallup Research Bureau. *A Study of Reader Interest in Sunday Newspapers, Made to Determine the Comparative Values of Advertising Space in Different Sections and the Relative Worth of Different Copy and Illustrative Techniques: Made for Kimberly-Clark Corporation by the Gallup Research Bureau.* Neenah, Wis.: Kimberly-Clark Corporation, 1935. 51 pp.

1600. Geisert, Harold L. *Circulation of Newspapers as an Index of Cultural Change* (Ph.D. thesis, sociology, North Carolina, 1938).

1601. Gosnell, Harold Foote; and Schmidt, Margaret J. "Relation of the Press to Voting in Chicago," *Journalism Quarterly,* 13: 129-48 (June 1936).

Two political scientists apply precision techniques to the measurement of newspaper influence.

1602. HADSEL, FRED LATIMER. "Propaganda in the Funnies," *Current History*, n.s. 1: 365-68 (December 1941).

"More people are reached through the comics than by any other part of a newspaper," says this University of Chicago fellowship holder. Comics of defense, army life, espionage, prototalitarianism, are briefly reviewed.

1603. LAZARSFELD, PAUL FELIX; and WYANT, ROWENA. "Magazines in 90 Cities—Who Reads What?" *Public Opinion Quarterly*, 1 no. 4: 29-41 (October 1937).

Magazine reading habits of the 90 American cities of more than 100,000 population (except Boston, Cambridge, and Somerville, Mass.) were correlated with geographical location, size of city, age distribution, occupational structure, educational expenditures, incomes, and number of movies.

1604. PUNKE, HAROLD H. "Cultural Change and Changes in Popular Literature," *Social Forces*, 15: 359-70 (March 1937).

Changes in amount and character of periodical material published in the United States since 1810, with tables and chart.

1605. WYMAN, PHILLIPS. *Magazine Circulation: An Outline of Methods and Meanings.* New York: The McCall Company, 1936. 191 pp.

By the Director of Circulation of the McCall magazines. "Every phase of the sale and distribution of magazines [in the U.S.] is covered," partly on the basis of tabulated findings of a force of field investigators who worked on newsstands recording behavior and preferences of magazine buyers.

III. EDUCATIONAL SYSTEM AND RESEARCH AGENCIES

1. CONTROL, ORGANIZATION, EQUIPMENT

1606. AIKIN, WILFORD MERTON. *The Story of the Eight-Year Study* (Adventure in American Education, vol. 1). New York: Harpers, 1942. 157 pp.

Results of Progressive Education Association's eight-year study (1933-41) of ways to improve secondary education.

1607. ALEXANDER, CARTER. *How to Locate Educational Information and Data: A Text and Reference Book*, 2nd ed., revised and expanded. New York: Teachers College, Columbia University, 1941. 439 pp.

Standard reference work on use of libraries by teachers. Author is Professor of Education, Teachers College, Columbia University. (First edition, 1935; 272 pp.)

1608. AMERICAN ASSOCIATION OF SCHOOL ADMINISTRATORS. *Youth Education Today* (Sixteenth Yearbook). Washington, D.C.: 1938. 509 pp.

Professional administrators evaluate different methods of civic training, through such devices as "life-centered" curricula, community centers, youth organizations, guidance services, youth-adult conferences. Both in-school and out-of-school youth are considered.

1609. AMERICAN ASSOCIATION OF SCHOOLS OF SOCIAL WORK. STUDY COMMITTEE. *Education for the Public Social Services.* Chapel Hill, N.C.: University of North Carolina, 1942. 324 pp.

Analysis of the U.S. schools of social work and their relation to the social services, sponsored by the American Association of Schools of Social Work under a grant from the Rockefeller Foundation. Bibliographic footnotes.

*1610. AMERICAN ASSOCIATION OF UNIVERSITY PROFESSORS. SPECIAL COMMITTEE Y. *Depression, Recovery, and Higher Education*, report prepared by Malcolm M. Willey (D,W). New York: McGraw-Hill, 1937. 543 pp.

Sociology of American higher education, 1930-36, by a group of well-known U.S. social scientists and educators. Includes data on size, incomes, depression problems, and "effectiveness" of faculty and students, and on relations of government to higher education. Chapter 14 is on "Student Ideologies and the Depression." Part 6, chapter 19, "Public Relations and the Depression," describes demands and pressures affecting the schools. Bibliographic footnotes.

1611. AMERICAN COLLEGE PUBLICITY ASSOCIATION. *Publicity Problems: Proceedings of the Annual Con-*

vention of the Association. Pittsburgh and elsewhere, 1936–.

1612. *American Teacher*, special 64-page issue, April 1940, on federal aid to education.

Articles by numerous authorities place federal aid proposals in a national political and economic context.

1613. ARNETT, TREVOR. *Recent Trends in Higher Education in the United States, with Special Reference to Financial Support for Private Colleges and Universities* (Occasional papers, no. 13). New York: General Education Board, 1940. 80 pp.

1614. ATKINSON, CARROLL. *Development of Radio Education Policies in American Public School Systems.* Edinboro, Pa.: Edinboro Educational Press, 1939. 279 pp.

"The attempt has been made to picture radio education development in American public schools both by recording the most important historical facts and by describing present policies of 126 (or 10.3%) of American public school systems representing population centers of eight thousand and more. A summary for each of these cities has been written. . . ." There is also evaluation of the policies of the networks, the U.S. Office of Education, the National Education Association, and other agencies of radio education.

1615. ATKINSON, CARROLL. *Radio Extension Courses Broadcast for Credit.* Boston: Meador, 1941. 128 pp.

Experiments of 13 universities and colleges in broadcasting correspondence-extension courses. Bibliographic footnotes.

1615a. BEALS, RALPH A.; and BRODY, LEON. *The Literature of Adult Education* (Studies in the Social Significance of Adult Education in the United States, no. 25). New York: American Association for Adult Education, 1941. 493 pp.

Extended bibliographic essay by two staff members of the Association. Covers materials that appeared between 1929 and 1939.

1616. BEESLEY, PATRICIA. *The Revival of the Humanities in American Ed-*

ucation. New York: Columbia University, 1940. 201 pp.

Data on the humanities courses that have been revived in some 30 U.S. colleges in the past dozen years, discussed from the point of view of a group of educators at Teachers College, Columbia University. Bibliography, pp. 136-90.

1617. BERNAYS, EDWARD L.; and FLEISCHMAN, DORIS E. *Universities: Pathfinders in Public Opinion.* New York: The authors, 1937. 38 pp.

Lists "Courses in Public Relations, Public Opinion, and Related Subjects Offered by American Universities."

1618. BINING, ARTHUR CECIL; and BINING, DAVID HENRY. *Teaching the Social Studies in the Secondary Schools*, 2nd ed. New York: McGraw-Hill, 1941. 378 pp.

Standard text by two professors of education. Bibliography at ends of chapters and pp. 357-59.

1619. BINING, ARTHUR CECIL; MOHR, WALTER H.; and MCFEELY, RICHARD H. *Organizing the Social Studies in the Secondary Schools.* New York: McGraw-Hill, 1941. 337 pp.

Analysis of alternative curricula and approaches. A companion to the volume of A. C. and D. H. Bining, cited above. Dr. A. C. Bining is professor of education in the University of Pennsylvania and his two coauthors are teachers in the George School. Bibliography at ends of chapters.

1620. BOND, HORACE MANN. *The Education of the Negro in the American Social Order.* New York: Prentice-Hall, 1934. 501 pp.

Comprehensive study of the relation of public policies and attitudes to concrete economic interests of the different classes in the South since the Civil War, together with an analysis of the cost and consequences of the separate systems of education. Bibliography, pp. 465-81.

1621. BOOTH, GEORGE C. *Mexico's School-made Society.* Stanford University: Stanford, 1941. 175 pp.

Account of Mexico's pattern of social reform through education, by a scholar who has studied it on the spot. Bibliographic footnotes.

1622. BRADBY, EDWARD, editor. *The University Outside Europe.* New York: Oxford University, 1939. 332 pp.

Essays on the development of university institutions in fourteen countries, by a group of prominent educators under the editorship of Mr. Bradby, General Secretary of International Student Service. Supplements *The University in a Changing World,* edited by Walter M. Kotschnig and Elined Prys (London: Oxford, 1932), which dealt mainly with European universities. Bibliographic footnotes.

1622a. (Pop.) BRYSON, LYMAN. *Adult Education.* New York: American Book Company, 1936. 208 pp.

History and analysis of goals and techniques of U.S. adult education movements, by a Teachers College professor nationally recognized as a specialist in this field. He has served for a number of years as chairman of the Adult Education Board of CBS. Bibliography at ends of chapters.

1622b. (Pop.) BRYSON, LYMAN. *A State Plan for Adult Education.* New York: American Association for Adult Education, 1934. 69 pp.

Outlines activity carried on through a score of channels when Professor Bryson was executive director of California Association for Adult Education.

1623. BURDETTE, FRANKLIN L., editor. *Education for Citizen Responsibilities: The Roles of Anthropology, Economics, Geography, History, Philosophy, Political Science, Psychology and Sociology.* Princeton, N.J.: Princeton University Press for National Foundation for Education in American Citizenship, 1942. 126 pp.

Essays by a dozen well-known educators and social scientists on the possible contributions of social science to secondary education. Bibliographic footnotes.

1624. CALIVER, AMBROSE; and GREENE, ETHEL G. *Education of Negroes: A Five-Year Bibliography, 1931-35* (U.S. Office of Education Bulletin, 1937, no. 8). Washington, D.C.: Government Printing Office, 1937. 63 pp.

Continues a previous bibliography for the period 1928-30, covering elementary, secondary, higher, vocational, health, adult, and religious education of Negroes in the U.S.

1625. CAMPBELL, DOAK SHERIDAN; BAIR, FREDERICK HAIGH; and HARVEY, OSWALD L. *Educational Activities of the Works Progress Administration* (U.S. Advisory Committee on Education, Staff study no. 14). Washington, D.C.: Government Printing Office, 1939. 185 pp.

1626. CARTWRIGHT, MORSE ADAMS. *Ten Years of Adult Education: A Report on a Decade of Progress in the American Movement.* New York: Macmillan, 1935. 220 pp.

By the Director of the American Association for Adult Education.

1627. CLARKE, E. L. "The Recruitment of the Nation's Leaders," *Sociological Review,* 28: 246-66, 333-60 (July, October 1936).

Statistical analysis of the probability that "a child of talent but of little wealth" can rise through the English universities to a position of leadership in the nation. The chances "are still small, in relation to the numbers of such children and the chances of the wealthier." The paper then sets out to answer the question: "How far is this due to a faulty system of selection by scholarship from the secondary schools, how far to the deliberate action of those who would lose by complete equality of opportunity?"

1628. COCKING, WALTER DEWEY; and GILMORE, CHARLES HAYGOOD. *Organization and Administration of Public Education* (U.S. Advisory Committee on Education, Staff study no. 2). Washington, D.C.: Government Printing Office, 1938. 183 pp.

"The legal boundaries of public education in America, and the place of education in the structure of government. State and local administration of education, and the interrelationships of the local, state, and Federal governments. Lists 14 fundamentals of educational organization and administration, and concludes with concrete suggestions for making the fundamentals operative."

1629. Coit, E. G. *Government Support of Workers' Education, With Special Reference to a Study of the Relation of Public and Private Agencies in the Field of Workers' Education in Denmark and Sweden.* New York: American Labor Education Service, Inc., 1940. 72 pp.

1630. Conant, James Bryant; and Spaulding, Francis Trow. *Education for a Classless Society: Three Essays on the Purposes and Problems of American Education.* Cambridge: Harvard University, 1940. 43 pp.

Dr. Conant is President of Harvard; Dr. Spaulding, Dean of the Harvard Graduate School of Education, was a member of the Regents' Inquiry on the Character and Cost of Education in the State of New York, title 1718 below.

1631. Council for Democracy. *America's Free Schools.* New York, 1941. Pamphlet.

"Though the consultants contributing to this pamphlet do not always agree as to particulars, they are in accord with the basic thesis that our schools must remain free. They insist that no teacher should take orders from outside groups, whether that group is the Communist Party or the National Association of Manufacturers."

1632. Counts, George Sylvester. *The Prospects of American Democracy.* New York: John Day, 1938. 370 pp.

Professor at Columbia University's Teachers College analyzes main outlines of the U.S. social structure and presents a comprehensive curriculum, centered on problems of democratic social integration, for "the twelve-year common school course."

1633. De Lima, Agnes; and the staff of the Little Red School House. *The Little Red School House,* introduction by John Dewey. New York: Macmillan, 1942. 355 pp.

Grade-by-grade study of goings-on in this well-known progressive school in New York City. Bibliography, pp. 289-323.

1634. Dent, Ellsworth Charles, editor. *The Audio-Visual Handbook,* 1942. Chicago: Society for Visual Education, 1942. 227 pp.

Contains announcements of technical developments, and articles by educators and others who have had personal experience in the use of visual aids. Lists sources of information on materials and equipment, pp. 199-227.

*1634a. D'Irsay, Stephen. *Histoire des universités françaises et étrangères depuis les origines jusqu'à nos jours.* Paris: Picard, 1933-35. 2 vols.

Volume 1: Middle Ages and Renaissance. Volume 2: 16th century to 1860. Copious bibliographic footnotes. Critical bibliographic essay, vol. 1, pp. 15-22. Bibliography, vol. 2, pp. 303-97.

1635. Douglass, Aubrey Augustus. *The American School System: A Survey of the Principles and Practices of Education,* rev. ed. New York: Farrar and Rinehart, 1940. 745 pp.

College text by associate superintendent, California State Department of Education. Bibliography at ends of chapters.

1635a. Dyson, Walter. *Howard University, The Capstone of Negro Education: A History, 1867-1940.* Washington, D.C.: Graduate School of Howard University, 1941. 553 pp.

By Howard University historian. Bibliography, pp. 500-25.

1636. Ebaugh, Franklin Gessford; and Rymer, Charles A. *Psychiatry in Medical Education.* New York: Commonwealth Fund, 1942. 612 pp.

Analytical survey of psychiatric teaching in the United States, 1934-40, by two U.S. psychiatrists. Discusses prevailing curricula, clinic facilities, conceptions of personality, diagnostic techniques. Bibliography at end of each chapter.

1637. Eells, Walter Crosby, editor. *American Junior Colleges.* Washington, D.C.: American Council on Education, 1941. 585 pp.

Directory compiled by executive secretary, American Association of Junior Colleges, with analysis of history and prospects of the junior college movement.

1638. ELY, MARY LILLIAN, editor. *Adult Education in Action.* New York: American Association for Adult Education, 1936. 480 pp.

Digests some 160 articles which have appeared from time to time in *Journal of Adult Education,* presenting a many-sided evaluation of adult education in the United States. Bibliography, pp. 459-63 and in index.

1639. FEDYAEVSKAYA, VERA; in collaboration with HILL, PATTY SMITH. *Nursery School and Parent Education in Soviet Russia.* New York: Dutton, 1936. 265 pp.

A Soviet specialist describes the daily routine of the "health, social, labor, and political education" of the Soviet citizen during the first three years of his life. Chapter 12 is entitled, "Health and Education Propaganda." Bibliography, pp. 254-65.

1640. FINE, BENJAMIN. *College Publicity in the United States* (Teachers College Contributions to Education, no. 832). New York: Teachers College, Columbia University, 1941. 178 pp.

History of growth of college publicity bureaus and an evaluation of present practices. Bibliography, pp. 168-72.

1640a. FINE, BENJAMIN. *Educational Publicity.* New York: Harpers, 1943. 320 pp.

Practical, nontechnical manual by education editor of New York *Times,* whose Ph.D. thesis (Teachers College, 1941) was on "College Publicity in the United States." Bibliography, pp. 311-13.

*1640b. FLEXNER, ABRAHAM (CB '41, D,W). *Universities: American, English, German.* New York: Oxford University, 1930. 381 pp.

Sets up criteria for a university that would answer the needs of the modern age, and evaluates in these terms the educational systems of England, Germany and U.S. Based on the author's first-hand inquiries over a period of 40 years, as a teacher and as an executive of large U.S. educational foundations.

1641. FOSTER, CHARLES RICHARD, JR. *Editorial Treatment of Education in the American Press* (Harvard Bulletins in Education, no. 21). Cambridge: Harvard University, 1938. 303 pp.

Examines all editorial comment on education appearing in 25 selected U.S. newspapers, January 1, 1930 to January 1, 1935. Makes suggestions for public relations of the educational system. Bibliographic footnotes.

1642. GABEL, RICHARD J. *Public Funds for Church and Private Schools.* Washington, D.C.: Catholic University of America, 1937. 858 pp.

History of public aid for church and private schools from Colonial times to the present, with arguments favoring such aid.

1643. GHOSE, AMALESH. "Mass Education in India," *Calcutta Review,* 80: 47-66 (July 1941).

Recent statistics.

1644. GRAHAM, GEORGE ADAMS. *Education for Public Administration: Graduate Preparation in the Social Sciences at American Universities* (Social Science Research Council, Committee on Public Administration, Studies in Administration, vol. 11). Chicago: Public Administration Service, 1941. 366 pp.

By Princeton professor of public administration.

1645. GRAY, GEORGE WILLIAM. *Education on an International Scale: A History of the International Education Board, 1923-38,* introduction by Raymond B. Fosdick. New York: Harcourt, Brace, 1941. 114 pp.

History of the activities of this far-flung Rockefeller philanthropy.

1646. GREENWOOD, MAJOR. "The Social Distribution of University Education," *Journal of the Royal Statistical Society,* 52: 355-72 (1939).

Using census data to determine the proportion of the British population in various classes, and using achievement of full-time students on Otis Group Advanced tests as an index of mental ability, it is concluded that 81.1 per cent of all the university students should come from among the graduates of the state-supported schools, and 18.9 per cent from among the graduates of private preparatory schools. The actual distribution is 40 per cent and 60 per cent, indicating that the free students have not quite half, and the fee-paying students more than three times, their proportionate share of the university population. Similar results have been obtained for Switzerland, Italy, Sweden, and Germany, where it has been found that families of high socioeconomic status have proportionally more children in the universities than families of low status as measured by occupation of father.

1647. HAMLIN, CHARLES HUNTER. *Educators Present Arms: The Use of the Schools and Colleges as Agents of War Propaganda, 1914-1918,* introduction by Harold E. Fey. Zebulon, N.C.: Record Publishing Company, 1939. 47 pp.

By professor of history, Atlantic Christian College, Wilson, N.C. Contains a number of minor inaccuracies, but presents the picture more adequately than previous publications. Bibliography, pp. 43-47.

1648. *Handbook of Adult Education in the United States, 1934–.* New York: American Association for Adult Education, at intervals, 1934–.

Details of facilities, programs, and bibliography.

1648a. HARRAL, STEWART. *Public Relations for Higher Education.* Norman: University of Oklahoma, 1942. 292 pp.

Practical, nontechnical manual. Bibliography, pp. 269-85.

1649. HARRIS, ARTHUR, compiler. *Governmental Research Organizations in the Western States: A Directory of Agencies and an Index to their Studies as of January 1, 1939.* Berkeley: University of California Bureau of Public Administration, 1939. 123 pp.

1650. HARTSHORNE, EDWARD YARNALL. *The German Universities and National Socialism.* London: Allen and Unwin, 1937. 184 pp.

Harvard tutor in sociology, who spent a year in the Third Reich, analyzes the Nazis' reorganization of the universities. A chapter on "The Recasting of the Academic Curriculum" contains a section on "Speculative Science and Propaganda." Bibliography, p. 5 and footnotes.

1651. HAWKINS, GAYNELL. *Educational Experiments in Social Settlements* (Studies in the Social Significance of Adult Education in the United States, no. 5). New York: American Association for Adult Education, 1937. 145 pp.

"Unabashedly personal" interpretation of adult education projects in settlements chosen because "their programs in some phase or another of adult education were either the most typical or the most distinct."

1652. HILL, DAVID SPENCE. *Control of Tax-Supported Higher Education in the United States,* preface by Howard J. Savage. New York: Carnegie Foundation, 1934. 385 pp.

1653. HOGBEN, LANCELOT, editor. *Political Arithmetic: A Symposium of Population Studies.* London: Allen and Unwin, 1938. 531 pp.

Part II, "The Recruitment of Social Personnel," includes elaborate statistical analysis of "Ability and Opportunity in English Education," by J. L. Gray and Pearl Moshinsky; "Ability and Educational Opportunity in Relation to Parental Occupation," by the same writers; and "Opportunity and the Older Universities," by David V. Glass and J. L. Gray. Bibliography at ends of chapters.

1654. HOLLIS, ERNEST VICTOR. *Philanthropic Foundations and Higher Education: The Role of the Philanthropic Foundation in the History of American Higher Education* (Ph.D. thesis, Teachers College). New York: Columbia University, 1938. 365 pp.

Bibliography, pp. 400-09.

1654a. *Index Generalis: Annuaire générale des universités et des grands écoles, académies, archives, bibliothèques, instituts scientifiques, jardins botaniques et zoologiques, musées, observatoires, sociétés savants,* 18th year, edited by S. de Montessus de Ballore. Paris: Masson, 1939. 2830 pp.

Guide to institutions of higher education and research in all countries. Includes directory of 115,000 intellectuals ("savants") all over the world, giving their titles and the institutions with which they are connected.

1655. JACKSON, SIDNEY L. *America's Struggle for Free Schools: Social Tension and Education in New England and New York, 1827-42,* introduction by Merle Curti (Ph.D. thesis, Columbia). Washington, D.C.: American Council on Public Affairs, 1941. 277 pp.

"The men who led the Common School Revival a century ago had to fight a real battle against both the privileged and the underprivileged." This volume traces attitudes and propagandist activities of the "intellectual leadership" of the times; of organized teachers; of spokesmen for agricultural interests; and of labor. Bibliography, pp. 175-269.

1656. JONES, VERNON AUGUSTUS. *Character and Citizenship Training in the Public School: An Experimental Study of Three Specific Methods.* Chicago: University of Chicago, 1936. 404 pp.

Results of experimental civic training programs in the United States, by Clark University professor of educational psychology. Bibliography, pp. 391-400.

1657. JUDD, CHARLES HUBBARD. *Research in the United States Office of Education* (U.S. Advisory Committee on Education, Staff study no. 19). Washington, D.C.: Government Printing Office, 1940. 133 pp.

Former head of department of education, University of Chicago, points out many new studies which he feels the U.S. Office of Education should undertake, and recommends enlarged support and additional personnel. Contains bibliography.

1658. KANDEL, ISAAC LEON. *The Making of Nazis* (Studies of the International Institute of Teachers College, no. 17). New York: Columbia University, 1936. 143 pp.

Theory and practice of civic training in the Third Reich, by a Columbia University professor of comparative education. Bibliography, p. 138.

1659. KAULFERS, WALTER VINCENT; KEFAUVER, GRAYSON N.; and ROBERTS, HOLLAND D. *Foreign Languages and Cultures in American Education.* New York: McGraw-Hill, 1942. 405 pp.

Reports from teachers in 23 representative high schools on programs in foreign languages and foreign culture, edited and evaluated by three Stanford University professors of education. Includes specimen teaching materials, curricula, tests, and bibliography.

1660. KELLY, ROBERT LINCOLN. *The American Colleges and the Social Order.* New York: Macmillan, 1940. 380 pp.

By Executive Director, Association of American Colleges, 1917-37. Bibliography, pp. 347-69.

1661. KING, BEATRICE. *Changing Man: The Education System of the U.S.S.R.* New York: Viking, 1937. London: Gollancz, 1936. 319 pp.

Impressions of a British educator who claims "a fluent knowledge of the language," and who has traveled extensively in the U.S.S.R.

1662. KING-HALL, STEPHEN. *Chatham House: A Brief Account of the Origins, Purposes and Methods of the Royal Institute of International Affairs.* New York and London: Oxford University, 1937. 144 pp.

Published under the auspices of the Institute's Endowment Committee, of which the author is chairman.

1663. KNELLER, GEORGE FREDERICK. *The Educational Philosophy of National Socialism* (Ph.D. thesis, education, Yale). New Haven: Yale University, 1941. 299 pp.

Study of the educational system and theories of Nazi Germany. Bibliography, pp. 257-84.

1664. KOON, CLINE MORGAN. *Sources of Visual Aids and Equipment for Instructional Use in Schools* (U.S. Office of Education Pamphlet no. 80). Washington, D.C.: Government Printing Office, 1937. 44 pp.

A fairly comprehensive list of U.S. distributors of objects, specimens, models, pictures, photographs, maps, charts, slides, film strips, movies, etc. Also contains a list of composite lists of educational films.

1665. KOON, CLINE MORGAN; and NOBLE, ALLEN W. *National Visual Education Directory: A List by States of 8,806 School Systems, Including an Inventory of Audio-Visual Equipment.* Washington, D.C.: American Council on Education, 1936. 269 pp.

Approximately 17,000,000 students attend the elementary and secondary schools covered by this study.

1666. KOTINSKY, RUTH. *Adult Education Councils* (Studies in the Social Significance of Adult Education, no. 20). New York: American Association for Adult Education, 1940. 172 pp.

By a U.S. specialist in educational research (Ph.D. Teachers College, Columbia).

1667. KOTINSKY, RUTH. *Elementary Education of Adults: A Critical Interpretation* (Studies in the Social Significance of Adult Education in the United States, no. 26). New York: American Association for Adult Education, 1941. 205 pp.

1668. KOTSCHNIG, WALTER MARIA. "Educating the Élite in Europe," *Journal of Educational Sociology,* 13: 70-81 (October 1939).

Compares secondary and college curricula of England, France, Germany and U.S., emphasizing growth of secondary curricula diversified to produce "several élites," each skilled for its particular function in society.

1669. KRIECK, ERNST. *Nationalpolitische Erziehung,* 20th ed. Leipzig: Armanen, 1936. 186 pp.

"National Political Education." An officially approved statement on Nazi education.

1669a. LEAGUE OF NATIONS ASSOCIATION OF JAPAN. NATIONAL COMMITTEE ON INTELLECTUAL COOPERATION. *Academic and Cultural Organizations in Japan.* Tokyo: Kokusai Bunka Shinkokai (Society for International Cultural Relations), 1939. 527 pp.

"This is believed to be the first English publication of the kind in Japan. . . . The compilation has been arranged primarily for the convenience of foreigners, while titles, addresses, and an index in Japanese have been added for the Japanese users. This handbook comprises about 600 organizations, such as the principal academic and cultural organizations, the universities and the special colleges as at about the end of 1938." *Data given*: Address; Officers' names; Year of establishment; Membership; Object; Activities; Finances; Publications; Facilities accorded to foreigners.

1670. LEARNED, WILLIAM SETCHEL; and WOOD, BEN D. *The Student and His Knowledge.* New York: Carnegie Foundation, 1938. 69 pp.

Summarizes the results and conclusions drawn from a 10-year study of the relations of higher and secondary education in Pennsylvania. 55,000 individuals were tested by means of an "objective-type inventory of the baccalaureate mind."

1670a. LEDERER, MAX. *Secondary Education in Austria, 1918-38* (U.S. Office of Education Bulletin, 1941, no. 9). Washington, D.C.: Government Printing Office, 1941. 41 pp.

The "democratic" period of Austrian education. "The author was an Austrian secondary school teacher from 1906-1920 and a *Hofrat* concerned with secondary education in the pedagogical division of the Federal Ministry of Education at Vienna from 1920 to 1938." —Introduction.

1671. LEMAN, GRANT WILLIAM. *Visual Aids in Education: A Syllabus for Use in Classes in Schools and Colleges of Education.* Paterson, N.J.: State Teachers College, 1941. 75 pp.

The New Jersey State Committee for the Improvement of Visual Instruction assisted Dr. Leman in planning and formulating this syllabus.

1672. LINDEGREN, ALINA MARIE. *Education in Germany* (U.S. Office of Education Bulletin, 1938, no. 15). Washington, D.C.: Government Printing Office, 1939. 145 pp.

Bibliography, pp. 143-45.

1673. LIN, MOUSHENG HSITIEN. *A Guide to Chinese Learned Societies and Research Institutes.* New York: China Institute in America, 1936. 48 pp.

Data on organizational forms, activities, and publications of 286 learned societies and research institutes, not including colleges and universities, libraries, and museums.

1674. *A List of Free and Inexpensive Teaching Materials* (W.P.A. Technical Series, Community Service Circular no. 8, Education Circular no. 3). Washington, D.C.: Educational and Training Section, Division of Professional and Service Projects, Works Progress Administration, 1940. 131 pp., mimeo.

"Bibliography of free and low-cost pamphlets, booklets and visual aids for use in adult education classes. Includes sections on consumer education and other related fields."

1675. LOVEJOY, CLARENCE EARLE. *So You're Going to College,* including *The Lovejoy College Rating Guide.* New York: Simon and Schuster, 1940. 384 pp.

Data on U.S. colleges, including cost, endowment per student, size of library, number of scholarships, proportion of self-supporting students, financial aids for students, numbers of Ph.D.'s, numbers of alumni in *Who's Who*; compiled by Columbia University's Alumni Secretary. Bibliography, pp. 341-51.

1676. LOWNDES, GEORGE ALFRED NORMAN. *The Silent Social Revolution: An Account of Expansion of Public Education in England and Wales, 1895-1935.* New York: Oxford University, 1937. 274 pp.

Bibliography, pp. 249-60.

1677. LUND, RAGNAR. "Adult Education in Sweden," *Annals of the American Academy of Political and Social Science*, 197: 232-42 (May 1938).

1678. LYND, ROBERT STAUGHTON. *Knowledge for What?: The Place of Social Science in American Culture.* Princeton: Princeton University, 1939. 268 pp.

Columbia sociologist, coauthor of the well-known *Middletown* studies, advises social scientists to "take sides" in molding opinion favorable to peace and democracy.

1679. McKOWN, HARRY CHARLES; and ROBERTS, ALVIN B. *Audio-Visual Aids to Instruction.* New York: McGraw-Hill, 1940. 385 pp.

Principles and techniques of use of pictures, models, strip film, sound equipment, field trips, etc., described by two specialists. "Sources of Materials and Equipment" are discussed in Chapter 16. Bibliography at ends of chapters.

***1680.** MACK, EDWARD CLARENCE (D). *Public Schools and British Opinion since 1860: The Relationship Between Contemporary Ideas and the Evolution of an English Institution.* New York: Columbia University, 1941. 511 pp.

Analysis of the nearly fatal narrowing of the focus of attention of a ruling class, due largely to an irrelevant school system. This is the second half of a study, of which the first half appeared under the title, *Public Schools and British Opinion, 1780 to 1860* (Ph.D. thesis, philosophy, Columbia). (London: Methuen 1938. U.S. edition, 1939. 432 pp. Bibliography, pp. 405-22.) Method used in both volumes: "I have recorded, in historical periods, the ideas of a large proportion of those who have expressed themselves on the subject of public school education, and have classified these ideas into significant groups. Further, I have attempted to understand the quality of the emotional relationship of the writer to the system. . . . Finally, I have tried to analyze the more obvious psychological, economic, or other motives that underlay the ideas and attitudes." Conclusions of this monumental and heavily documented study: "In 1919 the world was crying for a new order of things, but the public schools, clinging to a tradition . . . not only failed to provide the leaders necessary to make that new order, but stood squarely in the way of its realization. Though many others must share the responsibility for social and political failure, the conclusion is irresistible that, had the public school actually produced real social sympathy among its graduates there would have been more unity in the nation and fewer men in high places willing to sacrifice Spain, Czechoslovakia, France, and ossibly the empire, rather than face the possibility of social progress at home. As Garratt wrote, the greatest ally of the Fascist has been 'the snobbishness which corrupts so much of England's life,' and that snobbishness . . . was to a large extent bred by the public schools. . . . Even this, however, is not the whole indictment. To making a new world, here was at least a conceivable alternative: reparing to save this one. But the upper lasses and the public schools, preferring to ompromise with rather than to defy liberalm, were equally unwilling to create leaders apable of meeting the challenge of barbarism which their own policies had in the past voked." By an instructor in English, College f the City of New York. Bibliography, pp. 67-85.

1681. MARRARO, HOWARD ROSARIO. *The New Education in Italy*. New York: S. F. Vanni, 1936. 506 pp.

By a Columbia University professor of Italian Literature. Published under the auspices of the Italian Historical Society, this is a general survey of Italian educational theory nd practice, largely superseding the author's *Nationalism in Italian Education* (1927). Bibliography, pp. 467-506.

1682. MARSH, CLARENCE STEPHEN, editor. *American Universities and Colleges*, 4th ed. Washington, D.C.: American Council on Education, 1940. 1120 p.

Standard handbook of factual information. Has appeared every four years since 1928.

1683. MAYHEW, ARTHUR. *Education in the Colonial Empire*. New York and London: Longmans, Green, 1938. 291 pp.

Evolution of educational policy in the British empire.

*1683a. MERRIAM, CHARLES EDWARD (D,W). *The Making of Citizens: A Comparative Study of Methods of Civic Training*. Chicago: University of Chicago, 1931. 371 pp.

University of Chicago political scientist summarizes the nine volumes of the *Civic Training Series*, dealing with the problem of civic education, the social composition of civic cohesion, and a comparison of techniques of civic training. Bibliographic footnotes.

1684. MILES, J. ROBERT. "Radio and Elementary Science Teaching: Ohio State University's Evaluation of School Broadcasts," *Journal of Applied Psychology*, 24: 714-20 (December 1940).

1685. MOEHLMAN, ARTHUR BERNARD. *Social Interpretation: Principles and Practices of Community and Public School Interpretation*. New York and London: Appleton-Century, 1938. 485 pp.

Treatise on public relations of public schools by Professor of School Administration and Supervision, University of Michigan, who is editor of *The Nation's Schools*. Bibliography, pp. 461-78.

1686. MORT, PAUL R. *Federal Support for Public Education*. New York: Columbia University, 1936. 350 pp.

Educational deficits of states, studied under the general supervision of the Columbia University Council for Research in the Social Sciences.

1687. MORT, PAUL R.; and CORNELL, FRANCIS GRIFFITH. *American Schools in Transition: How Our Schools Adapt Their Practices to Changing Needs: A Study of Pennsylvania*. New York: Teachers College, Columbia University, 1941. 546 pp.

Two Columbia University professors of education analyze factors affecting the diffusion of nine innovations "generally accepted as desirable": kindergarten, adult leisure activities, classes for mentally handicapped, etc. Bibliographic footnotes.

1688. NATIONAL COUNCIL FOR THE SOCIAL STUDIES. *Yearbook*. Philadelphia, 1931–.

Organized in 1921, the Council is the Department of Social Studies of the National Education Association. Its *Yearbooks* are devoted to symposia of specialists in civic training. The 1937 *Yearbook* is on "Education against Propaganda: Developing Skill in the Use of Sources of Information about Public Affairs." See also its *Publications* series, *Curriculum* series, and *Bulletins*, many of which deal with the content of civic training programs and with measurement of students' predisposition and response.

The Council also publishes two journals for teachers: *Social Education* (Crawfordsville, Indiana, 1937–; published jointly with American Historical Association) and *Social Studies* (Philadelphia, 1909–; formerly entitled *History Teacher's Magazine* [1909-18] and *Historical Outlook* [1918-33]).

1689. NATIONAL EDUCATION ASSOCIATION. EDUCATIONAL POLICIES COMMISSION. *A Bibliography on Education in the Depression.* Washington, D.C., 1937. 118 pp.

1690. NATIONAL EDUCATION ASSOCIATION. EDUCATIONAL POLICIES COMMISSION. *Learning the Ways of Democracy: A Case Book of Civic Education.* Washington, D.C., 1940. 486 pp.

1691. NATIONAL EDUCATION ASSOCIATION. EDUCATIONAL POLICIES COMMISSION. *The Purposes of Education in American Democracy.* Washington, D.C., 1938. 157 pp.

Official formulation of objectives by important committee of the largest U.S. professional association in the field of education.

1692. *The Nazi Primer: Official Handbook for Schooling the Hitler Youth,* translated by Harwood Lawrence Childs, commentary by William E. Dodd. New York: Harpers, 1938. 280 pp.

Indicates doctrines being taught to German youth.

1693. NEW YORK CITY. BOARD OF EDUCATION. *Men and Women at School: An Interim Report on Adult Education.* New York, 1936. 361 pp.

A special report submitted with the 37th Annual Report of the New York City Superintendent of Schools. "A complete account of what is being done in the field of Adult Education in the City of New York." Pp. 271-79 discuss the publicity for these services.

1694. NORTON, JOHN KELLEY; and NORTON, MARGARET ALLTUCKER. *Wealth, Children and Education,* 2nd ed. New York: Teachers College, 1938. 138 pp.

Teachers College professors analyze inequalities in educational opportunity in the U.S., citing studies of Moulton, Loeb, Nourse, Mort, Strayer and Haig, and others to show that inequality is unnecessary. Includes a plan of federal assistance to the states, without centralized control.

1695. PINKEVICH, ALBERT PETROVICH. *Science and Education in the U.S.S.R.* London: Gollancz, 1935. New York: Putnam's Sons, 1935. 176 pp.

Standard Soviet teacher-training text.

1696. PINKEVICH, ALBERT PETROVICH. *The New Education in the Soviet Republic,* translated under auspices of International Institute, Teachers College, by Nucia Perlmutter; introduction by George Sylvester Counts. New York: John Day, 1929. 403 pp.

Standard treatise by prominent Soviet professor of education.

1697. PROCTOR, WILLIAM MARTIN, compiler. *Annotated Bibliography on Adult Education.* New York: American Association for Adult Education, 1934. 124 pp.

Lists 839 titles, extensively annotated.

1698. RAUP, (ROBERT) BRUCE. *Education and Organized Interests in America.* New York: Putnam's Sons, 1936. 238 pp.

A study of the efforts of 88 organized pressure-groups to influence the classroom. By a Teachers College professor of education. Based on the work of the Commission on the Social Studies of the American Historical Association. Contains extended quotations from the platforms and declarations of the pressure-groups concerned, and charts indicating their attitudes on a number of issues.

1699. ROPE, FREDERICK T. *Opinion Conflict and School Support* (Ph.D. thesis; Teachers College Contributions to Education, no. 838). New York: Teachers College, Columbia University, 1941. 164 pp.

Considers public opinion as a force affecting education, summarizes research methods, and, by describing a study conducted in Pittsburgh, shows how public relations officers of public schools may use the techniques of opinion polling. Bibliography, pp. 149-53.

1700. ROUCEK, JOSEPH SLABEY; and associates. *Sociological Foundations of Education: A Textbook in Educational Sociology.* New York: Crowell, 1942. 771 pp.

By a score of U.S. professors. Bibliographic footnotes.

1701. RUSSELL, JOHN DALE; and associates. *Vocational Education* (U.S. Advisory Committee on Education, Staff study no. 8). Washington, D.C.: Government Printing Office, 1938. 325 pp.

A "critique and evaluation of the federally reimbursed program of vocational education, the place of vocational education in modern society, and the place of the Federal Government in vocational education in America." An appendix deals with the experience of organized labor with trade and industrial education. Includes texts of the principal Federal statutes in force regarding vocational education grants to States.

1702. SALVEMINI, GAETANO. "The Teachers' Oath in Italy," *Harvard Educational Review*, 7: 523-36 (October 1937).

Ex-Italian historian describes the purge of teachers and professors unsympathetic to the government; Ministry of Education control of all publications by teachers; military service required of university professors.

1703. SAMPER-ORTEGA, DANIEL. "Mass Education in Colombia," *Quarterly Journal of Inter-American Relations*, 1:71-76 (April 1939).

By Counselor of Colombian Embassy, Washington.

1704. SÁNCHEZ, GEORGE I. *Mexico: A Revolution by Education.* New York: Viking, 1936. 211 pp.

Civic training in Mexico. A study made under the auspices of the Rosenwald Fund by a New Mexican specialist in educational research.

1705. SCHNEIDER, FLORENCE HEMLEY. *Patterns of Workers' Education: The Story of the Bryn Mawr Summer School*, introduction by Hilda

W. Smith. Washington, D.C.: American Council on Public Affairs, 1941. 158 pp.

Plutocratic women's college makes its campus available, in summer, for women factory workers, "many of them deprived through economic circumstances of any schooling beyond the most elementary grades." This study analyzes experiences of the school and its impact in the trade union movement and elsewhere. Bibliography on workers' education, pp. 149-53.

1706. SEASHORE, CARL EMIL. *The Junior College Movement.* New York: Henry Holt, 1940. 160 pp.

Evaluation of the movement in nontechnical language. By Dean Emeritus, State University of Iowa. Bibliographic footnotes.

1707. SMITH, HENRY LESTER. *Comparative Education.* Bloomington, Ind.: Educational Publications, 1941. 529 pp.

By Dean of University of Indiana School of Education. Bibliography at ends of chapters.

*1708. SMITH, PAYSON (W); WRIGHT, FRANK WATSON; and associates. *Education in the Forty-Eight States* (U.S. Advisory Committee on Education, Staff Study no. 1). Washington, D.C.: Government Printing Office, 1939. 199 pp.

The panorama of American education at all levels from kindergarten to the graduate school and adult education. Historical sketch of the century 1830-1930, and a look at the future. Statistics of enrollments and institutions at all levels. The curriculum, health education, teaching service, and the school plant. Education for children in rural areas, for Negroes, and for handicapped children.

1709. *Social Research*, vol. 4 no. 3 (September 1937).

In a series of discussions held in April 1937, the Graduate Faculty of Political and Social Science ("University in Exile") at the New School for Social Research, together with some of their colleagues from other schools, took stock of themselves. The discussions, printed in this issue of *Social Research*, deal with: (1) the general nature of "intellectual freedom" and "intellectual responsibility"; (2) the interrelations of cultures and the influence of the exiled intellectual; (3) surveys of the educational systems of Germany, Great Britain, Italy, U.S.A., and U.S.S.R.

1710. SOLIS-COHEN, ROSEBUD LOTTA TESCHNER. *A Comparative Study of the History Program in English and American Secondary Schools* (Ph.D. thesis, Pennsylvania). Philadelphia: The author, 1939. 198 pp.

1711. STUDEBAKER, JOHN WARD; and WILLIAMS, CHESTER S. *Forum Planning Handbook: How to Organize School Administered Forums, Prepared for Study and Discussion for Planning Groups of Educators and Civic Leaders.* Washington, D.C.: American Association for Adult Education and Office of Education of U.S. Department of the Interior, 1939. 71 pp.

By two officials of U.S. Office of Education. Includes a survey of U.S. forum demonstrations and projects. Select bibliography, pp. 69-71.

1712. SWIFT, FLETCHER HARPER. *European Policies of Financing Public Educational Institutions* (University of California Publications in Education, vol. 8). Berkeley: University of California, 1939. 5 parts.

Covers France, Czechoslovakia, Austria, Germany, England, Wales. The author is a specialist in public school finance.

1713. TOWNSEND, MARY EVELYN; and STEWART, ALICE GERTRUDE. *Audio-Visual Aids for Teachers in Junior and Senior High Schools, Junior Colleges, and Adult Education Classes* (Social Science Service Series, no. 2). New York: Wilson, 1937. 131 pp.

A guide to atlases, maps, charts, pictures, posters, slides, motion pictures, and other illustrative materials of use to social science teachers.

*1714. U.S. ADVISORY COMMITTEE ON EDUCATION. *Report of the Committee.* Washington, D.C.: Government Printing Office, 1938. 243 pp.

Report and recommendations of an Advisory Committee appointed by President Roosevelt to give "extended consideration to the whole subject of Federal relationship to State and local conduct of education." Contains many charts and tables dealing with public support of education in the U.S. Recommends a new Federal aid program for elementary and secondary schools and for youth-serving agencies.

*1715. U.S. ADVISORY COMMITTEE ON EDUCATION.

Publication of the 19 staff studies of the Advisory Committee on Education is now completed. They constitute "a library on many of the most important topics in education for the modest sum of $4.80."

1716. U.S. NATIONAL RESOURCES COMMITTEE. *Research: A National Resource* (Report of the Science Committee). Washington, D.C.: Government Printing Office, 1938. 255 pp.

The Federal Government spent $120,000,000 on research in 1937, of which $50,000,000 went to social sciences and social statistics. Report deals with some 125 federal agencies engaged in research, and has brief sections on university, state government, and private activities.

1717. U.S. OFFICE OF EDUCATION. *To Promote the Cause of Education* (Bulletin, 1938, Misc. No. 2). Washington, D.C.: Government Printing Office, 1938. 80 pp.

Pictures and charts dealing comprehensively with the objectives, methods, and services of the U.S. Office of Education. Published originally as February 1938 issue of *School Life*, the Office's official organ.

1718. UNIVERSITY OF THE STATE OF NEW YORK. REGENTS' INQUIRY OF CHARACTER AND COST OF EDUCATION IN THE STATE OF NEW YORK. *Education for American Life: A New Program for the State of New York.* New York: McGraw-Hill, 1938. 167 pp.

General report of the 10-volume study recently completed by this influential group of educators.

1719. WALTERS, RAYMOND. "Recent Trends in Collegiate Enrollment," *School and Society,* 50: 321-33 (September 9, 1939).

Statistics covering the period from 1930 through 1938, compiled from attendance records of 355 approved institutions. Dr. Walters, President of University of Cincinnati, interprets the fluctuations in terms of business depression and of population trends, and describes the effects of financial aid from the National Youth Administration. Tables summarize enrollments according to types of institutions, geographical distribution, and freshman enrollment; also show public elementary and secondary school enrollment since 1930.

1720. WARE, EDITH ELLEN. *The Study of International Relations in the United States: Survey for 1937.* New York: Columbia University, 1938. 567 p.

Brings up to date this U.S. political historian's survey for 1934, covering foundations, institutes, councils, associations, religious groups, journals, conferences, forums, courses, seminars, research projects, etc.

1721. WATSON, GOODWIN BARBOUR. *How Good Are Our Colleges?* (Public Affairs Pamphlet, no. 26). New York: Public Affairs Committee, 1939. 31 pp.

By a Teachers College social psychologist. Based on Bulletin 29 of the Carnegie Foundation for the Advancement of Teaching (*The Student and His Knowledge*, by William Setchel Learned and Ben D. Wood), cited above, title 1670. Bibliography, p. 31.

1722. WILSON, IRMA. *Mexico: A Century of Educational Thought* (Ph.D. thesis, philosophy, Columbia). New York: Hispanic Institute in the United States, 435 West 117th Street, 1941. 576 pp.

Educational theory in Mexico from colonial days to 1910. By a U.S. educator. Bibliography, pp. 335-61.

1723. WOODYARD, ELLA. *Culture at a Price: A Study of Private Correspondence School Offerings* (Studies in the Social Significance of Adult Education in the United States, no. 23). New York: American Association for Adult Education, 1940. 125 pp.

1724. WONG, PEARL H. "Mass Education in China," *Sociology and Social Research*, 22: 38-44 (September 1937).

Graphic description of government-sponsored adult education in Fukien.

1725. *Workers' Education: A Quarterly Journal of American Workers' Education.* New York, 1923-.

"Fifteenth Anniversary Issue" (vol. 13, no. 4, October 1936) contains history, chronology, and bibliography of Workers' Education Bureau of America, and evaluations of its work by such writers as Charles Austin Beard and Abraham Epstein.

1726. WORKS, GEORGE ALAN; and MORGAN, BARTON. *The Land-Grant Colleges* (U.S. Advisory Committee on Education, Staff Study no. 10). Washington, D.C.: Government Printing Office, 1939. 141 pp.

How the Federal Government subsidizes the 69 universities and colleges founded by the States in pursuance of the Morrill Act of 1862. Bibliographic footnotes.

1727. WASHBURNE, CARLETON WOLSEY. *A Living Philosophy of Education.* New York: John Day, 1940. 583 pp.

Comprehensive statement of experience and theories of President of Progressive Education Association. Includes views on physical and emotional development of the child; on mental hygiene, subject-matter fields, educational administration, practice and teaching of democracy, and personal habits of the teacher.

1728. ZIEMER, GREGOR ATHALWIN. *Education for Death.* New York: Oxford University, 1941. 208 pp.

Report on Hitlerite education. The author was for 11 years headmaster of the American Colony School (for children of U.S. parents) in Berlin, and remained in Germany until the outbreak of World War II. Bibliography, pp. 201-02.

2. PERSONNEL

1729. AGRESTI, OLIVIA ROSSETTI. *David Lubin: A Study in Practical Idealism,* 2nd ed. Berkeley, Calif.: University of California, 1941. 372 pp.

Biography of the founder of the International Institute of Agriculture. First edition: Boston: Little, Brown, 1922. 372 pp.

*1729a. ARNETT, CLAUDE ELIAS. *The Social Beliefs and Attitudes of American School Board Members* (Ph. D. thesis, Columbia). Emporia, Kansas: Emporia Gazette Press, 1932. 237 pp.

Sponsored by the American Historical Association's Commission on the Investigation of the Social Studies in the Schools. Bibliography, p. 235.

1730. BEELEY, ARTHUR L. "A Clinical Technique for the Selection of Prospective Teachers," *School and Society*, 50: 183-85 (August 5, 1939).

Advances reasons for selecting students for teacher training on the basis of personality. Procedures employed at the University of Utah include results of medical examinations, reports from the ortho-psychiatric clinic, intelligence test scores, college grades, and high school records.

1731. BEYLE, HERMAN CAREY. "Research Trends in Political Science," *Public Opinion Quarterly*, 1 no. 2: 87-92 (April 1937).

U.S. political scientist describes current focus of attention of political scientists, as shown by their professional journals and conventions.

1732. BORNEMANN, ALFRED. *J. Laurence Laughlin: Chapters in the Career of an Economist.* Washington, D.C.: American Council on Public Affairs, 1940. 97 pp.

Biography of first head of Department of Political Economy, University of Chicago— an austere classicist. By economist, New York University. Bibliographic footnotes.

1733. BRINTON, CRANE. *Nietzsche.* Cambridge: Harvard University, 1941. 266 pp.

By Harvard historian. Bibliography, pp. 245-59.

1734. *Britain without Capitalists: A Study of What Industry in a Soviet Britain Could Achieve, By a Group of Economists, Scientists, and Technicians.* London: Lawrence and Wishart, 1936. 474 pp.

The authors are anonymous. Chapter 10, "Science and Education," deals with the recruitment and training of skilled scientific workers under capitalism, and proposes a plan for the reorganization of scientific training and of opportunities for publication.

1735. BUTLER, NICHOLAS MURRAY. *Across the Busy Years: Recollections and Reflections.* New York: Scribner's, 1940. 2 vols.

1735a. CENTRE D'ÉTUDES DE POLITIQUE ÉTRANGÈRE, GROUPE D'ÉTUDES DES SCIENCES SOCIALES. *Les sciences sociales en France: Enseignement et recherche.* Paris: Hartmann 1937. 379 pp.

Survey of the state of the social sciences in France by well-known scholars. Raymond Aron writes on sociology; Jean Meuvret, on history; Gérard Milhaud, on education; Roger Picard, on economics; A. Jordan, on political science; Jacques Lambert, on international relations; Henri Lemaître, on centers of documentation; and other writers cover human geography, ethnology, linguistics, folklore, sociology of religion, history of art, statistics, jurisprudence.

1736. CHUGERMAN, SAMUEL. *Lester F. Ward: The American Aristotle.* Durham, N.C.: Duke University, 1939. 591 pp.

Biographical materials on this well-known U.S. sociologist are included in this extensive critique of his theories. Bibliography, pp. 559-60.

1737. COLE, LUELLA WINIFRED. *The Background for College Teaching.* New York: Farrar and Rinehart, 1940. 616 pp.

Study of college life, college students, and college instruction for prospective teachers. Includes statistical data on college populations, curricula, teaching loads, economic conditions, etc., and analysis of teachers, students, procedures, and social-economic consequences of higher education. Heavily documented. Bibliographic footnotes.

1738. COULBOURN, JOHN. *Selection of Teachers in Large City School Systems* (Teachers College Contributions to Education, no. 740). New York: Columbia University, 1938. 177 pp.

"Endeavors to present a comprehensive survey of practices in the largest [U.S.] cities in the field of teacher selection, project these practices in the light of basic criteria, and recommend standards." Bibliography, pp. 175-77.

*1739. CURTI, MERLE EUGENE (D, W). *The Social Ideas of American Educators* (Report of the Commission on the Social Studies of the American Historical Association, part 10). New York: Scribner's, 1935. 613 pp.

U.S. historian's description of attitudes toward nationalism and internationalism, war, peace, and patriotism, the wealthy and the underprivileged, among educators in the fields of primary and secondary education. Bibliography, pp. 593-600.

1740. *Directory of American Scholars,* edited by Jaques Cattell. Lancaster, Pennsylvania: Science Press, 1942. 928 pp.

A biographical directory of several thousand scholars in the humanities and social sciences. The first such directory to appear in the U.S.

*1741. DONOVAN, FRANCES R. *The Schoolma'am.* New York: Stokes, 1942. 356 pp.

Study of the 853,967 U.S. schoolma'ams. Includes material on teachers' social characteristics, incomes, professional standards, professional organizations, and tenure, and on "The Schoolma'am of Tomorrow," whose training, it is said, "will include, besides her special interest, psychology, sociology and psychiatry, as well as economics and civics. She will be a highly skilled person. . . ." Based on the author's twenty years as a teacher and as manager in a large teachers' agency. Bibliography at ends of chapters.

1742. ELDRED, LEWIS. "Traits of a Group of Prospective Teachers," *School and Society,* 50: 477-80 (October 7, 1939).

In 1937 the author conducted a study of the 127 Cornell graduates of the years 1935, 1936, and 1937 who were preparing for secondary school teaching. Their ages ranged from 19 to 26 years. Data on home backgrounds indicate a rather privileged group; their high school records reveal high scholastic rank; and their college rating is above the university average.

1743. ELSBREE, WILLARD SLINGERLAND. *The American Teacher: Evolution of a Profession in a Democracy.* New York: American Book Company, 1939. 566 pp.

Nationwide survey of U.S. teachers from colonial times to 1937, by Teachers College Professor of Education. Chapter 34 is on "Public Attitude toward the Teaching Profession"; chapter 35 on "Social Composition of the Teaching Population." Bibliography at ends of chapters.

1744. FISHER, HERBERT ALBERT LAURENS. *An Unfinished Autobiography.* New York: Oxford University, 1941. 163 pp.

The author was an historian and liberal statesman, warden of New College, Oxford, and highly influential in setting up Britain's present public educational system.

1745. FREDERIC, KATHERINE AMELIA. *State Personnel Administration: With Special Reference to Departments of Education* (U.S. Advisory Committee on Education, Staff Study no. 3). Washington, D.C.: Government Printing Office, 1940. 271 pp.

"The first extensive study of personnel administration for key units in the educational system, the 48 State departments of education. An up-to-date summary of general provisions for State government personnel administration. New data on the qualifications, experience, salaries, selection, and tenure of chief State school officers and their staffs. Suggestions for improving the adequacy of personnel."

1746. GREENHOE, FLORENCE GRACE. *Community Contacts and Participation of Teachers: An Analysis of the Community Relationships of 9,122 Public School Teachers Selected as a National Sample.* Washington, D.C.: American Council on Public Affairs, 1941. 91 pp.

Bibliography, pp. 90-91.

1747. GUMBEL, E. J., editor. *Freie Wissenschaft: Ein Sammelbuch aus der deutschen Emigration.* Strasbourg: Sebastian Brandt, 1938. 283 pp.

Symposium by eminent German scientists now outside Germany. See especially Theodor Geiger on the coming tasks of the intellectual; Julius Lips on public opinion among the Indians of Labrador; Arthur Rosenberg on the task of the emigrant historian.

1748. GUNDLACH, RALPH H. "The Psychologists' Understanding of Social Issues," *Psychological Bulletin*, 37: 613-20 (October 1940).

"For nearly ten years we have suffered through a national social and economic crisis; yet, from an examination of our professional journals and the programs of our professional meetings, one might conclude that psychologists were oblivious of the fact that our social institutions are rattling about our ears." A questionnaire study was made among members and associates of American Psychological Association and among University of California students. The questions measured attitudes toward "items of general social significance." *Conclusions*: (1) In every case, a plurality or a majority of psychologists select "liberal, progressive, democratic" answers. (2) Views of students differ considerably from those of psychologists, being less "liberal, progressive, democratic." (3) Intercorrelation shows that "apparently, the more fascistic ideas and attitudes one has, the less one recognizes them as fascistic." (4) If this questionnaire's outcome indicates the intentions of psychologists, "we can expect at least something of a shift in the emphasis in the teaching of psychology and in the press releases of the organizations of psychologists."

1749. HADDOW, ANNA. *Political Science in American Colleges and Universities, 1636-1900* (based on Ph.D. thesis, George Washington University), with introduction and supplementary chapter by William Anderson. New York: Appleton-Century, 1939. 308 pp.

U.S. specialist in educational research tells who the political scientists were, "what courses they offered, what books they used, what ideas influenced them, what things each one particularly emphasized in his work, how the teaching changed from time to time, and how political science finally became disentangled from . . . other subjects. . . ." A chapter by William Anderson, Professor of Political Science, University of Minnesota, deals with the period since 1900, concluding that "American political science today is a long step ahead of where

it stood even a generation after the Civil War" (p. 266). Bibliography, pp. 269-96.

1750. HARTSHORNE, EDWARD YARNALL. "Metabolism Indices and the Annexation of Austria: A Note on Method," *American Journal of Sociology*, 45: 899-917 (May 1940).

U.S. sociologist describes University of Vienna faculties before and during the process of Nazification. In the course of the first year, 49.5 per cent of the faculty were dropped, according to data obtained by comparing faculty lists in successive University of Vienna catalogues.

★1751. HERZBERG, ALEXANDER. *Psychology of Philosophers*. New York: Harcourt, Brace, 1929. 228 pp.

German philosopher's study of private lives of 30 world-famous philosophers, using psychoanalytic concepts. See especially pp. 175-90, which state concisely the findings and interpretations. Bibliography, pp. 223-25.

1752. HOBSON, JOHN ATKINSON. *Confessions of an Economic Heretic*. London: Allen and Unwin, 1938. New York: Macmillan, 1938. 217 pp.

Autobiography of well-known British economist.

1753. JANDY, EDWARD D. *Charles Horton Cooley: His Life and His Social Theory*. New York: Dryden, 1942. 319 pp.

Biography of well-known U.S. sociologist. By Wayne University sociologist. Dr. Jandy had complete access to Cooley's records, files, correspondence, "Journals" (covering 46 years), and library. Bibliography, pp. 270-310.

1754. KENNEDY, MILLARD FILLMORE; and HARLOW, ALVIN F. *Schoolmaster of Yesterday: A Three-Generation Story*. New York: Whittlesey House, 1940. 359 pp.

Biography of a dynasty of Indiana school teachers.

1755. KOTSCHNIG, WALTER MARIA. *Unemployment in the Learned Professions: An International Study of Occupational and Educational Planning.*

London: Oxford University, 1937. 347 pp.

World survey of the employment conditions affecting intellectuals, begun by the International Student Service at Geneva in 1932 and completed with the assistance of the International Institute of Teachers College, Columbia University. Bibliographic footnotes.

1755a. *Leaders in Education: A Biographical Directory*, 2nd ed., edited by James McKeen Cattell, Jaques Cattell and E. E. Ross. Lancaster, Pennsylvania: Science Press, 1941. 1134 pp.

A Who's Who of "those in North America who have done the most to advance education, whether by teaching, administration, publication or research . . . the first edition of *Leaders in Education,* published nine years ago, contained about 11,000 names. The present edition contains about 17,500 names and most of the biographical sketches in the first edition have been revised."

1756. LEAGUE OF NATIONS. HIGH COMMISSION FOR REFUGEES (JEWISH AND OTHER) COMING FROM GERMANY. *A Crisis in the University World.* London, 1935.

Record of the work of organizations dealing with problems of refugee scholars.

1757. LASSWELL, HAROLD DWIGHT. "What Psychiatrists and Political Scientists Can Learn from One Another," *Psychiatry*, 1: 33-39 (February 1938).

1758. MENDIETA Y NÚÑEZ, LUCIO. "The Integration of Social Research in the Americas," *American Sociological Review*, 7: 166-75 (April 1942).

Reviews focus of attention of Western Hemisphere sociologists, and suggests creation of an Inter-American Sociological Society. Outlines program for such a Society. The author is Director of the Institute for Social Research at the National University of Mexico, and editor of the *Revista Mexicana de Sociología.*

1759. MEYER, ADOLPHE E. *Modern European Educators and Their Work.* New York: Prentice-Hall, 1934. 241 pp.

By New York University professor of education. Bibliography, pp. 231-36.

1760. MYERS, ROBERT C. "Some Notes on the 1942 Membership of the American Sociological Society," *American Sociological Review*, 8: 203-06 (April 1943).

Questionnaire answered by 310 out of 926 members (1942) of the Society. Covers age; sex; residence; occupation; country of birth of self, father, mother; father's occupation; subject's teaching experience, honors, degrees.

1761. NATIONAL COUNCIL FOR THE SOCIAL STUDIES. *In-Service Growth of Social Studies Teachers* (10th *Yearbook* of the Council), edited by Burr W. Phillips. Cambridge, Massachusetts, 1939. 187 pp.

Nine essays by educators on means of aiding the personal and intellectual development of social studies teachers. Bibliographic footnotes.

1762. ODEGARD, PETER H. "The Political Scientist in the Democratic Service State," *Journal of Politics*, 2: 140-64 (May 1940).

By U.S. political scientist.

1763. OVERSTREET, HARRY ALLEN; and OVERSTREET, BONARO WILKINSON. *Leaders for Adult Education* (Studies in the Social Significance of Adult Education in the United States, no. 24). New York: American Association for Adult Education, 1941. 202 pp.

1764. QUEEN, STUART ALFRED. "Can Sociologists Face Reality?" *American Sociological Review*, 7: 1-12 (February 1942).

President of American Sociological Society reviews certain indicators of foci of attention of sociologists during the past quarter of a century. In the earlier period, "On the whole, papers were of a general nature, idealistic in tone, hortatory in purpose. . . . The 1939 and 1940 programs of our Society showed no concentration of attention upon any particular subject. The 1941 program looks much the same. . . ." However, there seems to be a mild trend toward integration and activism.

1765. REED, THOMAS HARRISON. "Report of the Committee on Policy of the American Political Science Association for the Year 1935," *American Political Science Review*, 30: 142-65 (February 1936).

Public-relations activities of an academic group. See especially the work of the Subcommittee on Political Education through "conferences, meeting privately and without publicity, resolutions, or action of any kind, in which academic political scientists" are "brought directly in contact with men in public office and with laymen active in political affairs." This report also gives details of the "You and Your Government" series of broadcasts (adult civic training).

1766. RESNICK, LOUIS. "Social Work Interpreters of the Future: Where Will They Come From?" *The Compass* (organ of American Association of Social Workers), 19 no. 5: 10-13 ff. (February 1938).

Clear-cut analysis by director of Social Security Board's Informational Service. Discusses educational background and work experience of efficient publicity writers; U.S. Civil Service Commission standards for Informational Service Representatives; different types of personnel required for money-raising campaigns as contrasted with public information services; etc.

1767. SALOMON, ALICE. *Education for Social Work: A Sociological Interpretation Based on an International Survey.* Zurich: Verlag für Recht und Gesellschaft, 1937. 265 pp.

Evaluates the achievements and psychology of this profession in practically all of the civilized countries except U.S.S.R., on the basis of the author's careful investigation of some 250 institutions in more than 30 countries. Bibliography, pp. v-vi.

1768. *Selective Admission of Prospective Teachers* (Research Studies in Admission, no. 1). Detroit: Wayne University, College of Education, 1939. 157 pp.

Handbook based on procedures and testing techniques applied to 1620 candidates for admission to the College of Education of Wayne University, February 1936 to June 1938. Of the total number 789 students were unconditionally accepted, 515 were conditionally accepted, and 316 were denied admission. Eighty-

five tables classify these three groups according to such categories as birthplace, family background, age, marital status, high school record, personality and achievement tests, health, extra-curricular program, self-support, vocational preference, college preference, college scholarship, and faculty ratings.

1769. SIMS, LEWIS B. "Social Scientists in the Federal Service," in *Public Policy* (first *Yearbook* of Harvard Graduate School of Public Administration, 1940, edited by Carl Joachim Friedrich and Edward S. Mason), pp. 280-97.

Job opportunities for social scientists, described by U.S. Census official. See also the author's "The Social Science Analyst Examinations," *American Political Science Review*, 33: 441-50 (June 1939).

1770. SULLIVAN, JOHN CAVANAUGH. *A Study of the Social Attitudes and Information on Public Problems of Women Teachers in Secondary Schools* (Ph.D. thesis; Teachers College Contributions to Education, no. 791). New York: Columbia University, 1940. 144 pp.

Bibliography, pp. 121-22.

1771. TAFT, HORACE DUTTON. *Memories and Opinions.* New York: Macmillan, 1942. 336 pp.

Autobiography of the founder of the Taft [private preparatory] School, a brother of the late President and Chief Justice Taft.

1772. U.S. WORKS PROGRESS ADMINISTRATION. *Government Aid During the Depression to Professional, Technical, and Other Service Workers.* Washington, D.C., 1936. 75 pp., reproduced from typewritten copy.

1773. WATTENBERG, WILLIAM W. *On the Educational Front: The Reactions of Teachers' Associations in New York and Chicago.* New York: Columbia University, 1936. 218 pp.

Carefully documented study prepared at Columbia University. Bibliography, pp. 209-10.

1774. (Pop.) WELLS, HERBERT GEORGE. *The Fate of Man.* New York: Alliance Book Corporation, 1939. 263 pp.

Mr. Wells, surveying world events anew, again recommends formation of a "World Brain"—the few thousand men with sufficient intelligence and integrity to rescue mankind from imminent catastrophe.

1775. (Pop.) WELLS, HERBERT GEORGE. *World Brain.* London: Methuen, 1938. New York: Doubleday, Doran, 1938. 130 pp.

A program for the organization of the world's intellectual resources. "The highly educated section, the finer minds of the human race are so dispersed, so ineffectively related to the common man, that they are powerless in the face of social and political adventurers of the coarsest sort. We want a reconditioned and more powerful Public Opinion . . . conscious of itself."

1776. WHITE, KENNETH B. "Selection of Prospective Teachers," *Educational Administration and Supervision,* 25: 120-26 (February 1939).

Discusses the trend toward professionalization of teaching, especially the idea that it is a privilege rather than a right to prepare for teaching. Explains the plan of selection in effect at the State Teachers College at Paterson, New Jersey.

1777. WILLIAMS, BLAINE T. *An Analysis of the Personnel of an Iowa School Board: A Study in Social Control* (M.A. thesis, sociology, Iowa, 1938).

***1778.** WILSON, LOGAN (D). *The Academic Man: A Study in the Sociology of a Profession.* New York and London: Oxford University, 1942. 248 pp.

By professor of sociology, Tulane University. Bibliographic footnotes.

1779. ZNANIECKI, FLORIAN. *The Social Role of the Man of Knowledge.* New York: Columbia University, 1940. 212 pp.

Broadly generalized statement by Polish sociologist now in U.S. Bibliographic footnotes.

3. QUANTITATIVE STUDIES OF AUDIENCES, COVERAGE AND EFFECTS

[See also Part 6.]

1780. BOLTON, FREDERICK ELMER; and CORBALLY, JOHN EDWARD. *Educational Sociology* (American Education Series). New York: American Book Co., 1941. 632 pp.

Introductory college textbook, by two University of Washington professors. Includes sections on U.S. Office of Education, National Education Association, press, motion pictures, radio, and certain effects of curricula on attitudes. Bibliography at ends of chapters.

1781. CHAMBERLIN, DEAN; CHAMBERLIN, ENID; DROUGHT, NEAL E.; and SCOTT, WILLIAM E. *Did They Succeed in College?: The Follow-up Study of the Graduates of the Thirty Schools* (Adventure in American Education, vol. 4), preface by Max McConn. New York: Harpers, 1942. 291 pp.

Comparative study of total college experience of 1475 matched pairs of students, half of whom graduated in 1936-39 from "conventional" high schools and half from the "Thirty Schools" which adopted special curricula drawn up by committees of Progressive Education Association. In college, the Thirty Schools' graduates made better grades, "were more often judged to be precise, systematic and objective in their thinking," showed more resourcefulness, took more part in extracurricular activities. The "more experimental" of the Thirty Schools had "strikingly" more successful graduates than the "less experimental." In general, "progressive education" is found to be vindicated in terms of the common-sense criteria used in this study. Evaluation schedules are reproduced in Appendix.

1782. DROSTE, EDWARD P.; and SEYFERT, WARREN CROCKER. "Attitudes and Activities of Graduates of a Military School," *School Review,* 49: 587-94 (October 1941).

Data from activities and from Thurstone-Droba Scale for Attitude toward War. "On the basis of the interpretations of scores developed by [Thurstone and Droba], less than one in nine among the graduates of this military school showed any degree of militarism in their point of view, and . . . even their militarism was of a very mild variety. . . . Both the mean and the median scores fall in the category entitled 'mildly pacifistic.' "

1783. FOSTER, ROBERT GEIB; and WILSON, PAULINE PARK. *Women After College: A Study of the Effectiveness of Their Education.* New York: Columbia University, 1942. 305 pp.

Analysis of case histories on careers and personality problems of 100 representative Detroit women who were college graduates, with some discussion of the role of the college in relation to their numerous neurotic difficulties. Bibliography of "related studies," pp. 273-75.

1784. HOBSON, C. V. "How Much Do Teachers Know About Mental Hygiene?" *Mental Hygiene*, 21: 231-42 (April 1937).

Supervisor of a state teachers' college reports on teachers' knowledge of "forty principles of mental hygiene" which are considered basic by a group of authorities in the field. This article contains a clear statement of a method for testing awareness of "the mental hygiene point of view," and also a concise statement of some "fundamental principles."

1785. ROGERS, AGNES. *Vassar Women: An Informal Study.* Poughkeepsie, N.Y.: Vassar Cooperative Bookstore, Vassar College, 1940. 223 pp.

Based on statistics relating to Vassar graduates for the past 75 years.

1786. THOMAS, M. E. "An Enquiry into the Relative Efficacy of Broadcast and Classroom Lessons," *Educational Research Series*, no. 48, pp. 1-48 (Melbourne, 1937).

IV. MOTION PICTURES AND THEATER

1. CONTROL, ORGANIZATION, EQUIPMENT

1787. AMERICAN COUNCIL ON EDUCATION. *The Other Americas through Films and Records*, 2nd ed. Washington, D.C., 1943. 48 pp.

Compilation of films and phonograph records available for classroom and other uses. Prepared in collaboration with Pan-American Union.

1788. AMERICAN COUNCIL ON EDUCATION. COMMITTEE ON MOTION PICTURES IN EDUCATION. Series of "Publications on Motion Pictures in Education." Washington, D.C., 1937–.

A series of books and brief monographs by educators and researchers. Representative titles: Vol. 1, no. 1: *The Motion Picture in Education: Its Status and Its Needs.* 24 pp. (Preliminary report of the Committee.) 1937. Vol. 1, no. 2: Dale, Edgar; and Ramseyer, Lloyd L. *Teaching with Motion Pictures: A Handbook of Administrative Practice.* 59 pp. 1937. Bibliography, pp. 58-59. Vol. 4, no. 3: *A School Uses Motion Pictures.* By the staff of the Tower Hill School. (This evaluation center report suggests means by which motion pictures can be adapted to the school curriculum.) 1940. Vol. 4, no. 4: Cochran, Blake. *Films on War and American Policy.* (Detailed descriptions of a selected group of films bearing upon war issues and American national defense.) 1940. 63 pp. Vol. 4, no. 5: Noel, Francis W. *Projecting Motion Pictures in the Classroom.* (Projecting the film, planning the projection room, selecting the projector, and other practical problems are discussed in this report based on the experience of public schools in Santa Barbara, Calif.) 1940. Vol. 5, no. 6: *Motion Pictures in a Modern Curriculum: A Report of Film Use in the Santa Barbara Schools.* 1941. Vol. 5, no. 7: *Students Make Motion Pictures.* (Tells how Denver high school students produced their own films and reports on their educational value.) 1941. Brooker, Floyde E.; Cochran, Blake; and Sackett, Robert S. *Selection, Use and Evaluation of Motion Pictures.* (Basic criteria that may be applied to the use of motion pictures in the school curriculum.) 1941. *Motion Pictures in the General College: A Research Report.* 1941.

1789. AMERICAN COUNCIL ON EDUCATION. COMMITTEE ON MOTION PICTURES IN EDUCATION. *Selected Educational Motion Pictures: A Descriptive Encyclopedia.* Washington, D.C., 1942. 372 pp.

Lists over 500 sixteen-millimeter films selected by cooperating schools and evaluation centers. Each film is described, and its purpose, source, and length are also indicated.

1790. BAIRD, THOMAS. "Films and the Public Services in Great Britain," *Public Opinion Quarterly*, 2: 96-99 (January 1938).

By a producer of documentaries, on the staff of the British General Post Office Film Unit, a celebrated agency in this field.

1791. BARDÈCHE, MAURICE; and BRASILLACH, ROBERT. *The History of Motion Pictures*, translated and edited by Iris Barry. New York: W. W. Norton and Museum of Modern Art, 1938. 412 pp.

A comprehensive treatise. Certain minor errors of fact were pointed out by Edward Wagenknecht in *New York Times Book Review*, May 15, 1938, p. 9. French edition: *Histoire du cinéma* (Paris: Denoël et Steel, 1935. 421 pp.).

1792. BELLING, CURT; and STRACHWITZ, CARL ERNST, GRAF VON. *Der Film in Staat und Partei*, with a foreword by Reichsamtleiter Carl Neumann. Berlin: Der Film, 1936. 143 pp.

Movies for government and party propaganda. Bibliography, p. 143.

1793. BERTRAND, DANIEL; EVANS, W. DUANE; and BLANCHARD, E. L. *The Motion Picture Industry: A Pattern of Control* (U.S. Temporary National Economic Committee, Investigation of Concentration of Economic Power, Monograph no. 43). Washington, D.C.: Government Printing Office, 1941. 92 pp.

Economics of the industry.

1794. BOWEN, CATHERINE DRINKER. "Ballet with Red Flags: 'Partisan Days,' the New Soviet Ballet," *Atlantic*, 161: 479-87 (April 1938).

Propaganda through revival of the romantic ballet tradition.

1795. BOX, SYDNEY. *Film Publicity: A Handbook on the Production and Distribution of Propaganda Films*. London: Lovat, Dickson, 1937. 143 pp.

A guide for the advertiser who is thinking of selling his wares with the help of the screen. The author is scenarist for a corporation which produces commercial advertising films. Contains a glossary of terms used in film production (pp. 123-42).

1796. BRUNSTETTER, MAX RUSSELL. *How to Use the Educational Sound Film*. Chicago: University of Chicago, 1937. 174 pp.

Both pedagogical and mechanical aspects of audio-visual education are explained in practical language for the use of teachers. Based on the author's researches under the auspices of Erpi Picture Consultants, Inc., a pioneer producer of educational films. Bibliography, pp. 108-09, 165, and in footnotes.

1797. CARTER, JEAN, compiler. *Annotated List of Labor Plays*. New York: Labor Education Service of Affiliated Schools for Workers, 1938. 36 pp.

1797a. CARTER, JEAN; and OGDEN, JESS. *Everyman's Drama: A Study of the Non-Commercial Theatre in the United States* (Studies in the Social Significance of Adult Education, no. 12). New York: American Association for Adult Education, 1938. 136 pp.

1798. COCHRAN, BLAKE. *Films on War and American Policy*. Washington, D.C.: American Council on Education, 1940. 63 pp.

1799. DALE, EDGAR. "Motion Picture Industry and Public Relations," *Public Opinion Quarterly*, 3: 251-62 (April 1939).

By a U.S. professor of education who has specialized in research on social and educational consequences of the movies.

1800. DALE, EDGAR; and RAMSEYER, LLOYD L. *Teaching with Motion Pictures*. Washington, D.C.: American Council on Education, 1937. 59 pp.

Concrete answers to questions most frequently asked by teachers and administrators who are introducing motion pictures and other visual aids into the classroom.

1801. DANA, HENRY WADSWORTH LONGFELLOW. *Handbook of Soviet Drama*. New York: American Russian Institute, 1938. 158 pp.

Bibliography of theaters, plays, operas, ballets, films, and books and articles about them.

1802. Davy, Charles, editor. *Footnotes to the Film*. London: Dickson, 1937. 346 pp.

The motion picture as an art, as a technical job, and as an industry. Prominent producers, directors, color technicians, and others contribute chapters on their respective skills. Part 4, "Films and the Public," contains articles on "Censorship and Film Societies," "The Film in Education," etc. "Contributors' Who's Who," pp. 334-39.

1803. *Educational Film Catalog*, with supplements. New York: H. W. Wilson, 1936–.

Lists producers, distributors; annotates several thousand films. Book review section gives brief reviews of recent books on the cinema. This *Catalog*, it is announced, will be kept up to date by supplements.

1804. Devine, John E. *Films as an Aid in Training Public Employees*. New York: Committee on Public Administration of the Social Science Research Council, 1937. 114 pp.

By an expert on public administration. Contains general discussion of the use of instructional films, outside the public service as well as in it. Appendix contains a "Catalog of Films Related to the Public Service." Bibliographic footnotes.

1805. Eisenstein, Sergei Mikhailovich. *The Film Sense*, translated and edited by Jav Leyda. New York: Harcourt, Brace, 1942. 288 pp.

Famous Soviet director-producer discusses his techniques and working habits. "Bibliography of Eisenstein's writings available in English," pp. 269-75. "Sources," pp. 276-81.

1806. Elliott, Godfrey. *The County Film Library: A Handbook on Organization, Administration, and Maintenance*. Morgantown, W. Va.: Harry L. Barr, 1941. 46 pp.

Problems of securing, criticizing, and using educational motion pictures. By Director, Audio-Visual Aids Service, Mercer County Schools, Princeton, West Virginia. Bibliography, p. 44.

1807. Ezickson, Aaron J. *Get That Picture! The Story of the News Cameraman*. New York: National Library Press, 1938. 200 pp.

Graphic description of the life of a newspicture man, with technical details about his craft, by a staff member of Wide World Photos.

1808. Feild, Robert Durant. *The Art of Walt Disney*. New York: Macmillan, 1942. 290 pp.

Profusely illustrated study of studio procedures in the production of animated cartoons.

1809. *Film Daily Year Book*. New York, annually, 1918(?)–.

One of the two standard U.S. data books on the industry.

1810. *The Film Index: A Bibliography: Volume 1: The Film as Art*. New York: Museum of Modern Art Film Library and H. W. Wilson Company, 1941. 723 pp.

Annotated bibliography of 8600 items, by more than 2000 authors, on the development of the motion picture. Compiled by workers on WPA Writers' Program, New York City.

1811. Flanagan, Hallie. *Arena*. New York: Duell, Sloan, and Pearce, 1940. 475 pp.

Account of the Federal Theatre, 1935-39. On this project an average of 10,000 people supported an average of four dependents for four years, while grossing a revenue of over two million dollars from box-office receipts, providing entertainment to over thirty million people in twenty-nine states, and giving approximately twelve hundred productions, exclusive of radio programs. The author was an administrator of the project. Bibliography, pp. 439-47.

1812. Forester, Max. "The Coming Revolution in Films," *Public Opinion Quarterly*, 3: 502-06 (July 1939).

The author has had experience with *Tide*, *Architectural Forum*, and the *March of Time* newsreel, and has organized a course on the documentary film at the New School for Social Research.

*1813. Freedley, George (Reynolds) (D); and Reeves, John A. *A History of the Theatre*. New York: Crown, 1941. 688 pp.

This reference book "provides as complete a record as can be condensed into a single large volume. Ranging from ancient Egypt to our own day, it considers an imposing number of playwrights, plays, actors, theatre architects, scene designers and directors. It reviews a large variety of movements, trends and forms of theatre, no matter how exotic, and overlooks no nation, past or present, except ancient Mesopotamia. Even the frequently neglected Latin-American theatre is included."—John Gassner in the *New York Times Book Review*, March 2, 1941. Copiously illustrated. Bibliography, pp. 620-28.

1813a. GIESE, HANS-JOACHIM. *Die Film Wochenschau im Dienste der Politik* (Leipziger Beiträge zur Erforschung der Publizistik, Band 5). Dresden: M. Dittert, 1940. 163 pp.

"The Weekly Newsreel in the Service of Politics." A study of political use of newsreels in the U.S.A. and various countries of Europe, Asia, and Latin America up to 1939, written by Dr. Giese for the Institut für Zeitungswissenschaft, University of Leipzig. Bibliography, pp. 160-63, cites German sources almost exclusively.

1814. GREGOR, JOSEPH. *Weltgeschichte des Theaters*. Zurich: Phaidon, 1933. 829 pp.

By German historian, a specialist on history of the theater, author of half a dozen other treatises and editor of *Theater der Welt* (monthly, 1937–). Bibliography, pp. 741-43.

1815. HARLEY, JOHN EUGENE. *World-Wide Influences of the Cinema: A Study of Official Censorship and the International Cultural Aspects of Motion Pictures*. Los Angeles: University of Southern California, 1941. 320 pp.

By University of Southern California professor of international relations. Pp. 96-199 deal with cases of censorship around the world, country by country. "Select list of cultural, documentary, and educational films and film sources," pp. 281-91. Bibliography, pp. 271-77.

1816. HENDRICKS, BILL L.; and WAUGH, HOWARD. *Charles "Chick" Lewis Presents the Encyclopedia of Ex-* *ploitation*. New York: Showman's Trade Review, 1937. 432 pp.

A thousand and one "tried and tested . . . lessons in how to attract public notice to a theater and its attractions," by two tried and tested publicity men. Appendix includes "Barnum's Lexicon," a list of words which have been found to be "super-charged" when used in theatrical advertising.

1817. HOBAN, CHARLES FRANCIS, JR. *Focus on Learning: Motion Pictures in the School*. Washington, D.C.: American Council on Education, 1942. 172 pp.

Director of the Council's Motion Picture Project summarizes and interprets findings of its five-year investigation. Foreword describes the half-dozen other books which have appeared in the course of this project. Bibliographic footnotes.

1818. "Hollywood in Uniform," *Fortune*, April 1942.

War effort of the movie industry.

1819. HOUGHTON, NORRIS. *Moscow Rehearsals: An Account of Methods of Production in the Soviet Theatre*. New York: Harcourt, Brace, 1936. 291 pp.

The author was a participant in the Russian theater for six months, as a Guggenheim fellow.

1820. *International Motion Picture Almanac*. Annual, New York, 1929–.

One of the two standard U.S. data books on the industry.

1821. ISTITUTO NAZIONALE LUCE. *Catalogo generale dei soggetti cinematografici*. Rome: Istituto Poligrafico dello Stato, 1937. 421 pp.

Catalogue of all cinema subjects which the Italian National Cinema Institute has produced or released in Italy under the Fascist regime. Indexed and extensively annotated.

1822. JACOBS, LEWIS. *The Rise of the American Film: A Critical History*. New York: Harcourt, Brace, 1939. 585 pp.

Bibliography, pp. 541-64.

1823. JOHNSTON, WINIFRED. *Memo on the Movies: War Propaganda, 1914-1939.* Norman, Oklahoma: Cooperative Press, 1939. 68 pp.

By U.S. journalist and English professor. Surveys the intensification of hate propaganda in the movies of all the Great Powers over a 25-year period. Bibliography, p. 65.

1823a. KALBUS, OSKAR. *Vom Werden deutscher Filmkunst.* Altona-Behrenfeld: Cigaretten-Bilderdienst, 1935. 2 vols.

"Development of the German Film." Bibliography, vol. 1, p. 136; vol. 2, pp. 135-36.

1824. *Kinematograph Yearbook.* London: Kinematograph Publishers, 1913(?)–.

1825. KLINGENDER, F. D.; and LEGG, STUART. *Money Behind the Screen: A Report Prepared on Behalf of the Film Council,* preface by John Grierson. London: Lawrence and Wishart, 1937. 79 pp.

Study of interlocking financial relations governing the cinema in England and U.S. as of the end of 1936.

1825a. KRACAUER, SIEGFRIED. *The Conquest of Europe on the Screen: The Nazi Newsreel, 1939-40* (Library of Congress, Experimental Division for Study of War Time Communications, Document no. 50). Washington, D.C., 1943. 33 pp.

By an ex-German sociologist and motion picture critic, now in U.S. Also appeared in *Social Research,* 10: 337-57 (September 1943).

1826. KRACAUER, SIEGFRIED. *Propaganda and the Nazi War Film.* New York: Museum of Modern Art Film Library, 1942. 90 pp.

1827. LANE, TAMAR. *A New Technique of Screen Writing: A Practical Guide to the Writing and Marketing of Photoplays.* New York: McGraw-Hill, 1936. 342 pp.

The author has been a screen editor and scenarist for several large producers.

1828. LEAGUE OF NATIONS. INTERNATIONAL INSTITUTE OF INTELLECTUAL COOPERATION. *Le rôle intellectuel du cinéma.* Paris, 1937. 289 pp.

Contains an historical essay by Valerio Jahier, "Quarante-deux ans du cinéma" in 11 countries (151 pp.), and eleven brief essays, by well-known writers in the motion picture field, on relations between the cinema and public opinion.

1828a. LIPSCHUETZ, RITA. *Der Ufa-Konzern: Geschichte, Aufbau und Bedeutung des deutschen Filmgewerbes.* (Dissertation, Berlin, 1932).

"The Ufa Concern: History, Structure and Significance of the German Film Business."

1829. MARTIN, OLGA JOHANNA. *Hollywood's Movie Commandments: A Handbook for Motion Picture Writers and Reviewers.* New York: H. W. Wilson, 1937. 301 pp.

Deals with pressures for various kinds of movies, citing the author's experiences as a worker in the Production Code Administration of the Association of Motion Picture Producers, Inc., which has attempted to formulate rules for dealing with movies' treatment of controversial topics like crime, sex, militarism, alcoholic drinks, animals, profanity, suicide, foreigners, etc.

1830. MASON, JOHN BROWN. "Germany's Leadership in School Films," *California Journal of Secondary Education,* January 1939, pp. 46-49.

"Germans have, within a few years' time established leadership in the field of educational films. Today, 30,000 of Germany's 60,000 school houses have their own projection machinery for 16 mm. films. All of these machines are of recent date. . . . In contrast we find that, of 100,000 American schoolhouses equipped with electric current, only 10,000 had motion picture projectors in the summer of 1937. . . . German schools have now available 564 educational films. . . . 325 more films are in the process of production. . . . But while National Socialist ideology leaves its decisive imprint on films dealing with certain subjects—such as 'The Life of the Führer' and 'National Socialist Party Congresses'— most films are remarkably free from onesided propaganda . . . educational films are excepted from the regular government censorship."

Author is a social scientist at Fresno State College, California, and a well-known specialist on public forums.

1831. METCALFE, LYNE SHACKLEFORD; and CHRISTENSEN, HAROLD GLOY. *How to Use Talking Pictures in Business*, foreword by Roy S. Durstine. New York: Harpers, 1938. 246 pp.

1832. *Motion Pictures of the World: Non-Theatrical Source Directory*. Boston, Mass. (40 Mt. Vernon Street), quarterly, February 1938–.

Classified and indexed directory, with annotations.

1833. NICOLL, ALLARDYCE. *Film and Theatre*. New York: Crowell, 1936. 255 pp.

Discusses techniques of the screen and stage in many countries. The author is professor of the history of drama at Yale. Bibliography, pp. 193-249.

1834. NOTCUTT, L. A.; and LATHAM, G. C., editors. *The African and the Cinema: An Account of the Work of the Bantu Educational Cinema Experiment During the Period March 1935 to May 1937*. London: Edinburgh House, 1937. 256 pp.

The Bantu Educational Cinema Experiment, financed by the Carnegie Corporation of New York and by the governments of Tanganyika, Kenya, and Uganda, produced a number of films employing natives as actors, for the purpose of making clear to illiterate African tribesmen the problems confronting them as a result of the diffusion of Western culture.

1835. PERLMAN, WILLIAM J., editor. *The Movies On Trial: The Views and Opinions of Outstanding Personalities*. New York: Macmillan, 1936. 254 pp.

A symposium. Includes an essay by Upton Sinclair, on "The Movies and Political Propaganda," giving details of the campaign in opposition to his candidacy for Governor of California.

1836. POLANYI, MICHAEL. "Economics by Motion Symbols: A Moving Picture Exposition of the Monetary System," *Review of Economic Studies*, 8: 1-19 (October 1940).

1837. PROGRESSIVE EDUCATION ASSOCIATION. COMMISSION ON HUMAN RELATIONS. *The Human Relations Series of Films*. New York, 1939. 87 pp.

Catalog of a collection of films on social problems which have been edited for teaching use by this group of educators. Includes plot résumés and examples of classroom discussions that were stimulated by the films.

1838. PRYOR, WILLIAM CLAYTON; and PRYOR, HELEN SLOMAN. *Let's Go to the Movies*. New York: Harcourt, Brace, 1939. 183 pp.

Popular account of moviemaking and distribution.

1839. RICKETSON, FRANK H., JR. *The Management of Motion Picture Theaters*. New York: McGraw-Hill, 1938. 376 pp.

Practical and explicit manual. "The sole purpose of theater operation is to make money. On that premise this book is written." Contains much material on advertising, architecture, color, lighting, "added attractions," etc.

1840. ROBINSON, T. C. "Fascism and the Political Theatre," *Sewanee Review*, 44: 53-67 (January 1936).

1841. ROSS, MURRAY. *Stars and Strikes: The Unionization of Hollywood*. New York: Columbia University, 1941. 233 pp.

Analysis of industrial relations in Hollywood by Brooklyn College professor. Bibliography, pp. 221-24.

*1842. ROSTEN, LEO CALVIN (CB '42, W) *Hollywood: The Movie Colony, The Movie Makers*. New York: Harcourt, Brace, 1941. 436 pp.

First comprehensive survey of the motion picture industry to be undertaken by a social scientist. Based on three years of research (1937-40). Bibliography, pp. 415-26.

1843. ROTHA, PAUL. *The Documentary Film*, revised and enlarged edition. New York: Norton, 1939. London: Faber and Faber, 1939. 320 pp.

A standard work on the history, principles, and technique of the documentary (informational) motion picture, by a well-known producer.

1844. SELDES, GILBERT VIVIAN. *Movies for the Millions: An Account of Motion Pictures, Principally in America,* preface by Charlie Chaplin. London: Batsford, 1937. 120 pp.

1845. SOBEL, BERNARD, editor. *The Theatre Handbook and Digest of Plays.* New York: Crown Publishers, 1939. 908 pp.

Encyclopedic handbook, in which alphabetically arranged articles deal with theatrical history and techniques, digests of famous plays, and biographies of theatrical personalities. See such topics as "Acting," "Censorship," "Direction," "Motion Picture," "Press Agentry," "Psychoanalysis in the Drama," "Radio Writing," "Television." Annotated bibliography, pp. 867-96.

1846. SOMMERICH, JANE, editor. *Films of the Pacific Area.* New York: American Film Center and American Council of Institute of Pacific Relations, 1939. 77 pp.

1847. *Soviet Films, 1938-1939.* Moscow: State Publishing House for Cinema Literature, 1940. About 100 pp.

Commentary and many pictures on Soviet films and their social role.

1848. SPENCER, DOUGLAS ARTHUR; and WALEY, H. D. *The Cinema Today* (Pageant of Progress series). New York: Oxford University, 1940. 191 pp.

Deals mainly with technique of making pictures, but contains a chapter on "The Film Industry and the Film as a Social Force." Mr. Spencer is past president, the Royal Photographic Society; Mr. Waley, Technical Director, British Film Institute. Bibliography, p. 187.

1849. "Survey of the Motion Picture Industry in Turkey," *Industrial Reference Service,* part 8, no. 48 (October 1941), pp. 1-3.

1850. STRASSER, ALEX. *Amateur Movies and How to Make Them.* New York: Studio Publications, 1937. 80 pp.

1851. STUBBS, STANLEY GEORGE BLAXLAND; MORTIMER, F. J.; and MALTHOUSE, GORDON S., editors. *The Modern Encyclopedia of Photography.* Boston: American Photographic Publishing Company, 1938. 2 vols.

Reference work for amateurs and professionals.

1852. THORP, MARGARET FARRAND. *America at the Movies.* New Haven: Yale University, 1939. 313 pp.

Data on the 85,000,000 persons who buy admissions every week to 17,000 movie houses in 9,000 U.S. communities; on the psychological techniques used by producers; and on the activities of reform and censorship agencies. Chapter 9, "The Lure of Propaganda," discusses Hollywood's experiments with propaganda for a big navy, for the British, and for "social justice."

1853. THRASHER, FREDERIC MILTON, editor. *Educational Aspects of Motion Pictures* (November 1937 issue of *Journal of Educational Sociology*).

Contains articles on such topics as "The Film as an Agency of British-American Understanding" (by Frank Darvall, Research Director of the English-Speaking Union of the British Empire); "The League of Nations' Interest in Motion Pictures in Relation to Child Welfare" (by Ruth Bloodgood, Children's Bureau, U.S. Department of Labor); "Civic Education by Radio" (by Thomas Baird, British General Post Office Film Unit); "Educational Possibilities of Motion Pictures" (by Mark A. May, Director of the Institute of Human Relations, Yale University); etc. Book reviews, pp. 190-92.

1854. "United Artists," *Fortune,* December 1940.

1855. U.S. BUREAU OF FOREIGN AND DOMESTIC COMMERCE. *Review of Foreign Film Markets, 1936–.* Washington, D.C., March 1937–.

A world survey, published annually. Inside back cover lists a number of the Bureau's other publications on the world motion picture situation.

1856. U.S. FILM SERVICE (Division of National Emergency Council). *Directory of U.S. Government Films.* Washington, D.C., December 1938. 17 pp. mimeo.

The U.S. Film Service assists in obtaining government-made films and in planning educational motion picture programs.

1857. U.S. SENATE. INTERSTATE COMMERCE COMMITTEE. *Propaganda in Motion Pictures: Hearings, 77th Cong., 1st sess., on S. Res. 152, Authorizing Investigation of War Propaganda Disseminated by Motion-Picture Industry.* Washington, D.C.: Government Printing Office, 1942. 449 pp.

1858. VREELAND, FRANK. *Foremost Films of 1938: A Yearbook of the American Screen.* New York: Pitman, 1939. 347 pp.

First of a proposed series of yearbooks, including reviews of films, production trends, problems, throughout the world. The editor is an experienced New York screen critic and adviser to Hollywood companies.

1859. WATTS, STEPHEN, editor. *Behind the Screen: How Films Are Made.* New York: Dodge Publishing Company, 1938. 176 pp.

Essays by well-known practitioners of every phase of movie-making from scenario writing to distribution. Pp. 158-66 are on "Public Relations," by Howard Dietz.

1860. WEHBERG, HILLA. "Fate of an International Film Institute," *Public Opinion Quarterly*, 2: 483-85 (July 1938).

International Educational Cinematographic Institute, described by a University of Chicago student of political science.

1861. WHITMAN, WILLSON. *Bread and Circuses: A Study of Federal Theatre.* New York and London: Oxford University, 1937. 191 pp.

Thoroughgoing study of the Federal Theater in the United States. Bibliography, pp. 173-74.

1862. WISE, HARRY ARTHUR. *Motion Pictures as an Aid in Teaching American History.* New Haven: Yale University, 1939. 187 pp.

Statistical analysis of methods and results of educational experiments with the "Chronicles of America" series of photoplays. Evaluates earlier studies of motion-picture effects. Bibliography, pp. 144-46.

1863. WOLF, KURT. *Entwicklung und Neugestaltung der deutschen Filmwirtschaft seit 1933* (inaugural dissertation, Heidelberg). Heidelberg: H. Meister, 1938. 79 pp.

Bibliography, pp. 77-78.

1864. WRIGLEY, M. J.; and LEYLAND, ERIC. *The Cinema: Historical, Technical and Bibliographical: A Survey for Librarians and Students.* London: Grafton, 1939. 198 pp.

Carefully organized reference work by two English librarians. Contains a chronology of the film industry. Bibliography, pp. 125-63.

2. PERSONNEL

1865. BIRDWELL, RUSSELL. *I Ring Doorbells.* New York: Messner, 1939. 253 pp.

Reminiscences of California ex-journalist, now a public relations man for movie producers.

1866. GIBBS, WOLCOTT. "The Customer is Always Wrong," *New Yorker*, 17: 27-32 ff. (October 11, 1941).

Profile of Richard Sylvester ("Dick") Maney, Broadway press agent.

3. QUANTITATIVE STUDIES OF AUDIENCES, COVERAGE AND EFFECTS
[See also Part 6.]

1867. "Boy Meets Facts," *Time*, July 21, 1941, p. 73.

On Audience Research Institute, a polling agency set up by Dr. George H. Gallup and headed by "a bright young Scot named David Ogilvy," for the purpose of surveying audience-reaction to Hollywood movies—"the most thorough study of the cinemaudience ever made."

1868. DALE, EDGAR. *The Content of Motion Pictures* and *Children's Attendance at Motion Pictures*, bound in one volume. New York: Macmillan, 1935. 234 + 81 pp.

Two studies in the Payne Fund series. The first monograph rather exhaustively analyzes symbols which appeared in 1655 films between 1920 and 1930. The second gives age and sex distributions, frequency of attendance, etc., derived from questionnaires in 50 Ohio communities. 36.7 per cent of movie-goers were estimated to have been minors.

1869. HEINDEL, RICHARD HEATH-COTE. "American Attitudes of British School Children," *School and Society*, 46: 838-40 (December 25, 1937).

Report by British school children, aged 13 to 16, on channels through which they received their impressions of the U.S. shows that cinema is by far the most influential. An attitude questionnaire confirmed the suspicion that many British school children assume that the cinema gives an accurate picture of U.S. life.

1870. ROSENTHAL, SOLOMON P. *Change of Socio-economic Attitudes under Radical Motion Picture Propaganda* (Ph.D. thesis, Columbia; Archives of Psychology, no. 166). New York, 1934. 46 pp.

Bibliography, p. 46.

1871. WESTFALL, LEON H. *A Study of Verbal Accompaniments to Educational Motion Pictures* (Teachers College Contributions to Education, no. 617). New York: Columbia University, 1934. 68 pp.

Evaluates the relative merits of several forms of verbal accompaniment to educational motion pictures, namely: 0. No explanation, 1. Average length titles, 2. Long titles, 3. Average length titles plus teacher comment, 4. Teacher lecture, 5. Talking picture, 6. Teacher prepared explanation.

Conclusion: 1. For films of the science or expository type originally constructed with the usual captions for silent projections: A. An explanation which the teacher prepares from materials furnished with the film, a lecture furnished with the film and read by the teacher, and the usual captions were about equal as an aid to understanding the contents of the film. B. These three forms of verbal accompaniment were superior to long captions by a statistically significant difference and superior to the regular captions supplemented by teacher explanation, by a difference that is nearly significant statistically. C. For each of the three films, when the regular captions were materially lengthened to increase the amount of explanation, they not only failed to increase the understanding of the picture, but actually lowered it.

2. For films of the science or expository type originally constructed for use with sound accompaniment: A. A mechanically produced lecture was significantly superior to any other form of verbal accompaniment used in the experiment. B. A lecture that is furnished with the film and read by the teacher was significantly superior to the same material printed on the film or to an explanation which the teacher prepared from materials furnished with the film. C. An explanation which the teacher prepared from material furnished with the film was slightly but not significantly superior to long captions printed on the film.

3. Oral forms of verbal accompaniment were especially helpful to low ability pupils. When oral explanations were offered, low ability pupils came nearer to keeping up with the average of the class in understanding than when the reading of titles was required.

4. Pupils expressed a five-to-one preference for talking pictures over any other form of verbal accompaniment.

5. As measured by the interest questions on the tests there was a large amount of difference in interest aroused by the different films but almost no difference in the amount of interest aroused by the several forms of verbal accompaniment.

1872. YOUNG, KIMBALL. Review of ten books on attitudes created by the movies (the Payne Fund Studies on Motion Pictures and Youth), *American Journal of Sociology*, 41: 249-55 (September 1935).

This reviewer, a U.S. social psychologist, finds that the author of the summary volume on the Payne Fund Studies departs considerably from the findings of the scientists who wrote the original monographs, so that "we have here a good case of the psychology of myth-making itself. . . . And we are now witnessing, partly as a result of this sort of misinterpretation or partial interpretation, a wave of sentiment against the movies which is likely to prove a boomerang when all the factors making for change in conduct are better known and understood by the man on the street."

V. RADIO, TELEPHONE, TELEGRAPH, CABLE, POSTAL SYSTEM, TELEVISION

1. CONTROL, ORGANIZATION, EQUIPMENT

1874. ABBOT, WALDO MACK. *Handbook of Broadcasting: How to Broadcast Effectively*, 2nd ed., rev. New York: McGraw-Hill, 1941. 422 pp.

By Assistant Professor of Speech and Director of Broadcasting, University of Michigan. Bibliography, pp. 371-77 and 393-409.

1875. *Air Law Review.* New York, 1930–.

This journal contains many articles on both technical and legal aspects of the control of radio, and occasional articles on the weight of opinions in determining policy.

1876. ARCHER, GLEASON LEONARD. *Big Business and Radio.* New York: American Historical Company, 1939. 503 pp.

History of the corporate control of U.S. radio, based on document files of the corporations. Dr. Archer, a lawyer and historian, is President of Suffolk University; has also published a *History of Radio to 1926* (New York: American Historical Company, 1938. 421 pp.).

1877. ATKINSON, CARROLL. *American Universities and Colleges That Have Held Broadcast License* (Hattie and Luther Nelson Memorial Library). Boston: Meador, 1941. 127 pp.

Bibliographic footnotes.

1878. ATKINSON, CARROLL. *Broadcasting to the Classroom by Universities and Colleges* (Hattie and Luther Nelson Memorial Library, no. 5). Boston: Meador, 1942. 128 pp.

Bibliographic footnotes.

1879. ATKINSON, CARROLL. *Radio Network Contributions to Education* (Hattie and Luther Nelson Memorial Library, no. 4). Boston: Meador, 1942. 128 pp.

History, development, and production methods of 40 radio programs which the author considers to have educational values. Bibliographic footnotes.

1880. ATKINSON, CARROLL. *Public School Broadcasting to the Classroom* (Hattie and Luther Nelson Memorial Library, no. 3). Boston: Meador, 1942. 144 pp.

History and development of the broadcasting of radio programs for classroom use by 29 public school systems. Bibliographic footnotes.

1881. ATKINSON, CARROLL. *Radio Programs Intended for Classroom Use* (Hattie and Luther Nelson Memorial Library, no. 6). Boston: Meador, 1942. 128 pp.

Bibliographic footnotes.

1882. "Bad News for the Networks," *Time*, June 24, 1940, p. 66.

Federal Communications Commission's Committee on Monopolism produces its long-awaited report on the radio industry, finding "undertones of monopoly all through the $165,000,000-a-year (1938) broadcasting industry," claiming that RCA "is controlled by three persons who between them have only 5829 shares of a total of 9,864,502 voted by them," and recommending extensive reorganization and government supervision of the whole system.

1883. (Pop.) BARNOUW, ERIK. *Handbook of Radio Writing: An Outline of Techniques and Markets in Radio Writing in the United States.* Boston: Little, Brown, 1939. 306 pp.

Tricks of the trade described from the wide experience of Dutch-born, Princeton-graduated author, dramatist, trouper, script-writer who teaches radio writing at Columbia. Includes examples from popular programs; pointers on background music and sound effects; lists of tabooed words and subjects.

1884. BARR, A. S.; EWBANK, H. L.; and McCORMICK, T. C. *Radio in the Classroom.* Madison: University of Wisconsin, 1942. 203 pp.

Report of the Wisconsin Research Project in School Broadcasting, "experimental studies in the production and classroom use of lessons broadcast by radio." It included the broadcasting of a series of well-planned lessons in music, nature study, geography, social studies, English, and speech. There were control groups studying essentially the same materials in each of these fields, selected from what appeared to be the same types of populations. Sampling method has been criticized by Charles C. Peters, *American Sociological Review*, 8: 242 (April 1943).

1885. BEALES, H. L. "The B.B.C.," *Political Quarterly*, 7: 522-37 (October 1936).

1886. BRINDZE, RUTH. *Not To Be Broadcast: The Truth About Radio.* New York: Vanguard, 1937. 310 pp.

Sweeping attack on results of private broadcasting, and proposal for a chain of government-operated stations.

1887. *Broadcasting and Peace.* Paris: International Institute of Intellectual Cooperation, 1934. 200 pp.

*1888. CANTRIL, HADLEY; and ALLPORT, GORDON WILLARD (W). *The Psychology of Radio.* New York and London: Harpers, 1935. 276 pp.

Two U.S. social psychologists analyze the social consequences of radio, of program preparation, and of listeners' habits and preferences as revealed by questionnaire. Comparisons are made of the specific advantages of the radio, the visible speaker, and the printed page in compelling attention and in affecting attitudes.

1889. CARLILE, JOHN S. *Production and Direction of Radio Programs.* New York: Prentice-Hall, 1939. 397 pp.

By production manager of CBS. A thoroughgoing treatise and handbook. Bibliography, pp. 381-83.

1890. CHURCH, GEORGE F. "Short Waves and Propaganda," *Public Opinion Quarterly*, 3: 209-22 (April 1939).

Rapid survey of the world's short-wave activities by a U.S. professor of journalism.

1891. CLARKE, W. HARVEY, JR. "Radio in Japan Now Housed in New Magnificent Home," *Far Eastern Review*, 35: 275-82 (July 1939).

Equipment, policy, and programs of Broadcasting Company of Japan. Japan now has 35 stations and 24 per cent of the households have receivers.

1892. COLUMBIA BROADCASTING SYSTEM. *Radio and Television Bibliography*, 6th ed. New York, 1942. 96 pp.

Prepared by CBS Reference Library. Not annotated, except for pp. 62-79, which are a bibliography of publications issued by CBS.

1893. CONNAH, DOUGLAS DUFF. *How to Build the Radio Audience.* New York: Harpers, 1938. 271 pp.

Publicity man's practical rules.

1894. DAVIS, ELMER. "Broadcasting the Outbreak of War," *Harpers*, 179: 579-88 (November 1939).

Vivid account of events in CBS news studios amid the torrent of incoming news from Europe; by U.S. journalist and radio commentator who later became head of Office of War Information.

1895. DE FOREST, LEE. *Television: Today and Tomorrow.* New York: Dial Press, 1942. 361 pp.

Economic, social, and technical analysis by well-known electrical engineer and inventor.

1896. DENISON, MERRILL. "Editorial Policies of Broadcasting Companies," *Public Opinion Quarterly*, 1 no. 1: 64-82 (January 1937).

By a specialist on radio drama who has been a program adviser for CBS and NBC.

1897. DENISON, MERRILL. "Soap Opera," *Harpers*, 180: 498-505 (April 1940).

"Sob-in-the-throat radio dramas . . . known to the trade as 'soap operas' or 'strip shows' " (the first because soap manufacturers bear the brunt of the cost; the second, apparently because of the resemblance of the shows to a comic strip). "Six manufacturers are now paying for more than two-thirds of all the soap operas. . . . In 1938, a single advertising agency, Blackett, Sample and Hummert, bought 53 per cent of the daytime and 8 per cent of all radio time sold by both networks and local stations in the United States. The cost was about $9,000,000; the agency commission $1,350,000." Article includes description of plots and symbols.

1898. Dryer, Sherman Harvard. *Radio in Wartime.* New York: Greenberg, 1942. 384 pp.

Discussion of current and possible uses of radio as a prodemocratic force, by director of radio productions at the University of Chicago. The author submitted his manuscript to a number of well-known specialists, whose comments, sometimes adverse, are printed in the text. Bibliographic footnotes.

1899. Dunlap, Orrin Elmer, Jr. *The Future of Television.* New York: Harpers, 1942. 194 pp.

Probable effects of television upon the radio industry, described by radio editor of New York *Times.*

1900. (Pop.) Dunlap, Orrin Elmer, Jr. *Talking on the Radio: A Practical Guide for Writing and Broadcasting a Speech.* New York: Greenberg, 1937. 216 pp.

States 50 practical rules; emphasizes the techniques of the politician.

1901. *The Educational Role of Broadcasting.* Paris: International Institute of Intellectual Co-operation, 1935. 294 pp.

1902. Engel, Harold A. "The Wisconsin Political Forum," *Public Opinion Quarterly*, 2: 309-12 (April 1938).

By production manager of a station operated by the State of Wisconsin which sells no time and is "free to operate with the interests of the listener, rather than a sponsor, as the primary concern."

1903. Evans, S. Howard. "National Conference on Educational Broadcasting," *Public Opinion Quarterly*, 1 no. 2: 125-29 (April 1937).

By secretary of National Committee on Education by Radio.

1904. "Farmers' Hour," *Time*, August 4, 1941, p. 54.

"The 4000 broadcasts of the [*National*] *Farm and Home Hour* have held the national air for 13 years. Six days a week, the program goes out over 100 stations, is heard by some 6,000,000 listeners. The Hour finds a front seat for the U.S. farmer at all big agricultural events, keeps him posted about weather and current markets, provides him with tips from the Department of Agriculture and half a hundred other farm organizations."

1905. "FCC *versus* Networks," *Fortune*, May 1943.

"The five-year legal and propaganda battle between the Federal Communications Commission and the broadcasting companies over the Commission's proposed network monopoly regulations."

1906. Federal Council of Churches of Christ in America. Department of Research and Education. *Broadcasting and the Public: A Case Study in Social Ethics.* New York: Abingdon Press, 1938. 220 pp.

A report "addressed primarily to the membership of the Protestant churches," on "The development of the broadcasting industry with particular reference to the cultural, social, moral, and spiritual values . . . ; to throw some light on the problem of achieving a wholesome balance of liberty and social control in broadcasting." Bibliography, pp. 211-14.

1907. Fly, James Lawrence. "FCC Monitoring Set-Up," *Radio News*, 27: 71 (January 1942).

FCC chairman describes Foreign Broadcast Monitoring Service.

1908. Friedrich, Carl Joachim. *Controlling Broadcasting in Wartime* (Harvard Studies in the Control of Radio, vol. 1). Cambridge: Harvard University, 1940. 34 pp.

By Harvard political scientist. See title 1911, below.

1909. Friedrich, Carl Joachim. "The FCC 'Monopoly' Report: A Critical Analysis," *Public Opinion Quarterly*, 4: 526-32 (September 1940).

1910. Friedrich, Carl Joachim. "Foreign-language Radio and the War," *Common Ground*, 3 no. 1: 65-72 (1942).

Analysis of possibilities of more pro-democratic foreign-language broadcasting in the

U.S. Dr. Friedrich, political scientist, is director of the Radio Broadcasting Research Project at Harvard University.

1911. FRIEDRICH, CARL JOACHIM; MASON, EDWARD S.; and HERRING, E(DWARD) PENDLETON, editors. *Public Policy: A Yearbook of the Graduate School of Public Administration, Harvard University, 1941.* Cambridge: Harvard University, 1941. 458 pp.

Symposium on major national problems by specialists. Dr. Friedrich writes on "Controlling Broadcasting in Wartime: A Tentative Public Policy" (pp. 374-401), and recommends appointment of a central programming board, "in close touch with, but not a part of, the Federal Communications Commission." This essay has been published as vol. 1 in the Harvard Studies in the Control of Radio series. Bibliographic footnotes.

1912. FROST, S. E., JR. *Education's Own Stations: The History of Broadcast Licenses Issued to Educational Institutions.* Chicago: University of Chicago, 1937. 480 pp.

Factual record of the experience of the 202 U.S. stations which were granted educational broadcasting licenses during the period 1921-36, with some analysis of the reasons why only 38 of them have survived. The author, whose recommendations are in his *Is American Radio Democratic?* (cited below), is Assistant Professor of Education, Adelphi College, and an associate of National Advisory Council on Radio in Education.

1913. FROST, S. E., JR. *Is American Radio Democratic?* Chicago: University of Chicago, 1937. 234 pp.

Extensively documented survey of technical and legal factors affecting the possible development of "a more democratic broadcast structure" in the U.S. Bibliographic footnotes.

1914. GORDON, DOROTHY. *All Children Listen.* New York: G. W. Stewart, 1942. 128 pp.

A study of radio programs for children in all parts of the world, by a U.S. producer of such programs. Bibliography, p. 128.

1915. GRANDIN, THOMAS BURNHAM. *The Political Use of the Radio* (Geneva Studies, vol. 10, no. 3). Geneva: Geneva Research Center, 1939. 116 pp.

Basic data on extent and character of long and short wave broadcasting and listening in Europe as of 1939. Author monitored broadcasts for Geneva Research Center for one year. Bibliographic footnotes.

1916. GRAVES, HAROLD NATHAN, JR. *War on the Short Wave* (Headline Books). New York: Foreign Policy Association, 1941. 64 pp.

Radio's role in the present war, described by former head of Princeton University Listening Center, later with Federal Communications Commission's Foreign Broadcast Monitoring Service.

1917. HADAMOVSKY, EUGEN. *Der Rundfunk im Dienste der Volksführung* (Gestalten und Erscheinungen der politischen Publizistik, Heft 1). Leipzig: Noske, 1934. 29 pp.

"Radio in the Service of National Leadership." By Nazi radio chief, author of the standard treatise, *Propaganda und Nationale Macht* (Oldenburg: Stalling, 1933, 153 pp.).

1918. HARRIS, CURETON. "$67,000 for Radio Research," *Market Research*, 7: 3-6 (December 1937).

Princeton Radio Research Project (on social effects of radio) to be started by School of Public Affairs, Princeton University.

1919. HEDIN, NABOTH. "Learning on the Air: Development of Educational Broadcasting in Sweden," *American Swedish Monthly*, July 1937, pp. 8-10.

1920. HERRING, JAMES MORTON; and GROSS, GERALD CONNOP. *Telecommunications: Economics and Regulation.* New York and London: McGraw-Hill, 1936. 544 pp.

Mr. Gross has been an engineer on staff of Federal Communications Commission and its predecessors since 1928.

1921. HERZOG, HERTA. *Survey of Research on Children's Radio Listening.* New York: Columbia University, Office of Radio Research, 1941. 86 pp.

"Deals with the programs listened to by children and is not limited to the so-called 'children's programs,' i.e., programs designed for a child audience. . . . Bibliography on children's radio listening (exclusive of school and strictly educational broadcasts)," pp. 67-72.

1922. HETTINGER, HERMAN STRECKER. "Marketing of Radio Broadcasting Service," *Harvard Business Review*, 17: 301-17 (Spring 1939).

Surveys the market positions of broadcasters, networks, transcription companies, advertisers, advertising agencies, station representatives, program builders, talent bureaus in recent years.

1923. HETTINGER, HERMAN STRECKER; and NEFF, WALTER J. *Practical Radio Advertising*. New York: Prentice-Hall, 1938. 372 pp.

Outlines the successive stages in the execution of a radio program and a campaign. Contains tabulated data on the mechanics of broadcasting, on geographical distribution of set owners, on volume of broadcast advertising matter by classes, and on network structure and rates. Dr. Hettinger, assistant professor of marketing, Wharton School, University of Pennsylvania, was for several years director of research for National Association of Broadcasters. Mr. Neff, president of the Neff-Rogow Agency, was formerly sales manager of station WOR, Newark.

1924. HILL, FRANK ERNEST. *Listen and Learn: Fifteen Years of Adult Education on the Air* (Studies in the Social Significance of Adult Education in the United States, no. 1). New York: American Association for Adult Education, 1937. 248 pp.

General treatise based on extensive study and observation. The author recommends establishment of an "educational network" to supplement the existing commercial networks. Bibliographic footnotes.

1925. HILL, FRANK ERNEST; and WILLIAMS, WILLIAM EMRYS. *Radio's Listening Groups: The United States and Great Britain*. New York: Columbia University, 1941. 270 pp.

This is a study not of individual listeners but of group listening for educational and cultural purposes in the United States and Great Britain. Characteristics of listening groups are described and the conditions for adult education through group listening are discussed. Mr. Hill is author of a number of books issued by American Association for Adult Education; Mr. Williams is connected with British Institute of Adult Education.

1925a. HOGAN, JOHN VINCENT LAWLESS. "Tomorrow's Problems for Broadcasters," *Yale Review*, 31: 132-41 (Autumn 1941).

By President of Interstate Broadcasting Company (WQXR).

1926. HUTH, ARNO. *Radio Today: The Present State of Broadcasting in the World* (Geneva Studies, vol. 12, no. 6), translated by Hélène Héroys. Geneva: Geneva Research Centre, 1942. 160 pp.

Bibliography, p. 159.

1927. HUTH, ARNO. *La Radiodiffusion—Puissance Mondiale*, 8th ed. Paris: Gallimard, 1937. 508 pp.

Treatise on technology and social and political influence of radio. Bibliography, pp. 466-82.

1928. HYLANDER, CLARENCE JOHN; and HARDING, ROBERT, JR. *An Introduction to Television*. New York: Macmillan, 1941. 207 pp.

Moderately technical. Profusely illustrated.

1929. INSTITUTE FOR EDUCATION BY RADIO. *Education on the Air: Yearbook of the Institute*. Columbus: Ohio State University, 1930–.

Contains articles by specialists.

1930. KERBY, PHILIP. *The Victory of Television*. New York: Harpers, 1939. 120 pp.

Describes the television studio and shows how a play is staged and acted and how its performance is managed in the control room. By member of staff of NBC.

1931. LAMBERT, R. S. *Ariel and All His Quality: An Impression of the BBC From Within*. London: Gollancz, 1940. 318 pp.

The author was for ten years a member of the BBC staff, editor (1929-39) of its publication, *The Listener*. He finds that "BBC has chiefly succeeded in fitting itself to be an instrument of government—for intellectual and cultural purposes—in the totalitarian state of the future."

1932. LAMBERT, R. S. "What About the Canadian Broadcasting Company," *Food for Thought*, February 1940, pp. 3-18.

Men, policies, programs of Canada's national radio.

1933. LANDRY, ROBERT J. "Wartime Radio Showmanship Survey," *Variety*, May 20-June 17, 1942.

Radio editor of *Variety* supplies a running commentary, week by week, evaluating the manner in which commercial programs carry out suggestions given in the *Radio War Guide* issued by the Office of Facts and Figures.

1934. LANDRY, ROBERT J. "Wanted: Radio Critics," *Public Opinion Quarterly*, 4: 620-29 (December 1940).

Radio Editor of *Variety* makes a plea for professional radio criticism, and draws up specifications for the perfect critic. See comment by Charles A. Siepmann, title 1968, below.

1935. LANDRY, ROBERT J. *Who, What, Why is Radio?* (Radio House book). New York: George W. Stewart, 1942. 128 pp.

Analysis of the broadcasting industry in relation to democracy.

1936. LAZARSFELD, PAUL FELIX. "Audience Building in Educational Broadcasting," *Journal of Educational Sociology*, 14: 1-9 (May 1941).

1937. LEATHERWOOD, DOWLING. "Outline of a Course in Radio Journalism," *Journalism Quarterly*, 16: 259-63 (September 1939).

News broadcasting has led to a new academic specialty, now offered by 14 schools. This article describes the Emory University offering. Included are new techniques of speech training, news "processing," making and analysis of transcriptions, a practice studio, actual broadcasts from local stations.

1938. LOHR, LENOX RILEY; and others. *Television Broadcasting: Production, Economics, Technique*, preface by David Sarnoff. New York: McGraw-Hill, 1940. 274 pp.

Presents complete operating technique of television, its equipment, program considerations, legal and economic aspects; by the president of NBC and associates. Includes actual television script, with marginal notations; illustrated.

1939. LOWDERMILK, R. R. *The School-Radio Sound System*. Washington, D.C.: Federal Radio Education Committee, U.S. Office of Education, 1942. Pamphlet.

Selection and proper use of equipment.

1940. LUNDBERGH, HOLGER. "Radio Broadcasting in Sweden," *American Scandinavian Review*, 29: 56-59 (March 1941).

1941. McGILL, EARLE. *Radio Directing*, foreword by H. Clay Harshbarger. New York: McGraw-Hill, 1940. 370 pp.

Comprehensive manual, including instructions for studio arrangement, sound effects, casting, rehearsal, production, glossary of terms, and a script for student use. The author, instructor in New York University's Radio Workshop, has had wide experience as a CBS director and producer.

1942. McNAIR, W. A. *Radio Advertising in Australia*, with a foreword by A. H. Martin. Sydney: Angus and Robertson, 1937. 461 pp.

Bibliography, pp. 451-53.

1943. MILLER, NEVILLE. "Radio's Code of Self-Regulation," *Public Opinion Quarterly*, 3: 683-88 (October 1939).

President of National Association of Broadcasters discusses the Association's Code of Ethics.

1944. MOSELEY, SYDNEY ALEXANDER; and BARTON-CHAPPLE, HARRY J. *Television Today and Tomorrow*, 5th ed., rev., foreword by John L. Baird. New York: Pitman, 1940. 179 pp.

"This book, while much of it is of a technical nature, is sufficiently descriptive to be followed in a general way by the man in the street . . . , in addition to which the chapters devoted entirely to technicalities deal with the latest advances in a manner useful to the technician."—Foreword. The authors were pioneer specialists in television with BBC.

1945. NATIONAL ADVISORY COUNCIL ON RADIO IN EDUCATION. *Radio and Education: Proceedings* [of the Council's annual assembly]. Chicago: University of Chicago, 1931–.

1946. NEUMEYER, MARTIN HENRY. "Radio and Social Research," *Sociology and Social Research*, 25: 114-24 (November 1940).

*1947. *New Horizons in Radio: Problems and Progress of Sound Broadcasting and Future Developments in the Radio Field* (Annals of the American Academy of Political and Social Science, vol. 213, January 1941, edited by Herman Strecker Hettinger).
Articles by a score of specialists.

1948. NIESSEL, A. "Propaganda par radio," *Revue des deux mondes*, 8 no. 47: 829-43 (1938).

1949. OBOLER, ARCH. *Fourteen Radio Plays*, with a foreword by Lewis H. Titterton, an introduction "On Reading a Radio Play" by Irving Stone, and an essay on "The Art of Radio Writing" by Arch Oboler. New York: Random House, 1940. 257 pp.
By celebrated U.S. radio playwright.

1950. O'BRIEN, TERENCE HENRY. *British Experiments in Public Ownership and Control.* New York: Norton, 1938. 304 pp.
Detailed study of Central Electricity Board, British Broadcasting Corporation, and London Passenger Transport Board, all of which are semi-independent public businesses. Contains material on controversial political broadcasts and on the social composition of the governors of BBC.

1951. PORTERFIELD, JOHN; and REYNOLDS, KAY, editors. *We Present Television.* New York: Norton, 1940. 298 pp.
Eleven experts describe television equipment, programs, personnel, financing.

1952. PRINGLE, HENRY FOWLES. "WQXR: Quality on the Air," *Harpers*, 180: 508-12 (April 1940).
By U.S. journalist. Station WQXR of New York City, owned and operated by Interstate Broadcasting Company, "has been making a vital contribution to the cultural status of radio during the past three years . . . broadcasts nothing but fine music, excellent lectures, intelligently presented news summaries and other programs aimed at the fit though few." Article describes financial status of the station and results of its listener-interest surveys.

1953. "QRX," *Time*, May 16, 1938, pp. 25-28.
The background of hearings before the House Naval Affairs Committee on Rep. Celler's Pan-American Broadcasting Station Bill, which would authorize the U.S. Navy to construct and operate a broadcasting station for educational and entertainment programs to be arranged by the U.S. Commissioner of Education.

1954. "Radio," *Fortune*, May 1938.
Deals with the broadcasting industry, its economic basis, the talent on which it draws, the owners of receiving sets (87 per cent of American families), and the manufacture of receiving sets. In the same issue is an article on Federal Communications Commission.

1955. *Radio Annual 1938–.* Jack Alicoate, editor. New York: *Radio Daily*, 1938–.
A yearbook of the radio industry.

1956. *Radio Directory: Programs and Production, Laws and Government, Physical Facilities, Agencies and Sponsors.* New York, Annual, 1937–.
Standard reference work for the radio industry. Includes data on program popularity, network tie-ups, advertising agency appropriations, radio law, Who's Who of radio actors and producers, etc. Published by *Variety*, news organ of the entertainment industry.

1957. *Radio: The Fifth Estate* (Annals of the American Academy of Political and Social Science, vol. 177, January 1935), edited by Herman Strecker Hettinger.

Articles by a score of specialists.

1958. "Radio Turns South," *Fortune*, April 1941.

New 64-station CBS network in South America.

1959. REED, THOMAS HARRISON. "Commercial Broadcasting and Civic Education," *Public Opinion Quarterly*, 1 no. 3: 57-67 (July 1937).

This well-known U.S. political scientist has done extensive research in this field as chairman, 1932-36, of the Committee on Civic Education by Radio (of the National Advisory Council on Radio in Education and the American Political Science Association). Article includes a report on experience with the "You and Your Government" series of radio programs.

1960. "Revolution in Radio," *Fortune*, October 1939.

On new invention, frequency modulation. "After years of battle a fighting inventor (Edwin Howard Armstrong) is in a position to cause replacement of 40,000,000 radio sets and $75,000,000 worth of broadcasting equipment." For results of FCC's licensing hearings on frequency modulation, see the Commission's releases, especially Press Release no. 41,117 (May 20, 1940).

1961. RIXON, ALEC T. "Telecommunications of China with Foreign Countries," *Public Opinion Quarterly*, 2: 478-83 (July 1938).

1961a. ROBINSON, THOMAS PORTER. *Radio Networks and the Federal Government* (Ph.D. thesis, political science, Columbia). New York: Columbia University, 1943. 278 pp.

Dr. Robinson, economist and former public relations man, on staff of the Office of Price Administration, submits a history of network broadcasting and a scholarly diagnosis of current differences between the broadcasters and the FCC. Bibliography, pp. 265-67.

1962. ROBSON, WILLIAM ALEXANDER, editor. *Public Enterprise: Developments in Social Ownership and Control in Great Britain* (New Fabian Research Bureau Publications). Chicago: University of Chicago, 1937. London: Allen and Unwin, 1937. 416 pp.

British public enterprise includes two major channels of communication: the British Broadcasting Corporation (chapter 3, by William A. Robson, British political scientist), and the Post Office (chapter 8, by John Dugdale). The volume also contains a chapter on "The Organization of the Cooperative Movement" by George Walworth. Bibliographic footnotes.

1963. ROLO, CHARLES J. *Radio Goes to War: The "Fourth Front,"* introduction by Johannes Steel. New York: Putnam's Sons, 1942. 293 pp.

How radio has been used by the belligerent nations, including the United States. By a onetime staff member of Princeton Radio Research Project. Bibliographic footnotes.

1964. ROSE, CORNELIA BRUÈRE, JR. *A National Policy for Radio Broadcasting*. New York: Harpers, 1940. 289 pp.

A comprehensive study dealing with both commercial structure and program content of American broadcasting. Prepared as a report of National Economic and Social Planning Association. Bibliography, pp. 279-83.

1965. SAERCHINGER, CESAR. *Hello, America!: Radio Adventures in Europe*. Boston: Houghton Mifflin, 1938. 393 pp.

Reminiscences of a pioneer in the organization of transatlantic broadcasting, including comments on famous broadcasts and on technical facilities.

1966. SAERCHINGER, CESAR. "Radio in Europe," *Atlantic*, 161: 509-18 (April 1938).

Factual summary.

1967. SAUER, JULIA LINA, editor. *Radio Roads to Learning: Library Book Talks Broadcast to Girls and Boys*. New York: H. W. Wilson, 1939. 236 pp.

Scripts of a series of library book talks broadcast to boys and girls, grades 5-12, as part of the Rochester (N.Y.) School of the Air, sponsored by the Board of Education. A preface explains the underlying educational theory.

1968. SIEPMANN, CHARLES A. "Further Thoughts on Radio Criticism," *Public Opinion Quarterly*, 5: 308-12 (June 1941).

Criticism of Robert Landry's article, *Public Opinion Quarterly*, 4: 620-29 (December 1940), advocating development of professional radio critics. By a U.S. specialist, formerly a director of BBC, later a lecturer at Harvard on radio and education.

1969. STANTON, FRANK. "Factors Involved in 'Going on the Air,'" *Journal of Applied Psychology*, 23: 170-87 (February 1939).

By CBS research director. "To present a brief outline to the social scientists of some of the things known regarding the radio audience and the use which the advertisers make of these data, this article is organized around the steps taken by a radio sponsor once he has decided to 'go on the air.'"

1969a. STEHMANN, OTTO. *Geschichte und Bedeutung der Leipziger Sender: Ein Beitrag zur Publizistik des Rundfunks* (Leipziger Beitraege zur Erforschung der Publizistik). Dresden: Dittert, 1939. 108 pp.

"History and Significance of the Leipzig Radio."

1970. STEWART, IRVIN, editor. *Local Broadcasts to Schools*. Chicago: University of Chicago, 1939. 239 pp.

Symposium on experiences of six representative U.S. cities—Detroit, Cleveland, Rochester (N.Y.), Portland (Ore.), Akron, Alameda (Calif.)—in presentation of local broadcasts to schools. Covers such factors as time, length, subject, cost, treatment, and results of broadcasts. The authors are officials in charge of the programs, who answered questionnaires and wrote essays suggested by the editor on behalf of the National Research Council's Committee on Scientific Aids to Learning.

1971. STOKER, WILLIAM HENRY. "The Broadcasting Report," *Contemporary Review*, 149: 582-88 (May 1936).

1972. STRANGER, RALPH (pseud.). *Dictionary of Radio and Television Terms*. Brooklyn: Chemical Publishing Company, 1942. 252 pp.

Technical; for radio and television engineers.

1973. SUMMERS, HARRISON BOYD, compiler. *Radio Censorship* (Reference Shelf, vol. 12, no. 10). New York: H. W. Wilson, 1939. 297 pp.

Debate manual.

1974. *Television: The Future of the New Art, and Its Recent Technical Developments*, vol. 2. New York: RCA Institute's Technical Press, October 1937. 435 pp.

Twenty-four papers on television engineering, and four papers of more general interest under the titles: "What of Television?" by David Sarnoff, president of RCA; "Television Among the Visual Arts"; "Television Problems: A Description for Laymen"; and "Commercial Television and Its Needs."

1975. THOMSON, DAVID CLEGHORN. *Radio Is Changing Us: A Survey of Radio Development and Its Problems in Our Changing World*. London: Watts, 1937. 143 pp.

General analysis of the social role of radio, especially in democracies, by BBC official.

1976. "T.P.," *Time*, August 1, 1938, p. 20 ff.

Transradio Press, news agency serving almost 300 radio stations.

1977. U.S. BUREAU OF THE CENSUS. CENSUS OF BUSINESS, 1935. *Radio Broadcasting*. Washington, D.C.: Government Printing Office, October 1936. 75 pp.

1978. U.S. FEDERAL COMMUNICATIONS COMMISSION. *Annual Reports*, 1935–. Washington, D.C.: Government Printing Office, 1936–.

1979. U.S. FEDERAL COMMUNICATIONS COMMISSION. SPECIAL INVESTIGATING COMMITTEE ON TELEVISION. *Report* on the television industry. 2 parts, 1939.

*1980. U.S. Federal Communications Commission. Special Committee on Monopoly Abuses in Broadcasting. *Report* of the Committee, June 12, 1940. 1300 pp., mimeo.

Comprehensive survey of U.S. radio industry. "Based on more than 10,000 pages of testimony and nearly 800 exhibits, largely obtained through hearings which continued for 73 days, . . . the Report discusses in detail practices" which are said to "reveal at every turn the dominant position of the network organizations in the field of broadcasting. . . . More and more of the applications filed with the Commission for authority to own stations show the applicants to be persons of other large business interests, such as manufacturing, banking, publishing, natural resources development, public utility, etc. . . . Two-thirds of the nation's standard broadcast stations are operated as incidental to other businesses. . . . Two-thirds of all standard broadcast stations are licensed to corporations or are under their control." Committee recommends that Commission "redefine" its licensing policy and "require the elimination of inequitable and arbitrary contractual arrangements which affect the duty of the licensee to serve the public interest." For summary, see FCC Press Release no. 41,550 (June 12, 1940).

1981. U.S. Library of Congress. *Television: A Selected List of Recent Writings* (Select list of references, no. 1414). Washington, D.C., March 21, 1938.

1982. U.S. Senate Committee on Interstate Commerce. *Development of Television* (hearings April 10-11, 1940, on SR 251, requesting the Committee on Interstate Commerce to investigate the actions of the Federal Communications Commission in connection with the development of television; 76th Congress, 3rd session). Washington, D.C.: Government Printing Office, 1940. 81 pp.

1983. Wagner, Paul H. *Radio Journalism.* Minneapolis: Burgess Publishing Company, 1940. 135 pp.

Text by instructor in radio and journalism, Indiana University. Bibliography, pp. 133-35.

1984. Waldrop, Frank C.; and Borkin, Joseph. *Television: A Struggle for Power.* New York: Morrow, 1938. 292 pp.

Analysis of the struggle for control of the television industry, involving giant rival corporations, a pool of 15,000 patents, the division of the market into spheres of influence by different groups, and possible government efforts to promote democratization. Exhaustively documented. Bibliography, pp. 277-81.

1985. Western, John. "Television Girds for Battle," *Public Opinion Quarterly,* 3: 547-63 (October 1939).

Financial, technical, artistic, and regulatory aspects of television are described by a University of Southern California graduate student who has specialized in experiments with this medium.

1986. Whipple, James. *How to Write for Radio.* New York: McGraw-Hill, 1938. 425 pp.

By a member of the Radio Department, Lord and Thomas advertising agency. Bibliography, pp. 415-16.

1987. (Pop.) Wylie, Max. *Radio Writing,* introduction by Lewis Titterton. New York: Farrar and Rinehart, 1939. 550 pp.

Text for script writers. By director of script and continuity of Columbia Broadcasting System. Introduction by manager, script division, National Broadcasting Company.

1988. Yenezawa, Yososhichi. "The Present Status of Broadcasting Installations in Japan," *Far Eastern Review,* 32: 269-75 (June 1936).

2. PERSONNEL

1989. Arnold, Frank Atkinson. *Do You Want to Get Into Radio?,* introduction by Levering Tyson. New York: Stokes, 1940. 140 pp.

Brief occupational survey of the radio industry, including its public relations specialists. Bibliography, pp. 135-40.

1990. DeHaven, Robert; and Kahm, Harold S. *How to Break into Radio.* New York: Harpers, 1941. 162 pp.

Advice on radio jobs. Mr. DeHaven is a radio production man, Mr. Kahm associate editor of *Radio Showmanship.* Includes results of a questionnaire study made at Ohio State University by W. W. Charters and Norval N. Luxon, in which 108 station executives indicated the college subjects and other prerequisites they preferred in the record of a job applicant.

1991. CARLISLE, NORMAN V.; and RICE, CONRAD C. *Your Career in Radio.* New York: Dutton, 1941. 189 pp.

Jobs in radio described in semifictional form. Program direction, the intricate organization of a broadcasting station, and the business side are discussed, with details as to salaries and qualifications. An appendix lists colleges and universities which offer radio courses.

1992. HORNUNG, JULIUS LAWRENCE. *Radio as a Career* (Kitson Career Series). New York: Funk and Wagnalls, 1940. 212 pp.

Thorough survey of radio vocations, for students and counselors. The author is a specialist in radio operation. Bibliography, pp. 211-12.

1993. KNIGHT, RUTH ADAMS. *Stand By For the Ladies!: The Distaff Side of Radio,* with introduction by Lenox R. Lohr. New York: Coward, McCann, 1939. 179 pp.

Opportunities and requirements for women in the field of radio, described by a celebrated U.S. script writer whose life (see *Current Biography,* August 1943) has been a vivid illustration of the advice she gives.

3. QUANTITATIVE STUDIES OF AUDIENCES, COVERAGE AND EFFECTS
[See also Part 6.]

1994. "Audimeter," *Time,* May 16, 1938, p. 30.

New attachment for radio sets will record with a stylus on moving tape every twist of the dials, furnishing advertisers with an infallible record of listeners' habits.

1995. BEVILLE, H. M., JR. "The ABCD's of Radio Audiences," *Public Opinion Quarterly,* 4: 195-206 (June 1940).

Research manager of NBC discusses the popularity of well-known programs among different socio-economic strata.

1996. BIRD, WIN(FRED) W. *The Educational Aims and Practices of the National and Columbia Broadcasting Systems* (University of Washington Extension series, no. 10), Seattle: University of Washington, 1939. 82 pp.

Dr. Bird is a professor of speech, University of Washington. In consultation with experts, educational criteria were applied to a sample of "educational" radio programs. *Findings*: 12.7 per cent of all CBS programs and 7.2 per cent of NBC programs were judged to be "educationally significant." Rated highest: *American School of the Air* (CBS); *Music Appreciation Hour* and *America's Town Meeting of the Air* (NBC); *University of Chicago Round Table; National Farm and Home Hour* (U.S. Department of Agriculture). This report also contains summaries of the educational philosophies of the radio networks, based on interviews with their officials.

1997. BRUNER, JEROME S.; and SAYRE, JEANETTE (i.e., SMITH, JEANETTE SAYRE). "Short-Wave Listening in an Italian Community," *Public Opinion Quarterly,* 5: 640-56 (Winter 1941).

A polling study of a group of marginal Americans in Boston's Italian North End furnishes a clue to the motivation and behavior of the recent immigrant short-wave listener. By two U.S. specialists in psychology of radio, working under auspices of Princeton Radio Research Project. See also Jeanette Sayre Smith's study, cited below, no. 2019.

1998. CANTRIL, HADLEY. "The Role of the Radio Commentator," *Public Opinion Quarterly,* 3: 654-62 (October 1939).

Why audiences like commentators. Based on data of the Princeton Radio Research Project.

1999. CHAPPELL, MATTHEW N. "Factors Influencing Recall of Radio Programs," *Public Opinion Quarterly,* 6: 107-14 (Spring 1942).

By a U.S. market research specialist.

2000. CHILDS, HARWOOD LAWRENCE. "Short-Wave Listening in the

United States," *Public Opinion Quarterly*, 5: 210-26 (June 1941).

Listening practices, program preferences, and personal characteristics of short-wave listeners are discussed on the basis of surveys to date.

2001. CLARK, WESTON R. "Radio Listening Habits of Children," *Journal of Social Psychology*, 12: 131-49 (August 1940).

2002. *Cooperative Analysis of Broadcasting.* New York, fortnightly, 1934–.

Reports the percentage of radio sets theoretically tuned in on leading U.S. radio programs, based on actual checks of homes in key areas. Findings are summarized in "Ten Years of Network Program Analysis," in *Variety Radio Directory*, vol. 3 (1939-40), pp. 36-158.

2003. CURTIS, ALBERTA. *Listeners Appraise a College Station: Station WOI, Iowa State College, Ames, Iowa.* Washington, D.C.: Federal Radio Education Committee, 1940. 70 pp.

Study by a Rockefeller Fellow under direction of Dr. Paul Felix Lazarsfeld, director of Office of Radio Research. Tells how different classes of listeners reacted to book programs, music, vocational guidance, market news, etc. Bibliographic footnotes.

2004. DE BOER, JOHN JAMES. "The Determination of Children's Interests in Radio Drama," *Journal of Applied Psychology*, 21: 456-63 (August 1937).

Specially designed programs were produced; groups of listening children were observed by various techniques for the measurement of attention.

2005. DE BOER, JOHN JAMES. *Emotional Responses of Children to Radio Drama* (abstract of Ph.D. thesis, education, Chicago). Chicago: University of Chicago Libraries, 1940. About 30 pp.

Children's responses were measured through a study of continuous records of circulatory, respiratory, and dermal changes occurring during programs. Children's statements as to their preferences were compared with these data, as were their other responses in group listening to programs.

2006. EISENBERG, AZRIEL L. *Children and Radio Programs: A Study of More Than Three Thousand Children in the New York Metropolitan Area.* New York: Columbia University, 1936. 240 pp.

Habits, preferences, and conscious attitudes of children and parents in the New York metropolitan area, with regard to radio programs heard at home. Bibliography, pp. 233-34.

2007. GAUDET, HAZEL. "High School Students Judge Radio Programs," *Education*, 60: 639-46 (June 1940).

Preferences of a panel of 600 high school students who listened to a specially prepared series of scripts. Author was on staff of Office of Radio Research.

2008. JOINT COMMITTEE ON RADIO RESEARCH. *The Joint Committee Study of Rural Radio Ownership and Use in the United States,* sponsored by National Broadcasting Corp. and Columbia Broadcasting Corp. New York, 1939. 2 vols.

Data on U.S. rural radio ownership, station availability, and listening habits, compiled for the use of the broadcasters.

2009. KAROL, JOHN J. "Measuring Radio Audiences," *Public Opinion Quarterly*, 1 no. 2: 92-96 (April 1937).

Techniques are discussed by CBS Director of Market Research.

2010. LAZARSFELD, PAUL FELIX; and STANTON, FRANK N., editors. *Radio Research, 1941.* New York: Duell, Sloan and Pearce, 1942. 333 pp.

Report of some of the researches directed in 1941 by Drs. Lazarsfeld and Stanton. Rudolf Arnheim and Martha Collins Bayne write on contents and appeals of foreign-language U.S. radio programs over local American stations. Duncan MacDougald, Jr., writes on "The Popular Music Industry," pointing out that in many cases a "hit" is created by smart public relations rather than by spontaneous audience-response to a tune. T. W. Adorno writes on the aesthetics of radio symphonies. Edward Suchman writes on the "Invitation to Music" program and its effect on those who may be discovering "highbrow" music for the first time. Frederick J. Meine reports a field study of effects of radio and press on 1200 young people's knowledge of the news. Dr. William S. Robinson, Columbia University sociologist, contributes a careful and elaborate analysis of what happened to interests, attitudes, and habits of midwestern farm families when they bought radios. Findings of this study concerning National Farm and Home Hour will be of especial importance to students of public opinion. Bibliographic footnotes.

2011. LIKERT, RENSIS. "Method for Measuring the Sales Influence of a Radio Program," *Journal of Applied Psychology*, 20: 175-82 (April 1936).

2012. LONGSTAFF, HOWARD PORTER. "Effectiveness of Children's Radio Programs," *Journal of Applied Psychology*, 20: 208-20 (April 1936).

2013. LONGSTAFF, HOWARD PORTER. "Mothers' Opinions of Children's Radio Programs," *Journal of Applied Psychology*, 21: 265-79 (June 1937).

Based on interviews with several hundred mothers in Minneapolis and St. Paul.

2014. "Progress in Radio Research," special issue of *Journal of Applied Psychology*, 24: 661-853 (December 1940), edited by Paul Felix Lazarsfeld.

Symposium on the commercial and educational results obtained in radio broadcasting, and on techniques of radio research. Contributors include Raymond Franzen, Hazel Gaudet, D. B. Lucas, Boyd McCandless, Seerley Reid, Malcolm G. Rollins, Elias Smith, Frank Stanton, Edward A. Suchman, Elmo C. Wilson, and others.

2015. "Radio Research," special issue of *Journal of Applied Psychology*, 23: 1-215 (February 1939), edited by Paul Felix Lazarsfeld.

Among the articles in this symposium of the Office of Radio Research are: P. F. Lazarsfeld, "The Change of Opinion During a Political Discussion"; Edward A. Suchman, "Radio Listening and Automobiles"; Francis Holter, "Radio Among the Unemployed"; and a "Bibliography on Program Preferences of Different Groups."

2016. "Radiovoter Offers New Plan to Measure Public Opinion," *Sales Management*, 40: 630 (April 1, 1937).

National Electric Ballots, Inc., of New York, are undertaking to manufacture an attachment for radio receiving sets, enabling the listener to "vote" by pressing a button at a moment specified by the announcer.

2017. SAYRE, JEANETTE (i.e., SMITH, JEANETTE SAYRE). "Progress in Radio Fan-Mail Analysis," *Public Opinion Quarterly*, 3: 272-78 (April 1939).

Fan-mail responses to America's Town Meeting of the Air.

2018. SCHULER, EDGAR ALBERT; and EUBANK, WAYNE C. "Sampling Listener Reactions To Short-Wave Broadcasts," *Public Opinion Quarterly*, 5: 260-66 (June 1941).

Based on a sample of telephone subscribers in Baton Rouge, Louisiana, this study by two Louisiana State University sociologists gives data on characteristics and reactions of listeners to European short-wave broadcasts.

2019. SMITH, JEANETTE SAYRE. "Broadcasting for Marginal Americans," *Public Opinion Quarterly*, 6: 588-603 (Winter 1942).

Field study of local Italian-language broadcasting in Boston. An outgrowth of the Bruner and Sayre study of "Short-Wave Listening in an Italian Community," *Public Opinion Quarterly*, 5: 640-56 (Winter 1941), cited above, title 1997.

2020. STANTON, FRANK. "Commercial Effects of Radio: A Two-way Check on the Sales Influence of a Specific Radio Program," *Journal of Applied Psychology*, 24: 665-72 (December 1940).

By CBS research director. "The investigation was carefully worked out with the manufacturer's advertising agent and a field research agency. For the experimental sample, two markets were selected in which all of the advertiser's sales factors were exactly comparable except that his program was broadcast in Market A and was not broadcast in Market B. . . . In brief, the investigation found that an average radio program—with an average audience—sells a branded product and builds a measurable degree of buying consistency among its listeners. In this case, the selling-edge of a radio program was isolated and measured for the sponsor perhaps more closely than it had ever been before. It is illuminating to examine the results separately and in greater detail."

2021. WELD, LOUIS DWIGHT HARVELL. "The Problem of Measuring Radio Coverage," *Journal of the American Statistical Association*, 33: 117-25 (March 1938).

Statistician evaluates recent studies of the Joint Committee on Radio Research, of which he is a member.

VI. BOOKS AND OTHER PRINTED MATTER; LIBRARIES AND MUSEUMS

1. CONTROL, ORGANIZATION, EQUIPMENT

2022. ADAM, THOMAS RITCHIE. *The Museum and Popular Culture* (Studies in the Social Significance of Adult Education in the United States, no. 14). New York: American Association for Adult Education, 1939. 177 pp.

2023. (Pop.) ARKIN, HERBERT; and COLTON, RAYMOND R. *Graphs, How to Make and Use Them*, 3rd ed., rev. New York: Harpers, 1940. 236 pp.

Revision of standard treatise illustrating nearly every type of graphic presentation.

2024. BARKER, TOMMIE DORA. *Libraries of the South: A Report on Developments, 1930-35*. Chicago: American Library Association, 1936. 215 pp.

Library development in 13 southern states, where in 1935 20,000,000 people were without access to public libraries. Discusses the arousing of public opinion through conferences, federal library projects, foundation-financed demonstrations, etc.

2025. BINKLEY, ROBERT C.; and others. *Manual on Methods of Reproducing Research Materials*. Ann Arbor: Edwards Brothers, 1936. 207 pp.

Report of Joint Committee on Materials for Research set up by Social Science Research Council and American Council of Learned Societies. Surveys costs of book publishing,

printing, multigraphing, offset processes, blueprinting, photostating, and other techniques.

2026. (Pop.) BRINTON, WILLARD COPE. *Graphic Presentation*. New York: Brinton Associates, 1939. 512 pp.

Most complete collection available of examples of every known type of graphic presentation: classification charts, organization charts, flow charts, bar charts; route, relief, aerial, symbolic, flow, contour, area maps; photos; slides; displays; exhibits; etc.

2027. BROWN, STEPHEN JAMES MEREDITH. *Libraries and Literature from a Catholic Standpoint*. Dublin: Brown and Nolan, 1937. 323 pp.

A study of Catholic literature and of Catholic censorship policies, written with a view to promoting the Catholic Library Movement. The author is editor of the Catholic Bibliographical Series, and Lecturer in the School of Library Training, University College, Dublin.

2028. BURNS, NED J. *Field Manual for Museums*. Washington, D.C.: Government Printing Office, 1941. 426 pp.

Manual for monument custodians, park naturalists, historians, and curators who operate National Park Service museums in the field.

2029. CANNON, CARL LESLIE, editor. *Guide to Library Facilities for National Defense*, rev. ed. Chicago: American Library Association, 1941. 448 pp.

2029a. CHANDLER, HENRY BRAMWELL; and CROTEAU, JOHN TOUGAS. *A Regional Library and its Readers: A Study of Five Years of Rural Reading*. New York: American Association for Adult Education, 1940. 136 pp.

2030. CHENEY, ORION HOWARD. *Economic Survey of the Book Industry 1930-31*. New York: National Association of Book Publishers, 1931. 337 pp.

The author continued this survey in a *Supplementary Report of the Economic Survey of the Book Industry* (1932).

2031. CIBELLA, ROSS C., compiler. *Directory of Microfilm Sources, includ-*

ing Photostat Service. New York: Special Libraries Association, 1941. 56 pp.

2031a. COLEMAN, LAURENCE VAIL. *The Museum in America: A Critical Study*. Washington, D.C.: American Association of Museums, 1939. 3 vols.

By a leading U.S. specialist, Director of American Association of Museums, who is author of half a dozen books on museums. Contains much material on public relations, including a chapter (17) devoted to that subject.

2032. DOWNS, ROBERT BINGHAM. *Resources of New York City Libraries: A Survey of Facilities for Advanced Study and Research*. Chicago: American Library Association, 1942. 442 pp.

Libraries of every description are covered in this survey by Director of Libraries, New York University. There are special chapters on sources for the history of books; journalism; government publications; history; geography and maps; social sciences; economics; languages; religion; law; medicine; technology. Bibliography in text and pp. 309-403.

2033. FRARY, IHNA THAYER. *Museum Membership and Publicity* (American Association of Museums, Publications, n.s. no. 13, pp. 1-35). Washington, D.C., 1935.

A brief discussion of publicity by the secretary of publicity at the Cleveland Museum of Art.

2034. FUSSLER, HERMAN HOWE. *Photographic Reproduction for Libraries: A Study of Administrative Problems* (University of Chicago Studies in Library Science). Chicago: University of Chicago, 1942. 218 pp.

Report on recent use of microphotography, by Head, Department of Photographic Reproduction, University of Chicago Libraries. Bibliography, pp. 205-07.

2035. GAUM, CARL GILBERT; GRAVES, HAROLD F.; and HOFFMAN, LYNE S. S. *Report Writing*, rev. ed. New York: Prentice-Hall, 1942. 332 pp.

Revision of a 1929 textbook for students in technical colleges, by three teachers of English.

2036. GLEASON, ELIZA ATKINS. *The Southern Negro and the Public Library: A Study of the Government and Administration of Public Library Service to Negroes in the South* (University of Chicago Studies in Library Science), foreword by Louis Round Wilson. Chicago: University of Chicago, 1941. 218 pp.

"It is one thing to say that the residents of New Orleans (population 458,762, 1930 Census) had access to 273,683 volumes in its public library in 1939. It is quite another thing to know, however, that 129,632 Negroes in New Orleans had only 14,697 volumes for their exclusive use ... and they constituted the only collection of books directly available to Negroes in the city. . . .

"The present study was made to determine just what public library service was available in 1939 to the 8,805,635 Negroes in 13 southern states in which segregation of service is prevalent." Mrs. Gleason has been librarian of Talladega College and was under appointment as director of the Library School of Atlanta University at the time of publication of this volume. Bibliography, pp. 199-202.

2037. GRAY, WILLIAM SCOTT, editor. *Proceedings of the Conference on Reading held at University of Chicago*. Chicago: University of Chicago, 1939, 1940, 1941. 3 vols.

Recent trends in reading are discussed by specialists.

2038. GÜLICH, WILHELM. "Politik und Forschung: Die dynamische Bibliothek als Quelle politischer Erkenntnis," *Zeitschrift für Politik*, January 1941, pp. 3-32.

"Politics and Research: The Dynamic Library as a Source of Political Insight." By organizer of the Library of the Kiel Institute of World Economics (Kieler Institut für Weltwirtschaft).

2039. HILL, DAVID SPENCE. *The Libraries of Washington: A Study of the Governmental and Non-Governmental Libraries in the District of Columbia in*

Relation to the Units of Government and Other Organizations Which They Serve. Chicago: American Library Association, 1936. 312 pp.

2040. HOLMSTROM, JOHANNES EDWIN. *Records and Research in Engineering and Industrial Science: A Guide to the Production, Extraction, Integrating, Storekeeping, Circulation and Translation of Technical Knowledge.* London: Chapman and Hall, 1940. 302 pp.

Deals with many phases of the problem of communication in the engineering and industrial fields. By British engineer and economist.

2041. INTER-AMERICAN BIBLIOGRAPHICAL AND LIBRARY ASSOCIATION. *Proceedings of the First and Second Conventions, Washington, D.C., 1938 and 1939.* New York: H. W. Wilson, 1938 and 1939. 267 and 330 pp.

Addresses and papers on Hemisphere intellectual cooperation. Includes material on library facilities, newspaper collections, government publications, children's books, etc., of the various American countries.

2042. JOECKEL, CARLETON BRUNS, editor. *Current Issues in Library Administration* (University of Chicago Studies in Library Science). Chicago: University of Chicago, 1939. 392 pp.

Papers before the Library Institute, 1938. Includes "Public Relations in Public Administration," by James L. McCamy; "Interpretation of the Public Library," and "Practical Publicity Methods," by J. A. Lowe. Bibliography, pp. 371-85.

2043. JOECKEL, CARLETON BRUNS. *The Government of the American Public Library* (Ph.D. thesis, University of Chicago). Chicago: University of Chicago, 1935. 393 pp.

The first factual survey of library government in the United States. The libraries of the 310 American cities having a population over 30,000 are studied, and suggestions for regional administration emerge. Bibliography, pp. 356-66.

2044. JOHNSON, ALVIN SAUNDERS. *The Public Library: A People's University.* New York: American Association for Adult Education, 1938. 85 pp.

General essay on U.S. libraries in terms of their possible functions in the diffusion of democratic practices; by Director of the New School for Social Research.

2045. JOHNSON, ISABEL SIMERAL. "Cartoons," *Public Opinion Quarterly,* 1 no. 3: 21-44 (July 1937).

Mrs. Milbank Johnson (Ph.D. Columbia), who has specialized in the collection and analysis of cartoons for many years, discusses use of cartoons since 1360 B.C.

2045a. LAUBACH, FRANK CHARLES. *Toward a Literate World,* foreword by Edward Lee Thorndike. New York: Columbia University, 1938. 178 pp.

Survey of world literacy problems, with convenient charts on extent of literacy, and with teaching suggestions. Dr. Laubach (Ph.D. Columbia 1915) has served for more than 25 years as a missionary and educator in the Philippines and has made extended studies on literacy in all parts of the world under auspices of World Literacy Committee.

2046. *Lexikon des gesamten Buchwesens,* edited by Karl Löffler, Joachim Kirchner and Wilhelm Olbrich. Leipzig: Hiersemann, 1935-37. 3 vols.

Encyclopedia of books and publishers, bibliophiles and libraries, copiously indexed and cross-referenced.

2047. LOIZEAUX, MARIE D. *Publicity Primer; an A B C of "Telling All" about the Public Library,* 2nd ed. rev. New York: H. W. Wilson, 1939. 72 pp.

Bibliography, pp. 67-68.

2048. *London Bibliography of the Social Sciences,* introduction by Sidney Webb. London: London School of Economics and Political Science, 1931-34. 4 vols. and supplements.

Comprehensive bibliography of materials available in London libraries.

2049. LOW, THEODORE LEWIS. *The Museum as a Social Instrument: A Study Undertaken for the Committee* on Education of the American Association of Museums. New York: Metropolitan Museum of Art and American Association of Museums, 1942. 70 pp.

Mr. Low, a Harvard graduate student in Fine Arts, wrote this study during a two-year period on a Carnegie grant as a Field Representative of American Association for Adult Education. Bibliography, pp. 67-70.

2050. MANLEY, MARIAN CATHERINE, editor. *Business and the Public Library: Steps in Successful Cooperation.* New York: Special Libraries Association, 1940. 83 pp.

Series of essays by librarians on services performed by public business libraries. Contains lists of publications and book selection aids.

2050a. MERRITT, LEROY CHARLES. *The United States Government as Publisher* (University of Chicago Studies in Library Science). Chicago: University of Chicago, 1943. 179 pp.

A general picture of the material to be found in United States public documents, and a study of their distribution and utilization, by a staff member of Farmville, Virginia, State Teachers College. Data are presented in terms of federal departments sponsoring the publications; functions of the publications; and subject-matter. Bibliography, pp. 175-76.

2051. MILES, ARNOLD; and MARTIN, LOWELL. *Public Administration and the Library* (University of Chicago Studies in Library Science). Chicago: University of Chicago, 1941. 313 pp.

Mr. Miles was staff member, Public Administration Service, at the time of writing; Mr. Martin in the Chicago Public Library. This is the last of three studies of the library in relation to government, sponsored by the Graduate Library School, University of Chicago. Bibliography in footnotes and pp. 293-98.

2052. (Pop.) MODLEY, RUDOLF. *How to Use Pictorial Statistics,* with one chapter on symbols by Franz C. Hess. New York: Harpers, 1937. 170 pp.

How to use pictorial statistics and how to make the layouts. The author (Ph.D. Vienna) is head of an American firm specializing in this craft. Bibliography, pp. 158-66. Theory

of Modley's pictorial statistics and those of Neurath (cited below, title 2055) is discussed by Bruce Lannes Smith in a review of their books and activities, *Public Opinion Quarterly,* 2: 148-50 (January 1938).

2053. MODLEY, RUDOLF. "Pictographs Today and Tomorrow," *Public Opinion Quarterly,* 2: 659-64 (October 1938).

Rules for pictorial statistics.

2054. MOORE, ELEANOR M. *Youth in Museums.* Philadelphia: University of Pennsylvania, 1941. 115 pp.

Study of the work for young people in more than a hundred museums in the U.S. and Canada, by a member of the staff of University Museum, Philadelphia.

2055. (Pop.) NEURATH, OTTO. *International Picture Language: The First Rules of Isotype* (Psyche Miniatures). London: Kegan Paul, 1936. 117 pp.

Theory of a picture-vocabulary suitable for world-wide communication is elaborated by the founder and former director of the Social and Economic Museum of Vienna. Bibliography, pp. 116-17.

*2056. (Pop.) OGDEN, CHARLES KAY. *The System of Basic English.* New York: Harcourt, Brace, 1934. 320 pp.

Advocates and explains the use of a basic English vocabulary of 850 selected words which may be used to clarify and simplify almost anything anyone has to say, and also to communicate with those who do not know much English. One of several works by the leading promoter of the Basic English movement. See also Professor Ogden's *General Basic English Dictionary* (London: Evans Bros., Ltd., 1940. New York: Norton, 1942. 438 pp.), a reference book which defines thousands of words.

2057. OUTERBRIDGE, PAUL. *Photographing in Color.* New York: Random House, 1940. 204 pp.

Lucid and comprehensive text.

2058. (Pop.) PUBLIC AFFAIRS COMMITTEE, INC. *More Than a Million,* rev. ed. New York, August 1939. 16 pp.

Summary of the three years' activities of Public Affairs Committee, the group which publishes *Public Affairs Pamphlets*: how they select their topics; how they make their pamphlets readable; how they promote distribution through bookstores, colleges, public schools, conferences, etc.; how they measure the size of the publics they are reaching. "One-third of our 3,400 subscribers are individuals, not otherwise identifiable; 592 are school and college faculty or Board of Education members; 544 are libraries; 305 are organizations and clubs; 230 are business firms." Promotion is also carried on through syndicated newspaper mats, radio programs, and a leading textbook firm.

2059. (Pop.) PUBLIC AFFAIRS COMMITTEE. *Two Million Public Affairs Pamphlets*. New York, July 1940. 12 pp.

The Committee has sold 2,000,000 of its pamphlets, covering 46 topics. Promotion also includes newspaper layouts, bookstore displays, and "Public Affairs Weekly," an NBC broadcast.

2060. *Public Affairs Pamphlets: An Index to Inexpensive Pamphlets on Social, Economic, Political, and International Affairs* (United States Office of Education, Bulletin, 1937, no. 3). Washington, D.C.: Government Printing Office, 1937. 83 pp. Supplement, 1938; 67 pp.

An aid to those who are studying the increasing use of pamphlet campaigns.

2061. RANDALL, WILLIAM MADISON; and GOODRICH, FRANCIS LEE DEWEY. *Principles of College Library Administration* (2nd ed.). Chicago: American Library Association and University of Chicago, 1941. 249 pp.

By two professors of library science. Bibliography at ends of chapters.

2062. RAUTENSTRAUCH, WALTER. *Industrial Surveys and Reports*. New York: Wiley, 1940. 189 pp.

Text for engineers on the preparation of engineering and financial reports on large enterprises. By Columbia professor of industrial engineering.

2063. RUBIN, I. N. "Book Production in the USSR," *Research Bulletin*

on the Soviet Union, 2: 101-10 (October 1937).

Tables showing categories of books. This *Research Bulletin* is a monthly published by American-Russian Institute for Cultural Relations with the Soviet Union, Inc.

2064. SAUNDERS, ALTA GWINN; and ANDERSON, CHESTER REED. *Business Reports: Investigation and Presentation*, rev. ed. New York: McGraw-Hill, 1940. 468 pp.

A standard text on preparation of questions, questionnaires, data sheets, and reports on large-scale business operations, by two University of Illinois professors of English. Bibliography, pp. 455-61.

2065. SHAW, MARIAN, editor. *Library Literature, 1933-35*. New York: H. W. Wilson, 1936. 435 pp.

"An author and subject index-digest to current books, pamphlets, and periodical literature relating to the library." Supplements Harry George Turner Cannons' *Bibliography of Library Economy, 1876-1920* and the American Library Association's *Library Literature, 1921-32*.

2066. SHELDON, CYRIL. *A History of Poster Advertising, Together with a Record of Legislation and Attempted Legislation Affecting Outdoor Advertising*. London: Chapman and Hall, 1937. 316 pp.

Study of English experience with outdoor advertising, by a former president of the British Poster Advertising Association. Bibliography in text.

2067. SHOVE, RAYMOND HOWARD. *Cheap Book Production in the United States, 1870 to 1891* (M.A. thesis, library science, Illinois). Urbana: University of Illinois Library, 1937. 155 pp.

Early efforts to publish lower-priced books. Bibliography, pp. 131-36.

2068. THOMPSON, JAMES WESTFALL. *The Medieval Library* (University of Chicago Studies in Library Science). Chicago: University of Chicago, 1939. 682 pp.

History of books and libraries from beginning of Christian era to the invention of printing, by a veteran U.S. historian. Bibliographic footnotes.

2069. U.S. NATIONAL RESOURCES PLANNING BOARD (formerly NATIONAL RESOURCES COMMITTEE). *Suggested Symbols for Plans, Maps, and Charts.* Washington, D.C.: Government Printing Office, June 1938. 12 pp.

A guide to those who employ graphic presentation, with the aim of encouraging uniformity of practice in the use of symbols and in other details of map preparation. Bibliography, pp. 9-10.

2070. VORMELKER, ROSE L., editor. *Special Library Resources, vol. 1: United States and Canada.* New York: Special Libraries Association, 31 East Tenth Street, 1941. About 900 pp.

Descriptive list of 765 special research libraries and their collections; covers private, public, and university libraries in the United States and Canada. "It is planned eventually to cover as nearly as possible every research library collection in this hemisphere. Work is already under way for Volume II."

2071. VREELAND, F. McL. "The Teaching Uses of a Sociological Museum," *American Sociological Review,* 3: 32-38 (February 1938).

2072. WALRAVEN, MARGARET KESSLER; and HALL-QUEST, ALFRED L. *Library Guidance for Teachers.* New York: John Wiley, 1941. 308 pp.

Comprehensive manual on school library procedures, with discussion of the principles of building a reference collection. Bibliography at ends of chapters.

2073. WAPLES, DOUGLAS. *The Library.* Chicago: University of Chicago, 1936. 82 pp.

Analyzes the contents, finances, and extent of use of American college libraries. A publication of the Committee on Revision of Standards, of the Commission on Higher Institutions.

2074. WARD, GILBERT OAKLEY. *Publicity for Public Libraries: Principles and Methods for Librarians, Library Assistants, Trustees, and Library Schools,*

2nd ed. New York: H. W. Wilson, 1935. 439 pp.

Supersedes 1924 edition. Bibliography, pp. 299-309.

2075. WELLARD, JAMES HOWARD. *The Public Library Comes of Age.* London: Grafton, 1940. 204 pp.

Based on Ph.D. thesis, library science, Chicago. Part I. The public library as a social force. Part II. The sociology of the public library. Part III. The practice of public librarianship.

2076. WILSON, LOUIS ROUND, editor. *Library Trends* (Papers presented before the Library Institute at the University of Chicago, August 3-15, 1936). Chicago: University of Chicago, 1937. 388 pp.

Papers by social scientists, librarians, and others on recent social trends and their implications for libraries.

2077. (Pop.) WILSON, LOUIS ROUND, editor. *The Practice of Book Selection.* Chicago: University of Chicago, 1940. 368 pp.

Papers presented before Library Institute at University of Chicago, August 1939. Includes "Community Analysis and the Practice of Book Selection," by Leon Carnovsky; "Important Books of the Last 100 Years in Political Science, Economics and Sociology," by Max Lerner; "Literature as Propaganda," by Henry Hazlitt; "Popularizing Science," by Waldemar Kaempffert; etc. Bibliography, pp. 344-56.

2078. WILSON, LOUIS ROUND, editor. *The Role of the Library in Adult Education* (Papers presented before the Library Institute at the University of Chicago, August 2-13, 1937). Chicago: University of Chicago, 1937. 321 pp.

2. PERSONNEL

2079. BOOK AND MAGAZINE GUILD. *Report of the Salary Survey of the Book Publishing Industry.* New York, 1940. 15 pp.

2080. MANLEY, MARIAN C., editor. *The Special Library Profession and*

What It Offers: Surveys of Fifteen Fields. New York: Special Libraries Association, 1938. About 100 pp.

Collection of about two dozen essays from *Special Libraries,* dealing with the services and personnel of this profession. Written by special librarians and others acquainted with chemical, newspaper, banking, municipal reference, and other types of libraries. Bibliography at ends of essays.

2081. SAVORD, RUTH. *Special Librarianship as a Career.* New London, Conn.: Institute of Women's Professional Relations, Connecticut College, 1942. Pamphlet, 15 pp.

An article sponsored by the Special Libraries Association. Bibliography, pp. 14-15.

2082. SCHMECKEBIER, LAURENCE FREDERICK. *Government Publications and Their Use,* 2d. ed. rev. Washington, D.C.: Brookings Institution, 1939. 479 pp.

Comprehensive manual. "These publications have long been the terror of librarians and the despair of almost everyone who has attempted to make use of them, and this manual furnishes a much needed description of the guides required. . . ."—*Foreword,* by A. P. Tisdel, U.S. Superintendent of Documents.

3. QUANTITATIVE STUDIES OF AUDIENCES, COVERAGE AND EFFECTS
[See also Part 6.]

2083. BERREMAN, J. V. *Factors Affecting the Sale of Modern Books of Fiction: A Study in Social Psychology* (Ph.D. thesis, Stanford, 1940).

2084. BRANSCOMB, BENNETT HARVIE. *Teaching with Books: A Study of College Libraries.* Chicago: American Library Association for the Association of American Colleges, 1940. 239 pp.

Under a Carnegie Corporation grant, a number of U.S. college libraries were studied to determine how much the students and faculty use them, how to make their facilities more useful and better understood, and how to select their books. The author is Director of the Libraries and Professor of Early Christian Literature, Duke University. Bibliographic footnotes.

2085. (Pop.) FLESCH, RUDOLF F. "Estimating the Comprehension Difficulty of Magazine Articles," *Journal of General Psychology,* 28: 63-80 (January 1943).

Semantic experiments at Readability Laboratory, Teachers College. Includes a critique and bibliography of previous efforts to determine statistically the factors that make a passage readable.

2086. GALLUP, GEORGE HORACE. "The Favorite Books of Americans," *New York Times Book Review,* January 15, 1939, pp. 2 ff.

Survey by American Institute of Public Opinion reveals that "Fiction leads non-fiction in public interest in all sections of the country . . . the public is inclined to overlook the serious thinkers . . . the first hint of history or economics is H. G. Wells's *Outline of History,* thirtieth on the list and a best-seller long before the depression. . . . Even in fiction the novel of 'social significance' is less likely to rank high in popular interest than the romantic kind." Leading choices in the 1938 study: (1) The Bible (named by nearly one voter in every five); (2) Gone With the Wind (named by 12 per cent); (3) Anthony Adverse; (4) The Citadel; (5) How to Win Friends and Influence People; (6) The Good Earth; (7) Ben-Hur; (8) Northwest Passage; (9) Little Women; (10) A Tale of Two Cities; (11) Les Misérables; (12) Magnificent Obsession; (13) Adventures of Tom Sawyer; (14) Treasure Island; (15) Count of Monte Cristo; (16) Robinson Crusoe; (17) Ivanhoe; (18) The Green Light; (19) David Copperfield; (20) Call of the Wild. "One thing comes immediately to mind about the leading books in the list. Nearly all of them have been seized upon by Hollywood as motion picture material. Even the Bible has been screened in part, and *Gone With the Wind* has been in casting pains for two years."

2087. (Pop.) GRAY, WILLIAM SCOTT, editor. *Reading in General Education: An Exploratory Study: A Report of the Committee on Reading in General Education.* Washington, D.C.: American Council on Education, 1940. 464 pp.

Information and guidance materials to aid schools and colleges in developing reading programs adapted to their needs. Bibliography at end of each chapter.

2088. (Pop.) GRAY, WILLIAM SCOTT; and HOLMES, ELEANOR. *The Development of Meaning Vocabularies in Reading: An Experimental Study*, with the cooperation of the faculty of the University Elementary School, the University of Chicago. Chicago: University of Chicago, 1938. 140 pp.

Two University of Chicago specialists in education review and summarize previous studies by educators relating to the nature and early development of vocabulary and of meaning in various subject-matter fields. The authors' own experiments with fourth graders are then reported. Bibliography in footnotes and pp. 130-35.

*2089. (Pop.) GRAY, WILLIAM SCOTT (W); and LEARY, BERNICE ELIZABETH. *What Makes a Book Readable, with Special Reference to Adults of Limited Reading Ability: An Initial Study*. Chicago: University of Chicago, 1935. 358 pp.

By two University of Chicago specialists in education. *Purpose*: "to make an initial survey of current opinion concerning what makes a book readable for adults of limited reading ability; to study objectively a small but important area of readability commonly designated 'case' or 'difficulty'; and to suggest possible applications of the findings to the work of librarians in selecting the right book for adult readers, as well as to the task of writers and publishers in preparing readable materials for different reading groups." Mathematical formulae (the "Gray-Leary formulae") are developed for determining degrees of readability. "Predicted Indexes of Difficulty of Three Hundred and Fifty Books," pp. 339-51. Bibliographic footnotes. See also 2089a.

2089a. (Pop.) GRAY, WILLIAM SCOTT; and MUNROE, RUTH. *The Reading Interests and Habits of Adults*. New York: Macmillan, 1929. 305 pp.

A digest of the investigations of reading and related subjects that have a bearing on adult education, with case studies of about 300 adults representing various social groups, to determine their reading habits. Bibliography, pp. 275-98.

2090. HAYGOOD, WILLIAM CONVERSE. *Who Uses the Public Library?: A Survey of the Patrons of the Circula-tion and Reference Departments of the New York Public Library*. Chicago: University of Chicago, 1938. 137 pp.
Bibliography, pp. 128-29.

2091. JOECKEL, CARLETON BRUNS. *Library Service* (U.S. Advisory Committee on Education, Staff study no. 11). Washington, D.C.: Government Printing Office, 1940. 107 pp.

"Public library service is accessible to 92 per cent of our urban people, but to only 26 per cent of rural residents. The Northeast and the Far West have more than their share of our 15,000 libraries and their quarter of a billion volumes, while the South is very much undersupplied. Ten specific recommendations are made as to what the Federal Government might properly do to improve this important educational service throughout the nation." Author is a University of Chicago professor of library science.

2092. JOECKEL, CARLETON BRUNS; and CARNOVSKY, LEON. *A Metropolitan Library in Action: A Survey of the Chicago Public Library* (University of Chicago Studies in Library Science). Chicago: University of Chicago, 1940. 466 pp.

Elaborate study by two specialists in Graduate Library School, University of Chicago. Includes a study of social composition of cardholders and of each group's attitudes toward the library.

2093. LIND, KATHERINE NILES. "The Social Psychology of Children's Reading," *American Journal of Sociology*, 41: 454-69 (January 1936).

Forty-four documents were secured from interviews and life histories. The isolating and socializing effects of reading were found to be closely related to a prior condition of frustration or adjustment. Other attitude changes were also noted. This article is based on a master's thesis (sociology), entitled "A Study in the Sociology of Reading" (University of Chicago, *ca.* 1936).

2094. MILLER, ROBERT A. "The Relation of Reading Characteristics to Social Indexes," *American Journal of Sociology*, 41: 738-57 (May 1936).

Reading interests of a middle-class census tract in Chicago are compared with those of a tract which is the home of industrial laborers.

2095. Punke, Harold H. "Cultural Change and Changes in Popular Literature," *Social Forces*, 15: 359-70 (1936-37).

2096. Punke, Harold H. "The Home and Adolescent Reading Interests," *School Review*, 45: 612-20 (October 1937).

Supplements the author's report in *Library Quarterly*, July 1937, on reading habits of pupils in 11 Georgia high schools and 11 Illinois high schools. Replies to questionnaires indicated preferred parts of newspapers, favorite types of magazines, names of magazines read, etc.

2097. Punke, Harold H. "Sociological Factors in the Leisure-Time Reading of High School Students," *Library Quarterly*, 7: 332-42 (July 1937).

Questionnaire study relating reading interests to sex differences, school year, employment status, size of family, and radio programs. Subjects were pupils in 11 Georgia high schools and 11 Illinois high schools.

2098. University of Chicago. Graduate Library School. *The Reference Function of the Library: Papers Presented before the Seventh Annual Library Institute at the University of Chicago, 1942*, edited by Pierce Butler, foreword by Louis Round Wilson. Chicago: University of Chicago, 1943. 366 pp.

*2099. Waples, Douglas (D,W). *People and Print*. Chicago: University of Chicago, 1937. 228 pp.

U.S. social scientist, author of a number of studies in reading-habits, analyzes statistics of the production, distribution, and consumption of reading matter, 1929-35, on the assumption that changes in those variables may indicate changes in public opinion. Presents a partial theory of depression psychology, and suggests a line of analysis for research in "the rich acres of newspaper files," which Dr. Waples regards as a fertile but virgin source of social insight. For an elaborate application of this author's methods to an election situation, see 2400.

2100. Waples, Douglas; Berelson, Bernard; and Bradshaw, Franklin R. *What Reading Does to People: Effects of Reading and a Statement of Problems for Research*. Chicago: University of Chicago, 1940. 222 pp.

States that "the responsible authorities and even academic students of the question have oversimplified their theories of reading influence to the point of serious error." The volume is an elaborate review of the literature, and also analyzes the social conditions affecting the publication and distribution of reading matter. Bibliography in footnotes and pp. 177-79.

2101. Waples, Douglas; and Carnovsky, Leon. *Libraries and Readers in the State of New York*. Chicago: University of Chicago, 1939. 160 pp.

Study of book and magazine reading of students and parents, and sources of supply of reading material, together with analysis of administration of public and school libraries.

2102. Waples, Douglas; and Lasswell, Harold Dwight. *National Libraries and Foreign Scholarship: Notes on Recent Selections in Social Science*. Chicago: University of Chicago, 1936. 152 pp.

A study of social science books and journals and of their international circulation. By two U.S. social scientists.

2102a. (Pop.) Waples, Douglas; and Tyler, Ralph Winfred. *What People want to Read About: A Study of Group Interests and a Survey of Problems in Adult Reading*. Chicago: University of Chicago, 1931. 312 pp.

Includes forms for determination of reading interests of a group, with instructions for their use.

VII. OTHER CHANNELS AND THEIR PERSONNEL

2103. *American Foundations and Their Fields*, vol. 5, compiled by Geneva Seybold. New York: Raymond Rich Associates, 1942. 274 pp.

1940 data. Earlier surveys were made by Twentieth Century Fund, 1930, 1931, and 1934, and by Miss Seybold in 1939. "An especially valuable departure is the analysis of the investment portfolios of the various foundations. . . ."

2104. *American Foundations for Social Welfare*, rev. ed. New York: Russell Sage Foundation, 1938. 66 pp.

Revision of a directory that has been out of print for several years. Lists 157 foundations and 31 community trusts.

2105. AUGUR, HELEN. *The Book of Fairs*, introduction by Hendrik Willem Van Loon. New York: Harcourt, Brace, 1940. 308 pp.

General history of fairs, beginning with the fairs of the Biblical city of Tyre, in 593 B.C. and so on down to the New York World's Fair and the Golden Gate International Exposition of 1939.

2106. BAIRD, ALBERT CRAIG. *Discussion: Principles and Types* (McGraw-Hill Series in Speech). New York and London: McGraw-Hill, 1943. 348 pp.

Treatise on leadership, participation, and language-use in discussion. By professor of speech, State University of Iowa. Bibliography, pp. 333-41.

2107. BAIRD, WILLIAM RAIMOND, 1858-1917, original editor. *Baird's Manual of American College Fraternities: A Descriptive Analysis with a Detailed Account of Each Fraternity*. New York: at intervals, 1879 to date.

1940 (14th) edition: 848 pp.

2108. BLOOMFIELD, LEONARD. *An Outline Guide to the Practical Study of Foreign Languages*. Baltimore: Linguistic Society of America, 1942. 16 pp.

Psychological and technical pointers for Americans who must learn foreign languages in a hurry. By Yale professor of linguistics.

2109. CLOKIE, HUGH McDOWALL; and ROBINSON, JOSEPH WILLIAM. *Royal Commissions of Inquiry: The Significance of Investigations in British Politics*. Stanford University: Stanford University, 1937. London: Oxford, 1937. 242 pp.

Comprehensive study of one of the most important British channels for multipartisan discussion and publicity on major social controversies. Some analysis is given of cases in which the Royal Commission is alleged to have whitewashed or to have concealed the evidence before it. Professor Clokie is a Canadian-American political scientist, at University of Manitoba since 1938. Dr. Robinson (Ph.D. Stanford) is a political scientist at Purdue.

2110. *Club Members of New York.* New York: Club Members of New York, Inc. (232 Madison Avenue), annual, 1913–.

A directory.

2111. COFFMAN, HAROLD COE. *American Foundations: A Study of their Role in the Child Welfare Movement*. New York: Association Press, 1936. 213 pp.

"Expenditures for the decade 1921-30 of seventy-five foundations, with a combined capital of over one billion dollars, are analyzed and depicted, and their organization and methods are described."

2112. COMMUNIST PARTY OF U.S.A. ORGANIZATIONAL-EDUCATIONAL COMMISSION. *How to Organize Mass Meetings*. New York: Workers Library, 1940. 48 pp.

How to conduct and publicize a meeting, how to appeal for funds, how to obtain publicity, singers, musicians, films, etc.

2113. COON, HORACE CAMPBELL. *Money to Burn: What the Great American Philanthropic Foundations Do with their Money*. London and New York: Longmans, Green, 1938. 352 pp.

By a U.S. journalist.

2114. DENNY, GEORGE VERNON, JR. *A Handbook for Discussion Leaders*. New York: Town Hall, 1938. 32 pp.

Prepared for use in connection with programs of America's Town Meeting of the Air. By the director of that celebrated forum.

2115. DOVIFAT, EMIL. *Rede und Redner: Ihr Wesen und Ihre Politische Macht*. Leipzig: Bibliographisches Institut, 1937. 150 pp.

"Oratory and Orators: Their Nature and Political Power." Comparative analysis of famous orators and oratorical techniques by a director of the Nazi Public Speaking School. Bibliography, pp. 148-51.

2116. ELLIOTT, EDWARD CHARLES; and CHAMBERS, MERRITT MADISON. *Charters of Philanthropies: A Study of the Charters of Twenty-Nine American Philanthropic Foundations.* New York: Purdue University and Carnegie Foundation for the Advancement of Teaching, 1939. 744 pp.

2117. ELY, MARY LILLIAN. *Why Forums?* (Studies in the Social Significance of Adult Education in the United States, no. 2). New York: American Association for Adult Education, 1937. 220 pp.

2118. "Forty-eight Years of Public Issues: Town Hall of New York Becomes No. 1 Forum of America," *Newsweek*, 18: 72 (October 20, 1941).

George V. Denny, Jr., head of America's Town Meeting of the Air, proposes a nationwide "Town Hall Movement."

2119. GIST, NOEL PITTS. *Secret Societies: A Cultural Study of Fraternalism in the United States*, foreword by Melville J. Herskovits. Columbia, Mo.: University of Missouri, 1941. 184 pp.

Scholarly analysis of the cultural patterning of U.S. secret societies, by associate professor of sociology, University of Missouri. Bibliography, pp. 173-76.

2120. GREGORY, WINIFRED, editor. *International Congresses and Conferences, 1840-1937.* New York: H. W. Wilson, 1938. 229 pp.

A list of congresses with a schedule of their publications and of American libraries that own their publications in whole or in part. Indexed.

2121. GRISIER, ORVILLE J. *How To Make Sign Advertising Pay.* Philadelphia: McKay, 1941. 166 pp.

Rules for sign makers. The author is editor of *National Sign Journal* and secretary of National Sign Association.

2122. HILL, FRANK ERNEST. *Man-Made Culture: The Educational Activities of Men's Clubs* (Studies in the Social Significance of Adult Education in the United States, no. 8). New York: American Association for Adult Education, 1938. 166 pp.

"The chief types explored . . . are men's discussion clubs; city clubs and policy associations; service clubs; advertising clubs; chambers of commerce; associations of credit men; art, music, and crafts groups; and certain clubs of an industrial character."—Foreword.

2123. (Pop.) INTERNATIONAL CONGRESS OF ESPERANTISTS. *Kongreslibro* (Proceedings) of the Congress, London, 1938.

The agenda of this year's session of the Congress were devoted almost entirely to the problem of popularizing Esperanto.

2124. JONES, JOHN PRICE, editor. *The Yearbook of Philanthropy, 1941-42.* New York: The Inter-River Press, 1942. 148 pp.

Information and statistics covering American philanthropy since 1920, with numerous charts and tables.

2125. LESTER, ROBERT MacDonALD. *Forty Years of Carnegie Giving: A Summary of the Benefactions of Andrew Carnegie and of the Work of the Philanthropic Trusts Which He Created.* New York: Scribner's, 1942. 186 pp.

Secretary of the Carnegie Corporation provides factual summary of Carnegie gifts from 1901 to 1941. The book does not attempt to appraise the results of the use of the $679,000,000 spent by the trusts, but it shows for each major trust the circumstances leading to its establishment, the nature of its organization and work, and a list of the trustees and officers who have executed the trust.

2126. LINDEMAN, EDUARD CHRISTIAN. *Wealth and Culture: A Study of One Hundred Foundations and Community Trusts and Their Operations During the Decade 1921-1930.* New York: Harcourt, Brace, 1936. 135 pp.

Charts, tables, and pictorial statistics in addition to socio-ethical evaluations. Bibliographic notes, pp. 51-54, include a list of magazine articles.

2127. Littell, Robert; and Mc-Carthy, J. J. "Whispers for Sale," *Harpers*, 172: 364-72 (February 1936).

Methods of the handlers of whispering campaigns.

2128. Mercer, F. A.; and Fraser, Grace Lovat, editors. *Modern Publicity in War (Modern Publicity, 1941)*. New York: Studio Publications, 1941. 128 pp.

Tells how the British, after two-and-a-half years of war, had mobilized the graphic arts in their struggle. Hundreds of government posters, advertising lay-outs, camera "shots," display schemes, booklets, leaflets, and colored advertisements are reproduced.

2129. "Mr. Junior's Beneficences: An Audit," *Fortune*, 14: 39-46, 116-40 (July 1936).

Discussion of the $167,000,000 paid out by John D. Rockefeller, Jr., in the interest of religion, education, science, arts, letters, conservation, and preservation of historic relics.

2130. *Modern Group Discussion* (Reference Shelf, vol. 11, no. 6). New York: H. W. Wilson, 1937. 200 pp.

How to organize, conduct, and take part in public and private meetings.

2131. Overstreet, Harry Allen; and Overstreet, Bonaro Wilkinson. *Town Meeting Comes to Town*. New York: Harpers, 1939. 268 pp.

Account of well-known radio forum, America's Town Meeting of the Air, by two U.S. specialists in adult education.

2132. Peabody, George E. *How to Speak Effectively, With Some Simple Rules of Parliamentary Practice*. 2nd ed., revised and enlarged. New York: Wiley, 1942. 108 pp.

By professor of extension teaching, Cornell University.

2133. Picard, Roger. *Les salons littéraires et la société française, 1610-1789* (Bibliothèque Brentano's: Etudes d'histoire et de critique littéraires). New York: Brentano's, 1943. 361 pp.

Literary salons as channels of communication. Bibliography at ends of chapters.

2134. Runion, Howard L. "An Objective Study of the Speech Style of Woodrow Wilson," *Speech Monographs*, 3 no. 1: 75-94 (October 1936).

Based on Ph.D. thesis, University of Michigan. Quantitative study of such factors as sentence length, sentence order, grammatical structure.

*2135. (Pop.) Shenton, Herbert Newhard. *Cosmopolitan Conversation: The Language Problems of International Conferences*. New York: Columbia University, 1933. 803 pp.

By U.S. sociologist (Ph.D. Columbia 1925). Basic data are derived from observation of language barriers at 1415 private and semi-public conferences held between 1923 and 1929. The study was sponsored by the International Auxiliary Language Association. Bibliography, pp. 488-89.

2136. Studebaker, John Ward. *The American Way: Democracy at Work in the Des Moines Forums*. New York and London: McGraw-Hill, 1935. 206 pp.

The United States Commissioner of Education reviews with enthusiasm the adult education experiments in Des Moines.

2137. Studebaker, John Ward; and others. *Forums for Young People* (U.S. Office of Education Bulletin, 1937, no. 25). Washington, D.C.: Government Printing Office, 1938. 113 pp.

A bulletin prepared for teachers and administrators in high schools and colleges; deals with forums for youth in secondary schools and colleges, and on an all-community basis.

2138. Twentieth Century Fund. *American Foundations and Their Fields—1934*. New York, 1935. 60 pp.

The third analysis of foundation disbursements to be published by the Twentieth Century Fund. Previous issues: 1931, 1932.

2139. U.S. Office of Education. Series of 8 Bulletins dealing with public forums. Washington, D.C.: Government Printing Office, 1935-37.

(1) *Choosing Our Way* (Bull., 1937, Misc. No. 1) surveys programs of the 19 U.S. demonstration centers and 431 other forums in the U.S., outlining their history, management, promotion, and financing. (2) *Forums for Young People* (Bull., 1937, No. 25) analyzes programs for high-school and out-of-school youth. (3) *Printed Page and the Public Platform* (Bull., 1937, No. 27) discusses library service in connection with forums, quoting opinions expressed by 400 forum leaders and administrators. (4) *Safeguarding Democracy through Adult Civic Education* (Bull., 1936, No. 6) evaluates the philosophy of adult education. (5) *Education for Democracy* (Bull., 1935, No. 17) is a handbook for leaders, devoted mainly to techniques and methods. Contains bibliography. (6) *A Step Forward for Adult Civic Education* (Bull., 1936, No. 16) is the story of the first ten demonstration centers conducted by the Office of Education. (7) and (8) *Public Affairs Pamphlets* (Bull., 1937, No. 3, and Supplement thereto) provide an annotated bibliography of many hundreds of inexpensive pamphlets dealing with forums and with issues frequently raised in forums.

2140. VERNON, ROLAND VENABLES; and MANSERGH, NICHOLAS, editors. *Advisory Bodies: A Study of their Uses in Relation to Central Government, 1919-39*, preface by Sir Arthur Salter. London: Allen and Unwin, 1940. 520 pp.

Use of advisory bodies by British government agencies is surveyed by a dozen specialists in public administration. Bibliographic footnotes.

*2141. AMERICAN MARKETING SOCIETY. *The Technique of Marketing Research*. New York and London: McGraw-Hill, 1937. 432 pp.

A practical manual prepared by a committee of experienced commercial consultants. Bibliography, pp. 403-22.

PART 6. MEASUREMENT

A. BIBLIOGRAPHIES AND GENERAL TREATMENTS

2142. BRETHERTON, RACHEL, compiler. *Market Research Sources: A Guide to Information on Domestic Marketing* (United States Department of Commerce, Bureau of Foreign and Domestic Commerce, Domestic Commerce series, no. 55). Washington, D.C.: Government Printing Office, 1936. 253 pp.

2143. BUROS, OSCAR KRISEN, editor. *Educational, Psychological, and Personality Tests of 1933, 1934, 1935, 1936*. New Brunswick, N.J.: Rutgers University, 1937. 3 vols.

Annual classified list, with title and author indexes. Supplements Gertrude H. Hildreth's *A Bibliography of Mental Tests and Rating Scales* (New York: Psychological Corporation, 1933, 242 pp.). Superseded by *Mental Measurements Yearbook of School of Education, Rutgers University*, 1938–, *q.v.*

*2144. BUROS, OSCAR KRISEN, editor. *Mental Measurements Yearbook of the School of Education, Rutgers University*. New Brunswick, N.J.: Rutgers University, 1938–.

A comprehensive and up-to-date bibliography, copiously annotated and with many critical reviews, of tests of intelligence, aptitude, interest, character, personality, information, attitude and opinion. Compiled by some 250 psychologists and technicians. Contains bibliography of recent books on measurement, statistics, and social science methodology in general, with excerpts from the reviews they received in the scientific journals.

2145. CANTRIL, HADLEY. "Reports of Research on: Symbols, Political Appeals, Measuring Attitudes, Testing Propaganda, Journalism," *Public Opinion Quarterly*, 1 no. 1: 105-09 (January 1937).

Summary of current research conducted by Ross Stagner, Selden C. Menefee, George W. Hartmann, Douglas McGregor, Richard L. Schanck, Frank Luther Mott.

2146. CATTELL, RAYMOND BERNARD. *A Guide to Mental Testing for Psychological Clinics, Schools, and Industrial Psychologists*, with a foreword by William Moodie. London: University of London, 1936. 312 pp.

"A handbook of tests of intelligence, attainment, special aptitudes, interest, attitude, temperament, and character." Bibliographic footnotes.

2147. CHASSELL, JOSEPH. "A Clinical Revision of the Experience Variables Record," *Psychiatry*, 1: 67-77 (February 1938).

A valuable tool for research, this is a questionnaire which constitutes a comprehensive inventory of "total personality." Dr. Chassell (Ph.D. Columbia; M.D. Rochester) has utilized it successfully in guidance units, vocational counseling and student health service. It can also be used as a guide by the scientific collector of life histories.

2148. DAY, DANIEL. "Methods in Attitude Research," *American Sociological Review*, 5: 395-410 (June 1940).

Bibliographic article citing 200 references on attitude- and opinion-research, by sociologist, Ohio State University. Classifies and analyzes the methods used, and tabulates their frequency, 1925-39.

2149. GOOD, CARTER VICTOR; BARR, ARVIL SYLVESTER; and SCATES, DOUGLAS EDGAR. *The Methodology of Educational Research* (Appleton Series in Supervision and Teaching). New York: Appleton-Century, 1936. 882 pp.

Text- and reference-book by two professors of education and a public school research director. Extensive bibliography at ends of chapters.

2150. GOSNELL, HAROLD FOOTE. "The Improvement of Present Public Opinion Analyses," essay in *Print, Radio and Film in a Democracy* (pp. 118-

32), edited by Douglas Waples (Chicago: University of Chicago, 1942).

2151. KIRKPATRICK, CLIFFORD. "Assumptions and Methods in Attitude Measurements," *American Sociological Review*, 1: 75-89 (February 1936).

2152. LASSWELL, HAROLD DWIGHT. "Intensive and Extensive Methods of Observing the Personality-Culture Manifold," *Yenching Journal of Social Studies*, 1: 72-86 (June 1938).

*2153. LUNDBERG, GEORGE ANDREW (D). *Social Research: A Study in Methods of Gathering Data*, rev. ed. New York: Longmans, Green, 1942. 426 pp.

Revision of textbook first published in 1929, by Bennington College sociologist. Bibliography at end of each chapter. Pp. 415-16 are a "Bibliography of Bibliographies" on research in the measurement of attitudes and personality traits.

2154. NELSON, MARTIN JOHAN. *Handbook of Educational Psychology and Measurement.* New York: Dryden Press, 1941. 174 pp.

Dictionary of terms, definitions, concepts, names, and principles with a survey of the subject, by head of Department of Education, Iowa State Teachers College. Annotated bibliography, pp. 151-74.

2155. NELSON, MARTIN JOHAN. *Tests and Measurements in Elementary Education.* New York: Cordon, 1939. 351 pp.

Bibliography at ends of chapters.

2156. SLETTO, RAYMOND FRANKLIN. *Construction of Attitude Scales by the Criterion of Internal Consistency.* Minneapolis, Minn., and Hanover, N.H.: Sociological Press, 1937. 92 pp.

Bibliography, p. 89.

2157. STRANG, RUTH MAY. "Methodology in the Study of Propaganda and Attitudes Relating to War," *School and Society*, 54: 334-39 (October 18, 1941).

General essay by Teachers College specialist in attitude analysis. Heavily documented from recent scientific literature.

2158. WANG, CHARLES K. A. *An Annotated Bibliography of Mental Tests and Scales*, vol. 2. Peiping, China: Catholic University, 1941. 698 pp.

This volume is devoted to tests concerned with the "measurement of educational achievement." Explanations of about 1800 different tests are given.

2159. YOUNG, PAULINE VISLICK. *Scientific Social Surveys and Research* (with chapters on statistical method by Calvin Fischer Schmid). New York: Prentice-Hall, 1939. 619 pp.

Text on research techniques by U.S. sociologists. Reviewed with reserve by Clark Tibbitts (University of Minnesota sociologist) in *American Journal of Sociology*, 45: 807-10 (March 1940). "The bibliography . . . [pp. 533-98] is second to none which the reviewer has seen on this subject . . . practically all the important references, and they are usefully classified."

B. MEASURING PREDISPOSITION AND RESPONSE

I. POLLS

One of the most prominent developments in this field since the publication of our 1935 bibliography has been the profusion of contributions to the measurement of audience predisposition, communication contents, and audience response. It has proved to be physically impossible, within the space and time available, to do justice to this increasingly refined and elaborate mass of literature. Of necessity the titles here listed are limited to those which appeared most representative and suggestive, while the reader is referred to the two principal sources of cumulated material on the subject: *Psychological*

Abstracts and the annual *Mental Measurements Yearbook of the School of Education of Rutgers University* (see titles 2143 and 2144, above). The former contains abstracts of nearly all the technical books and articles in the field. The latter contains abstracts together with critical evaluation of the validity and reliability of the measurement methods used. The critique is often written by two or more independent reviewers representing different methodological approaches.

A next step in the development of scientific research on public opinion will no doubt involve the systematic charting and contemporary reporting of *who* has been tested, by *what methods*, with respect to *which* of his *predispositions* and *which* of his *responses* toward *which socio-political symbols* and *practices*. Only thus will it be possible to ascertain the net result of the measurement studies now being carried forward by an army of diligent if disconnected investigators.

2160. "A.D. 1940: A Review of Public Opinion," *Fortune*, January 1941.

Review of shifts in U.S. opinion on foreign policy during 1940, based on Gallup and Roper surveys and other data.

2161. BELDEN, JOE. "Measuring College Thought," *Public Opinion Quarterly*, 3: 458-62 (July 1939).

By editor of Student Opinion Surveys of America, the opinion-measuring organization described in this article.

2162. BENSON, LAWRENCE E.; CROSSLEY, ARCHIBALD M.; ROPER, ELMO; and RUGG, DONALD. "Recent Experiments in Polling Techniques," *Public Opinion Quarterly*, 5: 79-92 (March 1941).

These articles deal with experiments conducted by the Gallup, Crossley, and *Fortune* polls, during the 1940 campaign, on the problem of question-wording.

2163. BLANKENSHIP, ALBERT B. "Choice of Words in Poll Questions," *Sociology and Social Research*, 25: 12-18 (September 1940).

2164. BLANKENSHIP, ALBERT B.; and MANHEIMER, DEAN I. "Whither Public Opinion Polls?", *Journal of Psychology*, 12: 7-12 (July 1941).

An analysis of the closeness of the past ten presidential elections to determine the predictive limitations of poll forecasts with a four per cent margin of error.

2165. CANTRIL, HADLEY. "Experiments in the Wording of Questions," *Public Opinion Quarterly*, 4: 330-32 (June 1940).

Fortune poll results show significant differences in response when a question is worded in different ways.

2166. COOK, STUART W.; and WELCH, ALFRED C. "Methods of Measuring the Practical Effects of Polls of Public Opinion," *Journal of Applied Psychology*, 24: 441-54 (August 1940).

2167. CROSSLEY, ARCHIBALD M. "Straw Polls in 1936," *Public Opinion Quarterly*, 1 no. 1: 24-35 (January 1937).

How to construct a sample for election prediction. By founder (1926) of Crossley, Incorporated, a commercial research organization best known for the Crossley Political Poll and for the Cooperative Analysis of Broadcasting.

2168. FIELD, HARRY H.; and CONNELLY, GORDON M. "Testing Polls in Public Election Booths," *Public Opinion Quarterly*, 6: 610-18 (Winter 1942).

Consistency in Colorado was tested by two staff members of National Opinion Research Center. "This report discloses the opinions secured from a sample of Boulder's electorate on three public issues, and comparable opinions secured in the actual polling stations on election day on the three identical questions, which were presented to all voters. Also . . . the representative respondents were asked their pre-election preferences in the senatorial and gubernatorial contests." Margin of error of prediction poll was in no case more than 4.2 per cent.

2169. *"Fortune* Quarterly Survey," *Fortune*, July 1935–.

Public opinion poll conducted for *Fortune* magazine by the firm of Elmo Roper.

2170. GALLUP, GEORGE HORACE. "The Public Rings the Bell," *Market Research*, February 1937, pp. 3-4.

In October 1936, American Institute of Public Opinion asked voters: "Regardless of how you yourself plan to vote, which presidential candidate do you think will win?" Result was "the most accurate state-by-state presidential poll ever conducted." Average error was less than five per cent. Article gives returns by states.

2171. GALLUP, GEORGE HORACE. "Reporting Public Opinion in Five Nations," *Public Opinion Quarterly*, 6: 429-36 (Fall 1942).

Dr. Gallup discusses his polling agencies in Australia, Canada, England, Sweden, U.S., which sample the opinions of an aggregate population of nearly 200,000,000.

2172. GALLUP, GEORGE HORACE. "What We, The People, Think About Europe: A Cross-Section of Opinion on Our World Role," *New York Times Magazine*, April 30, 1939, pp. 1-2 ff.

According to the Gallup polls, "nearly all American thinking sums up to two great purposes: The American people want to stay out of war. They want to give all possible assistance to the British and French, short of going to war, in the event that war does come. . . . And the people think that they should have the right, in a national vote, to say whether United States troops should ever be conscripted for fighting abroad."

*2173. GALLUP, GEORGE HORACE (CB '40, W); and RAE, SAUL FORBES. *The Pulse of Democracy: The Public Opinion Poll and How It Works.* New York: Simon and Schuster, 1940. 290 pp.

Standard treatise on the polls. Dr. Gallup is Director of American Institute of Public Opinion; Dr. Rae a member of his staff. Bibliography, pp. 326-28.

2174. GOSNELL, HAROLD FOOTE. "How Accurate Were the Polls?" *Public Opinion Quarterly*, 1 no. 1: 97-105 (January 1937).

Technical research paper comparing poll predictions and actual votes in the 1936 Presidential election.

2175. GOSNELL, HAROLD FOOTE. "The Improvement of Present Public Opinion Analyses," essay in *Print, Radio and Film in a Democracy* (pp. 118-32), edited by Douglas Waples (Chicago: University of Chicago, 1942).

2176. GOSNELL, HAROLD FOOTE; and DE GRAZIA, SEBASTIAN. "A Critique of Polling Methods," *Public Opinion Quarterly*, 6: 378-90 (Fall 1942).

By two U.S. political scientists.

2177. KATZ, DANIEL. "Do Interviewers Bias Poll Results?" *Public Opinion Quarterly*, 6: 248-68 (Summer 1942).

The experiment here reported compared the findings of white-collar interviewers of the American Institute of Public Opinion with the findings of working-class interviewers. Though both interviewing staffs worked under the same instructions they did not find the same public sentiment on labor and war issues. The author, a professor of psychology, Princeton, is a member of the Princeton Office of Public Opinion Research.

2178. KATZ, DANIEL. "The Public Opinion Polls and the 1940 Election," *Public Opinion Quarterly*, 5: 52-78 (March 1941).

Social psychologist's careful review of factors affecting poll predictions.

2179. KATZ, DANIEL; and CANTRIL, HADLEY. "Public Opinion Polls," *Sociometry*, 1: 155-79 (July-October 1937).

General evaluation of several methods currently used in opinion polls.

2180. LAZARSFELD, PAUL FELIX. " 'Panel' Studies," *Public Opinion Quarterly*, 4: 122-28 (March 1940).

A "panel" is a group of people who are

given repeated interviews by public opinion pollers. This specialist on polling discusses advantages and disadvantages of panel technique.

2180a. LAZARSFELD, PAUL FELIX; and DURANT, RUTH. "National Morale, Social Cleavage and Political Allegiance," *Journalism Quarterly*, 19: 150-59 (June 1942).

Analysis of relation of party allegiance to attitudes on Administration domestic and foreign policy, as shown by Gallup polls. Includes a pioneering discussion of "opinion turnover": "This phenomenon of turnover, in itself worthy of investigation, has been so far neglected in public opinion research. It is possible for net change of opinion to be small between two time-periods; still, this might be the result of many persons' changing in one direction, while about as many change in the opposite direction. Such a situation could be called socially vulnerable. It would indicate that a people's attitudes are ambivalent, and that any major event could bring about sudden shifts in opinion."

2181. LAZARSFELD, PAUL FELIX; and ROBINSON, WILLIAM S. "Some Properties of the Trichotomy 'Like, No Opinion, Dislike' and Their Psychological Interpretation," *Sociometry*, 3: 151-78 (1940).

Statistical techniques for treating such data are worked out and a new measure for stating the "average attitude of a group" is offered by these two specialists in polling technique.

2182. LINK, HENRY C.; and FREIBERG, A. D. "The Problem of Validity vs. Reliability in Public Opinion Polls," *Public Opinion Quarterly*, 6: 87-98 (Spring 1942).

Dr. Link, vice-president of the Psychological Corporation, and Dr. Freiberg, technical director of its Market Research Division, apply the experience of their organization to the problem of the validity of poll results, and suggest methods for establishing the soundness of answers to poll questions.

2183. LIVINGSTONE, DAME ADELAIDE; and JOHNSTON, MARJORIE SCOTT. *The Peace Ballot: The Official History, with a Statistical Survey of the Results by Walter Ashley and Conclu-*

sion by Viscount Cecil. London: Gollancz, 1935. 64 pp.

Opinion-poll conducted by British League of Nations Union, in which about 11,500,000 persons balloted on (1) Should Great Britain remain in the League? (2) Arms reduction; (3) Prohibition of profit-making armament production; (4) Economic and military sanctions.

2184. MOSTELLER, FREDERICK; and McCARTHY, PHILIP J. "Estimating Population Proportions," *Public Opinion Quarterly*, 6: 452-58 (Fall 1942).

Technical study of poll procedures, using data from Princeton Office of Public Opinion Research.

2185. NATIONAL OPINION RESEARCH CENTER, UNIVERSITY OF DENVER (COLORADO).

Incorporated October 27, 1941, with a grant from the (Marshall) Field Foundation, this is "the first non-profit, non-commercial organization to measure public opinion in the United States. Through a national staff of trained interviewers, representative cross-sections or samples of the entire population will be personally interviewed on questions of current importance." Director: Harry H. Field. Its series of publications, available for 5c or 10c a copy, includes: (1) Announcement of Purposes. (2) National Survey, Report No. 1: Opinions and Attitudes of the American People toward the War in Europe (December 1941). 24 pp. (3) National Survey, Report No. 2: Attitudes of the American People toward Important Post-War Problems (March 1942). 32 pp. (4) Rocky Mountain Survey, Report No. 3: Regional Opinions on Post-War Problems and on Foreign Products of Particular Importance to the Mountain Area (April 1942). 24 pp. (5) Supplement to Report No. 3: Regional Opinion on Federal Regulation of Gas and Electric Companies, Banks, Labor Unions, Chain Stores, and Railroads; also, Federal *versus* State Control of Old Age Pensions, Unemployment Insurance, Public Schools and Water Rights (May 1942). 8 pp. (6) National Survey, Report No. 4: Anti-Inflation Measures (June 1942). 24 pp. (7) Supplement to Report No. 4: Opinion toward Federal Regulation, After the War, of Gas and Electric Companies, Banks, Labor Unions, and Railroads; and on Federal versus State Control of Old Age Pensions, Unemployment Insurance, and Public Schools (June 1942). 8

pp. (8) National Survey, Report No. 5: Post-War Problems. 32 pp. (9) Special Graphic Supplement, Report No. 6: Current and Post-War Problems (October, 1942). 16 pp., 12 charts. (10) Distorted Maps: A. Outline Map of U.S., Showing States as They Would Appear if Area Were Proportional to Number of Persons 21 Years of Age and Over. B. Same, Based on Total U.S. Population, 1940 Census. C. Same, Based on Popular Vote for President, 1940.

2186. "The People's Choice: *Life* Survey Discloses Why People Voted as They Did in This Week's Election," *Life*, November 11, 1940, pp. 95-103.

Erie County, Ohio, was chosen for an investigation sponsored jointly by Columbia University's Office of Radio Research, the Elmo Roper organization, *Life*, and *Fortune*. Citizens of this highly representative county were interviewed repeatedly to determine reasons for their Presidential vote. Income, party preference, religion, age, rural or urban residence, occupation and sex were among the factors controlled. Basic results: "those who were in poor to middling economic circumstances, those who were young, those who were Catholic—all of these tended to vote Democratic." Those who were "undecided" in May, when the interview series began, tended by October to cast their votes according to these factors in the same proportion as those whose minds had been made up all the time.

2187. "O. F. F. Polling Public on War News," *Editor and Publisher*, March 28, 1942, p. 7.

U.S. Office of Facts and Figures has launched a poll to find out to what extent the public believes it is receiving news of the war effort; how true a picture the public has; what has been told the public through various media; and what reaction the public has. The results will not be released.

2188. POLL SUMMARIES: AMERICAN INSTITUTE OF PUBLIC OPINION AND *Fortune*.

Beginning with the July 1938 issue, the *Public Opinion Quarterly* has published summaries of all the published surveys conducted by the Institute. The July 1938 summary covered the first three years of the Gallup poll's existence. The next summary (*Public Opinion Quarterly*, 3: 581-607, October 1939) covered the Institute's polls of 1938 and part of 1939. Beginning with the October 1939 issue, each

issue of the *Quarterly* has contained summaries of both the Gallup and the *Fortune* polls.

*2189. "Public Opinion Polls: Dr. Jekyll or Mr. Hyde?" Symposium in *Public Opinion Quarterly*, 4: 212-84 (June 1940).

A dozen specialists on problems of public opinion express their views on reliability and social consequences of polls.

2190. ROBINSON, CLAUDE EVERETT. "Pre-Election Polls in the 1942 Elections," *Public Opinion Quarterly*, 7: 139-44 (Spring 1943).

"The off-year elections of November, 1942 are of special interest to students of polling procedures because scientific polls were confronted for the first time in a national election with a marked drop in turnout." By a U.S. political scientist specializing in opinion polls.

2191. ROBINSON, CLAUDE EVERETT. "Recent Developments in the Straw-Poll Field," *Public Opinion Quarterly*, 1 no. 3: 45-56 (July 1937); 1 no. 4: 42-52 (October 1937).

2192. ROPER, ELMO B., JR. "Neutral Opinion on the Court Proposal," *Public Opinion Quarterly*, 1 no. 3: 17-20 (July 1937).

Director of *Fortune's* opinion poll discusses characteristics of the "No opinion" and "Undecided" vote.

2193. ROPER, ELMO B., JR. "Sampling Public Opinion," *American Statistical Association Journal*, 35: 325-34 (June 1940).

2194. RUGG, DONALD; and CANTRIL, HADLEY. "Wording of Questions in Public Opinion Polls," *Journal of Abnormal and Social Psychology*, 37: 469-95 (October 1942).

2195. SCHREINER, SAM, JR. "China's First Public Opinion Poll," *Public Opinion Quarterly*, 7: 145-48 (Spring 1943).

"Similar in purpose to the early American straw ballots, the poll was conducted by the

Ta kang pao, a newspaper with a circulation of approximately ten thousand people in the city of Hengyang, Hunan Province, for the purpose of attracting reader interest in its anniversary edition. . . . The survey itself was conceived and conducted by the editorial staff of the newspaper, none of whom have been abroad or had any close personal contact with methods of public opinion measurement as developed in the United States."

2196. WARNER, LUCIEN. "The Reliability of Public Opinion Surveys," *Public Opinion Quarterly*, 3: 376-90 (July 1939).

Sources of possible error in polling are discussed by U.S. psychologist who has had practical experience as director of research for a public relations firm.

2197. WEAVER, LEON. "Polls of the Especially Competent: A Proposal," *Social Forces*, 21: 44-51 (October 1942).

Carefully documented analysis of the author's proposal for a series of polls of those who are "most competent" to express opinions, as shown by their ability to analyze and predict in their own fields of specialization. "If a continuous poll of what is supposed to be the most competent opinion were undertaken and published in conjunction with the current public opinion polls, it would seem only reasonable to suppose that it would have some educative effect on public opinion and government policy."

2198. WILLIAMS, DOUGLAS. "Basic Instructions for Interviewers," *Public Opinion Quarterly*, 6: 634-41 (Winter 1942).

Head of interviewing staff of National Opinion Research Center reproduces instructions issued to the Center's interviewers.

II. MORE INTENSIVE METHODS

2199. ALLPORT, FLOYD HENRY; and HANCHETT, GERTRUDE A. "The War-Producing Behaviors of Citizens: A Scale of Measurement, with Preliminary Results in Imagined Situations," *Journal of Social Psychology*, 11: 447-90 (May 1940).

By two social psychologists at Syracuse University.

2200. BALLIN, MARIAN R.; and FARNSWORTH, PAUL R. "A Graphic Method for Determining the Scale Values of Statements in Measuring Social Attitudes," *Journal of Social Psychology*, 13: 323-27 (May 1941).

In place of the Thurstone technique of equally appearing intervals for the determination of scale values, subjects allocated statements of opinion to points on an 11-inch line, with resulting values comparable to the Thurstone technique.

2201. BERNARD, WILLIAM S. "Student Attitudes on Marriage and the Family," *American Sociological Review*, 3: 354-61 (June 1938).

2202. BONNEY, M. E. "The Validity of Certain Techniques of Gathering Psychological Data, with Special Reference to Personality Questionnaires," *Journal of Social Psychology*, 13: 103-22 (1941).

2203. CHAMBERS, MERRITT MADISON; and BELL, HOWARD M. *How to Make a Community Youth Survey* (American Council on Education Studies, Series 4, American Youth Commission, no. 2). Washington, D.C.: American Council on Education, 1939. 45 pp.

How to select and coach interviewers; sample a public; conduct interviews; code and edit results; present, illustrate, publish, and follow up the data. Includes sample schedule used in the American Youth Commission's Maryland Survey, which investigated attitudes, among other factors.

2204. FERGUSON, LEONARD W. "A Study of the Likert Technique of Attitude Scale Construction," *Journal of Social Psychology*, 13: 51-57 (1941).

2205. "*Fortune* Forum of Executive Opinion," *Fortune*, September, October, December 1940.

Membership in this opinion forum, by invitation only, consists of (a) presidents of all businesses rated AA-1 by Dun and Bradstreet; (b) directors of the 750 largest corporations in the U.S.; (c) "executives of U.S. business whose salaries are at a level that assures that each of them is a man of high executive responsibility qualified to speak *for* Management." Topics considered include government, foreign policy, labor policy, and monopolistic pricing.

2206. FROMME, ALLAN. "On the Use of Certain Qualitative Methods of Attitude Research: A Study of Opinions on the Methods of Preventing War," *Journal of Social Psychology*, 13: 429-59 (May 1941).

An exploratory study in the use of projective methods which give the individual's own mental content rather than the arbitrary categories of the usual questionnaire. (For example, subjects selected captions to designate cartoons.) The results show that less violence is done by this new approach to the organization of attitude and the real reasons underlying the attitude.

2207. GARRETT, ANNETTE MARIE. *Interviewing: Its Principles and Methods.* New York: Family Welfare Association of America, 1942. 123 pp.

Rules of social case work interviewing discussed by Associate Director, Smith College School for Social Work.

2208. GILLILAND, ADAM RAYMOND; and KATZOFF, E. TAYLOR. "A Scale for Measurement of Attitudes Toward American Participation in the Present European Conflict," *Journal of Psychology*, 11: 173-76 (January 1941).

2209. HANCHETT, GERTRUDE A. *Construction and Use of a Telic Scale for the Measurement of War-Producing Behaviors* (Ph.D. thesis, social psychology, Syracuse University, 1939).

2210. HARDING, JOHN SNODGRASS. "A Scale for Measuring Civilian Morale," *Journal of Psychology*, 12: 101-10 (July 1941).

Questionnaire designed by Harvard psychologist.

2211. HART, HORNELL NORRIS. *Chart for Happiness.* New York: Macmillan, 1940. 198 pp.

Presents and explains the "Euphorimeter," a psychological scale for measuring happiness.

The author is professor of sociology, Duke University. Bibliography, pp. 191-93.

2212. HAYES, SAMUEL PERKINS, JR. "Probability and Beyle's 'Index of Cohesion,' " *Journal of Social Psychology*, 9: 161-67 (May 1938).

Social psychologist criticizes the statistical method proposed by Herman Carey Beyle, *Identification and Analysis of Attribute-cluster-blocs* (Chicago, 1931).

2213. JARVIE, LAWRENCE LEE; and ELLINGSON, MARK. *A Handbook on the Anecdotal Behaviour Journal.* Chicago: University of Chicago, 1940. 71 pp.

An "anecdotal behavior journal" is a series of weekly reports of examples of an individual's "significant" behavior, as observed by his associates. This book reports on experience with such a journal as a device of educational administration at Rochester Athenaeum and Mechanics Institute. Bibliography, pp. 66-67.

2214. JENNINGS, HUMPHREY; and MADGE, CHARLES, editors. *May the Twelfth: Mass-Observation Day Survey.* London: Faber and Faber, 1937. 431 pp.

British investigators have secured the voluntary cooperation of a large number of persons who supply written accounts of their observations on particular days. This volume presents vivid eyewitness descriptions of Coronation Day and also of March 12, a "normal working day," together with a scheme for social analysis of the observations.

2215. KARSLAKE, JAMES SPIER. "Purdue Eye Camera: Practical Apparatus for Studying the Attention Value of Advertisements," *Journal of Applied Psychology*, 24: 417-40 (August 1940).

2216. KIRKPATRICK, CLIFFORD. "Construction of a Belief Pattern Scale for Measuring Attitudes toward Feminism," *Journal of Social Psychology*, 7: 421-37 (November 1936).

2217. LAZARSFELD, PAUL FELIX. "Evaluating the Effectiveness of Advertising by Direct Interviews," *Journal* of *Consulting Psychology*, 5: 170-78 (July-August 1941).

2218. LAZARSFELD, PAUL FELIX. "Repeated Interviews as a Tool for Studying Changes in Opinion and Their Causes," *American Statistical Association Bulletin*, 2: 3-7 (January 1941).

2219. LUCAS, DARRELL BLAIN. "Rigid Technique for Measuring the Impression Values of Specific Magazine Advertisements," *Journal of Applied Psychology*, 24: 778-90 (December 1940).

2220. LURIE, WALTER A. "Study of Spranger's Value-Types by the Method of Factor Analysis," *Journal of Social Psychology*, 8: 17-37 (February 1937).

2221. MILLER, DELBERT CHARLES. "The Measurement of National Morale," *American Sociological Review*, 6: 487-98 (August 1941).

By sociologist, State College of Washington. "The following hypotheses are proposed as components of national morale: (1) belief in the superiority of the social structure of the in-group; (2) degree and manner by which personal goals are identified with national goals; (3) judgments of the competence of national leadership; (4) belief that resources are available to hurl back any threats to the in-group; (5) confidence in the permanence of the national goals." A 48-item scale for testing these was devised, using the methods of Likert, Rundquist, and Sletto. Split-half reliability coefficient was .69.

2222. OSGOOD, C. F.; and STAGNER, ROSS. "Analysis of a Prestige Frame of Reference by a Gradient Technique," *Journal of Applied Psychology*, 25: 275-91 (June 1941).

Occupational stereotypes were analyzed by separate ratings of occupational characteristics with resulting indices of occupational prestige. The technique can be applied to social and political attitudes to determine the significant factors in psychological judgment.

2223. MADGE, CHARLES; and HARRISSON, TOM (i.e., THOMAS HART-NETT). *Mass-Observation* (Mass-Observation series, no. 1), with a foreword by Julian Huxley. London: Muller, 1937. 64 pp.

Objectives of the Mass-Observation enterprise are stated by two of its leaders. Bibliography, p. 64.

2224. PACE, C. ROBERT. "A Situations Test to Measure Social-Political-Economic Attitudes," *Journal of Social Psychology*, 10: 331-44 (August 1939).

Instead of using the usual test, which measures agreement with stated opinions (Thurstone scales and the like), this author asked subjects what they would do in a variety of hypothetical situations. Test reliability centered around .80.

2225. RASKIN, EVELYN; and COOK, STUART W. "A Further Investigation of the Measurement of an Attitude toward Fascism," *Journal of Social Psychology*, 9: 201-06 (May 1938).

Experimental work testing validity of Ross Stagner's scale (see titles 2233, 2234, below).

2226. RUDOLPH, HAROLD J. *Four Million Inquiries from Magazine Advertising*, with a foreword by GEORGE HORACE GALLUP. New York: Columbia University, 1936. 101 pp.

Value of coupon responses as a means of judging the effectiveness of advertising. "In this analysis an attempt has been made to measure the effect of many factors never before measured in a coupon analysis" (p. 96).

2227. ROSANDER, ARLYN CUSTER. "Attitude Scale Based Upon Behavior Situations," *Journal of Social Psychology*, 8: 3-15 (February 1937).

2228. ROSANDER, ARLYN CUSTER. "The Measurement of Social Attitudes," *Social Studies*, 28: 65-69 (February 1937).

Analysis of applicability of Thurstone attitude scales.

2229. ROSLOW, SYDNEY; and BLANKENSHIP, ALBERT B. "Phrasing the Questions in Consumer Research," *Journal of Applied Psychology*, 23: 612-22 (October 1939).

*2230. Rundquist, Edward Alfred; and Sletto, Raymond Franklin (D). *Personality in the Depression: A Study in the Measurement of Attitudes* (Institute of Child Welfare Monographs, no. 12). Minneapolis: University of Minnesota, 1936. 398 pp.

The University of Minnesota's Institute of Child Welfare tested attitudes of adolescents (of both sexes, in and out of school, employed and unemployed) toward symbols of family, law, education, and the social-economic situation. "Morale and inferiority measures were included as checks." All measures were then related to a wide variety of other factors such as income-level, employment status of parents, and extent of family disorganization. "An important practical outcome of the study is the well-standardized Minnesota Scale for the Survey of Opinions, which can be given either to groups or to individuals. The results of the specific attitude scales, and of a very sensitive general adjustment scale incorporated in the total scale, can be quickly converted into standard scores which enable the examiner to determine the relative standing of the person examined and construct a psychograph that will picture his attitudinal relation to his environment in striking fashion" (p. vi). Dr. Rundquist is Assistant Director of the Psychological Laboratory, Cincinnati Public Schools; Dr. Sletto is Assistant Professor of Sociology, University of Minnesota. Appendix includes scale and scoring instructions. Bibliography, pp. 373-74.

2231. Schanck, R. L.; and Goodman, Charles. "Reactions to Propaganda on Both Sides of a Controversial Issue," *Public Opinion Quarterly*, 3: 107-12 (January 1939).

To two U.S. psychologists, "it seemed possible . . . to load a questionnaire in such a way that it might serve as a medium of indoctrination of individuals without their being aware of it." Innuendo favoring and attacking the prestige of Civil Service as a means of selecting public employees was inserted into three questionnaires. Differences in questionnaire response were calculated.

2232. Smith, Elias; and Suchman, Edward Allen. "Do People Know Why They Buy?" *Journal of Applied Psychology*, 24: 673-84 (December 1940).

2233. Stagner, Ross. "Fascist Attitudes: An Exploratory Study," *Journal of Social Psychology*, 7: 309-19 (August 1936).

University of Akron social psychologist collected statements relating to American conditions, but illustrating certain features which were thought to characterize Fascist movements in both Germany and Italy. "When these were presented in disguised form to [Midwestern] college students, evidence of a general attitude which might be called 'pro-Fascist' developed." A technically advanced method of study was used. See title 2225, above.

2234. Stagner, Ross. "Fascist Attitudes: Their Determining Conditions," *Journal of Social Psychology*, 7: 438-54 (November 1936).

*2234a. Thurstone, Louis Leon (W); and Chave, Ernest John. *The Measurement of Attitude: A Psychophysical Method and some Experiments with a Scale for Measuring Attitude toward the Church.* Chicago: University of Chicago, 1929. 96 pp.

An influential early study by two University of Chicago psychologists whose leads have been followed by many later analysts of attitude. See also Thurstone's later material on mental measurement, especially *The Vectors of Mind: Multiple-Factor Analysis for the Isolation of Primary Traits* (Chicago: University of Chicago, 1935. 266 pp.), which includes bibliography of the author's previous papers on multiple-factor problems.

2235. Willcock, H. D. "Mass-Observation," *American Journal of Sociology*, 48: 445-56 (January 1943).

"First comprehensive account presented to American readers" concerning this group of volunteer workers engaged in a continuing study of "all England's social institutions." Several book-length reports have been published, sampling methods developed, interviewers trained. Mr. Willcock is a member of "M.-O."

2236. Young, Pauline Vislick. *Interviewing in Social Work: A Sociological Analysis*, introduction by Joanna C. Colcord. New York and London: McGraw-Hill, 1935. 416 pp.

A sociologist formulates psychiatric, psychological, and sociological aspects of the problem, and presents twenty-four verbatim interviews. Annotated bibliography, pp. 385-403.

2237. WEINBERGER, JULIUS. "Money Spent for Play: An Index of Opinion," *Public Opinion Quarterly*, 2: 245-59 (April 1938).

Quantitative study of U.S. recreational habits. By radio engineer, associated with RCA for 20 years.

C. MEASURING CONTENTS OF COMMUNICATIONS

Includes only studies of contents of communication channels during the last generation. For earlier periods, see Part 4.

2238. ALBIG, (JOHN) WILLIAM. "The Content of Radio Programs, 1925-1938," *Social Forces*, 16: 338-49 (March 1938).

Table I. Percentages of Time Devoted to Various Types of Programs, Averages of Nine American Radio Stations, 1925-35. Table II. Same, London National of the BBC, 1925-35. Table III. Range of Program Type Percentages for 1934.

2239. AMES, JESSIE DANIEL. "Editorial Treatment of Lynchings," *Public Opinion Quarterly*, 2: 77-84 (January 1938).

Environment rather than personal inclination of editors determines the editorial treatment of lynchings, according to a survey, begun in 1930, of editorials on lynchings in every one of 13 Southern states. The author is Executive Director of the Central Council of the Association of Southern Women for the Prevention of Lynching, with offices in Atlanta. Efforts of the Council are directed toward the promotion of educational programs against lynching.

2240. *Analysis of Newspaper Opinion.* Washington, D.C., October 1939-. Weekly.

Statistical summary of U.S. newspaper contents, published by James S. Twohey, formerly statistician on the staff of Emil Hurja, of the Democratic National Committee (see title 2278, below).

2241. BRITT, STEUART HENDERSON; and LOWRY, ROYE L. "Conformity Behavior of Labor Newspapers with Respect to the AFL-CIO Conflict," *Journal of Social Psychology*, 14: 375-87 (November 1941).

2242. *Business Opinion.* New York, monthly, January 1938-.

Monthly bulletin for legislators, executives, and business executives; digested from business papers by members of National Conference of Business Paper Editors, 369 Lexington Avenue, New York City.

2243. CARPENTER, MARIE ELIZABETH (RUFFIN). *The Treatment of the Negro in American History School Textbooks: A Comparison of Changing Textbook Content, 1826-1939, with Developing Scholarship in the History of the Negro in the United States* (Ph.D. thesis, philosophy, Columbia). Menasha, Wis.: George Banta, 1941. 137 pp.

Annotated bibliography, pp. 130-37.

2244. DALE, EDGAR. "Need for Study of the Newsreels," *Public Opinion Quarterly*, 1 no. 3: 122-25 (July 1937).

Includes a common-sense classification of subject matter of newsreels, 1931-32 and 1935. By specialist in educational research, Ohio State University.

2245. EATON, HELEN SLOCOMB, compiler. *Semantic Frequency List for English, French, Spanish, and German.* Chicago: University of Chicago for the Commission of Modern Languages of the American Council on Education, 1940. 441 pp.

Lists in parallel columns the 6000 most frequently used words in these four languages. Valuable reference work for psychologists, popularizers, propagandists. An appendix undertakes a semantic analysis of the 6000 words.

2246. ELEAZER, ROBERT BURNS. *School Books and Racial Antagonism: A Study of Omissions and Inclusions that Make for Misunderstanding*, 3rd ed. Atlanta, Georgia: Executive Committee, Conference on Education and Race Relations, 1937. 8 pp.

2247. FOSTER, HARRY SCHUYLER. "Charting America's News of the World War," *Foreign Affairs*, 15: 311-19 (January 1937).

Excerpts from the author's study of news in the New York *Times* during the war years, originally *American News of Europe, 1914-1917* (unpublished Ph.D. thesis, political science, University of Chicago, 1931. 355 pp.).

2248. GELLER, A.; KAPLAN, DAVID; and LASSWELL, HAROLD DWIGHT. *The Differential Use of Flexible and Rigid Procedures of Content Analysis* (Library of Congress, Experimental Division for Study of War Time Communications, Document no. 12). Washington, D.C., 1943. 16 pp., mimeo.

Statistical study of effect of various kinds of instructions on reliability of symbol-counting procedures.

2249. GELLER, A.; KAPLAN, DAVID; and LASSWELL, HAROLD DWIGHT. "An Experimental Comparison of Four Ways of Coding Editorial Content," *Journalism Quarterly*, 19: 362-71 (December 1942).

2250. GUTTENBERG, KARL LUDWIG, FREIHERR VON. *Die zeitgenössische Presse Deutschlands über Lenin* (thesis, Würzburg). Würzburg: Becker, 1931. 122 pp.

How the contemporary German press treated Lenin. Bibliography, pp. 86-120. See also Walter Lippmann and Charles A. Merz, "A Test of the News," supplement to *New Republic*, August 4, 1920, in which two prominent U.S. journalists discuss New York *Times* handling of the Russian Revolution.

2251. GUTTINGER, FRITZ. "Distribution of Space in British and Swiss Newspapers," *Political Quarterly*, 10: 428-41 (July-September 1939).

Systematic comparison of British and Swiss papers, including a count of "relative space allotted to the various subjects dealt with, similar to the analysis of distribution of space carried out by the authors of the P. E. P. Report" (see title 1501). Six leading German-Swiss dailies for the week of July 11-17, 1938, were chosen, together with six English papers. *Conclusions*: Swiss papers are more "highbrow," and "Swiss readers' interest is focused on world events abroad to a far greater extent than that of English readers."

2252. HAMILTON, THOMAS. "Social Optimism and Pessimism in American Protestantism," *Public Opinion Quarterly*, 6: 280-83 (Summer 1942).

"A movement away from the 'social gospel' with the introduction of a note of social pessimism seems observable in the preaching of American Protestant ministers during the period from 1929 to 1940," according to this study of the contents of U.S. sermons.

2253. JANIS, IRVING L.; and FADNER, RAYMOND H. *A Coefficient of Imbalance for Content Analysis* (Library of Congress, Experimental Division for Study of War Time Communications, Document no. 31). Washington, D.C., 1942. 17 pp., mimeo.

Also appeared in *Psychometrika*, 8: 105-19 (June 1943). By two members of Special War Policies Unit, U.S. Department of Justice. "This article presents a Coefficient of Imbalance applicable to any type of communication that may be classified into favorable content, unfavorable content, neutral content, and non-relevant content. The combined influence of the average presentation of relevant content and the average presentation of total content is reduced to two components, the coefficients of favorable imbalance and of unfavorable imbalance. A precise definition of imbalance is developed and measured against ten criteria."

2254. JANIS, IRVING L.; FADNER, RAYMOND H.; and JANOWITZ, MORRIS. *Reliability of a Content Analysis Technique* (Library of Congress, Experimental Division for Study of War Time Communications, Document no. 32). Washington, D.C., 1942. 6 pp., mimeo.

By three specialists in employ of U.S. government. Also appeared in *Public Opinion Quarterly*, 7: 293-96 (Summer 1943).

2255. Jones, Dorothy Blumenstock. "Quantitative Analysis of Motion Picture Content," *Public Opinion Quarterly*, 6: 411-28 (Fall 1942).

An adaptation of Harold D. Lasswell's code for symbol analysis. Mrs. Jones, chief of the Motion Picture Analysis Division of O.W.I.'s Bureau of Motion Pictures in Hollywood, presents the results of an experimental study designed to provide an instrument capable of measuring with scientific exactness the content of each motion picture as it is released.

2256. Kaplan, Abraham; and Goldsen, Joseph M. *Reliability of Certain Categories for Classifying Newspaper Headlines* (Library of Congress, Experimental Division for Study of War Time Communications, Document no. 40). Washington, D.C., 1943. 37 pp., mimeo.

2257. Kingsbury, Susan Myra; Hart, Hornell Norris; and others. *Newspapers and the News: An Objective Measurement of Ethical and Unethical Behavior by Representative Newspapers* (Bryn Mawr College Series in Social Economy, no. 1). New York: Putnam's Sons, 1937. 238 pp.

Space-measurement study of U.S. newspapers in recent years. Bibliography, pp. 217-26.

2258. Lasswell, Harold Dwight. *Analyzing the Content of Mass Communication: A Brief Introduction* (Library of Congress, Experimental Division for Study of War Time Communications, Document no. 11). Washington, D.C., 1942. 39 pp., mimeo.

2259. Lasswell, Harold Dwight. "A Provisional Classification of Symbol Data," *Psychiatry*, 1: 197-204 (May 1938).

A suggested system of precise categories for the description and comparison of symbols. "Although the present discussion is conducted with reference to the psychoanalytic interview situation, the categories which are proposed

are often directly transferable to many other symbolic situations in society."

2260. Lasswell, Harold Dwight. "The World Attention Survey," *Public Opinion Quarterly*, 5: 456-62 (Fall 1941).

Brief statement on Dr. Lasswell's basic procedures of content analysis, including a reprint of a short form of his code of "indulgences" and "deprivations."

2261. Lasswell, Harold Dwight; and associates. "The Politically Significant Content of the Press: Coding Procedures," *Journalism Quarterly*, 19: 12-24 (March 1942).

Pioneer in systematic analysis of the contents of communications discusses technical problems connected with a "symbol-count" of politically significant press content.

2262. Lasswell, Harold Dwight; and Blumenstock, Dorothy. "The Volume of Communist Propaganda in Chicago," *Public Opinion Quarterly*, 3: 63-78 (January 1939).

A chapter from the authors' *World Revolutionary Propaganda* (1939).

2263. Leites, Natan C. *The Third International on its Changes of Policy: A Study of Political Communication* (Library of Congress, Experimental Division for Study of War Time Communications, Document no. 25). Washington, D.C., 1942. 80 pp., mimeo.

Careful analysis of verbal forms in which the Third International (CI) justified its changes of policy on six historic occasions between 1921 and 1941. Based on close study of verbatim reports of CI congresses, *International Press Correspondence*, and *Daily Worker*. By University of Chicago political scientist, now in U.S. government service. Bibliography in text.

2264. Leites, Natan C.; and Pool, Ithiel de Sola. *Communist Propaganda in Reaction to Frustration* (Library of Congress, Experimental Division for Study of War Time Communications, Document no. 27). Washington, D.C., 1942. 54 pp., mimeo.

Quantified analysis of contents of *International Press Correspondence* articles dealing with strikes and elections, 1919-41, "which were mentioned in the *Inprecorr* and also characterized by the New York *Times* as Communist dominated and as resulting in defeats" [for the Communists]. A very elaborate psychological code was used in quantifying the results. Bibliography, pp. 48-54.

2265. LEITES, NATAN C.; and POOL, ITHIEL DE SOLA. *On Content Analysis* (Library of Congress, Experimental Division for Study of War Time Communications, Document no. 26). Washington, D.C., 1942. 27 pp., mimeo.

General statement of methods and aims, by two U.S. social scientists.

2266. LOGAN, RAYFORD WHITTINGHAM, editor. *The Attitude of the Southern White Press Toward Negro Suffrage, 1932-40,* foreword by Charles H. Wesley. Washington, D.C.: The Foundation Publishers (P.O. Box 132), 1940. 115 pp.

Compilation of news articles and editorials. "In general, the expression of opinion reveals a continuing intolerance in the Deep South and a growing tolerance in the Border States. In the latter there is an occasional voice that goes beyond mere tolerance and demands the participation of at least some Negroes in the Democratic primary. . . . As the United States girds herself for the preservation of Democracy, it might not be a bad idea to have some Democracy to defend" (p. xii). Dr. Logan is Professor of History, Howard University.

2267. LUXON, NORVAL N. "3,206 Newspaper Editorials Studied," *Editor and Publisher,* 69: no. 15, p. 7 (April 11, 1936).

Statistical report of relative space devoted to national, local, and international affairs.

2268. McDIARMID, JOHN. "Presidential Inaugural Addresses: A Study in Verbal Symbols," *Public Opinion Quarterly,* 1 no. 3: 79-82 (July 1937).

By political scientist trained at University of Chicago.

2269. McKENZIE, VERNON. "Treatment of War Themes in Magazine Fiction," *Public Opinion Quarterly,* 5: 227-32 (June 1941).

Fifty-five short stories about the war are grouped according to character of material and attitude conveyed. On the whole, the type of presentation could be expected to influence the reader in favor of the British. By Director of School of Journalism, University of Washington.

2270. MORGAN, WILLIAM THOMAS. "The British General Election of 1935: A Study of British Public Opinion as Expressed in Ten Daily Newspapers," *South Atlantic Quarterly,* 37: 108-31 (April 1938).

2271. (Pop.) NOVAK, BENJAMIN JOSEPH. *An Analysis of the Science Content of the New York Times and of Selected General Science Textbooks* (Ed.D. thesis, Temple University, 1942). Philadelphia, 1942. 60 pp.

Bibliography, pp. 53-60.

2272. SARGENT, S. S. "Emotional Stereotypes in the Chicago *Tribune,*" *Sociometry,* 2: 69-75 (1939).

Psychologist in Central Y.M.C.A. College, Chicago, tested reactions of six groups of adults to some 40 terms selected from news columns of Chicago *Tribune* and New York *Times. Tribune* terms were found to be more emotional and stereotyped than *Times* terms for the same bits of news.

2273. SAUNDERS, DERO AMES. "Social Ideas in McGuffey Readers," *Public Opinion Quarterly,* 5: 579-89 (Winter 1941).

Contents and probable impact of the social ideas in the textbooks which were studied by nearly every U.S. child during the last century are discussed by executive secretary of League for Fair Play.

2274. SEVERSON, A. L. "Nationality and Religious Preferences as Reflected in Newspaper Advertisements," *American Journal of Sociology,* 44: 540-45 (January 1939).

An unusual method of public opinion research: "Evidences of nationality and religious preferences are found in the help-wanted and resort ads in the Chicago *Tribune* over a sixty-five year period." Frequency of ads indicating discrimination increased when considerable propaganda was current. "Analysis of the respective frequencies by sex and occupation indicates that the propaganda had little if any effect in the rise. The movement into the white-collar market of second-generation East European immigrants is the important factor . . . 'second-generation' characteristics."

2275. SHUMAN, RONALD B. "Identification Elements of Advertising Slogans," *Southwestern Social Science Quarterly*, 17: 342-52 (March 1937).

Study of 4022 well-known advertising slogans to determine degree of the observance or violation of the "Slogan Rule of Three" (mention of name, brand, and product in the motto). About 60 per cent were found to violate the "rule."

2276. STENE, E. O. "Newspapers in the [1936] Campaign," *Social Science*, 12: 213-15 (April 1937).

Space-measurement study of 21 U.S. newspapers in 1936 Presidential campaign showed that 15 out of the 21 papers gave more attention and space to Landon than to Roosevelt; 5 gave a relative advantage to Roosevelt; one (Baltimore *Sun*) was impartial, giving 50-50 coverage to the two candidates. New York *Times* gave Roosevelt 51 per cent of its political news space, "a close second to the Baltimore *Sun*."

2277. SYRJAMAKI, JOHN. "The Negro Press in 1938," *Sociology and Social Research*, 24: 43-52 (September 1939).

Based on "detailed examination of 61 Negro papers chosen by geographical and population distribution."

2278. TWOHEY, JAMES S. "An Analysis of Newspaper Opinion on War Issues [Summer 1941]," *Public Opinion Quarterly*, 5: 448-55 (Fall 1941).

Mr. Twohey conducts a continuing statistical survey of front pages and editorials of U.S. newspapers (see no. 2240, above).

2279. WALWORTH, ARTHUR. *School Histories at War: A Study of the Treatment of Our Wars in the Secondary School History Books of the United States and in Those of Its Former Enemies*, introduction by Arthur Meier Schlesinger. Cambridge: Harvard University, 1938. 92 pp.

Bibliography, pp. 87-92.

2280. WILSON, LOGAN. "Newspaper Opinion and Crime in Boston," *Journal of Criminal Law and Criminology*, 29: 202-15 (July-August 1938).

U.S. sociologist analyzes editorials on crime which appeared in Boston newspapers in 1935. Tabulation brings out the variety of reactions "in the public mind."

2281. WRIGHT, QUINCY; and NELSON, CARL J. "American Attitudes Toward Japan and China, 1937-38," *Public Opinion Quarterly*, 3: 46-62 (January 1939).

Dr. Wright, University of Chicago specialist in international relations, and one of his graduate students examine newspaper editorial contents, using a simple statistical method.

D. MEASURING RELATIONS AMONG CONTENT, PREDISPOSITION, RESPONSE

2282. ALDERFER, HAROLD FREED; and SIGMOND, ROBERT M. *Presidential Elections by Pennsylvania Counties, 1920-1940*. State College: Pennsylvania State College, 1941. 61 pp.

2283. ANNIS, A. D. "Relative Effectiveness of Cartoons and Editorials as Propaganda Media," *Psychological Bulletin*, 36: 638 ff. (1939).

2284. ASHER, R.; and SARGENT, S. S. "Shifts in Attitude Caused by Cartoon Caricatures," *Journal of General Psychology*, 24: 451-55 (1941).

Compares college students' reactions to (1) visual presentation of a word on a blank card; (2) verbal presentation of the same word; (3) visual presentation of the same word as a label on a cartoon. "The only other experimental study of cartoons was done by [A.D.] Annis . . ." ("Relative Effectiveness of Cartoons and Editorials as Propaganda Media," *Psychological Bulletin*, 36: 638 ff. [1939]).

2285. BATEMAN, RICHARD M.; and REMMERS, H. H. "A Study of the Shifting Attitude of High School Students When Subjected to Favorable and Unfavorable Propaganda," *Journal of Social Psychology*, 13: 395-406 (May 1941).

Both negative and positive propaganda appeals produced significant shifts in attitude which were still measurable after a lapse of two months.

2286. BEAN, LOUIS H. *Ballot Behavior: A Study of Presidential Elections*, introduction by Charles Edward Merriam. Washington, D.C.: American Council on Public Affairs, 1940. 101 pp.

Analysis of factors in Presidential elections by well-known U.S. statistician and agricultural economist.

2287. BENSON, EDWARD G. "Three Words," *Public Opinion Quarterly*, 4: 130-34 (March 1940).

Staff member of American Institute of Public Opinion discusses variable meaning of the terms "radical," "liberal" and "conservative," as shown by poll results.

2288. BENSON, EDWARD G.; and PERRY, PAUL. "Analysis of Democratic-Republican Strength by Population Groups," *Public Opinion Quarterly*, 4: 464-73 (September 1940).

Two staff members of American Institute of Public Opinion analyze Gallup poll data to show centers of, and shifts in, Democratic and Republican strength among component groups of the national population.

2289. BEYLE, HERMAN CAREY. "Checking Response to Municipal Publicity," *Public Management*, 18: 163-66 (June 1936).

2290. BEYLE, HERMAN CAREY; and PARRATT, SPENCER. "Approval and Disapproval of Specific Third Degree Practices," *Journal of Criminal Law and Criminology*, 28: 526-50 (1937-38).

Study of the "third degree practices which were deemed to be tolerable though extralegal" by U.S. policemen, prisoners, and free private citizens, late in 1934 and early in 1935. By two Syracuse University professors of political science. Police are much more severe than the others.

2291. BLANKENSHIP, ALBERT B.; and TAYLOR, HOWARD RICE. "Psychological Effects of Changing a Trade Name," *Journal of Applied Psychology*, 21: 94-101 (February 1937).

2292. BOLTON, EURI BELLE. "Measuring Specific Attitudes Towards the Social Rights of the Negro," *Journal of Abnormal Psychology*, 31: 384-97 (January 1937).

2293. BROMLEY, DOROTHY DUNBAR; and BRITTEN, FLORENCE HAXTON. *Youth and Sex: A Study of 1300 College Students*. New York: Harpers, 1938. 303 pp.

Two married U.S. women journalists collected information on sexual practices and attitudes from 1364 men and women students in 46 colleges.

2294. BURTON, WILLIAM HENRY. *Children's Civic Information, 1924-35* (University of Southern California Education Monograph no. 7). Los Angeles: University of Southern California, 1936. 300 pp.

The growth of civic information from grades five to nine is presented for the years 1924-35, together with analysis of the sources from which children's information is derived. Approximately ten thousand children were studied in many parts of the United States.

2295. CANTRIL, HADLEY. "America Faces the War: A Study in Public Opinion," *Public Opinion Quarterly*, 4: 387-407 (September 1940).

The Director of the Princeton Public Opinion Research Project presents the latest cross-section picture of American opinion on the war, and traces trends of public sentiment since the outbreak of war.

2296. CANTRIL, HADLEY. "Prediction of Social Events," *Public Opinion*

Quarterly, 1 no. 4: 83-86 (October 1937).

A questionnaire asking for 70 different predictions (on war, depression, election outcomes, labor unions and other public affairs) was circulated to several hundred people—— eleven varieties of specialists and one group of laymen. Effects of specialization on prediction were studied.

2297. CANTRIL, HADLEY; and RUGG, DONALD. "Looking Forward to Peace," *Public Opinion Quarterly*, 4: 119-21 (March 1940).

Two U.S. social psychologists interpret poll results on the question (asked in November 1939): "If England and France defeat Germany, should the peace treaty be more severe on Germany or less severe than the treaty at the end of the last war?"

2298. CANTRIL, HADLEY; RUGG, DONALD; and WILLIAMS, FREDERICK. "America Faces the War: Shifts in Opinion," *Public Opinion Quarterly*, 4: 651-56 (December 1940).

Members of Princeton Public Opinion Research Project trace shifts in American opinion on World War II.

2299. CATTELL, RAYMOND B. "The Measurement of Interest," *Character and Personality*, 4: 147-69 (December 1935).

2300. CAVAN, RUTH SHONLE; and RANCK, KATHERINE HOWLAND. *The Family and the Depression* (Social Science Studies, no. 35). Chicago: University of Chicago, 1938. 209 pp.

From the files of the Institute for Juvenile Research in Chicago, 100 families were selected, on whom considerable information had been accumulated since 1928-29. Crisis-time reaction patterns were analyzed. A special study was made of attitudes toward the depression, relief agencies, and social reform. Bibliography, pp. 205-08, includes discussion of similar depression studies.

2301. CHAVE, ERNEST JOHN. *Measure Religion: Fifty-two Experimental Forms for the Measurement of Religious Attitudes*. Chicago: University of Chicago Bookstore, 1939. 142 pp.

By U.S. psychologist.

2302. CHEN, WILLIAM KE-CHING. "Retention of the Effect of Oral Propaganda," *Journal of Social Psychology*, 7: 479-83 (November 1936).

2303. (Pop.) CLARKE, JAMES. "In the Language of the People," in *The Practice of Book Selection*, edited by Louis Round Wilson (Chicago: University of Chicago, 1940), pp. 179-89.

Professor of Education, Teachers College, reports on application of readability tests such as the Gray-Leary formula to the production of books for the ordinary man, like *The People's Library*, of which the author and Lyman Bryson are coeditors. "It is estimated, for example, that the average American adult has had about six years' schooling and reads about as well as is expected of a fifth-grade child. . . . [But] an adult reacts differently to material in print. His emotional response is more mature, his interest of a different kind, his understanding deepened and also, perhaps, narrowed, by experience." (P. 181.)

2304. CONARD, LAETITIA M. "Differential Depression Effects on Families of Laborers, Farmers, and the Business Class," *American Journal of Sociology*, 44: 526-33 (January 1939).

Interview and questionnaire study of 150 families of an Iowa town and surrounding farms in 1935-36 indicates that the depression "affected laborers, farmers, and business class very differently at several points." "The number of the business class expressing hope for a new social order was nearly twice as great as those who wished to return to the conditions of 1925-29; . . . among laborers the number was more nearly equal; . . . among farmers those who said they wanted a new social order were less than half as many as those who hoped to return to the later twenties. The fact that more of the business class than of the laboring class mentioned a new social order is . . . of interest."

2305. COTTRELL, LEONARD SLATER, JR.; and BURGESS, ERNEST WATSON. *Predicting Success or Failure in Marriage*. New York: Prentice-Hall, 1939. 472 pp.

Careful multiple-variable analysis of U.S. marriage by two University of Chicago sociologists. Bibliography, pp. 437-63.

2306. Cronbach, Lee J. "Measuring Students' Thinking about a Presidential Election," *School Review*, 49: 679-92 (November 1941).

Questionnaire study of tendency of students to consider favorably a series of arguments, some of which were regarded as "indicative of intelligent citizenship." By teacher in State College of Washington.

2307. Day, Daniel Droba. "Rural Attitudes of Mississippi College Students," *Sociology and Social Research*, 25: 342-50 (March 1941).

2308. Dearborn, Walter F.; and Rothney, John W. M. *Scholastic, Economic, and Social Backgrounds of Unemployed Youth* (Harvard Bulletins in Education, no. 20). Cambridge, Mass.: Harvard University, 1938. 172 pp.

Harvard Graduate School of Education's careful statistical study of a sample of 1360 New England young people, aged 17-23, with respect to a long list of sociological, psychological, anthropometric, medical, and attitude characteristics. Differences between the employed and unemployed were found to be statistically insignificant in nearly all items. Bibliography, pp. 167-72.

2309. DeWick, H. N. "Relative Recall Effectiveness of Visual and Auditory Presentation of Advertising Material," *Journal of Applied Psychology*, 19: 245-64 (June 1935).

2310. Doob, Leonard William. "Some Attitudes Underlying American Participation in War," *Journal of Social Psychology*, 13: 475-87 (May 1941).

Attitude scale on willingness to take part in war.

2311. Eldridge, Seba. *Public Intelligence: A Study of the Attitudes and Opinions of Voters*. Lawrence: Bulletin of the University of Kansas, 1936. 101 pp.

University of Kansas sociologist's true-false test of twenty questions on the League of Nations, the tariff, and compulsory arbitration of labor disputes, filled out in the years 1924 to 1927 by 1250 voters, 960 of whom lived in the state of Kansas. Reviewed by Harold F. Gosnell in *American Political Science Review*, 30: 412-13 (April 1936).

2312. Elkin, Adolphus Peter. *Our Opinions and the National Effort*. Sydney: Australasian Medical Publishing Co., 1941. 80 pp.

"For this survey of Australian opinion on various aspects of the war effort, opinions were obtained from various segments of the population on such things as the validity of Allied war aims, willingness to participate personally in civilian war projects, satisfaction with the government's conduct of the war, the adequacy and reliability of the news. The author concludes that the Australian public was, at the time of the survey (summer of 1941), far from united and not wholeheartedly behind the war effort."—Donald Rugg, *American Journal of Sociology*, 48: 297 (September 1942).

2313. Elliott, Frank R. "Attention Effects from Poster, Radio, and Poster-Radio Advertising of an Exhibit," *Journal of Applied Psychology*, 21: 365-71 (August 1937).

Public attention was attracted to an exhibit at a state fair by three different methods, and results were compared.

2314. Elliott, Frank R. "Eye vs. Ear in Moulding Opinion," *Public Opinion Quarterly*, 1 no. 3: 83-86 (July 1937).

Experiments indicating relative effectiveness of eye and ear modes of stimulation of an audience.

2315. Fay, Paul J.; and Middleton, Warren C. "Judgment of Occupation from the Voice as Transmitted over a Public Address System and over a Radio," *Journal of Applied Psychology* 23: 586-601 (October 1939).

2316. Fletcher, Ralph; and Fletcher, Mildred. "Consistency in Party Voting, 1896-1932," *Social Forces*, 15: 281-85 (December 1936).

2317. Foster, Harry Schuyler; and Friedrich, Carl Joachim. "Letters to the Editor as a Means of Measuring the Effectiveness of Propaganda," *American Political Science Review*, 31: 71-79 (February 1937).

Based on examination of several hundred published and unpublished letters to editors.

2318. GALLUP, GEORGE HORACE. "Youth Declares War," *Literary Digest*, 125: 13-15 (January 1, 1938).

"Surveys conducted throughout the U.S. by the American Institute of Public Opinion in the past year show . . . most clearly . . . that the old taboos which once surrounded the discussion of venereal diseases are breaking down. The public wants information. It is ready for a first-rate crusade." Article cites statistics collected throughout the U.S. 87 per cent of those interviewed said they would like to take Wassermann tests; in Chicago, 95 per cent favored them. The young, and especially those of college age, were slightly more willing than their elders.

2319. GAUDET, FREDERICK JOSEPH. *Individual Differences in the Sentencing Tendencies of Judges* (Archives of Psychology, no. 230). New York: Columbia University, 1938. 58 pp.

Bibliography, p. 58.

2320. GLEECK, LEWIS E. "96 Congressmen Make Up Their Minds," *Public Opinion Quarterly*, 4: 3-24 (March 1940).

A study, based on personal interviews, of the factors which determined the votes of 96 members of Congress on embargo repeal. The author was a University of Chicago graduate student in political science.

2321. GOLDSTEIN, HARRY. *Reading and Listening Comprehension at Various Controlled Rates* (Ph.D. thesis: Teachers College Contributions to Education, no. 821). New York: Columbia University, 1940. 69 pp.

Bibliography, pp. 64-67.

2322. GOSNELL, HAROLD FOOTE; and COLMAN, WILLIAM G. "Political Trends in Industrial America [1928-40]: Pennsylvania an Example," *Public Opinion Quarterly*, 4: 473-86 (September 1940).

Voting behavior is analyzed by University of Chicago political scientist and one of his advanced students.

2323. GOSNELL, HAROLD FOOTE; and PEARSON, NORMAN M. "Relation of Economic and Social Conditions to Voting Behavior in Iowa, 1924-1936," *Journal of Social Psychology*, 13: 15-35 (1941).

2324. GOSNELL, HAROLD FOOTE; and PEARSON, NORMAN M. "The Study of Voting Behavior by Correlational Techniques," *American Sociological Review*, 4:809-15 (December 1939).

1932 and 1936 Presidential elections.

2325. GOSNELL, HAROLD FOOTE; and SCHMIDT, MARGARET J. "Factorial and Correlational Analysis of the 1934 Vote in Chicago," in *Journal of the American Statistical Association* (September 1936).

Precision techniques applied by two political scientists.

2326. GUNDLACH, RALPH H. "Emotional Stability and Political Opinions as Related to Age and Income," *Journal of Social Psychology*, 10: 577-90 (November 1939).

Sample: 250 college students, 700 adults, living in Seattle. *Findings*: Neuroticism, radicalism increase with poverty. But usually the radicals are not neurotic.

2327. HALL, OLIVER MILTON. *Attitudes and Unemployment: A Comparison of the Opinions and Attitudes of Employed and Unemployed Men* (Ph.D. thesis, Columbia; Archives of Psychology, no. 165). New York, 1934. 65 pp.

Bibliography, p. 56.

2328. HARLAN, HOWARD HARPER. "Some Factors Affecting Attitude toward Jews," *American Sociological Review*, 7: 816-27 (December 1942).

Statistically significant correlations of anti-Semitism with sex, age, religious affiliation, education, size of home community, occupation, income, etc., as shown by questionnaire given to 502 representative U.S. college students.

2329. HARTMANN, GEORGE WILFRIED. "Contradiction between the Feeling-Tone of Political Party Names and Public Response to their Platforms," *Journal of Social Psychology*, 7: 336-57 (August 1936).

Teachers College professor found that party preferences of Pennsylvania voters did not correlate highly with their statements about the policies of which they approved.

2330. HARTMANN, GEORGE WILFRIED. "Field Experiment on the Comparative Effectiveness of Emotional and Rational Political Leaflets in Determining Election Results," *Journal of Abnormal and Social Psychology*, 31: 99-114 (April 1936).

2331. HAYES, SAMUEL PERKINS, JR. "Homogeneity in Voters' Attitudes, in Relation to Their Political Affiliation, Sex, and Occupation," *Journal of Social Psychology*, 9: 141-60 (May 1938).

8419 voters in 37 states answered questionnaires presented in interviews by members of National League of Women Voters during two weeks preceding presidential election of 1932. It is suggested that party differences in unanimity may give a practicable indication of the most effective issues to stress in a campaign.

2332. HAYES, SAMUEL PERKINS, JR. "Occupational and Sex Differences in Political Attitudes," *Journal of Social Psychology*, 8: 87-113 (February 1937).

2333. HAYES, SAMUEL PERKINS, JR. "Voters' Attitudes Toward Men and Issues," and "The Predictive Ability of Voters," *Journal of Social Psychology*, 7: 164-91 (May 1936).

Excerpts from the author's *Voters' Attitudes Toward Men and Issues* (Ph.D. thesis, Yale, ca. 1934).

2334. HAYES, SAMUEL PERKINS, JR. Series of studies on voters' attitudes, *Journal of Social Psychology*, 1936-1939.

Elaborate statistical studies in the interrelations of attitudes and in their etiology, by social scientist, Sarah Lawrence College.

2335. HERRING, E(DWARD) PENDLETON. "How Does the Voter Make Up His Mind?" *Public Opinion Quarterly*, 2: 24-35 (January 1938).

Harvard professor of government analyzes responses to a questionnaire on merit appointments to the civil service, circulated to professionals, employers, clerical employees, skilled workers, and housewives by National League of Women Voters.

2336. HOLLINGWORTH, LETA STETTER. *Children Above 180 IQ, Stanford-Binet: Origin and Development*. Yonkers-on-Hudson, N.Y.: World Book Co., 1942. 332 pp.

A posthumously published volume by a Columbia University professor of educational psychology. Contains reports on the history of 12 children carried through some years, followed by a number of the author's previously published papers and by chapters on general problems of the adjustment of gifted children. Bibliography at ends of chapters.

2337. HOROWITZ, EUGENE L. *The Development of Attitude Toward the Negro* (Ph.D. thesis, Columbia; Archives of Psychology, no. 194). New York, January 1936. 47 pp.

Attitude tests were administered to boys from kindergarten through eighth grade in various types of U.S. communities. Bibliography, p. 37.

2338. JACOB, PHILIP E. "Influences of World Events on U.S. 'Neutrality' Opinion," *Public Opinion Quarterly*, 4: 48-65 (March 1940).

A study of the shifts shown by the Gallup and *Fortune* polls, 1935-39, in four kinds of American "neutrality" opinion: personal, commercial, military, financial. By Princeton Instructor in Politics who formerly served as Field Secretary of American Friends Service Committee.

2339. JEWETT, ARNO JOSEPH. *A Study to Determine the Results of Instruction in the Detecting and Analyzing of Propaganda in the Eleventh and Twelfth Grades* (from Ph.D. thesis, Minnesota). Chicago, 1940. 10 pp.

Methods advocated by Institute for Propaganda were found successful in statistical study by associate professor of English, Arizona State Teachers College. Reprinted from *English Journal*, 29: no. 2, part 1 (February 1940). See also title 2363, below.

2340. KIRKPATRICK, CLIFFORD; and STONE, SARAH. "Attitude Measurement and the Comparison of Generations," *Journal of Applied Psychology*, 19: 564-82 (October 1935).

2341. KLINGBERG, FRANK LEROY. "Studies in Measurement of Relations Among Sovereign Nations," *Psychometrika*, 6: 335-52 (December 1941).

Part of Ph.D. thesis, political science, Chicago.

2342. KORNHAUSER, ARTHUR W. "Attitudes of Economic Groups," *Public Opinion Quarterly*, 2: 260-68 (April 1938).

Associate professor of business psychology analyzes interview results on attitudes of various income classes toward political and economic issues.

2343. LIN, C. T. *A Historiopsychometric Study of Thirty-four Eminent Chinese* (Fu Jen Studies in Psychology). Peiping: Catholic University, 1939. 72 pp.

Statistical study, patterned after Terman and Cox's *Genetic Studies of Genius*, vol. 2. Attempts to discover (1) the mental traits of eminent Chinese, 618-1911 A.D.; (2) reliability and validity of historiopsychometric method as applied to Chinese biographical data. Judges matching 10 sets of statistical data with 10 biographical sketches had 90 per cent success—demonstrating high validity for the method.

2344. LOCKE, HARVEY J. "Changing Attitudes Toward Venereal Diseases," *American Sociological Review*, 4: 836-43 (December 1939).

Study of propagandas and of poll results. By University of Indiana sociologist.

2345. LORGE, IRVING. "Prestige, Suggestion, and Attitudes," *Journal of Social Psychology*, 7: 386-402 (November 1936).

By U.S. social psychologist.

2346. LURIE, WALTER A. "The Measurement of Prestige and Prestige-Suggestibility," *Journal of Social Psychology*, 9: 219-25 (May 1938).

Items are submitted once without, and once with, prestige-carrying symbols. Items are scaled by the method of paired comparisons both times.

2347. MACCRONE, IAN DOUGLAS. *Race Attitudes in South Africa: Historical, Experimental and Psychological Studies*. New York: Oxford University, 1937. 328 pp.

Statistical and psychological studies of attitudes toward the African native and toward the African social situation, by social psychologist, University of the Witwatersrand. Bibliography, pp. 311-17.

2348. McGREGOR, DOUGLAS. "The Major Determinants of the Prediction of Social Events," *Journal of Abnormal and Social Psychology*, 9: 179-204 (April 1938).

Analysis of 3500 predictions made by 400 subjects in May 1936. When the stimulus situation was unambiguous, wishful factors were of negligible significance in determination of prediction. Besides *ambiguity, importance* was demonstrated to be a significant factor.

2349. McKINNEY, F. "Retroactive Inhibition in Advertising," *Journal of Applied Psychology*, 19: 59-66 (February 1935).

2350. MEIER, NORMAN C.; and LEWINSKI, ROBERT J. "Occupational Variation in Judging Trends in Public Opinion," *Public Opinion Quarterly*, 2: 442-49 (July 1938).

Two University of Iowa psychologists obtained estimates of Gallup poll results from members of various occupations, and compared these estimates with the actual figures.

2351. MENEFEE, SELDEN COWLES. "Experimental Study of Strike Propaganda: The Pacific Northwest Lumber Strike of 1935," *Social Forces*, 16: 574-82 (May 1938).

U.S. social psychologist analyzes press treatment of Pacific Northwest lumber strike of

1935. Effects of propaganda appeals were tested on groups of students.

2352. MELTZER, H. "The Development of Children's Nationality Preferences, Concepts, and Attitudes," *Journal of Psychology*, 11: 343-58 (April 1941).

A comparative measurement of the attitudes of children of different ages toward 21 nationalities.

2353. MIDDLETON, WARREN C. "Personality Qualities Predominant in Campus Leaders," *Journal of Social Psychology*, 13: 199-201 (1941).

2354. MILK RESEARCH COUNCIL, INC. *A Study of the Psychological Factors Influencing the Drinking of Plain Milk by Adults.* New York, January 1935. About 75 pp., mimeo.

A study made for the Milk Research Council, Inc., jointly by the Psychological Corporation of America and Dr. Paul Felix Lazarsfeld.

2355. MURPHY, JOHN C. *An Analysis of the Attitudes of American Catholics toward the Immigrant and the Negro, 1825-1925* (Ph.D. thesis, sociology, Catholic University). Washington, D.C.: Catholic University of America, 1940. 158 pp.

Bibliography, pp. 147-53.

2356. NATIONAL INDUSTRIAL CONFERENCE BOARD. *A Statistical Survey of Public Opinion Regarding Current Economic and Social Problems As Reported by Newspaper Editors in the First Quarter of 1936* (Studies, no. 222). New York, 1936. 56 pp.

2357. NELSON, ERLAND. *Radicalism-Conservatism in Student Attitudes* (Psychological Monographs, vol. 50, no. 4). Columbus: Psychological Review Company, 1938. 32 pp.

2358. NEWCOMB, THEODORE MEAD. "Determinants of Opinion," *Public Opinion Quarterly*, 1 no. 4: 71-78 (October 1937).

"This review attempts to bring together the results of recent attitude studies which throw light on the relationship between given opinions and certain personality and cultural influences." By Bennington College social psychologist.

2359. NEWCOMB, THEODORE MEAD; and SVEHLA, GEORGE. "Intra-Family Relationships in Attitude," *Sociometry*, 1: 180-205 (July-October 1937).

Thurstone scales of attitude toward various symbols were filled in by several different members of certain families, and the resulting attitude-constellations were analyzed.

2360. NEWLAND, HUBERT CHARLES. *The Change in Attitude toward Sex Freedom as Disclosed by American Journals of Opinion during the Years 1911 to 1930* (Ph.D. thesis, Chicago, 1932).

2361. OGBURN, WILLIAM FIELDING; and HUNT, ESTELLE. "Income Classes and the Roosevelt Vote in 1932," *Political Science Quarterly*, 50: 186-94 (June 1935).

2362. OGBURN, WILLIAM FIELDING; and JAFFE, ABE J. "Independent Voting in Presidential Elections," *American Journal of Sociology*, 42: 186-201 (September 1936).

Statistical analysis by counties, 1876-1932. "Counties that had the greatest increase in the fluctuation of voters from 1920 to 1932 were those that had (a) the largest proportion of young voters, (b) the largest proportion of men, (c) the smallest percentage of native-born citizens of native parents, (d) the greatest growth in population, (e) the greatest degree of urbanism, (f) the highest incomes, (g) the least increase in wages, and (h) the greatest lessening of the share of the manufactured product going to labor."

2363. OSBORN, WAYLAND WAYNE. "An Experiment in Teaching Resistance to Propaganda," *Journal of Experimental Education*, 8: 1-17 (September 1939).

Summary of Ph.D. thesis, University of Iowa. A carefully objective test used in seventeen Iowa high schools shows low results from use of procedures similar to those recommended by Institute for Propaganda Analysis. Also confirms findings of other research as to low correlation between information on certain subjects and response to propaganda about them. *Conclusions*: (1) "There are no shortcuts to propaganda resistance. Thorough study is necessary." (2) A study of propaganda tricks seems to be a strong motivating factor in propaganda study. (3) A pupil's intelligence and achievement are not a reliable index of his ability to resist propaganda. See also title 2339, above.

2364. PACE, C. ROBERT. "The Relationship Between Liberalism and Knowledge of Current Affairs," *Journal of Social Psychology*, 10: 247-58 (May 1939).

Based on Ph.D. thesis in University of Minnesota Library.

2365. PHILLIPS, MARGARET. "The Development of Social-Political Sentiments in Women," *British Journal of Educational Psychology*, 5: 266-98 (November 1935).

2366. "President Roosevelt Wins *Fortune* Poll in Spite of New Deal," *Life*, June 27, 1938, pp. 9-17.

Graphs and pictures explaining the poll on Franklin D. Roosevelt's popularity, as reported in *Fortune* for July 1938.

2367. PRESTON, HARLEY O. *Relationship of Eschatological Emphasis to Economic Status of Protestant Churches in Bloomington* (M.A. thesis, sociology, Indiana, 1938).

2368. PRINGLE, HENRY FOWLES. "What Do the Women of America Think?" *Ladies Home Journal*, 55: 14-15 ff. (February 1938).

Report of a quantitative opinion survey on "Marriage and Divorce," "Birth Control," "Money," "Morals."

2369. RACKLEY, JOHN RALPH. *The Relationship of the Study of History to Student Attitudes* (George Peabody College for Teachers, Abstract of Ph.D. thesis; Contribution to Education no. 260). Nashville, Tennessee: George Peabody College for Teachers, 1940. 5 pp.

2370. RAZRAN, G. H. S. "Conditioned Response Changes in Rating and Appraising Socio-political Slogans," *Psychological Bulletin*, 37: 481 ff. (1940).

2371. REMMERS, HERMANN HENRY. "Propaganda in the Schools—Do the Effects Last?" *Public Opinion Quarterly*, 2: 197-210 (April 1938).

Experiments with carefully designed pieces of propaganda are reported by well-known U.S. specialist in educational measurement.

2372. REMMERS, HERMANN HENRY. *Studies in Attitudes: A Contribution to Social Psychological Research Methods*, and *Further Studies in Attitudes*, series 2, 1936; series 3, 1938. Lafayette, Ind.: Purdue University, Division of Educational Reference. 298 and 151 pp.

Bibliography, series 1, pp. 110-12; series 2, pp. 296-98; series 3, pp. 149-51.

2373. ROBINSON, EDGAR EUGENE. *The Presidential Vote, 1896-1932*. Stanford University: Stanford University, 1934. 399 pp.

A tabulation of the Presidential election returns by counties, with little attempt at interpretation; comparable to such continental studies as Fritz Giovanili's *Statistik der Nationalratswahlen, 1919-1928* (Bern: Eidgenössischer Statistischen Amt, 1929. 150 pp.).

2374. ROBINSON, EDGAR EUGENE. *The Presidential Vote, 1936*. Stanford University, Calif.: Stanford, 1940. 91 pp.

Supplement to *The Presidential Vote, 1896-1932* (Stanford University, 1934. 403 pp.), standard compilation of voting statistics by counties.

2375. ROSKELLEY, R. WELLING. *Attitudes and Overt Behavior: Their Relations to Each Other and To Selection Factors* (Ph.D. thesis, sociology, Wisconsin, 1938).

2376. ROUCEK, JOSEPH SLABEY. "Social Attitudes of Native-Born Children of Foreign-Born Parents," *Sociology and Social Research*, 22: 149-55 (November 1937).

By U.S. sociologist.

2377. ROUCEK, JOSEPH SLABEY. "Social Attitudes of the Soldier in Wartime," *Journal of Abnormal and Social Psychology*, 30: 164-74 (1935-36).

2378. RUCH, FLOYD LEON; and YOUNG, KIMBALL. "Penetration of Axis Propaganda," *Journal of Applied Psychology*, 26: 448-55 (August 1942).

Survey of rumor acceptance in Boston and New York, by two U.S. social psychologists.

2379. RUGG, DONALD; and CANTRIL, HADLEY. "War Attitudes of Families with Potential Soldiers," *Public Opinion Quarterly*, 4: 327-30 (June 1940).

According to Gallup polls: "The opinions of persons with draft-age [18 to 30] family members and those without such members appear to be almost identical. . . ."

2380. SEELEMAN, VIRGINIA. *The Influence of Attitude upon the Remembering of Pictorial Material* (Archives of Psychology, no. 258). New York, 1940. 69 pp.

Bibliography, pp. 62-63.

2381. SHAFFER, LAURANCE FREDERIC. *Children's Interpretations of Cartoons: A Study of the Nature and Development of the Ability to Interpret Symbolic Drawings* (Teachers College Contributions to Education, no. 429). New York: Columbia University, 1930. 73 pp.

By a U.S. psychologist. Bibliography, pp. 72-73.

2382. SCHILLER, GWENDOLYN ANNE. "Experimental Study of the Appropriateness of Color and Type in Advertising," *Journal of Applied Psychology*, 19: 652-64 (December 1935).

2383. SIMPSON, RAY HAMILL. *A Study of Those Who Influence and of Those Who Are Influenced in Discussion* (Teachers College Contributions to Education, no. 748). New York: Columbia University, 1938. 89 pp.

Measured relationship between certain individual traits and the individual's ability to influence (1) immediate group decisions and (2) persistent individual attitudes. College women were organized into discussion groups, asked to reach decisions "agreeable to the group" on various controversial issues. Those most influential in discussion tend to (1) have high school marks; (2) have a "strong" religious background; (3) make high scores on Scholastic Aptitude Test of Verbal Ability; (4) be least influenced by discussion; (5) be widely dispersed (not necessarily dominant) on paper-and-pencil tests of dominance-submissiveness. Bibliography, pp. 88-89.

2384. SIMS, VERNER MARTIN. "Factors Influencing Attitudes Toward the TVA," *Journal of Abnormal and Social Psychology*, 33: 34-56 (January 1938).

Using a Thurstone scale, it was found that Southern adults, Southern students, and Northern students were in general more favorable to the TVA than Northern adults. Persons of business and industrial affiliation were less favorable than laborers, farmers, and professionals. Exposed to printed experimental propaganda, pro and con, matched groups changed their attitudes according to definite patterns.

2385. SMITH, (JAMES) MAPHEUS. "An Empirical Scale of Prestige Status of Occupations," *American Sociological Review*, 8: 185-92 (April 1943).

Average prestige status ratings for 100 representative occupations, as given by Kansas college and high school students, 1938-41, are presented by University of Kansas sociologist in the form of a numerical scale. Government officials and professional workers received the highest ratings; small business men, salesmen, clerical workers, and skilled workers were given medium ratings; unskilled workers were given lowest positions. Illustrations are presented of the use of the ratings in the identification of occupational strata, and in correlating prestige with other characterstics of occupational classes. Article includes critical bibliography on previous prestige and status studies.

2386. Smith, (James) Mapheus. "Spontaneous Change of Attitude Toward War," *School and Society*, 46: 30-32 (July 3, 1937).

Using the Droba *Attitude Toward War Scale*, 282 students in sociology classes at the University of Kansas were tested at intervals from 1932 to 1936. The group as a whole increased in antagonism toward war from year to year.

2387. Smith, (James) Mapheus. "University Student Intelligence and Occupation of Father," *American Sociological Review*, 7: 764-71 (December 1942).

A definite pattern of relations is shown between (1) scores obtained by 5487 University of Kansas students on American Council on Education intelligence tests and (2) occupations of their fathers.

2388. Stabley, Rhodes Rufus. *Newspaper Editorials on American Education* (Ph.D. thesis, education, Pennsylvania). Philadelphia: University of Pennsylvania, 1941. 283 pp.

Number and attitudes of editorials on U.S. education in ten metropolitan U.S. newspapers, 1910-37. Relation of editorial content to (1) social trends, (2) sectionalism, (3) political affiliations of newspapers and (4) control changes among papers. Bibliography, p. 283.

2389. Stagner, Ross. "Correlational Analysis of Nationalistic Opinions," *Journal of Social Psychology*, 12: 197-212 (August 1940).

2390. Stagner, Ross. "Marital Similarity in Socio-economic Attitudes," *Journal of Applied Psychology*, 22: 340-46 (August 1938).

2391. Stagner, Ross. "Measuring Relationships Among Group Opinions," *Public Opinion Quarterly*, 2: 622-27 (October 1938).

Political and economic stereotypes of a representative U.S. population (in Akron, Ohio) are statistically analyzed by U.S. social psychologist.

2392. Thomsen, Arnold. "What Voters Think of Candidates Before and After Election," *Public Opinion Quarterly*, 2: 269-74 (April 1938).

Attitudes toward Roosevelt and Landon before and after the 1936 election were measured by a member of the staff of the School of Citizenship and Public Affairs, Syracuse University.

2393. Thorndike, Edward Lee. "Facts vs. Opinions: An Empirical Study of 117 Cities," *Public Opinion Quarterly*, 2: 85-90 (January 1938).

Well-known Columbia psychologist compares facts about 117 cities with ratings given them on a series of scales by a large number of leaders in business and the professions. Leaders' opinions "suffer from grave inadequacies and errors," it was found, "because they are ignorant and neglectful of the facts. . . . The opinions of people in general will surely be no better than these and probably will be much worse. We, the people of the United States, are not much more competent judges of the cities we live in than of the stars we see." Correlation of opinions with the facts among Educators was .59; "Progressives" and "Reformers," .51; Clergymen and Social Workers, .36; Businessmen, .27.

2394. Timmons, William Murray. *Decisions and Attitudes as Outcomes of the Discussion of a Social Problem* (Teachers College Contributions to Education, no. 777). New York: Teachers College, Columbia University, 1939. 106 pp.

By a U.S. professor of English. Group discussion of alternative prison parole systems was conducted in a group of 672 high school juniors and seniors enrolled in social studies courses. Attitudes, intelligence, and choice of solutions were correlated. Discussion appeared to facilitate arrival at solutions that were acceptable to "experts," whether discussants were of high or low intelligence. Bibliography, pp. 91-93.

2395. Tingsten, Herbert Lars Gustav. *Political Behavior: Studies in Election Statistics*. London: P. S. King, 1937. 231 pp.

By a Swedish political scientist. Electoral participation and attitudes of voters in various countries are classified by sex, age, and occupation, and a number of "laws" of political behavior are formulated.

2396. Titus, Charles Hickman. *Voting Behavior in the United States: A Statistical Study* (Publications of the University of California at Los Angeles in Social Sciences, vol. 5, no. 1). Berkeley: University of California, 1935. 74 pp.

By University of California political scientist. Bibliography, pp. 73-74.

2397. Travers, R. M. W. *A Study in Judging the Opinions of Groups* (Archives of Psychology, no. 266). New York, 1941. 73 pp.

2398. Travers, R. M. W. "Who Are the Best Judges of the Public?" *Public Opinion Quarterly*, 6: 628-33 (Winter 1942).

"The present writer has been engaged for some time in conducting a series of researches in an attempt to discover, first, the factors in personality that result in erroneous judgments of public opinion and, secondly, the qualities that are associated with the ability to make accurate judgments of public opinion. It seems appropriate here to gather together the conclusions of these researches regarding the qualities that characterize good and bad judges." Article cites this U.S. psychologist's other writings on this subject.

2399. Tucker, Anthony Carter. *Some Correlates of Certain Attitudes of the Unemployed* (Ph.D. thesis; Archives of Psychology, no. 245). New York, 1940. 72 pp.

Case records of New York City Adjustment Service, 1933-1934, were analyzed for background data. Attitudes of older people were more stable and more conservative than those of younger. Men with higher earnings prior to unemployment were more conservative than less "successful" men; but "successful" women less conservative than those paid less.

2400. Waples, Douglas; and Berelson, Bernard. *Public Communications and Public Opinions*, and *What the Voters Were Told*. Chicago: Graduate Library School, University of Chicago, 1941. 76 and 77 pp. mimeo. (bound together).

The first study reports a careful effort to determine "under what conditions communications were more or less influential in determining public opinion." Two sample groups in Erie County, Ohio, were asked to identify and evaluate fourteen major 1941 Presidential campaign arguments. 497 persons typical of the community and 182 with some high-school training were interviewed.

What the Voters Were Told is an elaborate content analysis of four leading newspapers, seven magazines, 28 major political speeches, three newscasts, at the focus of attention of voters of Erie County during the 1941 Presidential election campaign. Subject matter, symbols of "action," intensity of action, sponsorship, preference, degree of sentimentalization were tabulated. "The communications favored the Republican candidate three to one until just before the election, when the Democrats campaigned most vigorously, then the preference fell to two to one. However, the communications centered on Roosevelt three to two. . . . The radio was the least partisan, the newspaper came next and the magazine was the most partisan. . . . The most important fact about the references to methods of fulfilling campaign promises is their scarcity. Only about 18 per cent of the content made any reference to methods (practicable or otherwise) whereby the advertised goals would be achieved." (P. 48.)

2401. Weld, Harry Porter; and Danzig, E. R. "Study of the Way in which a Verdict is Reached by a Jury," *American Journal of Psychology*, 53: 518-36 (October 1940).

2402. Williamson, A. C.; and Remmers, Herrmann Henry. "Persistence of Attitudes Concerning Conservation Issues," *Journal of Experimental Education*, 8: 354-61 (1940).

As a result of planned propaganda, attitudes of rural and urban high school students toward the issues were changed, and remained changed over a period as long as eight months. Rural group was less affected by the stimuli than urban group.

2403. Whisler, L. D.; and Remmers, Herrmann Henry. "Liberalism, Optimism, and Group Morale: A Study of Student Attitudes," *Journal of Social Psychology*, 9: 451-67 (November 1938).

Scales by Harper, Chant and Myers, and

Whisler and Remmers; also a questionnaire about social trends in the U.S.

2404. WYANT, ROWENA; and HERZOG, HERTA. "Voting via the Senate Mailbag," *Public Opinion Quarterly*, 5: 359-82, 590-624 (Fall, Winter 1941).

A pioneer attempt to ascertain statistically the nature of letters sent to congressmen on the issue of conscription, the extent to which the admonition is heeded, the content of the letters sent, who writes them, and why. By staff members of Office of Radio Research.

2405. YOUNG, KIMBALL; and OBERDORFER, DOUGLAS W. "Factors Influencing Student Political Opinion," *Public Opinion Quarterly*, 2: 450-56 (July 1938).

Careful statistical study of background factors that would be likely to show some reasons for expressed Presidential preferences in the 1936 election. By two U.S. sociologists, then at University of Wisconsin.

PART 7. CONTROL AND CENSORSHIP OF COMMUNICATION

Selections from the vast literature that seeks to interpret the function of promotion in all its varied forms in contemporary civilization, together with titles that summarize social experience in striving to abolish or to regulate certain forms of communication.

2406. *The Administration of the Foreign Agents Registration Act.* Washington, D.C.: Institute of Living Law (340 Woodward Building), June 1941. 45 pp.

This law ("the McCormack Act") requires disclosure of propaganda agents of foreign principals that seek to influence U.S. public opinion. This report by a group of U.S. attorneys and social scientists analyzes the Act and its administration, telling what it was intended to accomplish, what it had accomplished to date, and what changes might make it more effective.

2407. ALBERTY, HAROLD B.; and BODE, BOYD HENRY, editors. *Educational Freedom and Democracy* (Second Yearbook of the John Dewey Society). New York: Appleton-Century, 1938. 292 pp.

A group of educators strongly influenced by the philosophy of John Dewey examine the conception of "educational freedom in a democracy." Chapter 9 deals with "The Organization of the Profession," and Chapter 10 with "Protecting Freedom Through Organization." Appendix contains replies of certain patriotic and youth organizations to a questionnaire on educational freedom submitted by the authors of the book.

*2408. AMERICAN CIVIL LIBERTIES UNION.

Issues *Annual Reports* that summarize the year's developments in civil liberties, religious freedom, academic freedom, censorship. Only the three most recent *Annual Reports* are cited below (titles 2408a, 2409, 2410). Also issues pamphlets and select bibliographies on special cases as they arise.

*2408a. AMERICAN CIVIL LIBERTIES UNION. *Freedom in Wartime.* New York, June 1943. 80 pp.

Annual report of the Union. "The striking contrast between the state of civil liberty in the first eighteen months of World War II and in World War I offers strong evidence to support the thesis that our democracy can fight even the greatest of all wars and still maintain the essentials of liberty. The country in World War II is almost wholly free of those pressures which in the first World War resulted in mob violence against dissenters, hundreds of prosecutions for utterances; in the creation of a universal volunteer vigilante system, officially recognized, to report dissent to the F.B.I.; in hysterical hatred of everything German; in savage sentences for private expressions of criticism; and in suppressions of public debate of the issues of the war and the peace. . . .

"The government has not resorted to prosecution or censorship on any appreciable scale. War-time prosecutions brought by the Department of Justice for utterances, and publications barred by the Post Office Department as obstructive, have so far numbered about forty-five, involving less than two hundred persons, compared with over a thousand persons involved in almost as many cases in World War I. Even though some of the proceedings were hardly justified by any reasonable interpretation of the 'clear and present danger' test laid down by the Supreme Court, the Department of Justice has on the whole shown commendable restraint."

Bibliography, list of officers and addresses of Local Committees in all parts of the U.S., pp. 72-79.

*2409. AMERICAN CIVIL LIBERTIES UNION. *The Bill of Rights in War: A Report on American Democratic Liberties in War-time.* New York, June 1942. 80 pp.

Annual report of the Union. Bibliography, list of officers and addresses of Local Committees in all parts of the U.S., pp. 73-79.

*2410. AMERICAN CIVIL LIBERTIES UNION. *Liberty's National Emergency: The Story of Civil Liberty in the Crisis*

Year 1940-1941. New York, June 1941. 80 pp.

Annual report of the Union. "The . . . vastly increased tempo of national defense maintained the crisis psychology. . . . Pressure on strikers, on aliens, on Communists, and on Jehovah's Witnesses, markedly tightened. . . . Most striking of the casualties was the barring of the Communist Party from the ballot in fifteen states. Comment from the Union's correspondents in 36 states in May 1941 pretty uniformly agreed that there has been little actual interference with civil liberties . . . , but all reported . . . a great apprehension. Most apprehension was expressed concerning the rights of labor and the expanding functions of the FBI." Bibliography, pp. 71-73.

2411. AMERICAN CIVIL LIBERTIES UNION. *Minority Parties on the Ballot.* New York, April 1941. 24 pp.

Memorandum on legal restrictions on nominations by minority parties, together with a model statute proposed by the Union.

2412. AMERICAN CIVIL LIBERTIES UNION. *Religious Liberty in the United States Today: A Survey of the Restraints on Religious Freedom.* New York, 1939. 48 pp.

2413. AMERICAN CIVIL LIBERTIES UNION. *School Buildings as Public Forums.* New York, 1935. 12 pp.

Survey of restrictions upon unpopular minorities desiring use of school buildings.

2414. AMERICAN CIVIL LIBERTIES UNION. *Statement to Members and Friends, Concerning the Resolution Fixing Qualifications for Membership on Our Guiding Committees and Staff.* New York, May 1940. 15 pp.

Civil Liberties Union explains why it feels it did not violate principles of civil liberty when in 1940 it excluded Communists from its board and staff. See title 2461.

2415. AMERICAN CIVIL LIBERTIES UNION. *Thumbs Down! The Fingerprint Menace to Civil Liberties.* New York, February 1938. 20 pp.

Discusses current propaganda for and against fingerprinting, naming some of the pressure-groups involved.

2416. AMERICAN CIVIL LIBERTIES UNION. *What Freedom for American Students?* New York, 1941. 48 pp.

Survey of the practices in typical colleges.

2417. AMERICAN COMMITTEE FOR DEMOCRACY AND INTELLECTUAL FREEDOM. *The Text Books of Harold Rugg: An Analysis* by George H. Sabine, Arthur N. Holcombe, Arthur W. MacMahon, Carl Wittke, Robert S. Lynd. New York, 1942. 28 pp.

Statement by prominent U.S. social scientists concerning a series of textbooks regarded as controversial by certain conservative groups.

2418. AMERICAN COUNCIL ON PUBLIC AFFAIRS. *Freedom of Assembly and Anti-democratic Groups: A Memorandum of the Council for Democracy.* Washington, D.C., 1940. 27 pp.

Views of group of students and authorities on control of public meetings in a democracy. Obtainable on request from the Council. Bibliography, pp. 26-27.

2419. AMERICAN MUNICIPAL ASSOCIATION. *Regulation of Handbill Distribution: Legal Problems Involved* (Report no. 136). Chicago, May 1, 1940. 20 pp.

2420. ARTHUR, WILLIAM REED; and CROSMAN, RALPH L. *The Law of Newspapers: A Text and Case Book for Use in Schools of Journalism and a Deskbook for Newspaper Workers,* 2nd ed. rev. New York and London: McGraw-Hill, 1940. 615 pp.

Professor Arthur is a professor of law, University of Colorado; Professor Crosman, Director of University of Colorado's College of Journalism. Bibliography, pp. 473-74 and footnotes.

2421. BAKER, JOSEPH. *The Law of Political Uniforms, Public Meetings, and Private Armies.* London: H. A. Just, 1937. 205 pp.

2422. BALDWIN, ROGER NASH; and RANDALL, CLARENCE B. *Civil Liberties and Industrial Conflict* (The Godkin

Lectures, 1938). Cambridge: Harvard University, 1938. 137 pp.

Civil liberties of industrial workers are discussed in two essays by counsel for American Civil Liberties Union and two essays by official of Inland Steel Company.

2423. BARRETT, WILTON AGNEW. "The National Board of Review of Motion Pictures: How It Works," *Journal of Educational Sociology*, 10: 171-88 (November 1936).

By executive director of the National Board of Review.

2424. BARTHÉLEMY, JOSEPH. "Le Projet contre la presse," *Revue politique et parlementaire*, 44: 3-27 (January 1937).

Proposed legislation to regulate French press is analyzed by a prominent member of the University of Paris Faculty of Law.

2424a. BEALE, HOWARD KENNEDY. *Are American Teachers Free?* (Report of the American Historical Association's Commission on the Social Studies, part 12). New York: Scribner's, 1937. 856 pp.

Study of restraints upon academic freedom in American teachers' colleges and schools below the college level. There are chapters on freedom of expression on war problems, peace and internationalism, patriotism, politics, economic and social questions, history, religion, and science.

*2425. BEALE, HOWARD KENNEDY (D,W). *A History of Freedom of Teaching in American Schools* (Report of the American Historical Association's Commission on the Social Studies, part 16). New York: Scribner's, 1941. 343 pp.

Comprehensive analysis of U.S. practice from Colonial times to the present. By professor of history, University of North Carolina. Includes an elaborate attitude questionnaire on academic freedom. Bibliography, pp. 291-98.

2426. BELLAMY, PAUL; and others. "Cooperation between Press, Radio, and Bar in the Matter of Trial Publicity: Report of the Special Committee of the American Bar Association," *Journal of Criminal Law*, 28: 641-56 (January 1938).

2427. BERRY, TYLER. *Communications by Wire and Radio: A Treatise on the Law of Wire and Wireless Communications in Interstate and Foreign Commerce, based on the Federal Communications Act of June 19, 1934, as amended . . .* Chicago: Callaghan, 1937. 462 pp.

2428. BIDDLE, FRANCIS. "Civil Rights in Times of Stress," *Proceedings of National Conference of Social Work, 1941* (New York: Columbia University, 1941), pp. 158-72.

U.S. Attorney General summarizes current U.S. emergency legislation and administrative action affecting civil liberties.

2429. BROWN, R. JARDINE. "The Constitutional Law and History of Broadcasting in Great Britain," *Air Law Review*, 8: 177-200 (July 1937).

By the Business Manager of British Broadcasting Corporation.

2430. BUNTING, DAVID EDISON. *Liberty and Learning: The Activities of the American Civil Liberties Union in Behalf of Education.* Washington, D.C.: American Council on Public Affairs, 1942. 147 pp.

American Civil Liberties Union has pioneered, with the American Association of University Professors and the American Federation of Teachers, in defending the freedom of teachers and teaching, particularly since World War I. This is a handbook on cases, participants, issues, books, and articles related to the Union's work. The author is Dean of the University of Tampa. Bibliography, pp. 136-43.

2431. BURTON, WILBUR. "Ways of the Oriental Censor," *Fortnightly*, 147: 724-31 (June 1937).

Modern and ancient examples of Chinese and Japanese censorship.

2432. CALDWELL, LOUIS GOLDSBOROUGH. "Developments in Federal

Regulation of Broadcasting," *Variety Radio Directory*, 1: 269-303 (1937-38); 2: 525-53 (1938-39); 3: 896-976 (1939-40); 4: 409-54 (1940-41).

Prominent member of the Washington radio bar traces the precedents and philosophies in radio regulatory practice that culminated in the "anti-monopoly orders" of the FCC.

2433. CALDWELL, LOUIS GOLDS-BOROUGH. "The International Ether Lanes," *Air Law Review*, 8: 201-12 (July 1937).

General survey of problems of world allocation of wave-lengths and broadcasting facilities.

2434. CANADA, CENSORSHIP CO-ORDINATION COMMITTEE. *Handbook: Press and Radio Broadcasting Censorship.* Ottawa: J. O. Patenaude, I.S.O., Printer to the King, 1940. 23 pp.

2435. "Censorship of Motion Pictures," *Yale Law Journal*, 48: 87-113 (November 1939).

2436. CERF, WALTER. "Freedom of Instruction in War Time," *Public Opinion Quarterly*, 6: 576-87 (Winter 1942).

Northwestern University professor of philosophy advocates balanced discussion—presentation of both sides of controversial subjects—as an alternative to suppression, even in the midst of war.

*2437. CHAFEE, ZECHARIAH, JR. (CB '42, D,W). *Free Speech in the United States.* Cambridge: Harvard University, 1941. 634 pp.

Extensively revised edition of this standard treatise on the law and institutions of free speech, by Harvard professor of law, which first appeared in 1920. Bibliography in footnotes, text, and pp. 569-71.

2438. CHAMBERS, MERRITT MADI-SON. *The Colleges and the Courts, 1936-40: Recent Judicial Decisions Regarding Higher Education in the United States.* New York: Carnegie Foundation for the Advancement of Teaching, 1941. 126 pp.

2439. CHAMBERS, MERRITT MADI-SON, editor. *The Tenth Yearbook of School Law, 1942.* Washington, D.C.: American Council on Education, 1942. 96 pp.

A narrative topical summary of decisions of the higher courts in the U.S. in cases involving school law, as reported during the preceding year.

2440. CHAUDET, GUSTAVE. *La Règlementation administrative de la presse dans les principaux pays.* Vevey: Marchino, 1938. 158 pp.

Legal study of administrative regulation of the press in France, Germany, Great Britain, Italy, Switzerland, U.S.

2441. CLARK, GRENVILLE. "Civil Liberties: Court Help or Self-Help," *Annals of the American Academy of Political and Social Science*, 195 part 2: 1-11 (January 1938).

Address by prominent attorney before American Political Science Association on recent relations "between the judicial power and the power of public opinion, as effective forces for the maintenance of the basic civil liberties."

2442. CLARK, GRENVILLE. "The Limits of Freedom of Expression," *United States Law Review* (June 1939).

2442a. COGGESHALL, REGINALD. "Was There Censorship at the Paris Peace Conference?" *Journalism Quarterly*, 16: 125-35 (June 1939).

By a U.S. journalist.

2443. COLMAN, LOUIS, editor. *Equal Justice: Yearbook of the Fight for Democratic Rights, 1936-37*, with an introduction by Anna Damon. New York: International Labor Defense, 1937. 104 pp.

2444. COLMERY, HARRY W. "Defense of Freedom by the American Legion," *Bulletin of the American Association of University Professors*, 23: 32-34 (January 1937).

National Commander of the American Legion declares against use of "force or violence or intimidation to suppress any group." Extract from his article in the *National Legionnaire*, November 1936.

2445. "The Consumer and Federal Regulation of Advertising," *Harvard Law Review*, 53: 828-42 (March 1940).

2446. COUNCIL FOR DEMOCRACY. *Censorship* (Democracy in Action, no. 10). New York, 1942. 46 pp.

Views of the Council. Bibliography, pp. 44-45.

2447. COUNCIL FOR DEMOCRACY. *Defense on Main Street: A Guidebook for Local Activities for Defense and Democracy.* New York, 1941. 88 pp.

General rules every citizen can follow. "Answers to those stock attacks on youth, labor, the foreign-born, Jews, and refugees." Practical programs for local application; directory of organizations; list of radio recordings, motion pictures, and scripts available for community use.

2448. COUNCIL FOR DEMOCRACY. *Freedom of Assembly and Anti-Democratic Groups.* Washington, D.C.: American Council on Public Affairs, 1941. 28 pp.

A concise handbook of the legal and political principles of freedom of assembly and of speech in a democracy. Prepared by a committee of specialists.

2449. COWLES, WILLARD BUNCE. "Joint Action to Protect an American State from Axis Subversive Activity," *American Journal of International Law*, 36: 242-51 (1942).

2450. CRAIG, ALEC. *Above All Liberties.* London: Allen and Unwin, 1942. 205 pp.

Discussion of effects on literature, art, science, and society of laws against literary obscenity. Bibliography, pp. 191-95.

2451. CRAIG, ALEC. *The Banned Books of England,* foreword by E. M. Forster. London: Allen and Unwin,

1937. New York: Macmillan, 1937. 207 pp.

Analyzes the English law of "obscene libel," with references to corresponding attitudes in the United States and elsewhere. Discusses numerous specific cases. Tables in appendix list cases, statutes, witnesses, and the books in question. Bibliography, pp. 187-95.

2452. CREEL, GEORGE. "The Plight of the Last Censor: Voluntary Censorship Won't Work," *Collier's*, 107: 13 ff. (May 24, 1941).

Reminiscences and recommendations by head of U.S. government Committee on Public Information in the 1914-18 war. "Pin down any member of Army or Navy Intelligence, and he will admit that there is no single activity in the field today that can be kept secret or needs to be kept secret," except minor technical inventions. "Nothing stood more clearly proved than that the atmosphere produced by common knowledge that news was being suppressed, even in small degree, provided an ideal 'culture' for the propagation of the bacteria of enemy rumor."

2453. CREW, ALBERT; and MILES, E. *The Law Relating to Public Meetings and Processions.* London: Pitman, 1937. 116 pp.

2454. CUSHMAN, ROBERT EUGENE. "The American Government in War-Time: Civil Liberties," *American Political Science Review*, 37: 49-56 (February 1943).

Year-end summary of developments. By Cornell political scientist.

2455. CUSHMAN, ROBERT EUGENE. *Safeguarding Our Civil Liberties* (Public Affairs Pamphlet no. 43). New York: Public Affairs Committee, 1940. 31 pp.

Lucid statement of the American tradition of civil liberties. Bibliography, pp. 30-31.

2456. DALE, EDGAR; and VERNON, NORMA. *Propaganda Analysis: An Annotated Bibliography* (Bureau of Educational Research, Ohio State University, series 1, vol. 1, no. 2). Columbus, Ohio, 1940. 29 pp.

In 1935 there were *two* articles dealing with propaganda analysis in a list of standard educational journals. In 1936 there was *one*; in 1937, *seven*; in 1938, *seventeen*; in 1939, *thirty-five*. This bibliography abstracts them, "in such a way as to underline effective methods which various teachers and experts in this field have found useful."

2457. DAVIS, ELMER; and PRICE, BYRON. *War Information and Censorship.* Washington, D.C.: American Council on Public Affairs, 1943. 79 pp.

General observations. Mr. Davis is head of U.S. Office of War Information and Mr. Price is head of U.S. Office of Censorship.

2458. DILL, CLARENCE CLEVELAND. *Radio Law, Practice and Procedure.* Washington, D.C.: National Law Book Company, 1938. 353 pp.

By former U.S. Senator who was in active charge of the writing and passage of the Radio Act of 1927 and of the Communications Act of 1934.

2459. DOWELL, ELDRIDGE FOSTER. "Criminal Syndicalism Legislation, 1935-1939," *Public Opinion Quarterly*, 4: 299-304 (June 1940).

Brings up to date the author's *History of Criminal Syndicalism Legislation in the United States,* 1917-33 (Johns Hopkins University, 1939).

2460. DOWELL, ELDRIDGE FOSTER. *A History of Criminal Syndicalism Legislation in the United States* (Ph.D. thesis; Johns Hopkins Studies in Historical and Political Science, series 57, no. 1). Baltimore: Johns Hopkins University, 1939. 176 pp.

Bibliography, pp. 155-60.

2461. DUNN, ROBERT WILLIAMS; and others. *Crisis in the Civil Liberties Union.* New York: Corliss Lamont, 1940. 46 pp.

Statement, including the basic documents concerned, giving the Communist position in the controversy over permitting Communists to be staff and board members of American Civil Liberties Union. See title 2414.

2462. EATON, (WILLIAM) CLEMENT. *Freedom of Thought in the Old*

South. Durham: Duke University, 1940. 343 pp.

U.S. historian portrays the successful control of public opinion in the ante bellum South, 1790-1860, by a powerful minority. At the time of the Civil War there were less than 11,000 individuals, or about three-fourths of one per cent of the free population, numbered among the select Southern group whose members owned 50 or more slaves.

There was some debate on slavery in Southern States in the early Eighteen Thirties; but after 1835 silence was the general policy. By 1850 "a striking change had taken place in the quality of leaders produced by the South." They were "warped by strong sectional prejudices, they lacked a catholic point of view, and they had lost the magic glow of republicanism." Bibliographic footnotes.

2463. ECCARD, FREDERIC. "La Législation anticommuniste dans le monde," *Revue politique et parlementaire*, 176: 21-36 (July 1938).

Brief summary of statutory measures against communism passed in modern states.

2464. *Education against Propaganda* (7th Yearbook of the National Council for the Social Studies, edited by Elmer Ellis). Cambridge, Massachusetts: National Council for the Social Studies, 1937. 182 pp.

A collection of articles by specialists in propaganda research, designed specifically to aid elementary and high school students and their social studies teachers to orient themselves to the uses of propaganda in modern society. The first eight articles deal with basic concepts and relations. The remaining articles describe educational techniques which have been thought successful in teaching school pupils how to "resist" propaganda.

2465. EDWARDS, VIOLET. *Group Leader's Guide to Propaganda Analysis: Experimental Study Materials for Use in Junior and Senior High Schools, in College and University Classes, and in Adult Study Groups.* New York: Institute for Propaganda Analysis, 1938. 31 pp.

Revised edition of *Propaganda: How To Recognize It and Deal With It* (1938).

2466. ERNST, MORRIS LEOPOLD; and LINDEY, ALEXANDER. *The Censor*

Marches On: Recent Milestones in the Administration of the Obscenity Law in the U.S. New York: Doubleday, Doran, 1940. 346 pp.

By two U.S. attorneys who are specialists on civil liberties. Records cases, reprints important court decisions, discusses censorship in theory and practice, and concludes with the tentative outline of a twelve-point legislative program which, the authors say, "is moderate enough to warrant hope of success and yet sufficiently forward-looking to yield real gains." See pp. 256-70, on this legislative program; and pp. 313-28, which reproduce the Broadcasters' Code and the Motion Picture Code.

2467. "Federal Sedition Bills: Speech Restriction in Theory and Practice," *Columbia Law Review* (June 1935).

2468. FEINBERG, I. R. "Picketing, Free Speech, and 'Labor Disputes,'" *New York University Law Review*, 17: 385-405 (March 1940).

2469. FENWICK, CHARLES GHEQUIERE. "Intervention by Way of Propaganda," *American Journal of International Law*, 35: 626-31 (October 1941).

By U.S. professor of international law.

2470. FENWICK, CHARLES GHEQUIERE. "Use of the Radio as an Instrument of Foreign Propaganda," *American Journal of International Law*, 32: 339-43 (1938).

2471. FERGUSON, CHARLES K. "The *Los Angeles Times* Contempt Case," *Public Opinion Quarterly*, 4: 297-99 (June 1940).

Supreme Court case involving right of a newspaper to comment on court cases in process of trial.

2472. "Film Censorship: An Administrative Analysis," *Columbia Law Review*, 39: 1383-1405 (December 1939).

2473. FORTUNOFF, DANIEL G. "Liability of Radio Corporations for Defamatory Statements Made Over the Air," *Air Law Review*, 12: 316-33 (July 1941).

Heavily documented legal study by student at Columbia Law School.

2474. FOSTER, JAMES E. "Censorship as a Medium of Propaganda," *Sociology and Social Research*, 22: 57-66 (September 1937).

2475. FRASER, CHARLES FREDERICK. *Control of Aliens in the British Commonwealth of Nations.* London: Hogarth, 1940. 304 pp.

Bibliography, pp. 293-94.

*2476. *Freedom of Inquiry and Expression* (Annals of the American Academy of Political and Social Science, vol. 200, November 1938, edited by Edward Potts Cheyney (D).

"A collection of facts and judgments concerning freedom and suppression of freedom of all forms of intellectual life." Includes "Freedom and Restraint: A Short History," by Edward Potts Cheyney, and articles by specialists on freedom among inventors, physicians, newspapermen, literary men, artists, teachers, social scientists, clergymen, wage earners, and others. There are special articles on the situation in Germany, Italy, and Russia. Appendix, pp. 292-306, "Tributes to the Ideal of Freedom of Expression," includes quotations by authorities from the days of Plato to the 1937 decisions of the U.S. Supreme Court.

2477. FRIEDRICH, CARL JOACHIM; and SAYRE, JEANETTE (i.e., JEANETTE SAYRE SMITH). *The Development of the Control of Advertising on the Air* (Radiobroadcasting Research Project at the Littauer Center, Harvard University, Studies in the Control of Radio, no. 1). Cambridge: Harvard University, 1940. 39 pp.

2478. GIBBONS, ROBERT D. "Recent Attempts to Curb Subversive Activities in the United States," *George Washington Law Review*, 10: 104-26 (November 1941).

Lists and describes enacted and proposed federal legislation, including espionage and sabotage acts, Alien Registration, Foreign Agents Registration and Voorhis (Registration) Acts.

2479. *The Gillette Bill for Propaganda Exposure: Analysis of the Bill and Radio Discussion of the Problem.* Washington, D.C.: Institute of Living Law (340 Woodward Building), March 1941. 17 pp.

Radio discussion of bill proposed by Senator Guy Mark Gillette of Iowa, to require publication of the name of the issuer on every piece of propaganda, and to set up a special nonpartisan federal agency to conduct research into propaganda campaigns. Any published matter not bearing the required disclosures would be barred from the mails and from importation into the United States.

2480. Hamilton, Robert Rolla; and Mort, Paul R. *The Law and Public Education, with Cases.* Chicago: Foundation Press, 1941. 579 pp.

Text and casebook on school law.

2481. Hays, Arthur Garfield. *Let Freedom Ring,* rev. ed. New York: Liveright, 1937. 475 pp.

Revision of a standard treatise on U.S. civil liberties cases, by a leading attorney of the American Civil Liberties Union.

2482. Hettinger, Herman Strecker. "The Economic Factor in Radio Regulation," *Air Law Review,* 9: 115-28 (April 1938).

Adversely criticizes rate regulation of radio.

2483. Houben, Heinrich Hubert. *Verbotene Literatur von der Klassischen Zeit bis zur Gegenwart. Ein Kritisch-historisches Lexikon über verbotene Bücher, Zeitschriften und Theaterstücke, Schriftsteller und Verleger.* Vol. 1: Berlin: Rowohlt, 1924. Vol. 2: Bremen: Schünemann, 1928.

"A Critical-historical Lexikon on Forbidden Books, Newspapers and Theatrical Presentations, Authors and Publishers."

2484. Institute for Propaganda Analysis. "Let's Talk About Ourselves," issue of *Propaganda Analysis* (vol. 2, no. 13, September 1, 1939).

Continues the self-scrutiny by the Institute that began with an article in the issue of September 1, 1938. "The study program has developed tremendously since last year. The 300 cooperating high schools and colleges have grown to 550; the handful of adult groups has swelled to 300 . . . the Institute has been cooperating with many other educational organizations. . . . Its materials have been used in many newspapers and magazines . . . we had close to 5,500 subscribers in September 1938. We have about 7,000 now. . . . In addition, Institute subscribers (and non-subscribers, too) have bought thousands of copies of each issue of *Propaganda Analysis* to distribute. . . . More than 15,000 extra copies of *The Attack on Democracy,* the January 1, 1939 issue of *Propaganda Analysis,* were sold in this way . . . [so were] *Father Coughlin* (June 1, 1939), *'The Munich Plot'* (November 1, 1938), *War in China* (February 1, 1939), *Communist Party, U.S.A., 1939 Model* (March 1, 1939), and *Spain: A Case Study* (July 1, 1939) . . . total income in round numbers was $50,600. Total expenditures as of September 1 were approximately $44,800."

2485. Jones, Robert William. *Law of Journalism, Including Matters Relating to the Freedom of the Press, Libel, Contempt of Court, Property Rights in News, and Regulation of Advertising.* Brooklyn, N.Y.: Metropolitan Law Book Co., 1940. 395 pp.

By University of Washington professor of journalism, a member of the Missouri bar. Bibliographic footnotes.

2486. Kiefer, Alexander F. "Government Control of Publishing in Germany," *Political Science Quarterly,* 57: 72-97 (March 1942).

Analysis of published laws and regulations and of known instances of their application.

2487. Knode, Jay C. "Professors and Propaganda," *Journal of Higher Education,* 6: 345-52 (October 1935).

To overcome public reluctance to accept any one social scientist's findings on unfamiliar subjects, a college dean recommends that the results of social science research be published by commissions of experts.

2488. Krause, Heinz. *Die voelkerverhetzende Propaganda im Voelkerrecht* (Leipziger Beitraege zur Erforschung der Publizistik). Dresden: Dittert, 1939. 106 pp.

"International Law Concerning Propaganda that Incites Hatred of a People."

2488a. KRIS, ERNST. "Some Problems of War Propaganda: A Note on Propaganda New and Old," *Psychoanalytic Quarterly*, 12: 381-99 (July 1943).

U.S. psychoanalyst, faculty member of New School for Social Research and codirector of Research Project on Totalitarian Communication, surveys changes in the content of world-political propaganda during recent decades. "In this war . . . propaganda has not been able to 'do the job.' . . . Men went to war in sadness and in silence, not only in the democracies but even in the totalitarian states. The course of the war has not decidedly affected the picture. . . . The economic crisis in all countries . . . has heightened the disappointment in government into a feeling of general insecurity." Citing Lasswell, Mannheim, and others, Dr. Kris concludes that a new type of leadership is being produced by the crises of the times. "Talking down or inciting will no longer do. The task is to explain. H. D. Lasswell, one of its advocates, has lately stressed what he calls balanced presentation—a presentation which states alternatives and thus enables independent evaluation of facts . . . the essentially educational function of the new propaganda."

2489. "A Label for Propaganda," *Ken*, 1 no. 1: 122 ff.

Discusses propaganda currently released in U.S. on behalf of Japanese, Chinese, Spanish, Italian, and German interests, giving names and addresses of sources. Asserts that enactment of the Foreign Agents Registration Act (H. R. 1591, 75th Congress), a bill to require registration of all propagandists for foreign countries, would be a step toward further disclosure of sources of such propaganda.

2490. LADAS, STEPHEN PERICLES. *The International Protection of Literary and Artistic Property* (Harvard Studies in International Law, no. 3). New York: Macmillan, 1938. 2 vols.

Volume 1: International Copyright and Inter-American Copyright. Volume 2: Copyright in the United States of America and Summary of Copyright Law in Various Countries.

2491. LASSWELL, HAROLD DWIGHT.

Democracy Through Public Opinion. Menasha, Wis.: Banta, 1941. 176 pp.

U.S. political scientist analyzes factors that may lead U.S. public opinion to exert democratic control over basic decisions. "The sacrifice of democracy is not a fundamental trend of the times. . . . Indeed, democracy is one of the long-run requirements of the skill society. . . . America, almost alone among the continents, *can* meet the needs of the time without giving up the rule of the majority." Includes extensive analysis of the principles and implications of "balanced discussion" (presentation of alternative points of view in public discussion of basic decisions).

2492. LEE, ALFRED McCLUNG. "Freedom of the Press: Services of a Catch Phrase," in *Studies in the Science of Society*, edited by George Peter Murdock (New Haven: Yale University, 1937), pp. 355-75.

". . . A survey of the general status of the catch phrase during the last decades of the eighteenth century, of the major changes that have swept the industry during the succeeding century and a half, and of the present services of the slogan. . . ." The author is a U.S. specialist in the sociology of journalism.

2493. LEROY, HOWARD S. "Treaty Regulation of International Radio and Short Wave Broadcasting," *American Journal of International Law*, 32 no. 4 (October 1938).

2494. LOEWENSTEIN, KARL. *Contrôle législatif de l'extrémisme politique dans les démocraties européenes.* Paris: Librairie Générale de Droit et de Jurisprudence, 1939. 136 pp.

How "democratic" European governments have sought, by legislation, to safeguard themselves against the dissemination of rival ideologies. This study by an Amherst College political scientist appeared first in *Columbia Law Review*, 38: 591-622, 725-74 (1938) and in *American Political Science Review*, 31: 417-32, 638-58 (1937). French edition contains some additional paragraphs on events since Munich. Topics considered include excesses of political propaganda, curtailment of freedom of assembly and of press, legislation against disloyal public officials, and institution of political police.

2495. LOEWENSTEIN, KARL. "Legislative Control of Political Extremism in European Democracies," *Columbia Law Review*, 38: 591-622, 725-74 (April, May 1938). See also his "Militant Democracy and Fundamental Rights," *American Political Science Review*, 31: 417-32, 638-58 (June, August 1937).

2496. MACKLIN, J. H. "A Study in Pressure Politics" (unpublished thesis, Syracuse University, 1940).

Study of American Civil Liberties Union.

2497. MARTIN, KINGSLEY. "Public Opinion and the Wireless," *Political Quarterly*, 10: 280-86 (April 1939).

Controversy in letters to London *Times* over news selection by BBC leads this observer to the "first conclusion" that "the BBC monopoly is a mistake. I believe that the American wireless, urged by competition, gives a better and a less nationalistic news service than the British. . . . It may be that the Canadian method by which a government wireless may compete with private companies may be the right solution." He also suggests attempts to "link up with the wireless services of all democratic countries (and if it can be done without the loss of independence as far as possible with the Fascist systems, too), so that throughout the democratic world the truest and most direct possible picture of world events is given to the public. This is the best and only counter to Fascist propaganda. Here at last is the technical basis for the internationalism of which we have all dreamt."

2498. MASON, JOHN BROWN. "Public Forums versus Propaganda," *School and Society*, 46: 311-13 (September 4, 1937).

"The public forum experiment . . . is one of the most effective means of meeting the evil effects of unbalanced propaganda."

2499. MILLER, CLYDE RAYMOND. "Some Comments on Propaganda Analysis and the Science of Democracy," *Public Opinion Quarterly*, 5: 657-65 (Winter 1941).

Comment by executive secretary of Institute for Propaganda Analysis on article by Bruce Lannes Smith (*Public Opinion Quarterly*, 5: 250-59, June 1941).

2500. MILLER, NEVILLE. "Legal Aspects of the Chain Broadcasting Regulations," *Air Law Review*, 12: 293-98 (July 1941).

By president, National Association of Broadcasters. Further discussion (anonymous), 12: 301-16 (July 1941).

2501. MOCK, JAMES ROBERT. *Censorship, 1917.* Princeton: Princeton University, 1941. 250 pp.

Based mainly on material in U.S. National Archives. By U.S. historian, coauthor of *Words That Won the War*. Bibliography, pp. 233-40.

2502. MOCK, JAMES ROBERT; CREEL, GEORGE; MILLER, NEVILLE; CHAFEE, ZECHARIAH, JR.; CASEY, RALPH DROZ; and KROCK, ARTHUR. "The Limits of Censorship: a Symposium," *Public Opinion Quarterly*, 6: 3-26 (Spring 1942).

2503. MORIYAMA, TAKEICHIRO. "Rescuing Radicals by Law," *Contemporary Japan*, 6: 277-81 (September 1937).

By a high administrator of the "Law for the Protection and Observation of Ideational Offenders effective since November 20, 1936, which is intended to rehabilitate both the mental and the material life of such offenders in order that they may be converted from radical doctrine and restored as loyal and useful members of society." "The zeal, paternal feeling, and devotion with which those who apply the law are thus serving the nation, have an important bearing upon the reform of the existing order which is a watchword of the nation today." Twenty-two such Homes for Protection and Observation are said to exist in Japan, to afford "ideational offenders" an opportunity to "resume their studies."

2504. MUNRO, W. CARROLL. "Cameras Don't Lie: Suppressed Newsreels of the South Chicago Strike Massacre Pose a Censorship Question," *Current History*, 46: 37-42 (August 1937).

2505. "N.A.M. Textbook Survey Arouses Storm," *Publishers Weekly*, 139: 1023-24 (March 1, 1941).

"Publishers, leading educators, and textbook authors have rallied to the defense of standard social science textbooks now used in secondary schools, which have been attacked by Ralph West Robey, who has been surveying some 563 books for the National Association of Manufacturers."

2506. NATIONAL ORGANIZATION FOR DECENT LITERATURE. *The Drive for Decency in Print: Report of the Bishops' Committee Sponsoring the National Organization for Decent Literature.* Huntington, Ind.: Our Sunday Visitor Press, 1939. 218 pp.

Censorship by Catholic Church groups.

2507. NAFZIGER, RALPH OTTO. "World War Correspondents and the Censorship of the Belligerents," *Journalism Quarterly*, 14: 226-43 (September 1937).

2508. PATTERSON, GILES JARED. *Free Speech and a Free Press*, foreword by James G. Stahlman. Boston: Little, Brown, 1939. 261 pp.

Survey of civil rights cases since Middle Ages, by member of Jacksonville (Florida) bar. Bibliography, pp. 247-52.

2509. POLLARD, JAMES E. "Advertising Copy Requirements of Representative Newspapers," *Journalism Quarterly*, 14: 259-66 (September 1937).

Fourteen U.S. metropolitan papers and a score of nonmetropolitan papers were queried as to their advertising standards.

2510. PRICE, BYRON. "Governmental Censorship in War-time," *American Political Science Review*, 36: 837-49 (October 1942).

By chief of U.S. Office of Censorship.

2511. PRICE, BYRON; BENTON, WILLIAM B.; and LASSWELL, HAROLD DWIGHT. *Censorship.* Chicago: University of Chicago, 1942. Pamphlet.

Radio round-table discussion.

2512. PRITCHETT, VICTOR SAWDEN. "A Muzzle on Critics," *Fortnightly* (London), 147 (n.s. 141): 67-73 (January 1937).

Essay on Nazi suppression of critics of literature and art.

2513. "Propaganda and Censorship," *Psychiatry*, 3: 628-32 (November 1940).

A William Alanson White Psychiatric Foundation Memorandum, designed to define the functions of propaganda and censorship in the present world situation from a psychotherapeutic standpoint.

2514. "Propaganda Probe," *Time*, October 11, 1937, p. 59.

Story on the Institute for Propaganda Analysis and brief biography of its executive secretary, Clyde Raymond Miller.

2515. "Public Order and the Right of Assembly in England and the United States: A Comparative Study," *Yale Law Journal*, 47: 404-32 (January 1938).

Comprehensive summary of the law.

2516. QUIGLEY, MARTIN. *Decency in Motion Pictures.* New York: Macmillan, 1937. 100 pp.

Essay on principles of motion picture morality by the publisher of a number of influential motion picture trade journals.

2517. RIESMAN, DAVID. "Civil Liberties in a Period of Transition," pp. 33-96 in *Public Policy* (Yearbook of Harvard Graduate School of Public Administration), vol. 3 (1942).

Heavily documented survey of current legal and scientific theories of civil liberties, by University of Buffalo professor of law.

2518. RIESMAN, DAVID. "Democracy and Defamation," *Columbia Law Review*, 42: 727-80 (May 1942).

Finds that older concepts of libel and defamation of individuals cannot be made to serve as an adequate remedy against Nazi and Fascist techniques of group-libel. Explores the precedents and legal arguments required to obtain effective civil remedies for group-libel.

2519. RIESMAN, DAVID. "Government Education for Democracy," *Public Opinion Quarterly*, 5: 195-209 (June 1941).

An educative program of democratic meetings, conducted by the government, is urged as a strategic offensive against antidemocratic forces at home and abroad.

2520. RIGGS, ARTHUR STANLEY. "'Of Value to the Enemy,'" *Public Opinion Quarterly*, 6: 367-77 (Fall 1942).

U.S. censorship procedures discussed by lieutenant commander, U.S.N.R., on staff of Cable and Radio Censorship Division of U.S. Office of Censorship.

2521. ROBERTS, LESLIE. *We Must Be Free: Reflections of a Democrat.* New York: Macmillan, 1939. 248 pp.

Description of the decline of liberty in the Dominion of Canada and a plea to maintain civil rights unabridged, even during wartime. See also title 2536.

2522. ROPE, F. T. "Assembly Program on Propaganda," *Clearing House*, 13: 173-74 (November 1938).

School assembly program showing how propaganda is presented. Program: (1) Four five-minute talks by pupils, on "Communist Propaganda Techniques," "Propaganda in Nazi Germany," "Mussolini's Methods," and "Propaganda at Home." (2) Between these talks and at other appropriate times during the program, stirring military music was played by the school band. (3) The stage was decorated with flags, posters, etc., typical of a "regulation" propaganda meeting. (4) Pupil questions and discussion from the floor closed the program.

2523. ROTNEM, VICTOR W.; and FOLSOM, F. G., JR. "Recent Restrictions upon Religious Liberty," *American Political Science Review*, 36: 1053-68 (December 1942).

U.S. Department of Justice officials examine the law and the facts and conclude that recent Supreme Court decisions have restricted religious liberty and provoked a certain amount of violence, without gaining corresponding social benefits.

2524. SCHMIDT-LEONHARDT, ALBERT HANS ERNST; and GAST, PETER. *Das Schriftleitergesetz vom 4. october 1933 nebst den einschlägigen Bestimmungen*, 2nd ed. Berlin: Heymann, 1938. 251 pp.

Critique of Nazi press law, with cases.

2525. SCHROEDER, THEODORE ALBERT. *A Challenge to Sex Censors.* New York: The Author, 1938. 159 pp.

2526. SENO, TOKUJI (pseud.). "Cinema Censorship in Japan," *Contemporary Japan*, 6: 87-94 (June 1937).

Lists and comments on outstanding cases of censorship between 1930 and 1936.

2527. SHARP, EUGENE WEBSTER. *The Censorship and Press Laws of Sixty Countries* (University of Missouri Bulletin, vol. 37; Journalism series, no. 77). Columbia, Missouri, November 1, 1936. 50 pp.

Regulations and decrees are presented with brief comments.

2527a. SIEBERT, FREDRICK SEATON. *The Rights and Privileges of the Press.* New York and London: Appleton-Century, 1934. 429 pp.

Contemporary law in relation to the publication of news. By University of Illinois professor of journalism, a member of the Illinois bar. Table of cases, pp. 401-18.

2528. SIEGEL, SEYMOUR N. "Radio and Propaganda," *Air Law Review*, 10: 127-45 (1939).

2529. SMITH, BRUCE LANNES. "Democratic Control of Propaganda Through Registration and Disclosure," *Public Opinion Quarterly*, 6: 27-40 (Spring 1942); 7: 707-19 (Winter 1943).

U.S. political scientist discusses methods which might be developed for federal registration and disclosure of activities, finances, backers, and connections of "the hidden propagandist," so that the public might get all the facts it would need for a rational judgment on major political and economic issues. Discusses potentialities of Voorhis Act and Foreign Agents Registration Act in this connection.

2530. SNIDER, E. M. "The American Civil Liberties Union: A Sociological Interpretation" (unpublished thesis, University of Missouri, 1937). 170 pp.

2531. STEWART, IRVIN. "The Public Control of Radio," *Air Law Review*, 8: 131-52 (April 1937).

2532. STOKE, HAROLD W. "Executive Leadership and the Growth of Propaganda," *American Political Science Review*, 35: 490-500 (June 1941).

University of Wisconsin political scientist reviews some of the well-known facts on recent federal publicity. "Perhaps one of the less apparent effects of this transformation in our political processes is a peculiar, widespread sense of political fatalism. The popular consciousness of being in control has seriously deteriorated. Polls recently showed that while 90 per cent of the public opposed the entrance of the U.S. into the war, an overwhelming majority believed that we would enter it. In this is a vague realization that the executive has been given enormous powers, that it can act when it sees fit, and that, having acted, there will be little choice save to accept its action and the explanation given for it."

2533. SULLIVAN, HAROLD WADSWORTH. *Contempts by Publication: The Law of Trial by Newspaper*, 2nd ed. Dorchester, Mass.: Published by the author, 1940. 212 pp.

By a member of U.S. Supreme Court bar. Holding that "trial by newspaper is a shabby form of jury tampering," the author believes U.S. courts should cite newspapers for contempt, as in England. A long line of cases is analyzed. Contempts by radio, cinema, and television are also discussed.

2534. SUMMERS, ROBERT EDWARD, compiler. *Wartime Censorship of Press and Radio* (Reference Shelf, 15 no. 8: 1-297). New York: H. W. Wilson, 1942.

2535. SWINDLER, WILLIAM F. "Law of the Press: A Supplementary Bibliography," *Journalism Quarterly*, 17: 159-60 (June 1940).

Technical articles in legal periodicals since July 1938.

2536. SWINDLER, WILLIAM F. "Wartime News Control in Canada," *Public Opinion Quarterly*, 6: 444-49 (Fall 1942).

"In three years of war Canada has maintained an ever-tightening surveillance over the freedom of its minority press and over civil liberties generally. Although no major newspaper has yet suffered restrictions, several scores of American publications have been barred from the country, and an undetermined number of minor Dominion newspapers and periodicals have been confiscated and their publishers fined." See also title 2521.

2537. TCHOU, KOANG-MOU. *La Saisie des journaux et imprimés* (thesis, University of Paris). Paris: Domat-Montchrestien, 1938. 117 pp.

Press law in France. Bibliography, pp. 111-13.

2538. "Treaty Regulation of International Radio and Short Wave Broadcasting," *American Journal of International Law*, 32 no. 4 (October 1938).

2539. TRIBOLET, LESLIE BENNETT. "A Decade of American Air Policies, 1922-1932," *Air Law Review*, 9: 181-95 (April 1938).

Summary of aviation and radio policies.

2540. U.S. LIBRARY OF CONGRESS. LEGISLATIVE REFERENCE SERVICE. *Acts of Congress Regulating Advertising*. March 28, 1936. 4 pp., mimeo.

2541. U.S. LIBRARY OF CONGRESS. LEGISLATIVE REFERENCE SERVICE. *Civil Liberties in Great Britain since the First World War* (Public Affairs Bulletin No. 14). Washington, D.C.: Government Printing Office, 1942. 35 pp.

2542. U.S. LIBRARY OF CONGRESS. LEGISLATIVE REFERENCE SERVICE. *Fraudulent Advertising: Digest of Regulatory Legislation*. March 27, 1936. 13 pp., mimeo.

2543. U.S. HOUSE OF REPRESENTATIVES. COMMITTEE ON THE DISTRICT OF COLUMBIA. SUBCOMMITTEE ON EDUCATION. *Teaching of Communism in the Public School of the District of Columbia* (hearings, 74th Congress, 2nd session, February 25, March 2, and March 9, 1936, pursuant to H.R.

10391 and H.R. 11375). Washington, D.C.: Government Printing Office, 1936. 283 pp.

2544. U.S. HOUSE OF REPRESENTATIVES. COMMITTEE ON IMMIGRATION AND NATURALIZATION. *Exclude and Deport Aliens Who Are Fascists or Communists* (report and minority views to accompany H.R. 7120, 74th Congress, 1st session). Washington, D.C.: Government Printing Office, 1935. 12 pp.

See also hearings before this committee on this question.

2546. U.S. HOUSE OF REPRESENTATIVES. COMMITTEE ON THE JUDICIARY. *Crime to Promote Overthrow of Government* (hearings before subcommittee no. 2, 74th Congress, 1st session, on H.R. 4313 and H.R. 6417, respectively to make it a crime to advocate or promote overthrow of government of the United States by force and violence, and to prohibit statements and publications advocating overthrow of government by violence). Washington, D.C.: Government Printing Office, 1935. 126 pp.

2547. U.S. HOUSE OF REPRESENTATIVES. COMMITTEE ON THE JUDICIARY. *Registration and Regulation of Lobbyists* (hearings, 74th Congress, 1st session, on S. 2176, to define lobbyists, to require registration of lobbyists, and provide regulation thereof). Washington, D.C.: Government Printing Office, 1935. 24 pp.

2548. U.S. OFFICE OF EDUCATION. *Let Freedom Ring* (Bulletin 1937, Nos. 32 and 33). Washington, D.C.: Government Printing Office, 1938.

Series of 13 radio programs which dramatized civil liberties issues, now made available as supplementary teaching material, to be used in social studies classes, school dramatics, and radio presentations. No. 32 contains the 13 scripts, with production notes. No. 33 is a study guide.

*2549. U.S. SENATE COMMITTEE ON EDUCATION AND LABOR. *Violations of Free Speech and Rights of Labor, Hearings, Pursuant to Senate Res. 266 (74th Congress, 2nd session) a Resolution to Investigate Violations of Right of Free Speech and Assembly and Interference with Right of Labor to Organize and Bargain Collectively.* . . . Washington, D.C.: Government Printing Office, 1936–.

The "La Follette Committee." Hearings before this Committee run to thousands of pages, in 75 or more parts. *Reports* of the Committee are also available from the Government Printing Office.

2550. U.S. SENATE. COMMITTEE ON THE JUDICIARY. *Censorship* (hearing before the Committee on the Judiciary, 77th Congress, 2nd session, on H.R. 7151, an Act to Amend the First War Powers Act, 1941, by Extending the Authority to Censor Communications to Include Communications between the Continental United States and any Territory or Possession of the United States, or between any Territory or Possession, and Any Other Territory or Possession. December 14, 1942). Washington, D.C.: Government Printing Office, 1943. 32 pp.

2551. VAN DYKE, VERNON. "Responsibility of States for International Propaganda," *American Journal of International Law*, 34: 58-73 (January 1940).

Part of Ph.D. thesis, Chicago, 1937.

2552. VOLD, LAWRENCE. "Defamatory Interpretations in Radio Broadcasting," *University of Pennsylvania Law Review*, 88: 249-96 (January 1940).

2553. WILLERT, ARTHUR. "Publicity and Propaganda in International Affairs," with discussion, *International Affairs*, 17: 809-26 (November 1938).

2554. WILSON, HOWARD E.; and others. *Teaching the Civil Liberties.*

Washington, D.C.: National Council for Social Studies, 1942. 40 pp.

Guide for high school teachers. Dr. Wilson is on faculty of Harvard Graduate School of Education. Bibliography, pp. 32-40.

2554a. WILSON, QUINTUS C. "Voluntary Press Censorship During the Civil War," *Journalism Quarterly*, 19: 251-61 (September 1942).

By news editor of St. Paul *Pioneer Press*, who is teaching assistant, School of Journalism, University of Minnesota.

2555. WILSON, WALTER; and DEUTSCH, ALBERT. *Call Out the Militia! A Survey of the Use of Troops in Strikes*. New York: American Civil Liberties Union, April 1938. 31 pp.

Lists and discusses cases, 1933-37, inclusive.

2556. WITTKE, CARL FREDERICK. "Academic Freedom and Tenure: Report of Committee A, Presented at the Annual Meeting, December 29, 1936," *Bulletin of the American Association of University Professors*, 23: 103-08 (February 1937).

2557. YOUNG, EUGENE JARED. *Looking Behind the Censorships*. Philadelphia: Lippincott, 1938. 368 pp.

Cable editor of New York *Times* describes the censorship of foreign news.

2558. ZIEGLER, RUTH. *The Chicago Civil Liberties Committee, 1929-38* (M.A. thesis, sociology, Chicago, 1938).

AUTHOR AND SUBJECT INDEX